Child Development

Child Development
Contemporary Perspectives

Edited by
Stewart Cohen and Thomas J. Comiskey
University of Rhode Island

F. E. PEACOCK PUBLISHERS, INC.
ITASCA, ILLINOIS 60143

Contents

Preface

Childhood plays a significant role in each of our lives. During the first decade of life the child experiences many encounters and interactions with its environment. These include the child's first contacts with people and events which, over time, come to influence the development of ideas, attitudes, emotions and behaviors.

Children are frequently acknowledged as the most important resources of society. Childhood, in turn, offers society its most promising opportunity to instruct and foster those human attributes most vital to its continued functioning. As we learn more about how the child grows, and the particular role of childhood in the growth process, the future of children and their importance to society shall be more fruitfully realized.

This book attempts to acquaint the student of child development with current information and concepts which extend our knowledge of how children develop. In addition, it seeks to foster the reader's interest in contemporary issues which influence the child's development in its role as a member of society.

The world of childhood has dramatically changed over the last several centuries. However, the challenges of development facing children as they strive to achieve adulthood have not significantly altered. What we learn about children and how we apply our findings will influence the present world of children, as well as future generations of children.

The purpose of this book is twofold. First, it seeks to enhance the student's concern for the world of childhood, its joy and its sadness. Second, it is hoped that this volume will serve to further our humane treatment of children, and in turn, serve the welfare of our children and their children.

This book is dedicated to some very special adults in our lives, Muriel and Alice, and Bob and Vicki. And it is dedicated to some very special children, Joseph, Michelle, and David.

STEWART COHEN
THOMAS J. COMISKEY

I. The World of Children

The Children of Yesterday

The history of children, as childhood itself, is a recent discovery. Until quite recently, whether from historical neglect or absence of sustained interest, the world of children has been largely unknown to adults. As Kessen noted, "The history of child study is a history of rediscovery," a history in which philosophers, educators, and physicians sensed the importance of childhood, but relegated its significance to issues of adult concern (e.g., problems associated with the selection of a wet nurse, problems pertaining to the acquisition and, hence, teaching of information) (1965). Clearly, from an historical perspective, ideas about childhood have reflected the values and aspirations of adult society, rather than the needs of the growing child and its requirements for maximum growth (Kramer, 1970).

Our knowledge of childhood during the beginnings of civilization is rather limited. However, from documents describing family life, training, and educational practices, we find that attitudes about children and childrearing differed dramatically from current beliefs. Our modern use of age as a criterion in the assignment of roles and status was far less pronounced; the differentiation of persons into sex roles early in life was not practiced; and childhood was only dimly seen as a distinct period of life.

In ancient times children became adults either by surviving a harsh and often indifferent environment or through the completion of adult-created and supervised rites of passage. These events signified the successful transition from infancy to adulthood, while childhood itself remained ill-defined or ignored.

Among ancient civilizations entry into society referred to the attainment of adult status (traditionally viewed as the achievement of manhood). Survival itself was problematic, and rites of passage were often painful, involving flogging, circumcision, or armed combat. Spartan boys were viciously

1

flogged, while Arabian boys were circumcised without anesthetic. Nuer boys, in ritualistic ceremony, had their foreheads incised to the bone (Plumb, 1972).

Prior to the Renaissance, children were regarded as infants until they reached approximately seven years of age, when they entered the world of adults. For the young child of the pre-Renaissance era, childhood represented a state of dependency controlled by adults. Among the dominant European languages, viz., English, French, and German, words used to denote a young male, for example, referred to a person who occupied a dependent or subordinate position relative to others. Correspondingly, language provided no special distinction between the ages of seven and sixteen. Moreover, the word "child" referred to kinship rather than age.

Perhaps the most significant achievement associated with the period of the Renaissance was the emergence of childhood as a distinct period of life, a European discovery that has slowly evolved over the past four hundred years. The emphasis had shifted from a preliterate, warrior society to a more modern industrial-vocational orientation.

As childhood came to be recognized as a separate period of life, a growing awareness and concern for the plight of children developed. Rising infant mortality rates, reform of educational practices, and labor laws protecting children and prohibiting their exploitation attracted attention. These reforms, of course, occasioned new problems, particularly the emergence of the period of adolescence, changes in the nature of family life, greater stress on education as a central vehicle of socialization, formation of restrictive class boundaries, and the consequences of rising affluence.

Children of Today

The world of childhood today constitutes a curious phenomenon. Presently the child is held in greater esteem than perhaps at any other time in history. Contemporary views of childhood, for example, stress an acceptance of the inherent potential of the individual and the belief that at no other time in life is the individual capable of demonstrating his/her promise for creative development or the realization of such expectations. Yet for many children the stark realities of circumstances surrounding childhood only mock such expectations. For many, an attitude of hope has been replaced by despair. In reality, for many children of modern times, especially those on the fringes of society, circumstances offer few guarantees or opportunities for success. Moreover, the constant struggle for survival prohibits more than a rudimentary adaptation to their environment. In historical perspective, the realities of modern times for the poor, the hungry, the emotionally disabled, the ill-treated, the neglected, and the abused parallel the circumstances of life which confronted children of yesterday.

Keniston's paper awakens us to disruptions in development by many contemporary problems faced by children and the need to counteract their debilitating consequences effectively. For example, we are asked to examine the current and future role of the family in light of its changing structure and functions. We are also asked to review other important avenues of development, such as the school, and to clarify what new and perhaps more viable role education shall play as a means to the resolution of endemic social problems. Finally we need to inquire how we can change society so that it will fulfill its promise to youth by providing more equitable growth-inducing environments for all children.

References

Kessen, W. *The child.* New York: John Wiley and Sons, 1965.

Kramer, R. You've come a long way baby, in three centuries. *The New York Times Magazine,* March 1970.

Plumb, J. H. The great change in children. *Horizon,* Winter 1971.

1.

Kenneth Keniston

DO AMERICANS REALLY LIKE CHILDREN?

Do Americans *really* like children? This question can be plausibly answered with both an emphatic *yes*—and a very disturbing *no.*

YES—*if* our own sentiments are to be taken as evidence. YES, we do like children and even love them—if the test is in values we profess and the myths we cherish and celebrate and pass on from generation to generation. Yes, of course—these sentiments and these myths and our dutiful celebration of them have given us a reputation as not only a child-loving but a child-centered nation. I do not profess to question the sincerity of these deeply held sentiments.

But I wish to suggest that our admirable sentiments, far too often and for much too long, have been thwarted and frustrated and rendered ineffectual by certain subtle, persistent, complex social and economic forces. And so I am prepared to assert that NO—in spite of our tender sentiments we do *not* REALLY like children. We do not as a nation really love them: we do not love them in practice, that is, and I'm sure that all of you will agree that practice—what we do—finally must provide the evidence that answers the question.

Let me remind you of how scandalously high is our infant mortality rate: The U.S. stands fifteenth among the forty-two nations ranked by the United Nations, just below East Germany and just above Hong Kong. Infant mortality rates for American nonwhites are almost twice those of whites. And for groups like American Indians, they are three and four times higher. We are among the very few modern nations that do not guarantee adequate health care to mothers and children.

Or consider malnutrition. A United States Department of Agriculture survey showed that between 1955 and 1965, a decade of rising affluence and agricultural productivity, the percentage of diets deficient in one or more essential nutrients actually increased. Millions of American children today remain hungry and malnourished.

So it goes—our sentiment of caring to the contrary.

We say that children have a right to the basic material necessities of life. Yet of all age groups in America, children are the most likely to live in abject poverty. In fact, one-sixth of them live below the officially defined poverty line. One-third live below that level defined by the government as "minimum but adequate."

A third of mothers of preschool children are in the labor force. Half the mothers of school-age children work outside the home. And we have yet to assure that these children receive adequate care when their parents are working. Here, again, we are behind other nations.

Even our tax structure is stacked against the children who most need help. To a very rich family, the tax deduction makes two children worth the equivalent of $750 or more in a direct grant from the govern-

Source: *Childhood Education,* 1975, **52,** 4-12. Reprinted by permission of Kenneth Keniston and the Association for Childhood Education International, 3615 Wisconsin Avenue, N.W., Washington, D.C. Copyright © 1975 by the Association.

ment. A family too poor to pay any taxes receives no help at all.

Our school system, of course, is supposed to equalize opportunity for all children, poor and rich. In fact, twelve years of public schooling actually increases the gap between rich and poor students. The best research shows that our school system actually *exaggerates* the inequalities with which children enter the schools.

Other nations may look to us for technological advances and material achievements, but we must look to almost every other industrial nation in the world for more advanced comprehensive systems of supports for children and families. In this area we are an underdeveloped nation.

Why are such things so? I have suggested that the answer is to be found in the forces of our economic system. Let me examine this suggestion in the context of three problems, which I will call the depopulation of the family, the intellectualization of the child, and the perpetuation of exclusion.

DEPOPULATION OF THE FAMILY

Last year more than half of all school-aged children in two-parent families had mothers who worked outside the home, mostly full time. In two-parent families with children under six, the proportion of working mothers has reached one-third and continues to grow rapidly. In single-parent families, of course, mothers are even more likely to work for wages.

For the first time in our national history, *most children now have mothers who work outside the home,* and most of these mothers work full time.

A particularly depopulated set of families are those with only one parent. Divorce rates have risen more than 700% in the last century. In 1948 only one out of fourteen children under six was brought up in a single-parent family. In 1973 that proportion had doubled to one out of seven children.

Another trend is the disappearance of non-parental relatives from families. In 1949 about half of children under six in single-parent families lived with another relative who headed the family. By 1973 this proportion had dropped to one in five. In less than twenty-five years the number of other relatives—usually grandparents, aunts and uncles—in the single-parent family has dropped from 50% to 20%.

Brothers and sisters are also increasingly scarce. At the peak of the postwar baby boom, the median completed family size was 3.8. Today, completed family size is below the zero population growth rate, about 1.9. Sixteen years ago, the average child had almost three siblings; today, the average child has less than one.

Let me cite one final statistic, the increasing proportion of children born to unmarried women. In 1960 about one out of every twenty women giving birth was not married; by 1972 this figure had increased to one out of eight.

Taken together, these statistics mean that more and more children are spending more and more time in homes empty of people to look out for them.

What has replaced the people in the family? For one, television has become a kind of flickering blue parent for many children. The technological babysitter, indeed, occupies more of the waking hours of American children than any other single influence—including both *parents* and *schools.* A second replacement is, of course, the peer group. Other unrelated children play a larger and larger role in socializing the young. A third group of institutions that have replaced the child's family members are schools, preschools, and the various child-care arrangements that must be made by working parents.

Thus millions of American children are today being raised for larger and larger portions of time by nonrelatives, often completely outside of their family. And, finally, growing numbers of children are simply growing up with no care at all. These we call latchkey children. They stay alone in empty houses, often locked in, while their parents work. The street is their playground.

Such are some effects of the depopulation of the family. A side effect is that a majority of American mothers who work outside the home tend to feel guilty, inadequate and fearful of neglecting their children.

The highest rates of female labor force participation occur in families of average and below-average income. Most women today work not only for fulfillment but because they need money to subsist. Most husbandless mothers work because their income is their *only* source of sustenance. It is well known that women work mostly in underpaid, boring and menial occupations. And even when their jobs are better ones, they are paid less than men.

The entry of mothers and other women into the occupational system seems to me irreversible. In many cases it is desirable. Women are simply gaining a right that men have always had—the right to seek productive, rewarding and remunerative employment. To my knowledge, no one on our Council believes that women should not have the same opportunities for productive work that men have. Nor do we believe that we should pressure women to stay at home. Our effort is not to condemn but to try to understand.

Certainly one thing that we have come to understand is that the economic forces at play on us are sharply at odds with our sentiments that children should receive consistent care and nurturance in and

from the family. The sentiment is no doubt real and sincere; but it is blocked, left irrelevant and impotent in a society that declines to support parents as parents and thus leaves many no choice but to go hungry or go to work outside the home. The pity is that we define work only as paid participation in the labor force, ritually celebrating but leaving unrewarded the strenuous and indispensable work women and men also do in their homes in rearing their children.

If families in America become little more than dormitories, quick-service restaurants, recreation centers and consumption units, we must look not to the negligence of American parents but to the pressures of the economy for the main explanation. And if this is allowed to happen—and it is happening at a hastening rate—what does it say about our *real* attitude toward children?

INTELLECTUALIZATION OF THE CHILD

Now I move to another subject and ask: while we have been depriving our children of what they might obtain from a complete and vital family, what have we been doing to them at school?

I believe that we are witnessing a growing emphasis upon the child as a brain; upon the cultivation of narrowly defined cognitive skills and abilities; and above all upon the creation, through our preschools and schools, of a breed of children whose value and progress are judged primarily by their capacity to do well on tests of IQ, reading readiness, or school achievement. Although children are, like adults, whole people, full of fantasies, imagination, artistic capacities, physical grace, social relationships, cooperation, initiative, industry, love and joy, the overt and above all the covert structure of our system of preschooling and schooling largely ignores these other human potentials to concentrate upon the cultivation of a narrow form of intellect.

Most of the fundamental objectives of Head Start, for example, seemed to be overlooked by the critics when the program was being evaluated. I suggest that the critics were impelled to overlook these other factors by the veritable obsession of our educational system with cognitive development and with standard tests as a measurement of the educational well-being of the young.

Most critics of Head Start seemed to hold the notion that, to have succeeded, that program should have been able in a few hours each day to overcome permanently the overwhelming disadvantages of children born into poverty and segregation and squalor. I would only say that it is a tribute to our optimism, if to nothing else, that any of us ever thought that we could do so much for so many for so little.

The fashionable theory underlying much of the valuation of Head Start attributes the plight of those children to something called "cultural deprivation." The phrase evokes images of children simply bereft of the cultural stimulation available to middle-class children, of homes without books, and of families getting together without meaningful conversation. Whence cultural deprivation was to be remedied by cultural enrichment—which is to say, intellectual stimulation.

This view leaves us all blind to far more fundamental things. We need to get at what is causing the cultural deprivation— that is, what is doing the depriving. When we see that, then we can wonder whether the main deprivation is really cultural at all. And it seems clear, to me at least, that the reason some families cannot provide

their children with intellectual stimulation at breakfast and cultural riches at dinner is that they are blighted by and bogged down in the morass of old-fashioned poverty. Now I, for one, see poverty as a manifestation not of our cultural system but of our economic system.

The cost of not properly identifying the roots of our problem is manifold. In the case of Head Start, we paid the price of stigmatizing those whom the program was intended to benefit. And our limited view also paved the way for the evaluatory sabotage of a program that, in my own view, was extraordinarily successful—even given the inadequacy of the theory on which it was evaluated. For Head Start did indeed show that it is possible to increase the ability of children at the bottom of our society to do well on tests. Head Start did succeed in empowering at least some parents. And Head Start did provide desperately needed health, dental and other services to at least a few children.

I have emphasized Head Start, however, to underscore a broader tendency in our society. It is the tendency arising from our obsession with cognitive development, with test scores. It is that tendency to rank and rate children, to reward and stigmatize them according to their ability to do well in the narrow tasks that schools (or we psychologists) believe we can measure quantitatively. This tendency is to be found not only among the critics of Head Start.

At every level of our preschool and school system, etc., this same ability to do well on tests is a primary determinant of the child's progress and position in the world of school and, to a large degree, in the later world of adults. Access to the "high" tracks, "superior" ability groupings, and even to good schools themselves is primarily determined by ability to do well on tests. We talk a great deal about the other human qualities of children; but when push comes to shove—when it is a matter of promotions, credentials and praise—the child who has learned to master test-taking gets the goodies.

And this fact lives next door to our professed devotion to human qualities we say we value—physical vitality, caring, imagination, resourcefulness, cooperation, moral commitment.

We measure the effectiveness of education by whether or not it produces income increments, not by whether it improves the quality of life of those who are educated. And we measure the success of schools not by the human beings they promote, but by increases in reading scores. We have allowed quantitative standards, so central to our economic system and our way of thinking about it, to become the central yardstick for our definition of our children's worth.

THE PERPETUATION OF EXCLUSION

The two problems I have so far mentioned affect *all* American children. Now I turn to the problem of the excluded—children born in the cellar of our society and systematically brought up to remain there. Our sentiments in their behalf are always touching. Our treatment of them is merely heartbreaking. Our excluded include one-quarter of all American children, and the tragic truth is that this*one-quarter of all American children today are being brought up to fail.*

This figure is an estimate, but we believe it to be on the conservative side. I am talking about children who are being deprived of the opportunity to realize a significant portion of their human potential, who are being actively injured, hurt, deprived at times even of the right to live. This is happening to them for four

reasons: race, poverty, handicap and being born of parents too overwhelmed by life to be able to care responsively and lovingly for the child.

One out of every five children in America is nonwhite, and these children must somehow cope with the persistent institutional and psychological racism of our society. One out of every three children lives below the minimum adequate budget established by the Department of Labor, and each of these children must face the multiple scars of poverty. One out of every twelve children is born with a major or minor handicap, and all of these children face the stigmas and social disabilities that accompany any handicap. One out of every ten children has a learning disability. Approximately one-quarter of all American children do not receive anything approaching adequate health care, nor did their mothers before they were born—whence our disgraceful infant mortality rates. Millions of children live in substandard housing. Millions attend deplorable schools. How many parents are themselves so overwhelmed by life that they are unable to provide responsive care? We don't know, but there must be millions, rich and poor.

What makes these facts even more disturbing is the frequency with which they occur together. For both white and nonwhite children, the single-parent family is likely to be poor—and vice versa. Poverty is irrevocably linked to inadequate medical care. Children who most desperately need good schools usually wind up in bad ones. To speak of the poor and the hungry is almost redundant—and a hungry child can rarely do well in school.

But the most powerful forms of exclusion are not physical but social and psychological. A child of poverty is denied those needs that most Americans consider fundamental. The children of the poor live in a world more dangerous by far than that of the prosperous. The poor child's is a world of broken stair-railings; of hustlers, busy streets, lead paint and prowling rats. Or it may be a rural world, where families cannot maintain the minimal levels of public health considered necessary a century ago. Urban or rural, it is a world of aching teeth without dentists to fill them, of untreated colds that result in permanent deafness. It is a world wherein a child learns to be ashamed of the way he or she lives. Such a world teaches a child to suppress any natural impulse to explore, to reach out. It turns off the child's initiative and strips the child of the eagerness that children can bring to learning. And it teaches many children that the best defense against a hostile world is constant offense—belligerent aggressiveness, sullen (and justified) anger, deep mistrust, and readiness for violence.

Such children are systematically trained for failure. As people they are defined as no good, inadequate, dirty, incompetent, ugly, dumb and clumsy. They learn that the best strategy for coping is never to venture out, to take no risks, or constantly to be on the attack. This pathetic sense of self and this view of the world is in fact an accurate perception of the messages our society gives these children. It is also the perception that condemns them to lives of failure in social if not in human terms.

The themes that dominate our social and political history sing with our commitment to equality and fair play. Nothing in our constellation of basic values even hints that our society should impose special burdens upon special children. On the contrary, to each generation we continue to repeat the same promise: Your children will be included; all of you who live here will become full members of the community of Americans. And much of our history has been an effort to confirm that

promise, although in a painfully slow, erratic and incomplete way.

How, then, can we understand the perpetuation of exclusion? One answer, put forward for almost two centuries in America, is that those at the bottom belong there because they lack virtue, merit, industriousness or talent. Or because they are immoral—lazy, dependent, profligate or licentious.

But no thoughtful person can accept such an unjust explanation. And here I suggest, once again, that the excluded are amongst us not because of their individual inadequacy or immorality but rather because of the way our society works, the way it has worked for more than a century.

Let me point to one cold and significant fact: The distribution of wealth and income in this nation has not changed materially in 150 years. It has not been changed by our promises of equal opportunity, or by our efforts at schooling, or by all of the general increases in our national prosperity, or by all of our efforts to reform and change and uplift those at the bottom of our society.

But exclusion persists not because of the evil motives of robber barons or the wicked intentions of industrialists. It persists because we all live in a system driven by the relentless quest for innovation, growth, and profit. And we must acknowledge how well that system has worked, given its goals. It has made us the most prosperous and technologically advanced nation in world history—though probably not emotionally the happiest, nor spiritually the most serene, nor morally the most just. But materially, we have profited. Most Americans have shared in the profit.

But I think it is indispensable to appreciate that the profit has been reaped at costs that do not appear on corporate ledger sheets, or the gross national product. These are hidden costs (or at least they are not so often witnessed), and they consist of the misery and despair and neglect and hunger and want of that vast fraction of us whom I have called the excluded. Such costs cannot be quantified in IQ points or dollars and cents. And maybe that is one reason we have yet as a nation to take them into account.

Another reason may be that the great majority of us have been too busy enjoying our profitable lives to take a long, hard look at the human cost we pay to go on as we do—and to look at the structure and assumptions of the economic system that exacts that cost.

Some prices we should not be willing to pay. In the long run, the price of exclusion is enormous—not only in dollars laid out for remedial services, for prisons, for mental hospitals, but in the anguish and pain exacted by social tension and unrest and discontent. And, finally, this nation pays a continuing price far more serious, and also beyond quantifying: This is the moral and human price we pay simply by tolerating a system that wastes a significant portion of the potential of the next generation, and wherein the advantage of some rests upon the systematic deprivation of others.

NEEDED ACTIONS

In each of these three problems—the depopulation of the family, the intellectualization of the child, the perpetuation of exclusion—I have suggested that the search for causes leads us not to blame the individual but the workings of that economic system which, for better or worse, pervades our national existence.

While I don't intend to place a program for reform before you, I would like to mention that those changes I expect the Council will argue and work for include programs designed not to replace but to support and sustain parents as the people usually best suited to nurture and care for children. We hope to recommend ways schools might function to enhance and liberate the life of the child instead of fixing his destiny and relentlessly tracking him. We will doubtless advocate programs to *include* the excluded by recognizing that their plight is not a consequence of moral failings or cultural flukes but of the hard and inexorable forces of the economic system, and by directly remedying the effects of those forces.

The challenge is to begin removing the causes of the problems that bedevil families and children. We need to eliminate the barriers, job ceilings and caste lines that shut minorities out of full participation. We need not to reform the poor but to guarantee them adequate income. We need not merely job training programs but programs to create jobs—and all of this as part of a long-term effort to learn how to eliminate that secondary labor market that relies on condemning many parents and children to exclusion. And we need to begin now to develop comprehensive and universally accessible services to support all families in the rearing of their children—as in the crises of life—services that would be available to all families by right and not because some particular inadequacy or special need is demonstrated.

Some of these things could be done quickly. Income support, for instance, could be implemented if only we mustered the national will to enact it. Other remedies such as job creation may take longer and may require a time of experimentation. The important thing is that we begin.

POSTSCRIPT:
A WORD FOR TEACHERS

I believe that the very beginning of the job is to recognize the way families and children have become the victims of our system. We Americans have been profoundly influenced by a tradition of individualism which makes it hard for us to perceive the larger causes of social ills. Since our very founding we have emphasized the freedom of the individual, the opportunities of the individual, and the responsibilities of the individual. And, historically, we as well have invariably tended to credit primarily the individual for his place, high or low, on the social ladder. And this of course has given rise to our long custom of blaming individually those of us who have wound up suffering financial or social or moral perplexities. Out of that perception has come the long—and largely unsuccessful—history of our efforts to cure our social ailments by reforming and uplifting those individuals we have viewed as short on character or morality.

I believe it is time to see that there are certain social and economic forces that none of us individually can resist. And I think it is now indispensable for us to see that millions of American children who suffer unmet needs for care and opportunity should not be blamed, nor should their parents, for crippling situations that are in fact wrought by us all within this system. No doubt individualism can and should continue to be a cherished value of this society. But it is time for us to behave not like a collection of competing individuals but like a family of related people. It is time for old-style individualism to give way to some old-style sense of community.

All this would entail, in fact, is that we translate our abundant and tender statements about children into *practice*. Then it might be said that we *really* like children.

II. The Roots of Development: Biological, Psychological, and Sociocultural Origins of Growth

As we view the miracle of growth in the young child, a number of questions arise. How does development come about? Is change a function of maturation (i.e., biological processes) or of environmental interchange? Or is development a product of both?

The origins of development have interested educators, philosophers, and scientists for some time. Several questions about the nature of growth and its process of emergence have been raised. Is the child a creature of nature or a product of its environment? Is he or she an active, self-monitored explorer of the world or a passive receiver of information? A natural thinker or an acquirer of thinking ability through varied experiences in the environment (Kessen, 1965)?

These themes are highly complex and multifaceted issues. Three subtopics of these issues are: (1) What are the inherent capabilities of the child? (2) What kinds of interaction characterize relations between the child and its environment? and (3) How do these transactions advance or impede the child's development?

The Competent Organism

Research on the growth and development of infants has expanded dramatically over the last several decades. This research has altered significantly our concepts of infancy and increased our knowledge of the infant and the quality of its transactions with its environment (Appleton, Clifton, & Goldberg, 1975). From findings derived from a variety of studies, scientists have discovered that the infant is a highly competent and unique organism. In addition, it has become increasingly apparent that the more carefully we study the infant, by revising our traditional assessment techniques and procedures in a manner befitting the young organism, the more capable we are discovering the infant to be.

What is the nature of the infant's capabilities? In research studies reviewed by Korner (in the first selection of this series), infants have been found to demonstrate remarkable visual capabilities. For example, the newborn can discriminate among various intensities of brightness, is attracted by movement, and demonstrates a preference for complex over simple visual stimuli. Of special interest, these behaviors are not only evident during the first hours of life but become increasingly complex and sophisticated thereafter.

Newborns are also highly responsive to auditory stimuli, and they possess well-developed auditory skills at birth or soon after. For example, infants have been shown to be capable of discriminating among auditory stimuli by demonstrating different response patterns to various auditory tasks (e.g., problems involving intensity, duration, or location of sound). Other studies have suggested that the infant's ability to respond to auditory stimulation is quite advanced. Kearsley (1973) found that infants coordinate their orientation to sound by attending to or withdrawing from varying qualities of tone. In orienting to sound the infant reduced its head movements, opened its eyes and decelerated its cardiac rate, while disorienting (i.e., withdrawing) was evident by increased head movement, closing the eyes, and increased cardiac rate.

The infant's visual and auditory competence is supplemented by olfactory, kinesthetic, and tactile capabilities of similar maturity and sophistication. In addition, the infant has been found to demonstrate sensorimotor behaviors. Such actions necessitate the coordination of diverse sensory modalities (e.g., the integration of eye-hand movements in prehension or grasping), a behavioral sequence which suggests the operation of complex thought processes.

Infant-Environment Relations

The maturity and competence which the infant demonstrates in adaptation to its inanimate world is also characteristic of its relations with the human environment.

Past views of the young child, which have stressed its relative static contribution to the infant-parent dyad, have been replaced through recognition of the infant as an active force in interpersonal relationships (Cohen, 1976). As Bell (1968; 1971) has noted, the "parent-effect" model of socialization, in which the parent is regarded as the prime initiator and controlling agent of the relationship, is both an imprecise and limited perspective of the infant-parent relationship. Rather, an egalitarian view of each participant as a co-contributor to this union appears warranted. This more recent perspective of the infant-parent relationship has been supported by research cited by Korner, and is documented by Carew, Chan, and Halfar. It is of particular interest that these latter researchers view the significance of the parent-child relation in terms of the rich and varied interplay which transpires among participants. As Gordon (1975) has suggested, sustained social interaction is reciprocal in quality, each participant continuously influencing its environment, and in turn, being influenced.

Early Experiences

Each individual experiences numerous interactions with its social and non-social environment in the course of development. Some of these interactions possess special significance for the child while others do not. Scientists interested in determining which experiences are most critical to development have studied growth in a variety of contexts, including membership across different cultural and social affiliations. These studies have been helpful in providing us with a picture of the diversity of experiences which people encounter in interaction with their environment and the relative consequences of such interchanges.

In the study reported by Brazelton, the effects of giving birth and of being born in different cultures are described from the perspective of the mother and her infant. In this paper, Brazelton attempts to relate how both the infant and the mother are part of a cultural matrix which determines the parameters of the mother-infant relationship by setting limits on the nature of resources available to both parties in the formation of the first social bond. He also reviews the role which cultural membership plays in the creation of behavioral expectancies affecting the mother-infant pairing and how such expectancies are met across different cultures.

The culture of poverty is perhaps more familiar to most readers than the diverse life circumstances encountered among persons of different cultural memberships. In the essay prepared by Tulkin, the political and socio-economic ramifications of poverty are reviewed. While recognizing the significance of poverty as a pervasive impediment to growth (through prohibiting adequate diet, preventing access to health and medical care, and by limiting educational opportunities), Tulkin further extends our understanding of poverty by calling for a differentiation of the effects of poverty from those consequences associated with minority group membership. He observes that being poor, for example, does not imply an absence of values, as frequently assumed, nor adherence to non-functional values. In contrast, he suggests that our understanding of development within the culture of poverty be prefaced by an appreciation of different life experiences and how such events viewed nonjudgmentally affect individual growth.

Summary

From the preceding discussion several general principles concerning the roots of development may be advanced:

1. The infant is a competent organism capable of relating to its environment in a variety of ways.

2. Development is a transactional process in which the organism and the environment interact.

3. The infant influences its environment and is, in turn, influenced by its responses to initiated interaction.

4. There are many forms of infant care, some of which reflect diverse cultural memberships, while others are influenced by social or economic conditions. Infants adapt to a variety of different environments with amazing flexibility and resourcefulness.

References

Appleton, T., Clifton, R., & Goldberg, S., The development of behavioral competence in infancy. In F. D. Horowitz (ed.), *Review of child development research,* Vol. IV. Chicago: University of Chicago Press, 1975.

Bell, R. Q., A reinterpretation of the direction of effects in studies of socialization. *Psychological Review,* 1968, **75,** 81-95.

Bell, R. Q. Stimulus control of parent or caretaker behavior by offspring. *Developmental Psychology,* 1971, **4,** 63-72.

Cohen, S. *Social and personality development in childhood.* New York: The Macmillan Company, 1976.

Gordon, I. J. *The infant experience.* Columbus, Ohio: Charles E. Merrill Publishing Company, 1975.

Kearsley, R. B. The newborn's response to auditory stimulation: A demonstration of orienting and defensive behavior. *Child Development,* 1973, **44,** 582-590.

Kessen, W. *The child.* New York: John Wiley and Sons, Inc., 1965.

2.

Anneliese F. Korner

EARLY STIMULATION AND MATERNAL CARE AS RELATED TO INFANT CAPABILITIES AND INDIVIDUAL DIFFERENCES

Early infancy has increasingly become the focus of attention among developmental psychologists, clinicians, and educators. Interest has focused on many different aspects of early development and, as a consequence, several branches of investigative work have developed. Developmental psychologists are engaged in research demonstrating heretofore unsuspected capabilities of the newborn and the very young infant. Other investigators are systematically assessing individual differences in these early capabilities and in the earliest manifestations of individual temperament. Still others focus primarily on the effects of early experience on the infant's development. For the most part, this focus is concerned with environmental influences such as the quality of the mother–child relationship, the availability of sensory stimulation, and the effect of experience such as separations, father absence, etc. There is, in addition, a beginning awareness on the part of some investigators that early experience is also influenced by differences *within* the infants in the way they experience the mother–infant relationship, separations, and other events in their lives.

Source: *Early Child Development and Care,* 1973, **2,** 307-327. The author's infant research was supported by United States Public Health Service grants HD-00825 and HD-03591 from the National Institute of Child Health and Human Development and was conducted under the auspices of Grant RR-81 from the General Clinical Research Centers Program of the Divisions of Research Resources, National Institutes of Health.

There is a multitude of implications from the findings of these different branches of infancy research both for maternal care and the issue of sensory enrichment. It is the purpose of this paper to briefly review some of the most salient recent findings of the young infant's capability and of the individual differences which exist between infants and to discuss these findings in the light of their relevance for issues of maternal care and early stimulation.

THE INFANT'S CAPABILITIES AT BIRTH

Not long ago, it was thought that newborns could neither see nor hear to any extent. This view is still very prevalent among parents of newborns. Research with neonates has demonstrated that newborns not only are able to visually fixate objects from a certain distance but that they are capable of pursuing moving objects when they are in the right state (i.e., Wolff & White, 1965; Barten, Birns, & Ronch, 1971; Korner, 1970). More remarkably, newborns show preferences among visual stimuli as judged by their consistently longer fixations of certain configurations as compared with others (Fantz, 1963; Hershenson, Munsinger, & Kessen, 1965). Fantz, for example, found that infants less than forty-eight hours old looked significantly longer at a picture with the stimulus configuration of a human face than at any other visual stimulus.

Newborns are also highly responsive to auditory stimuli. They not only respond to such stimuli through autonomic reactions (i.e., Bridger, Birns, & Blank, 1965; Steinschneider, 1968), but they turn their eyes and heads toward the source of certain sounds provided they are in the right state (Wolff, 1959). As is the case with the visual modality, the newborn responds differentially to sound, depending on its stimulus configuration. Eisenberg (1965) in very carefully controlled studies demonstrated that a great deal depends on the sound pressure level, the duration, the frequency, and complexity of the sound as to whether or not it elicits a response. From Eisenberg's research (1965) and that of others, it appears that the newborn is most responsive to sound within the human speech range. Interestingly enough, the newborn appears to be programmed to respond more readily to the female than the male voice as suggested by Brazelton's (1970) observations. By four weeks of age, the infant is so sensitive to minor differences in speech sounds that he orients to the change of a consonant after being habituated to another (Eimas, Siqueland, Jusczyk, & Vigorito, 1971).

Newborns also are quite skilled at hand to mouth coordination (Hendry & Kessen, 1964; Wolff, 1966; Korner, Chuck, & Dontchos, 1968). In fact, judging from the fact that the infant touches his mouth significantly more often than his face even though the face represents a much larger surface, and judging from his persistence in maintaining this contact, hand-mouth coordination is a well-organized congenital behavior pattern (Korner & Kraemer, 1972). In addition, the newborn appears to show the rudiments of eye-hand coordination (Bower, 1971; Korner & Beason, 1972).

There has been a great debate about the extent to which newborns are capable of learning, particularly through conditioning. There is a large Russian literature on this subject. Brackbill (1962) published a table given to her by Kasatkin and other Russian scientists which summarizes the developmental sequence in which conditioned responses may be established, depending on the sensory modality used as a conditional stimulus. Apparently, by using a vestibular-proprioceptive conditional stimulus the Russian investigators were able to elicit a conditioned response by the eighth day of life. It took twice as long when an auditory conditional stimulus was used, and longer when tactile and visual conditional stimuli were employed. In the USA, Lipsitt (1966) in reviewing his own work on conditioning and that of others concluded that the human newborn definitely is a learning organism. Sameroff (1971), in a more recent review of the conditioning literature concluded that the growing evidence points to the fact that, while operant conditioning is feasible with the newborn, classical conditioning does not become effective until the infant is three weeks old or older. For the most part, conditioning experiments have used as response measures, changes in already existing behavior patterns. Thus, changes in sucking rates, (Kron, 1967; Siqueland & DeLucia, 1969; Butterfield & Siperstein 1972) increases in head-turning with reinforcement (Siqueland, & Lipsitt, 1966) have most frequently been taken as response measures. Of particular interest are the studies of Butterfield and Siperstein (1972) and by Siqueland (1969) because they suggest that the newborn, and the month old infant, may already be hungry for stimulation. Butterfield and Siperstein (1972) were able to demonstrate that newborns will modify their sucking rates in order to hear music. Siqueland (1969) found that one month old infants will suck hard when the presentation of visual stimuli is contingent upon their sucking, and will suppress sucking when sucking results in withdrawal of the projected stimuli.

In sum, all the above clearly points to the fact that the newborn and very young infant is a great deal more capable of organized responses than has hitherto been assumed.

INDIVIDUAL DIFFERENCES AMONG NEWBORNS

There are relatively few studies whose primary objective is to systematically assess individual differences in newborns. More often individual differences are merely mentioned because they emerge in the context of studies which primarily investigate the norm of general developmental trends or the effect of specific experimental interventions. In this context, individual variations are often viewed as a source of error or annoyance rather than as interesting findings in their own right, because such variations tend to obscure the generality of the study's findings. It has mostly been the clinically oriented investigator who has had an intrinsic interest in individual differences, because the clinician, more than others, is concerned with predisposition toward, and early detection of deviation in development. It is probably the child who holds an extreme position in any given reaction pattern rather than the norm who tends to be more vulnerable to such early deviation.

To establish statistically significantly individual differences in neonates, great care has been taken to ensure that the individual differences found are not an artifact of pre- or postnatal complications, of variations in the infant's momentary state or of differences in the conditions of observation. (For an elaboration of these issues, see Escalona, 1962; Korner, 1971, 1972.) Statistically significant differences have been found in many of the neonate's

functions discussed above. Specifically, the studies by Barten, Birns, and Ronch (1971) and by Korner (1970) demonstrated reliable differences in visual pursuit behavior among neonates. Infants also differ significantly in the frequency and durations of periods of spontaneous alertness (Korner, 1970) and in alerting behavior in response to maternal types of ministrations (Korner & Thoman, 1970). In the tactile–cutaneous modality, Bell, Weller, and Waldrop (1971) found highly self-consistent thresholds in newborns. There are also reliable differences in the infants' readiness to respond to auditory stimuli. In addition, those infants who readily respond to auditory stimuli also tend to be the infants who engage in a great deal of visual activity. Thus, infants tend to have high or low thresholds across sensory modalities (Birns, 1965; Korner, 1970).

In the area of activity, highly significant differences have been found in the frequency of motions (Campbell, 1968; Korner, Chuck & Dontchos, 1968) and in the types of motions infants rely upon (Korner et al., 1968). In the oral behaviors, newborns differ significantly from each other in the frequency of spontaneous mouthing and sucking (Balint, 1948; Bell et al., 1971; Hendry & Kessen, 1964; Korner et al., 1968) and in the frequency, skill, and persistence of hand–mouth coordinations (Korner & Kraemer, 1972). Significant individual differences have also been found in the irritability and soothability of newborns (Birns, Blank, & Bridger, 1966; Korner & Thoman, 1972). Also, in the area of autonomic reactivity, significant individual variations have been identified shortly after birth in heartrate (i.e., Richmond & Lustman, 1955; Grossman & Greenberg, 1957) and respiration rates (i.e., Bell et al., 1971).

As outlined in a previous paper (Korner, 1971), these differences at birth among babies may have both short-range and long-range implications for the beginning mother–infant relationship, the manner in which the infant will experience the earliest weeks of life, and for the vulnerabilities and strengths in his later development. Specifically, low sensory thresholds have been implicated as an etiological factor of colic (Benjamin, 1961; Carey, 1968) and in the development of a rich fantasy life (Escalona & Heider, 1959). Extremes in irritability and unsoothability among infants have been found to have devastating effects on the mother–infant relationship and to predict atypical development in some cases (Brazelton, 1962; Prechtl, 1963). Individual differences in autonomic reactivity in newborns have been studied in the hope of identifying the physiological antecedents to differing styles of affect management as well as the precursors of psychosomatic disease. Innate activity level has been centrally implicated as a determinant of infantile reaction to deprivation (Schaffer, 1966) and of the extent of contact seeking and the intensity of the infant's attachment behavior (Schaffer & Emerson, 1964). It is probably the integration and balance between the sensory threshold levels and the levels of activation and the resultant effects on personal tempo and on approach toward, and withdrawal from stimulation which have the greatest impact on both cognitive and affective development. This is strongly suggested by the findings of longitudinal studies, such as the Berkeley Guidance Study (Honzig, 1964), the studies by Thomas, Chess, Birch, Hertzig, and Korn (1963) and by Meili-Dworetzki (1959).

THE IMPLICATIONS OF THE NEWBORN'S CAPABILITIES FOR EARLY STIMULATION AND INFANT CARE

The recent discoveries of the extent and the variety of the newborn's capabilities leave little doubt that the very young infant is able to avail himself of and respond to a great many more forms of stimulation than had been suspected. Researchers and educators draw a wide range of differing conclusions from this evidence. Particularly the evidence that the infant can change his behavior as a function of contingent reinforcement has led to a lot of interest and enthusiasm regarding the infant's potential learning capacity. Personally, I feel that there is a great deal of fundamental interest in the discovery that the human brain is capable of functioning to the degree that it does at such an early stage of development. In addition to this intrinsic research interest, these findings also have an applied interest, in that they tell us that what we do with very young infants and what we expose them to may have a far greater impact on them than we have assumed. What these findings *do not imply,* to me at least, is that we should embark on programs of early stimulation to foster early learning. Yet all too frequently this is what these findings seem to imply to certain activists in the profession and to eager parents reading about these discoveries. My reticence to go along with this stems from several considerations: for one, I fail to see the advantage in the long-range scheme of achieving developmental spurts a few days before they would occur spontaneously. Also, from much of the evidence it is very doubtful that acceleration of development thus produced is maintained for any length of time. Furthermore, we know too little about the natural sequence of developmental changes to intervene in a functionally appropriate way; at the same time, we know enough from clinical experience that disordered developmental sequences can lead to serious consequences. For all these reasons, it seems safer and wiser to consolidate what the infant spontaneously is capable of doing rather than to push for acceleration of his development.

To be effective in this consolidation, we need to delineate the range and limits of appropriate forms of stimulation for any given stage of infant neurophysiological development. We also need to define the state of the infant during which such stimulation will be most effective (Escalona, 1962; Korner, 1972). A good deal of research is currently in progress which attempts to find the most relevant stimulus configurations both with respect to the sensory modalities and the formal quality of the stimulus presentation to which the young infant is most responsive. Thus we have learned that newborns respond more to speech sounds than to pure tones (Eisenberg, 1965); that a moving stimulus evokes more visual attention than a stationary one; that newborns are soothed more easily and become alert more readily with vestibular-proprioceptive stimulation than through body contact (Korner & Thoman, 1970, 1972). With respect to the formal quality of stimulation, we have begun to learn that the infant's responsiveness varies with the novelty, variety, and complexity of the stimuli. As infants get just a few weeks older, they respond more to the novel and complex stimuli than to familiar and simple ones. By the age of five months, variety of stimulation appears to be especially important for development (Yarrow, Rubenstein, & Pederson, 1971). By that age, too, the infant, if he is to progress and acquire a sense of effectance and competence, must experience that his actions have a predictable result both in the inanimate environment and in relation to his caretaker (White, 1959; Watson, 1966). While predictability of cause and effect is an absolutely essential ingredient for the infant's learning and growing sense of mastery, a degree of unpredictability also furthers his development. The growing infant is challenged to greater flexibility and adaptation when the stimulating object has a life of its own. There are interesting findings in the non-human primate literature which supports this contention. Mason (1968) provided swinging surrogate "mothers" to infant monkeys. In addition to getting the benefits of vestibular-proprioceptive stimulation the infant monkey, by jumping on the surrogate mother, predictably caused it to swing, but in unpredictable directions. By providing these swinging surrogate "mothers," Mason (1968) was able to offset the most severe developmental deficits typically shown by Harlow's (1958) infant monkeys reared on stationary "mother" surrogates.

One of the most fascinating aspects of the literature regarding the relative efficacy of various forms of stimulation for young infants is the fact that, one by one, the forms of stimulation to which the infants are most responsive are those which an adequate and sensitive mother inadvertently provides in the course of infant care. To illustrate, in talking to her baby, the mother makes the very speech sounds the infant is so responsive to. In her caretaking activities, she not only represents a continuously moving visual stimulus to him, but she also, by picking him up and moving him around, provides him with a good deal of vestibular-proprioceptive stimulation. She certainly is a complex stimulus, and one of infinite variety, and while she hopefully is predictable in response to the infant's signals, which should teach him that his actions have an effect on his environment, she also has a life of her own which constitutes a source of unpredictability for him. The researchers thus have unwittingly found through their non-naturalistic experiments, at least some of the stimulus components which are inherent in the mother and her care. This contribution is not as trivial as it sounds inasmuch as until now, we have known only in the most global terms, what stimulus components are involved in maternal care. In evolutionary terms, these research findings make good sense: it is not surprising that the infant is most tuned to those stimuli emanating from the very person on whose care his survival is most dependent. In practical terms, what the research findings add up to, for me at least, is that adequate maternal care during the first few months is a rich and sufficient source of sensory stimulation and perceptual experiences for the average infant. In these early months, the mother thus can rightfully be viewed as the primary source of both affective and cognitive stimulation for the infant.

But what about those conditions where there is a deficit of maternal care, either due to unavoidable circumstances or due to neglect? Perhaps a concerted effort at extra stimulation in these instances is more justified in that such stimulation is not intended to accelerate development but may be *compensating* for the specific ingredients in the infant's experience which he may otherwise be missing. The premature infant, for example, has missed the kind of stimulation prevalent *in utero* in the last few weeks of gestation which includes containment and the vestibular-proprioceptive stimulation inherent in floating in the amniotic fluid. Replacing this natural environment is a highly artificial one, the incubator, which provides no containment, no motion, but a bombardment of considerable unpatterned noise originating from the equipment and monotonous bright lights. We know from research with full-term infants that a monotonous environment of sound and light lowers the infant's arousal state. Perhaps, if the premature responds to monotonous stimulation in the same way, lowering his level of arousal may conserve

his energy. But he may also need some patterned stimulation, particularly the kind he would have received *in utero.* A recent study by Neal (1970) bears this out very nicely. Infants ranging from 28 to 32 weeks gestational age were provided complex vestibular stimulation in a small cot inside the incubator for 30 minutes three times a day. Their development was compared with a group of matched controls. The experimental subjects achieved significantly greater motor, visual and auditory development, and they weighed more than the control group at the end of the study. Fairly similar results were achieved when patterned sound in the form of a tape recording of the mother's voice was played in the incubator six times a day (Katz, 1970).

Much has been written about the deprivations of both the institutional infant and the ghetto child. From published research it seems clear that the deprivations in these two situations are quite different in kind. The institutional infant is not only deprived of a specific mother, who is available on demand and who responds predictably to the individual infant's signals, but he also frequently lives in a drab and monotonous environment depriving him of inanimate sensory stimulation as well. Much could be done to compensate for his deprivation by increasing the usually low caretaker–child ratio, by providing the stimulation emanating from the company of other babies, and by enriching his sensory environment through age-appropriate, movable toys, mobiles and other colorful things.

The ghetto infant, by contrast, is probably not sensorially deprived. If anything, the crowded conditions in which he lives provide an overload of stimulation. In his case, when there is a deficit, it may be a function of the chaotic conditions in which he lives which make it difficult for him to learn cause and effect relationships, to anticipate and to predict. Very early in life, the ghetto child may learn that his actions have little if any effect on his environment with a resultant sense of ineffectance, apathy, and lack of motivation. To offset his deficit, aside from eradicating the economic reasons for his ghetto existence and overcrowded housing, specific help to the mother and, at least part-time day care can be highly effective. Obviously, the day care should not be custodial in nature, but should be geared to compensating for the very types of experiences which are apt to be missing in his home environment. The ratio of infant to caretaker should be high so that the baby has an opportunity to relate to a few specific adults who can become tuned to his individual reactions and whose responses he could learn to anticipate. To counteract the confusion of ghetto conditions, it may be more important to provide sensory experiences during day care that are calming and binding rather than rousing in effect. Thus, a predictable routine which is important for any young infant, may be an even more important experience for the ghetto child who is more apt to live under chaotic conditions. Day care, in addition to compensating for specific experiences the infant might otherwise be lacking to some degree, provides a reprieve to an all too frequently harassed mother.

In addition to part-time day care, much can be accomplished by giving specific help to the mother. A number of interesting programs have been initiated which aim at awakening the mother's interest in providing age-appropriate stimulation for her infant (Gordon, 1969; Weichart & Lambie, 1969; Wittenberg, 1971). This is done through weekly or monthly visits to the home by trained paraprofessionals or professionals. One of the most important ingredients of such a program is to convey to the mother that her task is of tremendous worth and importance. By focussing on the child's behavior and expressing delight with his activities and reactions, the visitor provides a model of identification for the mother, fosters the mother's bond to her child, and increases her interest and capacity to observe her infant and her sensitivity to his needs.

In cases of deficit of maternal care one of the best ways of improving infant care may be by providing "mother care." Both socio-economic and psychological deprivation past or present may so deplete a mother's energies that she is quite incapable of giving to her child. By giving to the mother through interest and commitment or through material ways, she may become more capable of giving to her child. Empathy with the difficulty of her task rather than pointing up her mistakes may lead to renewed efforts on her part. Rather than evoking guilt in her for wishing to get away at times from the burdens of child care, this should be facilitated through moral support, partial day care, or other means. With a little bit of leisure and the opportunity to pursue an interest of her own, the mother is apt to replenish her drained energies and to return to the care of her child with renewed interest. Judging from recent research findings it is apparently not the quantity but the quality of mother-infant interaction which is most critical for the child's development (White, 1971). By supporting the mother in her need and effort to give to herself, we may be most instrumental in her giving to her child.

THE IMPLICATIONS OF INDIVIDUAL DIFFERENCES AMONG NEWBORNS FOR CHILD CARE

Most of the above discussion applies to the care of the "average expectable" infant.

The care of infants with special sensitivities and exceptional strength in their reactions may pose some additional problems. Unless a special effort is made to accommodate to these variations in endowment, the development of these infants may be much more vulnerable than that of the average child.

Researchers are just beginning to delineate the optimal levels of variety, complexity, intensity, and novelty of stimulation to which the average infant is most responsive at any given age. Very little is known regarding the optimal levels of stimulation for infants at the extremes of the continuum with respect to any given trait. Certainly, the optimal level of variety, complexity, intensity, and novelty of stimulation must vary greatly depending on whether an infant is overly sensitive and subject to being flooded by excitation, or whether he is extremely placid and difficult to rouse. The overly sensitive baby may function better at reduced levels of intensity, novelty, and complexity of stimulation. His needs for sameness, predictability, and routine may far exceed that of the average baby. Also, the range of his optimal functioning may be far narrower than that of the average infant.

Before birth, the maternal organism symbiotically regulates most of the infant's functions. After birth, the infant's first task is to function independently of his mother's body. Depending on his maturity, his birth history, and his basic endowment, he is more or less equipped to function independently. The mother's first interactions with her baby and her ministrations are largely serving to regulate his level of arousal. As Thoman (1972) put it: "The function of the mother–infant relationship . . . is to provide conditions which facilitate the infant's organization until it reaches the point of being an autonomous separate system." It is the mother's function in the first few weeks of life to aid in regulating the infant's sensory input and his motor responses. In a sense, she acts like a shield or like an external stimulus barrier. While this is important for the development of all babies, it is absolutely crucial for the development of those infants who have unusually low sensory thresholds. To fail to do so, may result in early colic (Benjamin, 1961; Carey, 1968) or a premature perception of separateness from the mother which may lead to severe pathology (Rubinfine, 1962; Korner & Osvig, 1966).

While care of a neonate always requires a good deal of adaptability on the mother's part, the demands on maternal flexibility are far greater in the case of an infant with unusual sensitivities. The maternal ministrations and interventions need to be delicately tuned to the infant's state at any given moment. Too often, unfortunately, maternal actions are dictated by factors external to the infant's needs such as maternal convictions regarding "good" child care practices or psychological needs within the mother. Frequently, these maternal factors cause a mismatch between mother and child. For example, a mother's intrusiveness in stimulating her infant stemming from a conviction that stimulation is good for babies may severely hamper an excitable baby's success in achieving any kind of homeostasis. A mother's fear of "spoiling" her infant may make her refrain from soothing efforts which her infant may sorely need. Or a mother, who in terms of her own psychological or symbiotic needs, may wish for a cuddly newborn to whom she can give a lot of contact comfort, may get off to a wrong start if she happens to have an active, uncuddly baby who resists physical restraint (Schaffer & Emerson, 1964).

Thus, individual differences among neonates should dictate just how much any given infant may benefit at any given moment from stimulating or rousing interventions or from ministrations which tend to inhibit or bind his excitation. Such differences in newborns should influence both the frequency and the kind of maternal interventions. Quite obviously, highly irritable infants will require more frequent soothing than placid babies. Infants who are difficult to soothe, will require not only more prolonged soothing efforts but also different methods of soothing. While some forms of soothing appear to be more effective than others for most babies (Korner & Thoman, 1972), certain ones are more consistently effective for some infants (Bridger & Birns, 1963). Infants who spontaneously engage in a great deal of oral activity and who, at the same time, do not have much skill in hand-mouth coordination (Korner *et al.*, 1968; Korner & Kraemer, 1972), may need the calming effect of a pacifier, while such a device may be entirely irrelevant in the care of an orally inactive baby. To facilitate the earliest forms of learning through visual prehension, the infrequently alert infant who rarely engages in spontaneous visual behavior, will need visual experiences more frequently than the baby who provides visual experiences for himself. As we have shown in our research (Korner & Grobstein, 1966; Korner & Thoman, 1970), one of the best ways this can be accomplished during the neonatal period is by picking the infant up for soothing. When a crying infant is put to the shoulder, he not only usually stops crying, but he also becomes bright-eyed and he scans his mother's face and other aspects of the environment.

Another good example of how innate differences may influence what is most beneficial in bringing forth optimal functioning in different infants, is Escalona's (1963) description of two markedly active

and two markedly inactive 28-week-old infants. Escalona (1963) found among other differences, that the inactive babies required a great deal of maternal stimulation to maintain active involvement with things and people and to bring forth their most mature behavior. By contrast, the markedly active infants required no such prodding; in fact, very strong stimulation tended to diminish the optimal level of functioning of these children, leading to less complex and less mature behaviors.

The study of individual differences in young infants, and especially the detection of extremes in reaction patterns is a most important aspect of preventive pediatric work. In addition to detecting potential vulnerabilities, studies of assessment of individual differences may eventually also lead to the detection of special strengths. We know next to nothing about this aspect of individual variation except that we can infer that such strength must exist judging from the fact that some individuals develop relatively normally in spite of the most adverse conditions. There is very little doubt from the psychiatric literature on depression, delinquency, and anti-social behavior that a high proportion of individuals affected have backgrounds reflecting either socio-economic deprivation, prolonged institutionalization, repeated or prolonged separations from parents, or parental loss. Yet, were one to take from a non-psychiatric population individuals with the same kinds of childhood experiences, one would probably not find a disproportionately high number of psychopaths or patients with severe depression in this group. At least reviews of the available research on this issue seem to be reasonably reassuring to that effect (Garmezy & Nuechterlein, 1972; Korner, 1968; Rutter, 1971). As is always the case, we seem to know much more about the individuals who "did not make it" and who come to the attention of the law or of psychiatry and from whom we can make reasonably good *postdictions,* than those individuals who "do make it" and for whom we would have to make *predictions.* Judging from the evidence from some prospective studies, we consistently underestimate the resilience and plasticity of the human organism in dealing with and in some instances in overcoming the effects of even the most traumatic childhood experiences. This undoubtedly is true because we know so little about how to identify those ingredients which make for this resilience.

In infants, we have a few inklings about those ingredients which predispose to difficulties. Thus, Thomas *et al.* (1963) demonstrated that children who were irregular in their sleeping and eating habits, who adapted slowly to novel situations, who reacted intensely to many situations, and whose mood was negative most of the time, were most likely to develop behavioral deviations. Schaffer (1966) showed that inactive infants were more likely to be adversely affected by the stress of a hospitalization experience than active infants. Bergman and Escalona (1949) demonstrated that young children with childhood psychosis frequently had a history of unusual sensory sensitivity. There are thus ingredients in the infant's make-up which are apt to make his development more vulnerable. The mechanisms by which this vulnerability actually becomes a developmental deviation, of course, are not clear. Quite likely, central nervous system differences yet to be delineated will account for differences in withstanding stress and in the subjective feeling as to what constitutes a stress. Such differences may thus explain why identical experiences are experienced differently by different individuals. What may of course also be involved, is that vulnerable infants are more difficult to raise, which may set

in motion, from the start, a less than optimal mother–infant interaction. Undoubtedly, this difficulty between parent and child, will, in turn, feed into the infant's vulnerability.

While we know some of the ingredients which predispose to developmental difficulties, does this imply that the oppositive characteristics embody those ingredients which make for unusual resilience to adversity? This is probably *not* the case. All we know is that less sensitive and intense and more active, more predictable infants are less apt to develop difficulties. To identify those ingredients which represent special strengths will require large-scale prospective studies which start out with an early and thorough evaluation of the subjects' autonomic and behavioral reaction patterns. One such study currently under way, could potentially give us some clues regarding those coping strategies and their underlying neurophysiological mechanisms which may make for a special kind of resilience. Mednick (1970), in a prospective, longitudinal study spanning over 20 years, has thoroughly evaluated 207 Danish children whose mothers are severe, chronic schizophrenics. According to psychiatric genetics, some 10 to 15% of these children could be expected to be hospitalized for schizophrenia and many more for other psychiatric disorders. In the cases who did break down, it was possible to look at the early evaluation to determine how those who became schizophrenic differed from those who did not. Mednick (1970) also studied a control group of low-risk children for schizophrenia. They were matched for sex, age, socio-economic class, education, and number of years in institutions. Mednick already has identified several factors which heavily contributed to the likelihood of psychiatric breakdown. They are mostly psychophysiological differences involving short latencies, an inability to habituate, and unusually fast recovery from the effects of stimulation. One other very important factor was that those high-risk children who were born with pregnancy and birth complications leading to anoxia were much more apt to break down than those who had no perinatal complications. Mednick's (1970) data thus has pointed to special sources of vulnerability in the high-risk group. In addition to the absence of these special vulnerabilities, it is reasonable to assume that Mednick's data would also contain clues of some of the *positive* factors within his subjects which would mitigate against breakdown. Such factors should exist not only in his high risk group but also in his control group which contains a good number of children who spent many years in institutions. Perhaps eventually, it will be possible to single out those children with unusually good coping strategies and look back at the early assessments to determine how these children differed from those who either broke down or made less adequate adjustments.

Once identified, it should be possible to develop methods which would foster and strengthen those adaptive mechanisms which underlies an unusual capacity to withstand stress.

REFERENCES

Balint, M. Individual differences of behavior in early infancy and an objective way of recording them. *Journal Genetic Psychology,* 1973, **73,** 57-117.

Barten, S.; Birns, B.; & Ronch, J. Individual differences in the visual pursuit behavior of neonates. *Child Development,* 1971, **42,** 313-319.

Bell, R.; Weller, G. M.; & Waldrop, M. E. Newborn and preschooler: organization of behavior and relations between periods. *Monograph of Society for Research in Child Development,* 1971, **36,** (1-2), Serial Number 142.

Benjamin, J. The innate and the experiential in development. In H. Brosin (ed.) *Lectures on experimental psychiatry.* Pittsburgh: University of Pittsburgh, 1961.

Bergman, P., & Escalona, S. K. Unusual sensitivities in very young children. In P. Greenacre *et al.* (eds.) *The psychoanalytic study of the child: 3/4.* New York: International Universities Press, Inc., 1949.

Birns, B. Individual differences in human neonates' responses to stimulation. *Child Development,* 1965, **36,** 249-256.

Birns, B.; Blank, M.; & Bridger, W. H. The effectiveness of various soothing techniques on human neonates. *Psychosomatic Medicine,* 1966, **28,** 316-322.

Bower, T. G. R. The object in the world of the infant. *Scientific American,* 1971, **225,** 30-38.

Brackbill, Y. Research and clinical work with children. In R. Bauer (ed.) *Some views of Soviet psychology.* Washington, D.C.: American Psychological Association, 1962.

Brazelton, T. B. Observations of the neonate. *Journal of the American Academy of Child Psychiatry,* 1962, **1,** 38-58.

Brazelton, T. B. Personal communication, October 19, 1970.

Bridger, W. H., & Birns, B. Neonates' behavioral and autonomic responses to stress during soothing. *Recent Advances in Biological Psychiatry,* 1963, **5,** 1-6.

Bridger, W. H.; Birns, B. M.; & Blank, M. A comparison of behavioral ratings and heart rate measurements in human neonates. *Psychosomatic Medicine,* 1965, **27,** 123-133.

Butterfield, E. C., & Siperstein, G. N. Influence of contingent auditory stimulation upon non-nutritional suckle. In J. F. Bosma (ed.) *Third symposium on oral sensation and perception: The mouth of the infant.* Springfield, Ill.: Charles C Thomas, 1972.

Campbell, D. Motor activity in a group of newborn babies. *Biology of Neonates,* 1968, **13,** 257-270.

Carey, W. B. Maternal anxiety and infantile colic: is there a relationship? *Clinical Pediatrics,* 1968, **7,** 590-595.

Eimas, P. D.; Siqueland, E. R.; Jusczyk, P.; & Vigorito, J. Speech perception in infants. *Science,* 1971, **171,** 303-306.

Eisenberg, R. B. Auditory behavior in the human neonate: I. Methodological problems and the logical design of research procedures. *Journal Auditory Research,* 1965, **5,** 159-177.

Escalona, S. K. The study of individual differences and the problem of state. *Journal of the American Academy of Child Psychiatry,* 1962, **1,** 11-37.

Escalona, S. K. Patterns of infantile experience and the developmental process. In R. S. Eissler *et al.* (eds.) *The psychoanalytic study of the child,* Volume 18. New York: International Universities Press, 1963.

Escalona, S. K., & Heider, G. M. *Prediction and Outcome.* New York: Basic Books, 1959.

Fantz, R. L. Pattern vision in newborn infants. *Science,* 1963, **140,** 296-297.

Garmezy, N., & Nuechterlein, K. Invulnerable children: fact and fiction of competence and disadvantage. Paper presented at the 49th Annual Meeting of the American Orthopsychiatric Association, Detroit, 1972.

Gordon, I. J. Early child stimulation through parent education. Final report to the Children's Bureau, Social and Rehabilitation Services, Department of Health, Education and Welfare, PHS-R-306, 1969.

Grossman, H. J., & Greenberg, N. H. Psychosomatic differentiation in infancy: I. Autonomic activity in the newborn. *Psychosomatic Medicine,* 1957, **19,** 293-306.

Harlow, H. F. The nature of love. *American Psychologist,* 1958, **13,** 673-685.

Hendry, L. S., & Kessen, W. Oral behavior of newborn infants as a function of age and time since feeding. *Child Development,* 1964, **35,** 201-208.

Hershenson, M.; Munsinger, H.; & Kessen, W. Preference for shapes of intermediate variability in the newborn human. *Science,* 1965, **147,** 630-631.

Honzig, M. P. Personality consistency and change: some comments on papers by Bayley, Macfarlane, Moss & Kagan, and Murphy. *Vita Humana,* 1964, **7,** 139-142.

Katz, V. *The relationship between auditory stimulation and the developmental behavior of the premature infant.* Doctoral dissertation, New York University, 1970; Ann Arbor, Mich.: University Microfilms.

Korner, A. F. Discussion of John Bowlby's paper on separation and loss. Symposium of the San Francisco Psychoanalytic Society, 1968.

Korner, A. F. Visual alertness in neonates: individual differences and their correlates. *Perceptual and Motor Skills,* 1970, **31,** 499-509.

Korner, A. F. Individual differences at birth: implications for early experience and later development. *American Journal of Orthopsychiatry,* 1971, **41,** 608-619.

Korner, A. F. State as variable, as obstacle, and as mediator of stimulation in infant research. *Merril-Palmer Quarterly of Behavior and Development,* 1972, **18,** 77-94.

Korner, A. F., & Beason, L. M. The association of two congenitally organized behavior patterns in the newborn: hand-mouth coordination and looking. *Perceptual and Motor Skills,* 1972, **35,** 115-118.

Korner, A. F.; Chuck, B.; & Dontchos, S. Organismic determinants of spontaneous oral behavior in neonates. *Child Development,* 1968, **39,** 1145-1157.

Korner, A. F., & Grobstein, R. Visual alertness as related to soothing in neonates: implications for maternal stimulation and early deprivation. *Child Development,* 1966, **37,** 867-876.

Korner, A. F., & Kraemer, H. C. Individual differences in spontaneous oral behavior. In J. F. Bosma (ed.) *Third symposium on oral sensation and perception: The mouth of the infant.* Springfield, Ill.: Charles C Thomas, 1972.

Korner, A. F., & Opsvig, P. Developmental considerations in diagnosis and treatment. *Journal of the American Academy of Child Psychiatry,* 1966, **5,** 594-616.

Korner, A. F., & Thoman, E. Visual alertness in neonates as evoked by maternal care. *Journal of Experimental Child Psychology,* 1970, **12,** 67-78.

Korner, A. F., & Thoman, E. B. The relative efficacy of contact and vestibular-proprioceptive stimulation in soothing neonates. *Child Development,* 1972, **43,** 443-453.

Kron, R. E. Instrumental conditioning of nutritive sucking behavior in the newborn. In J. Wortis (ed.) *Recent advances in biological psychiatry,* 1967, **9,** 295-300.

Lipsitt, L. P. Learning processes of human newborns. *Merrill-Palmer Quarterly of Behavior and Development,* 1966, **12,** 45-71.

Mason, W. A. Early social deprivation in the non-human primates: implications for human behavior. In D. C. Glass (ed.) *Environmental influences.* New York: The Rockefeller University Press, Russell Sage Foundation, 1968.

Mednick, S. A. Breakdown in individuals at high risk for schizophrenia: possible predispositional perinatal factors. *Mental Hygiene,* 1970, **54,** 50-63.

Meili-Dworetzki, G. Lust und Angst. Regulative Momente in der Persönlichkeitsentwicklung zweier Brüder. *Beiträge zur Genetischen Charakterologie,* Number 3. Bern: Hans Huber, 1959.

Neal, M. V. *The relationship between a regimen of vestibular stimulation and the developmental behavior of the premature infant.* Doctoral dissertation, New York University, 1967; Ann Arbor, Mich.: University Microfilms.

Prechtl, H. F. R. The mother-child interaction in babies with minimal brain damage. In B. M. Foss (ed.) *Determinants of infant behavior,* II. London: Methuen, 1963.

Richmond, J. B., & Lustman, S. L. Autonomic function in the neonate: implications for psychosomatic theory. *Psychosomatic Medicine,* 1955, **17,** 269-276.

Rubinfine, D. L. Maternal stimulation: psychic structure and early object relations. *The Psychoanalytic Study of the Child,* 1962, **17,** 265-282.

Rutter, M. Parent-child separation: psychological effects on the children. *Journal of Child Psychology and Psychiatry,* 1971, **12,** 233-260.

Sameroff, A. J. Can conditioned responses be established in the newborn infant: 1971? *Developmental Psychology,* 1971, **5,** 1-12.

Schaffer, H. R. Activity level as a constitutional determinant of infantile reaction to deprivation. *Child Development,* 1966, **37,** 595-602.

Schaffer, H. R. & Emerson, P. E. Patterns of response to physical contact in early human development. *Journal of Child Psychology and Psychiatry,* 1964, **5,** 1-13.

Siqueland, E. R. The developmental exploratory behavior during the first year of human life. Paper presented at the meeting of the Society for Research in Child Development, Santa Monica, California, 1969.

Siqueland, E. R., & DeLucia, C. A. Visual reinforcement of non-nutritive sucking in human infants. *Science,* 1969, **165,** 1144-1146.

Siqueland, E. R., & Lipsitt, L. P. Conditioned head-turning in human newborns. *Journal of Experimental Child Psychology,* 1966, **3,** 356-376.

Steinschneider, A. Sound intensity and respiratory responses in the neonate. *Psychosomatic Medicine,* 1968, **30,** 534-535.

Thoman, E. B. Some consequences of early infant-mother-infant interaction. Submitted for publication, 1972.

Thomas, A.; Chess, S.; Birch, H. G.; Hertzig, M. E.; & Korn, S. *Behavioral individuality in early childhood.* New York: New York Universities Press, 1963.

Watson, J. S. The development and generalization of "contingency awareness" in early infancy: some hypotheses. *Merrill-Palmer Quarterly of Behavior and Development,* 1966, **12,** 123-135.

Weichart, D. P., & Lambie, D. Z. Early enrichment in infants. Paper presented at the meeting of the American Association for the Advancement of Science, Boston, 1969.

White, B. L. *Human infants' experience and psychological development.* Englewood Cliffs, N.J.: Prentice-Hall, 1971.

White, R. W. Motivation reconsidered: the concept of competence. *Psychological Review,* 1959, **66,** 297-333.

Wittenberg, C. Infant stimulation as part of well baby care in a disadvantaged area. In J. Segal (ed.) Mental Health Program Reports-5, Department of Health, Education and Welfare Publication Number (HSM) 72-9042, 1971, 257-271.

Wolff, P. H. Observations of newborn infants. *Psychosomatic Medicine,* 1959, **21,** 110-118.

Wolff, P. H. The causes, controls and organization of behavior in the neonate. *Psychological Issues,* 1966, **5,** Monograph 17.

Wolff, P. H., & White, B. L. Visual pursuit

and attention in young infants. *Journal of the American Academy of Child Psychiatry,* 1965, **4,** 473-484.

Yarrow, L. J.; Rubenstein, J. L.; & Pedersen, F. A. Dimensions of early stimulation: dif-ferential effects on infant development. Paper presented at the meeting of the Society for Research in Child Development, Minneapolis, 1971.

3.

Jean V. Carew, Itty Chan, and Christine Halfar

OBSERVED INTELLECTUAL COMPETENCE AND TESTED INTELLIGENCE: THEIR ROOTS IN THE YOUNG CHILD'S TRANSACTIONS WITH HIS ENVIRONMENT

Twenty-five years ago Robert White (1959) drew attention to a class of behaviors which he felt were of profound biological significance because they formed "part of a process by which the animal or child learns to interact effectively with his environment." White chose the word "competence" to describe this learned ability to conduct effective transactions with the environment and described competent behaviors as those having an exploratory, experimental character, that are executed with considerable persistence and selective attention to parts of the environment that provide interesting feedback, and that are organized to produce effects on these parts. White deliberately excluded from this class of competent behaviors reflexes and other kinds of automatic responses, well learned patterns including complex and highly organized

ones, behaviors in the service of strongly aroused drives, and random or discontinuous activity. These were not "competent" behaviors in the sense meant by White. Their automatic, routine, or unstructured character made it unlikely that the subject was *learning* how to deal effectively with his environment.

The aim of the present study was to describe the young child's development of intellectual competence in terms similar to those advanced by White. Its general purpose was to delineate in detail the everyday transactions with the environment of a group of children observed longitudinally in their own homes and neighborhoods from age one to three. The observed experiences of these children were categorized in terms of a system which (1) distinguished experiences considered to be "intellectually valuable" from other types of experiences, (2) distinguished the child's own "competent" behaviors and various environmental inputs as "sources" of intellectually valuable experiences, and (3) distinguished between situations in which the child was relating to his human environment and

Source: Paper presented at the Annual Meeting of the Eastern Psychological Association, New York City, 1975, and at the Biennial Meeting of the Society for Research in Child Development, Denver, Colorado, 1975.

those in which he was involved solely with his non-human environment. These data permitted us to trace the relationships of intellectually valuable experiences occurring in different situations or coming from different sources to two measures of intellectual competence, namely, the child's spontaneous, intelligent or "competent" behavior and his tested intelligence. Insofar as one may infer probable causes and effects from correlation data, this research is designed to tell us: (1) what types of experiences are intellectually valuable to the young child, (2) whether and when it is important that he construct such experiences for himself as opposed to receiving them from his environment, and (3) whether and when it is important that he encounter such experiences in contexts in which he relates to the human as contrasted to the non-human environment.

METHODS

Data collection

The sample consisted of twenty-three white children from a variety of social class and ethnic backgrounds who were observed repeatedly in their own homes and neighborhoods between age one and three.[1] Each child was observed for about one hour on three to five separate occasions during each of four periods: age 12 to 15 months, 18 to 21 months, 24 to 27 months, and 30 to 33 months. The observer began her visits to the home by reminding the mother to follow her normal routine and to let the child do the same. In making an observation the observer used special

---

[1]Fifteen *S*s in this sample were included in a study described in White, Watts *et al.* (1973) in which the present authors analyzed only the child's interactive experiences with people. Their data were recoded for this study in terms of the HOME Scale which was applied to all of the child's experiences, not just his interactions with people.

coding sheets and a stop watch. She observed the child's activities for fifteen seconds, wrote down what she saw during the next fifteen seconds, and continued in this alternating fashion for ten minutes at a time. On a typical visit she completed four ten-minute observations, which were then coded in terms of a system called the HOME Scale (Watts, Barnett, & Halfar, 1972).

Observation instrument

The principal dimension of the HOME Scale is the *quality of the child's experience.* This dimension encoded the observer's judgment of the relevance and value of the child's experience for his development of intellectual competence, and to a lesser extent, for his social development. The content or topic of the child's experience was the major criterion used in making this judgment. Four types of experiences were judged to be intellectually valuable because they seemed to provide the child with clear opportunities to learn basic skills and content in four important domains: verbal/symbolic, spatial/fine motor, concrete reasoning, and expressive/artistic (see Table 1 for examples). The source of these intellectually valuable experiences might be the child's own active "competent" behavior or an environmental input to which he was attentive.

In the first type of experiences—experiences relevant to verbal and symbolic learning and the acquisition of novel, nonroutine information—the child's own behavior or the environmental input provided evidence that the child was learning to recognize, understand or use labels, grammatical forms, basic symbols such as letters and numbers, and two-dimensional representations of objects and events as in picture books. Typically, the child was engaged in labeling objects, counting,

TABLE 3.1. Categories of Experience in the HOME Scale

Experience	*Focus*	*Example*
1. Intellectually Valuable Experiences		
Verbal-symbolic learning	Acquisition of verbal skills.	Mother reads words "school bus" on the toy bus. *S* repeats "school bus".
Spatial-fine motor learning	Differentiation in perception or motor coordination.	*S*. fits toy figures in holes in the bus and turns them all to face the front.
Concrete reasoning	Concept formation or investigation of physical laws.	*S* makes an incline with a sofa cushion and lets the bus roll down from the top several times. Mother comments: "It goes all by itself on a hill, doesn't it?"
Expressive	Expression of imagination or creation of representational products.	*S* creates dialogue for imaginary children on the school bus.
2. Intellectually Less Valuable Experiences		
Play	Investigation and undifferentiated use of toys, household objects, or naturally occurring materials.	*S* scoops some dirt into the back of a toy truck and pushes the truck along the ground.
Play-work involving executive skills	Carrying out of patterned sequences.	*S* and mother put toys away in the playroom, placing some on shelves and some in the toy box.
Conversation	Gaining routine information.	*S* listens to mother talking on the telephone. Mother tells him: "Grandma's coming to see us."
Gross motor learning	Acquisition of gross motor skills.	*S* climbs up and down the stairs.
Basic care	Satisfaction of physical needs.	Mother diapers and dresses *S* after his lunch.
3. Socio-emotional Experiences		
Positive emotion and social games	Expression of affection or pleasure. Social–physical games or playful teasing.	*S* smiles and kisses baby sibling. *S* laughs as mother bounces her on her knee.
Social contact, attention, and distress	Seeking another's attention for its own sake.	*S* smiles shyly at visitor and walks after him when he and father leave the room.
	Demanding another's attention.	*S* sees sibling showing mother a drawing. *S* shoves her own drawing in mother's face and shouts "Look at mine!"
Preparatory	*S* prepares for an activity.	*S* lines up a set of blocks (later she builds with them).
Discouraged	*S* is discouraged or restricted from undertaking an activity or is punished or scolded for doing it.	*S* plays with pots and pans. Mother scolds her for making a mess.

reciting nursery rhymes or children's songs, or "reading" books, or he was attentive to another person or a television character who was doing these things.

In the second type of intellectual experience—perceptual, spatial, and fine motor experiences—the child's own behavior or the environmental input suggested that he was learning to make perceptual discriminations such as those involved in matching, distinguishing or ordering objects by size, shape, color or position; or learning about other spatial concepts such as angles and perspectives. In this category of experience the child was typically engaged in tasks of fitting, stacking, building, modeling, tying, or matching objects, and was often using materials especially designed for such activity, such as puzzles, shape boxes, nesting cups, blocks, tinker toys, scissors, crayons, and lotto cards. Or he might simply be attentive to another person or a television character doing these things.

In the third type of intellectual experiences, those labeled "concrete reasoning," the child's own behavior or the environmental input indicated that the child was likely to be learning basic reasoning and problem-solving skills such as those involved in finding out how mechanisms work or differentiating means from end and cause from effect; or learning about physical principles such as object permanence, conservation, volume, gravity, momentum, buoyancy, trajectory, equilibrium, reflection; or learning about concepts of order, classification and relationship (other than those involved in perceptual, spatial and fine motor experiences). In this type of experience, the child was typically engaged in "scientific experiments" with objects that sailed or sank, objects that plummeted or floated gently to the ground, objects that held more or less liquid, objects that cast shadows or provided reflection, and mechanisms that worked in interesting ways. His focus seemed to be on understanding basic physical regularities and relationships through varying his own actions on appropriate objects or noticing these as they occurred. As in other types of intellectual experiences, the source of the concrete reasoning experience might also be the behavior of another person or television character whom the child observed.

In the fourth category of intellectual experiences—those related to expressive/artistic/imaginative activities—the child's own behavior or an environmental input suggested that he was likely to be learning artistic skills, or how to express himself imaginatively. Typically he was involved in make-believe with toys, or in role play, or in making representational products such as painting a monster or building a sand castle, or in expressive activities such as

playing a musical instrument or singing a melody. If he did not engage in these activities himself, then he observed another person or a television character performing them.

It must be stressed that intellectually valuable experiences did not necessarily involve "lessons" or the use of "educational" materials. On the contrary, an intellectual experience might occur in any context of activity so long as the content of the experience related to one of the four categories previously discussed. Indeed, one of the more challenging of the observer's tasks was to be alert to intellectual experiences arising in mundane unstructured contexts which no one had planned as learning experiences and in which neither instruction nor educational toys were evident.

Only a minority of experiences of one- and two-year olds were judged to be clearly intellectually valuable on the basis of the content criteria referred to above. The majority were considered to be of less clear intellectual value, their content being relevant to one of the categories listed and exemplified in the second cluster of experiences in Table 1. Of these categories the most frequently used by observers were varieties of play-exploration with toys, household objects, natural objects; routine talk; basic care activities; and gross motor activities. Beyond content, the basic process difference between these experiences and those considered to be clearly intellectually valuable concerns the more automatic, routine, unfocused, and unorganized character of the child's or other person's behavior.

Sources and situations associated with intellectual experiences

A major aim of the study was to trace the relationships between the child's observed and tested intellectual competence and intellectually valuable experiences occurring in different situations and generated by sources intrinsic and extrinsic to the child. Four everyday situations in which intellectual experiences occurred were distinguished: the child interacting with another person, the child observing another person who was not interacting with him, the child in solitary play, and the child watching television. The first two of these are situations in which the child is relating to the *human environment*,

TABLE 3.2. Criteria for Judging the Child's Behavior as Competent

Type of Child Behavior	Behavior	Examples
Competent Verbal	S expresses complex idea.	S answers M: "Apples grow on apple trees and carrots grow in the ground." S tells peer: "Jenny-penny. I made your name rhyme."
	S expresses imaginative idea.	S says about a drawing: "This is a bubble that didn't pop yet and this one did." S, carrying a handbag: "I'm going to the store to get cookies."
	S tries to master a verbal skill.	S walks along a row of alphabet posters identifying the letter and picture for each, occasionally making mistakes. S repeats "rhinoceros" after mother, concentrating on sounding each syllable.
Fine motor	S constructs a product.	S builds a block tower and a low structure nearby.
	S conducts an experiment.	S fills three small bottles with water and then pours each into a larger bottle.
	S tries to master a fine motor skill.	S puts snap clothespins around the edge of a pail, takes them all off, and then replaces them.
Gross motor	S tries to master a gross motor skill.	S hits a ball with a hockey stick from one end of the hallway to the other.
Less Competent Verbal	S makes a routine statement.	S tells mother she will slide down the slide when they get to the playground.
	S asks a question.	S asks sibling: "What's that for? What are you making?"
Fine motor	S carries out patterned sequence that is routine.	Mother asks S to empty ashtray. S promptly carries ashtray to wastebasket and returns to mother.
	S explores the qualities of an object.	S strokes, pats, and pokes at the family cat.
	S engages in routine or undifferentiated activity.	S carries a toy car across the room, then kneels and pushes it along the floor.
Passive–attentive	S listens and/or looks attentively.	S looks on as mother repairs sibling's roller skate.
Passive–Inattentive	S wanders about and/or gazes vacantly.	S stares absently across the room and picks at the edge of his blanket.
Social	S expresses affection. S expresses delight in social–physical play. S expresses dependency or seeks social contact. S demands attention.	S runs to mother and hugs her. S shrieks with laughter as she runs from sibling. S follows after mother when she leaves the room. S shouts sibling's name when sibling does not respond to S's tug on his sleeve.

whereas the last two are situations in which he is involved solely with the *non-human environment.* Two major *sources* of intellectual experiences were also compared. The first was the *child* himself when he constructed intellectual experiences through his own competent behavior. The child could be the source of his intellectual experience in any of the four situations referred to above. The second source of intellectual experiences was human and non-human *environmental* inputs to which the child was attentive. These inputs varied with the four situations.

The Child's Behavior as a Source of his Intellectual Experiences. The child's behavior was judged to be a source of his intellectual experience when three conditions were met: the child played an active role in the experience, the inferred topic of his activity was intellectual (in the sense defined in the discussion of content criteria above), and the process aspects of his behavior indicated that he was dealing effectively with the environment, that is, his behavior was "competent." The criteria for judging competent child behaviors are set out in Table 2. As in Robert White's analysis (1959) discussed in the introduction to this paper, these criteria have to do with the child's selective and directed attention to aspects of the environment that produce interesting feedback, the systematic organization of his behavior toward some end, the varying of his actions on objects as if to understand their fundamental properties, the ordering, sequencing, and classification of materials as if to grasp their similarities and differences, the expression of new, difficult or imaginative ideas, the struggle to find solutions to problems, and the mastery of verbal and motor skills.

The cluster of competent child behaviors in Table 2 is contrasted with a class of behaviors that were more routine or unstructured and were judged to involve less productive transactions with the environment. Thus, the child's behavior was considered routine rather than "competent" when he carried out a well learned pattern of sequenced steps, when he merely requested routine information, made run-of-the-mill comments, engaged in relatively simple exploration or in routine motor activity, was passively attentive to incoming information, or simply seemed to be marking time. Intellectually competent and routine/unstructured behaviors are also distinguished in Table 2 from a cluster of socio-emotional behaviors. These behaviors were only coded when the socio-emotional aspect of the child's behavior was particularly salient as when the child was clearly trying to get someone's attention, was expressing or receiving affection, or was engaged in social–physical games as in bouncing on his mother's lap or rough-housing.

The distinctions between competent, routine or less competent, and socio-emotional child behaviors are perhaps best conveyed by concrete examples in which the child uses the same basic materials—a set of small animal toys—but in quite different ways.

Competent behavior (S is source of an intellectual experience)
S moves toy animal about. *S* announces: "This is a horse, but this is a zebra because it has lines." (Verbal/symbolic content; *S* makes a verbal distinction)
S lines up toy animals in decreasing order of size. (Perceptual, spatial, fine motor content; *S* organizes materials, constructs a product)

Less competent behaviors (S is not a source of an intellectual experience)
S puts away the toy animals in her toy box. (Play work involving executive skills; *S* carries out a well learned pattern of steps)
S moves the toy animals about. *S:* "I have lots of animals." (Routine talk; *S* makes routine comment)

S plays with toy animals, shaking, squeezing, and mouthing them. (Play with toys; simple exploration)

S and friend play at tickling each other with toy animals. (Social–physical game; *S* engages in game for sheer enjoyment)

The examples given above highlight the occasions when the child's own behavior can be judged to be the primary source of his intellectually valuable experiences. However the child also encounters a great many experiences which may also be considered intellectually valuable although his own behavior is less than "competent." In these experiences another person or thing in the child's environment provides the content that warrants the judgment that the child's experience is intellectually valuable. In this study three types of environmental inputs were found to occur fairly frequently. In the interactive situation this input came from the interactor, in the people-watching situation it came from the behavior of the person whom the child observed, and in the television-watching situation it came from the television program. In the interactive situation there was also the special case of true reciprocal interaction in which both the child's and the interactor's behavior met the criteria for providing the child with an intellectual experience. In other words, if the child's behavior were considered alone, he would have been judged the source of the intellectual experience, and if the interactor's behavior were considered alone, he would have been judged to be the source. In such cases, the child and the interactor were judged to be joint sources of the child's intellectual experience.

The Interactor as a Source of the Child's Intellectual Experiences. For the interactor to be judged as the sole or joint source of the child's intellectual experiences, four conditions had to be met: the child's behavior was judged as other than compe-

tent, the content of the interactor's behavior was intellectual, the child was attentive to the interactor's behavior and the interactor used a "participatory" technique of interaction. An interactor was thought to use a participatory technique when he taught the child, entertained him, joined in an activity with him, helped him perform an activity, or talked to him about it. The common feature of participatory techniques was that the interactor *actively* took part in an experience that might be judged to be intellectually valuable or not for the child. Here are two examples of another's use of a participatory technique. In the first the mother is the sole source of the child's intellectual experience, whereas in the second she and the child are judged to be joint sources.

M labels the pictures on *S*'s pajamas, "cow", "horse", "elephant". *S* listens attentively. (*M* is source of intellectual experience; *S*'s behavior is routine; *M*'s technique is participatory)

M labels the pictures. *S* repeats "cow", "horsie", "elephant" in response. (*M* and *S* are joint sources of intellectual experience; *S*'s behavior is competent; *M*'s technique is participatory)

The Non-interactor as a Source of the Child's Intellectual Experiences. A person whom the child observed but who was not interacting with him was considered to be the source of the child's intellectual experience if three conditions were met: the child's behavior was judged as other than competent, the child was attentive to the other person's behavior, and the content of that behavior was intellectual. Here is an example of a people-watching situation in which the other person's behavior is judged to be the source of the child's intellectual experience.

S observes his big sister conducting a flotation experiment, dropping heavy and light objects into a bowl of water to see which ones will float. (Sister is source of intellectual experience)

Television as a Source of the Child's Intellectual Experiences. The behavior of a television character (or other aspects of a television sequence) was considered to be the source of the child's intellectual experience if three conditions were met: the child's behavior was judged as other than competent, the child was attentive to the program, and the content of the program was intellectual. Here is an example of television-watching in which the television program is judged to be the source of the child's intellectual experience.

Television character shows difference between circle and square, pointing to their contours. *S* listens attentively. (TV is source of intellectual experience; *S*'s behavior is routine)

Reliability of observers

Two forms of agreement were checked to establish reliability of the HOME Scale: inter-observer agreement (between two observers making simultaneous observations on the same child), and inter-coder agreement (between two coders coding the same observation made by the third observer). For the inter-observer reliability check the three observers were paired with each other and each pair simultaneously observed six *S*s for 40 minutes apiece. Inter-observer agreement for each item or cluster of items of each dimension was then checked for each unit and the total agreement calculated. In the inter-coder reliability check each pair of coders coded sixteen observations on sixteen different *S*s originally made by the third observer, four at each period. For each reliability check scores for major items summed across observations coded by one observer/coder on a given *S* were correlated with the corresponding scores of the other observer/coder, and correlations for the three pairs were averaged. Agreement between observers/coders was high. For example, the

correlation between observers' scores was .97 for intellectually valuable experiences, between .92 and .95 for each of the four situations, and between .76 and .96 for each source of intellectual experience.

Intellectual competence: tested and spontaneous

Two types of measures of intellectual competence—tested and spontaneous—were obtained for each child toward the end of his third year. At 36 months the test measures were the Stanford Binet and tests of Receptive Language and Spatial Abilities. The Bayley Mental Scales (1969) were also given at 12 and 24 months and tests of Receptive Language and Spatial Abilities at 12, 15, 21, 24, 27 and 30 months. The latter tests are described in White, Watts *et al.* (1973).

Intellectual experiences which the child constructed for himself in his solitary play at age 30 to 33 months were the measure of the child's spontaneous display of intellectual competence. By definition, the child's behavior in such experiences was intellectually competent, and his behavior was also spontaneous in that he was not performing for anyone else's benefit (except, perhaps, the observer's) nor was he being helped or encouraged by another. Similar measures of the child's natural expression of intellectual competence were obtained from observations at age 12 to 15, 18 to 21, and 24 to 27 months.

RESULTS AND DISCUSSION

Three key questions were investigated in this research: (1) Are certain experiences encountered by the young child in his everyday life more important to his intellectual development than others? (2) If so, does it matter what is the source of these experiences, whether they come to the child from human or non-human environmental inputs or whether he constructs them for himself through his own active, intellectually competent behavior? (3) If certain sources matter more than others, is the question of timing important?

The results of this study suggested clear answers to each of these questions. First, they demonstrated that a class of observed experiences that we had deemed *a priori* to be intellectually valuable to the child were indeed so, at least insofar as their correlation with IQ and other test scores is evidence of their intellectual value. These experiences were considered intellectually valuable because they seemed to provide the child with clear opportunities to learn verbal/symbolic, spatial/fine motor, practical reasoning, and expressive skills or content that are considered variously by psychologists, educators, test constructors, and laypeople to be important intellectual achievements for a young child. This category of intellectually valuable experiences was distinguished from nine other types of everyday experiences, including simpler, unstructured, unfocused play, which were thought to offer less clear opportunities for the child to master intellectual skills or content. The validity of this distinction was demonstrated by the contrasting correlations with IQ and other test scores of intellectual and non-intellectual experiences. Intellectually valuable experiences were highly positively correlated with scores on the Binet and tests of Receptive Language and Spatial Abilities at age three (and earlier), whereas all other types of experiences were uncorrelated with or negatively correlated with test performance. We conclude from these and other supporting data that the class of intellectually valuable experiences that were observed in this study are more deeply implicated in the child's intellectual development than other types of everyday experiences, at least insofar as the criterion tests measure intellectual competence.

The next two questions intrigued us more than the first. Does it matter whether the child constructs these intellectually valuable experiences for himself or whether he receives them from his human or non-human environment? If so, is the question of timing important? The answers to these questions have profound theoretical and pedagogical implications. From Piagetian theory and the philosophy behind the open classroom it might be supposed that the child's active construction of his own experiences is central to his intellectual development, passive learning from the environment being relatively unimportant. In contrast, traditional learning theory and traditional classroom practice assumes that the child progresses intellectually by receiving information, by demonstrations, corrective feedback and reinforcement from the environment. More sophisticated versions of traditional learning theory emphasize the need for structure and appropriateness in environmental inputs and for precisely applied feedback and reinforcement contingencies, but there is not nearly the same stress on the active child fashioning his own knowledge as there is in Piaget's writings (Kohlberg & Mayer, 1972). The Piagetian philosophy is well exemplified by Piaget's claim that to teach a child something is to prevent him from discovering, that is, truly learning it. Learning theorists and traditional practitioners would find this assertion incomprehensible if not preposterous.[2]

The results of this research give some support to both camps, full comfort to

[2]In some of his writings (e.g., Piaget, 1951), Piaget has referred to the essential role of the social environment in the child's construction of cognitive concepts. But he has given relatively little attention to analyzing it in detail.

neither. Briefly, we found that it does matter a great deal how the child's intellectual experiences are derived but different sources of intellectually valuable experiences become important at different periods in the child's life. The earliest forms of intellectual experiences that are correlated with test performance at age three (and earlier) are experiences in which the *child interacts with another person.* These intellectual experiences include reciprocal interaction in which the child and the interactor contribute jointly to the child's intellectual experience, but equally important are encounters in which the interactor is the primary source of the intellectual experience and the child the attentive but basically non-contributing partner. Starting at about age two a second source of intellectual experiences begins to be significantly correlated with later test performance. This source is the *behavior of another person whom the child merely observes* and who is not tailoring his actions for the child's benefit but merely pursuing his own activities. It is only after these two sources have become prominent that a third source of intellectual experiences—the child himself—comes to the fore. At age two and a half but not before, intellectual experiences that *the child fashions through his own competent behavior in solitary or interactive play* begin to be significantly correlated with his tested intellectual competence.

These results may be summarized by saying that there is a definite sequence which places in time certain sources of the child's intellectual experiences before others in promoting the skills and knowledge that are reflected in test performance. Intellectual experiences in which another person plays an active, structuring, even a dominant part are the ones from which the younger child gains most. Intellectual experiences that this younger child constructs

for himself do not correspond nearly as well to the tasks set by tests. It is not until he is two and a half, that the experiences that he fashions through his own intelligent behavior begin to rival those he receives from his human environment in promoting the competencies that are assessed by tests.

We would be left decidedly uncomfortable if this pattern of relationships with *tested* intellectual competence was all that the results of our study demonstrated, since an equally important goal of this research was to investigate the experiential antecedents of the child's *spontaneous* expression of intellectual competence in his everyday life. It does not satisfy us merely to know more about the role played by experience in tested intellectual competence when this assessment, conducted in a contrived situation and employing an arbitrary and restricted range of items, is far from perfectly correlated with the child's display of intellectual competence in his day-to-day activities. A central question for us then was how this spontaneous display of intellectual competence, manifested in a large variety of activities in the natural setting of the child's home, related to environmental factors that impinged on the child's experiences. As was the case for tested intellectual competence, the most compelling way of answering this question is to consider the correlations between the older child's observed intellectual competence (that is, his tendency to create intellectual experiences for himself in solitary play at 30 to 33 months) and intellectual experiences he receives from different sources at earlier periods in his life.

The results of this analysis astonished us by their simplicity. Briefly, we found that the child's observed intellectual competence at 30 to 33 months was more highly and stably related to intellectual experiences provided to him *by other people* in the preceding year and a half than to intellectual experiences he fashioned for himself (that is, his previous observed intellectual competence). Further, we found that when the sample was divided into subgroups of children classified as relatively high or low in intellectual competence (either tested or spontaneous), the groups differed from each other only in interactive intellectual experiences up until age two. Striking differences in their self-generated intellectual experiences (that is, their observed intellectual competence) did not occur until age two and a half and this was preceded by clear differences in their intellectual interactions with other people that were evident as early as age 12 to 15 months. These results duplicated in essential details the findings for tested intellectual competence. In both cases it was the role played by the *interactor* in creating intellectual experiences for the child or reciprocally sharing in them that was first and most highly related to the child's later intellectual competence.

The interactor as participator in the child's intellectual experiences

To understand why early interactive intellectual experiences should play so critical a role in the child's intellectual development it is essential to remember how an interactor comes to be judged as a source of the child's intellectual experiences in this research. An interactor is considered to be the primary or joint source of the child's intellectual experiences only when he uses a *participatory* technique of interaction. The specific techniques defined as participatory include teaching, helping, entertaining, conversing and sharing in the intellectual activity like a playmate. The common feature of these techniques is that the interactor plays a direct, active, and integral role in creating, guiding and

expanding the child's intellectual experience. The interactor is responsible either solely or jointly with the child for the manifest intellectual content of the experience. His behavior is not merely facilitative (in the sense, say, of supplying needed materials), or reinforcing (in the sense, say, of praise or approval), or incidental to the intellectual experience. Rather, the interactor's behavior literally creates or helps to create the intellectual content. This content is often judiciously chosen, well structured and attractively presented. But the same or better can be said of certain children's television programs, the watching of which, in this research, seemed not to relate at all to the child's intellectual development. What seems to distinguish these two types of environmental inputs are two features that are highly salient in the interactor's behavior and seldom present in television programs. These are the *individualized and responsive* quality of the interactor's behavior and its *affective* subtext.

When an interactor engages in an intellectual activity with a child he typically tailors his input to the individual child's needs. He tries to match its content and style to what he knows of the child's capabilities and interests. He is responsive to questions, problems, inadequacies in the child's understanding. His behavior is geared to the particular not the average child. When this interactor is a parent who is in intimate contact with the child on a day-to-day basis, the potential power of such individualized treatment hardly needs further commentary.

An important, related aspect of the interactive situation is that it often links three distinct sources of intellectual experiences. Although for purposes of analysis we distinguish these three sources (the interactor, the interactor and child jointly, the child), in practice such experiences often occur as parts of a larger interactive sequence. The first two sources of experience were the ones that showed the earliest and most stable relationship to the child's intellectual competence, but it seems likely that the third type of experience (in which the child is the source and the interactor the approving but basically "non-contributing" partner) is an essential link to the child's later ability to generate intellectual experiences in his solitary play. Put more concretely, the child in this type of interactive situation is practicing the art of creating intellectual experiences for himself in the presence of an approving interactor who a minute before may have provided the model for his intellectually competent behavior. It is not unreasonable to suppose that these practice experiences make him more likely to engage in similar behavior when the interactor is no longer present.

This point brings us to the affective aspect of interactive experiences. By the very fact of sharing in intellectual experiences with the child the interactor conveys that such experiences are valued and pleasing. It is not necessary that the interactor express approval or affection overtly. The essential message is already transmitted by the sheer fact that the interactor participates positively in the experience. When this interactor is a parent, a sibling, or a friend to whom the child is emotionally attached, it seems very likely that the child will come to value and engage in such activities for the simple reason that these are the ones that people he likes prefer. When, for example, the interactor chooses to read a book to the child rather than to roughhouse with him, the child comes to understand what the other person's system of values is, and, trite though it may seem to say it, he will tend to reflect those values in his own self-directed activities.

The process of interaction: some concrete examples

It may not be easy for a reader to visualize from this abstract discussion what the process of intellectual exchange between a skillful interactor and a child actually looks like. The picture that comes to mind most readily is of an adult humorlessly pushing the child to achieve and forcing pre-packaged information on him willy nilly. This picture is entirely incongruous with our observations, but it is not an uncommon reaction to the labels that we have chosen to use in our conceptual system. In this section therefore we shall try to bring to life the process of intellectual exchange that we call an "intellectually valuable interaction." We shall do this by presenting a series of excerpts culled from our actual observations of young children's experiences.[3]

The Interactor as Teacher. The first two examples depict the interactor as *teacher.* The first portrays a fairly conventional teacher–pupil relationship, the mother playing the role of transmitter of knowledge and skills. The next excerpt shows a more subtle process at work. Here there is a conceptual problem that clearly seems to challenge the child, and the interactor's teaching skill consists of being able to cue into the child's concerns and to do something that helps him solve his problem through reorganizing his current mode of thinking.

First, the more conventional example.

Mother is arranging some flowers in a large vase. Janie (age 32 months): "Let me take one, Mommy." Mother suggests: "Why don't you smell this?" and puts a carnation to Janie's nose. Janie sniffs, smelling the flower. Mother:

---

[3]Much more detailed descriptions are to be found in Carew, Chan, and Halfar (in press) from which these excerpts were taken.

"These are carnations. Not much of a smell. And those are chrysanthemums." Janie looks on, solemnly taking it all in.

This conventional, though apparently effective, teaching technique may be contrasted with the following more unusual one.

Father is reading to John, age 33 months, Ezra Keat's story "Goggles." They turn to a picture showing the dog Willy running away with the goggles through a hole in a fence. In the picture the dog's face is half hidden behind the fence. John looks and tells Father: "Doggie face broken." Father explains: "No, it's not broken. It's hiding behind the fence." John looks puzzled. He asks: "Hiding?" Father demonstrates: "See my hand? Now, see it hide when I move it behind the book?" John watches intently. Father continues: "Now, see it come out again. It's not broken. It was hiding." John imitates Father's action several times, passing his hand behind the book and watching it reappear.

The Interactor as Entertainer. For some adults, especially those with the performer's instinct, the most pleasurable way of participating in intellectual activities with a child is to entertain him. Dramatization of stories, role playing, singing, dancing, strumming a guitar are all ways that novel material, original ideas, as well as skills involving the mastering of set sequences can be delightfully imparted. Consider Nancy's experience:

Nancy (age 30 months) calls to her mother: "Find me. I'm hiding." Mother tells her "all right" and walks over to the closet where Nancy is standing in full view. Mother calls out in mock distress: "Oh dear, I can't find my Nancy. I wonder where she's gone. Perhaps she's only gone out to buy some bread and milk, but I didn't hear the door. Oh dear, she's just disappeared." Nancy is chortling with delight. Mother pulls back the clothing and looks in at Nancy. She shakes her head and says: "I guess she isn't here. There is a little girl here but her name is Mary. I still don't know where Nancy

has gone." Nancy laughs and hides her eyes (presumably so her mother will not be able to see her!). Nancy continues chortling as Mother plays variations on the theme of "Where has Nancy gone?"

The Interactor as Playmate. Closely allied to the interactor's role as entertainer in terms of willingness to do "childish" things is his role as the child's playmate. Here, however, the interactor is not so much on the stage as on the floor. His role as playmate calls for getting down to the level of the one- to three-year-old and pitching into his childish but intellectually important activity. Here is an excerpt that captures the child-like, reciprocal, playful character of this role performed in the context of activities that are clearly of intellectual value to the child.

Mother and Jamie (13 months) are sitting on the floor. Jamie sees a little wooden pig lying on the floor. He picks it up and hands it to Mother calling, "Piggy, piggy." Mother asks, "Shall we hide the piggy?" Jamie smiles. Mother tells him, "I think your piggy is too big to fit under the cup. I'll get something to hide the piggy under." She shows him that the cup is too small. "See, your piggy sticks out. It can't hide under there." Mother goes to the kitchen and returns with pans for a three-tiered cake. Mother hides the pig under the largest pan and places the others on top in a tower. Jamie smiles and immediately takes down the pans one by one and uncovers the pig. He laughs and Mother claps, "Terrific." Jamie then covers the pig with the pan, but immediately uncovers it and grins. Mother: "Hey, you found the piggy. Hide him again." Jamie covers the toy pig and looks at Mother. Mother asks, "Well, where did that piggy go?" Jamie takes off the pan and giggles. Mother claps, "There he is. Hurray for Jamie. Jamie found the piggy."

The Interactor as Converser. The participatory role that comes most easily to many adults is that of the conversation partner. One can chat to a child while doing the ironing, or eating lunch, or walking to the bus stop. But only certain forms of conversation are thought, in this research, to create an intellectually valuable experience for the child. These include the use of language to teach (e.g., labeling objects or events or by expanding a child's statement into a structurally more complete form); to convey novel information; to make comparisons, contrasts, and classes; to explain; to revive past experiences; to anticipate future events; or to evoke a poetic or imaginary world. Many examples of this use of language occur in our observations as in the following excerpt:

Mother and Sonja, age two, are in the living room where Mother is about to blow up a balloon. Sonja says something to Mother about a circus. Mother tells her: "No, you didn't go to the circus—you went to the parade." Mother asks: "What did you see?" She thinks a moment and then shouts: "Big girls!" Mother smiles: "Big girls and what else?" Sonja says: "Drums!" and laughs. Mother asks: "What made all the loud noise at the end?" Sonja answers: "Trumpets." Mother tells her: "Yes, and fire engines. Do you remember the fire engines?" Sonja nods: "You hold my ears a little bit." Mother smiles: "Yes, I did, just like this," and puts her hands on Sonja's ears. Sonja laughs.

The Interactor Blends His Roles. We have methodically exemplified the several participatory roles that interactors play in their young children's intellectual experiences and yet we have not captured the essence of the part. The fault, we think, lies in compartmentalizing the roles for analytic presentation as if in real life they stood apart from each other. In fact, the most striking feature of the behavior of the effective participator is a remarkable blending of these roles. Read almost any of the excerpts that we have given under the four separate headings and the reader will find that many roles are combined in a single episode. The skillful participator

shifts from one to another blurring the lines of demarcation so much so that the ability to vary one's approach seems the quintessence of the part.

In our writings we have often used a metaphor of the theatre in describing the art of effective participation, and for good reason. Just as the skill of a good actor cannot be reduced to separate, quantifiable components, so too the art of stimulating and sustaining a child's intellectual interests cannot be captured by a formula. In the next excerpt, when we see Matthew's mother play an imaginary badminton match with her son, she is teacher, entertainer, conversation partner, and playmate all at the same time. Her roles are not blocked out in segments. They are combined and interwoven in a creative whole bound together by the mother's exquisite sense of her son's interests and capabilities.

Matthew (age 26 months) comes into the kitchen holding a child-size badminton racket. Matthew swings the racket. Mother: "Did you get it? Where did it go? Down there?" Matthew: "I got it!" and runs out of the kitchen after an *imaginary* shuttlecock. (Apparently, Mother and Matthew have played this game before, since her words are immediately taken as a signal to start the make-believe game.) Matthew swings the racket hitting the imaginary shuttlecock. Mother pretends to toss the "shuttlecock" back to Matthew. They continue, Matthew and Mother taking turns hitting the "shuttlecock."

The game continues, becoming more sophisticated. Matthew seems to be timing his imaginary shots to follow Mother's and looks up at the imaginary "birdie" each time it approaches. Matthew inadvertently drops the racket. Mother: "You lost your racket." Matthew: "Oh, I missed!" (As if dropping the racket really did cause him to miss the imaginary shuttlecock.) Matthew runs to the hallway and retrieves the "birdie." Matthew pretends to serve and Mother to return the serve. Matthew retrieves the imaginary shuttlecock from the hallway. They continue. Matthew calls: "Enough, enough!" . . . Matthew: "I want a drink of water." Mother gets a glassful: "Are you thirsty?" as she holds the glass for Matthew to drink.

This excerpt captures as beautifully as any we have seen what we mean by a mother's *active participation* in her young child's intellectual experiences. Remember that Matthew is only 26 months old and has probably never seen a badminton match. Think of the imagination and skill it requires of Matthew to synchronize his movements with his mother's, to anticipate the trajectory of the imaginary shuttlecock, to retrieve it when he has miscalculated, to reason that if he dropped his racket during the approach of the shuttlecock, then he couldn't have been able to hit it. Think too of the imagination and skill it requires of Matthew's mother to inspire this performance, making their tournament ever more challenging until, at last, Matthew staggers from the court begging for a glass of water much like a tennis player after a grueling match!

Matthew's experience is profoundly intellectual, his mother's behavior truly educative. She challenges Matthew to perform by performing herself; she inspires him to create wonderful images by creating them herself; she excites and pleases him by being excited and pleased herself. Like an actor at one with his audience, she closes all psychological distance between herself and Matthew. Intellectually and emotionally, they have *interacted*.

REFERENCES

Bruner, J. S. Nature and uses of immaturity. *American Psychologist,* 1972, **27,** 687-716.

Bruner, J. S. Organization of early skilled action. *Child Development,* 1973, **44,** 1-11 (a).

Bruner, J. S. *Patterns of growth.* Oxford: Clarendon Press, 1974.

Carew, J. V.; Chan, I.; & Halfar, C. *Observing intelligence in young children: Eight case studies.* Englewood Cliffs, N.J.: Prentice-Hall, in press.

Clarke-Stewart, K. Interactions between mothers and their young children: characteristics and consequences. *Monographs of the Society for Research in Child Development,* 1973, **38.**

Hollingshead, A., & Redlich, F. *Social class and mental illness.* New York: John Wiley & Sons, 1958.

Kagan, J. *Change and continuity in infancy.* New York: John Wiley & Sons, 1971.

Kohlberg, S., & Mayer, R. Development as the aim of education. *Harvard Educational Review,* 1972, **42,** 449-496.

Piaget, J. *The origins of intelligence in children,* 2nd Edition. New York: International University Press, 1952.

Singer, J. *The child's world of make believe: Experimental studies of imaginative play.* New York: Academic Press, 1973.

White, R. Motivation reconsidered: the concept of competence. *Psychological Review,* 1959, **66,** 297-333.

White, B.; Watts, J.; Barnett, I.; Kaban, B.; Marmor, J.; & Shapiro, B. *Experience and environment: Major influences on the development of the young child,* Vol. 1. Englewood Cliffs, N.J.: Prentice-Hall, 1973.

4.

T. Berry Brazelton

EFFECTS OF MATERNAL EXPECTATIONS ON EARLY INFANT BEHAVIOR

The behavior of the new infant can be a powerful influence in shaping the kind of reaction which the mother has to him. Her genetic endowment, her life experiences, her past experiences with being mothered, her cultural expectations must determine the limits on her capacity to become a mother. But the particular kind of infant with which she is faced in the neonatal period must determine which mothering reactions she will draw from her repertoire. Certainly, we see parents who can function well with one kind of infant, but not with another. Failures in mothering— such as are seen in the clinical syndromes of infantile autism, child abuse, failure to thrive, and repeated accidents (Heider, 1971), point to this in families where one child is the target for the family's pathology, while the other children are spared and even appear to be well mothered. Such pathological syndromes suggest that a diagnostic documentation of the early mother–child interaction might lead to measures which could prevent the development of pathology in this vital area in a stressed family. The father, the other

siblings, and the extended family are of vital importance to the dyad of which we shall speak, but for simplicity's sake, it is easier to speak of the mother–child dyad as of primary significance.

Although no member of a dyadic interaction is ever free or independent of the power of the dyad, it is important to understand the dynamics of each member which lead to the establishment of "attachment behavior." Ainsworth (1967) and Bowlby (1969) have been stressing the importance of attachment behavior as a way of measuring the kind of bonds which exist between a parent and a child. Behavioral assessments of each member in the dyad as they form this attachment might lead to better methods for determining the differences in dynamics and the strengths in their interaction.

In prenatal interviews with normal primiparas and their husbands, we uncovered anxiety which often seemed to be of pathological proportions (Brazelton, 1963). We felt that the earliest observable behavior of mothers and infants might be a clue to the influence each member of the dyad might have on the other. Instead, we found in our research at Putnam Children's Center that the prenatal interviews with normal primiparas, in a psychoanalytic interview setting, uncovered anxiety which often seemed to be of what appeared to be of pathological proportions (Brazelton, 1963). The unconscious material was so loaded and so distorted, so near the surface, that before delivery one felt an ominous direction for making a prediction

Source: *Early Child Development and Care,* 1973, **2,** 259-273. (The author is supported by a grant from the Carnegie Corporation of New York, Inc.)

Portions of this text were delivered at the March of Dimes Conference, Mount Zion Hospital, San Francisco, 1971—"Infants at Risk"—and will be published in a March of Dimes monograph of the proceedings.

The research in Zambia was supported by a grant from National Early Childhood Research Councils Incorporated, Princeton, New Jersey.

about the woman's capacity to adjust to the role of mothering. And yet when we saw her in action as a mother, this very anxiety and the distorted unconscious material could become a force for reorganization, for readjustment to her important new role. I began to feel that much of the prenatal anxiety and distortion of fantasy could be a healthy mechanism for bringing her out of the old homeostasis which she had achieved to a new level of adjustment. The "alarm reaction" we were tapping in on was serving as a kind of "shock" treatment for reorganization to her new role. I do agree with Bowlby's concept of attachment and of the necessity for a kind of "imprinting" of the mother on the new infant (Bowlby, 1969). I now see the shakeup in pregnancy as readying the circuits for new attachments, as preparation for the many choices which they must be ready to make in a very short critical period, as a method of freeing her circuits for a kind of sensitivity to the infant and his individual requirements which might not have been easily or otherwise available from her earlier adjustment. Thus, this very emotional turmoil of pregnancy and that in the neonatal period can be seen as a positive force for the mother's adjustment and for the possibility of providing a more individualized environment for the infant (Brazelton, 1963).

Prospective fathers seemed to be going through a similar upheaval. Each young man was forced to reevaluate his role as a provider for the family, as an adult male ready to adjust to the responsibility of a dependent, as a model for the new child's learning about masculinity, and as a major support for his wife as she adjusted to her role as a mother. In the process, he was forced back on self-examination and his experience with being fathered. If he was trying to free himself of ties to his own parents, it was hard for him to identify with them as models for his new role. He may have barely adjusted to being a husband, and the new, added expectations became difficult for him to encompass. In our lonely, nuclear family structure in the USA, the young father was often the only available support for his wife. They had moved away from their families, both in physical distance and in psychological expectations, and were unwilling to fall back on them for moral or physical support. There were rarely other supportive figures nearby—such as family physicians, ministers, close friends or neighbors who could help. The father was expected to assume the major supportive role.

In our research situation, we provided both new parents with important support—by listening to their concerns about themselves as parents, and by offering guidelines in a pediatric and group setting for developing their own child-rearing practices. Although these were not our research goals at the outset, the need for them was so great that we found ourselves placed in the role of substituting for the support which extended families provide in other cultures. Physicians and child care workers, who are available in the early months of the development of a new infant, have a unique and valuable opportunity to play such an interventive role in helping young parents to shape the environment for the baby.

As we began to document neonatal behavior, very powerful mechanisms seemed to dominate the neonate's behavior (Brazelton, 1962). In the tremendous physiological realignment that the changeover from intrauterine to extrauterine existence demanded, it has always amazed me that there was any room for individualized responses, for alerting and stimulus seeking or for behavior which indicates a kind of processing of information in the neonate. And yet there is.

Despite the fact that his major job is that of achieving homeostasis in the face of enormous onslaughts from his environment, we can see precursors for affective and cognitive responses in the immediate period after delivery. The two most exciting behavioral responses which can be observed reflect the strength of the neonate's capacity to control, and then to selectively interact with his environment. Since he might otherwise be at the mercy of a response to every stimulus, he is equipped with the capacity to shut out or habituate to repeated stimulation which is disturbing.

For example, we exposed neonates to a disturbing visual (bright operating room light) stimulus placed at a distance of 24 inches from their heads. The infants were lightly swaddled and resting quietly. The light stimulus was on for three seconds, off for one minute, for twenty stimuli. Monitored for cardiac, respiratory and electroencephalographic changes, we saw infants respond at first with behavioral startles which decreased rapidly after a few stimulus periods. By the tenth stimulus, no behavioral, cardiac or respiratory change could be noted. By the fifteenth stimulus, sleep spindles appeared on the EEG tracing although their occipital leads continued to demonstrate reception of the visual stimulus. After twenty stimuli, they awoke from this "induced" sleep to scream and thrash. We felt this represented the marvelous capacity of the neonate to use changing state to control responses to a disturbing stimulus. Certainly he is no longer at the mercy of the environment. Because of this capacity to shut out responses to stimuli which might otherwise overwhelm him, he can select and attend to stimuli with rather narrowly determined properties (for example, a neonate alerts and attends to a female voice in preference to a male voice) (Birns,

1965; Eisenberg, 1969; Korner, 1971). He prefers an ovoid stimulus and a human face to a distorted face, and will stare at it for surprisingly long periods immediately after delivery—long before he has had experience of mothering (Stechler *et al.,* 1966). He is set up with pathways for attention and, then, complex reactions to appropriate stimuli at birth. There is evidence that individual differences affect the narrow range of stimuli which call out this attention (Birns, 1965; Korner, 1971). These mechanisms set the stage for individual differences in infants—individual in their capacity to receive and shut out, and then individual in their ability to demonstrate responsive behavior to which the environment can respond with appropriate attachment behavior. Mothers who are responsive to these individualized responses shape their own reactions to account for them in their new babies. Thus, the individual infant's ability to imprint to a particular set of stimuli will set the tone of the mother–infant interaction in the neonatal period.

Cross-cultural work gives us an opportunity to see "natural experiments" without the constraint of manipulating people, and with an opportunity for seeing the strengths of a society as well as its differences from our own. It offers an opportunity to reevaluate the judgments which are likely to be made rather blindly in one's own culture. I found I was judging certain behavior in mother and infant as "good," others as "bad," which was leading to a self-perpetuating kind of research tool. In order to try to free myself of this kind of prejudice, I began to seek an opportunity to study the early mother–infant adjustment in other cultures.

My first opportunity was with Professor Vogt and his Harvard anthropologists in Southern Mexico. We were able to study an isolated group of Mayan Indians in the

Chiapas Highlands (Vogt, 1966). This was a strong, well-balanced group called the Zinacantecos who had managed to defend themselves for six hundred years from acculturating invasions of the Ladino society around them, the Catholic Church, and now modern medicine and the anthropologists. They were a pure genotype, were well nourished (we believed), as they were seen to eat protein two or three times a week, and had achieved what appeared to be a successful way of life in which they raised their own food, still using a hand plow, maintained their own curers and midwives, and had a strong patrilineal society based on extended families. Their beliefs in the "evil eye" and in their own religion and customs preserved their integrity as a culture. The emphasis in this culture was on equality, not on individuality, and all speech, dress, and ceremony was highly ritualized and structured. Overt aggression was not a factor in their lives—even a drunken adult regressed to an infantile level, not to an aggressive one. The children were expected to take adult roles in early childhood, and they learned by imitation in hunks of behavior. For example, at eight months, infants to whom we were administrating Bayley developmental scales (Bayley, 1969) watched the two red cubes which we presented to them. Their eyes, mouths, and entire bodies stretched eagerly toward the cubes, but there was no reaching for them with hands. After we demonstrated the test by reaching for a cube with one hand, reaching for the other with a second hand and banging them together, the Zinacanteco infant imitated our "hunk" of behavior precisely, then replaced the cubes without further exploration. They had absorbed our demonstration visually, had reconstructed it immediately and precisely without the exploratory experimentation which we deem necessary for skilled behavior in

our infants (Brazelton *et al.,* 1969). The economy of such imitative learning and the lack of exploration that went into it is also exemplified by the non-existence of tantrums and rebellious behavior, and by such things as a four-year-old who could imitate his father's hoeing in the fields for a four-hour stretch.

We had chosen these people for the pure genotype, the lack of acculturation, the apparent protein adequacy in their diets, and, most fortunately of all, for the major asset of having an "in" through the anthropologists who know them so well, and had worked with them for 16 years (Vogt, 1966). Despite this latter advantage, we were only able to see their newborns (who are always the most vulnerable part of any society) because of a rather magical trigger which occurred after the first two weeks of being shut out of their households. We were attempting to play with a five-month-old baby, but the mother turned to place herself between us and to cover his face. We asked our interpreter to tell her we were a curer in our culture, to which she nodded, saying she knew that already. "And," we added, "if I *have* the evil eye, I know how to cure it." With that, her eyes widened, and she handed her baby over to us. Our reputation as a curer rapidly spread and we were able to see deliveries and newborns, whom no one else had been able to see. This kind of magical thinking carries its own defensive protection! We learned a great deal from that experience about the importance of learning at all levels the "language" of people with whom one wants to communicate.

But what did their special kind of infants contribute to this culture? Birth was easy, no medication, no ingestion of any depressant or anesthesia used. It was truly a natural childbirth. The neonates in Zinacantan were very different from any group we have seen. They were tiny (five pounds), but very mature in appearance, not dysmature or post mature. Their faces and bone structure were Oriental and the behavior I shall describe has also been found in a group of Chinese-Americans in San Francisco (Freedmans, 1969). Their movements were smooth, circular, and very mature, free in arc of movement as well as in flexor-extensor balance. There were virtually no startles, tonic neck reflexes, or Moros which interfered with liquid motor activity. They lay for 30 minutes after delivery, undressed in front of the fire, while rituals were performed over them. In our US culture, the movements would have been interspersed with jerky, startle behavior. Also, our infants would not have been able to control their body temperature while undressed; as their temperature dropped they would have shivered or cried to raise body heat. The automatic stability demonstrated by these infants was very strikingly different from our neonates. While the Zinacanteco infants lay exposed, they attended repeatedly to auditory cues, and followed a visual stimulus in slow 180-degree arcs, with head turning to follow, for as much as 90 seconds at a time (our infants can and will follow for as much as 30 seconds without a break). These quiet, alert babies were then swaddled, their faces covered, and wrapped up with their mothers for a month. After an initial month of being taken care of by her own extended family, the infant's mother carried him on her back in a serape all day, and slept next to him at night. He was never played with, placed out on a bed to be talked to, or given toys to jazz him up. Before he could awaken and cry for hunger, he was fed. The thirty to forty feedings a day seemed to be aimed at keeping him quiet, as opposed to our US practice of allowing for a cycle of hunger, realization of it, the infant's re-

sponse of crying, being fed, and realization that his crying had produced the response from his environment which ended with satisfaction. This cycle must produce a sense of independent mastery in an infant; that of the Zinacantecos seems to generate quiet conformity and the habit of low-grade peaks of excitement. We did not feel that the quiet infants we saw were affected by clinical anemia or malnutrition, but the size of the infants and the 30 per cent infant mortality rate point to subclinical levels of protein malnutrition. We saw optimal neonatal behavior which was followed by infant development parallel in quantity to ours, but very different in its quality (Brazelton *et al.,* 1969). Our question, of course, was how much did these quiet, alert infants influence their culture and its childrearing practices to allow for the kind of expectation parents demonstrated—or for a five-year-old to tell you, without ever looking up, what kind of bird flew over and in what direction he flew?

We went to East Africa in the summer of 1970 to attempt to evaluate neonates at what we thought might be the other end of a spectrum of behavior. We had been influenced in our thinking by Geber and Dean (1959) who pointed to motor precocity in Ugandan neonates. We were not able to assess the sensory, cognitive responses in neonates from their work, nor obtain from any African neonatal studies any clues as to the range of their cognitive or affective responses at birth. We were able to see neonates in Lusaka, Zambia in a lying-in hospital setting (Brazelton *et al.,* 1971). These infants were the offspring of a group of urbanizing blacks who were coming to Lusaka from the surrounding bush, or escaping from South Africa. In the process of urbanizing, they not only were forced to live in slum-like cities all around the prosperous city of Lusaka, but they gave up old protective taboos for new ones which created poor conditions for the infants we saw. In the bush, the grandmother passed on the customs and advised her pregnant daughter to eat protein. In the city, although protein is not expensive or particularly difficult to come by, the young father needs to save his money and he says, "If you eat meat, your baby will bleed. If you eat an egg, he'll be bald. If you eat fish, he will drown" (Goldberg, 1971). In the bush, the husband has several wives, and it is the custom to sleep with one who is not pregnant or nursing her new baby. In Lusaka, he can afford but one wife, and she has a pregnancy every twelve months on the average (though fortunately not all of them are viable). Her uterus quickly becomes depleted. The neonates we saw were all less than 24 hours old when we examined them, since a mother will not stay in the hospital longer than that. They were not at all what we expected from reports we had read. Their births were "natural" also, without medication or anesthesia. They were six pounds at birth, 19 inches in length; they were not immature, but did show evidence of dysmaturity—dry scaling skin, poor subcutaneous fat stores, yellowing cord stumps— all pointing to some recent intrauterine depletion (as if the placenta had been inadequate in the last month). They were limp, poorly responsive, fragile-appearing neonates. We handled them with great care, and were stunned by their physiological state and their psychological unresponsiveness. The mothers breast fed them frequently and tended them in the nursery from the first. They came in to take them home within 24 hours after delivery. A mother would pick up the limp, wobbly infant, set him on her hips to sit upright, wind a dashica around hers and the infant's waists, leaving the infant's shoulders and head unsupported. The floppy infant would respond by adjusting

his head, and straightening his back and shoulders to her body, as she walked off to her village with him upright on her hip. By her expectation of his capacity to respond, she had changed him from a floppy, fragile neonate to one who was effectively supporting his shoulders and head as she walked along. By the time we made home visits at five days, her milk had come in. The infant was hydrated, his skin no longer dry, and his subcutaneous tissue stores were restored, and upon testing he had the vigor and more alertness than we see in control infants in our own culture at five days. By 10 days these neonates were ahead of our controls in alerting to voice and handling, in social interest and quieting when handled, in regulating motor adjustments, in maintaining alert states, and were demonstrating an exciting quality of motor response which we had labeled "directed" for want of a better term. We saw two five-month-old infants who took several steps without support. This five month walking was in response to their grandmothers' stimulating their walk reflexes and propelling them forward to a reflex walking response. Ainsworth (1967) describes the kind of constant motor and postural interaction that Ugandan mothers provide for their infants. The infants' experiences were certainly different from those we had seen in Mexico. Their faces were always uncovered, usually they were carried where they could look up at their mothers from her hip, or placed on her back to look around, and they were played with by every member of the extended family. Their early experiences were surely shaping them in a different direction from our Mayan infants.

We felt that we had seen neonatal behavior which was powerfully shaped by intrauterine experience—from depleted uteri, from protein and caloric malnutrition, from intra-uterine infection. But the expectation of their mothers generated responses which we had not dared to produce in these depleted neonates. This expectation, coupled with their inborn potential, served to produce the exciting sensory and motor precocity which surfaced with adequate breast milk and rehydration. In our neonatal evaluation, there were eight of twenty behaviors which were significantly different from a US control group by 10 days—social interest in examiner, alertness, consolability, cuddliness—all were higher; tempo of movement, rapidity of build-up, defensive movements, amount of activity were lower. The motor and sensory precocity we saw persisted throughout the first year, and was present in the older infants we observed.

The lesson from these observations was that in a place where mothers still had enough physical energy for the kind of interaction and cultural expectation that we saw in the Zambian mothers, infants could and did respond. The black mothers in Lusaka were straight, dignified, and caring about themselves in a depressing set of surroundings. They were able to convey this to their depleted infants, who responded with postural and motor response with the vigor that was necessary to perpetuate the interaction. To contrast this group, we have studied a group of nutritionally stressed Ladinos in Guatemala, with INCAP.[1] This group produces neonates who are immature, short in length, and dysmature at full term gestation. These infants reflect chronic malnutrition of the mothers and intrauterine protein-calorie deprivation of the fetuses throughout pregnancy. The behavior of the neonates was similar to the Mexican-Mayan

group, and their genotype is probably comparable, but their intrauterine conditions are not. In addition, these Guatemalan infants enter a depleted environment with a mother who is too stressed, too nutritionally depleted herself to be able to rise to an expectation for recovery in her baby. The cycle of maternal malnutrition, physiological depletion, and central nervous system depression in the infant, with less recovery in physiological or psychological parameters in the infant, makes for a much more hopeless situation for infancy in Guatemala. That there are only a small proportion of infants who end up with clinical maramus and qwashiorkor is the miracle. It seems possible now to predict from neonatal evaluations (Brazelton, 1971b) which infant of an overstressed household is predilected for these devastating diseases—the quiet, poorly responsive neonate (whose intrauterine depletion has contributed to such behavior).

Poverty reproduces itself with hopelessness from one generation to another. In Africa in the face of a potential for a hopeless cycle, the excitement which became obvious to us as a mother and her infant interacted with each other is self-perpetuating. We felt that there is a kind of reparability in the excitement from this relationship which can surmount tremendous obstacles—even those of poverty and ignorance.

The vicious cycle of poverty starts before birth: intrauterine depletion →genetically impaired neonates who grow up with limited motivation and potential in later childhood, and end up as poverty-stricken adults. The priorities for changing this are obvious: nutrition, housing, education, and creating a feeling of self-value in them. If society could make these available during pregnancy and immediately thereafter, their importance in reinforcing the strengths of the early mother–child rela-

[1]Instituto de Nutrition de Centro America y Panama, Guatemala City, Guatemala.

tionship might be a turning point in breaking into this cycle. From our cross-cultural studies, we have seen that the strengths of a culture are handed on from one generation to another in this early period. Perhaps the weaknesses could best be mitigated at such a time.

Under ideal intrauterine conditions, the epigenetic effects of chronic protein depletion will take two generations to eradicate in any given culture (Kaplan, 1964). The feeling of optimism and hope which is engendered in a mother who is presented with a new, vital, responsive infant might quickly improve her expectation for this baby, and even in the face of rather hopeless poverty for herself, she could reinforce his vitality and potential by her responses to him. I would like to advocate out-reach programs which attempt to reach pregnant mothers, to provide them with necessary nutrients—both food and a feeling of being cared for. If jobs can be offered their husbands and the environment into which the new infants will come can be provided with the fuel of calories and hopefulness, the outcome of these infants can be expected to change the vicious degrading cycle of poverty reproducing itself.

The problems of reaching women in early pregnancy are great. Their wish to deny such a pregnancy must certainly reinforce their resistance to any system which tries to "help" them at such a time. The value of prenatal care and of improving intrauterine conditions for the fetus behooves us to find ways of bridging personal and cultural resistance to being reached. We must start with the education of young girls and boys as to the vital importance of improving their diet and of taking care of themselves during the child bearing years. Cultural practices which protect the pregnant mother and her fetus in more natural settings must be revived and supported in the deprived ghettos of poverty areas around our cities. Education and provision of necessary ingredients at such a crucial time will provide a self-fulfilling outcome at the advent of an exciting, intact infant who is optimally equipped to demand and utilize an improved environment for his own children.

SUMMARY

Parents are prepared for their roles with the new infant during pregnancy, the anxiety and turmoil serving as a source of energy for reorienting them to their new roles. The individuality of the neonate then shapes their responses to him and

TABLE 4.1. Mean Scores on Measures for African and American Infants (9-Point Scale)

Neonatal Days	Africans			Americans		
	1	5	10	1	5	10
Alertness	3·4	6·3	7·4	4·2	5·1	4·8
Social interest	4·2	6·2	6·7	4·3	5·2	4·3
Visual tracking	2·4	4·6	4·6	4·7	4·7	5·1
Tempo	3·2	5·9	4·4	5·8	5·5	6·4
Activity	3·0	5·9	4·6	4·9	5·5	5·9
Rapidity of buildup	3·2	5·6	3·5	4·8	4·5	5·5
Irritability	2·5	4·4	3·8	4·9	4·7	5·0
Quiet with intervention	6·6	5·0	6·2	5·6	4·6	4·8
Reactivity to stimulation	3·3	5·3	4·1	4·4	4·7	5·7
Defensive movements	3·2	5·1	4·9	4·4	5·5	6·1
Cuddliness	3·3	5·2	6·3	4·4	5·6	5·1

essentially creates an environment which is suitable to his particular needs. Rather than being at the mercy of the environment, the kind of infants a culture produces may perpetuate the culture and its outcome. But the powerful intrauterine experiences of malnutrition, infection, and uterine depletion can seriously affect the genotype as it is reflected in neonatal behavior. When the mother can respond with expectation for his recovery and when proper nutrition can be provided in the neonatal period, the infant is more likely to live up to his genetic potential. When the extrauterine environment does not provide necessary nutrients and parents cannot respond to their psychological needs, the cycle of poverty and malnutrition must reproduce itself via infants who will be impaired—somatically, as well as psychologically.

REFERENCES

Ainsworth, M. D. S. *Infancy in Uganda.* Baltimore: Johns Hopkins Press, 1967.

Bayley, N. *Manual for the Bayley Scales of Infant Development.* New York: Psychological Corporation, 1969.

Birns, B. Individual differences in human neonates' responses to stimulation. *Child Development,* 1965, **30,** 249-254.

Bowlby, J. Attachment and loss, Vol. I Attachment. New York: Basic Books, 1969.

Brazelton, T. B. Observations of the neonate. *Journal of Psychiatry,* 1962, **1,** 38-47.

Brazelton, T. B. The early mother–infant adjustment. *Pediatrics,* 1963, **32,** 931-938.

Brazelton, T. B.; Robey, J. S.; & Collier, G. A. Infant development in the Zinacantan Indians of Southern Mexico. *Pediatrics,* 1969, **44,** 274-285.

Brazelton, T. B.; Koslowski, Barbara; & Tronick, E. Infant development in a group of urbanizing blacks in Zambia, in preparation, 1971.

Brazelton, T. B.; Koslowski, Barbara; Main,
M.; & Bruner, J. S. Origins of mother–infant reciprocity, in preparation, 1971 (a).

Brazelton, T. B. Neonatal behavioral assessment. In press, 1971 (b).

Bridger, W. Sensory habituation and discrimination in the human neonate. *American Journal of Psychiatry,* 1961, **117,** 991-998.

Bruner, J. S. Competence in infants. Lecture at SRCD meetings (L. K. Frank Symposium), Minneapolis, 1971.

Eisenberg, R. B. Auditory behavior in the human neonate: functional properties of sound and their ontogenetic implication. *Ear, Nose and Throat Audiology,* 1969, **9,** 34-40.

Freedman, D. G., & Freedman, N. Behavioral differences between Chinese-American and American newborns. *Nature,* 1969, **224,** 1227-1230.

Geber, M., & Dean, R. F. A. The state of development of newborn African children. *Lancet,* 1959, **1,** 1216-1222.

Goldberg, S. Infant care in Zambia: measuring maternal behavior. *HDRU Reports,* No. 12, Human Development Research Unit, University of Zambia, 1970.

Heider, G. M. Factors in vulnerability from infancy to later age levels. In J. Hellmuth (ed.), *Exceptional infant,* **2,** Bruner/Mazel, New York: 1971.

Kaplan, S. Clinical contribution to the study of narcissism in infancy. *Psychoanalytic Study of Child,* 1964, **19,** 398-410.

Klein, R. E.; Habicht, J. P.; & Yarbrough, C. Effect of protein-calorie malnutrition on mental development. To be published in *Advances in Pediatrics,* INCAP publication No. I-571, 1971.

Korner, A. State as a variable, as obstacle and as mediator of stimulation in infant research. Personal communication, 1971.

Stechler, G.; Bradford, S.; & Levy, H. Attention in the newborn: Effect on motility and skin potential. *Science,* 1966, 1246.

Viteri, F.; Behar, M.; & Arroyave, G. Clinical aspects of protein malnutrition. In H. N. Munio and J. S. Allison (eds.), *Mammalian protein metabolism,* Vol. 2, New York: Academic Press, 1964.

Vogt, E. Los Zinacantecos. Instituto Nacional Indegenesta, 1966.

5.

Steven R. Tulkin

AN ANALYSIS OF THE CONCEPT OF CULTURAL DEPRIVATION

The term "cultural deprivation" is commonly used to summarize the presumed reasons why lower-class and minority group children show deficits in the development of "intellectual skills." However, there are serious limitations to the validity of the concept of cultural deprivation, and psychologists and educators should reevaluate their roles in programs which attempt to "enrich" the lives of "deprived" populations. The cultural deprivation concept is limited in that (*a*) it does not advance psychology as a science because it does not focus attention on how specific experiences affect developmental processes, (*b*) it ignores cultural relativism, and (*c*) it neglects political realities, which are likely to be primarily responsible for many of the traits observed in deprived populations. The limitations described under *a* are discussed only briefly, since they are likely to be most familiar to social scientists.

THE IMPORTANCE OF PSYCHOLOGICAL PROCESSES

The concept of cultural deprivation has often made it easy for social scientists to

Source: Reprinted from and copyrighted as part of *Development Psychology*, 6(2), copyright © 1972, by the American Psychological Association, Inc. Portions of the paper were presented at the meeting of the Inter-American Society of Psychology, Panama City, December, 1971. The author wishes to thank Jerome Kagan, Murray Levine, A. M. Graziano, Edward S. Katkin, and Sydney Perry for their encouragement and helpful suggestions on the present article.

overlook the importance of the *processes* by which environmental experiences influence development. Jessor and Richardson (1968) stated:

To speak, for example, of maternal deprivation as an explanation is to attempt to account for certain characteristics of infant development by the absence of the mother rather than by the presence of some specifiable set of environmental conditions. While mother absence may be a useful and convenient way to summarize or symbolize the conditions which will likely be present, the important point is that development is likely to be invariant with or related to the conditions which are present, not with those which are absent (p. 3).

Research concluding that social class or racial differences are found on particular developmental or intellectual tasks does not further understanding of development, unless we examine the actual processes that contributed to the differences. Wolf (1964) urged researchers to distinguish between status variables (class, race, etc.) and process variables (the actual *experiences* of children which contribute to their cognitive growth). He rated parents on 13 process variables descriptive of interactions between parent and child. The items fell under the headings of parental press for academic achievement and language development, as well as provision for general learning. He found a correlation of .76 between these process variables and IQ measures of fifth-grade students. Similarly, Davé (1963) obtained a multiple correlation of .80 between process variables and school achievement. These are substantially higher than the correlations of .40 to .50 which are typically reported between socio-economic status and measures of intelligence or school achievement.

NEED FOR CULTURAL RELATIVISM

Many authors who discuss deprived populations appear to disregard cultural relativism, despite the attempts—predominantly from anthropologists—to emphasize the importance of cultural relativism in understanding minority subcultures in the United States. Writers have enumerated certain charactersitics of black American culture, for example, which can be traced to the cultural patterns of its African origin (Herskovits, 1958). Other authors have argued that particular minority groups possess cultures of their own, which have "developed out of coping with a difficult environment" here in the United States (Riessman, 1962). Despite the recognition of the need for relativism, middle-class Americans, including professionals, have difficulty remaining relativistic with regard to minority cultures. Gans (1962) discussed the difficulties encountered by middle-class "missionaries" in understanding the Italian-American subculture he studied in Boston's West End. He observed that West End parents made frequent use of verbal and physical punishment, and commented that "to a middle-class observer, the parents' treatment often seems extremely strict, and sometimes brutal." Gans, however, felt that

the torrents of threat and cajolery neither impinge on the feelings of parental affection, nor are meant as signs of rejection. As one mother explained to her child, "We hit you because we love you." People believe that discipline is needed constantly to keep the child in line with and respectful of adult rules, and without it he would run amok [pp. 59-60].

Another example of a subcultural pattern which is foreign to middle-class observers was reported by Lehmer (1969). She noted that Navajo children would not compete for good grades in school, and explained that Navajo customs emphasized cooperation, not competition: "In Navajo tradition, a person who stands out at the expense of his brother may be considered a 'witch' [p. D-4]." Does this low need for achievement reflect cultural deprivation or cultural difference?

Why is it so difficult for outsiders to acknowledge subcultural behavior patterns? Gans (1962) believed that the difficulty stemmed from the observers' missionary outlook:

[They] had to believe that the West Enders' refusal to follow object-oriented middle-class ways was pathological, resulting from deprivations imposed on them by living in the West End. They could not admit that the West Enders acted as they did because they lived within a social structure and culture of their own [pp. 151-152].

In fact, Gans had earlier stated that one of the tenets of West End life was a rejection of "middle-class forms of status and culture." In other words, it was culturally valued to be culturally deprived.

The difficulty of achieving a relativistic approach to the study of subcultures has made research difficult, because minority group children are constantly evaluated by middle-class standards. One issue of current interest to psychologists is whether black ghetto residents are less able to communicate verbally or are simply less proficient in "standard English." It is claimed by many researchers that lower-class subjects are verbally deficient, and the deficits are "not entirely attributable to implicit 'middle-class' orientations [Krauss & Rotter, 1968]." Other experts have argued that black English is a fully formed linguistic system in its own right, with its own grammatical rules and unique history (Baratz & Shuy, 1969; Labov, 1967; Stewart, 1967, 1969a). These critics have stated that black language is "different from standard American English, but no less complex, communicative, rich, or sophisticated [Sroufe, 1970]"; and argued that research reporting language "deficits" among black children reflects only the middle-class orientation of the research instruments and procedures. Supporting this argument, Birren and Hess (1968) concluded that

studies of peer groups in spontaneous interaction in Northern ghetto areas show that there is a rich verbal culture in constant use. Negro children in the vernacular culture cannot be considered "verbally deprived" if one observes them in a favorable environment—on the contrary, their daily life is a pattern of continual verbal stimulation, contest, and imitation (p. 137).

Similarly, Chandler and Erickson (1968) observed *naturally occurring* group interaction and reported data which disputed the findings of Bernstein (1960, 1961) and others that middle-class children more commonly used "elaborated" linguistic codes while lower classes typically spoke with "restricted" codes. Chandler and Erickson found that the use of restricted or elaborated linguistic codes was not as closely related to the social class of speakers as had been suggested by other researchers.

Both inner-city and suburban groups . . . were found to shift back and forth between use of relatively "restricted" linguistic codes and relatively "elaborated" codes. These shifts were closely related to apparent changes in the degree of shared context between group members. Examples of extremely abstract and sophisticated inquiry among inner-city Negro young people were found in which a highly "restricted" linguistic code was employed (p. 2).

If black English and standard English are simply different languages, one cannot be seen as more deficient than the other (Sroufe, 1970). Most schools, however, demand that students use standard English, and frequently black children who have been classified by their schools as "slow learners" are able to read passages of black English with amazing speed and accuracy (Stewart, 1969b). Similarly, Foster (1969) found that the introduction of nonstandard English dialect increased the ability of tenth-grade disadvantaged students "to comprehend, to recall, and to be fluent and flexible in providing titles for verbal materials." Black students ($N=90$) also scored higher than white students ($N=400$) on Foster's (1970) Jive Analogy Test (H. L. Foster, personal communication, 1971).

This argument does not imply that the teaching of standard English is an infringement of the rights of minority cultures. It is necessary that students learn standard English, but there is a development of positive skills which may facilitate a successful adaptation to a particular majority culture versus devaluating a group of people who may not emphasize the development of these particular skills. As Baratz and Baratz (1970) suggested, research should be undertaken to discover the *different* but not pathological forms of minority group behavior. "Then and only then can programs be created that utilize the child's differences as a means of helping him acculturate to the mainstream while maintaining his individual identity and cultural heritage [p. 47]."

An objective look at the middle class

The cultural bias of middle-class America has not only hindered an appreciation of the attributes of minority cultures, but it has also prevented an objective evaluation of middle-class culture. Psychologists do not write about the "deficiencies" of the middle class, but the cultural relativist might find a great deal to write about. Coles (1969) suggested that it may be appropriate to label middle-class children deprived, because

they're so nervous and worried about everything they say—what it will mean, or what it will cost them, or how it will be interpreted. That's what they've learned at home, and that's why a lot of them are tense kids, and, even worse, stale kids with frowns on their faces at ages 6 or 7 (p. 277).

Similarly, Kagan (1968) hypothesized that middle-class children were more anxious about failing than lower-class children. He noted that lower-class children may be less anxious about making a mistake and, therefore, more likely to answer questions and make decisions "impulsively." Most people would agree that an impulsive style could be a hindrance to the development of abstract analytical thinking, but researchers have paid little attention to the possible virtues of an impulsive (or "spontaneous," "nonanalytical") style, and have not considered the consequences of attempting to discourage this style. Maccoby and Modiano (1966) spoke to this point in their discussion of differences among children in Mexico City, Boston, and a rural Mexican village. They noted that, people socialized into the modern industrialized world often lose the ability to experience. "They are," the authors suggested, "like people who see a painting immediately in terms of its style, period, and influences, but with no sense of its uniqueness [p. 268]." Maccoby and Modiano concluded by cautioning that

as the city child grows older, he may end by exchanging a spontaneous, less alienated relationship to the world for a more sophisticated outlook which concentrates on using, exchanging, or cataloguing. What industrialized man

gains in an increased ability to formulate, to reason, and to code the ever more numerous bits of complex information he acquires, he may lose in decreased sensitivity to people and events (p. 269).

But it is quite doubtful if psychologists would call him culturally deprived.

Relativism toward other cultures

Psychologists frequently label American minority groups as culturally deprived, but they are less likely to make value judgments about other cultures. In fact, social scientists are reasonably tolerant of child-rearing practices observed in other cultures which would be devaluated if they were found in a minority group in the United States. Rebelsky and Abeles (1969), for example, observed American and Dutch mothers with their 0-3 month-old infants. They found that a Dutch baby typically slept in a low closed bed with a canopy overhead. Dutch mothers kept the infant's room cool—"for health reasons"—necessitating infants being "tightly covered under blankets, often tied into the crib with strings from their sheets." Further, the authors reported comparisons showing that "American mothers looked at, held, fed, talked to, smiled at, patted, and showed more affection to their babies more often than did Dutch mothers." These findings, however, were not used to condemn Dutch mothers. The authors related the differences in parental behavior to cultural variations in the parents' conceptions of infancy. For example, they noted that

Even if a [Dutch] parent sees a child awake and wanting to play or look around, . . . he is not likely to respond to this wish or to the behavior which implies this wish because of fear of "spoiling" the baby (stated by 9 of the 11 mothers in Holland), or because of the belief that a baby in this age range should sleep and not play or stay awake (pp. 16-17).

Observations also revealed that Dutch infants had fewer toys with which to play. By 3 months of age, almost half of the Dutch babies still had no toys within sight or touch. The authors explained that Dutch mothers were concerned that "toys might keep the babies awake or overstimulate them." There were also cultural differences in the mothers' reactions to their infants crying.

Crying meant a call for help to U.S. mothers; they often reported lactating when they heard the cry. In Holland, crying was considered a part of a baby's behavior, good for the lungs and not always something to stop. In addition, though a mother might hear the cry in Holland and interpret it as a hunger cry, she still would not respond if it was not time for the scheduled feeding (pp. 7-8).

Rebelsky and Abeles did not suggest that Dutch mothers were rejecting or depriving their infants. They did not argue that intervention was necessary to change the patterns of mother–infant interaction. They concluded, instead, that both United States and Dutch cultures "may be training very different kinds of people, yet with each culture wanting the ones they produce." Such data reported for a group of lower-income American mothers might be followed by a call for a massive intervention program, or possibly the removal of the infants from their homes.

A similar cultural comparison was reported by Caudill and Weinstein (1966, 1969) who investigated maternal behavior in Japan and in the United States. The authors reported that American mothers talked more to their infants, while Japanese mothers more frequently lulled and rocked their infants. These differences were seen as reflecting different styles of mothering:

The style of the American mother seems to be in the direction of stimulating her baby to respond . . . whereas the style of the Japanese mother seems to be more in the direction of soothing and quieting her baby (1966, p. 18).

In both cultures, the "style" of mothering was influenced by the prevailing conception of infancy. Caudill and Weinstein (1969) reported that in Japan

The infant is seen more as a separate biological organism who from the beginning, in order to develop, needs to be drawn into increasingly interdependent relations with others. In America, the infant is seen more as a dependent biological organism who, in order to develop, needs to be made increasingly independent of others (p. 15).

American mothers, following their conception of infancy, pushed their infants to respond and to be active; Japanese mothers, also following their conception of infancy, attempted to foster reduced independent activity and greater reliance on others. As a part of this pattern, the Japanese tended to place less emphasis on clear verbal communication. Caudill and Weinstein reasoned that "such communication implies self-assertion and the separate identity and independence of the person" which would be contrary to the personality which Japanese mothers were attempting to build into their children. Thus, in Japan, as in Holland, mothers related to their infants in a manner consistent with their beliefs and values.

Caudill and Weinstein (1966) also reported data showing that according to American "standards," the Japanese infants might be considered "deficient." They engaged in less positive vocalization and spent less time with toys and other objects: "The Japanese infant," they said, "seems passive—he spends much more time simply lying awake in his crib or on a *zabuton* (a flat cushion) on the floor [p. 16]." The authors further reported that a study by Arai, Ishikawa, and Toshima (1958) found that—compared to American norms—Japanese infants showed a steady decline on tests of language and motor development from 4 to 36 months of age. Caudill and Weinstein, however, remained relativistic. They commented that although Arai, Ishikawa, and Toshima seemed somewhat distressed that the "Japanese mothers were so bound up in the lives of their infants that they interfered with the development of their infants in ways which made it difficult to meet the American norms," Caudill and Weinstein (1969) did not share the Japanese authors' concern over the lack of matching the American norms: "We do not believe that the differences we find are necessarily indications of a better or a worse approach to human life, but rather that such differences are a part of an individual's adjustment to his culture [p. 41]." Again, it is doubtful if the same conclusion would have been reached had the data been collected from a minority subculture in the United States.

A final example of the need for cultural relativism involves a study of Ashkenazic and Sephardic Jews in Brooklyn (Gross, 1967). Both groups were solidly middle class, and lived only two blocks apart. Both had been long established in this country and spoke English in their homes. On entering school, however, the Ashkenazic children averaged 17 points higher on a standard IQ test, a disparity similar in magnitude to that often reported between children of white suburbs and black slums.

Gross pointed out that it is generally assumed that inferior performance in school necessarily reflects deprivation and lack of opportunity. He argued, on the contrary, that each culture has its own ideas of what is important—some emphasize one skill, some another. Despite their children's lower IQ scores the Sephardic mothers were not deprived, however one defines the term: "In many cases they had minks, maids, and country homes." The Sephardic mothers were all native born, high school graduates, and none worked. The children "were blessed with privilege, money and comfort, but their level of academic readiness was similar to that of their underprivileged Israeli counterparts."

Gross explained that the difference was related to cultural tradition: The two communities represented different routes into the middle class—the Ashkenazim through success in school and the Sephardim through success in the marketplace. The author concluded that educational unpreparedness could be found among the "financially well-to-do" as well as among the lower classes, and suggested that this finding should be a "caution signal to social engineers." Gross questioned those who advocate changing lower-class blacks to conform to the life styles and values of middle-class whites, and suggested that there was an element of "white colonialism" in the attempt to "reshape the economically underprivileged in the image of the education-minded intellectually oriented academicians."

Gross's final point merits expansion, because intervention is becoming a big business in the United States today. The federal government is spending large amounts of money on intervention programs, and some social scientists fear that the interventionists will totally disregard subcultural systems in their attempts to "save" the "deprived" children.

When we force people of another culture to make an adjustment to ours, by that much we are destroying the integrity of their personalities. When too many adjustments of this sort are required too fast, the personality disintegrates and the result is an alienated, dissociated individual who cannot feel really at home in either culture (Lehmer, 1969).

Why is it so common for researchers to remain relativistic in their discussions of socialization practices in other nations, while being intolerant of subcultural differences among lower-income and minority groups in this country? One could propose that each nation socializes its children according to prevailing cultural values so that regardless of the fact that practices in other nations are different, children in each country develop the personalities and intellectual skills needed for success in their own particular social systems. This theory would argue that it is inappropriate to apply cultural relativism to subcultures because a person's success remains defined by the majority culture. Keller (1963), for example, argued that "cultural relativism ignores the fact that schools and industry are middle class in organization and outlook."

Cultural relativism and success in "schools and industry," however, are *not* mutually exclusive. It is possible to teach children the skills needed for articulation with the majority culture, while encouraging them to develop a pride in their own family or cultural heritage, and to utilize the particular skills which their own socialization has strengthened. A majority culture can, however, promote a narrow definition of success in order to ensure that the power of the society remain in the hands of a relatively select group within the society. Thus, by maintaining that any deviation from the white middle-class norm represents cultural deprivation, the white middle class is guarding its position as *the* source of culture—and power—in this nation. Cultural deprivation, then, is not just a psychological or educational issue; it is also very much a political issue.

POLITICS AND CULTURAL DEPRIVATION

Subcultural influences may represent a legitimate explanation for some of the behavior observed in particular lower-income or minority populations, but these influences should not be regarded as the sole determinant of life styles in these groups. Social scientists must also consider the way in which the majority culture, by its tolerance for social, political, and economic inequality, actually contributes to the development, in some subgroups, of the very characteristics which it considers "depriving." Responsibility, then, lies not with the subpopulations—for being "deprived"—but rather with the "total environmental structure that disenfranchises, alienates [and] disaffects [Hillson, 1970]." Fantini (1969) echoed this argument when he suggested that the "problem" of disadvantaged school children may not be rooted in the learner's "environmental and cultural deficiencies" but rather with the system—"the school and its educational process." He suggested the need for reorientation "from our present 'student-fault' to a stronger 'system-fault' position."

One of the most obvious system faults—and one that is quite relevant to child development—is inadequate medical care for the poor. Social scientists investigating cultural deprivation have paid insufficient attention to the ways in which poor physical health, both of mothers during pregnancy and of infants early in life, can influence the child's developmental progress. The incidences of inadequate prenatal nutrition, premature births, and complications of delivery which can lead to brain injuries, are all greater among lower-income and non-white groups (Abramowicz & Kass, 1966; Knoblock & Pasamanick, 1962). The effects of these medical differences are not unknown. Kagan (1965), for example, noted that one of the possible consequences of minimal brain damage during the perinatal and early postnatal periods is "increased restlessness and distractability, and inability to inhibit inappropriate responses during the pre-

and early school years." The effects of malnutrition on developing cognitive skills have also been reported (Brockman & Ricciuti, 1971). We do not know the extent to which developmental "deficits" of lower-income and minority-group children can be traced to these differences in their *medical* histories. This is a clear-cut case where responsibility for deprivation falls mainly on the *majority* culture.

Society as a whole is also responsible for other behavior patterns observed in deprived groups. Liebow (1967) argued that many of the behavior patterns he observed among lower-class blacks were "a direct response to the conditions of lower-class Negro life. . . ." His most cogent example involved the "delay of gratification" variable. The frequent finding that lower-class (usually black) children prefer a smaller reward given immediately rather than a larger reward given later is often cited as a serious handicap to their schoolwork. It is often hypothesized that the child-rearing practices employed by lower-class parents lead children to prefer immediate gratification; and attempts are being made to change these practices and to teach the children to defer gratification. Liebow demonstrated that, although socialization patterns may encourage behaviors which are seen as reflecting a preference for immediate gratification, the socialization patterns do not represent the primary determinant of this pattern. He argued that the so-called preference for immediate gratification derives from the conditions of life encountered in this population. The *realities of life* represent the causal agent; the child-rearing patterns are only intermediary variables. The importance of Liebow's argument merits thorough examination.

What appears as a "present-time" orientation to the outside observer is, to the man experi-

encing it, as much a future orientation as that of his middle-class counterpart. The difference between the two men lies not so much in their different orientations to time as in their different orientations to future time or more specifically, to their different futures.

As for the future, the young streetcorner man has a fairly good picture of it. . . . It is a future in which everything is uncertain except the ultimate destruction of his hopes and the eventual realization of his fears. The most he can reasonably look forward to is that these things do not come too soon. Thus when Richard squanders a week's pay in two days it is not because, like an animal or a child, he is "present-time oriented," unaware of or unconcerned with his future. He does so precisely because he is aware of the future and the hopelessness of it all.

Thus, apparent present-time concerns with consumption and indulgences—material and emotional—reflect a future-time orientation. "I want mine right now" is ultimately a cry of despair, a direct response to the future as he sees it (pp. 64-68).[1]

To encourage greater delay of gratification, interventionists should focus on the conditions causing the "hopelessness" and "despair" in lower-income populations, rather than emphasizing the necessity of changing child-rearing patterns. Other researchers have also noted that "conditions of life" represent major causal factors

---

[1]Liebow also pointed out that there is no intrinsic connection between "present-time" orientation and lower-class persons:

Whenever people of whatever class have been uncertain, skeptical or downright pessimistic about the future, "I want mine right now" has been one of the characteristic responses. . . . In wartime, especially, all classes tend to slough off conventional restraints on sexual and other behavior (i.e., become less able or less willing to defer gratification). And when inflation threatens, darkening the future, persons who formerly husbanded their resources with commendable restraint almost stampede one another rushing to spend their money. . . . [Thus] present-time orientation appears to be a *situation-specific phenomenon* rather than a part of the standard psychic equipment of cognitive lower-class man (pp. 68-69).

contributing to parental practices and child development. Minturn and Lambert (1964) interviewed mothers in six cultural settings (New England, Mexico, Philippines, Okinawa, India, and Kenya) and found that situational constraints in the mothers' immediate life space were primary determinants of their responses. Hess and Shipman (1966) analyzed situational constraints among lower-income Americans and noted that

a family in an urban ghetto has few choices to make with respect to such basic things as residence, occupation, and condition of housing, and on the minor points of choice that come with adequate discretionary income. A family with few opportunities to make choices among events that affect it is not likely to encourage the children to think of life as consisting of a wide range of behavioral options among which they must learn to discriminate (p. 4).

The same authors (Shipman & Hess, 1966) spoke specifically about language development:

The lower-class mother's narrow range of alternatives is being conveyed to the child through language styles which convey her attitude of few options and little individual power, and this is now being reflected in the child's cognitive development (p. 17).

Gordon (1969) reported specific data. He found that within the "poverty group" the amount of verbal interaction directed toward an infant was related to the "mother's view of her control of her destiny." The extent to which an individual feels he has some control over his destiny is also related to a whole myriad of variables associated with educational achievement. Coleman, Campbell, Hobson, McPartland, Mood, Weinfeld, and York (1966) found that, among minority group students, this factor was the best predictor of academic success. Similarly, Rotter (1966) argued that:

the individual who has a strong belief that he can control his own destiny is likely to (*a*) be more alert to those aspects of the environment which provide useful information for his future behaviors, (*b*) take steps to improve his environmental position, (*c*) place greater value on skill or achievement reinforcements and be generally more concerned with his ability, particularly his failures, and (*d*) be resistive to subtle attempts to influence him (p. 25).

There is little doubt that the realistic perception of the poor that they have little control over their lives leads not only to the "hopelessness" and "despair" observed by Liebow, but also to less concern with education and reduced academic success.

Interventionists must concern themselves with these social, economic, and political realities of lower-class life and see the relations between these realities and indexes of parental behavior and intellectual development. Several interventionists have moved in this direction. Schaefer (1969) reported that "current stresses and the absence of social support influence maternal hostility, abuse and neglect of the child." He suggested that intervention programs hoping to change a mother's behavior toward her child needed to "alleviate the stress and increase the support of mothers at the time the initial mother–child relationship is developed."

Similarly, Kagan (1969) spoke of the "need for ecological change" to improve the conditions of life among lower-class populations. He emphasized that the interventionists needed to be sensitive to "the communities' belief as to what arrangements will help them," and that the changes should be directed toward facilitating the development of a "sense of control over the future."

Other researchers have come to the same conclusion. Pavenstedt (1967) reported that every member of her staff concurred "in the conviction that far-reaching social and economic change must take place in order to fundamentally alter the lives of the families" they observed. Stodolsky and Lesser (1968) suggested that intervention programs "would probably be a lot more successful if we were to modify the conditions which probably lead to many of these [parental] behaviors; namely, lack of money and of access to jobs." Liebow (1967) presented the most convincing argument:

We do not have to see the problem in terms of breaking into a puncture proof circle, of trying to change values, of disrupting the lines of communication between parent and child so that parents cannot make children in their own image, thereby transmitting their culture inexorably, ad infinitum. No doubt, each generation does provide role models for each succeeding one. Of much greater importance for the possibilities of change, however, is the fact that many similarities between the lower-class Negro father and son (or mother and daughter) do not result from "cultural transmission" but from the fact that the son goes out and independently experiences the same failure, in the same areas, and for much the same reasons as his father. What appears as a dynamic, self-sustaining cultural process is, in part at least, a relatively simple piece of social machinery which turns out, in rather mechanical fashion, independently produced look-alikes. The problem is how to change the conditions which, by guaranteeing failure, cause the son to be made in the image of the father (p. 223).

Intervention programs must effect changes in the conditions of life and not ignore these issues by merely attempting to change behavior patterns. Intervention programs which do attempt to change the "conditions of life," however, may encounter political opposition, simply because to change the conditions of life necessitates a wider distribution of power and wealth. While it is beyond the scope of the present discussion to closely examine the politics of poverty, it is necessary to understand why poverty may be difficult to eliminate.

All poor peoples do not share the characteristics which Lewis (1965) calls the "culture of poverty" or which researchers have labeled "deprived." Lewis reported that these characteristics are found only among the poor people who occupy a "marginal position in a class-stratified, highly individuated, capitalistic society" in which there is a "lack of effective participation and integration of the poor in the major institutions of the larger society." He reported, for example, that:

many of the primitive or preliterate peoples studied by anthropologists suffer from dire poverty which is the result of poor technology and/or poor natural resources, or of both, but they do not have the traits of the subculture of poverty. Indeed, they do not constitute a subculture because their societies are not highly stratified. In spite of their poverty they have a relatively integrated, satisfying and self-sufficient culture (p. 48).

Where a "culture of poverty" exists, however, the poor are less than poor: They are poor while others are rich, and they do not have the power to demand their "fair share." Thus, Lewis aptly characterized the fight for equality in this country as a "political power struggle" and pointed out that, rather than allowing poor people to participate effectively in society, many of those currently holding power "emphasize the need for guidance and control to remain in the hands of the middle class. . . ." The culture of poverty will not be obliterated, however, until power is shared. The elimination of physical poverty per se may not be enough to eliminate the culture of poverty; more basic political changes may be necessary. Some might even argue that a political revolution is the only means of redistributing power and wealth, thus eliminating the culture of poverty. Lewis noted that:

by creating basic structural changes in society, by redistributing wealth, by organizing the poor and giving them a sense of belonging, of power and of leadership, revolutions frequently succeed in abolishing some of the basic characteristics of the culture of poverty even when they do not succeed in abolishing poverty itself (p. 53).

To illustrate, Lewis went on to report:

On the basis of my limited experience in one socialist country—Cuba—and on the basis of my reading, I am inclined to believe that the culture of poverty does not exist in the socialist countries. After the Castro Revolution I found much less of the despair, apathy, and hopelessness which are so diagnostic of urban slums in the culture of poverty. The people had a new sense of power and importance. They were armed and were given a doctrine which glorified the lower class as the hope of humanity (p. 49).

The purpose of this discussion is not to encourage political revolution, but rather to point out the complexities of attempting to understand the behavior of people who differ from us—culturally, financially, or any way. It is easier to think of these other people as "groups," and more difficult to think of them as individuals who differ a great deal among themselves—just as members of our own group do. It is easier to think of them as wanting to be like us and needing us to help them; it is more difficult to reject the philosophy of the "white man's burden" and allow people the freedom to retain life styles which differ from the ones we know. It is easy to blame people for what we have defined as their "deficits," but more difficult to consider how we as a society might have contributed to the problems we have defined as "theirs."

REFERENCES

Abramowicz, M., & Kass, E. H. Pathogenesis and prognosis of prematurity. *New England Journal of Medicine,* 1966, **275,** 878.

Arai, S.; Ishikawa, J.; & Toshima, K. Developpement psychomoteur des enfants Japonais. *La revue de neuropsychiatrie infantile et d'hygiene mentale de l'enfance,* 1958, **6,** 262-269. Cited by W. Caudill & H. Weinstein, Maternal care and infant behavior in Japan and America. *Psychiatry,* 1969, **32,** 41.

Baratz, J. C., & Shuy, R. W. (eds.) *Teaching black children to read.* Washington, D. C.: Center for Applied Linguistics, 1969.

Baratz, S. S., & Baratz, J. C. Early childhood intervention: The social science base of institutional racism. *Harvard Educational Review,* 1970, **40,** 29-50.

Bernstein, B. Language and social class. *British Journal of Sociology,* 1960, **11,** 271-276.

Bernstein, B. Social class and linguistic development: A theory of social learning. In A. H. Halsey; H. Floud, & C. A. Anderson (eds.), *Education, economy and society.* Glencoe, Ill.: Free Press, 1961.

Birren, J. E., & Hess, R. Influences of biological, psychological, and social deprivations on learning and performance. In *Perspectives on human deprivation.* Washington, D. C.: Department of Health, Education, and Welfare, United States Government Printing Office, 1968.

Brockman, L. M., & Ricciuti, H. N. Severe protein-calorie malnutrition and cognitive development in infancy and early childhood. *Developmental Psychology,* 1971, **4,** 312-319.

Caudill, W., & Weinstein, H. Maternal care and infant behavior in Japanese and American urban middle class families. Bethesda, Md.: National Institute of Mental Health, 1966. (Mimeo)

Caudill, W., & Weinstein, H. Maternal care and infant behavior in Japan and America. *Psychiatry,* 1969, **32,** 12-43.

Chandler, B. J., & Erickson, F. D. *Sounds of society: A demonstration program in group inquiry.* (Final Rep. No. 6-2044) Washington, D. C.: United States Government Printing Office, 1968.

Coleman, J. S., Campbell, E. Q., Hobson, C. J., McPartland, J., Mood, A. M. Weinfeld, F. D., & York, R. L. *Equality of educational opportunity.* Washington, D.C.:

United States Government Printing Office, 1966.

Coles, R. Violence in ghetto children. In S. Chess & A. Thomas (eds.), *Annual progress in child psychiatry and child development.* New York: Brunner/Mazel, 1968.

Davé, R. H. The identification and measurement of environmental variables that are related to educational achievement. Unpublished doctoral dissertation, University of Chicago, 1963.

Fantini, M. D. Beyond cultural deprivation and compensatory education. *Psychiatry and Social Science Review,* 1969, **3**, 6-13.

Foster, H. L. Dialect-lexicon and listening comprehension. Unpublished doctoral dissertation, Teachers College, Columbia University, 1969.

Foster, H. L. Foster's Jive Lexicon Analogies Test. Series II. Buffalo: Office of Teacher Education, State University of New York, 1970. (Mimeo)

Gans, H. J. *The urban villagers: Group and class in the life of Italian-Americans.* New York: Free Press of Glencoe, 1962.

Gordon, I. J. *Early child stimulation through parent education.* (Final Rep. No. PH5-R-306) Washington, D.C.: Department of Health, Education and Welfare, United States Government Printing Office, 1969.

Gross, M. *Learning readiness in two Jewish groups.* New York: Center for Urban Education, 1967.

Herskovits, M. *The myth of the Negro past.* Boston: Beacon Press, 1958.

Hess, R. D., & Shipman, V. C. Maternal attitude toward the school and the role of pupil: Some social class comparisons. Paper presented at the Conference on Curriculum and Teaching in Depressed Urban Areas, Columbia University, 1966.

Hillson, M. The disadvantaged child. *Community Mental Health Journal,* 1970, **6**, 81-83.

Jessor, R., & Richardson, S. Psychosocial deprivation and personality development. In *Perspectives on human deprivation.* Washington, D. C.: United States Government Printing Office, 1968.

Kagan, J. Information processing in the child. In P. H. Mussen, J. J. Conger, & J. Kagan (eds.), *Readings in child development and personality.* New York: Harper & Row, 1965.

Kagan, J. On cultural deprivation. In D. C. Glass (ed.), *Environmental influences.* New York: Rockefeller University Press, 1968.

Kagan, J. Social class and academic progress: An analysis and suggested solution strategies. Paper presented at the meeting of the American Association for the Advancement of Science, Boston, 1969.

Keller, S. The social world of the urban slum child: Some early findings. *American Journal of Orthopsychiatry,* 1963, **33**, 823-834.

Knoblock, H., & Pasamanick, B. Mental subnormality. *New England Journal of Medicine,* 1962, **266**, 1092-1097.

Krauss, R. M., & Rotter, G. S. Communication abilities of children as a function of status and age. *Merrill-Palmer Quarterly of Behavior and Development,* 1968, **14**, 161-174.

Labov, W. Some sources of reading problems for Negro speakers of nonstandard English. In A. Frazier (ed.), *New directions in elementary English.* Champaign, Ill.: National Council of Teachers of English, 1967.

Lehmer, M. Navajos want their own schools. *San Francisco Examiner and Chronicle,* December 14, 1969.

Lewis, O. *La Vida: A Puerto Rican family in the culture of poverty.* New York: Random House, 1965.

Liebow, E. *Tally's corner: A study of Negro street-corner men.* Boston: Little, Brown, 1967.

Maccoby, M., & Modiano, N. On culture and equivalence. I. In J. S. Bruner, R. R. Olver, & P. M. Greenfield (eds.), *Studies in cognitive growth.* New York: John Wiley and Sons, 1966.

Minturn, L., & Lambert, W. W. *Mothers of six cultures.* New York: John Wiley and Sons, 1964.

Pavenstedt, E. (ed.) *The drifters.* Boston: Little, Brown, 1967.

Rebelsky, F., & Abeles, G. Infancy in Holland and in the United States. Paper presented at the meeting of the Society for Research in Child Development, Santa Monica, 1969.

Riessman, F. *The culturally deprived child.* New York: Harper & Row, 1962.

Rotter, J. B. Generalized expectancies for internal versus external control of reinforcement. *Psychological Monographs,* 1966, **80** (1, Whole No. 609).

Schaefer, E. S. Need for early and continuing education. Paper presented at the meeting of the American Association for the Advancement of Science, Boston, 1969.

Shipman, V. C., & Hess, R. D. Early experiences in the socialization of cognitive modes in children: A study of urban Negro families. Paper presented at the meeting of the Conference of Family and Society, Merrill-Palmer Institute, 1966.

Sroufe, L. A. A methodological and philosophical critique of intervention-oriented research. *Developmental Psychology,* 1970, **2,** 140-145.

Stewart, W. A. Sociolinguistic factors in the history of American Negro dialects. *The Florida FL Reporter,* 1967, **5**(2).

Stewart, W. A. Linguistic and conceptual deprivation—fact or fancy? Paper presented at the meeting of the Society for Research in Child Development, Santa Monica, 1969. (a)

Stewart, W. A. On the use of Negro dialect in the teaching of reading. In J. C. Baratz & R. W. Shuy (eds.), *Teaching black children to read.* Washington, D. C.: Center for Applied Linguistics, 1969. (b)

Stodolsky, S., & Lesser, G. Learning patterns in the disadvantaged. In S. Chess & A. Thomas (eds.), *Annual progress in child psychiatry and child development.* New York: Brunner/Mazel, 1968.

Wolf, R. M. The identification and measurement of environmental process variables related to intelligence. Unpublished doctoral dissertation, University of Chicago, 1964.

III. Intelligence and Thought

The development and enhancement of intelligent behavior has concerned philosophers and educators since the dawn of civilization. Evidence of this is borne witness historically by a rich, if at times confusing, dialogue in which the origins, performance, and encouragement of intellect have been vigorously debated. Among the significant issues that have been identified are: (1) Is intelligence a product of biological or environmental events? (2) What is intelligence, and how should it be measured? and (3) How shall intellectual capacity be fostered?

Intelligence and Cognition

Scientists interested in the development of thought have centered their inquiries on two facets of intellectual growth: the child's acquisition of information (intelligence), and the child's formulation and use of rules or principles of thought in the construction of intelligence (cognition). By focusing on the concept of intelligence, scientists have sought to determine *what* children know (i.e., the content or product of the child's intellectual strivings) and those circumstances contributing to the child's attainment of knowledge (e.g., the effects of exposure to formal bodies of information in scholastic settings). In contrast, studies of cognition have asked *how* the child comes to know its environment. This latter concern focuses on the underlying structure of the child's intellect, principally upon explaining how the child arrives at an understanding of its world.

While the interests of scientists involved in defining the intellectual perimeters of children's thought parallel those of colleagues concerned with discovering how children arrive at this information, research on intelligence has concentrated on defining and assessing learning outcomes from the perspective of environmental input (viz., what is taught). Cognitive research, in contrast, has attempted to specify learner–environmental outcomes in which the child's experience and construction of reality provides the major focus for evaluating intellectual growth. Further differences in approach are also evident. Conceptually, the study of intelligence has generated a cumulative model of intellectual growth which focuses on continuities in intellectual attainment across age (i.e., growth achieved through the extension and expansion of existing knowledge), whereas cognitive research has stressed changes in the quality of intelligence over time by concentrating on the discontinuities (i.e., dramatic transformations and shifts in how information is processed) characteristic of thought at different ages (Gagne, 1968; Piaget, 1963). This latter approach assumes that thought changes at different stages of development as a function of maturational and environmental conditions which become evident through the child's restructuring of its experiences.

The first selection of this series of readings examines several traditional and contemporary issues frequently raised in the assessment of intellectual growth in children. In addition, the reader is provided a unique historical account of changes and refinements associated with the construction and use of the intelligence test as an instrument for appraising intellectual maturity.

Thought in the Young Child

Thought represents a distinct human achievement. In no other species is the ability to seek solutions to problems through the use of intellectual resources so well developed or so frequently evident in the conduct of behavioral transactions. Yet thought is also an emergent property, one in which experience over time plays a central role. Certainly, the young infant provides us with clear evidence of its ability to process and sort out different forms of information, as well as its capacity to employ effective solutions to adaptation. Yet the quality of human thought is such that among individuals of different age, as well as within the same individual over time, we find that the nature of intelligence differs dramatically. Two issues may be raised concerning this observation. First, it may be asked how does thought differ across individuals. Second, we may inquire why these differences exist.

From naturalistic observations, as well as more formal assessment, it is evident that a child does not think like an adult. While we may take account of this difference by recognizing that a child's experience and knowledge of its environment is more restricted than that of an adult, differences in the intellectual productivity of individuals across time appear only partially attributable to experiential factors. In contrast, it has become increasingly evident that the manner in which a child perceives, organizes, and structures its environment differs from that of an adult. For example, in infancy the game of peek-a-boo is made cognitively meaningful insofar as the parent's hiding or "out of sight," behavior is literally synonymous with the infant's "out of mind" response. This reaction is predictable, since the young infant has not developed a concept of object permanence (i.e., an understanding that things exist apart from our perception of them). Similarly, in the preschool child, one cookie broken in half often fulfills the child's request for two cookies since the child has not achieved the idea of conservation of matter (i.e., the recognition that matter remains the same despite alterations in appearance if nothing is added or subtracted). What does a school-age child see? How are its perceptions different from that of an adult? These questions are explored in the paper by Sigel. As discussed in this reading, a child's perceptions, and thereby its understanding of its world, are incomplete. Yet this world is not random. Rather it consists of a subjective perspective which is dictated by the child's efforts at constructing a view of events which conforms to its perceptions. These observations, as Sigel notes, suggest that our assessment of children's knowledge requires an acute sensitivity and recognition that the child's thought is not capricious, but reflects a different and unique awareness of its environment.

The role of cognition, and our understanding of its contribution to the child's development has become recognized relatively recently. This perspective has been advanced largely through the research and writing of J. Piaget. His theories of development, which view children's thought as an organized system of beliefs, have assumed a critical role in the way in which developmentalists have come to regard children's intelligence. In the paper by Weis, Piaget's ideas and the postulates of his theory are reviewed. In addition, Weis attempts to provide the reader with pragmatic suggestions for enhancing children's cognitive potential.

While Piaget's ideas have extended our understanding of children's thought in many ways, several key concepts have been subject to rigorous investigation. These include Piaget's concepts of animism (i.e., the child's understanding of living things) and egocentrism (i.e., the child's inability to understand the perspective held by another person). The concept of animism is explored in second-grade children in the paper by Looft. From this research it may be noted that the child's understanding of life, as Looft concludes, is founded upon knowledge acquired gradually, and integrated by the child in conjunction with the unfolding of cognitive structures necessary for effective information processing.

The paper written by Borke examines Piaget's concept of egocentrism. This report introduces Borke's attempt at replicating and reanalyzing a classic experiment performed by Piaget and Inhelder (1956). The final paper in this series of selections, by Bronfenbrenner, is a particularly critical reading which evaluates no single theory of intelligence, but rather examines the role of environmental intervention in the fostering of intellect, an issue of major concern in our attempt to translate theory into practice.

REFERENCES

Gagne, R. M. Contributions of learning to human development. *Psychological Review,* 1968, **75**, 177-191.

Piaget, J. The attainment of invariants and reversible operations in the development of thinking. *Social Research,* 1963, **30**, 284-299.

Piaget, J., and Inhelder, B. *The child's conception of space.* London: Routledge & Kegan Paul, 1956.

6.

Robert L. Thorndike

MR. BINET'S TEST 70 YEARS LATER

Unlike a human infant, a psychometric device has no clearly defined and annually celebrated birthday. The moment of conception is unspecified, and attended by no particular ecstasy; the period of gestation is variable and ill-defined; and the date of parturition is usually unknown. So in looking for a birthdate for the Binet Intelligence Scales, we have some room for maneuver. However, a reasonable case can be made for 1905, the year in which L'Annee Psychologique published the account of a workable version of an individual intelligence test. And so, we may define 1975 as the 70th anniversary of that event—an event that, as much as any in the early years of this century, determined the shape and course of subsequent psychological and educational research, and of psychological and possibly educational practice. For my remarks today, I have chosen to look at a few aspects of that 70-year career.

That first set of tasks proposed by Binet stemmed from no elegant theory, nor from any precise definition of intelligence. Binet made no assumptions about the causes or origins of the intellectual deficits that he proposed to study (for his initial concern was primarily with intellectual deficiency), nor about their prognostic significance for future development. He undertook to describe objectively, in the here and now,

levels of development of what he described in a very general way as "judgment." The basis of his selection of tasks was very largely empirical—try-out with groups of children of various ages in regular school, and comparison of their performance with that of those who were in institutions for the mentally retarded.

In his own country of France, Binet's efforts appear to have been received with what our late colleague Alexander Wesman used to describe as "modified rapture," but in the United States the rapture was more immediate and complete. By 1916 there were at least three translations and adaptations of Binet's scales—one by Goddard at the Vineland Training School, one by Kuhlmann at Minnesota, and one by Terman at Stanford—but of these only Terman's Stanford-Binet has survived to the present day. It has not only survived but flourished. According to figures provided by the publisher on sales of the test record form, Terman's version appears to have been administered to about 150,000 persons a year during its first incarnation from 1916 to 1937, to about 500,000 a year during the reincarnation from 1937 to 1960, and to about 800,000 a year during the third coming from 1960 to 1972.

It is interesting to speculate why this version won out in the competition. Was it because it was a better test, better standardized, with a more discriminating, more administrable set of tasks? Was it that it provided adequate "top" so that it was able to assess the ability not only of the deficient but also the intellectually gifted? Or was it due to Terman's professional

Source: *Educational Researcher,* 1975, **4,** 3-7. Thorndike, Robert L., "Mr. Binet's Test 70 Years Later." *Educational Researcher,* vol. 4, pp. 3-7. Copyright © 1975, American Educational Research Association, Washington, D.C.

reputation and personal enthusiasm, together with his massive and widely publicized "Genetic Studies of Genius" in which he followed over 1,000 very bright California youngsters through 35 years of their lives and all that remained of his?

Be that as it may, it was the Stanford-Binet that survived, that was revised in 1937 and again modestly in 1960, that was renormed in 1972, and that has been for most of the past 60 years the workhorse of psychometric appraisal of cognitive development, the standard against which other tests of cognitive abilities have been evaluated, and more recently a prime target for the social critics of ability testing.

Binet was concerned with an over-all appraisal of mental functioning. It was not that he failed to recognize that functions were involved other than the "judgment" to which he accorded a central role—functions of perception, discrimination and memory—and that each might be separately evaluated. It was rather that he felt it most important to provide a unitary over-all appraisal of level of mental functioning, and believed that a judicious pooling of a variety of different tasks provided the best basis for such an appraisal. This unitary over-all appraisal has been carried forward to the present as the central feature of the successive versions of the Stanford-Binet—the lineal descendant of Binet's original efforts.

A good deal of test development in the past 40 years has tended to move away from single-score composite measures, just as factor analyses of abilities have moved their focus away from Spearman's original conception of a general intellectual g factor of perceiving relationships. But it is worth standing back for a moment and asking whether the latter-day urge to fractionate abilities into smaller and smaller splinters always represents either sound theory or effective practice.

Since the basic pool of exercises used in the Binet includes tasks of a spatial nature as well as verbal tasks, tasks calling for short term retention as well as tasks demanding the application of more remote past experiences, it is possible both rationally and statistically to identify several components in the Binet score. Factor analyses of the exercises of the 1937 and 1960 versions of the Binet, starting with McNemar's original 1942 analyses of the revised test, have generated multiple factors that have been more or less interpretable. But it is also true that in these analyses a very large proportion of the common-factor variance (approximately 80% in some analyses that we have recently carried out) is extracted by the first factor. This large common core is what gives meaning to a single score and support for Binet's original notion of pooling performance on a diverse array of tasks into a single assessment of cognitive ability.

One feature of the over-all assessment by the Binet that has given it practical significance to users has been its stability in an individual over a span of years. My very first article published as a graduate student 42 years ago related that stability to the interval over which the forecast was made, and a host of subsequent analyses affirm the dependence of the stability on not only time interval but also the age level at initial testing. As we consider fractionating cognitive abilities into more narrowly defined bits and pieces, it is appropriate to ask whether those narrower abilities show comparable stability, and especially whether the individual patterning of strengths and weaknesses is maintained from one time to another, especially in young children.

This question is better attacked using those tests that are specifically designed to yield more than a single score, such as, for example, the Wechsler Intelligence Scale for Children.

Thanks to the kindness of Dr. Robert

Osborne of the University of Georgia, who made available his data on repeated WISC testing of children in grades 1, 2, 4, and 6, we have been able to calculate the stability of the differences between various part scores on the WISC. Thus, one might look at the difference between Verbal and Performance IQ and undertake to interpret it in some way in relation to the potential or personality of a child. How stable is the difference score on whose basis such an interpretation is made? Comparing grade 1 with grade 6, Osborne's data yield a correlation of 0.38.

Clinicians have from time to time been tempted to interpret even more specific aspects of patterning in Wechsler profiles. How stable are these in young children? We calculated the stability coefficients for all possible pairs of sub-test differences over this grade 1 to grade 6 time span. The correlations range from − 0.08 to 0.39, with a median value of 0.15. These very modest relationships may be compared with the stability of WISC total IQ for these same children over the same time span of 0.79.

Of course, over shorter time spans and at later ages the stability of the differential measures is a bit better, as is that of total IQ, and the distinctions between some pairs of sub-scores may have value as a source of tentative hypotheses for the clinician studying a specific child. But the real stability of cognitive measures lies in the common core of general cognitive functioning. Especially with young children, Binet may have shown good judgment in focussing upon "judgment," this common core.

In his early test series, Binet was content to express individual cognitive performance in rather crude age equivalents, reporting to the nearest year the developmental level of the children whom he tested. However, as the tests were taken over in the United States and developed by

Terman and others, the attempt was made to achieve greater precision, reporting mental ages in years and months rather than in simple year units, and the ratio concept proposed by Stern in Germany was adopted as a form of score that displayed the individual's progress relative to his own age group. Thus, the IQ came to occupy a central role in our conceptions of testing of cognitive performance, and is perpetuated in our language to this day in that somewhat unhappy phrase "IQ tests." Next I will consider the wandering IQ in the special context of Terman's development of the Binet Scales.

In his 1916 test, Terman, by a judicious assignment of tasks to age levels and specification of scoring standards for evaluating performance, arranged things so that the average mental age on his test series would correspond to chronological age at each age level. Thus, the average IQ was made to remain firmly at 100, and appeared to do so rather consistently over the whole range of ages at least from 6 to 14. Beyond that age range, the 1916 test was not really adequately normed and it had inadequate top to tap the abilities of older children of high ability.

It so happened, not by any special plan or design, that the standard deviation of these 1916 IQ's was approximately twelve points, so that the middle fifty percent of youngsters fell between roughly 92 and 108 on this ratio index. Fortunately, this spread of scores turned out to be quite uniform over the age range, so that a given IQ value could be interpreted in much the same terms whether the individual was six years old or ten years old or twelve years old. Thus, the IQ became in effect a type of standard score with a mean of 100 and a standard deviation of twelve.

When the 1937 revision was produced, once again the tasks were chosen and scoring adjusted so as to yield an average IQ of approximately 100 at each age level in a representative population sample. The equivalence of the mean IQ's on the 1916 and 1937 versions of the test was fairly well documented by a study by Merrill in which some 1500 youngsters who had previously taken the 1916 test were tested with the 1937 version, and this is supported by the careful national surveys carried out in Scotland. To a very close approximation, on average the individual who earned an IQ of 100 on the earlier test also earned an IQ of 100 on the later test. However, for reasons which have never been quite clear to me, the standard deviation of the new test in the US was no longer twelve but somewhere in the range of 16 to 17. The spread of scores was increased by about a third. In the Scottish surveys the comparable figures were 15 and 20.

I've brooded a good deal about how this might have come to be. In both the early and late tests, the authors required that the items they retained in the test show an increase in percent passing from one age to the next. However, in both forms, attention was also paid to having test tasks that might reasonably be considered to have an intellectual component, and to including tasks that showed a substantial relationship to the total score for individuals of a given age. The last criterion corresponds to the conventional type of item analysis that has become completely familiar in test development over the past fifty years. It seems to me that there must have been a good deal more emphasis upon the item's relationship to total score *within* an age group in the development of the 1937 test than there had been in 1916. This, combined with a need to generate more than twice as many tasks in order to have two forms of the test, L and M, probably resulted in items that were less related to chronological age and that showed flatter profiles of improvement as one went from younger to older children. Items of this

sort would tend to show a greater spread of score values for children of a single age and to yield the larger standard deviation of scores.

The shift in variability of scores would have only a modest impact on the typical youngster who fell fairly close to the national average. However, the impact upon individuals at the extremes would be quite marked. This can be illustrated by instances at both extremes. For example, in Terman's longitudinal study of very bright children, to which I made earlier reference, the average IQ of the original gifted group was approximately 150 based upon the 1916 form of the Binet. The average IQ for these children based upon the 1937 form of the Binet was approximately 132. The difference between 150 and 132 suggests a relatively modest regression towards average in the offspring generation. On the other hand, if one realizes that the 150 on the 1916 form was fully four standard deviations above the general population mean, and represents approximately the equivalent of 165 on the 1937 form, the regression from the highly selected parent generation to their offspring becomes considerably more marked, the children being only about one half as extreme as their gifted parents.

At the other end of the scale the Binet critical score for defining mental deficiency had been set on the 1916 test at approximately an IQ of 70, or minus two and a half standard deviations. If one translates that into the scale of the 1937 Binet, it corresponds approximately to an IQ of 60, and educational and legal interpretations would need to be adjusted to correspond. I suspect that they were in part, but I am not sure that they ever were completely.

The 1960 edition was a consolidation of the two forms developed in 1937, where the consolidation took account of data accumulated during the 1950's but the basic standardization population was the same one that had been used in 1937. In 1960, frank recognition was made of the fact that an IQ functions as a standard score, and the IQ equivalents of mental ages were adjusted so that at every chronological age level the mean would be 100 and the standard deviation would be 16. This adjustment also took account of the fact that the original 1937 standardization population had been somewhat disproportionately drawn from middle and upper socioeconomic levels and that the obtained mean IQ's in the 1937 standardization sample were running two or three points above the 100 level.

The final journey of this wandering IQ occurred in 1972 when the form of the test assembled in 1960 was re-standardized on a new and current sample of cases. The standardization procedure was somewhat different from the one that had been used previously. The 1972 sample was based on the year-before standardization of the Cognitive Abilities Test on a large national sample, rather than being chosen to proportionally represent socioeconomic categories. A stratified sample of children was selected to be representative of those who had been included in the 20,000-per-grade group-test standardization. That child and/or one or more siblings were tested on the Binet. The sample was so chosen that at each age level the deviation IQ's of the group-tested siblings had a mean of 100 and a standard deviation of 16. If we can assume that the large-scale group-test standardization was appropriately carried out, then it would seem that by this procedure the individual tests should have been rather effectively anchored to a much larger base population than could possibly be tested directly with an individual test. Since the correlation between the group test and the Binet was of the order of .70, a

good deal of control over the characteristics of the Binet sample was achieved.

The first step was to look at the distribution of IQ's based upon the 1960 standard scores. These, it should be remembered, had been based upon the standardization testing for Form L and Form M in the early 1930's.

The shifts were fairly dramatic. At the preschool ages, the average deviation IQ of the 1972 sample was running close to 110. This, then, gradually dropped off to an IQ of about 102 at age 10 and gradually crept up again to 105 or 106 by the adolescent years. What makes these higher average values even more impressive is that the sample in 1972 included ethnic minorities as well as the white group that was the only group tested in the 1930's. If one allows for this fact, the actual shift is probably two or three points greater than it appears on the surface.

The general rise in IQ level is not surprising. Such a rise has been reported by test-makers on all sorts of ability tests both in this country and abroad. The thing that is perhaps a little surprising is the size of the shift in the preschool group. On the other hand, perhaps this isn't surprising when one considers how life has changed for a preschooler between 1932 and 1972. Certainly, the amount of verbal and visual stimulation that the preschooler of 1970 was getting was enormously more than that available to the typical preschool-age child in the 1930's. The child of 1970 was probably watching television three or four hours a day. Furthermore, he had parents with two or three years more education, on the average, and had a much wider and more varied stock of books, toys, and other materials available to him.

The question we immediately faced with respect to these preschoolers was whether they represented the "Sesame Street" generation who were brighter than their older siblings, and would maintain their higher IQ's as they got older, or whether longitudinal data would reproduce the cross-sectional results with the drop that we observed in 1972. Thanks to the Spencer Foundation, we have now finished retesting, after an interval of roughly three years, about 80% of the 750 children in the preschool norming group who were between three and one half and six years old at the time of the original testing, and I can report in a general way what has happened to these youngsters over a three-year period. The best quick summary is that they have lost about one IQ point per year, so that in this group the drop from age 4 to age 9 would be about five points; and this would come close to the difference that was observed in the cross-sectional data. The greater change from the 1930's to the 1970's at the pre-school level appears to be a genuine phenomenon and not a deficiency in our sampling procedures or a very recent bulge in measured ability.

Some have been inclined to point a finger of reproach at our schools and ask: Why isn't the preschool acceleration maintained through the school years? Perhaps, instead, the finger should be pointed at our forebears with the question: Why didn't you provide a stimulating world for your toddlers? But more realistically, we should recognize that with TV, the world of the child has changed, and that the beneficial aspects of that change are experienced primarily, perhaps even exclusively, in the preschool years.

These re-norming results are both intellectually interesting and practically significant. They indicate the extent to which the total impact of a changing culture can have an influence at least on the test performance that youngsters display, and probably on their basic cognitive functioning, and they reinforce our recognition

that the tests that we have produced measure developed abilities, developed in a particular cultural setting.

Of course, individual differences persist in the midst of this general shift, and the variability of IQ's in 1972 has remained at least as great as that established in 1960, based upon testing carried out in the period from 1932 to 1937. That is, the changes that have produced a general elevation of abilities have not reduced individual differences, but the current culture has maintained them at least at the level that they displayed in the earlier period.

We were interested to inquire whether the shifts that have taken place over the forty-year period have affected the test items, uniformly, or whether some systematic and meaningful description could be made of the items that show large changes and the items that show small ones. Dr. Robin Garfinkle has just finished a dissertation on this topic based upon the preschool results, and rather to our surprise the largest shifts in the direction of items becoming easier have taken place in the nonverbal, pictorial, perceptual, and memory items, rather than the ones that involve a good deal of semantic content. This phenomenon appears clearly only at the earlier age levels, that is, from about age three to about age four and one half, but it suggests that the impact of cultural change on the preschooler has not been primarily and fundamentally a verbal impact but has been at least as much a visual and perceptual enrichment.

Binet developed his scales 70 years ago in a France that was ethnically and culturally relatively homogeneous for a school system generally elitist in its orientation and unsympathetic and unresponsive to individual variability. In that setting he sought a procedure that could add objectivity and impartiality to the identification of children to be screened out of the regular school system for more appropriate placement in special classes. When Terman adapted the scales for use in this country, completion of high school was still the exception rather than the rule here, and schooling through most of the country was oriented toward the white English-speaking majority. Even in the 1930's it seemed to Terman more important to have a clearly defined all-white norming group than to have representation of the totality of the school-age population.

The United States of 1975 is different from France in 1905—or even the United States of 1930. We recognize and try to adapt to our ethnic and cultural pluralism, though not in full accord as to how best to do it. We undertake to provide education for all citizens at least through the secondary school years, and in many locations through some type of post-secondary program. We do this in a world in which the only thing that is constant is change at an ever increasing rate. How must our conception and use of Mr. Binet's test be modified for the educational scene of 1975?

Clearly, the normative interpretations must be adjusted to the changing times. But it seems equally clear that the prog-nostic interpretations must be adjusted to the particular place—that is, the setting and sub-culture in which a child has been reared and educated. Though the temporal change in a culture may facilitate test performance, sub-cultural differences may inhibit that performance. As a consequence, any rigid specification of level of test performance as the basis for decision or action—whether specified by law or by administrative ruling—seems unwise and perhaps pernicious. Binet's test—or any other—must guide, and not replace informed judgment.

Accepting the goal of maximizing the effectiveness of education for *all* children and youth, we must face up to the problem that we have long acknowledged but seldom dealt with effectively—the problem of providing for each individual the educational treatment that will be most effective in developing that person's potential. A good measure of scholastic aptitude is not automatically a good guide to the optimal educational treatment. Binet's test, like others used in education, must be judged in terms of its ability to facilitate constructive adaptations of educational programs for individuals. This is the challenge for the next 70 years.

7.

Irving E. Sigel

WHEN DO WE KNOW WHAT A CHILD KNOWS?

The title of this paper may appear facetious. It is serious because it forms a basic question for research in developmental psychology: namely, the question of valid determination of a child's knowledge base. The answer is difficult enough when asked in regard to adults, but when asked for children, the problem becomes more complicated. The additional complexity resides in the fact that the frame of reference for interpreting verbal and gestural messages among children is not the same frame of reference that is applicable for adults. For adults, a common level of discourse within a common level of meaning is shared. Although differences in shared meanings exist among adults and lead to communication problems, the probability is that the amount of overlap in consensual meaning between adults is significantly greater than that between adults and children. Piaget (1970), Werner (1957), and Freud (1938) point out that what a child says or what he knows or what a child does is not necessarily a veridical reflection of what he knows or believes. If each of these writers is correct in his basic

assumption that there is a discrepancy or a potential discrepancy between the child's communication and the adult's understanding of that communication, then important and profound questions arise for education where assessment of the knowledge of young children is necessary to evaluate achievement. The issue becomes equally critical when considered from the perspective of our understanding cognitive development of children, since the validation of our theory is dependent on a veridical data base.

At issue in this discussion is not *what* the child actually knows: at issue is *when* do we know the child knows. There are at least two ways to determine whether or not the child's knowledge is congruent with our expectation of that knowledge: the first is the overt behavior of children as we observe it in varying settings with little or no direct communication between child and observer. Here we rely heavily on inference to comprehend the "message." The second is direct, interpersonal communication (verbal, gestural, graphic, or written) which includes the language, its structure, and meaning. In effect, the utilization of an array of communicative acts expressed in various modalities becomes a major source of data offered by the child.

METHODS OF GETTING
TO KNOW CHILDREN
AND THEIR EXPERIENCES

Before proceeding to an elaboration of the above issues, it might be helpful to attempt a quasi-role play technique, an

Source: *Human Development*, 1974, **17**, 201-217.

The research reported herein is supported by the Office of Economic Opportunity grant No. CG8547, Early Childhood Education Project.

This paper is a revised version of one presented as part of the conference "New Perspectives in Developmental Assessment" held at University of Georgia, 1972, conducted by Dr. C. D. Smock and R. R. Cocking. Support for the conference was made possible by the Mathemagenic Activities Program— Follow Through, University of Georgia. The author wishes to express heartfelt thanks for the special editorial assistance of Rodney R. Cocking.

effort at recreating mentally the role of respondent in an evaluation situation.

The following are ways to get to know about children and their experience. The first is what one might call *introspective ethology*, a term coined in informal discussion by William Charlesworth. Introspective ethology derives from the fact that we can introspect in terms of our own behaviors, of our own actions, of our own intentions. Further, we can reflect on our own experiences, and relate them in various ways—to outcomes, to new situations, etc. Using oneself as an informant for possible responses to situations of others may yield meaningful data. The legitimacy of this type of advocacy rests on the basic proposition that humans do share certain common response tendencies by virtue of being members of the same species. The ranges of behavior and response capabilities are probably finite. We are all capable of anxiety, anger, love, excitement. We are all capable of some kind of reasoning. We all have experienced success or failure. It seems reasonable to assume that for all of us there are certain common shared response capabilities, and the ranges of responses or attendant feelings, attitude and actions overlap among individuals. In fact, is this not basic to our conception of psychology as a science? The point will become relevant later, but just for now think of how any of you reading this must have felt when you were given an IQ test, either in a group or as an individual. What kind of feelings did this generate in you? What kinds of feelings did it generate that you feel or felt were relevant to the outcome? Why did you think you were being given these sorts of tasks, etc.?

Another analogue here is the way Katherine Wolf, years back at Yale, would train observers in what she called "motor empathy," a system in which the individual

observer recorded observations in a non-verbal way, using a graphic system so as to exclude the bias automatically generated by verbal labels. Reconstruction was through role play, using the graphic descriptions as guides to one's motor actions. She called the system *motor empathy* because she postulated that one feels akin to the subject being observed by trying to get into his posture, move his way, etc. These behaviors generate motor impulses and feelings that may approximate those of the subject. The objective is the same as introspective ethology, namely, to get to understand someone of our own species. The argument offered is that perhaps it can be facilitated by addressing ourselves to introspections in action states.

This brings us to a second data-gathering procedure with children which is *observational*. Here we are maximally inferencers. Even when describing what we see and when we do it in purely verbal terms, the words we use are selected and biased, fragmenting the subject being observed. If you were to read anecdotal narrative recordings of individuals, you would probably find a wide range of language used by observers to record behavior, varied objects selected for recording, etc. I remember vividly when one of my colleagues and I were observing children years ago: it came to us suddenly that one of us apparently was expert in describing hand movements, while the other was expert in describing the total torso movements, but neither of us ever recorded any highly detailed statements of hand-eye coordination. Where one observer focussed on the details of particular aspects of a total individual, the other had a broader perspective, the net outcome was a differential picture of the child. It is much like the classic story of the blind men and the elephant. Defining particular classes of behavior in advance would of course reduce disagreements between observers. However, it does not resolve the issue of the validity of the selected classes of behavior. Thus while resolving problems of observer reliability, validity issues are still present. It is evident that data obtained by observations are always dealing with selected aspects of behavior, simply because our limits as research observational instruments express the theoretical bias of the investigator.

Perhaps more important is that observations, while seemingly descriptions of behavior, are in fact inferential. This is particularly true when dealing with social-emotional or cognitive types of behaviors. An example of this would be a definition of a mood or an expression of an effect such as anger. Actually, this is not behavioral description, but rather is an inference of a mood quality. To literally describe what that is would merely mean a statement of the physical changes on the face or any other body parts and movement of that body, but to imply that it is anger or happiness or sadness or whatever is indeed inferential.[1]

METHODS OF ASSESSMENT

To enhance objectivity and comparability, investigators created tests which are not tests in the strict sense of the term, but rather tasks given to subjects in order to assay their competence in performing with the particular materials in that particular context. These tasks tend, as we know, to be either methods to determine the knowledge or competence level of an individual, that is, to assess what he can do or attempt to assess the processes employed by indi-

viduals in solving certain classes of problems. There is a variety of familiar tests both objective and projective, which vary in a variety of characteristics, from high structure with right or wrong answers to free and open-ended with unspecified correctness. All of these tests, however, share certain commonalities, which will become the central discussion of this paper. It is the shared commonality of tests and their underlying philosophy and rationale that raises a variety of issues which are contra-indicated by the usual definition or designation of tests.

Tests, as we all know, are efforts at objectively measuring individual capability or an individual's strategy in dealing with classes of problems. A test is a measurement device and is treated as an objective instrument allowing for quantifiable data. It attempts to remove inference and bias, to provide a standardized set of tasks and conditions in which responses are produced. In this way, presumably, the responses of individuals become comparable simply because the tasks presented to each person are standard or identical. My contention is that we tend to take for granted many of the sources of error in test construction, administration, and interpretation which cloud or mislead our perspective regarding the value of tests. This remark is in no way to be construed as advocating rejection of tests or this type of measurement. Rather, the intention is to provide a perspective by which we can conceptualize the role of tests, the sources of error, and then alter some of our conceptions about their utility.

TESTS AND CONTEXT

A test as a task is usually taken out of any rational context and presented in a specified set of conditions on the assumption that this sample of items (i.e., the test

---

[1]Application of *any* verbal label to any behavior is an interpretation but here would take us far afield. The issue, however, should not be dismissed lightly since it is basic to the descriptive language of science.

item) represents a sample of a universe of tasks. The response to this task is the knowledge, and the response is construed as a sample of the individual's ability. Thus, if an individual is asked how far it is from Paris to New York, this is assumed to assess social comprehension or maybe geography knowledge, and the response is assumed to be a sample of the individual's knowledge of that universe of knowledge, be it geography or general social questions. In effect, tests and the test procedure involve sampling in areas of (1) the class of items, and (2) the class of responses.

Items are selected out of context and presented to the individual in standardized social situations, and responses are coded in predetermined ways. An array of such decontextualized statements or tasks is presented. At issue is the basic question: if one samples an individual's knowledge base with a decontextualized item or items, what does that response to that item mean?

One could argue that it is exactly in this type context that we would have maximal certainty that the respondent knows something. For example, if I present you with an algebraic equation for solution, would solution to this be a better indication of your knowledge of algebra than if I gave you a specific problem involving the same mathematical processes, but in the context of two differentially speeding trains going a particular distance, with the requirement that you determine which train will arrive first at a particular point? In other words, the problem changes when the first problem is an algebraic equation with no designated content and in algebraic form demanding solution, whereas the other is a problem put into a verbal context with meaningful content. The processes involved in each require identical mathematical operations. Which one is the test of

mathematical knowledge, which one is a "better" test, and if they are equivalent why give different ones—what makes the difference?

Another example of a decontextualized situation is more extreme: when asking individual questions, e.g., in geography, and then moving on into arithmetic or other items, in contrast to asking questions in the context of the discussion or the teaching situation for geography. In other words, we may have two settings, each of which demands a similar process, but the context in which the process is to be expressed varies.

In testing, it may be argued, the decontextualized response is a better indication of knowledge since it is not dependent on extra dimensional support, but rather is pure or independent of concrete types of associations. The response reflects generalization not tied to a particular context. Generalization of phenomena across situations may well be considered the better test of the person's knowledge state.

On the other hand, one could argue that if tasks demand similar processes, but vary in form of presentation, we should examine the meaning and significance of form. The form in which an item occurs may be a critical feature, for it contributes to a definition of context. I would like to propose, *the principle of contextualization, which argues that the context in which the item is presented alters the very nature of that item by virtue of necessitated situational constraints or facilitators.*

There is another question regarding context which resolves itself into a decision of how much of a context must be included in the evaluation and what that context should be. In experimental psychology or psychometric test-taking or research involving tasks, everyone must face this issue. Is paired associate learning a test of learning in general and will it produce laws of learning applicable to all learning? Or will it yield highly specific sets of laws which are particular to paired associate learning in that particular context? In psychology the issue is not usually addressed in these terms. Rather, methodological discussion emphasizes research design, which is necessary but not sufficient since it ignores the psycho-logic of research contexts. The context in which an experiment is run and the particular tasks involved are critical because a complex array of behaviors (overt and covert) are elicited and not taken into account in the interpretation of responses. The analysis of the experimental situation is usually done in linear S-R terms, when in reality it is a complex set of field forces interacting simultaneously to influence the response, the responses being an interpretive statement of these conditions.

TEST PERFORMANCE
AND CLASSROOM BEHAVIOR

Let me review how I became concerned about this issue, relating some distinct experiences I had in analyzing test data and observational data, thereby illuminating the fundamental complexities discussed above. For three years I was the director of an Early Childhood Education Project involving children aged two. As in all these projects, evaluations of the child's status were done prior to his entry into the program and periodic evaluations during and at the end of three academic years. In addition, considerable observational data were gathered to describe the social and cognitive behaviors of the children in classroom settings. In other words, formal test data and detailed observational data were collected. Among the tasks in the formal test situation was one called the *Concept of One* taken from the Bayley Infant Scale. On the initial testing most of

the children failed, and they also failed eight months later. This was surprising, for in the judgment of the teachers, the children knew the concept of one. The observations were examined, and the teachers were asked to try to recollect experiences with the children involving number concepts. It was found that the children understood the concept "one" and in most cases even the concept "two."

To grasp the import of the problem more clearly, it is necessary to describe the two situations. The concept of one in the psychometric task involves the child's presenting on demand one block from an array of blocks. In the classroom we discovered that the children knew the concept one and two when integrated with the taking of cookies, or passing cookies, or giving the teacher cookies. In many other "play" areas the concept of one and two seemed clear. Granted, the concept of one was not general to every situation and seemed to be specific to a class of events. These observations lead, then, to the questions, how do we know when a child knows the concept of one, or two, or anything; and secondly, what does it mean in terms of his knowledge base, i.e., when a child seems to know something in one context and not in another?

Lest it be thought that the item has only to do with quantity, we found a similar phenomenon in visual memory. A visual memory task is involved when the child is presented with a picture of a familiar item, and it is removed, and 10 seconds later he is asked to find the item among an array of choices. Again the children had difficulty with this. The question now is not why the difference, nor why the difficulty with visual memory; the question is, why the difficulty in visual memory in the formal testing situation when visual memory seems to be well articulated in the classroom. The children remember who was present, will identify those who were absent, and will find materials or games and move directly toward them. They will mentally reconstruct these while riding the bus to school and then proceed to follow through. In other words, whatever the memory components are, they certainly seem to have an idea or image of how their nursery school world is structured.

The same discrepancy was found with language tests. The children were given a number of such tasks in the testing situation. They seemed to master words involving their own body, such as labeling parts of the face and head and hands, and did quite well on this type of task. They failed on understanding prepositions which are, admittedly, relational terms and frequently pose some problems. However, the failure of the prepositional terms, in contrast to some of the success on the body figure terms, poses a contradiction that is further heightened by the performance of the children on language tasks involving prepositions. In the classroom context we had no question that children understood such prepositions as *on* or *under* or *beside* or *in* or *out*. In the test situation this was not true. They had considerable difficulty understanding these relational terms outside of certain kinds of associated contexts or actions. The question, again, is—what does it mean when we contend that the child has limited comprehension of prepositional language, or that the child has differential receptive or expressive language? It is these kinds of contradictions between test performance and classroom behavior that force us to ask the questions: Does the child have a concept of one? Does the child have deficiencies in visual memory? Does the child understand, or not, certain prepositions? Precisely, when do we know when the child knows? From experience, these distinctions suggest that the child's knowledge is contingent upon certain classes of environmental events, and these environmental events interact with other unanticipated, unassessed cognitive processes, which in their totality enable appropriate action and/or comprehension by the child.

IMPLICATIONS FOR PSYCHOMETRICS

Is this an important issue, or is it a straw man? This becomes a legitimate concern. For me the issue is not a straw man, but is a basic epistemological question that demands understanding if we are to grasp the essence of the child's knowledge. Keep in mind how important test results are, for in fact our data base rests on such accumulation of knowledge. Traditionally, we are concerned about the validity and validation criteria for tests. We ask, Do tests, in fact, measure what they purport to measure? What does the concept of one task measure? The child's knowledge of *one*. If so, what is my validating criterion? Is it performance in another context? If it fails, then there is no correlation and consequently no validity. Is there reliability? In this case, yes. Consistently, children fail, but it is in this particular context. How do we determine validity of our measure if it is so? Every day for a month, this may show high consistency, but then the child comes in and solves the problem. Is that the reliability of the test, or that the child is aging rapidly and acquiring considerable knowledge at a considerable rate? For us, in this field, it seems that construct validity is not sufficiently relevant. We are more concerned with predictive validity, that is, the ability to predict from test performance to other classes of competence in relevant areas of functioning. Thus, the first task is to establish validation criteria for tests with young children.

Secondly, the significance of the issue rests on its implication for our conceptualization of psychometrics tests. It seems self evident that each task is complex and multidimensional, but it may be the lack of consideration of this simple notion may be one of the sources of error; or, to put it another way, contributes to the increased variance we find. For example, all tests do share certain commonalities, in spite of their ostensive differences. Let me give an illustration involving comparisons in tasks and settings. Let us take the particular situation addressed in this discussion, namely the concept "one" in the classroom and the concept "one" in the test situation. Each involves number; there is an overlap in that informational domain. Each involves counting which is a serial activity. Third, each involves a distinction or a discrimination of an item from an array of identical items. In the cookie basket, all the cookies are alike. In the test situation, all the blocks are alike. But, in spite of these shared similarities, there is also an array of discrepancies, so that the overlap is partial. The discrepancies are such things as the social context. In one situation, there is a child and an adult away from the group, away from any relevant activity and involved in what may seem to the child a legitimate achievement-assessing situation. There is seriousness about it, in spite of the adult's assertion that "we are here to play games." In the classroom, there are familiar surroundings and a familiar kind of social support in activity and high association to previous experiences in which this same act occurred.

The content of the items becomes a second discriminating situation. Now the content of the items is a meaningful object with which the child has had experience and has some affective relationships. He knows about the objects involved, he knows about cookies, that you put them in the mouth, you eat them, and they taste good. He knows something about their characteristics. Therefore, he is now dealing with a familiar content item in a social context. In the block situation in the formal test, the blocks have no relevance. They are, in fact, merely representative of instances of oneness, where "one" has no relevance for these children. Consequently, the content of the item is different.

And perhaps, more important, the outcome of the activity is different. In the cookie situation, the outcome is consumption of an object. It is internal, it is to give pleasure to the person involved. Or if it is giving the cookie to someone else, this kind of sharing may also have its own symbolic significance, because the child is aware of the fact that the cookie has value. The blocks have no value. The task has no value. This is merely an adult asking for a silly thing, "give me one block," and that is it. The lack of meaningful outcome may be a significant factor here.

This type of analysis is only a preliminary one, suggesting that content similarity is not enough to expect correlations between performance in one setting and the other.

NONCOGNITIVE TASK DEMANDS

The analysis offered above, while merely preliminary in nature, speaks primarily to certain kinds of logical and cognitive factors that are involved. In addition to the cognitive factor, attention must be given to the noncognitive demands in the situation which I believe influence outcome. The task demands which are present exist in terms of relationships between participants, one an examiner, the other the child, with materials, with a sense of freedom, with a sense of being evaluated. These are but some of the noncognitive relevant factors that are operating constantly from the moment the child walks into the room until he is through. There are considerable differences in the quality of their experience, so that the participants—examiner and child—have a built-in expectation of each other. Children quickly become aware of the fact that they are being examined and evaluated in spite of our dishonest statements to the contrary. We eliminate and reduce the sense of freedom for the children to come or to go and we use certain kinds of pressures or seductions to keep them "playing games." Even young children may find themselves conflicted about these social demands. Finally, children from many backgrounds, including very deprived ones, must get some feeling that they are in an evaluative situation where they are being judged by the adult in the testing situation. In the classroom situation, these noncognitive elements are different. Materials may be shared by other peers, and there is a struggle about that. Children may, in other programs, have a greater sense of freedom to move in and out of situations, and in their moving in and out they may not feel as though they were being evaluated for this and every act. In other words, these cognitive and noncognitive variables mentioned provide sources of error; or, to put it another way, my analytic perspective readily tells me what factors are involved in influencing the kinds of responses that children give.

Critical as I appear regarding predictive validity of psychological assessment procedures in formal testing situations, there is a solution to the problem implicit in the above analysis. I offer it for consideration because I firmly believe the testing movement, and what it has to offer, does have significance. Our task is to place it in the proper perspective so that we are interpreting responses consistently within frameworks appropriate and relevant for test procedures, and perhaps for particular program evaluations. Before unfolding this analysis, I must raise some other restrictions, that is, the types of responses elicited by any inquiry and how these shall be treated. Although an issue of a different genre, I do believe that the type of response expected through the kinds of questions posed and the kinds of tasks selected create another set of factors influencing the quality of the response.

TOWARD A DEFINITION OF CONTEXT VARIABLES

Returning now to the main thrust of the argument, it goes something like this: Since performance varies with content and with problems presented to the child, since consistency is a criterion of knowledge utilization, then our task is to define the context variables in order to discover what questions influence the expression of that knowledge. In effect, why does the child solve a problem in one context and not in another?

The answers will come from task and situational analyses. To achieve this goal, however, we must identify the relevant dimensions. This task, I confess, I have not worked out fully, but I have alluded to it and I would like to elaborate on it somewhat now.

First, examination of "task" demands, as expressed in instructions or other types of structuring: for example, do instructions orient a child? How is the task structured if and when the child shows deviant or irrelevant behavior? Tasks involve a variety of demands, e.g., cognitive and motoric involvement, or nonmotoric involvement and/or cognitive demands, perceptual activity, etc. Building a tower involves cognitive and motoric activity, while digit spans involve purely verbal responses. The variety of demands made in a task and the way in which these demands are expressed become very important determinants of subsequent responses. I am not only referring here to mood quality or warmth of relationship, but rather getting the child to know what he is supposed to do. You will note how complicated some of the instructions are that psychologists dream up for children. It makes one raise the question as to how much of our knowledge of children's knowledge is influenced by such impoverished and insensitive question-asking.

Second, the social definition of the situation also generates a class of variables that must be considered in the analysis. Testing situations are essentially achievement-oriented in spite of our euphemisms "let's play a game" or "I just want to see how children play with these types of toys," etc. We have found children as young as two from impoverished homes asking "Is that right?" or "Is that good?" Our good old mythology of the lack of active orientation and achievement evaluation in very young children is not a valid generalization. The children, however, do not seem to see the classroom situation as evaluative, nor have they made comments to that effect which they make in the testing situation.

Contextual relevance and embeddedness in the social context are other factors that must guide our construction and analysis of testing situations. Taking a cracker embedded in a familiar social scene which has continuity must have some kind of significance for the child. Tests alone describe how they respond to a decontextualized task, but it's like coming from nowhere and going nowhere. The degree to which the task demands are embedded and the characteristics of this embeddedness pose some important factors for consideration.

Meaningfulness in relationship to experience is a third consideration. Granted that the psychometric tasks are supposed to be novel and hence neutralize effects of differential practice, this very point may be counter-productive in revealing what children know. If this is a variable, then we can learn what the child knows in terms of its familiarity, but perhaps not in terms of its generalization yield. Thus, what the child does *not* know is the generality then in question, but yet he does know the item sometimes. For example, do I know Mr. Doe? If I only identify him in one context, but I cannot identify him in Washington or elsewhere, you may say I do not know him, essentially. This is relevant to what we might talk about as object constancy or object permanence, namely, that the knowledge of the object exists independent of context or symbolic form. It is the question of whether or not the object remains or does not remain when you cannot see it or you see it in an otherwise unfamiliar context. The question is, Does the child still respond to some dimension of that object independent of the object's presence or its context? The issue is not settled by any means. Getting back to our problem: if you grant that there is partial knowledge of an item or an event, does this suggest a different mode of analysis to determine a knowledge base? Does this perhaps not lead to the idea of levels of knowledge, levels not only in hierarchical complexity, but in extension of situational contexts?

A fourth factor is in the task demand itself: Is it recognition or reconstruction? Where recognition is the criterial response to determine the knowledge base, it may be appropriately responded to because of morphological similarities with no inference; where reconstruction is required, a retrieval system that has its own criterion for identification has to be employed. It is important to distinguish between recognition and reconstruction to ascertain the knowledge base. If I ask a child to define something with no structure present, he has to engage in an entirely different set of processes to respond. Thus, for example, when we ask children to reconstruct or to recapture something from memory, we are setting demands which are different from recognizing. How we ask the question and how we communicate the type of response desired poses critical procedural issues, the resolution of which will inevitably influence results. I believe it is relevant for any item which requires the examiner to ask questions. It is a sensitive issue and one to which we must attend.

The above criteria are task-oriented. Now let us turn to a discussion of motivational elements. These are communicated differentially, in various social situations. In a testing situation a child is being tested where the entire format is perhaps school-like, or at least the orientation is set by an adult. The child is asked a question; there is obviously an answer or if not, why would this grown-up spend time doing this? There are varying types of reinforcement used by examiners in these situations to communicate the quality of a child's response, or transition from one task to another, etc. Also in this context, there is the inevitable time constraint, sometimes made obvious and sometimes subtle.

The above motivational elements are the traditional achievement aspects. Achievement, however, is only one of many types of personality manifestations. Other types of personal-social behavior that occur are help-seeking: In playing games with an adult can the child ask for help? Help is rejected even if nicely so. Suppose the child says, "I want to see how you do it" or "Let's bring Johnny in here and see if he too can play like me." There is a variety of

issues that comes up in this, and I think it is very important to understand some of these questions. In addition to help-seeking and achievement, we also have intention, will, and fatigue. These are very common elements in all tasks, and there is no reason to go on discussing them.

PRELIMINARY DATA: RELATIONS BETWEEN PERSONALITY CHARACTERISTICS AND PERFORMANCE

It is appropriate to conclude with a focus on an issue which is implied in all the above; that is, what is the relationship between personality characteristics and performance? Our research indicates that as young as age two, there are considerable significant relationships obtained between observations of a child in a testing situation and his test performance.

As the child was given a battery of tests, a variety of attentional, motivational, verbal, and manipulatory behaviors was recorded. Thirteen tester behaviors, involving giving instructions, presenting test materials, giving the child reinforcement and personal attention, were systematically observed. Thirty-six child behaviors, such as looking at the tester or material, handling items, wandering, staring, etc., were observed in relation to the tester behaviors which were presumed to be probable elicitors. One tester behavior and two child behaviors were recorded every 5 seconds throughout the test sessions. Two to four observers recorded these behaviors with an overall reliability of 85%.

Of these tester-child behaviors, only six tester and twenty child behaviors occurred with enough frequency to warrant statistical treatment. Three types of responses were analyzed: (1) attentional and interpersonal responses; (2) orientation and manual responses to materials, and (3) verbal responses. Comparisons along these dimensions were then made between those children who scored in the first and fourth quartile of the test battery.

Attentional and interpersonal responses

It was found that high and low scorers seem to differ in their orientation to the material and to the tester. Low scorers stare away while being watched, sit still during instructions and throughout the test sessions; high scorers smile when material is presented and smile at the tester throughout the session more than low scorers do.

Boys appear more distracted than girls as evidenced by staring away from either the tester or the task, but there are some indications of greater dependence as seen in going to the teacher's lap while girls moved close to the tester and boys seemed to smile more during instructions. This latter observation is particularly interesting, since it is the high scorers rather than the low scorers who smile more during instructions, and it will be recalled that the high-scoring group contains more females than males.

Orientation and manual
responses to test materials

The differences in this category reflect the nature of high- versus low-scoring groups and indicate a possible source of this difference. Obviously correct and incorrect gestural responses, such as pointing to the correct picture or placing a form into the correct slot, differentiate high- from low-scoring groups. In addition, low scorers show greater absence of responding. Low scorers engage in more tactile manipulation of material during instructions and throughout all tester-child combinations. This may indicate some impulsivity since

instructions were given with the command not to touch the material until told to do so. It may also be an indication of a more primitive mode of response to the material since tactile manipulation was defined as random touching and fingering rather than any exploratory constructive handling of the materials.

The differences in this area that are at lower levels of statistical significance, but also very suggestive, are as follows: high scorers looked at the materials more than low scorers, although boys appear to look more than girls as a group, even though boys require more orientation to the materials. This may be a confounding factor in the looking response. While boys responded to the initial instructions with the correct gesture more often than girls, the girls improved significantly when instructions were repeated. Girls were better at piling blocks and aligning them laterally.

Verbal responses

Girls and high scorers clearly verbalize more and respond correctly to test questions, whereas boys remain silent rather than make errors.

In summary, then, the high scorers were predominantly female, were more active, enjoyed the task more, and evidenced more smiling, perhaps because of greater interpersonal ease. They sit still more, vis-à-vis the low scoring group only when instructions are repeated, indicating once again perhaps a response to a personal demand from an adult or possibly need for achievement or social desirability, etc. The low scorers who were predominantly male seem to show less motivated interaction within the materials, stare away and engage in tactile manipulation of materials as opposed to an exploratory response.

When we looked at the comparison of boys' versus girls' behaviors, irrespective of their scoring status, we found that the boys were quiet, more unresponsive, less verbal, less drawn to test materials, and required more orientation. The girls were more restless, more verbal, better at piling and aligning blocks.

Thus, we find that there is some obvious relationship between performance and attendant behaviors.[2] As one examines these results, one should be cautioned that some of the attendant behaviors and test performance are confounded. However, there are indications that the attendant test behaviors seem to be in the service of test performance rather than just a concomitant.

To resolve the issues raised in this dis-

cussion will require specification of variables (or dimensions) and subsequent investigations examining the relationship implied herein. In effect, we do need empirical validation of these intuitions.

This paper will have accomplished its purpose if it has communicated a perspective that will contribute to increased veridicality of our knowledge of what a child knows.

REFERENCES

Freud, S. *The basic writings of Sigmund Freud.* New York: Modern Library, 1938.

Piaget, J. Piaget's theory. In Mussen, *Carmichael's manual of child psychology.* New York: John Wiley and Sons, 1970.

Werner, H. The concept of development from a comparative and organismic point of view. In Harris, *The concept of development.* Minneapolis: University of Minnesota Press, 1957.

[2]Attendant behaviors are those which are an integral part of the activated cognitive structures and thus "causally" associated with other dimensions of performance.

8.

Diane P. Weis

CHILDREN'S COGNITIVE DEVELOPMENT— OR HOW CHILDREN DRAW "MAPS"

One can liken the impressions, opinions, and conclusions people reach in response to their experiences in the world to maps that serve to guide their decisions and behavior. Simon has described the phenomenon in terms of the principle of bounded rationality:

The first consequence of the principle of bounded rationality is that the intended rationality of an actor (one who commits an act)

requires him to construct a simplified model of the real situation in order to deal with it. He behaves rationally with respect to this model, and such behavior is not even approximately optimal with respect to the real world. To predict his behavior we must understand the way in which this simplified model is constructed, and its constructions will certainly be related to his psychological properties as a perceiving, thinking, and learning animal (1957: 198)

Research data in the field of children's behaviors that might appear random or irrational are quite logical if one is aware

Source: *Child Welfare,* 1975, **54,** 567-580.

of certain regularities in the way children structure their understanding of the world.

This paper describes the ways in which understanding how children draw "maps" can contribute to the promotion of children's social and emotional well-being, and proposes ways of applying this understanding.

Premise 1: Cognitive structures (or maps) mediate between what happens to a child and how these influences affect him. For example, Serot and Teevan found that children's perceptions of their parent–child relationships were correlated with adjustment. There was, however, little agreement in perception between the children and their parents, and the parents' perceptions of the parent–child relationships were not related to the children's adjustment (Serot & Teevan, 1961). The point this study demonstrates is that the environmental conditions alone are not necessarily what directly affect a child, but rather how he experiences or perceives his environment, which is in large part a cognitive function.

Premise 2: Certain cognitive skills are necessary in managing one's social and emotional life. Several studies have shown positive correlations between conceptual skills in the social and emotional spheres and more effective interpersonal behavior (Feffer & Suchotliff, 1966). In a comprehensive survey of research findings related to predicting adult mental health from childhood indicators, Kohlberg found not only that childhood IQ scores were one of the best predictors of adult mental health, but that the degree of cognitive maturity relative to one's own age group was related to the degree of social maturity and adjustment (Kohlberg, LaCrosse, & Ricks, 1972).

Although one cannot be certain of the causal direction of these correlations (Does greater social participation lead to more experiences and practice, or does cognitive maturity lead to greater social skills?) it is our contention that many of the skills necessary for more effective interpersonal relationships can be learned.

THEORETICAL MODEL FOR UNDERSTANDING CHILDREN'S MAPS

Piaget has provided a basic model of how people develop cognitive structures. Two of his key concepts are assimilation and accommodation. According to his theory, people are able to use only information they can assimilate into their cognitive structures. Other stimuli either will not be perceived at all or will be distorted to fit the individual's overall organization of conceptual understanding.

Obviously, people continue to develop increasingly complex ideas to explain what they perceive and experience, which is where the concept of accommodation comes in. If a person perceives something that is a little like other things he already knows but is a little different, he can modify his cognitive structures to accommodate them to the information he has perceived. Accurate accommodation cannot occur, however, if the information presented requires cognitive skills too far beyond the person's present capacities. Thus, cognitive growth is cumulative and certain basic steps must be mastered before others can be reached.

The principles discussed in the foregoing can be illustrated by the following conversation with a 4-year-old:

Child: What's that picture?

Adult: That's a bird.

Child: No, it's a chicken. (Failure to assimilate the answer)

Adult: A chicken is a bird.

Child: Is a bird a chicken? (Attempted accommodation of this new information)

Adult: All chickens are birds, but not all birds are chickens. There are other kinds of birds like robins, ducks, etc. (Attempting to aid the accommodation)

Child: That's not true! A chicken is a bird and a bird is a chicken. (Assimilation)

The concept the adult is trying to explain requires the ability to comprehend schemes for classifying things into hierarchical groups, a skill children usually do not have until they are 6 or 7 years old.

What is the motivation?

A basic question behind Piaget's model of cognitive development is why the 4-year-old asked what the picture was in the first place. What motivates people to learn or develop? Piaget attributes mental growth to the maturation of the nervous system, experiences with the physical world, socialization pressures, and a general organismic tendency to seek organization and structure (Piaget & Inhelder, 1969). Berlyne (1966) and White (1963) have reviewed research with both animals and humans to indicate that living organisms tend to be curious, to want to explore, and to test what kinds of effects they can have

on their environment. These tendencies may be called proactive in that they function autonomously without necessarily being a reaction to some kind of tension or direct stimulus, although it is necessary to have environmental stimuli to which to attach one's exploratory behavior. Reaction to environmental conditions that require adaptive cognitive development can also "motivate" learning. A classic example is the chimpanzee who "learns" he can get a banana that is out of reach by using a stick to extend his reach.

Keeping in mind the basic ideas discussed thus far about how and why people develop increasingly complex cognitive structures, let us look at some cognitive characteristics of various developmental stages. Table 8.1 summarizes some of the key points. The developmental stages, presented down the side of the table, are approximate in terms of chronological ages. Cognitive-developmental theory postulates that there is a general sequence of stages and that one must move through each lower stage before he can reach the next one, but the exact timing of the stages varies among different individuals and among different cultural groups. The

TABLE 8.1. Characteristics of the Stages of Cognitive Development

Developmental Stage (Ages Approximate)	New Cognitive Skills	Cognitive-Developmental Tasks
Sensorimotor (0-18 months)	Born with grasping, sucking, and arousal responses and perceptual apparatus.	To mentally coordinate different sensory impressions of the physical world; to develop object constancy.
Preoperational (18 months-6 years)	Use of mental images; beginning concepts of specific cause and effect.	To differentiate between symbols or images and the external world.
Concrete Operational (6-12 years)	Structures of classification, conservation, reversibility; capacity for logical reasoning.	To differentiate between logical thought and events in the external world; to learn social expectations.
Formal Operational (After 12 years)	Capacity for abstract thought and hypothetico-deductive reasoning.	To differentiate between how things theoretically should be and how they really are.

cognitive capacities listed in the second column of the table are developmental milestones whose presence is a necessary defining characteristic of the stages of development. Typically a given individual does not represent a pure stage type. An individual would usually be more advanced in some content areas than in others, due to differential experiences and to the complexity of the particular content area. The third column presents developmental tasks associated with the various stages.

The newborn infant comes into the world without having collected information from which to build maps. He does have, however, certain fundamental equipment that will enable him to begin to make some sense out of the world. If you hold a bottle in front of a baby's eyes, it is something he sees. If you put it on his cheek, it is something to try to suck, whether or not it contains milk. If you put it in his hand, it is something to grasp. It will take several months of practice and maturation before the baby can draw a "map" that will allow him to see a bottle and know he can reach for it, pick it up, and put it in his mouth. This process presents in rudimentary terms the building of a coordinated concept of an object. The way an object looks and feels and what it can do are all elements that go together to describe the same object.

Developing attachments

In the social sphere the infant's most crucial task is to develop attachments to social objects. He begins to do so primarily as a result of the association of care, comfort, and tension reduction to the presence of his caretakers. In order to form attachments to specific persons, he has to learn to recognize differences in persons. In terms of concept formation, to be able to do so would seem to presuppose a capacity to recall some kind of sensory

image of essential characteristics of a given person against which to compare current perceptions.

The results of a capacity to recognize differences in persons illustrate a typical feature of stage developmental theories— that is, new skills bring on new problems to be solved. The baby who has formed attachments to specific persons is now subject to two new sources of anxiety. He may be surprised and frightened on seeing a stranger, and he may become upset to the point of panic if mother disappears to go get him a bottle when he is hungry. Fortunately, he has probably also been developing two other skills that can help him solve these problems. One is rudimentary communication skills, which he has probably acquired through the process of selective reinforcement. Crying draws attention to needs and smiling or laughing elicits interest, responsiveness, and stimulation from persons around him. On seeing a stranger he may cry for help or may smile to try to elicit a positive response.

In relation to mother's disappearance, he may also cry for help. A more effective and flexible solution requires that he develop the concept of object constancy. Initially a baby has no idea that an object exists unless he can immediately perceive it by seeing, touching, or hearing it. After repeated experiences with objects appearing and disappearing, the baby gradually becomes aware that an object can continue to exist even if he does not see it. The importance of object constancy is profound in terms of expanding the realm of potential problem-solving skills. On a simple level, if a child knows his favorite toy exists even when he can not see it, he can look for it or indicate to a caretaking person that he wants it. On a more complex level, object constancy can help a child resolve conflicts about how the same person can sometimes be good and rewarding and sometimes be bad and punishing. Although in the latter example the child's definition of what is constant about the object is much more complex and abstract than a mere constancy of physical existence of the object, the basic capacity to conceptualize constancy is equally important in both examples.

Opening new worlds

During the sensorimotor stage of development the child's explorations and manipulations of the world are primarily limited to the world of physical objects. He gathers and coordinates information about how things look, feel, smell, and sound. He finds he can affect objects through touching, pushing, pulling, lifting, and various other forms of physical activity. By the time he is about 18 months old he is beginning to develop skills that open new worlds for him to understand. In addition to manipulating physical objects and activities, he can now explore and modify mental images and mental symbols in the form of words. He can try to affect a world within his own mind through play, imitation, and fantasy. He can affect his external world through verbal as well as physical activity. He can use his imitative skills to try out and practice new roles and new forms of behavior.

At this point the child faces a major cognitive task to coordinate his internal and external manipulations. He has to learn more about the nature of images and symbols. A word or image is not the same as the thing it represents, and he cannot magically cause an external change or event by just changing a name, thought or symbol.

During the preschool years a child also acquires certain basic social and emotional concepts. He can learn to label such directly experienced feelings as happiness,

sadness, or fear. He can also make some judgments about the feelings of others through such readily apparent cues as tears, smiles, and loud, angry voices. He has some capacity to see connections between specific actions on his part and the reactions of specific persons to what he does. After he has stored enough connections, he can begin to form ideas to help him guide his behavior.

Assume, for example, that a child wants a piece of candy from his mother. Suppose he uses his new verbal skills to ask her for one, but he has some idea that she may not want him to have it because she has "a funny look on her face." This situation presents a problem to the child. What will his map tell him to do? That depends on what information he has gathered from past experiences. Will she give in if he demands enough? If he cries? Does she so rarely give in that it is useless to try? Has the child seen an older sibling use some behavior successfully with her that he might want to try? Although the content of each child's maps may vary, it is important to be aware that maps can not be elaborated or amended unless the child has the capacity to construct maps in the first place.

Operational thought

Around the age of six or seven a child begins to move away from the world of idiosyncratic and highly specific modes of thinking into the world of what Piaget calls concrete operational thought. A major characteristic of operational thought is that it is not peculiar to the individual, but is based on a system of logic common to all individuals of the same mental level. The two most important cognitive structures that enable a child to think in operational terms are conservation and classification.

Conservation involves the recognition that things may change, but some defining quality about them remains the same. A classic Piagetian experiment that demonstrates the principle of conservation is one in which water is poured from a tall, slender container into a short, wide container. If one asks a preschool child whether the amount of water stays the same, he will say no. He may say the fatter container has more water or he may say the taller one has more, but he will think the amount is different because it looks different. Only when he is ready and after repeated observations does he realize that the amount stays basically the same and that the action is reversible; that is, the water can be poured back into the tall container if he wants to get it back to its original form.

The ability to classify means the capacity to abstract certain qualities of objects that will place them in general categories. This can be done along any of a number of dimensions such as color, size, shape or function. In the social world, the ability to classify enables a child to learn to understand systems of rules or norms that govern interpersonal behavior. For example, it is all right to do certain things at home, but one does not do them in public; if you want to get along with others you have to share and compromise sometimes; interrupting other people when they are talking is an example of rudeness; and all of these activities belong to larger classifications of socially desirable or undesirable behaviors.

RULES—AND NEW CONFLICTS

The child in the stage of concrete operational thought is concerned with learning what the rules are. Major conflicts are generated for him in situations where things in the real world do not work out the way his logic tells him they should. Consider the child who has just shared a toy with his sibling. A child who has not yet reached the stage of concrete operations might say if asked that he did so because Mommy told him to. Once a child has some consistent idea of a more pervasive system of rules governing the behavior of all people, he might say he shared because it would be bad or selfish not to. How can he resolve his desire not to share with a rule that orders him to share, especially when he sees other people who do not play by the rules?

A later and more flexible conceptual development has occurred when a child says the reason he shares is because others may then also share with him, and agreeing to do so provides a means for people to get along with each other to their mutual benefit. He can then be free to decide not to share in instances when it appears that sharing is not going to be of any mutual benefit. This solution indicates the child is trying to understand the reasons behind the rules, rather than just learning what the rules are. When this tendency begins to take the ascendancy in a child's cognitive life, he is entering what Piaget has called the stage of formal operational thought. The two major components of this stage in terms of cognitive structuring are the capacities for highly abstract thought and hypothetico-deductive reasoning.

Levels of abstraction

Abstract thought refers to how far removed a concept is from physical or tangible objects. To clarify the meaning of level of abstraction, one can look at the following ascending order of complexity: (1) physical objects or feeling states that can be directly perceived by one's sensory modalities; (2) symbols and images that represent physical objects or directly experienced emotions; (3) word symbols that represent theoretical abstractions such as the structural logic of thought, the nature of psychological makeup, or systems of justice.

The capacity to manipulate high-level abstractions is valued in many academic and occupational settings. It is also common for adolescents to apply this kind of thinking to try to understand their own personalities and to build philosophical systems conceptualizing how the world should be. The major conflict inherent in formal operational thought is to resolve discrepancies between how things ideally should be and how they are, or to explore the limits of the extent to which logic can alter the "real world."

Theoretically, hypothetico-deductive reasoning helps to solve the problem. Hypothetico-deductive reasoning refers to the capacity to conduct mental experiments or to think through the likely implications of several alternatives without having to directly experience them first, *and* an understanding of probability—that there is no guarantee things will work out the way one plans and hopes. The best one can do is to predict likely outcomes. It should be noted, however, that mankind still has a long distance to travel in developing the full utility of hypothetico-deductive reasoning. Slovic has aptly described man's cognitive condition:

Our basic perceptual and motor skills are remarkably good, the product of a long period of evolution, and thus we can process *sensory* information with remarkable ease. This may fool us into thinking that we can process *conceptual* information with similar facility. Anyone who tries to predict where a baseball will land by calculating its impact against the bat, trajectory of flight, etc., will quickly realize that his analytic skills are inferior to his perceptual-motor abilities. Another reason for our confidence is that the world is structured in such a complex, multiply-determined way that we can usually find some reason for our failures, other than our inherent inadequacies—

bad luck is a particularly good excuse in a probabilistic world. (Slovic, 1972)

PROPOSED MEANS TO HELP CHILDREN CONSTRUCT MAPS

The two aspects of planning interventions considered are: (1) Who should be the primary interveners? and (2) What are some maps to guide the behavior of those who are attempting to implement the implications of the foregoing analysis?

The response to the first issue is derived from pragmatic considerations of feasibility and likelihood of impact, rather than from cognitive-developmental theory. The recommendation is that the primary interveners should be primary caretakers, whether they be parents, foster parents, or guardians. The reasons for this are:

(1) Practitioners have better access to modifying the necessary individualized facilitating behavior of primary caretakers than of other sources of influence in the child's life, such as school personnel and peer groups.

(2) Ties with primary caretakers, more than with anyone else, usually afford continuity over a longer time and offer more extended opportunities to explore a child's reasoning.

(3) Children ordinarily have strong affective ties to their caretakers, whether positive or negative. For reasons suggested later, a program geared toward the modification of cognitive structures can contribute to the establishment of more positive affective ties between child and caretaker.

Reaching the child

The major assertion underlying a coordination of the first and second issues is that caretakers can learn certain principles that can guide their behavior in transactions with the children. The following specific principles should be helpful:

(1) A child is inherently motivated to explore the world and to understand its organization. To do so also helps him develop adaptive problem-solving skills. Pressing states of arousal such as hunger, pain, or fear can block the motivation to explore and, thus, should be eliminated insofar as possible. It is also more effective to follow and gradually lead a child's spontaneous interests than to try to impose interests on him.

(2) It is essential that caretakers who try to explore and understand their children's view of things do so consistently, and not just at times of stress and disagreement. When both caretaker and child are emotionally aroused or upset, it is difficult to achieve genuine interest in each other's points of view. Both parties to the discussion are all too likely, under these conditions, to view mutual exploration of reasons as necessitating self-justification and defensiveness. If a general systematic attempt to understand each other prevails at other times, however, it should be easier to reestablish temporarily broken channels of communication.

(3) Concept formation involves an exploration and coordination of the different qualities of the object, emotion, or idea to be conceptualized. Such exploration is most readily comprehended through the sensory modalities. The manipulation of objects, pictures, diagrams, and actions (e.g., drama or fantasy) can be a powerful technique for facilitating concept development.

(4) Each stage of cognitive development carries new cognitive capacities and new cognitive tasks. An awareness of what the child is working on and what he has to work with can help one focus on the forms of exercise and practice that would be most useful. The specific content should be geared to the problem area the child is working on—such as social skills, behavioral control, emotional control.

(5) Trying to explain something to a

TABLE 8.2. Suggested Phase-Specific Activities

Developmental Stage	Key Cognitive Structures	Suggested Activities
Sensorimotor	Coordinated sensory impressions.	Provide varied objects to see, touch, move, manipulate.
	Object constancy.	Peek-a-boo and hide-and-seek games.
Preoperational	Understanding words and symbols.	Talking about what words mean to the child; mutual story-telling activities.
	Beginning concepts of cause and effect.	Role-playing games to illustrate results of different behaviors.
Concrete Operational	Conservation and reversibility; classification.	Mutual discussion of what concepts mean, how they are alike and not alike.
	Learning the "rules"	Willingness to talk about and negotiate behavioral expectations; thinking through hypothetical problems—What would you do if . . .?
Formal Operational	Abstract thought, hypothetico-deductive reasoning.	Same as above; support exposure to and discussion of a variety of ideas.

child that is beyond his cognitive grasp will not hurt him, but it will indicate that one needs to seek a different level of communication. Otherwise he will assimilate the information in his own form and may conclude, as the 4 year old did, that a chicken is a bird and a bird is a chicken.

Table 8.2 presents some phase-specific suggested activities.

In conclusion, it can be said that caretakers who are willing and able to explore their children's understanding of the world can more truly empathize with the child. They can give him a sense that what he thinks is important and valuable, a positive association to have with the caretaker. Another advantage to children's caretakers of the activities described here is that they add some fun to child rearing. Adult motivation need not be based in guilt or fear, nor is this kind of activity as physically or emotionally draining as diapering, fixing meals, laundering, or staying up all night with a sick child. It can be an adventure to re-explore the world through the eyes of a child, and his excitement with the process can be contagious.

REFERENCES

Berlyne, David. Curiosity and exploration. *Science.* 1966. **43.**

Feffer, Melvin, & Suchotliff, Leonard. Decentering Implications of Social Interactions, *Journal of Personality and Social Psychology,* 1966, **4.** Also, Robert King. The Development of Some Intention Concepts in Young Children and Their Relation to Interaction Skills. Unpublished doctoral dissertation, University of Colorado, 1968; Arne Korstvedt. Role-taking behavior in normal and disturbed children: a developmental analysis of cognitive processes. Unpublished doctoral dissertation, Clark University, 1962; Barbara Rothenberg. Children's ability to comprehends adults' feelings and motives: its development and relationship to interpersonal competence, intrapersonal comfort, and intellectual level. Unpublished doctoral dissertation, Cornell University, 1967.

Kohlberg, Lawrence; LaCrosse, Jean; & Ricks, David. The Predictability of adult mental health from childhood behavior. In Benjamin Wolman (ed.) *Manual of child psychopathology.* New York: McGraw-Hill, 1972.

Piaget, Jean, and Inhelder, Barbel. *The psychology of the child,* New York: Basic Books, 1969.

Serot, Naomi, and Teevan, Richard. Perception of the parent–child relationship and its relation to child adjustment, *Child Development.* 1961, **32.**

Simon, Herbert A. *Models of man: social and national.* New York: John Wiley & Sons, 1957.

Slovic, Paul. From Shakespeare to Simon: speculations—and some evidence—about man's ability to process information. *Oregon research institute monograph,* 1972, **12.**

White, Robert. *Ego and reality in psychoanalytic theory.* New York: International Universities Press, 1963.

9.

William R. Looft

ANIMISTIC THOUGHT IN CHILDREN: UNDERSTANDING OF "LIVING" ACROSS ITS ASSOCIATED ATTRIBUTES

INTRODUCTION

One of the characteristics of thought in the young child is that of *animism,* or the tendency to attribute life-like qualities to inanimate objects (e.g., "A cloud is alive because it moves.") Previous research by Piaget and many others (reviewed in detail by Looft and Bartz [1969]) has shown that this animistic tendency gradually drops out of the child's thinking, and his concept of "life" assumes more and more the form held by educated adults.

The purpose of the present research was to explore the extent or generalizability of a child's understanding when he correctly classifies an object as "living" or "not living." That is, does the child have knowledge of the attributes or qualities that are implied by the "living" status? In Piaget's (1929) clinical method, after the subject has made a judgment about the living/not-living status of an object, further questions are posed to obtain his justification or explanation for his decision. Piaget found that reference to usefulness and movement characterized the animistic child's explanations; older children made more frequent reference to biological criteria. The present study focused upon this latter aspect by determining the degree to which nonanimistic children, identified by their accuracy on alive/not-alive classification of objects, could generalize this understanding over three related biological criteria—respiration, ingestion of nutriments, and reproduction.[1]

METHOD

Subjects

Fifty-nine second-grade children (eighteen males, forty-one females) from two parochial schools in a medium-sized Midwestern city comprised the initial sample. The mean age was 7.15 years ($SD = .36$).

Procedure and test materials

Sixteen stimulus items were selected; eight were living things (turkey, tree, frog, turtle, fish, flower, woman, honeybee), and eight were nonliving things (automobile, television, chair, airplane, watch, camera, coffee cup, gloves). Although this aspect was not a major focus of attention in this study, children were randomly assigned to one of two testing conditions in an attempt to replicate the findings of a previous study (Looft, 1972) that compared the prevalence of animistic answers obtained in diverse response modes. In the

Source: *The Journal of Genetic Psychology,* 1974, **124**, 235-240.

Acknowledgment and thanks are extended to Marc Baranowski for his considerable assistance in this study.

[1]The selection of these biological attributes was not entirely arbitrary. A film entitled "Living and Nonliving Things" (distributed by Coronet Instructional Films, Chicago) presents an explicit delineation of these three "life-indicating" attributes, in addition to another, labeled "movement."

verbal condition, an adaptation by Looft and Charles (1969) of the Russell and Dennis (1939) animism interview procedure was used. After a series of warm-up questions (e.g., "Do you know what it means to be alive, to be living?" "Name some things that are living.") were asked to acclimate the child to the testing situation, four different sets of questions were posed. One set was the standard animism question—"Is a frog [television, etc.] alive?"—and the accompanying request to explain the answer given (although this latter information was not germane to the purpose of this study). The other three sets of questions pertained to the biological criteria. At the beginning of each set the subject was asked "Do you know what *breathing* means? Can you name some things that breathe or that need to have air?" Other terms or phrases were also suggested (e.g., "to take in air," "respiration"). Then for each of the 16 items the subject was asked, "Does a frog [chair, etc.] breathe, or need air?" Parallel questions were framed for each of the other two concepts: After the introductory comments and questions, the child was asked "Does a [item] need food, or nutrition?" or "Do [item] reproduce, or make more things just like themselves?" for each of the sixteen items. The order of presentation of these four sets of questions was varied across subjects (i.e., the alive/not-alive concept was not always given first), and the living and nonliving items were mixed together and given in a different order of presentation to each subject. Responses were recorded by a second examiner in the room.

In the nonverbal condition, the testing session began with the same warm-up questions. Then the subject was told that he was about to be shown a series of pictures and that he was to decide which of the things shown on those pictures are alive and which are not alive (or breathe/don't breathe, need food/don't need food, reproduce/don't reproduce). On the table in front of the subject were placed two cards—one marked ALIVE and the other NOT ALIVE (and so forth for the other concepts). (Assurance was made that each subject understood the distinction between these printed words.) He was then handed a stack of sixteen cards, each of which contained a picture (obtained from magazines) of one of the same living and nonliving objects used in the verbal condition. Altogether, each subject sorted the cards four times: alive/not alive, breathes/does not breathe, needs food/does not need food, reproduces/does not reproduce. For each concept, the subject was told he could take as much time as he wished to sort the pictures into the two piles. No other oral communication took place while the subject carried out this task. As in the verbal condition, presentation orders were varied across subjects.

RESULTS

As in previous studies ([Looft, 1972; Looft & Charles, 1969] see also Looft and Bartz [1969] for a review of earlier studies), there was no difference between the animism scores (expressed as correct living/not-living judgments) of boys and girls (their means were virtually identical), and therefore the data were combined for the remaining analyses. There was also no significant difference between the mean animism scores of the verbal ($\bar{X}=14.67$) and the nonverbal ($\bar{X}=15.52$) groups ($t<1$, $df=57$), in congruence with the earlier Looft (1972) study. In light of this finding that different response modes elicit essentially identical frequencies of animistic answers, the data from both conditions were combined for the generalization analyses. The mean life-concept score for the entire group was therefore 15.22 (SD=1.49), indicating a high level of accuracy among these children, at least for this particular set of items. Thirty-nine of the fifty-nine subjects correctly classified all ten items.

The generalization analysis was carried out only on the data from the thirty-nine completely "nonanimistic" responders. A generalization score for each subject was obtained in the following way: For each correct response on each of the three biological attributes, one point was assigned, an incorrect judgment was given a negative point. Thus, for each item a child's score could range from to -3 to $+3$, and over the entire set of sixteen items his score could range from -48 to $+48$.

The mean generalization score over the three biological attributes was 32.89 (SD=89), which was quite high when one considers that the highest possible score was 48. Closer scrutiny of the data, however, gives more insight into the nature of the children's understanding of the interrelationships of these concepts. For example, none of the subjects gave correct responses for all sixteen objects across all three biological attributes. The need-for-nutriment concept was best understood by these supposedly nonanimistic subjects; twenty-three (or 59%) responded correctly across all items for this attribute. The respiration and reproduction aspects, at first glance, seemed to be of considerable and equal difficulty; only three subjects correctly indicated which of these objects respired, and four knew which reproduced and which did not. However, additional examination indicated that the living forms of *Plants* (tree and flower in this list) caused the greatest difficulty for these second graders: When plants were excluded from the analysis, 72% of the sample indicated correct choices on *both* the nutriment and respiration dimensions

for the remaining fourteen items and 21% correctly generalized on the mutual presence or absence of the nutriment and reproduction attributes. There was strong indication that a high degree of familiarity with any given object was related to accuracy and extent of generalization. The stimulus item that without doubt had greatest similarity to the subjects themselves—the woman—elicited the highest degree of generalization: Sixty-nine percent of the sample attributed to her conjointly the need to eat and breathe and the ability to reproduce.

One final analysis indicated that large differences existed in the subjects' understanding of these biological concepts as they apply to living and nonliving objects. The mean generalization score on the eight nonliving items ($\bar{X}=19.64$) was significantly higher than that for the eight living items ($\bar{X}=13.26$). This difference was significant ($t=2.80$, $df=38$, $p<.01$; test for correlated means). Fourteen of the subjects obtained perfect generalization scores across the three attributes for all nonliving items; none of the subjects obtained perfect scores across all living items.

DISCUSSION

The major findings from this study (which can, of course, be generalized only to children of this age) were that subjects who were identified as "nonanimistic," according to the usual criterion based upon alive/not-alive classification of objects, possessed an incomplete understanding of the concept of "living" according to associated biological attributes; that the attribute of need for nutriment was better understood than that of respiration, and that respiration was better understood than that of reproduction; and that the generalization of these biological attributes was greater for nonliving objects than for living objects. Minor findings were that there were no sex differences, and that there was no difference in concept understanding as indicated in either verbal or nonverbal response modes.

The import of this study would seem to be that although a child may indicate a "correct" understanding of a concept according to usual task criteria, his single judgmental response (i.e., in this study, "living" *vs.* "not-living") may not be indicative of a complete and thoroughgoing understanding of what this concept implies. That is, a child may at some point be able to make the distinction that a frog is alive and that a coffee cup is not, but he is not likely to understand at this early stage what else is implicated by the "life" status. This is suggestive of the notion of *horizontal décalage* proposed by Piaget (1952); that is, a concept is not acquired in a saltatory manner, but rather there is always some degree of gradualness in attaining consummate comprehension.

Not to be overlooked in this discussion is the role of familiarity. Research by Nass (1956) and Berzonski (1971) has convincingly indicated that there is a high degree of relationship between subjects' familiarity with various objects and the sophistication of their understanding of these objects. There can be little doubt that the stimulus objects in this study were quite common to the experience of these children. Moreover, the concepts of need for nutriment, respiration, and reproduction most likely can be placed on a greater-to-lesser continuum of familiarity for children; the findings from this study, certainly, would suggest this *horizontal décalage* of concepts related to the larger concept of "living." The activity of eating is unquestion-ably more salient in the lives of children than that of breathing, and despite the increasing number of sex education classes in elementary schools, it is likely that second graders understand the meaning of reproduction least well of all among these three activities.

This study is best viewed as a preliminary endeavor, one that suggests many future avenues for investigation. The obvious questions pertain to the issues of the *horizontal décalage* of the associated attributes of living, the extent of familiarity or experience with stimulus objects, and the nature of the developmental progression toward the construction of a mature concept of life.

REFERENCES

Berzonski, M. D. The role of familiarity in children's explanations of physical causality. *Child development,* 1971, **42,** 705-715.

Looft, W. R. Animistic thought in children: Effects of two response modes. *Perceptual and motor skills,* 1972, **27,** 443-448.

Looft, W. R., & Bartz, W. H. Animism revised. *Psychological Bulletin,* 1969, **71,** 1-19.

Looft, W. R., & Charles, D. C. Modification of the life concept in children. *Developmental psychology,* 1969, **1,** 445.

Nass, M. L. The effects of three variables on children's concepts of physical causality. *Journal of abnormal & social psychology,* 1956, **53,** 191-196.

Piaget, J. *The child's conception of the world.* New York: Harcourt, Brace, 1929.

Piaget, J. *The origins of intelligence in children.* New York: International Universities Press, 1952.

Russell, R. W., & Dennis, W. Studies in animism: I. A standardized procedure for the investigation of animism. *Journal Genetic Psychology,* 1939, **55,** 389-400.

10.

Helene Borke

PIAGET'S MOUNTAINS REVISITED: CHANGES IN THE EGOCENTRIC LANDSCAPE

Piaget and Inhelder's (1956) mountain experiment is most frequently cited in the literature as support for the theory of early egocentrism. In this experiment, Piaget and Inhelder investigated perceptual role-taking ability in children between 4 and 12 years of age. The children were asked to imagine how a doll would view a mountain scene from several different positions. The subjects communicated their ability to visualize the doll's viewpoint by (a) selecting one picture from a group of pictures to show how the mountains looked to the doll from different perspectives, (b) selecting one picture and placing the doll in an appropriate position for taking an identical snapshot, or (c) arranging three cardboard replicas of the mountains to reconstruct the doll's view. Piaget and Inhelder reported that when asked to indicate what the doll saw, the 4- and 5-year-old subjects invariably responded by giving their own perspective. Although the 6-year-old subjects appeared to show some awareness that the doll's viewpoint was different from their own, like the younger children, they were unable to reproduce the doll's view successfully. Not until 9 years of age did the children demonstrate a real comprehension of the doll's perspective. Piaget and Inhelder concluded that the young child "appears rooted in his own viewpoint in the narrowest and most restricted fash-

ion so that he cannot imagine any perspective but his own" (p. 242).

Another possible conclusion is that the task presented to the children for communicating their perceptual role-taking skills was beyond the cognitive capabilities of most children below 9 years of age (Borke, 1971, 1972, 1973). The effect of the task on the relationship between age and role-taking ability is evident in several experiments by Flavell, Botkin, and Fry (1968). In one study modeled after Piaget and Inhelder's mountain experiment, a series of four geometric configurations of increasing difficulty was presented to subjects between 7 and 17 years of age. The subjects were given a duplicate set of geometric forms and asked to reconstruct the model so that it looked just the way the examiner saw it from various positions. The results showed that the youngest subjects had difficulty reproducing the examiner's view on the easiest displays and only a minority of the 17-year-old subjects could reconstruct the most difficult configuration correctly.

On another series of tasks designed by Flavell et al. to investigate role-taking ability in children between 3 and 6 years of age, the 6-year-old subjects made relatively few errors. The younger children showed considerable variation in performance, but on the two easiest tasks (e.g., orienting a picture for the examiner to look at upside down and predicting which of two pictures the examiner was viewing) even the majority of the 3-year-old subjects demonstrated an ability to take into

Source: Reprinted from and copyrighted as part of *Developmental Psychology*, Vol. 11, No. 2, copyright © 1975, by the American Psychological Association, Inc.

account the other person's perspective. While Flavell interpreted his results as supporting Piaget's conclusions that children under 6 years of age are either "wholly or almost wholly unaware of perspective differences," his data suggest that the complexity of the task may well be a critical variable in determining at what age children demonstrate role-taking ability.

Recently a number of investigators (Fishbein, Lewis, & Keiffer, 1972; Hoy, 1974; Huttenlocher & Presson, 1973) studied the effects of altering both the task and the mode of responding on children's ability to reproduce another person's perspective.

All of these researchers found that success in demonstrating perceptual role-taking by preschool and elementary school children varies with both the dimensions of the task and the type of response required. In two of these studies (Fishbein *et al.*, 1972; Huttenlocher & Presson, 1973), the researchers had subjects rotate a three-dimensional scene to reproduce the other person's point of view. This procedure resulted in significantly fewer errors than when children were asked to indicate another person's perspective by selecting a picture. Fishbein *et al.* reported that on the rotation task even their 3- to 5-year-old

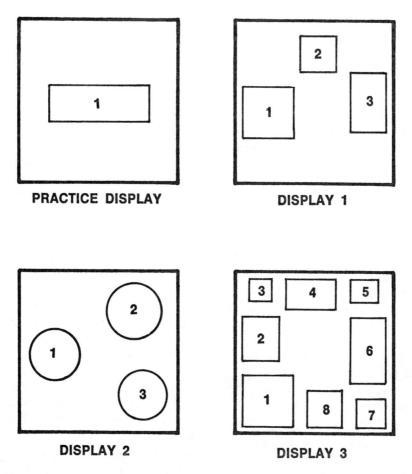

Figure 10.1. Displays as viewed from above

subjects predicted the other's perspective correctly over 90% of the time.

If young children's ability to succeed on perceptual role-taking tasks is a function of both the nature of the task and the type of response required, then both of these variables should be controlled in any research investigating the ability of young children to predict another person's viewpoint. By replicating Piaget and Inhelder's basic experimental design but substituting a more age-appropriate task, it was hypothesized that children as young as 3 and 4 years of age would demonstrate perceptual role-taking ability.

METHOD

The subjects were eight 3-year-old children and fourteen 4-year-old children attending a child care center sponsored by a large urban university. The majority of the subjects were the children of students. Approximately one fourth of the youngsters in each group came from the neighboring community. White children predominated with no more than 2 black subjects in each age group.

The task presented to the children consisted of four three-dimensional displays. The children were first shown a practice display to orient them to the task and then three experimental displays. As each subject entered the room, he or she was seated at a table facing the practice display which consisted of a large red fire engine (see Figure 10.1). An exact duplicate of the fire engine appeared on a revolving turntable to the subject's left. Each youngster was then introduced to Grover, a character from Sesame Street, and told,

Grover is going to play this game with us. He will drive his car along the road. Sometimes Grover likes to stop and look out of his car. Now the fire engine on this other table turns so you can look at it from any side. When Grover stops to look out of his car, I want you to turn the scene that moves so you are looking at it the same way Grover is.

The examiner then parked Grover in turn at each of the three sides which presented a view different from the subject's. If a subject incorrectly predicted how the fire engine looked to Grover for any of the three positions, the examiner said, "Sometimes it is hard to tell what Grover sees. Let's go over and look at the fire engine the way Grover sees it." The subject was then asked to go back and "move the turntable so that the fire engine looks the way Grover sees it." If the children again gave an incorrect response, the examiner moved the turntable to the correct position explaining, "This is the way Grover sees the fire engine from where he is parked."

After completing the practice trial with the fire engine, each subject was shown the three experimental displays one at a time (see Figure 10.1). Display 1 consisted of a small lake with a toy sailboat (1), a miniature horse and cow (2), and a model of a house (3). Display 2 was a papier-mâché replica of Piaget and Inhelder's three mountains: the mountain with a cross on top (1), the mountain with a snow cap (2), and the mountain with a small house on top (3). Display 3 contained a wide variety of miniature people and animals in natural settings: cowboys, Indians, and trees (1), a lake with ducks (2), a windmill (3), cows pulling a wagon (4), a dog and a doghouse (5), a barn with farm animals and a farmer (6), a woman feeding chickens (7), two rabbits and a pig pen with pigs (8).

The procedure for these three displays was similar to that used in the practice task except that the child was not given any further opportunity to look at the scene from Grover's point of view. If the subject gave an incorrect response, it was simply accepted and the experimenter moved Grover to the next position. For every display, Grover parked in turn at each of the three sides which presented a view different from that of the subject. The sequence of stops was varied randomly for the three scenes. A subject's response was scored correct if the revolving display was turned so that it matched Grover's perception and scored egocentric if the display conformed to the subject's own view.

RESULTS

A 3x2 (Scene x Age) analysis of variance of the total number of correct responses revealed significant differences in the accuracy of the children's perception on the three displays, $F(2, 64)=8.32$, $p>.001$. No other effects were significant.

All subjects were highly accurate in their prediction of Grover's perception on the two scenes containing toy objects, but made significantly more errors when responding to Piaget and Inhelder's mountain scene. On Display 1 showing a lake with a sailboat, animals, and a house, the 3- and 4-year-old subjects rotated the duplicate scene so that it accurately reflected Grover's perspective for all three positions over 80% of the time. On Display 3 containing a wide variety of different objects, the 3-year-olds predicted Grover's viewpoint correctly for all three positions over 79% of the time, and the 4-year-olds predicted Grover's perspective correctly 93% of the time. In contrast, on Piaget and Inhelder's mountain scene, the 3-year-old subjects gave only 42% correct responses for the three positions and the 4-year-olds gave 67% correct responses. There were no significant differences in the children's ability to predict Grover's perspective for any of the three positions. Of the total number of errors on all three displays, almost one third or 31% were egocentric and slightly over two thirds or 69% were random.

DISCUSSION

The nature of the task appears to have a significant effect on the role-taking ability of young children. The children's considerably greater success on both the simple and complex scenes containing small toy figures as compared with the three mountains suggests that one important factor affecting role-taking ability is the ease with which the subject can discriminate cues for visualizing the other person's perspective. Discrete, easily differentiated objects provide more cues for young children to identify and remember than essentially similar configurations such as Piaget and Inhelder's three mountains.

Another critical variable appears to be the way the child is expected to communicate an awareness of the other person's perspective. Having subjects revolve an exact duplicate of the experimental display to indicate the other person's viewpoint resulted in a very low error rate on the two scenes depicting discrete objects. The 4-year-olds even achieved some degree of success on Piaget and Inhelder's three mountains. This confirms the observations of other researchers (Fishbein *et al.*, 1972; Huttenlocher & Presson, 1973) that children find it much easier to communicate their awareness of another person's point of view when asked to turn an identical display than when asked to select a picture or build a model. While young children can recognize pictures of objects from a fairly early age, they seem to experience considerable difficulty when asked to make the transition from a three-dimensional display to a two-dimensional picture. Reconstructing a model of the other person's viewpoint also appears to involve conceptual skills beyond the capacity of most children under 6 or 7 years of age. The relatively small proportion of egocentric responses to all three scenes, compared with the predominance of such responses in children under 6 years of age reported by Piaget and Inhelder, suggests that the more difficult it is for subjects to solve a task, the greater the likelihood that they will give their own perspective in an attempt to perform successfully in the situation.

Data from the present study and from previous investigators exploring perceptual role-taking skills in 4- to 6-year-olds (Fishbein *et al.*, 1972; Flavell *et al.*, 1968) raise considerable doubt about the validity of Piaget's conclusion that young children are primarily egocentric and incapable of taking the viewpoint of another person. When presented with tasks that are age appropriate, even very young subjects demonstrate perceptual role-taking ability. If one accepts the premise that the capacity to understand another person's perspective is a basic component of empathy, then the evidence indicates that the potential for empathic understanding is already present in children as young as 3 and 4 years of age.

REFERENCES

Borke, H. Interpersonal perception of young children: Egocentrism or empathy? *Developmental Psychology,* 1971, **5,** 263-269.

Borke, H. Chandler and Greenspan's "ersatz egocentrism": A rejoinder. *Developmental Psychology,* 1972, **7,** 107-109.

Borke, H. The development of empathy in Chinese and American children between three and six years of age: A cross culture study. *Developmental Psychology,* 1972, **9,** 102-108.

Fishbein, H. D., Lewis, S., & Keiffer, K. Children's understanding of spatial relations: Coordination of perspectives. *Developmental Psychology,* 1972, **7,** 21-33.

Flavell, J. H., Botkin, P. T., & Fry, C. L., Jr. *The development of role-taking and communication skills in young children.* New York: John Wiley and Sons, 1968.

Hoy, F. A. Predicting another's visual perspective: A unitary skill? *Developmental Psychology,* 1974, **10,** 462.

Huttenlocher, J., & Presson, C. Mental rotation and the perspective problem. *Cognitive Psychology,* 1973, **4,** 277-299.

Piaget, J., & Inhelder, B. *The child's conception of space.* London: Routledge & Kegan Paul, 1956.

11.

Urie Bronfenbrenner

IS EARLY INTERVENTION EFFECTIVE?

The 1960s saw the widespread adoption in this country of early education programs aimed at counteracting the effects of poverty on human development. Although some of these programs produced dramatic results during the first few months of operation, the question of long-term impact has remained unanswered for lack of extended follow-up data. Recently, however, research results have become available which shed some light on five questions of considerable scientific and social import:

1. Do children in experimental early education programs continue to gain in intellectual development so long as the education continues, or at least do they maintain the higher level achieved in the initial phase?
2. Do children continue to improve, or at least to hold their own, after termination of the program, or do they regress to lower levels of function once the program is discontinued?
3. Is development enhanced by intervention at early ages, including the first years of life?
4. In terms of long-range impact, what kinds of programs are most effective?
5. Which children from what circumstances are most likely to benefit in the long run from early education programs?

Source: This article is a condensed version of a longer report, *Is Early Intervention Effective?* published by the United States Department of Health, Education, and Welfare, Office of Child Development, 1974.

THE NATURE AND LIMITATIONS OF THE DATA

Follow-up data are available from two types of early education projects: those conducted in group settings outside the home and those which involve regularly scheduled home visits by a trained person who works both with the child and his parents, usually the mother. We have attempted to insure comparability in our analysis by reviewing only those studies which (1) include follow-up data for at least two years after the termination of intervention, (2) provide information on a matched control group, and (3) provide data which are comparable to results in other studies.

With respect to the third criterion, it is regrettable that the only comparable measures available from most studies are IQ scores (usually the Stanford-Binet) and, for older children, school achievement tests. This circumstance seriously qualifies the conclusions that can be drawn. Thus we have no systematic information about effects of intervention programs outside the cognitive realm, and, even within that sphere, standardized tests of intelligence and achievement are limited in scope and subject to a marked middle-class bias. Not only are they typically administered by middle-class professionals in middle-class settings, but the kinds of objects, facts, and activities with which the tests are concerned are far more common in middle-class than in less favored environments. As a result, the scores obtained inevitably underestimate the potential of children from disadvantaged families.

TABLE 11.1

Identifying Data	Sample	Nature of Intervention	Experimental and Control Groups
Howard University Preschool Program Washington, D.C. Elizabeth Herzog (Herzog, Newcomb, and Cisin, 1972a, 1972b; Kraft, Fuschillo, and Herzog, 1968)	Black children in generally good health from families selected at random from four census tracts in Washington inner-city neighborhoods. All parents had to agree in advance to have their children attend the pre-school program if selected. No other requirements. Approximately 68% of families below poverty line; 18% on welfare; median income about $3,500 but extending up to $10,000. About 25% of parents graduated from high school, 90% unskilled labor, remainder skilled and semi-profes-sional. 28% of the mothers worked, and apparently all of the fathers when present. No father in 40% of the homes. Median number of children in the family 4. The "no-show" rate was over 30% during the recruitment phase, but attrition was very low thereafter.	"A well-run middle class nursery school, with no specific 'enrich-ment' features." Children attended full day for 5 days a week. Each group of twelve had its own teacher and two or three teachers' aides. Weekly parent meetings were held at the university plus individual contacts with families, usually unscheduled. In the hope of consolidating any benefits . . . a series of special school situations was arranged for the 30 experimental children during the three years immedi-ately following nursery school. These included being in the same class in kindergarten, extra teachers and aides, an enriched curriculum, special trips, and assignment of a social worker to the children's families.	Thirty children from one census tract were designated as the experimental group and 69 from the other three tracts as the control group. The experimental group ended up with a higher percentage of intact families (66% versus 16%), and slightly smaller families.
Perry Preschool Project, Ypsilanti, Michigan David P. Weikart (Weikart, D. P., et al., 1970; Weikart, 1967)	Black children from disadvantaged homes residing in a city of 50,000 on the fringe of metropolitan Detroit. To qualify all children had to have IQ's between 50 and 85 with no discernible organic involve-ment. In addition, families had to fall below a low cutting point on a cultural deprivation scale based pri-marily on parents' education and occupation, and also number of persons per room in the home. Parents' education averaged below tenth grade; occupations over 70% unskilled; half the families are on welfare; no information on income; 14% of fathers unemployed. Average number of children in the family 4.8. 48% of the children have no	Half-day classes, 5 days a week, from mid-October through May for two years. Curriculum derived mainly from Piagetian theory and focused on cognitive objectives. Four teachers for each group of 24 children with emphasis on individual and small group activities. Teachers made weekly 90-minute home visit "to individualize instruction through a tutorial relationship with the student and to make parents knowledgeable about the educative process . . . mothers were encouraged to observe and participate in as many teaching activities as possible during the home visits."	Children from the total sample were divided at random into experimental and control groups with some adjust-ments to assure matching on social class, IQ, boy/girl ratio, and percent of working mothers. The groups appear to be well matched on other variables as well. Although there were 5 waves of experimental and control groups initiated over a period of years, the waves have been pooled in reporting follow-up data.

TABLE 11.1 (Continued)

III. Intelligence and Thought 107

Identifying Data	Sample	Nature of Intervention	Experimental and Control Groups
	father in the home; about 28% working mothers. There appears to have been little self-selection of families in the sample and attrition during the course of the project has been low.		Sixty-one children from the same large city were divided at random into two experimental groups (E1 and E2) and one control group (C1). The remaining control group (C2), consisted of twenty-seven children from like backgrounds residing in a similar city 65 miles away. Group E1 attended the ten-week intervention program for three years of weekly meetings with a trained home visitor when preschool was not in session. Group E2 began the program a year later with only two years of exposure.
Early Training Project Nashville, Tennessee Susan W. Gray (Gray and Klaus 1970; Klaus and Gray 1968)	Black children from families "considerably below" the poverty line. Selected on the basis of parents' occupation (unskilled or semi-skilled), education (average below eighth grade), income (average $1,500), and poor housing conditions. No data on welfare status or percent of parents unemployed; one-third of the homes with no father; median number of children per family 5. Both self-selection of families at entry and attrition over the course of the study appear to have been minimal.	In summer, daily morning classes emphasized the development of achievement motivation, perceptual and cognitive activities, and language. Each group of nineteen had a black head teacher and three or four teaching assistants divided equally as to race and sex. In dealing with the children, staff emphasized positive reinforcement of desired behavior. The weekly home visit stressed the involvement of the parent in the project and in activities with the child. Home visits lasted through the year.	
Philadelphia Project Temple University E. Kuno Beller (1972)	Children from urban slum areas of north Philadelphia, 90% black. Families in target mainly employed in unskilled or semi-skilled labor with median income of $3,400. Children admitted to the nursery group were selected from families responding to a written invitation, who also met the following criteria; "dependency of family on public services, mothers working, and broken homes." Kindergarten group consisted of children from the same classroom attended by nursery children, but without prior nursery experience. First grade group was composed of children entering the same classrooms but without prior nursery or kindergarten experience. Attrition was 10% by the time the original groups reached fourth grade.	Nursery groups composed of fifteen children with one head and one assistant teacher for four half days a week, with a fifth day devoted to staff meetings, teacher training, and parent conferences. "The program was a traditional one" emphasizing "curiosity for discovery . . . creativity . . . warm, personalized handling of the child . . . balance of self-initiated, instructed activities." Kindergarten and first grade classes consisted of 25 to 30 children, meeting five half days a week, with one head teacher and an aide or assistant teacher. Work with parents and home visits were conducted by a home-school coordinator.	A major purpose of the research was to examine the effect of age at entry into school by examining intellectual development of three comparison groups starting in nursery, kindergarten, and first grade respectively. Groups were matched on age, sex, and ethnic background. No data are available on comparability of the three groups in terms of education, socioeconomic status, or family structure. Comparison at time of entry into school on three different tests of intelligence and on other psychological measures, however, revealed no significance differences. The children from all three groups attended the same classrooms through Grade II, but by Grade III children were dispersed over many schools.

TABLE 11.1 *(Continued)*

Identifying Data	Sample	Nature of Intervention	Experimental and Control Groups
Indiana Project Indiana University Bloomington, Indiana Walter L. Hodges (Hodges et al. 1967)	Five-year-old children in good health predominantly white from Bloomington and from small semi-rural Indiana communities selected on the basis of low-rated "psychosocial deprivation" and Binet intelligence score between 50 and 85. Average length of schooling for parents just below tenth grade. No information on welfare status or income. Fathers' occupation approximately 70% unskilled and 8% semi-skilled; 12% unemployed; one-third of the mothers work; 20% of the homes have no father present; average number of children in the family 5; no information is available on the degree of self-selection among sample families. There was only one slight attrition over the course of the study.	Group E1 was exposed to a special "diagnostically-based curriculum" designed to remedy specific deficits of individual children through "an intensive, structured, cognitively-oriented" program. The children met daily for morning sessions. To increase the likelihood of adoption of the program by the public schools, "the teacher to child ratio was smaller in the present study than that reported in the other preschool projects. . . For the same reason, no work was done with the families of the subjects."	One experimental group (E1) and control group (C2) were constituted by random assignment, Group E1 attended one year of the specially designed kindergarten program in Bloomington, C2 was composed of at-home controls from the same city. Children in Group C1 attended regular kindergartens newly established in several semi-rural Indiana towns. This was a "traditional kindergarten," providing facilities and equipment similar to those for C2 but without the special "diagnostically evolved" curriculum. Group C3 consisted of at-home controls in these same localities. In general, the families in the experimental group were rated by investigators as more disadvantaged than those in the control group but this difference is not reflected in indices of socioeconomic status, family size, parents' education, or occupation.
Infant Education Research Project Washington, D.C. Earl S. Schaefer (Schaefer 1972a, 1968; Schaefer and Aaronson 1972; Infant Education Research Project, undated)	Fifteen-month old black male infants selected from door-to-door surveys of families in two low socioeconomic inner-city neighborhoods in Washington. To be accepted families had to meet four criteria: (1) income under $5,000; (2) mother's education under twelve years; (3) occupation either unskilled or semi-skilled; and (4) willingness to have infant participate in either the experimental or control group. In addition, "an attempt was made to choose participants from relatively stable homes, not so noisy or over-crowded as to interfere with the	Trained tutors worked with each child in the home for one hour a day, five days per week, from the time the child was 15 months old until 3 years of age. The main emphasis was on development of verbal and conceptual abilities through the use of pictures, games, reading, and puzzles. "Participation of the mother and of other family members in the education of the infant was encouraged but not required."	Chosen from different neighborhoods to avoid contamination. "Comparisons between the groups revealed only small differences, many of which favored the control group, on the family variables that might be expected to influence the child's intellectual development."

TABLE 11.1 (*Continued*)

Identifying Data	Sample	Nature of Intervention	Experimental and Control Groups
	home tutoring sessions." No other background information available. Of the 64 subjects in the original sample, 48 (equally divided between experimental and control group) were available for the final followup.		
Verbal Interaction Project Mineola, New York Phyllis Levenstein (1972a, 1970)	Infants 2 to 3 years of age, 90% black, from disadvantaged families in three Long Island suburbs. To qualify mothers had to be eligible for low income housing with an education not higher than high school graduation. About 25% of the families were on welfare. Average education of parents was eleventh grade; fathers apparently all employed; about 65% unskilled or semi-skilled. About 35% of mothers work; 30% of the fathers absent. Average number of children per family, 3-4. Self-selection involved in willingness of mothers in experimental group to participate. Attrition especially high in untreated control groups. Average IQ of mothers of children in the experimental groups was 83; in the control group 88.	Semi-weekly half-hour visits in the home for 7 months each year by trained worker who stimulated interaction between mother and child with the aid of a kit of toys and books referred to as VISM (Visual Interaction Stimulus Materials).	Randomized by housing project. The several experimental and control groups differ on age of entry into the program (2 vs. 3, see Table 11.3), length and intensity of intervention, and prior experience. Groups E1 and E2 had one year of the regular program at two years of age followed by a much abbreviated program in the second year as follows. Group E1 received 7 visits in which the focus of attention was on the kit of materials with no involvement of the mother in interaction with the child. Group E2 was given the regular program but with half as many visits as in the first year. Group E3 received the full program for 2 years beginning at 2 years of age. Groups E4 and E5 were both given 1 year of the regular program at age 3, but Group E5 had served the previous year as a "placebo" control group which had received the semi-weekly visits but without exposure to the special kit of materials or encouragement of mother–child interaction. The visitor simply brought a gift and played records for the child. Seven of the 8 groups are generally comparable on major background variables, but one control group (C2) was far out of line—with better educated mothers, smaller families, higher occupational status, no absent fathers, etc.

Nevertheless, few scientists or citizens would dismiss as unimportant the demonstration that a particular strategy of early intervention had enabled children from disadvantaged backgrounds to solve problems of the type presented on tests of intelligence at a level of competence comparable to that of the average child of the same age. Whereas performance below the norm on tests of this kind cannot be taken as firm evidence that the child lacks mental capacity, attainment of the norm year after year does mean that the child possesses both intellectual ability and the skill to use it. It is from this perspective that the present analysis was undertaken.

METHODOLOGICAL PROBLEMS

Before turning to an interpretation of the results, several methodological complications must be noted.

1. If low IQ is used as a criterion for admission to the program (as in the Weikart and the Hodges studies[1]), the initial gains are appreciably inflated by regression to the mean. This phenomenon is responsible for the mistaken but often cited conclusion that the most deprived children are the ones who profit most from intervention programs. In fact, the opposite is the case (see below).

2. A child whose parents are interested in his development and are eager to take advantage of opportunities for him is likely to be more advanced in and to gain more from an intervention program. Thus failure to control for differences in parents' motivation leads to spurious results.

3. Recent evidence indicates that programs involving children from relatively less deprived homes are likely to achieve more favorable results.[2] In comparing effects from different projects, this source of variation must be taken into account.

4. In evaluating results of intervention, other possible sources of confounding include age (the effects of deprivation increase as the child gets older) and diffusion effects from experimental to control group (i.e., the latter begins to adopt the practices of the former).

SOME EFFECTS OF PRESCHOOL INTERVENTION IN GROUP SETTINGS

The results of group intervention studies are summarized in Table 11.2. For each study the table records the number of subjects, IQs achieved in successive years by experimental and control groups, and the differences between them. The scores given first are those obtained by both groups before the program began. A double line indicates the point at which intervention was terminated. At the bottom, major changes over time are summarized in terms of initial gain (before-after difference in the

---

[1] D. P. Weikart. *Preschool Intervention: A Preliminary Report of the Perry Preschool Project.* Ann Arbor, Mich.: Campus Publishers, 1967; D. P. Weikart, "A Comparative Study of Three Preschool Curricula," a paper presented at the biannual meeting of the Society for Research in Child Development, Santa Monica, Calif., March 1969; D. P. Weikart *et al. Longitudinal Results of the Ypsilanti Perry Preschool Project.* Ypsilanti, Mich.: High/Scope Educational Research Foundation, 1970; D. P. Weikart, C. K. Kamii, and M. Radin. *Perry Preschool Progress Report.* Ypsilanti, Mich.: Ypsilanti Public Schools, 1964; D. P. Weikart, L. Rogers, C. Adcock, and D. McClelland. *The Cognitively Oriented Curriculum.* Washington, D.C.: National Association for the Education of Young Children, 1971; and W. L. Hodges, B. R. McCandless, and H. H. Spicker. *The Development and Evaluation of a Diagnostically Based Curriculum for Preschool Psychosocially Deprived Children.* Washington, D.C.: U.S. Office of Education, 1967.

[2] E. Herzog, C. H. Newcomb, and I. H. Cisin. But some are poorer than others: SES differences in a preschool program. *American Journal of Orthopsychiatry,* 1972, **42,** 4-22.

TABLE 11.2. Effects on Later Intellectual Development of Intervention Programs in Preschool Setting
(Double line designates point at which intervention was terminated.)

	Herzog			Weikart			Gray					Beller			Hodges				
No.	1	2	3	4	5	6	7	8	9	10	11	12	13	14	15	16	17	18	19
	E	C	E-C	E	C	E-C	E_1	E_2	C_1	C_2	$\bar{E}-C_1$[b]	C_1	C_2	C_3	E	C_1	C_2	C_3	$\bar{E}-C_2$
N	30	66-62		58-13[a]	65-15[a]		19	19	18	23		57-50	53-46	57-53	11	11	13	13	13
Age 3 Before	81	85	-4	79.7	79.1	.6	87.6	92.5[c]	85.4	86.7	-1.4[c]								
After	91	85	6	95.8	83.4	12.4**	102.0	92.3[c]	88.2	87.4	11.8*[c]								
Age 4 Before	96	88	8**	94.7	82.7	12.0**	96.4	94.8	89.6	86.7	6.0	92.1							
After							97.1	97.5	87.6	84.7	9.7*								
Kindergarten Before	97	90	7	90.5	85.4	5.1*	95.8	96.6	82.9	80.2	13.3**	98.6	91.2		74.5	75.0	74.5	72.5	0
After							98.1	99.7	91.4	89.0	7.5*				93.8	87.5	80.9	81.3	12.9*
Grade I	95	89	6	91.2	83.3	7.9**	91.2	96.0	87.9	84.6	5.7*	98.4	94.4	89.9	97.4	83.2	91.7	84.8	5.4
Grade II	92	87	5	88.8	86.5	2.3	—	—	—	—	—	97.8	92.8	88.6	94.9	85.5	89.2	86.5	5.7
Grade III	87	87	0	89.6	88.1	1.5	—	—	—	—	—	97.6	93.1	89.3					
Grade IV							86.7	90.2	84.9	77.7	3.5**	98.4	91.7	88.6					
Initial Gain	10	0	10	16.1	4.3	11.8	14.4	5.0	2.8	.7	6.9	6.5*	3.2	-1.3	19.3	12.5	6.4	8.8	12.9
Gain 2 Years After	14	4	10	11.5	4.2	7.3	3.6	3.5	2.5	-2.1	1.1	6.3[d]	1.6[d]	-.6[d]	20.4	10.5	14.7	12.0	5.7
Overall gain	6	2	4	9.9	9.0	.9	-.9	-2.3	-.5	-9.0	1.3	6.3[d]	.5[d]	-1.3[d]					
Achievement Level	no difference			2.1	.6	1.5*[f]	3.7	4.0	3.8	3.4	.2	—	—	—	2.1	2.0	1.8	1.5	.4

[a] N's decrease because only earlier waves reached grade school (see Table 11.1).
[b] Published significance level includes C_2.
[c] Intervention began one year later in E_2; hence C_1 includes E_2 for this age group only.
[d] Significance of difference not tested.
[e] Difference significant for the distal control group (C_3) only.
[f] Difference significant for girls only.
[g] A reduced parent intervention program was continued through grade one.

first year of treatment), gain two years after all intervention was terminated (shown because it permits a comparison of all seven studies), and overall gain (difference between initial IQ and last follow-up score three to four years after the children left the program). Also shown are differences between these gains for the experimental and control group. Finally, the bottom row records the average grade equivalent attained on a test of academic achievement administered in the final year of follow-up. Unless otherwise noted, significant differences between experimental and control groups for each year are designated by asterisks, one for the 5 percent level and two for 1 percent. The absence of asterisks indicates that the difference was not reliable. Ordinarily no significance tests are available for gain scores, but these are shown in the few instances when they were computed by the original investigator.

Two striking patterns become apparent. First, early intervention produces substantial gains in IQ as long as the program lasts. But the experimental groups do not continue to make gains when intervention continues beyond one year, and, what is more critical, the effects tend to "wash out" after intervention is terminated. The longer the follow-up, the more obvious the latter trend becomes.[3] There appear to be some exceptions to the generally regressive trend, but these are faulted by methodological artifacts—regression to the mean in the Hodges and Weikart programs,[4] inadequate control for parents' motivation

in the nonrandom comparison groups of the Beller and Gray projects.[5]

Additional support for our conclusion comes from DiLorenzo's evaluation of long-term effects of preschool programs in New York State. Although DiLorenzo still found significant differences between experimental and control groups on achievement tests administered in first grade, these differences were no longer present at the end of second grade.[6]

The DiLorenzo study also adds some new evidence on the comparative effectiveness of different types of preschool programs. The data presented suggest that most significant differences between experimental and control groups were found in highly structured, cognitively oriented programs. Furthermore, these programs produced the most pronounced long-term effects. Karnes reports similar findings.[7] In comparing Montessori programs to structured, cognitively oriented programs, she concludes that structure *per se* is not crucial. Rather, the greatest and most enduring gains are made in structured programs which include an emphasis on verbal and cognitive training.

The intervention programs reported herein were carried out over a period of one or two years. Deutsch reports results of more extended intervention conducted with severely disadvantaged inner-city children over a five-year period.[8] After five

[3]Weikart, *op. cit.;* S. W. Gray and R. A. Klaus. Experimental preschool program for culturally-deprived children. *Child Development,* 1965, **36,** 887-898; and S. W. Gray and R. A. Klaus, The early training project: The seventh-year report. *Child Development,* 1970, **41,** 909-924.

[4]Hodges, *op. cit.;* Weikart, *op. cit.*

[5]E. K. Beller, Impact of early education on disadvantaged children. In S. Ryan (ed.) *A report on longitudinal evaluations of preschool programs.* Vol. 1, Washington, D.C.: Office of Child Development, 1974; E. K. Beller, personal communications, 1973; and Gray, *op. cit.*

[6]L. T. DiLorenzo. *Pre-kindergarten programs for educationally disadvantaged children: Final report.* Washington, D.C.: U.S. Office of Education, 1969.

[7]M. B. Karnes. *Research and development program on preschool disadvantaged children: Final report.* Washington, D.C.: U.S. Office of Education, 1969.

[8]M. Deutsch *et al. Regional research and resource*

years in the program, the difference between the experimental and control groups in the third grade was a nonsignificant four points.

These findings raise the important issue of the effect of program length. Of the programs reported in Table 11.2, four extended longer than one year. Of these, only one (Herzog) showed some rise after the first year. Two indicated no change (Weikart and Gray E_2) and the third (Gray E_1), like Deutsch's, exhibited a decline. It is significant, in light of Herzog's conclusion "The less they have, the less they learn,"[9] that the Gray and Deutsch samples were the most economically depressed of any included in the analysis.

The hope that group programs begun in the earliest years of life would produce greater and more enduring gains is also disappointed. In a project directed by Caldwell, children entering intervention programs before age three did no better than later entrants, with duration of participation held constant.[10]

One ray of hope emanates from Follow-Through, a nationwide, federally sponsored program, which extends the basic philosophy of Head Start into the primary grades. Some early findings indicate that Follow-Through children made significantly larger fall-to-spring gains in achievement than did children in the control group. Furthermore, greatest gains were made by participants who were below the OEO poverty line and by children who had previously participated in Head Start. Finally, highly structured curricula produced the greatest gains. These findings,

though encouraging, must be viewed with caution because of inadequate matching between experimental and control families in socioeconomic characteristics and parental motivation. Nevertheless, the possibility exists that the comprehensiveness of the Head Start and Follow-Through programs—including family services and health and nutritional care—accounted for the more enduring gains.

The long-term effectiveness of Follow-Through is yet to be determined. Many of the declines apparent in Table 11.2 occurred after first grade. Other studies report a drop in IQ beyond the first-grade level, even while the program was still in operation.[11] It has been fashionable to blame the schools for the erosion of competence in disadvantaged children after age six. The decline in Deutsch's experimental subjects, who were at the time in an innovative and enriched educational program, suggests that the fault lies in substantial degree beyond the doors of the school. Additional findings lend support to this conclusion. The children who profited least from intervention programs and who showed the earliest and most rapid decline were those who came from the most deprived social and economic backgrounds. Especially relevant in this regard were such variables as the number of children in the family, the employment status of the head of the household, the level of parents' education, and the presence of only one parent in the family.

The impact of such environmental factors is reflected in a study by Hayes and Grether.[12] Rather than assessing academic gains from September to June, as is done

center in early childhood: Final report. Washington, D.C.: U.S. Office of Economic Opportunity, 1971.

[9]Herzog, *op. cit.*

[10]S. J. Braun and B. Caldwell. Emotional adjustment of children in daycare who enrolled prior to or after the age of three. *Early Child Development and Care,* 1973, **2,** 13-21.

[11]Deutsch, *op. cit.;* Gray, *op. cit.*

[12]D. Hayes and L. Grether. "The school year and vacation: when do students learn?" paper presented at the Eastern Sociological Convention, New York, 1969.

conventionally, they looked at changes from June to September—that is, over the summer. They found that during summer vacation white children from advantaged families either held their own or continued to gain, whereas youngsters from disadvantaged and black families reversed direction and lost ground. Hayes and Grether conclude that differences over the summer months account for 80% of the variation in academic performance between economically advantaged whites and children from nonwhite families. Accordingly, they argue that intervention efforts are best directed at the home. Our analysis of home-based programs, however, did not lead to such a verdict. Rather, as indicated below, it suggested combining elements from both strategies in a sequential manner.

SOME EFFECTS OF HOME-BASED INTERVENTION

The form of Table 11.3 is the same as that of Table 11.2, but the substance is happily different. The experimental groups in most home-based programs not only made substantial initial gains, but these gains increased and continued to hold up rather well three to four years after intervention had been discontinued. The fact that matched controls also exhibited gains in IQ over time is probably due to the special characteristics of the families who participated in home-based intervention. First, the parents were all volunteers who were then randomly assigned to experimental or control groups. Thus, all were motivated to provide educational experiences for their children and were willing to accept a stranger into their homes. Second, participants in these programs were from relatively less disadvantaged backgrounds, thus providing some corroboration for Herzog's sobering verdict, "The less they

have, the less they learn."[13] But other important factors distinguished these home-based programs: They began working with children at an earlier age, and they emphasized one-to-one interaction between the child and adult.

This one-to-one interaction, however, appears to require special participants. For example, a tutor visiting on a daily basis produces only temporary gains.[14] From their analyses of the reasons for the failure of this type of program, Schaefer and Aaronson concluded that a necessary and crucial component was maternal interest and direct involvement in the teaching process.[15] Schaefer's insistence on a "family-" rather than a "child-centered" approach[16] is exemplified in a project developed by Levenstein. She developed strategies to maximize mother–child interaction around educational materials which she provided. Viewed as a whole, the results from Levenstein's five differentially treated experimental groups suggest that the earlier and more intensely mother and child were stimulated to engage in communication around a common activity the greater and more enduring the gain in IQ achieved by the child.

To facilitate this mother–child interaction, Levenstein trained home visitors,

[13]Herzog, *op. cit.*

[14]E. S. Schaefer. *Progress report: Intellectual stimulation of culturally-deprived parents.* Washington, D.C.: National Institute of Mental Health, 1968; S. A. Kirk. The effects of early education with disadvantaged infants. In Karnes, *Research and development program on preschool disadvantaged children: Final report, op. cit.*

[15]E. S. Schaefer and M. Aaronson. Infant education research project: Implementation and implications of the home-tutoring program. In R. K. Parker (ed.) *The preschool in action.* Boston: Allyn and Bacon, 1972.

[16]Schaefer, personal communication, 1972; E. S. Schaefer, Parents as educators: Evidence from cross-sectional longitudinal and intervention research. *Young Children,* 1972, **27,** 227-239.

TABLE 11.3. Effects on Later Intellectual Development of Home-based Intervention Programs
(Double line designates point at which intervention was terminated.)
(Single broken line designates point of entry into school.)

	Schaefer[a]			Levenstein I[c]					Levenstein II				
	1	2	3	4	5	6	7	8	9	10	11	12	13
	E	C	$E\text{-}C$	E_1	E_2	E_3	C_1	$\bar{E}\text{-}\bar{C}$[d]	E_4	E_5	C_2	C_3	$\bar{E}\text{-}\bar{C}$
N	24	24	—	6	7	21	8	—	8	15	7	10	10
Age 1 Before	105.9	109.2	−3.3[b]										
After	95.3	89.4	5.9										
Age 2 Before	99.6	90.2	9.4	82.8	82.6	90.1	91.4	−8.7					
After				101.8	101.1	101.8	89.8	11.6*					
Age 3 Before	105.6	89.4	16.2						91.1	87.6	91.3	91.0	−3.5
After				102.6	105.0	108.6			101.3	102.4	95.8	—	6.4
Age 4 Before	99.1	90.1	9.0										
After													
Kindergarten Before													
After	97.8	92.8	5.0	98.5	103.6	107.2	85.0	16.0[b]	106.6	103.8	101.1		—
Grade I	100.6	96.9	3.7	98.8	100.6	108.2	88.8	10.9[b]	104.5	94.4	104.3	96.3	—
Initial Gain	−10.6	−19.8	9.2	19.0*	18.5*	11.7*	−1.6	20.4*	10.2	14.8*	4.5		0
Gain 2 Years After	−8.1	−16.4	8.3	15.7*	21.0*	17.1*	−6.4	24.8[b]	15.5*				8.7[b]
Overall Gain	−5.3	−12.3	7.0	16.0*	18.0*		−2.6	19.6	13.4[b]	6.8[b]	12.9	5.3	2.2
Achievement Level	.7	.7	0	1.2	1.4		1.2	.1	2.1	1.5	1.6		.2

[a] Bayley Infant Scale was used for first three testing periods; Binet thereafter.
[b] No significant tests available for this value and rest of column.
[c] Cattell Test used at age 2.
[d] $\bar{E} = 1/2(E_1 + E_2)$.

whom she called toy demonstrators. After first using professionals, she found that nonprofessional, low-income mothers were equally competent in this role. Their task was to demonstrate the use of toys, but far more importantly, to "treat the mother as a colleague in a joint endeavor in behalf of the child."[17] Levenstein strongly emphasized that the demonstators "keep constantly in mind that the child's primary and continuing educational relationship is with his mother."[18] The task of the demonstrator was to enhance this relationship. Thus Levenstein not only created a structured cognitive program, but directed it at the mother–child system. Furthermore, the mother, rather than a stranger-expert, was the primary agent of intervention.

The resulting reciprocal interaction between mother and child involves both cognitive and emotional components which reinforce each other. When this reciprocal interaction takes place in an interpersonal relationship that endures over time (as occurs between mother and child), it leads to the development of a strong emotional attachment which, in turn, increases the motivation of the young child to attend to and learn from the mother. It is important, as demonstrated in the Levenstein project, that this process be reinforced when the child's dependency on the mother is greatest—that is, in the second year of life.[19] In addition, Levenstein reports that

neither a friend's visit with mother and child nor the provision of instructional materials alone was sufficient by itself to produce the major effect; the critical element involved mother–child interaction around a common activity.

This reciprocal process may explain the enduring effectiveness of home intervention programs. Since the participants remain together after intervention ceases, the momentum of the system insures some degree of continuity for the future. As a result, the gains achieved through this kind of intervention strategy are more likely to persist than those gained in group preschool programs, which, after they are over, leave no social structure with familiar figures who can continue to reciprocate and reinforce the specific adaptive patterns which the child has learned. In emphasizing the primary role of the parent, and in carrying out the intervention at home, Levenstein maximizes the possibility that gains made by the child will be maintained.

But is it necessary to involve both the mother and child? Perhaps the same result can be obtained by working mainly with the mother. Karnes *et al.* developed a program which included home visits but emphasized weekly group meetings of the mothers and lasted fifteen months instead of seven as in the Levenstein study.[20] At the end of the program, the experimental group obtained a mean IQ of 106, sixteen points higher than the comparison group. To control for factors associated with home and family, Karnes *et al.* also compared IQ scores of the experimental subjects with those that had been obtained by older siblings when they were of the same

[17]P. Levenstein. Cognitive growth in preschoolers through verbal interaction with mothers. *American Journal of Orthopsychiatry;* 1970, **40,** 429.

[18]*Ibid.*

[19]U. Bronfenbrenner. Early deprivation: A cross-species analysis. In S. Levine and G. Newton, (eds.), *Early experience in behavior.* Springfield, Ill.: Charles C Thomas, 1968; U. Bronfenbrenner. When is Infant Stimulation Effective? In D. C. Glass, (ed.), *Environmental influences.* New York: Rockefeller University Press, 1968.

[20]Karnes. *Research and Development Program on Preschool Disadvantaged Children: Final Report, op. cit.*

age. A twenty-eight IQ point difference in favor of the experimental group was found.

Encouraged by these findings, Karnes and her colleagues sought to create an optimal intervention strategy by combining the mother-intervention with a preschool program for the children themselves. The results were disappointing, at least by comparison. The children entered the program at age four. After two years there were no differences in IQ between the experimental and control group, and the latter actually scored reliably higher in tests of language development. Why the marked difference in effectiveness? The authors cite one crucial change in the program: the introduction of a group preschool experience. This new element, combined with a reduction in the number of at-home visits, may have led the mothers to believe that they no longer played the critical role in furthering the development of their children.

The effectiveness of parent intervention also appears to vary as a function of age. Evidence from a number of studies indicates that the greatest gains are obtained with two-year-olds and tend to be smaller with older preschoolers, becoming negligible when children are not enrolled until age five.[21] Further support for this conclusion comes from Gilmer *et al.* in an investigation of the effects of home-based intervention on siblings of the target child.[22] Results indicated that younger siblings of those in the parent-intervention groups benefited even more from the program than did the target children.

In the same study Gilmer and her colleagues also demonstrated a further complexity as a function of age. In addition to looking at effects on siblings, these investigators compared the relative effectiveness of group, home, and combined programs with four- and five-year-old participants. They found that the group program was most effective initially, but scores rapidly declined after discontinuation of the program. The parent intervention groups, while not exhibiting as dramatic gains, nevertheless sustained their advantage longer than the group-centered children. Thus although parent intervention did not achieve as high gains in the later preschool period, it appeared to retain its power to sustain increases attained by whatever means, including group programs in preschool settings.

A SEQUENTIAL STRATEGY FOR EARLY INTERVENTION

Gilmer's results suggest the possibility of a phased sequence beginning with parent intervention in the first two years of life, followed by the addition of group programs in the late preschool and early school years. A program involving such a phased sequence is currently being conducted by Gordon with indigent families from twelve Florida counties.[23] A weekly

[21]B. Gilmer, J. O. Miller, and S. W. Gray. *Intervention with Mothers and Young Children: A Study of Intra-Family Effects.* Nashville, Tenn.: DARCEE (Demonstration and Research Center for Early Education), 1970; M. B. Karnes, W. M. Studley, W. R. Wright, and A. S. Hodgins. An Approach to Working With Mothers of Disadvantaged Preschool Children. *Merrill-Palmer Quarterly,* 1968, **14**, 174-184; M. B. Karnes, A. S. Hodgins, and J. A. Teska. The effects of short-term instruction at home by mothers of children not enrolled in a preschool. In Karnes. *Research and Development Program on Preschool Disadvantaged Children: Final Report, op. cit.;* and Levenstein, *op. cit.*

[22]Gilmer, *op. cit.*
[23]I. J. Gordon. *A Home Learning Center Approach to Early Stimulation.* Gainesville, Fla.: Institute for Development of Human Resources, 1971; I. J. Gordon. *A Home Learning Center Approach to Early Stimulation.* Gainesville, Fla.: Institute for Develop-

home visit is made for the first two years of life, with a small group setting being added in the third year. About 175 children were randomly distributed into eight groups, systematically varied with respect to age at entry and length of exposure to the program, with one group receiving no treatment whatsoever.

Although no measures of intellectual level were obtained at the beginning of the program, Gordon has recently reported Binet IQs for each group five years after intervention was started; that is, from two to four years after "graduation."[24] Of the seven experimental groups, the only three that still differed from controls by more than five IQ points (with means from ninety-five to ninety-seven in the last year of follow-up) were those that had received parent intervention in the first year of life and continued in the program for either one or two consecutive years. Groups which started parent intervention later, whose participation was interrupted for a year, or who were exposed to parent and group intervention only simultaneously did not do as well. Moreover, the addition of group intervention in the third year did not result in a higher IQ for those groups that had this experience. Indeed, in both instances in which parent intervention in the second year was followed by the addition of preschool in the third, the mean scores showed a drop over the two-year follow-up period. In contrast, the two groups for whom parent intervention was continued for a second year without the addition of a group program either held their own or gained during the follow-up period, despite the fact that they were tested three rather

than only two years after intervention had ended.

Taken as a whole, Gordon's results lend support to the following conclusions:
1. The generalization that parent intervention has more lasting effects the earlier it is begun can now be extended to the first year of life.
2. When parent intervention precedes group intervention, there are enduring effects after completion of the program, at least throughout the preschool years.
3. The addition of a group program after parent intervention has been carried out for a one- or two-year period clearly does not result in additional gains, and may even produce a loss, at least when the group intervention is introduced as early as the third year of life.

But what if the preschool component is not added until the children are four or five years old? A partial answer comes from the evaluation of a Supplementary Kindergarten Intervention Program (SKIP) developed by Weikart et al.[25] The program involved disadvantaged kindergarten children of high ability and consisted of two components in various experimental combinations: (1) a special class supplementing the regular kindergarten session with a Piagetian, cognitively oriented curriculum, and (2) a home visit program to plan similar activities with the mother which she subsequently carried out with her child. The children who experienced the full program—both group and home—exhibited higher IQ gains than those who experienced the supplementary program plus kindergarten or kindergarten only. But more importantly, an analysis comparing children who had attended a

ment of Human Resources, 1972; and I. J. Gordon. *An Early-Intervention Project: A Longitudinal Look.* Gainesville, Fla.: University of Florida, Institute for Development of Human Resources, College of Education, 1973.
[24]Gordon. *An Early Intervention Project, op. cit.*

[25]N. Radin. The impact of a kindergarten home counseling program. *Exceptional Children,* 1969, 36, 251-256.

preschool program involving intensive parent intervention with those who had not revealed that children who had had the earlier parent involvement experience gained more in IQ during the SKIP program. Furthermore, children who experienced no parent intervention, either in preschool or school, but who spent a full day first in regular kindergarten and then in the SKIP Piaget course fell six points in IQ during the kindergarten year. The impact of the classroom program was negative in the absence of any previous or concomitant parent intervention—particularly since it kept the child away from home for a full day.

Radin has just replicated her findings in a second study designed to provide a direct test of the hypothesis that prior exposure to parent intervention enhances the impact of subsequent group programs.[26] Three matched groups of 21–28 four-year-olds from lower-class homes were exposed to a preschool program supplemented with biweekly home visits. In one group, the visitor worked directly with the child, and the mother was not present. In a second group, the visitor employed the same activities as a basis for encouraging mother–child interaction. In the third group, mother–child intervention was supplemented by a weekly group meeting led by a social worker and focusing on child-rearing practices conducive to the child's development. At the end of the first year, all three groups made significant gains in IQ but did not differ reliably from each other. In addition, the mothers in the two treatments involving parent intervention showed changes in attitude interpreted as more conducive to the child's development, with the greatest shift observed in the group receiving home visits supplemented by weekly meetings.

During the following year, when the children were attending regular kindergarten (with no parent intervention program), the children who had been tutored directly in the preceding year made no additional gains in IQ, whereas the two groups exposed to prior intervention achieved further increases of ten to fifteen points. Radin concludes:

> In general the findings of this study suggest that a parent education component is important if the child is to continue to benefit academically from a compensatory preschool program, although there may be no immediate effect on the youngsters. . . . A parent program does appear, however, to enhance the mothers' perception of themselves as educators of their children and of their children as individuals capable of independent thought. Thus, perhaps, new maternal behaviors are fostered which are conducive to the child's intellectual functioning.[27]

It is to be emphasized that Radin's parent program, like all the other effective parent strategies we have examined, focuses attention on interaction between parent and child around a common activity. This approach is to be distinguished from the widespread traditional forms of parent education involving courses, dissemination of information, and counseling addressed only to the parent. There is no evidence for the effectiveness of the latter approaches.[28]

Radin's data indicate that the beneficial influence of parent intervention is substantial if it is introduced before the child enters school, but the effect is reduced if

---

[26]N. Radin. Three degrees of maternal involvement in a preschool program: Impact on mothers and children. *Child Development,* 1972, **43,** 1355-1364.

[27]*Ibid.,* p. 1363.

[28]A. Amidon and O. G. Brim. What do children have to gain from parent education? Paper prepared for the Advisory Committee on Child Development, National Research Council, National Academy of Science, 1972.

home visits are not begun until the kindergarten year. But what of the influence of parent intervention in the later school years? Smith demonstrated that parent involvement in a slightly different form, continues to be effective through the sixth grade.[29] Her project included 1,000 children from low-income housing projects, most of them black. Smith asked parents to support the child's educational activities without being actively involved in teaching, as in the preschool programs. Support consisted of such things as insuring household quiet during homework time, reading books themselves in the presence of the children, and listening to children read. This program produced significant gains in scores on reading achievement in both the second and fifth grades. Once again the family emerges as the system which sustains and facilitates development, spurred by educational experience outside the home. These findings, however, do not displace our earlier conclusion: The optimal time for parent intervention is in the first three years of life.

In summary, intervention programs which place major emphasis on involving the parent *directly* in activities fostering the child's development are likely to have constructive impact at any age, but the earlier such activities are begun and the longer they are continued, the greater the benefit to the child.

One major problem still remains, nevertheless. Given that the optimal period for parent intervention is in the first three years of life, or at least before the child enters school, implementation of this strategy still requires the cooperation of the parents at home. But many disadvantaged families live under such oppressive circumstances that they are neither willing nor able to participate in the activities required by a parent intervention program. Inadequate health care, poor housing, lack of education, low income, and the necessity for full-time work all continue to rob parents of time and energy to spend with their children. Does this mean that the best opportunity for the child must be foregone? Is there an alternative course? In our last section we turn to an examination of the problem and some possible solutions.

THE ECOLOGY OF EARLY INTERVENTION

One radical solution to this problem, which is being tried by Heber in his Milwaukee project, involves removing the child from his home for most of his waking hours, placing him in an environment conducive to his growth, and entrusting primary responsibility for his development to persons specifically trained for the job.[30] The sample for this study consisted of black mothers with newborns who were living in a severely depressed area of Milwaukee and who had IQs of seventy-five or less. The experimental group of children attended an intensive, cognitively structured program taught by paraprofessional-teachers selected from the children's own neighborhood. The children entered the program at the age of three months and stayed at the center from 8:45 a.m. until 4:00 p.m. Each child remained with his primary teacher on a one-to-one basis until he reached twelve to fifteen months. Later, children were placed in small

[29]M. B. Smith. School and home: Focus on achievement. In A. H. Passow (ed.), *Developing programs for the educationally disadvantaged.* New York: Teachers College Press, 1968.

[30]R. Heber, H. Garber, S. Harrington, and C. Hoffman. *Rehabilitation of families at risk for mental retardation.* Madison, Wis.: Rehabilitation Research and Training Center in Mental Retardation, University of Wisconsin, October 1972.

groups of two to four per teacher. A parallel program conducted for the mother involved two phases: job training and instruction in home economics and child-rearing skills.

With respect to the cognitive development of the children, the program has been astoundingly successful and will probably continue to be so as long as intervention lasts. At age 5½, the control and experimental groups were separated by thirty IQ points, with a mean of 124 for the latter.

Given our frame of reference, the success is not unexpected, since the program fulfills the major requirements we have stipulated as essential or desirable for fostering the cognitive development of the young child. With one particular person remaining the primary agent of intervention, group experiences were gradually introduced emphasizing language and structured cognitive activities. The entire operation was carried out by a group of people sharing and reinforcing a common commitment to young children and their development.

But what will happen when intervention is discontinued remains an open question. In addition, the costs of the program are prohibitive in terms of large-scale applicability. Nor have the ethical questions of removing a child from home been dealt with. Is there another approach which does not entail these problems?

An affirmative answer to this question is suggested by Harold Skeels in his report of a follow-up study[31] of two groups of mentally retarded, institutionalized children, who constituted the experimental and control groups in an experiment

Skeels had initiated thirty years earlier.[32] The average IQ of the children and of their mothers was under seventy. When the children were about two years old, thirteen of them were placed in the care of female inmates of a state insitution for the mentally retarded with each child being assigned to a different ward. The control group was allowed to remain in the original—also institutional—environment, a children's orphanage. During the formal experimental period, which averaged a year and a half, the experimental group showed a mean rise in IQ of 28 points, whereas the control group dropped 26 points. Upon completion of the experiment, it became possible to place eleven of the experimental children in legal adoption. After 2½ years with their adoptive parents, this group showed a further nine-point rise to a mean of 101. Thirty years later, all of the original thirteen children, now adults, in the experimental group were found to be self-supporting; all but two had completed high school, with four having one or more years of college. In the control group, all were either dead or still institutionalized. Skeels concludes his report with some dollar figures on the amount of taxpayer's money expended to sustain the institutionalized group in contrast to the productive income brought in by those who had been raised initially by mentally deficient women in a state institution.

The Skeels experiment is instructive on two counts. First, if Heber demonstrated that disadvantaged children of mothers

[31]H. M. Skeels. Adult status of children from contrasting early life experiences. In *Monographs of the Society for Research in Child Development,* Vol. 31, Serial No. 105, 1966.

[32]H. M. Skeels, R. Updegraff, B. L. Wellman, and H. M. Williams. A study of environmental stimulation: an orphanage preschool project. *University of Iowa Studies in Child Welfare,* 1938, **15**; H. M. Skeels and H. B. Dye. A study of the effects of differential stimulation on mentally retarded children. In *Proceedings and Addresses of the American Association on Mental Deficiency,* 1939, **44**, 114-136.

with IQs under seventy-five could, with appropriate intervention, attain an IQ well above the norm, Skeels showed that retarded mothers themselves can achieve the same gains for children under their care at substantially less expense. How was this accomplished? First, Skeels points out that almost every experimental child was involved in an intense one-to-one relationship with an older adult. Not only did the children enjoy this close interpersonal relationship, but the girls and the attendants "spent a great deal of time with 'their children' playing, talking, and training them in every way."[33] The grounds and house also afforded a wide range of toys and activities, and all children attended a nonstructured preschool program as soon as they could walk.

Thus three of the essential components of the sequential strategy we previously identified are included in the Skeels research: the initial establishment of an enduring relationship involving intensive interaction with the child; priority, status, and support for the "mother–child" system; and the introduction, at a later stage, of a preschool program, but with the child returning "home" for half the day to a highly available mother substitute. The only element missing is the systematic involvement of the child in progressively more complex activities, first in the context of the mother–child relationship, and later, in the curriculum of the preschool program. Had these elements of cognitively challenging experience been present, it is conceivable that the children would have shown even more dramatic gains in IQ, approaching the levels achieved by Heber's experimental group.

Both the Skeels and Heber experiments demonstrate the effectiveness of a major transformation of the environment for the child and the persons principally responsible for his care and development. We shall refer to this kind of reorganization as *ecological intervention.* The aim is to effect changes in the *context* in which the family lives which enable the family as a whole to exercise the functions necessary for the child's development.

The need for ecological intervention arises when the conditions of life are such that the family cannot perform its child-rearing functions, even though it may wish to do so. Under these circumstances no direct form of intervention aimed at enhancing the child's development is likely to have much impact. For children living in the most deprived circumstances, the first step in any strategy of intervention must be to provide the family with adequate health care, nutrition, housing, and employment. It is clear that ecological intervention is not being carried out today because it almost invariably requires institutional changes.

But even when the basic needs for survival are met, the conditions of life may be such as to prevent the family from functioning effectively in its child-rearing role. As we have seen, an essential prerequisite for the child's development is an environment which provides not only the opportunity but also support for parental activity. Once this is established, the style and degree of parent-child interaction becomes a crucial factor.

Skodak and Skeels demonstrated this point in a study of the effects of adoption on the development of 100 children whose true parents were both socioeconomically disadvantaged and mentally retarded.[34]

---

[33]Skeels, Updegraff, Wellman, and Williams, *op. cit.*, pp. 16-17.

[34]M. Skodak and H. M. Skeels. A final follow-up study of 100 adopted children. *Journal of Genetic Psychology,* 1949, **75**, 85-125.

The children were placed in foster families who were above average in economic security and educational and cultural status. The average IQ of the children's true mothers was 86; by the age of thirteen the mean IQ of their children placed in foster homes was 106. A thorough analysis revealed that among the group of adopted children those who made the greatest sustained gains were those who had experienced "maximal stimulation in infancy with optimum security and affection following placement at an average of three months of age."[35]

These three investigations demonstrate the extraordinary effectiveness of massive ecological intervention. But two of them involved placing institutionalized children in foster homes. When the child remains a member of his family, such a course is problematic. Can anything be done for such disadvantaged families, whose basic needs for survival are being met but whose lives are so burdened as to preclude opportunity for effective fulfillment of the parental role?

No answers are available to this question from our analysis of the research literature, for as we have indicated, ecological intervention is, as yet, a largely untried endeavor both in our science and in our society. It seems clear, however, that certain urgent needs of families will have to be met in ways which provide support and status for parents in their child-rearing activities. Possibilities exist in four major areas:

1. The world of work—part-time jobs and flexible work schedules.
2. The school—parent apprentice programs in the schools to engage older children in supervised care of the young, involvement of the parents in work at school.

3. The neighborhood—parent-child groups for mutual assistance, family centers for discussions and demonstrations.
4. The home—prenatal training in nutrition, medical care, homemaker service, emergency insurance, television teaching.[36]

Programs focused on these themes, addressed to both children and adults, would contribute to making parenthood a more attractive and respected activity in the eyes of children, parents, and society at large.

SOME PRINCIPLES OF EARLY INTERVENTION: A SUMMARY

Although further research is needed to replicate results and eliminate alternative interpretations, some principles can be stated specifying the elements that appear essential for the effectiveness of early intervention programs.

First, the family seems to be the most effective and economical system for fostering and sustaining the child's development. Without family involvement, intervention is likely to be unsuccessful, and what few effects are achieved are likely to disappear once the intervention is discontinued.

Secondly, ecological intervention is necessary for millions of disadvantaged families in our country—to provide adequate health care, nutrition, housing, employment and opportunity, and status for parenthood. Even children from severely deprived backgrounds of mothers with IQs below seventy or eighty are not doomed to inferiority by unalterable constraints either of heredity or environment. But it is certain that ecological intervention will require major changes in the institutions of our society.

Thirdly, a long-range intervention pro-

[36]For a more extensive discussion, see U. Bronfenbrenner. The origins of alienation. *Scientific American.* August 1974, **231**(2), 53-61.

gram may be viewed in terms of five uninterrupted stages:

1. Preparation for parenthood—child care, nutrition, and medical training.
2. Before children come—adequate housing, economic security.
3. The first three years of life—establishment of a child–parent relationship of reciprocal interaction centered around activities which are challenging to the child; home visits, group meetings to establish the parent as the primary agent of intervention.
4. Ages four through six—exposure to a cognitively oriented preschool program along with a continuation of parent intervention.
5. Ages six through twelve—parental support of the child's educational activities at home and at school, parent remains primary figure responsible for the child's development as a person.

In completing this analysis, we re-emphasize the tentative nature of the conclusions and the narrowness of IQ and related measures as aspects of the total development of the child. We also wish to reaffirm a deep indebtedness to those who conducted the programs and researches on which this work is based, and a profound faith in the capacity of parents, of whatever background, to enable their children to develop into effective and happy human beings *once our society is willing to make conditions of life viable and humane for all its families.*

REFERENCES

Bee, H. L.; Van Egeren, L. F.; Streissguth, A. P.; Nyman, B. A.; & Leckie, M. S. Social class differences in maternal teaching strategies and speech patterns. *Developmental Psychology,* 1969, **1,** 726-734.

Bell, R. Q. A reinterpretation of the direction of effects in studies of socialization. *Psychological Review,* 1968, **75,** 81-95.

Bereiter, C., & Engelman, S. *Teaching disadvantaged children in the preschool.* Englewood Cliffs, N.J.: Prentice-Hall, 1966.

Bissell, J. S. *The cognitive effectives of preschool programs for disadvantaged children.* Washington, D.C.: National Institute of Child Health and Human Development, 1971.

Bissell, J. S. *Implementation of planned variation in Head Start: First year report.* Washington, D.C.: National Institute of Child Health and Human Development, 1971.

Bloom, B. S. *Compensatory education for cultural deprivation.* New York: Holt, Rinehart & Winston, 1965.

Bogatz, G. A., & Ball, S. *The second year of Sesame Street: A continuing evaluation,* Vols. 1 and 2. Princeton, N.J.: Educational Testing Service, 1971.

Bronfenbrenner, U. The changing American child: A speculative analysis. *Merrill-Palmer Quarterly of Behavior and Development,* 1961, **7,** 73-84.

Bronfenbrenner, U. *Two worlds of childhood: U.S. and U.S.S.R.* New York: Russell Sage Foundation, 1970.

Bronfenbrenner, U. Developmental research and public policy. In J. M. Romanshyn (ed.), *Social science and social welfare.* New York: Council on Social Work Education, 1973.

Bronfenbrenner, U., & Bruner, J. The President the children. *New York Times,* January 31, 1972.

Caldwell, B. M. & Smith, L. E. Day care for the very young—prime opportunity for primary prevention. *American Journal of Public Health,* 1970, **60,** 690-697.

Coleman, J. S. *Equality of educational opportunity.* Washington, D.C.: U.S. Office of Education, 1966.

Deutsch, M. Minority group and class status as related to social and personality factors in scholastic achievement. In *Society for applied anthropology monograph No. 2.* Ithaca, N.Y.: New York State School of Industrial and Labor Relations, Cornell University, 1960.

Deutsch, M.; Taleporos, E.; & Victor, J. A brief synposis of an initial enrichment program in early childhood. In S. R. Ryan (ed.), *A report on longitudinal evaluations of preschool programs.* Washington, D.C.: Office of Child Development, 1972.

Gardner, J. & Gardner, H. A note on selective imitation by a six-week-old infant. *Child Development,* 1970, **41,** 1209-1213.

Hebb, D. O. *The organization of behavior.* New York: John Wiley and Sons, 1949.

Hertzig, M. E. ; Birch, H. G.; Thomas, A.; & Mendez, O. A. Class and ethnic differences in responsiveness of preschool children to cognitive demands. In *Monograph of the Society for research in child development.* 1968, **33.**

Herzog, E.; Newcomb, C. H.; & Cisin, I. H. Double deprivation: The less they have the less they learn. In S. Ryan (ed.), *A report on longitudinal evaluations of preschool programs.* Washington, D.C.: Office of Child Development, 1972.

Herzog, E.; Newcomb, C. H.; & Cisin, I. H. *Preschool and postscript: An evaluation of the inner-city program.* Washington, D.C.: Social Research Group, George Washington University, 1973.

Hess, R. D.; Shipman, V. C.; Brophy, J. E.; & Bear, R. M. *The cognitive environments of urban preschool children.* Chicago: University of Chicago Graduate School of Education, 1968.

Hess, R. D.; Shipman, V. C.; Brophy, J. E.; & Bear, R. M. *The cognitive environments of urban preschool children: Follow-up phase.* Chicago: University of Chicago Graduate School of Education, 1969.

Hunt, J. McV. *Intelligence and experience.* New York: Ronald Press, 1961. Infant Education Research Project. Washington, D.C.: U.S. Office of Education Booklet No. OE-37033.

Jones, S. J., & Moss, H. A. Age, state, and maternal behavior associated with infant vocalizations. *Child Development,* 1971, **42,** 1039.

Kagan, J. On Cultural Deprivation. In D. C. Glass (ed.), *Environmental influences.* New York: Rockefeller University Press, 1968.

Kagan, J. *Change and continuity in infancy.* New York: John Wiley and Sons, 1971.

Karnes, M. B., & Badger, E. D. Training mothers to instruct their infants at home. In M. B. Karnes. *Research and development program on preschool disadvantaged children: Final report.* Washington, D.C.: U.S. Office of Education, 1969.

Karnes, M. B.; Hodgins, A. S.; & Teska, J. A. The impact of at-home instruction by mothers on performance in the ameliorative preschool. In M. B. Karnes. *Research and development program on preschool disadvantaged children: Final report.* Washington, D.C.: U.S. Office of Education, 1969.

Karnes, M. B.; Teska, J. A.; Hodgins, A. S.; & Badger, E. D. Educational intervention at home by mothers of disadvantaged infants. *Child Development,* 1970, **41,** 925-935.

Karnes, M. B.; Zehrbach, R. R.; & Teska, J. A. An ameliorative approach in the development of curriculum. In R. K. Parker (ed.), *The preschool in action.* Boston: Allyn and Bacon, 1972.

Kirk, S. A. *Early education of the mentally retarded.* Urbana, Ill.: University of Illinois Press, 1958.

Klaus, R. A., & Gray, S. W. The early training project for disadvantaged children: A report after five years. In *Monographs of the Society for Research in Child Development,* 1968, 33 (4), Serial No. 120.

Kraft, I.; Fushillo, J.; & Herzog, E. Prelude to school: An evaluation of an inner-city school program. In *Children's Bureau research report number 3.* Washington, D.C.: Children's Bureau, 1968.

Levenstein, P. *Verbal interaction project.* Mineola, N.Y.: Family Service Association of Nassau County, Inc., 1972.

Levenstein, P. But does it work in homes away from home? *Theory Into Practice,* 1972, **11,** 157-162.

Levenstein, P. personal communication, 1972.

Levenstein, P., & Levenstein S. Fostering learning potential in preschoolers. *Social Casework,* 1971, **52,** 74-78.

Levenstein, P., & Sunley, R. Stimulation of verbal interaction between disadvantaged mothers and children. *American Journal of*

Orthopsychiatry, 1968, **38,** 116-121.

Moss, H. A. Sex, age, and state as determinants of mother–infant interaction. *Merrill-Palmer Quarterly of Behavior and Development,* 1967, **13,** 19-36.

Radin, N., & Weikart, D. A home teaching program for disadvantaged preschool children. *Journal of Special Education,* 1967, **1,** 183-190.

Resnick, M. B., & Van De Riet, V. *Summary evaluation of the learning to learn program.* Gainesville, Fla.: University of Florida, Department of Clinical Psychology, 1973.

Rheingold, H. L. The social and socializing infant. In D. A. Goslin. *Handbook of socialization theory and research.* Chicago: Rand McNally, 1969.

Schaefer, E. S. Need for early and continuing education. In V. H. Denenberg (ed.), *Education of the infant and young child.* New York: Academic Press, 1970.

Schoggen, M., & Schoggen, P. *Environmental forces in home lives of three-year-old children in three population sub-groups.* Nashville, Tenn.: George Peabody College for Teachers, DARCEE Papers and Reports, 1971, 5 (2).

Skeels, H. M. Adult status of children from contrasting early life experiences. In *Monographs of the Society for Research in Child Development,* Vol. 31, Serial No. 105, 1966.

Soar, R. S. An integrative approach to classroom learning. NIMH Project Number 5-R11MH01096 to the University of South Carolina and 7-R11MH02045 to Temple University, 1966.

Soar, R. S. *Follow-through classroom process measurement and pupil growth (1970-71).* Gainesville, Fla.: College of Education, University of Florida, 1972.

Soar, R. S., & Soar, R. M. Pupil subject matter growth during summer vacation. *Educational Leadership Research Supplement,* 1969, **2,** 577-587.

Sprigle, H. Learning to learn program. In S. Ryan (ed.), *A report of longitudinal evaluations of preschool programs.* Washington, D.C.: Office of Child Development, 1972.

Stanford Research Institute. *Implementation of planned variation in Head Start. Preliminary evaluation of planned variation in Head Start according to follow-through approaches (1969-70).* Washington, D.C.: U.S. Department of Health, Education, and Welfare, Office of Child Development, 1971.

Stanford Research Institute. *Longitudinal evaluation of selected features of the national follow-through program.* Washington, D.C.: U.S. Department of Health, Education, and Welfare, Office of Education, 1971.

Tulkin, S. R., & Cohler, B. J. Child rearing attitudes on mother–child interaction among middle and working class families. Paper presented at the meeting of the Society for Research in Child Development, 1971.

Tulkin, S. R., & Kagan, J. Mother–child interaction: Social class differences in the first year of life. In *Proceedings of the 78th annual convention of the American Psychological Association,* 1970, pp. 261-262.

Van De Riet, V. *A sequential approach to early childhood and elementary education.* Gainesville, Fla.: Department of Clinical Psychology, University of Florida, 1972.

IV. Language and Communication

Language represents a truly remarkable human achievement. While evidence is available that animals, especially the chimpanzee, have some ability to use language to manipulate their environment, in humans this capacity far exceeds that of any other species. As the child grows, language becomes a cornerstone for advanced cognitive processes not yet evidenced in any other species.

Even before the child begins to speak, however, he is expected to understand and comprehend language. Parents rely on language as a prime training tool. Raising a child would be much more difficult if parents relied only on what the child could see them do. This communication between parents and child comes not simply through the words themselves but through the particular arrangement of those words and through the intonations used. This complex combination of words, arrangement, and intonation soon becomes part of the child's repertoire. As his facility with language increases, so does his world.

Language serves the child well. As a fundamental tool of human interaction, language provides the child with the power to understand its world in a truly distinct fashion. For example, language allows the child to make fine discriminations between objects and situations as well as to generalize from one situation to another. Thus, to call someone "friend" quickly and efficiently conveys acceptance of that person. This ability to discriminate or to generalize acts as a guide to different reactions and behaviors which may be extended to new situations. For example, when a child understands the word "hot," his behavior, directed toward a new object such as a radiator, can be guided by reference to the word "hot." A repertoire of behavior accompanying this word is set in motion. Language also helps the child structure his behavior. After completion of an action, language may serve to evaluate the appropriateness of a given behavior, *viz.*, as a reward or punishment. "Good" and "no" both have extensive use as simple, quick messages of acceptance or rejection.

In addition to the ability to discriminate, guide, and reward which language provides a child, language frees him from temporal and spatial restrictions. Through language the child learns to substitute verbal symbols for future consequences. Through language, alternatives may be examined; plans may be established relative to the past and the future. The child is freed to touch base with the past and reach out for the future.

Language and Thought

Language plays an integral role in the expanding world of the child. In particular, language development is closely tied to the child's emerging thought processes. This link raises important developmental questions concerning the relationship between these two critical functions. While language and thought are intimately related, less is known about how this relationship develops. Some theorists propose that thought is dependent on language while others argue that language is dependent on thought. The former position is best evidenced in the work of Russian psychologists following the Pavlovian tradition. This view holds that language is the foundation of thought and is what makes man conscious of his world. Language is the means by which thought is formulated. While language is a system of words and meanings, thought refers to the relationships established between words and meanings. Benjamin Whorf, in advancing a more radical form of this position, suggests that the child's view of its world is shaped by its spoken language. Thought is largely determined by our language, and thoughts which cannot be verbalized cannot be thought. Thus, language restricts our view of the world.

In contrast to this view, cognitive theory has suggested that language is dependent on thinking. The use of language is viewed as dependent on the child's emerging intellect, and this theory stresses that language is contingent upon events which precede its appearance. Thought and experience are viewed as primary and sequential, with language serving to represent prior conceptual thinking (Jenkins, 1969).

The etiology of the relationship between thought and cognition may lie in the origins of each component. Jenkins (1969) suggests that children likely possess an inherent set of rules which govern both actions and thoughts. Within this schema, language may be one manifestation of an overall system of rules, serving as a cornerstone for the organization of thought. Research on children's language lends support to this idea. It has been found that language development does not simply reflect the acquisition of words and sentences by a process of imitation and reinforcement. Rather, the child has been observed to produce sentences which possess an unlearned structure. Moreover, children from different cultures develop language along similar structural lines. Finally, children's speech, while different from that of adults, provides evidence of a rule-generating principle.

The fact that a child has an internal system of rules sets the general framework for his language development. His experience fleshes out that framework. The specifics of what is learned (i.e., a particular language in a particular context) is subject to that environment. This "fleshing out" within a particular environment effects the development of both language and cognition.

Language and Its Development

Boyd's article discusses the development and use of syntax by children. She notes that the child is a "rule inducer" who generates language following rule formation principles. She explores the relationship between children's speech and adult speech. In this context, speech differences and the role of imitation is reviewed. It is noted that even though the child demonstrates an internal rules structure, his/her immediate surrounding also plays an essential role in the language acquisition process. Finally, the relationship between particular types of language communication and their effectiveness with regard to cognitive performance is explored.

Eveloff views the child as a social organism. His paper explores the complex interweaving of emotional and cognitive factors within the parent–child interaction as they jointly affect the development of language. As each stage of language unfolds, various cognitive and emotional events emerge simultaneously. Eveloff finds that the parents' emotional involvement with the child has both cognitive and linguistic consequences for the child, while the child's responses elicit and reinforce particular parental behaviors. The integration of parent–child communication appears essential to emerging language, and the breakdown of any one aspect may seriously hamper language development. Eveloff points to the importance of the child's emerging cognitive ability, e.g., his/her recognition of maternal separation and the emotional reaction attendant to separation, as providing the personal impetus to the child's word learning. He also notes that as the child becomes more experienced, cognitive functions begin to play a more active role in language acquisition. The emphasis within this complex developmental sequence is placed on the interaction between the developing child and a caring adult.

Anderson and Vietze explore the preverbal, vocal interactions between parent and child, finding that a significant proportion of vocal interactions between parent and child entail the simultaneous vocalization of mother and child. They suggest that these interactions signal a linguistic attachment between the mother and infant.

Reference

Jenkins, J. J. Language and thought. In Voss, J. F. *Approaches to Thought.* Columbus, Ohio: Charles E. Merrill, 1960.

12.

Gertrude A. Boyd

DEVELOPMENTAL PROCESSES IN THE CHILD'S ACQUISITION OF SYNTAX

The complex system of speech sounds that is called language is the basic channel for human intellectual and social interaction. The birth cry signals the entrance of the human into a complicated social world in which language is the primary tool of communication.

At some time in the second six months of life most children say their first intelligible word. But the child's ability to pronounce sounds and to order them into words does not mean he has learned a language. This kind of imitating is readily taught to birds, and many other kinds of animals can be trained to respond to words or word combinations. During the first four years the child moves from mere vocalizing to creative, meaningful, purposeful language use. He produces new sentences never heard before, going well beyond imitation of those around him. Only when the child generates and comprehends sentences he has never heard before, can it be said he has learned a language.

EARLY STAGES

Children throughout the world originally have the capacity for making all speech sounds. Some of these sounds are encouraged by the specific language heard, and others drop out because they are not part of the child's environment.

Psycholinguists view the child more as a "rule inducer" than as a learner of discrete items, from the early steps of word acquisition and naming (the base of all symbolization) to complex sentence development. Roger Brown and Ursula Bellugi have stated the hypothesis of the psycholinguists well:

> One must somehow account for the fact that, when children have heard a lot of speech, they start to talk, whereas, if apes hear the same noises, they do not talk. A "language generator" must be built into the brain and set to operate independent of any natural language. The character of possible language, or the set of possible grammars, must somehow be represented in the brain. In the broadest sense the language generator must contain the information-processing procedures which any human organism will use when exposed to some speech community. . . . The particular language, particular grammar, and phonological system, are learned. When we talk of language acquisition, it is often in the sense of the child's internalization of the particular grammar to which he has been exposed.[1]

Babbling

The first stage in the acquisition of language is marked by the appearance of babbling. According to Otto Jespersen, babbling may start as early as the third week of life, but it usually starts around the seventh or eighth week.[2] The first

Source: *Linguistics in the Elementary School.* Itasca, Ill.: F. E. Peacock Publishers, 1976.

[1]Roger Brown & Ursula Bellugi. Three processes in the child's acquisition of syntax," *Harvard Educational Review,* 1964, **34,** 133.
[2]Otto Jespersen, *Language: its nature, development, and origin.* London: Allen & Unwin, 1922.

babbling sounds probably have no referent but are merely muscular exercises. Babbling continues until the child starts to use words in a meaningful manner and persists more than a year after the child starts to talk.

A popular explanation of babbling is that it is a period in which the child refines those phonemes used by the adults with whom he associates and drops those phonemes that are unnecessary in the language he soon will speak, a phenomenon called *phonemic contraction.* This babbling is a period of practice during which the child perfects and completes his phonemic repertoire.

The earliest vocalizations of infants are vowel saturates; their cooing becomes interspersed with consonants by the age of five months. At six months the frequency and types of sounds uttered by deaf children become distinct from those of their age-mates.

In the first year of life the vowel speech sounds vocalized by infants are composed mainly of front and middle vowels. By 30 months, however, the distribution of percentages is similar to that for the English-speaking American adult. In studies of consonant articulation it is found that young infants use mainly voiceless, fricative, and plosive sounds; rarely do they use nasals, semivowels, and glides. Vowel sounds exceed consonants for the first year, after which there are more consonants than vowel types. At two and a half years almost all vowel sounds used by the adult and about two-thirds of the consonants used by the adult are present.[3]

How a child manages to make a match between his sounds and those of speakers in his environment is still an open and interesting question. All things considered, such as the infant's immature vocal and brain structures, it is an enormous feat for a baby to match his sound to that produced by another human being.

Vocabulary

The appearance of a baby's first word is a much recorded event. But there are differences in the definition of a word. It is difficult to state whether the child is actually using an utterance meaningfully—as a word—or the utterance is merely part of his normal babbling, with no definite referent intended. As noted above, most children say their first intelligible word some time in the second six months of life.

Between the ages of one and one and a half, a child speaks in single-word utterances. These early words do not have part-of-speech value to the child, although the adult calls them nouns, verbs, and adjectives, the contentives of lexical items of a vocabulary. Words take on value as a part of speech only when combined with other words, when their position or privilege of occurrence in a string of words identifies them as nouns, verbs, and adjectives. To the one-year-old child, all words are contentives and merely stand for and call to mind categories of similar events that have been abstracted cognitively from the flux of sensimotor experience: *shoe, spoon, car, drink, walk, go, pretty, dirty, all gone.* All words in the beginning vocabulary are on the same level of abstraction: They are labels for the developing categories of experience.[4]

[3]Freda G. Rebelsky *et al.* Language development—the first four years. In Yvonne Brackbill (ed.), *Infancy and early childhood.* New York: Free Press, 1967, p. 300.

[4]Laura L. Lee. The relevance of general semantics to the development of sentence structure in children's language. In Lee Thayer (ed.), *Communication: General semantics perspectives.* New York: Spartan Books, 1970, p. 118.

SYNTAX IN CHILD LANGUAGE

Language does not come about by simple imitation. The child can repeat only that which is formed by rules he has already mastered. The child abstracts regularities or relations from the language he hears, which he then applies to building up language for himself as an apparatus of principles.

The child's one-word utterances, or holophrases, have semantically and syntactically a different range than the single-word utterances of older children and adults. First words tend to be nouns, verbs, and interjections. Their form is sometimes that of the repeated syllable, as in the child's modification of *flower* to *fa-fa*. This illustrates how children's comprehension precedes production.

Sometimes the syntactic devices the child has at his disposal are too primitive (at least from an adult perspective) to serve as vehicles for the expression for his ideas. In such cases it is interesting to observe how the child overcomes his syntactic deficiencies. In the stage of one-word utterances, however, the child does manage to express relations among several ideas. He may say: "Train. Train. Bump." "Cow. Moo." "Beep Beep. Trucks. Beep. Trucks. Trucks." There are pauses between words, often accompanied by falling intonation. Thus, speech is more than a collection of remarks—it is an act of communication wherein the speaker selects from his repertoire whatever symbols and syntactic structures seem to him to be adequate and appropriate.

Patricia Carlson and Moshe Anisfeld report that at 29 months a boy they were studying had begun to use "because" in his sentences, as in "I can't clap because I'm a boy." Asking for a forbidden jar which was out of reach, the boy said, "I need a honey girl. Because I *need* it." At this age he could deliberately manipulate segmental phonemes in some ways, as in substituting one for another in songs. To the tune of "The Bear Went over the Mountain," he sang "Da de de doder da doundin"; to the tune of "I've Been Working on the Railroad," he sang "I pin purkin' on a pail poad." Soon afterwards he was able to control rhymes by giving a rhyming word on command or in a song which required it.[5]

The rapid development of language is also evident in that a child who is not able to produce initial *s* plus consonant clusters may begin to produce them all at approximately the same time (thus distinguishing for the first time between *cool* and *school,* for example), and characteristically will do this in just the right words. This indicates that the correct phonemic representation of these words was present to the mind at the stage where it did not appear in speech.

One cannot assume that a child's grammar is a form of the adult's. When a child's remarks are understood by an adult whose awareness of structure is explicit, it is possible for that adult to assign an immediate constituent analysis to those remarks. Hazel Francis, in analyzing the utterances of her son from the ages of two years seven months to two years ten months, found that many utterances could be matched with sentences having immediate constituents of noun phrase and verb phrase, where these in turn contained further elements. In strings of sentence patterns (noun phrase + *be* + adjective or further noun phrase), the main verb *be* was omitted from the verb phrase, although in other remarks it was included. The development of the auxiliary was much more

---

[5]Patricia Carlson & Moshe Anisfeld. Some observations on the linguistic competence of a two-year-old child. *Child Development*, 1969, **40**, 572, 574.

complicated, as noted in these grammatical errors and omissions: "A police car go up there." "He be sick." "Mine gone up there." "I going on a horse."[6]

Research seems to indicate that young children classify words into parts of speech according to the adult model before they begin to use these words in parts of speech other than those in which they heard them. A noise which was "loud" was later used in an utterance as "a louding plane" by Francis' son. The -*ing* form was applied in an utterance at bath time, "Don't wash that poor little sore, because it's still soring."

The child between the ages of one and a half and two years appears to have a repertoire of noun phrase, verb, prepositional phrase, adjective, and adverb, based on operational categories. Francis's child was able to arrange these in sentence form according to his perceptions of a situation and his acceptance of the simple order used in the fragments of adult speech that he could understand. . . .

In the natural situation of the child with his family, the best evidence that the child possesses construction rules is the occurrence of systematic errors, according to Roger Brown and Colin Fraser. So long as a child speaks correctly, he may be saying only what he has heard. In general, it is not possible to know what the total input has been or how to eliminate the possibility of an exact model for each sentence that is uttered. When a young child says, "I digged in the yard" or "I saw some sheeps" or "Johnny hurt hisself," however, it is unlikely that he is imitating. Furthermore, his mistake is not a random one. Many verbs ending in voiced consonants form the simple past with -*d,* and many

nouns ending in voiceless consonants form the plural with -*s.* The sets of forms *me, my, myself* and *you, your, yourself* strongly suggest *he, his, hisself.* As it happens, actual English usage breaks with these simple regularities, and in the child's examples, *dug, sheep,* and *himself* would be preferred.[7]

By smoothing the language into a simpler system than it is, the child reveals his tendency to induce rules. The child systematizes his language in his early utterances, and irregularities inherent in the adult language usually appear later. For example, internal borrowing or *analogy* is the kind of change employed when a child says *foots* instead of *feet, oxes* instead of *oxen, sticked* instead of *stuck,* or *breaked* instead of *broke.* Through such "errors" the child is revealing a knowledge of one of the rules of forming plurals: He is simply not aware of all the exceptions. If instead the child had said "feet," one could not be certain that the plural rule was understood. The child could actually know the plural as an irregular form, or he could just be imitating an adult.

The child has heard and learned many "regular" formations—plural formations such as *root-roots, hat-hats, book-books, map-maps* and past formations like *kick-kicked, rake-raked,* in the hundreds. He has made his new formation of a plural for *foot* or *ox* by abstracting the "regular" ending -*s* or -*es* and adding it to *foot* or *ox.* Likewise, he has added the "regular" past ending -*ed* to *break* on the analogy of other past tenses like *kicked, raked.* Thus the child is making what may be termed analogical new formations.

[6]Hazel Francis. Structure in the speech of a 2½-year-old. *British Journal of Educational Psychology,* 1969, **39,** 293.

[7]Roger Brown & Colin Fraser. The acquisition of syntax. In Ursula Bellugi & Roger Brown (eds.), *The acquisition of language. Monographs of the Society for Research in Child Development,* 1964, **39,** 43-49. Chicago: University of Chicago Press, 1964.

Such observations of "errors" have been helpful in studying grammatical development. "Errors" such as these occur infrequently in the child's speech, so the amount of speech that has to be examined in order to gain a thorough knowledge of the child's morphological rules is very large.

In an effort to avoid this problem, James Berko devised a method for testing a child's knowledge of grammatical rules involved in forming plurals, past tenses, diminutives, derived adjectives, third-person singulars, possessives, comparatives and superlatives, progressive and derived compounds, and compounded or derived words. Pictures were presented, and the child was told something about the picture and given a sentence to complete. In testing plurals the child was shown a picture of a birdlike object and then a picture of two of them. He was told: "This is a wug. Now there is another one. There are two of them. There are two _____." Variants of the plural morpheme were tested by using different nonsense names. Thus *wug* should elicit -z, while *tass* should elicit *ez*. The subjects included children four to seven years and adults. Subjects were able to form plurals, verb forms, and possessives with a relatively high degree of skill but were not so successful in inflicting adjectives, deriving and compounding new words, or analyzing compound words.[8]

Morphology (patterns of word formation) is relatively unimportant in English, while syntax (patterns of formation of sentences and phrases from words) is quite important. An English-speaking child can say "five boy" instead of "five boys" and still be understood; however, ambiguity as to meaning would result if he says "boys five."

Roger Brown, Courtney Cazden, and Ursula Bellugi documented striking similarities in sequence of acquisition, regardless of large differences in the rate of grammatical acquisition. They also indicated that the young children studied did not combine words randomly; their errors were those of omission and overgeneralization. In both instances, the children were thought to be in the process of developing patterns of their own instead of imitating adult patterns.[9]

Cazden studied the errors in noun and verb inflections in the speech of three Cambridge children, studied longitudinally by Roger Brown, and twelve black children in a Roxbury, Massachusetts, day care center: "The overgeneralizations made by the two groups (Cambridge and Roxbury) are strikingly similar in kind, though not of course in absolute numbers. The Roxbury children not only make the same kind of errors; they even make them with some of the identical words. While we cannot assume that similar or even identical forms necessarily have the same status in different language systems, the similarities across these fourteen children, despite differences in their home dialect, are too numerous to be dismissed . . .

"To the extent that analogical errors indicate children's syntactic rules, these data suggest that dialect differences do not make much difference at these early stages. It seems likely that those parts of the structure of English which children learn first are the same across dialects, and it seems even more likely that the strategies or processes by which children learn that structure are also the same."[10]

[8]J. Berko. The Child's Learning of English Morphology. *Word*, 1958, **14**, 150-77.

[9]Roger W. Brown, Courtney B. Cazden, & Ursula Bellugi, The child's grammar from 1 to 111. In J. P. Hill (ed.), *Minnesota symposium on child psychology*, 5 vols. Minneapolis: University of Minnesota Press, 1969.

[10]Courtney B. Cazden. *Child Language and Education.* New York: Holt, Rinehart and Winston, 1972, p. 48.

Although many research workers expected to find pervasive differences in grammatical skills as a function of social class to substantiate further the linguistic deficiency hypotheses, the differences that emerge are limited. There is evidence to support the position that children in different dialect communities have identical grammars up to a point (though their parents do not). These might be rules which in fact disappear in later stages of development.

GRAMMATICAL SYSTEMS FOR ENCODING AND DECODING

Some research shows that an individual has two grammatical systems, one for encoding and another for decoding, or an active and passive grammatical system. The assumption underlying this view is that the speaker's behavior should be modeled by one sort of system and the hearer's by another. There appears to be no precise characterization for a "grammar for the encoder" or a "grammar for the decoder" that is not convertible, by a notational change, into the other. For the adult, then, a single grammar can normally account for almost all of both systems. The adult can interchange his encoding and decoding systems at will.

However, a child in the beginning stages of learning his language must understand a grammatical pattern before he can produce it. This understanding may be almost instantaneous, or it may develop gradually. This learning stage indicates the interdependence of the encoding and decoding systems; it appears that one is derived from the other. The grammar that represents the speaker's competence is, of course, involved in both his speaking and his interpretation of speech, and there seems to be no reason to assume that there are two different underlying systems, one

involved in speaking, one in understanding.

Sentences

Before the child utters his first two-word sentence, there is a long period during which he passively understands sentences, although he does not use them. The child's first true sentence is a shortened, telegraphic version of adult speech. These sentences usually contain only content words and require the listener to add the function words he considers necessary on the basis of his knowledge of the child and the situation. The utterance *I go* could mean *I am going* or *I want to go*, depending on whether the child is getting ready to go some place with his parents or is watching them go some place without him.

Imitation and reduction

The transcribed dialogue of two young children designated by Roger Brown and Ursula Bellugi as "Adam" and "Eve" offers interesting comparisons with adult speech. The mother's speech to her child

TABLE 12.1. Section from "Adam's" First Recording

Adam	Mother
See truck, Mommy	
See truck.	
	Did you see the truck?
No I see truck.	
	No, you didn't see it?
	There goes one.
There go one.	
	Yes, there goes one.
See a truck.	
See truck, Mommy.	
See truck.	
Truck.	
Put truck, Mommy.	
	Put the truck where?
Put truck window.	
	I think that one's too large to go in the window.

differs from the speech that adults use to one another. Her sentences are short, simple, and often repetitive. Thus the child's introduction to English comes in the form of a simplified, repetitive, and idealized dialect.

A section from "Adam's" first recording is given in Table 12.1. Notice that the imitations preserve the word order of the model sentences. Words are often missing, but the preservation of order suggests that the model sentence is processed by the child as a total construction rather than as a list of words. This kind of reduction was very common in the speech of the two children studied.

Imitation with expansion

Adult expansion of child speech is quite common. The words spoken by the mother preserve the order of the words in the child's sentences. Words and inflections are added, but they are fitted in—before, after, and between the words the child uses. In Table 12.2, also based on Brown and Bellugi's study, notice the character of the forms added by the mother to the child's utterances. They include the auxiliaries *is* and *will;* the prepositions *in, on, to,* and *up;* the verb forms *is, have, had,* and *having;* the articles *a* and *the;* and the pronouns *he, her,* and *it.*

In Table 12.2 the first set of utterances produced by the child are all of the same grammatical type; all four consist of a proper noun followed by a common noun, but each is expanded in different ways. The form of the verb added changes: in the first case it is the simple present tense; in the second, the simple past; in the third, the present progressive; in the last, the simple future. Each of the second set of utterances consists of a verb followed by a noun. The expansions are all grammatical but quite unalike, especially with regard to the preposition supplied.[11]

There appears to be little evidence that expansions are necessary for learning either grammar or sentence construction. Some parents and nursery school teachers do expand, and children do learn from it. Most expansions are responsive not only to the child's words but also to the circumstances attending their utterance. By adding something to the words the child has just produced, one confirms his response insofar as it is appropriate. Expansions add meaning at a moment when the child is most likely to be attending to the cues that can teach that meaning.

In fact, when the child is not talking with adults he reflects in his speech his own mode of operating in the world, although he may at times repeat well-rehearsed items of songs, rhymes, and snatches of adult language. Exposure to more adult speech presents him with the opportunity of acquiring a little more than he expects or understands, and if the heard remark refers to ongoing, meaningful activity then the little extra may be attended to, considered, and eventually

TABLE 12.2. Expansions of Child Speech Produced by Mothers

Child	Mother
Baby highchair	Baby is in the highchair
Mommy eggnog	Mommy had her eggnog
Eve lunch	Eve is having lunch
Mommy sandwich	Mommy'll have a sandwich
Sat wall	He sat on the wall
Throw Daddy	Throw it to Daddy
Pick glove	Pick the glove up

Source: Roger Brown and Ursula Bellugi. Three processes in the child's acquisiton of syntax. *Harvard Educational Review,* 1964, **34,** 144.

[11]Brown & Bellugi. Child's Acquisition of Syntax. pp. 133-51.

tried out to see what happens. Slowly the child adds to his repertoire, not using simply the syntax of language but what might be called the syntax of experience of the relations between his functioning brain and body and the rest of the world.

Studies of early child language show that the child's speech is intimately linked to the immediate behavioral setting. The conversations are tagged on to contemporaneous objects and events. These studies show no speech of the sort that Leonard Bloomfield called "displaced," that is, speech about other times and other places.[12] The conversations were very much in the here and now.

Imitation and construction

So long as a child speaks as correctly as the adults he hears, there is no way to tell whether he is simply repeating what he has heard or whether he is actually constructing. However, when he says something like "I digged a hole," he can be assumed to be constructing, because it is unlikely that he would have heard *digged* from anyone.

Acceptance of the concept that a child's grammar is simply an abbreviated form of adult grammar supports the finding that imitated sentences become more like the original ones (those spoken by the adult) with increasing age. There is also a tendency for the same morphemes to be omitted by different children but for the word order to be preserved—indicators of the strength of syntax in English. The fact that the child's first sentences preserve the word order of their models partially accounts for the ability of an adult to "understand" these sentences and to feel that he is in communication with the child.

As the child repeats the sentences of the

[12]Leonard Bloomfield, *Language.* New York: Henry Holt & Co., 1933.

adult and makes utterances of his own, he is likely to retain the "open" classes of words as nouns, verbs, and adjectives. Thus the words used have semantic content and are called "contentives." This telegraphic transformation of English generally communicates very well. It does so because it retains the high-information words that carry meaning. Then, too, it appears the child retains the words on which the heavier stresses fall. In a construction such as *Push car* programmed as a single utterance, the primary stress falls on *car*, thus unifying the two words. With sentences such as *Want baby, Want horsie, It horsie*, it is quite possible that the sentence *It baby* would be used in the future.

USE OF PIVOTS
IN WORD COMBINATIONS

The use of syntax begins somewhere between 18 months and two years. Several separate psycholinguistic studies have announced similar findings that a set of rather abstract words called "pivots" appears in children's first word combinations, usually in the initial position, with the contentive or open-class word following. These pivots include the articles, *a* and *the;* quantity words such as *some, all, no, more;* designative words such as *here, there, this, that, it;* and position words in combination with verbs, such as *fall down, stand up, put on, take off.* The pivot plus open-class combination has become recognized as a child's first grammatical structure. It allows such typical word combinations as *a doggie, the car, more cookie, no milk, there shoe, here baby, that truck, sit down, turn off.* Occasionally two open-class words are combined. Two nouns make an immature possessive, *Daddy hat;* an adjective and a noun make an immature noun phrase, *big car;* a verb and noun make a short verb phrase, *see horse, turn wheel, read book.* While these are not subject–predicate sentences by adult grammatical standards, they are complete sentences in child grammar. They express an entire, unified bit of information, and the child seems to consider them complete statements.[13]

A step in syntactic development is the recognition of the noun phrase as an independent grammatical unit. There is a cohesiveness about the noun and its modifiers that allows them to be moved about in a string of words, preserving their grammatical integrity. The pivot combinations are now expanded to include noun modifiers in their proper sequence. *That doggie* becomes *that a doggie* or *that a big doggie; car dirty* becomes *the car dirty* or *Daddy car dirty; read book* becomes *read a book* or *read more book.* Such constructions are usually developed before the age of three. The next step in grammatical structure is the addition of the subject to form a subject–predicate, actor–action sentence. Laura Lee identifies typical three-year-old sentences as: designative (*There's a car, It is a house, That's a doggie*); predicative (*The light is on, The dress is pretty, Spot is a good dog*); actor–action (*The boy sit down, Me put on a hat, The doggie run away*).[14]

EXPANDING KERNEL SENTENCES

Several researchers indicate that the child's language development does not stop with the formation of basic subject--predicate sentences.[15] The three-year-old child embarks upon another stage of language growth. His basic kernel sentences are transformed into other types through the use of negatives, interrogatives, passives, and so on. He learns to conjoin two sentences, to subordinate some sentences to others, or to include one sentence within another by means of infinitives, participles, and gerunds. He learns the elaborate English verb tenses and modifies the "*is* of identity" and the "*is* of predication" (see below) from *it is* into *it was, it should be, it could have been.*

Always as the substrate of any transformational structure, however, lies the kernel sentence, a basic linguistic unit, a bit of verbal information all children learn between the ages of two and three. All adult sentences can be reduced from their transformational complexity into one or more of three underlying kernel sentence types. The classification of developmental sentence types described below closely parallels the kinds of sentences that Alfred Korzybski describes as "*is* of identity" (*This is a knife*), "*is* of predication" (*The knife is sharp*), and "subject–predicate" (*The knife cuts*).[16]

Types of statements

Three distinct types of statements have been described by Lee.[17] With considerable uniformity, normally developing children seem to have three different kinds of things to say, three varieties of verbal observations. The first of these is "designative construction," which merely points out and names an item of attention: *Here a*

---

[13]Braine, Ontogeny of English Phrase Structure; Brown & Fraser, Acquisition of Syntax; Miller & Ervin, Grammar in Child Language.

[14]Lee, Relevance of General Semantics, pp. 119-20.

[15]*Ibid.,* pp. 120-21; Noam Chomsky, *Syntactic structures.* The Hague, Netherlands: Mouton, 1957.

[16]Alfred Korzybski, *Science and sanity: An introduction to non-aristotelian systems and general semantics,* 4th ed. Lakeville, Conn.: International Non-Aristotelian Library Publishing Co., 1958, p. 371.

[17]Lee, Relevance of General Semantics, p. 119.

horsie, That a big car, It a funny hat. The designative words *here, there, this, that,* and *it,* which were pivot words in an earlier stage, seem now to serve as verbal replacements for a pointing gesture, accompanied by the naming of objects. Designative statements are common in the speech of children two and a half years old.

The second type of statement, called the "predicative construction," includes a noun phrase followed by an adjective, prepositional phrase, or another noun, as: *The milk all gone, The car in garage, Billy a good boy.* These constructions are noun phrase expansions of their earlier two-word counterparts.

The third type of statement contains a verb but is a verb phrase only; the subject is missing. The child who says *Have a cookie* is not inviting you to take one; rather, he is announcing that he himself has a cookie. He accompanies his play with predicates describing his own activities: *See a big car, Put it here.* These constructions are expansions of the two-word, verb-object combinations.

STYLES OF COMMUNICATION

Separate conversations may deal with the very same objects and be oriented toward precisely the same task but nevertheless differ markedly. This is clearly shown in a systematic analysis of maternal teaching styles by R. D. Hess and V. C. Shipman.[18] Black mothers and children, of both low and middle classes, were brought to the laboratory at the University of Chicago Early Education Research Center. Each mother was to teach the same content to her child. The wide range of individual

differences in linguistic and interactional styles can be illustrated by excerpts from recordings of these transactions. The task of the mother was to teach the child how to group or sort a small number of toys. To be effective, the mothers had to be able to communicate specific meanings clearly and precisely, as in the following example:

First Mother: All right, Susan, this board is the place where we put the little toys; first of all you're supposed to learn how to place them according to color. Can you do that? The things that are all the same color you put in one section; in the other section you put another group of colors, and in the third section you put the last group of colors. Can you do that? Or would you like to see me do it first?
Child: I want to do it.
Second Mother (introducing the same task): Now I'll take them all off the board; now you put them all back on the board. What are these?
Child: A truck.
Second Mother: All right, just put them right here; put the other one right here; all right put the other one there.[19]

The first mother (middle class) introduced the particular toys with the abstract definite article plus noun groups of words ("the toys," "the things") while the second mother (lower class) made sole use of purely deictic (or demonstrative) words ("them," "these"). In the first case references are made to subsets of objects ("things that are the same color," "another group of colors," "the last group of colors"), which also involve abstract conceptual strategies. The second mother's reference to subsets as "the other" and "the other one" is devoid of such strategies.

Ragnar Rommetveit points out that the board in this experiment is also dealt with in distinctively different ways. In the first

[18]R. D. Hess & V. C. Shipman. Early experience and the socialization of cognitive modes in children. *Child Development,* 1966, **36,** 869-86.

[19]*Ibid.,* p. 881.

conversation there is an abstract linguistic elaboration of its spatial functional properties ("this board," "the place where we put the little toys," "one section," "the other section," "the third section"). The second mother, on the other hand, sticks very closely to what is perceptually given ("the board," "right here," "there"). Then note how the first mother presupposes (and exploits) the child's capacity to tag "pro words" such as "do" and "that" onto cognitions introduced by previous speech. The first "do that" refers to "place them according to color." When "do that" is said the second time, this cognition has been further elaborated by reference to three sections of the board and three color groups. The "do it" in the child's "I want to do it" is thus actually the sixth link in an anaphoral deictic chain, initiated by the phrase "place them according to color."[20] ("Them" was already at the very beginning partly emancipated from unique perceptual characteristics by the mother's identifying phrases "the little toys" and "the things.")

Such differences in conversation styles were frequently found in this study between upper-middle-class (as illustrated by the first mother) and culturally deprived (the second mother) homes. Hess and Shipman maintained that "the meaning of

deprivation is a deprivation of meaning."[21]

Further evidence of different conversation styles was noted in the Hess and Shipman study in the praise and encouragement of successful mothers and the criticism and coercive control of others to motivate their chldren. When the child made a mistake, some mothers simply said, "That's not right," "Pay attention now and get it right," or "No, that's not what I showed you!" leaving him in the dark as to what to do next. In contrast other mothers would point to the erroneously placed block and the other blocks and say, "No, see, this block has an O on it and these have X's. You don't want to mix up the O's and the X's, so you have to put this block where there are some other blocks that have O on them, too." or "No, . . . That's a big one. Remember we're going to keep the big ones separate from the little ones." Children of mothers who explained the task were more successful in completing it than were children whose mothers could not transmit information specifically enough to teach the child what to do.

Teachers and other adults working with young children can discover ways of helping children accomplish goals by giving specific explanations and encouraging any attempt to reach a goal or solve a problem.

[20]Ragnar Rommetveit, *Words, meanings, and messages.* New York: Academic Press, 1968, p. 195.

[21]Hess & Shipman, Early Experience and Cognitive Modes, p. 885.

13.

Herbert H. Eveloff

SOME COGNITIVE AND AFFECTIVE ASPECTS OF EARLY LANGUAGE DEVELOPMENT

In this paper, I will attempt to elucidate and synthesize some cognitive and affective aspects of early human language development. For the purposes of this paper, I will limit my definition of language to the following, recognizing that any concise definition of language may well exclude much that is important. With this in mind, language is defined as: the means by which one human being intentionally contacts another in a mutually understood, representational manner in order to convey an ideational or affective message.

Thus, for example, a blow delivered in anger would not here be considered language, as it is the literal expression of affect itself. Neither would the words or actions of someone in the throes of a psychomotor seizure be considered as examples of language, since intent is not involved. Lastly, the enigmatic idiosyncratic jargon of the regressed schizophrenic would also be excluded from the definition, since mutual understanding between the sender and receiver would be absent.

However, the angry exchange of words and threatening gestures that routinely accompany the neighborhood sandlot baseball game would be considered examples of language, since either represents (symbolizes) something other than itself.

While this broad definition includes

nonverbal communication—as it properly should—the discussion will be largely confined to the development of speech. Before turning to this task, I will make several introductory comments emphasizing the phylogenetic and ontologic importance of speech.

While it is true that many animals have a surprising ability to communicate, there exists a large gap in the developmental scale between the most complex animal interaction and the language of even a preschool child (Hochett, 1966). The acquisition of speech may have been the deciding mutation in elevating man above his simian ancestors.

Perhaps the cardinal aspect of this new ability was that it allowed man to free himself from the confines of time. While with other animals, the development of unique adaptive techniques was largely limited to experience spanning but one generation, this new primate was able to transmit to his successors accumulated secrets of survival wrung from the struggles of his own lifetime. He alone became aware of his past legacy, his current existence (Kaplan, 1966), and his future responsibilities.

This unique biologic ability to rapidly substitute verbal symbols for concrete perceptions lies dormant in the mind of every normal infant (Lenneberg, 1964), but the realization of this language potential is not developed mysteriously as the result of some vague maturational process; it must be developed by others of the species who must relate to the infant within certain

Source: *Child Development,* 1971, **42,** 1895-1907.
© 1972 by the Society for Research in Child Development, Inc.

emotional and cognitive limits (Lewis, 1954).

By interpreting the world around him in an organized, logical manner, the adult reflects facets of reality for the child that are incomparably deeper and more complex than those he would have gleaned from his own experimentations. The incorporated words of the parent become a tremendous factor which helps to form the very substance of mental activity.

When the child verbally establishes complex connections and relations between perceived phenomena with the help of an adult, the child introduces at each moment essential qualitative changes in the receptivity and interpretation of sensory input to his brain, that is, in the perception and cognition of his world. Thus, the word not only makes possible the coding of information but modifies the nature of that which is to be coded.

This reorganization of perception, this transference of human consciousness from the stage of direct sensory experience to the stage of generalized rational understanding, by no means exhausts the influence of the word in the formation of mental processes; language also permits the elaborate development of internal modifiers of behavior (Luria, 1961). When a child acquires a word which isolates a particular thing and serves as a signal for a particular action, the child, as he carries out an adult's verbal instruction, is subordinated to this word. The adult's word, associated with love and authority, is incorporated into the child's mental processes and becomes a regulator of his behavior. This subordination to the word of an adult helps the child formulate, at first consciously and then unconsciously, control of voluntary activity. By these means, the child advances to a new level of internal order, one that represents a triumph over the action potentials gene-

rated by the immediacy of his perceptions. Thus, individual speech provides the reflexive structure for the channeling of impulses so that they may be discharged in a manner consistent with the culture. This patterning reduces the necessity of continually struggling with impulse discharge, freeing up time and energy for the child's further development.

Lastly, language aids the child in the mastery of himself and his environment by enabling him to mentally anticipate challenging situations. By allowing him to create intricate, imaginative play plans, words permit the child to safely assimilate bits of reality by internal trial action that are otherwise unacceptable, inaccessible, or too dangerous to experience "firsthand."

Unlike his fellow animal neophytes who largely depend on perceptual recall for the solution of problems, the child can utilize symbols for precepts and rapidly compute these symbols into an expanding hierarchy of possible solutions. Within the context of a protected, predictive, and emotionally gratifying relationship, the parents utilize symbols to teach the child efficient methods of reducing the unknown (novelty), thereby increasing the probability of survival (Shands, 1969). Language can thus be seen to be perhaps the most significant adaptive measure available to the developing human.

Now that we have considered the symbol and some of its relationships to language and the thinking process, we can proceed to the development of language per se.

Language can be viewed as evolving along three separate but highly related developmental hierarchies; neurophysiologic, cognitive, and affective. As previously indicated, this paper will be largely concerned with some aspects of the latter two parameters. An exhaustive review of all facets of language development is neither intended nor possible within the context of this paper.

The development of speech seems to fall into several recognizable but overlapping phenomenological stages, namely, (*a*) prelingual, (*b*) random articulation or babbling, (*c*) lalation, (*d*) imitation (echolalia), and (*e*) articulate utterance (including symbol formation).

In the earlier phases of the prelingual stage (0 to 3 months) there is no language as earlier defined. However, since the acquisition of a language is at least a dyadic process (that is, involving at least two people), this process can be considered to begin with the first attempts by the mother to contact her child.

The baby's initial contribution to this dyadic process consists mainly of nonspecific crying. Since the child has no knowledge of objects, including himself, and therefore no concept of an inside or an outside, a "me" or "not me," these initial utterances have only a sign value in that they are nondirective reflections of a homeostatic imbalance that have no intentional communicative value (Ervin, Tripps, & Slobin, 1966). The alleged ability of a mother to differentially recognize the needs of the infant in the infancy period (0 to 1 month) is debatable (McCarthy, 1954) and may be due to her perception of cues other than the baby's crying, such as the time of crying, position of the baby, temperature of the room, etc.

Though debatable, the mother's feeling that she "knows" what is wrong in this early period is significant. Empathizing with her infant's cry, she feels the child is attempting to "tell" her something. In a sense, the mother's emotional need to contact her child, to assign a signal or "appeal" value to the infant's nondirective sign expressions of disequilibrium, is part of her contribution to the dyadic process that forms the anlage of future communication.

Gradually, by simple association, the baby learns that his cries are followed by (i.e., cause) a pleasurable or tension-reducing response, and the mother begins to differentiate her infant's sounds. However, the mode of interaction is still essentially one of active maternal action on a passive infant; that is, it is still unidirectional.

The beginning of a true bidirectional communications system, in my opinion, has its inception toward the middle of this phase with the appearance of the human social smile. Since, as I view it, the social aspect of this complex response is a prime ingredient involved in the change from the unidirectional to the bidirectional mode of interaction upon which language development will depend, a brief digression is necessary for further elaboration of this important parameter.

While it is true that the presentation of the human face in social context or otherwise is not crucial for this smiling behavior to occur (it can be elicited by even inanimate objects, particularly if certain face parts are represented), I feel it may be justified to call it both "human" and "social." This is so with respect to the former because in my opinion the smile is the first interaction between mother and child that has no counterpart in other species, and with respect to the latter because it fosters the mother's illusory belief that "my baby really knows me" (Solley, 1966), thereby providing increased emotional impetus to keep the dyadic process fueled.

Soon, the child's sounds and gestures progress from merely having a sign function to that of possessing a signal function (in the sense that a signal is being intentionally sent from the transmitting baby to the receiving mother).

It appears to me, then, that this crucial progression is more under the influence of social rather than biologic forces. Thus, in my opinion, the first attempts on the part of the infant to intentionally convey something from within himself to something outside himself are not primarily related to pain, hunger, bodily discomfort, or other noxious stimuli. Nor does it involve the vicissitudes of some vague sexual energy. These biologic forces continue to fall within the response range if paired with a noxious stimulus overwhelming the organism, or if the stimulus itself is noxious, the organism will likewise turn away. However, in these latter overloading situations, if the organism cannot escape, it will often attempt again and again to approach the overloading situation in a repetitive, compulsive manner, trying in some way to assimilate or master it.

Now, to apply these concepts to the mother–child relationship, it is proposed that mother, unlike an inanimate object, presents a complex stimulus that can neither be avoided nor entirely assimilated. That is, she (face in particular) has so many facets of novelty (presentation from different angles, expression, pairing with different emotional sets) that in a sense, the child is continually fascinated with her and is compelled to gravitate toward her, provided that the conditions indicated are met, namely, that the stimulation she presents falls within the infant's capability of response. The role of this rich source of stimulation can be appreciated more fully when, for a variety of reasons, mother is not optimally available, as, for instance, with insufficient presentation (analytic depression, marasmus, etc.), excessive presentation (anxious overstimulation, overfeeding, etc.), presentation paired with noxious stimuli (pain on feeding as in oral thrush, or pain on holding as with infantile eczema, noisy chaotic home, etc.). A similar unsatisfactory net effect may prevail if the infant cannot perceive that which the mother may be optimally

providing, as, for instance, with faulty reception (blindness, mental retardation, perceptual inconstancy [Ornitz & Ritvo, 1968], etc.) or excessive internal discomfort which binds the child's attention onto himself (as in severe infantile asthma, pyloric stenosis, or other painful somatic conditions).

This consideration of the importance of the infant's response to novelty may represent one contribution from the area of cognitive development to those already understood emotional factors that combine to constitute the infant's attraction or "love" for his mother. These contributions from the neurophysiologic, affective, and cognitive spheres of development within the child blend with the mother's increasing involvement to generate the symbiotic bond. The importance of this bond with respect to speech will become evident over the ensuing months.

The next stage, the stage of lalation, can probably be called the latter phase of babbling. It occurs around the seventh or eighth month. In this stage, the child begins to repeat over and over again, sometimes for hours, certain phones such as "ba ba da da" which have as yet not reached the status of the phoneme (sound unit with meaning). Theorists have speculated on the cause for these repetitive sounds, but these will not be discussed, because we are concerned here with their emotional significance. For, once again, the interest of the eager, loving parents adds impetus to the process of language development. The parents, feeling that the child is beginning to talk ("da da, ma ma") enter into the cycle, repeating over and over again to the child "mommy" or "daddy" or whatever else the sound approximates as they point to the object "named" by the infant. Thus, as earlier, the parental desire to communicate with their child provides the substrate for the conversion of a nonspecific sign phenomenon (i.e., the autistic pleasure of making a sound) to a signal one (the intentional assignment of a sound to an external event or object). An optimum emotional climate, which has been important for language acquisition from the very first days of life, becomes increasingly significant. If a parent is not pleased, but bored, angry, punitive, emotionally or physically absent, then the necessary stimulation from the environment for the production and shaping of these early sounds may hamper language development from both a mechanical and an emotional viewpoint.

In the stage of imitation (10 to 12 months), the child begins to repeat the sounds he hears someone else make, provided they bear a reasonable resemblance to those he has already made himself. Therefore, when the mother interjects her "mamma" into the mama verbalizations that the child is randomly making, the child may attempt to imitate them. However, no symbolic significance is initially attached to his occasional imitative utterances; this inclination to imitate an interested adult appears to be an innate property, requiring only the proper emotional substrate and a central nervous system of normal maturation for its elaboration. (This latter includes the extremely important property of being able to maintain perceptual and cognitive constancy [Ornitz & Ritvo, 1968].) Again, one can speculate that this "innateness" is in part one reflection of the infant's primitive sensory motor attempt to assimilate the novel (this time a sound), utilizing the vocal equipment that now becomes available by maturation of the neurologic and motor apparatus of speech.

Although he cannot yet vocalize understandable symbols, a major cognitive advance has begun to take place. The child begins to globally understand simple spoken commands by 9 to 10 months, especially if they are supplemented by gestures, tonal inflection, and other environmental cues; that is, the child begins to comprehend even though he cannot articulate (McCarthy, 1966). This ability to vaguely understand symbolic reference to objects is predicated on the increasing ability to differentiate objects from himself, an ability that had its first indication of emergence with the bidirectional mode of interaction as initiated with the social smile. The child has learned so many facets of the objects (the most important being mother) with which he has come in contact during the previous months of primitive concrete sensory motor experimentation (in concert with a maturing central nervous system) that he arrives at a consideration of them as something apart from himself (Piaget, 1954).

In my view, this ability represents a major advance in the development of a higher-order intelligence—even if, for only a moment, the child can now rise above the perceptual and concrete to form mental images. The infant has gone beyond the mere passive recognition of objects as in the past to the active reconstruction of them in his mind.

Once this has been achieved, it allows goals to be conceptualized and means–ends activity to commence. Prior to this, objects ceased to exist when not in view or when not being acted upon. Now, with this separateness from and internalization of objects, the child can observe them and their actions without feeling that the object is part of himself; he can experience action by observation instead of having to be part of the action. This ability to internalize images and mentally manipulate them to solve problems is a forerunner of true symbolic thinking. (This nonverbal type of abstract thinking probably is not entirely replaced by the latter in adult life [Mowrer,

1958]; that is, a part of normal adult cerebration almost certainly involves the direct comparison of stored preverbal sensory motor and perceptual memory traces rather than the verbal symbols of these traces.)

This advance also has crucial emotional significance for language development. It is hypothesized that the process of individuation both stimulates language development and reflects it. Individuation, while permitting the infant to see his mother as separate from himself, also dispenses with his prior omnipotent union with her; he becomes painfully aware that she is susceptible to loss. The potential of words to represent and therefore replace the lost mother is a primary stimulus for their acquisition. (That is, language represents a special aspect of "identification as a defense against separation" [Sears, 1957].) "Mama"—spoken or thought— can, when needed, become mama in the flesh, a "remembered" mother there to temporarily comfort baby when she is not present. Thus, it is suggested that all early verbalizations, for whatever else they may represent, are also initially one aspect of a loosely united constellation of sensations (McCarthy, 1966), a vague nexus of affective and cognitive experiences that *is* mother. By this I mean that they are much like transitional objects, less palpable perhaps than the familiar blanket or teddy bear but no less valued. Thus, in my view, the first words are learned because they have a very intense meaning to the child. Things that do not have this intense personal meaning either directly or by association with the mother will tend not to be named. Words then are learned because they are meaningful, since the child does not cathect a preexisting objective world. He relates to objects and their associated words via their meanings as related by adults (principally mother),

and they then *become* objects (Church, 1961).

Some disturbed children who, for a variety of physical and emotional reasons, do not form a maternal relationship may be mute, as in autism (Lenneberg, 1964). Those who do not completely negotiate the next developmental task of individuation may reflect this arrested development by abnormally prolonging the use of words for their transitional rather than communicative function, as in symbiotic types of childhood schizophrenia. This is postulated as one etiology of echolalia (see the excellent article by Griffith [1967] for a complete discussion of this symptom).

The next step in language development, that of articulate utterance (12 to 18 months), reflects the period of separation itself. If successfully completed, thereby allowing the child to recognize mother as a separate and reliable object, both internally and externally, the next affective stimulus for the acquisition of words increasingly involves the need for affectionate care and attention as intentionally expressed by the child to the mother. The child says the words as much "for" mother to interact with her as he does to allay separation anxiety. That is, words are used to enhance the relationship with mother (via praise, delight, pride, etc.) rather than as a substitute for this relationship. Consequently, words tend to get repeated in a flexible, nonstereotypic (i.e., nonecholalic) manner if they are used in the context of a positive relationship(Mowrer. 1958) that has value in "welcoming" the child into a "safe" environment.

As the child matures, words slowly assume properties that transcend (but do not entirely replace) the emotional functions that initially stimulated their acquisition; they increasingly become tools of communication and accommodation to the environment. The use of syntax begins.

This signifies an ability to clearly distinguish subject from object and to indicate the type of action between them (that is, verbs develop, allowing an animate comparison of objects). Words are less repeated in a passive, imitative manner (to conquer the anxiety of relating to a mother who comes and goes or to indicate simple needs) and more used in an active manner (to assimilate novel situations in the environment). The child gradually learns by parental example and by trial and error that words are indeed useful extensions of himself. For example, he can ask for a toy on a high shelf rather than be frustrated in his attempts to get it himself.

The crucial shift from a passive, unstable, expressive mode to an active, descriptive, stable mode is marked by the ability of the word to maintain its valence despite distracting circumstances. For example, a child will pay attention to a less interesting toy farther away from him rather than an interesting toy closer if he is directed to do so (Luria, 1959). Now parents, other adults, sibs, peers, and so forth are increasingly able to help the child perfect the connections between his desires and the words he uses to satisfy them. These perfected words can then be reincorporated into the child's mind to facilitate the organization of his thoughts. With increasingly efficient symbols of external reality, he can more accurately manipulate these internal objects (that is, think) in consonance with his observations; that is, his thoughts are validated by his perceptions, and vice versa.

It can be seen that, although words in my view are first learned in part to deal with separation anxiety, this powerful stimulus later begins to lose its predominance because of the repetition of the word with decreasing external reinforcement (i.e., the child spends less and less time with mother as the predictability of

his relationship with her allows him to become more independent). In a sense, emotional stimuli for language development begin to decrease as other, more cognitive reinforcements increase. Words allow him to master his environment more efficiently, to obtain objects, to influence others, to codify and therefore more efficiently explore and master his immediate surroundings. If the feedback is good, that is, if words serve as efficient tools with which to adapt to environmental challenges, they eventually tend to get used without a great deal of deliberate parental reinforcement.

Language pathology that has its roots in an arrested development in this stage may reflect the advancements made in that the child *can* communicate but that he limits communication to contacting his internal world (hallucinated speech). Harshly spoken words that have no adaptive value (i.e., either do not further cement the parent–child relationship, or are insufficiently related to external events, or both) may be repeated, but they tend not to be used for communication with others (Robson, 1967). Thus, an important reason for the failure of language as a tool to adapt to the environment at this level is that words learned in this fearful or confusing context lost their function as effective devices with which to cement the dependent relationship with parents or accommodate to the external world and are withdrawn, like amoebic pseudopods contracting from a noxious stimulus. Language is now restricted to the inner world of the child, repetitively attempting to somehow ameliorate the fear emanating from the hostile, unreliable, internal mother—one that threatens from within to revert him back to a complete state of helplessness.

Although affect for the first time begins to have a decreasing effect on perception (Solley, 1966), the necessity for having an interested adult available in subsequent stages continues unabated because the child must repeatedly refine and elevate global concepts. This whole process of the transmission and conceptualization of information allows the adult to influence the child's intellectual development not only by influencing the content of the child's conscious activity but also by modifying its form. This is important because the form of the particular language the child learns materially modifies his conceptual view of the world and consequently his ability to adapt to it (Whorf, 1956). (In fact, certain problems cannot even be solved unless an appropriate language exists to conceptualize them [Rimaldi, 1967].) Therefore, although children may learn to attach words to objects and actions on their own or from other children, this does not mean that parental influence becomes relatively unimportant. Selective coding guided by adults is a significant, if not crucial, factor in acquiring a facile and consensual language (i.e., cognitively consonant with the environment—that is, nonidiosyncratic). Children can learn to attach words to things and events, but this does not guarantee understanding, since quantitative coding cannot be equated with qualitative connotation (Furth, 1964).

Once again, pathologic use of language may be related to a developmental level. The child has now gone beyond the muteness of the autistic phase, the echolalia of the early object-constancy phase, and the limited communication with internal objects (hallucinated speech) of the separation phase, to a more subtle distortion of language. Now the distortions involve the use of language between people after the symbol formation process has a firm beginning (18 months or older). If symbols do not reflect reality as it is, if the child's perceptual system constantly invalidates the symbols (i.e., conceptual system) that

the parents are transmitting, a great deal of inner confusion can occur. For example, if a child endorses his perceptual system, he is possibly threatened by disapproval of his parents. If he endorses the distorted communication, he may invalidate in some way his perceptual system. Certainly, the child has enough cultural distortions to deal with anyway, for instance, religious practices, cultural mores, and so forth. Obviously, the earlier such dissonance occurs, the more fundamental will be the distortions in obtaining a true symbolic language for the purposes of negotiating with reality or with self. Thus, constant meaningful communication with adults is of decisive significance because the acquisition of a language system involves a continuous reorganization of all the child's mental processes in accord with his expanding universe.

The first 18 months, then, are seen as the most crucial for symbolic language development. Further development of communication with others and with one's internal world rests on this cornerstone. If this process is seriously flawed, it is possible that it may never be repaired. Certainly, if the child does not develop a communicative language by the age of 5, the probability of any further language development is greatly reduced.

One can see that learning language is more than a complex series of computer-like conditioned responses that are made possible by maturing pathways and an innate ability to imitate (Ervin *et al.*, 1966). A theory of language development must take into account the emotional consequences of a prolonged dependence of the human organism on nurturing adults to explain the use of words for more than a sign or signal value. It is these nurturing adults, making regular and gratifying emotional contact, who help the infant overcome anxieties that the human organism feels when facing the unknown (the seemingly chaotic, nonperiodic events that flood in upon him at birth). These repetitive, predictive encounters with the parents make it possible to acquire a set of internalized, organized, predictive responses to the environment that increase the probability of survival. Further parental efforts make it possible to learn a superior method of coding these experiences for the exploration of new vistas beyond the realm of experience itself.

In summary, man's great capacity to represent the elements of his world by symbols was probably his most significant developmental advancement. It led him from the darkness of his prehistoric cave into the dawning light of civilization.

The early cognitive and emotional factors involved in acquiring a language have been the focus of this paper.

The human infant must have certain prerequisites met to protect him from his vulnerability as a physically inferior animal who, but for his ability to think, would be doomed to succumb to a hostile environment.

The first of these prerequisites is the possession of an intact central nervous system that has the phylogenic anlage for sophisticated perception. The second is an even greater capacity to integrate these perceptions and express them in a way that no other creature can. The third is the opportunity to have one of his species care enough for him to act as an interpreter for the confusing deluge of stimuli that flood in upon him at birth.

The first two prerequisites are there as a birthright, hard won by eons of grim, countless evolutionary struggles with predators and the elements. Only the third, his parents' love, is a gift from his own generation. This gift alone will insure the infant of his right to fully realize his potential for human symbolic language.

REFERENCES

Church, J. *Language and the discovery of reality.* New York: Random House, 1961.

Ervin, S.; Tripps, S.; & Slobin, D. Psycholinguistics. *Annual Review of Psychology,* 1966, **17,** 435-474.

Furth, H. G. Research with the deaf: implications for language and cognition. *Psychological Bulletin,* 1964, **62,** 145-165.

Griffith, R. J., & Ritvo, E. R. Echolalia: concerning the dynamics of the syndrome. *Journal of the American Academy of Child Psychiatry,* 1967, **6**(1), 184-193.

Hochett, C. F. The problem of universals in language. In J. H. Greenberg (ed.), *Universals of language.* Cambridge, Mass.: M.I.T. Press, 1963. Pp. 1-22.

Kaplan, B. The study of language in psychiatry. In *American handbook of psychiatry.* Vol. 3. New York: Basic Books, 1966. Pp. 658-659.

Lenneberg, E. H. A biologic perspective of language. In E. H. Lenneberg (ed.), *New directions in the study of language.* Cambridge, Mass.: M.I.T. Press, 1964. Pp. 65-88.

Lewis, M. D. *How children learn to speak.* New York: Basic Books, 1954.

Luria, A. R. The directive function of speech in development and dissolution. *Word,* 1959, **15,** 341-352.

Luria, A. R. *The role of speech in the regulation of normal and abnormal behavior.* Oxford: Pergamon, 1961.

McCarthy, D. Language development in children. In L. Carmichael (ed.), *Manual of child psychology.* New York: John Wiley and Sons, 1954.

McCarthy, D. In A. H. Kidd & J. A. Rivoire (eds.), *Perceptual development in children.* New York: International Universities Press, 1966. Pp. 305-341.

Mowrer, O.H. Hearing and speaking: an analysis of language learning. *Journal of Speech and Hearing Disorders,* 1958, **23,** 143-151.

Ornitz, E. M., & Ritvo, E. R. Perceptual inconstancy in early infantile autism. *Archives of General Psychiatry,* 1968, **18,** 76-98.

Piaget, J. *The construction of reality in the child.* New York: Basic Books, 1954.

Rimaldi, H. J. Thinking and language. *Archives of General Psychiatry,* 1967, **5,** 568-575.

Robson, K. S. The role of eye-to-eye contact in maternal–infant attachment. *Journal of Child Psychology and Psychiatry and Allied Disciplines,* 1967, 8(1), 13-25.

Sears, R. R. Identification as a form of behavioral development. In D. B. Harris (ed.), *The concept of development.* Minneapolis: University of Minnesota Press, 1957. Pp. 149-161.

Shands, H. C. Coping with novelty. *Archives of General Psychiatry,* 1969, **20,** 64-70.

Solley, E. M. Affective processes in perceptual development. In A. H. Kidd & J. L. Rivoire (eds.), *Perceptual development in children.* New York: International Universities Press, 1966. Pp. 275-304.

Whorf, B. L. *Language, thought and reality.* New York: John Wiley and Sons, 1956.

Winnicot, D. W. Transitional objects and transitional phenomena. *International Journal of Psychoanalysis,* 1953, **34,** 89-97.

14.

Barbara J. Anderson, and Peter M. Vietze

EARLY DIALOGUES: THE STRUCTURE OF RECIPROCAL INFANT-MOTHER VOCALIZATION

Contemporary reviews of theories of language development indicate that attention to the development of conversational behavior has been tied to the onset of meaningful child speech (Dale, 1972; Menyuk, 1971). However, in a recent effort to reconceptualize early language development in terms of the growth of "communicative competence," Ryan (1974) has pointed out that socialization experiences for learning how to talk begin with the "nonverbal but vocal dialogues often observed between mothers and infants" (p. 210), in which the element of vocal reciprocity first appears.

While compelling anecdotal descriptions of the conversation-like quality of infant–

caregiver vocal exchanges have been offered (Bowlby, 1969; Brazelton, Koslowski, & Main, 1974; Freedman, 1974), there have been no systematic investigations of the structure and course of these naturally-occurring vocal interactions. In a preliminary report, Bateson (1971) presented initial evidence for an early, preverbal conversational pattern between very young infants and their mothers. Most observational coding systems, however, have isolated pairs of adjacent mother and infant vocal responses from the on-going flow of vocal activity, arbitrarily imposing on them the designations of antecedent (stimulus) and consequent (contingent response) (e.g., Lewis, 1972; Lewis & Freedle, 1972). This methodological convention has precluded any understanding of the process of early vocal exchanges. The purpose of the present research was to investigate in more detail the structure of the dialogues between mothers and their

Source: Paper presented at the Biennial Meeting of the Society for Research in Child Development, Denver, Colorado, 1975. The preparation of this paper was supported in part by NIE Contract No. NE-C-00-3-0260.

infants and the roles of each dyad member in initiating and ending vocal interactions.

METHOD

Subjects

Twenty-four dyads, each composed of a 3-month-old infant and its mother, served as subjects. The sample included 12 dyads with a male infant ($\bar{X}$=97.5 days) and 12 with a female infant ($\bar{X}$=91.6 days). Names of families were selected initially from public birth records according to the following criteria: all infants were first-born, full-term, of single births, with birth weights 5.5–9.5 pounds, and were free of significant health complications at birth; parents of these infants were married, with each parent over 20 years of age and at least a high-school graduate.

Parents of infants who met the above criteria were contacted in random order by telephone, and the purposes and requirements of the research were introduced. If the parents were interested in participating and it was also established that the infant had no serious illnesses since birth and the mother was the primary daytime caretaker, a date was set for a home observation visit.

Apparatus

Data were collected using a portable, electronic digital recording system (Datamyte, Electro-General Corporation). This system consists of a hand-held numeric keyboard connected to a cassette tape recorder which is worn over the shoulder. The observer presses keyboard push buttons, representing digits 0-9, to generate a signal which is silently recorded on cassette tape. The unit also contains a digital clock which can record the cumulative elapsed time, in seconds, for each code entered.

Once an observation visit was made, the cassette tape was played back through an interface and entered directly onto a PDP-11/40 computer magnetic tape system. Each original data file was then edited for errors to prepare the data file for reduction and analysis.

Observation system

The observation system was designed to carry out two major functions: (1) continuous recording of the behavior of both

TABLE 14.1. Outline of Observation Categories

Infant Behavior Patterns	*Maternal Behavior Patterns*	*Caregiving*
1. Vocalize	1. Vocalize to infant	1. Feed
2. Look at mother	2. Look at infant	2. Bathe/Diaper/Dress
3. Look/Smile	3. Look/Smile	3. Put to sleep
4. Vocalize/Look	4. Vocalize/Look	4. No caregiving
5. Vocalize/Look/Smile	5. Vocalize/Look/Smile	
6. Vocalize/Smile	6. Vocalize/Tactile-play	*Infant State*
7. Smile	7. Look/Smile/Tactile-play	
8. Cry	8. Voc/Look/Smile/Tactile-play	1. Active-awake
9. Cry/Look	9. Tactile-play	3. Quiet-awake
10. No signaling behavior	10. No behavior to infant	3. Drowsy
		4. Asleep
		Maternal Proximity
		1. Holds infant
		2. Within three feet
		3. Greater than three feet
		4. Out of room

infant and mother, and (2) coding patterns of responses (as opposed to coding one response modality in isolation from the response configuration within which it was embedded). The observation system consisted of sets of numeric codes representing five areas: patterns of infant behavior, patterns of maternal behavior, caregiving activities, infant states of arousal, and maternal proximities to infant. The categories in each area are listed in Table 14.1.

The on-going behaviors of each dyad member were coded continuously as onsets of one of a set of mutually exclusive and exhaustive behavior patterns. As indicated in Table 14.1, each infant and maternal behavior pattern was defined as a composite of one or more response modalities. For infants, five response modalities were of interest: visual attention to mother, non-distress vocalization, smile, fret/cry, and no distance receptor signaling to mother. There were five maternal response modalities which contributed to the maternal behavior patterns: visual attention to infant, verbalization/vocalization to infant, smile at infant, tactile-play stimulation, and *no* behavior directed to infant. Each behavior pattern was entered as a unique two-digit code. When an inanimate object was involved in the interaction, a zero was added to the end of the two-digit behavior pattern code.

Procedure

Each mother was asked to suggest a time for the observation just prior to the infant's awakening. On the day of the observation visit, the observer arrived at the home before the infant woke up, with the intention to observe from the time of the infant's wakening for 90 minutes or until the infant fell asleep, whichever happened first. The mother was told that observing the baby during a feeding, as well as in a variety of situations such as a bath and playtime alone or with the mother, was of interest. However, the observer emphasized that the mother should maintain her normal routine as much as possible.

Observation visits were divided between two observers. Prior to data collection, inter-observer reliabilities were established for each maternal and infant behavior modality for frequency of occurrence using a percentage agreement index and for duration of behavior using a Pearson product-moment correlation coefficient. Results for each behavior on both reliability indices ranged between .86 and .99. Reliability checks made mid-way and near the end of data collection indicated that this level of agreement was maintained throughout the study. (See Strain, 1975, for details on computation of inter-observer agreement indices and results for specific behavior categories.)

RESULTS AND DISCUSSION

The present discussion reports primarily on the continuously recorded vocal behavior of infants and mothers when they were together in the same room. As the amount of the observation session in which the dyad was together varied across families, proportional scores were required. In view of the fact that proportional scores may be distributed differently from non-proportional scores, descriptive characteristics of the distributions were derived. An examination of the distributions formed from the proportional vocalization scores for mothers and infants revealed no significant deviations from normality.

Each observation record, excluding portions when mother was out of the infant's room, was divided into consecutive one-second intervals. One of the following mutually exclusive dyadic vocal states was

TABLE 14.2. Mean Proportion of Time in Dyadic Vocal States

Member Vocal State		Dyadic Vocal State	$\bar{X}$ Male Dyads	$\bar{X}$ Female Dyads	$\bar{X}$ All Dyads
Mother	*Infant*				
Present	Present	1. Simultaneous vocalization	.082	.111	.096
Present	Absent	2. Mother vocalize only	.467	.469	.468
Absent	Present	3. Infant vocalize only	.036	.046	.041
Absent	Absent	4. Mutual silence	.415	.374	.395

assigned to each one-second interval: Simultaneous mother–infant vocalization, Mother vocalizing only, Infant vocalizing only, or Mutual silence. As outlined in Table 14.2, the behavior of each dyad member contributes to the definition of a dyadic state classification. For example, if the infant was vocalizing, the dyadic system could be in one of two dyadic states, depending on the mother's behavior. If the mother was also vocalizing, the one-second interval was classified as Simultaneous vocalization; if the mother was silent when the baby was vocalizing, the interval was classified as Infant vocalizing only.

The proportion of time spent in each of the four dyadic vocal states is presented in Table 14.2. No significant sex differences were found. Across all dyads, the dyadic state Mother vocalizing only dominated the dyadic state Infant vocalizing only by a ratio of 10 to 1. Simultaneous vocalization occurred 9.6% of the time. Notice in Table 14.2 that *twice* as much infant vocalization occurred in the state of Simultaneous vocalization as in the state of Infant vocalizing only.

To determine the effect of the infant's vocalization on the initiation and termination of maternal speech to infant, and likewise the effect of maternal speech on the infant's beginning and ceasing to vocalize, comparisons of specific pairs of transition probabilities were tested using a series of Sex (2)X Transition (2) repeated measures analyses of variance. These comparisons are reported in Table 14.3. First, comparisons were made of the probability with which each dyad member initiated vocalizations given the antecedent condition of partner's vocalization versus silence. Comparison #1 considered the effect of infant vocalization on the onset of maternal speech to infant. Mothers were significantly more likely to begin to talk to the infant when the infant was already vocalizing than when the infant was quiet

TABLE 14.3. Effects of Ongoing Partner Vocalization vs. Partner Silence on the Initiation and Termination of Vocalization Episodes by Mothers and Infants

Comparisons of Transitions Between Dyadic States	Mean Probabilities	F	P
1. (Ongoing Infant Voc → Onset Mother Voc) > (Silence → Onset Mother Voc)	.065 > .039	11.10	.003
2. (Ongoing Mother Voc → Onset Infant Voc) > (Silence → Onset Infant Voc)	.017 > .010	24.24	.001
3. (Ongoing Simultaneous → End Mother Voc) < (Ongoing Mother Voc → End Mother Voc)	.025 < .035	14.63	.001
4. (Ongoing Simultaneous → End Infant Voc) = (Ongoing Infant Voc → End Infant Voc)	.100 = .116	2.03	n.s.

($F=11.10$, 1/22 df, $p<.003$). A parallel analysis for infants, Comparison #2, revealed that significantly more infant vocal onsets occurred when the mother was speaking to the infant than when the mother was silent ($F=24.24$, 1/22 df, $p<.001$). Thus a symmetrical relationship is revealed in which both dyad members are likely to begin vocalizing when the partner is also vocalizing.

A second set of comparisons concerned the effect of ongoing vocalizations by one dyad member on the termination of the partner's vocalization. Comparison #3 indicates that mothers were less likely to stop vocalizing when the infant was vocalizing than when the infant was silent ($F=14.63$, 1/22 df, $p<.001$). In other words, mothers tended to maintain and prolong simultaneous vocal episodes with their infants. Infants' termination of vocal activity, as indicated in Comparison #4, did not differ between antecedent conditions of maternal vocalization or maternal silence ($F=2.03$, 1/22 df, $p>.05$). In contrast to mothers, the infants' termination of vocal activity was not differentially affected by the presence or absence of his partner's vocal behavior.

To summarize the structure and course of vocal interactions for these dyads: first it was demonstrated that simultaneous vocalization occurred an unexpectedly high proportion of the time and was the dominant dyadic state when the infant was vocalizing. Second, infant vocalization affected the mother's beginning to talk and the mother's speech affected the infant's beginning to vocalize. This "joining in" pattern indicated a co-participant relationship between the two dyad members in the initiation of vocal exchanges. Finally, mothers continued rather than terminated their talking if the infant was also vocalizing. Cessation of infant vocalization, however, was not affected by the

mother's vocal behavior. All analyses consistently failed to find any effect on sex of infant on transitions between vocal states.

Similar findings have been reported recently in two different research efforts. First, the observational methodology developed for the present research was replicated in a larger, longitudinal study. Data analyzed for fifty-one mothers and their infants at 2 1/2 months of age revealed that durations of the four dyadic vocal states and transition probability relationships between infant and maternal vocalizations were almost identical to those found in the present research with 3-month-old infants (Vietze, Strain, & Falsey, 1975).

Secondly, Stern, Jaffe, Beebe, and Bennett (1975) investigated vocalization patterning between mothers and their 3-month-old twin infants using stop-frame analysis of interactions filmed in the home. Similar to the present results, Stern and colleagues reported a surprising predominance of simultaneous or "co-actional" mother–infant vocalization. They found an intriguing relationship between co-actional vocalization and a high level of infant arousal and suggested that this vocalization-in-unison is an important behavioral representation of attachment between mother and infant.

Maternal vocal dominance in the present data, as evidenced by the tendency for mothers not only to create but also to prolong simultaneous vocalization episodes, may have reflected efforts by the mother to stimulate infant attention to her. This is one strategy by which a mother can regulate the intensity or duration of positive dyadic contact with her infant. This suggestion is supported by additional analyses of the data which considered the multi-sensory patterns of behavior coded for mother and infant. When the dyad members were in close proximity, 96% of maternal speech to infant was accompanied by visual attention to the infant, while only 50% of infant vocalizations occurred while looking at the mother.

It should also be pointed out that the vocal response serves multiple functions for the young infant (see Piaget, 1952; Hulsebus, 1973; Jones & Moss, 1971; Kagan, 1971). With the present data, when observation sessions were partitioned according to maternal proximity to infant, additional analyses indicated that amount of infant vocalization was significantly affected by maternal proximity ($F=4.99$, 3/66 *df*, $p<.001$). Newman-Keuls comparisons indicated that significantly more infant vocal activity occurred when the mother was out of the infant's room than when the mother held the infant. Also, infants vocalized while interacting with an inanimate object significantly more often when the mother was absent than when she was present ($F=39.95$, 1/22 *df*, $p<.001$). This suggests that the infants' vocalizations indexed information processing to various sources of stimulation in the natural environment.

Within this perspective that vocalization is a complex communicative and cognitive response in the young infant, the present data document that in a social context, both infant and maternal vocalizations are interrelated determinants of the process of their interactions. The predominance of simultaneous vocalization in their interactions suggests that an initiator–responder model tends to over-simplify mother–infant vocal interactions. Both of these conclusions point out the importance of a methodology which preserves the behaviors in sequence for each participant and allows for consideration of simultaneous and overlapping patterns of dyadic responding. The present results are limited in that the vocal response was isolated from the ongoing behavior patterns of

mothers and infants (see Condon & Ogston, 1967). The next step is to include visual attention to the partner in the definitions of dyadic vocal states to understand vocal and visual regulation of early dialogues.

REFERENCES

Bateson, M. C. Speech communication. Quarterly Progress Report, No. 100, Massachusetts Institute of Technology Research Laboratory of Electronics, Cambridge, Mass.: 1971. Pp. 169-176.

Bowlby, J. *Attachment and loss.* Vol. 1. *Attachment.* New York: Basic Books, 1969.

Brazelton, T. B.; Koslowski, B.; & Main, M. The origins of reciprocity: The early mother–infant interaction. In M. Lewis & L. A. Rosenblum (eds.), *The origins of behavior.* Vol. 1. *The effect of the infant on its caretaker.* New York: John Wiley and Sons, 1974. Pp. 49-76.

Condon, W. S., & Ogston, W. D. A segmentation of behavior. *Journal of psychiatric research,* 1967, **5,** 221-235.

Dale, P. S. *Language development: Structure and function.* Hinsdale, Ill.: Dryden Press, 1972.

Freedman, D. G. *Human infancy: An evolutionary perspective.* Hillsdale, N.J.: Lawrence Erlbaum Associates, 1974.

Hulsebus, R. C. Operant conditioning of infant behavior: A review. In H. W. Reese (ed.), *Advances in child development and behavior.* Vol. 8. New York: Academic Press, 1973. Pp. 112-158.

Jones, S. J., & Moss, H. A. Age, state, and maternal behavior associated with infant vocalizations. *Child Development,* 1971, **42,** 1039-1051.

Kagan, J. *Change and continuity in infancy.* New York: John Wiley and Sons, 1971.

Kemeny, J. G., & Snell, J. L. *Mathematical models in the social sciences.* New York: Blaisdell, 1963.

Lewis, M. State as an infant–environment interaction: An analysis of mother–infant interaction as a function of sex. *Merrill-Palmer*

Quarterly of Behavior and Development, 1972, **18**, 95-121.

Lewis, M., & Freedle, R. Mother–infant dyad: The cradle of meaning. Paper presented at a Symposium on Language and Thought: Communication and Affect, Toronto, 1972.

Menyuk, P. *The acquisition and development of language.* Englewood Cliffs, N.J.: Prentice-Hall, 1971.

Piaget, J. *The origins of intelligence in children.* New York: International Universities Press, 1952.

Ryan, J. Early language development: Towards a communication analysis. In M. P. M. Richards (ed.), *The integration of a child into a social world.* London: Cambridge University Press, 1974. Pp. 185-213.

Stern, D. N.; Jaffe, J.; Beebe, B.; & Bennett, S. L. Vocalizing in unison and in alternation: Two modes of communication within the mother–infant dyad. Paper presented at the Conference on Developmental Psycholinguistics and Communication Disorders, New York Academy of Sciences, New York, 1975.

Strain, B. A. Early dialogues: a naturalistic study of vocal behavior in mothers and three-month-old infants. Doctoral dissertation, George Peabody College, 1975; Ann Arbor, Mich.: University Microfilms.

Vietze, P. M.; Strain, B. A.; & Falsey, S. Contingent responsiveness between mother and infant: Who's reinforcing whom? Paper presented at the meeting of the Southeastern Psychological Association, Atlanta, 1975.

Wolff, P. The natural history of crying and other vocalizations in early infancy. In B. M. Foss (ed.), *Determinants of infant behavior.* Vol. 4. London: Methuen, 1969. Pp. 81-109.

V. Social and Personality Development

Attachment

Attachment refers to the binding of one person to another in the formation of a love bond. This tie, which is established between the infant and its primary caretaker at approximately seven months of age, serves as a model for the development of early affectional relations which extend through early childhood, and likely beyond.

Attachment denotes a developmental model of early infant–caretaker social relations. Conceptually, the phenomenon of attachment offers us a theoretical framework for viewing the occurrence of an encompassing social-love bond, whose value ensures the infants' survival, as well as allows us, through comparative inquiries, to establish a link between the human infant and the young of other higher order species (Bowlby, 1958; Ainsworth, 1969). Behaviorally, attachment refers to a series of initially, independently appearing responses (crying, sucking, clinging, smiling, and following), which become integrated over time as they are directed exclusively toward the caretaker by the infant. This behavioral focus, which increases in intensity over the second half of the first year of life, leads to the emergence of a pattern of progressively more mature relations which appear relatively enduring over the course of childhood.

The developmental importance of attachment is severalfold. First attachment develops over time, demonstrating behavioral stability in the wake of structural change. Specifically, during the course of the first year of life the infant passes through four distinct phases in the establishment of affectional bonds (indiscriminate responsiveness to people; differential responsiveness to the mother, but with continued interest in other people; sharply defined attachment to the mother; extension of attachment behaviors to familiar persons). Second, the attachment bond underscores the interactive and egalitarian character of infant-caretaker relations. That is, attachment directs attention to both the infant and the caretaker as coequal participants and contributors to the formation of this bond. Finally, early attachments appear to serve as a prototype (i.e., primary model) for the development of later love bonds.

In the first selection of this series of readings, Ainsworth and Bell examine the attachment bond in relation to exploratory behavior and the child's reactions to separation. In addition, they discuss how changes in attachment over the course of the first year of life come to influence the infants' establishment of successive patterns of interaction, as well as the changing quality of its reactions to its environment. In the selection by Lamb which follows, the importance of both mothers and fathers in the development of attachment is reviewed. In this paper, Lamb describes the roles assumed by each parent as complementary, rather than competitive, suggesting that each parent, through their independent interactions with the infant, supplements the contributions of the other.

Aggression

Interest in the child's acquisition and performance of aggressive behavior has become of increasing concern to parents, educators, and the community. This concern, correspondingly, has drawn unparalleled focus among researchers, leading to the development of a comprehensive literature on aggression. Two forms of inquiry have emerged from this literature: (1) the enumeration of probable antecedents of aggression, and (2) the search for methods leading to the modification and control of aggression.

Aggression has been defined as behavior directed toward another person leading to the infliction of injury (Berkowitz, 1973). While this definition transcends a strict behavioral description, by alluding to the goal-oriented intentions of the actor, it nevertheless directs our attention to aggression as a high amplitude response capable of sustaining injury to others, whether intended or accidental in consequence. Behaviorally, illustrations of such responses in children would include the exhibition of unprovoked physical aggression, provoked physical aggression, unprovoked verbal aggression, provoked verbal aggression, indirect forms of aggression, and outburst aggression.

The origins of aggressive behavior in children have been viewed historically from a number of theoretical perspectives. These differing perspectives include views which stress aggression as being founded on instinctual origins, as well as oppositional positions which regard aggression as being acquired through social learning opportunities. Within this latter theoretical framework, researchers have examined the course and maintenance of such responses over time. Specifically, they have asked what facets of the child's experiential background and current life circumstances lead to the likelihood of the child displaying such response patterns. From this latter concern, as discussed in the Cohen paper, aggression appears to be correlated with the child's encounter of frustration, its exposure to aggressive models, and its experience of conditions which either sanction or reinforce the continued expression of such behavior. Supplementing these concerns, researchers have also begun to examine conditions allowing for the adoption of behavioral alternatives to the use of aggression in the resolution of conflict situations.

The child's performance of aggression is prefaced by situational and personal considerations. Among the latter, the sex of the child is an important factor in observing the frequency and form of aggressive responses. For example, males tend to employ physical aggression more frequently in interpersonal relations, while girls more often resort to verbal and indirect forms of aggression in social interchanges. While these differences may possess biological roots, as Sandidge and Friedland find, aggression is strongly influenced by social expectations. Specifically, boys and girls appear to equate the use and display of aggression with high regard for social expectations and the requisites for role enactment inclusive to each sex. For boys and girls, the performance of aggression appears to mirror the child's interpretation of appropriate behavior to his/her sex.

Sex-Role Development

With the advent of birth the child becomes a member of society. Among humans this entrance occasions the beginning of an extended period of socialization, one in which the child will be exposed to many social learning opportunities, some of which will culminate in its acquisition and performance of social roles representative of its society of membership.

The child's learning of social roles is founded upon its exposure to the teachings of its culture, including the social expectations which each society creates for its members. For young males and females in American society, as in other cultures, the implementation of social expectations begins at birth. By tradition, the young boy, early in its life, learns that to be a male requires an active, assertive, and exploratory orientation to its human and material surroundings. Conversely, the young female learns that femininity, traditionally defined, requires a less active, affiliative, and more structured orientation to its environment.

The learning of sex roles is neither accidental nor momentary. Each child, from the moment of birth, via the assignment of color of dress (i.e., blue *vs.* pink), provision of toys, and the nature of infant–parent relations, will assume a social role contingent upon its sexual status. As discussed in the selection by Chafetz, these initial assignments are extended over time, serving to insure the performance of social roles, contingent upon sexual distinctions, throughout life.

The process of sex-role learning is a long and arduous one. As reviewed by Biller, the child initially acquires a sex-role orientation, learning what is appropriate sex-role behavior for each sex. A second aspect of this process entails the expression of a sex-role preference. Here the child demonstrates a desire to be of one sex rather than the other. Finally, the child shows evidence of a formal acceptance of its sexual status through the adoption of roles congruent with social standards and expectations of masculine or feminine behavior.

The learning of sex roles is a continuous process, one in which the child receives extensive support throughout its life. It is also a multifaceted process, involving parents, peers, and society at many levels of interchange. As discussed by McGhee, the child is the recipient of varied forms of guidance and influence. One such source of input is television. In an analysis of program content, McGhee finds that children are provided ample opportunities to acquire attitudes and behavior which guarantee the learning of social roles congruent with the child's sexual membership.

Moral Development

Each society is founded upon ethical principles which govern the behavior of its members. How, and under what circumstances, the child acquires and applies moral principles with regard to its behavior has been studied under the rubric of moral development.

The formal study of morality in children has involved three separate dimensions of inquiry: (1) the formation of conduct or moral action, (2) the study of emotional responses accompanying moral behavior, and (3) the child's acquisition of moral decision-making processes. Supplementing these concerns, recent studies of moral development have focused attention on prosocial aspects of morality, viz., generosity, altruism, and empathic responses.

Studies of children's conduct have sought to determine the antecedents of moral action. In response to this interest, researchers have attempted to discover how such pervasive conditions as the quality of parent–child relations supplemented by specific training practices, influence the child's acquisition and use of moral principles in the course of behavioral transactions. Research in this area has found that children's moral behavior is related to both continuous (i.e., enduring) and situational (i.e., transitional) factors surrounding his/her behavioral performance. To illustrate, continuous variables such as the use of reasoning and the expression of concern for others, which characterize parent–child interchange, have been found to correlate with children's moral activity (Sears, Maccoby & Levin, 1957; Hoffman & Saltzstein, 1967). Complementing these findings, it has also been demonstrated in laboratory settings that situational variables, such as the timing and intensity of punishment, as well as the quality of affective and cognitive interchange shared by the child and the adult also appear related to the child's moral behavior (Parke & Walters, 1967; Parke, 1969).

Interest in the child's expression of emotional–affective responses accompanying moral behavior represents a second component of moral development. This constituent of moral action has been studied in the belief that the child's feelings, as evident by his/her experience of shame, guilt, and confession, plays an integral role in the formation of attitudes surrounding morality.

A third component of children's morality is judgmental. This aspect of moral development refers to the child's ability to make moral decisions based upon ethical principles. To amplify, this component reflects the child's exercise of decision-making capacities in situations where varying behavioral alternatives, leading to different moral outcomes, may be offered.

Understanding how the child acquires and employs rules in the derivation of ethical decisions has both practical and theoretical value. For example, in terms of the former, it may be asked whether moral judgments generalize across situations. Or, it may be inquired how such decisions correlate with the child's behavior. Theoretical interests, on the other hand, have raised questions pertaining to how the child acquires rules, under what circumstances rules become part of the child's decision-making process, and what role experience plays in enhancing the child's ability to make moral judgments. These and related issues are discussed in this series of readings. In the first selection by Berg and Mussen, the origins and development of children's concepts of justice are examined from several alternative theoretical perspectives, viz., social learning theory, psychoanalysis, and cognitive development theory. In the following paper by Denney and Duffy, children's responses to moral dilemmas are examined. Of particular interest, this article focuses on correlates appearing among children's moral judgments and maternal child rearing practices. In the final paper of this series, Hoffman explores children's responses to the distress of others, attempting to equate the child's ability to respond to sympathetic distress in terms of his/her actualization of altruistic behavior.

References

Ainsworth, M. D. S. Object relations, dependency, and attachment: A theoretical review of the infant–mother relationship. *Child Development,* 1969, **40,** 965-1025.

Berkowitz, L. Control of aggression. In B. M. Caldwell and H. N. Ricciuti (eds.), *Review of child development research,* Vol. 3. Chicago: University of Chicago Press, 1973.

Bowlby, J. The nature of the child's tie to his mother. *International Journal of Psychoanalysis,* 1958, **39,** 350-373.

Hoffman, M. L., & Saltzstein, H. D. Parent discipline and the child's moral development. *Journal of Personality and Social Psychology,* 1967, **5,** 45-57.

Parke, R. D. Effectiveness of punishment as an interaction of intensity, timing, agent nurturance and cognitive structuring. *Child Development.* 1969, **40,** 213-236.

Parke, R. D., & Walters, R. H. Some factors determining the efficacy of punishment for inducing response inhibition. *Monographs of the Society for Research in Child Development,* 1967, **32,** 1.

Sears, R. R., Maccoby, E. E., & Levin, H. *Patterns of child rearing.* New York: Harper & Row, 1957.

A. ATTACHMENT

15.

Mary D. Salter Ainsworth and Silvia M. Bell

ATTACHMENT, EXPLORATION, AND SEPARATION: ILLUSTRATED BY THE BEHAVIOR OF ONE-YEAR-OLDS IN A STRANGE SITUATION

Within the last decade the term "attachment" has appeared with increasing frequency in both empirical and theoretical segments of the developmental psychological literature (see Cairns, 1966; Gewirtz, 1961, 1969; Maccoby & Masters, in press; Robson, 1967; Schaffer & Emerson, 1964; Schwarz, 1968). The term, as originally introduced by Bowlby (1958, 1969) and as used by Ainsworth (1963, 1964, 1967), implies an ethological and evolutionary viewpoint, and hence has connotations not necessarily shared by those with other theoretical orientations. Infant–mother attachment has been conceived as related to separation anxiety (see Bowlby, 1960), fear of the strange and strangers (see Morgan & Ricciuti, 1969; Schaffer, 1966), and exploration (see Ainsworth, 1967; Ainsworth & Wittig, 1969). It is believed that the interrelationships between these behaviors throw light upon the biological function of infant–mother attachment; that they do is strongly suggested by field studies of ground-living nonhuman primates. Although comparable reports of human infants in their natural home environment are not yet forthcoming, interaction between attachment behavior, exploration, separation anxiety, and fear of the strange may be observed in a controlled laboratory environment—the strange or unfamiliar situation.

It is the purpose of this paper to highlight some distinctive features of the ethological-evolutionary concept of attachment, by citing reports of the interactions between the infant's attachment behavior and other behaviors mentioned above; to illustrate these interactions by a report of the behavior of one year olds in a strange situation; and to note parallels between strange-situation behavior and behavior reported in other relevant observational, clinical, and experimental contexts.

Let us begin with some definitions and key concepts distinctive of the ethological-evolutionary viewpoint, as proposed by Bowlby (1958, 1969) and Ainsworth (1964, 1967, 1969). An *attachment* may be defined as an affectional tie that one person or animal forms between himself and another specific one—a tie that binds them together in space and endures over time. The behavioral hallmark of attach-

Source: *Child Development*, 1970, **41**, 49-67. © 1970 by the Society for Research in Child Development, Inc.

An earlier version of this paper was prepared while the first author was a fellow of the Center for Advanced Study in the Behavioral Sciences. It was presented at the annual meeting of the American Psychological Association, at San Francisco, September 1968, in a symposium, "Attachment Behaviors in Humans and Animals." The extended project which yielded the data has been supported by grant 62-244 of the Foundations' Fund for Research in Psychiatry, and by USPHS grant RO1 and HD 01712; this support is gratefully acknowledged. We are also appreciative of help given by the following in various aspects of the "strange situation" study: George D. Allyn, John Conklin, Elizabeth A. Eikenberg, Edwin E. Ellis, William C. Hamilton, Mary B. Main, Robert S. Marvin II, Eleanor S. McCulloch, and especially Barbara A. Wittig who helped in the original planning of the strange situation.

ment is seeking to gain and to maintain a certain degree of proximity to the object of attachment, which ranges from close physical contact under some circumstances to interaction or communication across some distance under other circumstances. *Attachment behaviors* are behaviors which promote proximity or contact. In the human infant these include active proximity- and contact-seeking behaviors such as approaching, following, and clinging, and signaling behaviors such as smiling, crying, and calling.

The very young infant displays attachment (proximity-promoting) behaviors such as crying, sucking, rooting, and smiling, despite the fact that he is insufficiently discriminating to direct them differentially to a specific person. These initial behaviors indicate a genetic bias toward becoming attached, since they can be demonstrated to be either activated or terminated most effectively by stimuli which, in the environment of evolutionary adaptedness, are most likely to stem from human sources. When these behaviors, supplemented by other active proximity-seeking behaviors which emerge later—presumably through a process of learning in the course of mother–infant interaction—become organized hierarchically and directed actively and specifically toward the mother, the infant may be described as having become attached to her.

The intensity of attachment behavior may be heightened or diminished by situational conditions, but, once an attachment has been formed, it cannot be viewed as vanishing during periods when attachment behavior is not evident. Therefore, it seems necessary to view attachment as an organization of behavioral systems which has an internal, structural portion that endures throughout periods when none of the component attachment behaviors have been activated.

Viewed in the context of evolutionary theory, infant–mother attachment may be seen to fulfill significant biological functions, that is, functions that promote species survival. The long, helpless infancy of the human species occasions grave risks. For the species to have survived, the infant has required protection during this period of defenselessness. It is inferred, therefore, that the genetic code makes provision for infant behaviors which have the usual (although not necessarily invariable) outcome of bringing infant and mother together.

Exploratory behavior is equally significant from an evolutionary point of view. As Hamburg (1968) has pointed out, a prolonged infancy would miss its adaptive mark if there were not also provisions in the genetic code which lead the infant to be interested in the novel features of his environment—to venture forth, to explore, and to learn. The implication is that the genetic biases in a species which can adapt to a wide range of environmental variations provide for a balance in infant behaviors (and in reciprocal maternal behaviors) between those which lead the infant away from the mother and promote exploration and acquisition of knowledge of the properties of the physical and social environment, and those which draw mother and infant together and promote the protection and nurturance that the mother can provide.

The interaction between exploratory and attachment behaviors has been highlighted in field studies of ground-living nonhuman primates (e.g., Southwick, Beg, & Siddiqi, 1965; DeVore, 1963; Goodall, 1965; Schaller, 1965) as well as studies of such species in captive colonies (see Hinde, Rowell, & Spencer-Booth, 1964, 1967) and in laboratories (e.g., Harlow, 1961; Harlow & Harlow, 1965; Mason, 1965.) Although at first infant and mother are in almost continuous close contact, soon they are in collusion to make more elastic the bonds that unite them. The infant ventures forth to investigate his environment and to play with other infants, and gradually spends more and more time "off" his mother. His expeditions take him further and further away from her, and she becomes increasingly permissive and retrieves him less promptly and less frequently. Alarm or threat of separation, however, quickly bring mother and infant together again.

Naturalistic studies of the attachment-exploration balance are very time consuming; the interaction between the two sets of behaviors must be observed over a wide range of situations. A short-cut alternative is to utilize a controlled strange or unfamiliar situation in which the child, with and without his mother, is exposed to stressful episodes of different kinds. So powerful is this technique in evoking behavioral changes that it is likely to be used with increasing frequency in studies of mother–infant interaction. The ethological–evolutionary view of the attachment–exploration balance is a useful model to use when planning and when interpreting the findings of strange-situation studies.

Of strange-situation studies already reported in the literature, only two have been guided by an ethological–evolutionary point of view. Harlow (1961) used a strange situation to demonstrate the security function of surrogate cloth mothers for infant rhesus macaques. Ainsworth and Wittig (1969) made a preliminary report of the attachment–exploration balance in human 1 year olds. Other studies—Arsenian (1943), Cox and Campbell (1968), Rheingold (1969)—focused on exploratory behavior and reported that the presence of the mother supports it, but paid scant attention to attachment behavior and its

hierarchical manifestations in reunion episodes as well as during separation.

The strange-situation procedure provides more than an opportunity to observe how exploratory behavior is affected by mother-present, mother-absent, or other conditions. It is a laboratory microcosm in which a wide range of behaviors pertinent to attachment and to its balance with exploratory behavior may be elicited. Attachment behaviors may be seen as complicated by "negative" behaviors, such as avoidance and aggression. And yet, since the laboratory situation provides but a very small sample of mother–infant interaction, strange-situation findings are not self-interpreting. Perception of the implications of the behaviors that occur in it is facilitated by reference to the findings of other studies—naturalistic, clinical, and experimental. For this reason the ensuing report of a strange-situation study is presented as a useful *illustration* of the shifting balance between exploratory and attachment behavior implicit in the ethological–evolutionary view of attachment. The discussion which follows the presentation refers to relevant findings of other studies. The propositions offered in conclusion comprehend these other relevant considerations as well as the findings of the illustrative strange-situation study.

THE STRANGE SITUATION

In the course of a longitudinal, naturalistic investigation of infant–mother attachment during the first year of life, there was little opportunity in the home environment to observe the balance of attachment and exploratory behaviors under conditions of novelty and alarm. Therefore, a laboratory situation was devised as a test situation to which the Ss were introduced when nearly 1 year old. It was desired to observe the extent to which the infant could use his mother as a secure base from which he could explore a strange environment, with fear of the strange kept in abeyance by her presence. It was also intended to observe the extent to which attachment behavior might gain ascendancy over exploratory behavior under conditions of alarm introduced by the entrance of a stranger and under conditions of separation from and reunion with the mother.

Method

Subjects. The fifty-six *S*s were family-reared infants of white, middle-class parents, who were originally contacted through pediatricians in private practice. One subsample of twenty-three *S*s, who had been observed longitudinally from birth onward, were observed in the strange situation when 51 weeks old. The second subsample of thirty-three *S*s, studied in the context of an independent project (Bell, in press), were observed when 49 weeks old.

Procedure. The strange situation was comprised of eight episodes which followed in a standard order for all subjects. The situation was designed to be novel enough to elicit exploratory behavior, and yet not so strange that it would evoke fear and heighten attachment behavior at the outset. The approach of the stranger was gradual, so that any fear of her could be attributed to unfamiliarity rather than to abrupt, alarming behavior. The episodes were arranged so that the less disturbing ones came first. Finally, the situation as a whole was intended to be no more disturbing than those an infant was likely to encounter in his ordinary life experience. A summarized account of the procedure has been given elsewhere (Ainsworth & Wittig, 1969) but will be reviewed here.

The experimental room was furnished—not bare—but so arranged that there was a 9 × 9-foot square of clear floor space,

marked off into sixteen squares to facilitate recording of location and locomotion. At one end of the room was a child's chair heaped with and surrounded by toys. Near the other end of the room on one side was a chair for the mother, and on the opposite side, near the door, a chair for the stranger. The baby was put down in the middle of the base of the triangle formed by the three chairs and left free to move where he wished. Both the mother and the female stranger were instructed in advance as to the roles they were to play.

In summary, the eight episodes of the situation are as follows:

Episode 1 (M, B, O). Mother (M), accompanied by an observer (O), carried the baby (B) into the room, and then O left.

Episode 2 (M, B). M put B down in the specified place, then sat quietly in her chair, participating only if B sought her attention. Duration 3 minutes.

Episode 3 (S, M, B). A stranger (S) entered, sat quietly for 1 minute, conversed with M for 1 minute, and then gradually approached B, showing him a toy. At the end of the third minute M left the room unobtrusively.

Episode 4 (S, B). If B was happily engaged in play, S was nonparticipant. If he was inactive, she tried to interest him in the toys. If he was distressed, she tried to distract him or to comfort him. If he could not be comforted, the episode was curtailed—otherwise it lasted 3 minutes.

Episode 5 (M, B). M entered, paused in the doorway to give B an opportunity to mobilize a spontaneous response to her. S then left unobtrusively. What M did next was not specified—except that she was told that after B was again settled in play with the toys she was to leave again, after pausing to say "bye-bye." (Duration of episode undetermined.)

Episode 6 (B alone). The baby was left

alone for 3 minutes, unless he was so distressed that the episode had to be curtailed.

Episode 7 (S, B). S entered and behaved as in Episode 4 for 3 minutes, unless distress prompted curtailment. (Ainsworth & Wittig, 1969, planned a somewhat different procedure for Episode 7, which was attempted for the first 14 *S*s but, as it turned out, approximated the simpler procedure reported here, which was used for the remaining *S*s.)

Episode 8 (M, B). M returned, S left, and after the reunion had been observed, the situation was terminated.

The behavior of the *S*s was observed from an adjoining room through a one-way vision window. Two observers dictated continuous narrative accounts into a dual channel tape recorder which also picked up the click of a timer every 15 seconds. (This represents the procedure we now consider standard. For the first fourteen *S*s, however, the dual channel recorder was not available, so one observer dictated, while the other made written notes. For the second subsample of thirty-three *S*s, author Bell was the sole observer.) The protocols were subsequently transcribed and consolidated, then coded. Reliability of observation was checked by separate codings of the dictated reports made by the two authors in four cases observed by both. Product-movement coefficients of 0.99 were found for each of locomotor, manipulatory and visual exploration, and one of 0.98 for crying.

The narrative record yielded two types of measure. A frequency measure was used for three forms of exploratory behavior—locomotor, manipulatory, and visual—and for crying. A score of 1 was given for each 15-second time interval in which the behavior occurred. The maximum was 12 for an episode, since the standard length of an episode was 3 minutes, and longer or shorter episodes were prorated. Frequency measures were obtained for episodes 2 through 7. Product-moment reliability coefficients for two independent coders for eight randomly selected cases were as follows: exploratory locomotion, 0.99; exploratory manipulation, 0.93; visual exploration, 0.98; crying, 0.99.

The second measure was based upon detailed coding of behaviors in which the contingencies of the mother's or stranger's behavior had to be taken into consideration. The codings were then ordered into 7-point scales on the assumption that not only could the same behavior be manifested in different degrees of intensity, but that different behaviors could serve the same end under different intensities of activation. There were five classes of behavior thus scored.

Proximity- and contact-seeking behaviors include active, effective behaviors such as approaching and clambering up, active gestures such as reaching or leaning, intention movements such as partial approaches, and vocal signals including "directed" cries.

Contact-maintaining behaviors pertain to the situation after the baby has gained contact, either through his own initiative or otherwise. They include: clinging, embracing, clutching, and holding on; resisting release by intensified clinging or, if contact is lost, by turning back and reaching, or clambering back up; and protesting release vocally.

Proximity- and interaction-avoiding behaviors pertain to a situation which ordinarily elicits approach, greeting, or at least watching or interaction across a distance, as when an adult entered, or tried to engage the baby's attention. Such behaviors include ignoring the adult, pointedly avoiding looking at her, looking away, turning away, or moving away.

Contact- and interaction-resisting be-

haviors included angry, ambivalent attempts to push away, hit, or kick the adult who seeks to make contact, squirming to get down having been picked up, or throwing away or pushing away the toys through which the adult attempts to mediate her interventions. More diffuse manifestations are angry screaming, throwing self about, throwing self down, kicking the floor, pouting, cranky fussing, or petulance.

These four classes of behavior were scored for interaction with the mother in episodes 2, 3, 5 and 8, and for interaction with the stranger in episodes 3, 4, and 7.

Search behavior was scored for the separation episodes 4, 6, and 7. These behaviors include: following the mother to the door, trying to open the door, banging on the door, remaining oriented to the door or glancing at it, going to the mother's empty chair or simply looking at it. Such behaviors imply that the infant is searching for the absent mother either actively or by orienting to the last place in which she was seen (the door in most cases) or to the place associated with her in the strange situation (her chair.)

In scoring these five classes of behavior, the score was influenced by the following features: the strength of the behavior, its frequency, duration, and latency, and by the type of behavior itself—with active behavior being considered stronger than signaling. Detailed instructions for scoring these behaviors as well as for coding the frequency measures are provided elsewhere.[1]

Reliability coefficients (rho) for two independent scorers for fourteen randomly

selected cases were, for behaviors directed to the mother, as follows: proximity- and contact-seeking, 0.93; contact-maintaining, 0.97; proximity- and interaction-avoiding, 0.93; contact-resisting, 0.96; search, 0.94.

Findings

The findings to be reported here are of behaviors characteristic of the sample as a whole. Individual differences were conspicuous, instructive, and significantly correlated with other variables. Some of these have been reported elsewhere (Ainsworth & Wittig, 1969; Ainsworth & Bell, in press; Bell, in press), but they cannot be considered here.

Exploratory Behavior. Figure 15.1 shows how three forms of exploratory behavior vary in successive episodes from 2 through 7. There is a sharp decline in all forms of exploratory behavior from Episode 2 when the baby was alone with his mother to

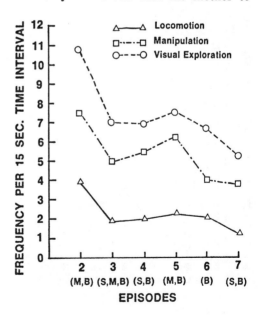

Figure 15.1. Incidence of exploratory behavior

---

[1]The following materials have been deposited with the National Auxiliary Publications Service: instructions for conducting the strange situation procedure, instructions to the mother, instructions for coding behaviors for frequency measures, and instructions for coding socially interactive behaviors.

Episode 3 when the stranger was present also. (This and all other interepisode differences reported here are significant at the .01 level or better, as tested by the binomial test, unless noted otherwise.) Exploration remains depressed through Episode 4 when the baby was left with the stranger. Visual and manipulatory exploration (visual at the .02 level) recover significantly in Episode 5, aided by the mother's attempts to interest the baby again in play, although similar efforts by the stranger in episodes 4 and 7 were ineffective. Visual and manipulatory exploration decline again in Episode 6 after the mother departs for a second time, leaving the baby alone. All forms of exploratory behavior decline to their lowest point in Episode 7 after the stranger had returned but while the mother was still absent.

To supplement the visual exploration score, which measured visual orientation

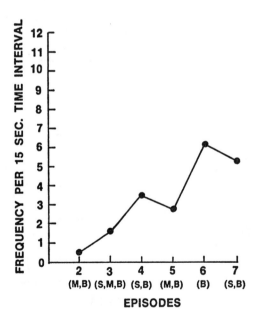

Figure 15.2. Incidence of crying

to the physical environment, visual orientation to the mother and to the stranger were also coded. The only noteworthy findings may be summarized as follows: In Episode 2, the baby looked at the toys and other aspects of the physical environment much more frequently than at the mother, at whom he glanced only now and then, keeping visual tabs on her; in Episode 3, the stranger, the most novel feature of the environment, was looked at more than the toys, and the mother was looked at no more frequently than before.

Crying. Figure 15.2 suggests that the strange situation does not in itself cause alarm or distress, for crying is minimal in Episode 2. Crying does not increase significantly in Episode 3 ($p = .068$), which suggests that the stranger was not in herself alarming for most Ss, at least not when the mother was also present. The incidence of crying rises in Episode 4 with the mother's first departure; it declines upon her return in Episode 5, only to increase sharply in Episode 6 when she departs a second time, leaving the baby alone. It does not decrease significantly when the stranger returns in Episode 7, which suggests that it is the mother's absence rather than mere aloneness that was distressing to most of the babies, and that the greater incidence of crying in Episode 6 than in Episode 4 is largely due to a cumulative effect.

Search Behavior During Separation. The mean strength of search behavior was moderate in Episode 4 (3.0), significantly stronger in Episode 6 (4.6), and moderate again in Episode 7 (2.5). Although this might suggest that search behavior is especially activated by being left alone and reduced in the presence of the stranger, this interpretation is not advanced because of the contingencies of the stranger's behavior and her location near the door. Some infants (37%) cried minimally if at all in Episode 6, and yet searched strongly. Some (20%) cried desperately, but searched weakly or not at all. Some (32%) both cried and searched. All but four *S*s reacted to being left alone with either one or other of these attachment behaviors.

Proximity-Seeking and Contact-Maintaining Behaviors. Figure 15.3 shows that efforts to regain contact, proximity, or interaction with the mother occur only weakly in episodes 2 and 3 but are greatly intensified by brief separation experiences. Contact-maintaining behavior is negligible in Episodes 2 and 3, rises in the first reunion Episode (5), and rises even more sharply in the second reunion Episode (8). In the case of both classes of behavior the increase from Episodes 2 through 5 to 8 is highly significant ($p < .001$). Some *S*s showed these behaviors in relation to the stranger also. Thus, for example, a few infants approached the stranger in each of the episodes in which the stranger was present, but substantially fewer than those who approached the mother. Some infants were picked up by the stranger in Episodes 4 and 7—in an attempt to comfort them— and some of these did cling to her and/or resist being put down again. Nevertheless proximity-seeking and contact-maintain-

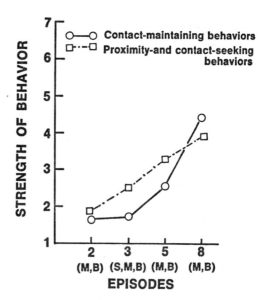

Figure 15.3. Strength of proximity-seeking and contact-maintaining behaviors directed toward the mother.

ing behaviors were displayed much less frequently and less strongly to the stranger than to the mother.

Contact-Resisting and Proximity-Avoiding Behaviors. Table 15.1 shows the incidence of contact-resisting and proximity-avoiding behaviors directed to both mother

TABLE 15.1. Incidence of Contact-Resisting and Proximity-Avoiding Behavior to Mother and Stranger

Strength of Behavior	Behavior to Mother		Behavior to Stranger		
	Episode 5	*Episode 8*	*Episode 3*	*Episode 4*	*Episode 7*
	Resist Contact				
6-7	4	6	0	6	7
4-5	5	8	5	3	12
2-3	9	13	2	3	3
1	38	29	49	44	34
	Avoid Proximity				
6-7	7	5	4	1	1
4-5	17	13	7	3	6
2-3	3	7	7	1	2
1	29	31	38	51	45

and stranger. Contact-resisting behavior directed toward the mother occurred very rarely in the preseparation episodes because the mother had been instructed not to intervene except in response to the baby's demands, and therefore Episodes 2 and 3 are omitted from the table. In the reunion episodes, some Ss resisted contact with the mother, but many did not. Therefore Table 15.1 shows the incidence of this behavior rather than its mean strength.

About one third of the sample showed contact-resisting behavior to the mother in Episode 5, at least to some degree, and about one half showed it in Episode 8. All but one infant who scored relatively high (4 or higher) in contact-resisting behavior received a comparably high score on contact-maintaining behavior. Thus, at least when directed to the mother, contact-resisting behavior seems to represent classic ambivalence—wanting to be held, wanting to be close, and at the same time angrily resisting contact.

Contact and interaction with the stranger were also resisted but somewhat less frequently than with the mother. Six Ss showed fairly strong contact- or interaction-resisting behavior (scores of 4 or higher) with both stranger in Episode 7 and with mother in Episode 8, but, for the most part, babies who tended to resist the mother did not resist the stranger and vice versa.

Proximity- and interaction-avoiding behavior did not occur in relation to the mother in the preseparation episodes, for the mother's nonparticipant role made no claim on the baby's attention. But, as shown in Table 15.1, it occurred to some degree in about half the sample in each of the reunion episodes, 5 and 8. About one third of the sample avoided the stranger at some time in Episode 3—ignoring her, avoiding meeting her eyes, or moving further away from her. The incidence of

these behaviors declined in Episode 4, and even in Episode 7 remained less than in Episode 3. About half the sample avoided neither mother nor stranger, but those who showed this behavior in any strength (score of 4 or over) to one did not show it to the other.

DISCUSSION

These findings illustrate the complex interaction between attachment behavior, response to novel or unfamiliar stimulus objects and situations, and responses to separation from the attachment object and to subsequent reunion. First, let us consider response to novelty. It is now commonly accepted that novelty may elicit either fear and avoidance or approach and exploration, depending both on the degree of novelty and upon circumstances. One of the conditions which facilitates approach and exploration of the novel is the presence, in reasonable but not necessarily close proximity, of the mother—the object of attachment. The infants of the present sample showed little alarm in the preseparation episodes of the strange situation. Their attachment behavior was not activated; they tended not to cling to the mother or even to approach her. They used her as a secure base from which to explore the strange situation. This finding is not new. Similar observations have been reported by Arsenian (1943), Cox and Campbell (1968), Ainsworth and Wittig (1969), and Rheingold (1969) for human subjects, and by Harlow (1961) for rhesus macaque infants. The presence of the mother can tip the balance in favor of exploring the novel rather than avoiding it or withdrawing from it.

Absence of the mother tends to tip the balance in the opposite direction with a substantial heightening of attachment behavior and concomitant lessening of exploration. During the mother's absence, proximity-promoting behaviors (crying and search) are evident. The mother's return in the reunion episodes did not serve to redress the balance to its previous level. Attachment behaviors—proximity- and contact-seeking and contact-maintaining behaviors—remained heightened. Crying did not immediately subside in many cases and, despite the mother's attempts to evoke a renewed interest in exploring the properties of the toys, exploration remained depressed below its initial level.

It was assumed that separation episodes totaling 9 minutes at most would not have any lasting effect on the balance between attachment and exploratory behavior, and indeed the posttest behavior of the infants tended to confirm this assumption. Nevertheless these minuscule separations evoke behaviors which are similar in kind to those provoked by longer separations, although differing in duration and intensity. The behavior of these 1-year-old humans in response to separations lasting only a few minutes bears remarkable resemblance to the behavior of infant monkeys in response to separation for longer periods—a week (Spencer-Booth & Hinde, 1966) or a month (Kaufman & Rosenblum, 1967). In these experiments the mother was removed, and the infant left in his familiar social group. Attachment behavior, including distress calling and search for the mother, was heightened, and exploratory and play behavior was depressed during the separation. The infants responded more intensely to frightening stimuli during separation than when the mother was present. As separation continued, there was some lessening of the intensity of distress and search, and some recovery of exploration and play—a recovery not manifest by the human infants in this sample in their very brief separations. When the mother was restored, however, the infant monkeys clung to her more and explored less than they had before separation—differing in this from nonseparated controls—and these effects lasted for three months or more.

The response of infant monkeys to experimental separations strongly resembles the behavior of young children, aged from 8 months to 3 years, when they undergo separations of several days, weeks, or even months away from home in hospitals or residential nurseries. Robertson and Bowlby (1952), Bowlby (1953), Schaffer (1958), and Heinicke and Westheimer (1965) have shown that the child is at first acutely distressed, protests the separation, and attempts to regain the mother by all means at his disposal. This initial phase of response tends to give way to despair, which in turn may give way—if the separation endures long enough—to a brightening of affect and renewed responsiveness to companions and to things in the environment. Attachment behavior directed toward the mother may have disappeared, but reunion with the mother tends to reactivate it and indeed to intensify it beyond its preseparation level. This heightened level tends to persist for a more or less prolonged period, usually much longer than the separation itself. During the period after reunion when the child's attachment behavior is heightened, he is focused on his mother, attends less to other people and to things in his environment, explores less, and presumably learns less. An unduly prolonged heightening of attachment behavior may be viewed as a distortion of the attachment-exploration balance. Some long-term follow-up studies (e.g., Bowlby, Ainsworth, Boston, & Rosenbluth, 1956) suggest that this kind of behavior, often described as over-dependent, may in some instances be a lasting effect of long, depriving separations.

Let us turn from attachment behavior to consider those behaviors that work against contact- and proximity-seeking, namely, contact-resisting and proximity- and interaction-avoiding behaviors. Contact-resisting behavior, as directed toward the mother, usually occurred in conjunction with contact-seeking behavior, and hence, as suggested earlier, implies an ambivalent response. Ambivalent or rejecting and angry responses are reported as common in young children returning home after brief separations (e.g. Heinicke & Westheimer, 1965). Separation heightens aggressive behavior of this kind as well as attachment behavior and predisposes the child toward angry outbursts upon minimal provocation. Spencer-Booth and Hinde (1966) report similar increase of aggression in monkeys: Unusually intense tantrums occur in response to any discouragement of contact-seeking behavior during the period of reunion after separation. Some of our strange-situation *S*s showed contact-resisting behavior toward the stranger. Although in some cases this may indicate fear of the strange person, it seems likely that in some, perhaps most, it is a manifestation of aggression evoked by the mother's departure.

Proximity-avoiding behavior, on the other hand, seems likely to stem from different sources in the case of the stranger than in the case of the mother, even though the overt behavior seems the same in both cases. Ignoring the stranger, and looking, turning, or moving away from her probably imply an avoidance of the unfamiliar and fear-evoking person. This is suggested by the fact that these responses are more frequent (as directed toward the stranger) in Episode 3, when the stranger has first appeared, then in later episodes. Similar avoidance of the mother cannot be due to unfamiliarity, and seems unlikely to be caused by fear. Such behavior occurs in the reunion episodes, and is more frequent than avoidance of the stranger.

Proximity- and interaction-avoiding behavior in relation to the mother is shown in striking form by some young children upon reunion after separations lasting for weeks or months. Robertson and Bowlby (1952) and Heinicke and Westheimer (1965) report that some children do not seem to recognize their mothers upon reunion, and that for a longer or shorter time they remain distant from her and treat her like a stranger. Bowlby (1960) has termed this kind of distanciation "detachment." During a prolonged separation, detachment tends to succeed protest and despair reactions, and after reunion it may persist for a long time—even indefinitely in cases in which separations have been very long and depriving. Such behavior has not yet been reported in nonhuman primates—perhaps because their experimental separations have been brief, perhaps because of species differences.

Avoidance responses of the kind observed in the strange situation in relation to the mother—looking away, turning away—may be detachment in the making and so constitute a primitive kind of defense. The constellation of individual differences in the strange-situation sample supports this hypothesis, although it is impossible here to present detailed evidence.

It may be pertinent, however, to refer to a similar looking-away response found in two experiments on the conditioning and extinction of attachment behaviors. Brackbill (1958) worked with the smiling response. During the conditioning period she provided contingent reinforcement for smiling by responding socially to the baby each time he smiled—and smiling increased in frequency. During the extinction period she met the baby's smile with an impassive face. Not only did the frequency of smiling decrease, but when the experimenter failed to respond to a smile, the baby fussed and looked away. It became increasingly difficult to catch the baby's eye. He looked away from the person who had previously reinforced his attachment behavior but who no longer did so. Similar results are reported for an experiment on babbling by Rheingold, Gewirtz, and Ross (1959).

These findings highlight the fact that in extinction—as indeed learning theorists have often themselves emphasized—there is an active process of blocking the response by another, antithetical behavior, rather than or in addition to the weakening of the strength of smiling (or babbling) behavior itself. This suggests that detached behavior may consist of responses, incompatible with attachment behavior, which have, often temporarily, gained the greater strength. That attachment can endure despite a period of detachment is shown by the strength with which attachment behavior can break through into overt expression in the case of young children who do not at reunion seem to recognize their mothers, but who subsequently manifest much heightened proximity-seeking and contact-maintaining behavior.

In summary, continuities have been noted between attachment and exploratory behavior and their activating and terminating conditions, observed in the microcosm of the laboratory strange-situation, and similar behaviors and conditions as reported by field studies, clinical studies, and experimental studies for both humans and nonhuman primate subjects. It is urged that the concept of attachment and attachment behavior employed as a guide in future studies be given a broad

enough perspective to comprehend the spectrum of findings relevant to attachment which have been sampled in this discussion.

PROPOSITIONS FOR A COMPREHENSIVE CONCEPT OF ATTACHMENT

The following propositions are suggested as essential to a comprehensive concept of attachment. They are based on an ethological-evolutionary point of view, and have been formulated on the basis of reports of a broad range of investigations, including naturalistic studies of mother–infant interaction, and studies of mother–child separation and reunion in both human and nonhuman primates, as well as the illustrative strange-situation study reported here.

1. Attachment is not coincident with attachment behavior. Attachment behavior may be heightened or diminished by conditions—environmental and intraorganismic—which may be specified empirically. Despite situationally determined waxing and waning of attachment behavior, the individual is nevertheless predisposed intermittently to seek proximity to the object of attachment. It is this predisposition—which may be conceived as having an inner, structural basis—that is the attachment. Its manifestations are accessible to observation over time; a short time sample may, however, be misleading.

2. Attachment behavior is heightened in situations perceived as threatening, whether it is an external danger or an actual or impending separation from the attachment object that constitutes the threat.

3. When strongly activated, attachment behavior is incompatible with exploratory behavior. On the other hand, the state of

being attached, together with the presence of the attachment object, may support and facilitate exploratory behaviors. Provided that there is no threat of separation, the infant is likely to be able to use his mother as a secure base from which to explore, manifesting no alarm in even a strange situation as long as she is present. Under these circumstances the relative absence of attachment behavior—of proximity-promoting behavior—can not be considered an index of a weak attachment.

4. Although attachment behavior may diminish or even disappear in the course of a prolonged absence from the object of attachment, the attachment is not necessarily diminished; attachment behavior is likely to reemerge in full or heightened strength upon reunion, with or without delay.

5. Although individual differences have not been stressed in this discussion, the incidence of ambivalent (contact-resisting) and probably defensive (proximity-avoiding) patterns of behavior in the reunion episodes of the strange situation are a reflection of the fact that attachment relations are qualitatively different from one attached pair to another. These qualitative differences, together with the sensitivity of attachment behavior to situational determinants, make it very difficult to assess the strength or intensity of an attachment. It is suggested that, in the present state of our knowledge, it is wiser to explore qualitative differences, and their correlates and antecedents, than to attempt premature quantifications of strength of attachment.

REFERENCES

Ainsworth, M. D. The development of infant–mother interaction among the Ganda. In B. M. Foss (ed.), *Determinants of infant behaviour II.* London: Methuen, 1963. Pp. 67-112.

Ainsworth, M. D. Patterns of attachment behavior shown by the infant in interaction with his mother. *Merrill-Palmer Quarterly of Behavior and Development,* 1964, **10,** 51-58.

Ainsworth, M. D. S. *Infancy in Uganda: infant care and the growth of love.* Baltimore: Johns Hopkins University Press, 1967.

Ainsworth, M. D. S. Object relations, dependency and attachment: a theoretical review of the infant–mother relationship. *Child Development,* 1969, **40,** 969-1025.

Ainsworth, M. D. S., & Bell, S. M. Some contemporary patterns of mother–infant interaction in the feeding situation. In J. A. Ambrose (ed.), *The functions of stimulation in early post-natal development.* London: Academic, in press.

Ainsworth, M. D. S., & Wittig, B. A. Attachment and exploratory behavior of one-year-olds in a strange situation. In B. M. Foss (ed.), *Determinants of infant behaviour IV.* London: Methuen, 1969. Pp. 111-136.

Arsenian, J. M. Young children in an insecure situation. *Journal of Abnormal and Social Psychology,* 1943, **38,** 225-249.

Bell, S. M. The development of the concept of the object as related to infant–mother attachment. *Child Development,* in press.

Bowlby, J. Psychopathological processes set in train by early mother–child separation. *Journal of Mental Science,* 1953, **99,** 265-272.

Bowlby, J. The nature of the child's tie to his mother. *International Journal of Psychoanalysis,* 1958, **39,** 350-373.

Bowlby, J. Separation anxiety. *International Journal of Psychoanalysis,* 1960, **41,** 69-113.

Bowlby, J. *Attachment and loss.* Vol. 1. *Attachment.* London: Hogarth, 1969; New York: Basic Books, 1969.

Bowlby, J.; Ainsworth, M. D.; Boston, M.; & Rosenbluth, D. The effects of mother–child separation: a follow-up study. *British Journal of Medical Psychology,* 1956, **29,** 211-247.

Brackbill, Y. Extinction of the smiling response in infants as a function of reinforcement schedule. *Child Development,* 1958, **29,** 115-124.

Cairns, R. B. Attachment behavior of mammals. *Psychological Review,* 1966, **73,** 409-426.

Cox, F. N., & Campbell, D. Young children in

a new situation with and without their mothers. *Child Development,* 1968, **39,** 123-131.

DeVore, I. Mother–infant relations in free-ranging baboons. In H. L. Rheingold (ed.), *Maternal behavior in mammals.* New York: John Wiley and Sons 1963. Pp. 305-335.

Gewirtz, J. L. A learning analysis of the effects of normal stimulation, privation and deprivation on the acquisition of social motivation and attachment. In B. M. Foss (ed.), *Determinants of infant behaviour.* London: Methuen, 1961. Pp. 213-299.

Gewirtz, J. L. Mechanisms of social learning: some roles of stimulation and behavior in early human development. In D. A. Goslin (ed.), *Handbook of socialization theory and research.* Chicago: Rand McNally, 1969. Pp. 57-212.

Goodall, J. Chimpanzees of the Gombe Stream Reserve. In I. DeVore (ed.), *Primate behavior: field studies of monkeys and apes.* New York: Holt, Rinehart & Winston, 1965. Pp. 425-473.

Hamburg, D. A. Evolution of emotional responses: evidence from recent research on non-human primates. In J. Masserman (ed.), *Science and psychoanalysis.* Vol. 12. New York: Grune & Stratton, 1968. Pp. 39-52.

Harlow, H. F. The development of affectional patterns in infant monkeys. In B. M. Foss (ed.), *Determinants of infant behaviour.* London: Methuen, 1961. Pp. 75-97.

Harlow, H. F., & Harlow, M. K. The affectional systems. In A. M. Schrier, H. F. Harlow, & F. Stollnitz (eds.), *Behavior of nonhuman primates.* Vol. 2. New York: Academic, 1965. Pp. 287-334.

Heinicke, C. M., & Westheimer, I. *Brief separations.* New York: International Universities Press, 1965.

Hinde, R. A., Rowell, T. E.; & Spencer-Booth, Y. Behaviour of socially living rhesus monkeys in their first six months. *Proceedings of the Zoological Society of London,* 1964, **143,** 609-649.

Hinde, R. A.; Rowell, T. E.; & Spencer-Booth, Y. The behaviour of socially, living rhesus monkeys in their first two and a half years. *Animal Behaviour,* 1967, **15,** 169-196.

Kaufman, I. C., & Rosenblum, L. A. Depression in infant monkeys separated from their mothers. *Science,* 1967, **155,** 1030-1031.

Maccoby, E. E., & Masters, J. C. Attachment and dependency. In P. Mussen (ed.), *Carmichael's manual of child psychology,* in press.

Mason, W. A. Determinants of social behavior in young chimpanzees. In A. M. Schrier, H. F. Harlow, & F. Stollnitz (eds.), *Behavior of nonhuman primates.* Vol. 2. New York: Academic, 1965. Pp. 287-334.

Morgan, G. A., & Ricciuti, H. N. Infants' responses to strangers during the first year. In B. M. Foss (ed.), *Determinants of infant behaviour IV.* London: Methuen, 1969. Pp. 253-272.

Rheingold, H. L. The effect of a strange environment on the behavior of infants. In B. M. Foss (ed.), *Determinants of infant behaviour IV.* London: Methuen, 1969. Pp. 137-166.

Rheingold, H. L.; Gewirtz, J. L.; & Ross, H. W. Social conditioning of vocalizations in the infant. *Journal of Comparative and Physiological Psychology,* 1959, **52,** 68-73.

Robertson, J., & Bowlby, J. Responses of young children to separation from their mothers. II. Observations of the sequences of response of children aged 16 to 24 months during the course of separation. *Courrier Centre International de l'Enfance,* 1952, **2,** 131-142.

Robson, K. S. The role of eye-to-eye contact in maternal–infant attachment. *Journal of Child Psychology and Psychiatry,* 1967. **8,** 13-25.

Schaffer, H. R. Objective observations of personality development in early infancy. *British Journal of Medical Psychology,* 1958, **31,** 174-183.

Schaffer, H. R. The onset of fear of strangers and the incongruity hypothesis. *Journal of Child Psychology and Psychiatry,* 1966, **7,** 95-106.

Schaffer, H. R., & Emerson, P. E. The development of social attachments in infancy. *Monographs of the Society for Research in Child Development,* 1964, **29,** (3, Serial No. 94).

Schaller, G. B. The behavior of the mountain gorilla. In I. DeVore (ed.), *Primate behavior: field studies of monkeys and apes.* New York: Holt, Rinehart & Winston, 1965. Pp. 324-367.

Schwarz, J. C. Fear and attachment in young children. *Merrill-Palmer Quarterly of Behavior and Development,* 1968, **14,** 313-322.

Southwick, C. H.; Beg, M. A.; & Siddiqi, M. R. Rhesus monkeys in North India. In I. DeVore (ed.), *Primate behavior: field studies of monkeys and apes.* New York: Holt, Rinehart & Winston, 1965. Pp. 111-159.

Spencer-Booth, Y., & Hinde, R. A. The effects of separating rhesus monkey infants from their mothers for six days. *Journal of Child Psychology and Psychiatry,* 1966, **7,** 179-198.

Walters, R. H., & Parke, R. D. The role of the distance receptors in the development of social responsiveness. In L. P. Lipsitt & C. C. Spiker (eds.), *Advances in child development and behavior.* Vol. 2. New York: Academic, 1965. Pp. 59-96.

16.

Michael E. Lamb

INFANT ATTACHMENT TO MOTHERS AND FATHERS

The assessment of the infant's attachment to his mother has been a topic of considerable interest to developmental psychologists in recent years (Ainsworth, 1973), but far less attention has been given to the nature of the relationship between the infant and his father. Since most children are raised in nuclear families containing both a mother and a father, it appears that in focusing so narrowly on the mother–infant interaction, we may have ignored a relationship which is of great importance (Lamb, 1975a).

In attempting to remedy this situation, I decided to examine the father–infant relationship by way of a longitudinal study based on a number of observations of the infants in their homes. The data I shall present are derived from the first two of these observations, which took place when the subjects were seven and eight months of age.

We chose this age as our starting point because, according to Bowlby's (1969) theory of attachment, the infants should have been forming their first (and primary) attachment to their mothers at this age. Thus, the preference for the mothers should be clearly evident, since the attachments to the fathers, if they existed at all, should be vastly inferior in quality. In addition, this is an age sometimes seen as the beginning of a period of "stranger anxiety," and our design permitted an evaluation of the sociability with strangers as well.

The subjects were twenty infants, ten boys and ten girls, recruited from the birth records of the Yale New Haven Hospital. They were equally distributed across the upper four of the five classes on Hollingshead's (1957) Two Factor Index of Social Position.

Each infant was visited at times when both parents were at home with the child. In general, this meant that most visits took place in the evening or on weekends, at the discretion of the parents. All visits were

Source: Paper presented at the biennial meeting of the Society for Research in Child Development, Denver, Colorado, 1975.

made by the same two persons, a male Observer and a female Visitor. The Observer dictated into a tape-recorder a detailed narrative account of the infant's behavior and the contingent behavior of others, taking particular care to note each time an attachment behavior (Ainsworth, 1964; Bowlby, 1969) was directed to one of the persons present. While the Observer withdrew completely from interaction with the parents and the child, the Visitor interacted with them, providing an alternative interactive partner for the child. It was hoped that this would assure us of a sampling of the typical interaction between the child and his parents when visitors were present. When subsequently questioned, most of the parents stated that we had managed to achieve this.

The narratives recorded by the Observer were subsequently transcribed by a typist, and analyzed by 15-second time periods. Infants were observed for a mean of 153.5 minutes, but the analyses reported today are based on the 122.25 minutes per infant (mean) during which both parents and the investigators were simultaneously present in the room, and could thus serve as targets for the display of attachment behaviors by the infants.

The transcripts were searched for each instance of one of the following attachment behaviors directed towards *Mother,*

Father, Visitor, or *Observer:* smiling to, vocalizing to, looking at, laughing at (with), touching, seeking to be picked up by, reaching to, and fussing to. It was also noted whether the infant was being held by or was within 3 feet of any of the adults. Thus, proximity to the adult was also regarded as an attachment behavior, as was approaching, which was defined as a movement from beyond to within 3 feet of the person. For looking, vocalizing, smiling and laughing, separate tallies were made for those behaviors which were directed when the child was close to (i.e., within 3 feet of) or distant from (beyond 3 feet from) the person concerned. Touching, being within proximity, and being held by were only coded once in every 15-second unit as a precaution against possible artificial inflation of the data. The estimate of proximity was adjusted (by subtraction) for the amount of time that the infants were being held.

Assessment of the data collection procedures was made by arranging for the Observer and a naive assistant to observe, simultaneously and independently, several mother–father–infant triads in a laboratory playroom, and then comparing the reports of the Observer with those of the assistant. In all categories except smiling, the rate of agreement was above 90%; in the case of smiling the agreement was

TABLE 16.1. Mean Rates Per Minute of Display of Attachment Behaviors

Behavior	Mother	Father	Visitor
Smiles	0.140	0.276	0.220
Vocalizes	0.052	0.108	0.064
Looks	0.868	1.240	1.196
Laughs	0.040	0.092	0.056
Approach	0.036	0.036	0.040
Proximity[a]	1.912	1.640	1.884
Reaches to	0.020	0.040	0.020
Touches	0.116	0.156	0.064
Seeks to be held	0.016	0.008	0.000
Fusses to	0.036	0.032	0.004

[a]Excluding time when the infants were being held

75%, with the Observer consistently reporting more smiling to both parents. Reliability in the tabulation of the behaviors was also high, ranging from 82% to 95% for the behavior categories. When the distinction between close and distant behaviors was eliminated, the rate of agreement was somewhat higher.

Though the data were derived from two observations of each child, there was no difference in behavior at the two ages, and consequently the data have been combined for the purposes of analysis.

To equalize the contribution of each infant to the group data, the scores for each infant on each measure were converted into rates per minute, and Table 16.1 displays the rates of attachment behaviors to Mother, Father, and Visitor.

A repeated-measures multivariate analysis of variance (MANOVA) using the rates of smiling, vocalizing, looking, laughing, touching, fussing, reaching, seeking to be held, approaching, and proximity (adjusted for the time that infants were being held) as variables was computed to determine whether there was a consistent preference for any person. The results showed a significant preference for the fathers over the other two persons ($p<.001$, $p<.014$ for the two roots). Fur-

ther MANOVAs comparing mother with Father, Mother with Visitor, and Father with Visitor, showed that the fathers were preferred to the mothers ($p<.05$) and to the Visitor ($p<.05$), while the mothers were preferred to the Visitor ($p<.01$). Univariate repeated measures ANOVAs were then computed on the individual measures. The infants smiled ($p<.05$), vocalized ($p<.001$) and looked ($p<.005$) at their fathers more often than at their mothers, and tended ($p<.10$) to reach to and laugh in interaction with them more often than with their mothers. The other measures showed no significant differences.

In comparing the Father–infant and Visitor–infant interaction, univariate tests showed that the infants vocalized to ($p<.05$), touched ($p<.01$) and fussed to ($p<.01$) their fathers more often than the Visitor, while also tending to reach towards him more often ($p<.10$).

Finally, the data showed that the infants sought to be held by ($p<.01$) and fussed to ($p<.001$) their mothers more often than the Visitor, and also tended ($p<.10$) to touch their mothers more often. On the other hand, they looked ($p<.01$) and tended to smile ($p<.10$) more often at the Visitor.

The preference patterns can be seen

TABLE 16.2. Patterns of Preferences in the Display of Attachment Behaviors

Behavior	M vs F	F vs V	M vs V
Vocalizes	F>M***	F>V*	—
Smiles	F>M*	—	V>M†
Looks	F>M**	—	V>M**
Laughs	F>M†	—	—
Approach	—	—	—
Proximity[a]	—	—	—
Reaches	F>M†	F>V†	—
Touches	—	F>V**	M>V†
Seeks to be held	—	—	M>V**
Fusses to	—	F>V**	M>V***

[a] Excluding time when infants were held
*** $p<.001$
** $p<.01$
* $p<.05$
† $p<.10$

more clearly on Table 16.2. Notice that the discrimination of the Visitor from the parents is clearest on those measures related to close physical contact and the desire for it. Both parents are preferred to the Visitor on such measures, but in addition to this, the fathers are preferred to both the Visitor and the mothers in the display of distal attachment behaviors.

It is valuable at this point to consider the distinction drawn by Bretherton and Ainsworth (1974) between affiliative and attachment systems. Whereas infants may affiliate with many familiar persons other than attachment figures, there are certain behaviors and certain types of interaction which are restricted largely to intercourse with attachment figures. On both conceptual and empirical grounds (Tracy, Lamb, & Ainsworth, 1974) the best examples would be the desire to be held by someone and the desire to be near someone when distressed. Inspection of Table 16.2 makes plain that neither parent is preferred to the other on measures of this nature, but both are preferred to the Visitor. Clearly, while the Visitor is an attractive person with whom to interact, the infants readily distinguish her from the parents.

The comparison between the two parents is also interesting. While neither Mother nor Father emerges as a preferred attachment object on these four measures, there is far more affiliative-type interaction with Father than with Mother. What this suggests is that neither mothers nor fathers are superior attachment figures in this situation, but that fathers are just more fun.

Thus far, I have made no reference to the parents' behavior. We did analyze the parent's contribution to the interaction in the contexts of *play* and *physical contact,* and these analyses have been reported elsewhere (Lamb, 1975b). To summarize them briefly: there was evidence that the

types of interaction in the Mother–infant and Father–infant dyads differed qualitatively. The response to play with Father was significantly more positive than with Mother, but this was clearly because fathers engaged the infants in more physically stimulating and unpredictable games. Likewise, the fathers picked up their infants mainly to play with them, not to perform caretaking functions, and consequently the response to physical contact was also more positive with fathers.

I began this research aiming to address the question with which most persons in this area appear to be concerned (e.g., Cohen & Campos, 1974; Kotelchuck, 1972) namely: Is there any evidence that mothers are preferred to fathers, as Bowlby's (1969) notion of monotropy predicts. As the project proceeds, I become increasingly convinced that this question is an inappropriate one to ask, and indeed one to which we are unable to formulate general conclusions because of the inadequacy of the measures at our disposal (Lamb, 1974; Weinraub, Brooks, & Lewis, 1975). The issue should not be: Is mother more important than father, for that depends on how you define and measure importance; rather the issue should be: *In what ways are fathers important.* Certainly, I think that the data we are gathering indicate that both parents are "important" but far more interestingly, they imply that the nature of mother–infant and father–infant interaction differ.

We intend to direct our attention in the course of this study to characterizing the relationships, and thereby determining in what ways mothers and fathers are contributing to social development. I believe we can no longer accept the implicit assumption that fathers are simply occasional mother-substitutes; rather, they may have an important role to play in socialization which is independent of the mothers'—a role which has been almost totally ignored by students of infancy. A tentative hypothesis (more fully detailed in Lamb, 1975a) based on the results of previous research and the present study, is that the prominence of play in the father–infant relationship contributes to a definition of the father as a person with whom interaction is pleasurable, varied, and unpredictable. Thus defined, the father serves to introduce the child to the world beyond the home and determines the attitude with which the child approaches the world. The tentative nature of the hypothesis underlines the need for further research on the role of the father in both infancy and childhood. I am convinced, though, that these efforts will substantiate my belief that the infant's social world is far more complex and multidimensional than we are accustomed to portraying it.

REFERENCES

Ainsworth, M. D. Patterns of attachment behavior shown by the infant in interaction with his mother. *Merrill-Palmer Quarterly of Behavior and Development*, 1964, **10**, 51-58.

Ainsworth, M. D. The development of infant–mother attachment. In B. M. Caldwell & H. N. Ricciuti (eds.), *Review of child development research III*. Chicago: University of Chicago Press, 1973.

Bowlby, J. *Attachment and loss*. Volume 1. *Attachment*. New York: Basic Books, 1969.

Bretherton, I., & Ainsworth, M. D. Responses of one-year-olds to a stranger in a strange situation. In M. Lewis & L. A. Rosenblum (eds.), *The origins of human behavior: Fear*. New York: John Wiley and Sons, 1974.

Cohen, L. J., & Campos, J. J. Father, mother, and stranger as elicitors of attachment behaviors in infancy. *Developmental Psychology*, 1974, **10**, 146-154.

Hollingshead, A. B. The two-factor index of social position. Unpublished manuscript (Yale University), 1957.

Kotelchuck, M. The nature of the child's tie to his father. Unpublished doctoral dissertation, Harvard University, 1972.

Lamb, M. E. A defense of the concept of attachment. *Human Development*, 1974, **17**, 376-385.

Lamb, M. E. Fathers: Forgotten contributors to child development. *Human Development*, 1975, **18**, 245-266.

Lamb, M. E. Infants, fathers, and mothers: Interaction at 8 months of age in the home and in the laboratory. Paper presented to the Eastern Psychological Association, New York, April 1975 (b).

Tracy, R. L.; Lamb, M. E.; & Ainsworth, M. D. Locomotor proximity seeking as related to attachment. Paper presented to the Southeastern Society for Research in Child Development, Chapel Hill, N.C., 1974.

Weinraub, M.; Brooks, J.; & Lewis, M. The social network: A reconsideration of the concept of attachment. Unpublished manuscript (Educational Testing Service, Princeton) 1975.

B. AGGRESSION

17.

Stewart Cohen

AGGRESSION IN CHILDREN: ITS DEVELOPMENT AND MODIFICATION

The development of aggression in children has been investigated from a variety of research and theoretical perspectives (Cohen, 1976). From research studies performed in this area major variables leading to the instigation, learning, and performance of aggressive behavior have been identified. Congruent with such efforts, we have witnessed the building of more tenable theories of aggression. Yet, while knowledge of the antecedents of aggressive behavior has accumulated, the delineation of strategies leading to its control and modifications has proceeded less rapidly. The present review attempts to synthesize research findings and theoretical perspectives directed toward a clearer understanding of mechanisms accounting for the display and control of aggression in children.

AGGRESSION AND CHILDREN

As a preliminary inquiry it may be asked, what role does aggression play in the lives of children? A cursory examination of the varied environments within which children develop in our society reveals that aggression occupies considerable prominence. Moreover, and perhaps most critical, the influence of aggression upon the present conduct of human affairs appears more pervasive than at any other time in history. Truly, our awareness of the reality of aggression as a copiously encountered facet of human interaction is only tempered in intensity by our concern for the ease in which aggressive responses are learned

and the frequency with which they are displayed.

The effects of exposure to aggression upon children are complex and varied. These include an assortment of direct and indirect effects upon the child's behavior and incorporate consequences of immediate and long-range importance. This outcome is based on the fact that while aggressive responses may be acquired quite readily, the full effects of exposure to aggression are generally not immediately known; often what the child learns through exposure to aggressive models is not performed, nor unless supported by situational sanctions, likely to be performed (Bandura, Ross, & Ross, 1963; Hicks, 1965). Moreover, the long-range behavioral consequences of continued exposure to a climate of violence likely produce results that extend beyond those experienced within the learning context responsible for the acquisition of aggressive responses.

Aggression is learned through personalized experiences and events involving others. On an experiential level, the young child learns that aggression, as a high amplitude response, is a powerful attention-getting device (Walters, 1964). Later the child discovers that aggression provides an effective mechanism for establishing control over other persons. Supplementing these observations, the child learns that aggression, among competing responses, may serve as a highly effective technique for the speedy resolution of complex social problems.

The child's experience of aggression involving others may incorporate events in which the child plays an observer or participant role. In the role of observer, the child becomes acquainted with aggression as a witness to the destructive behavior of people portrayed in fantasy and in reality. In the latter category media presentations provide reality-based observations of persons involved in territorial, racial, religious, or politically motivated aggression. These indirectly encountered experiences are supplemented locally through direct exposure to violence among peers. Moreover, in some instances, these events will involve adults as participants or perpetrators of aggression. Finally, it may be suggested that the child in American society experiences a culture in which aggression and assertion are not strongly distinguished (Staub, 1971). This failure to discriminate among competing responses, coupled with exposure to strong sanctions fostering competitive, rather than cooperative, behavior may be assumed to influence the child's choice of response in a variety of settings, particularly those in which limited resources or positions of status may be achieved.

AGGRESSION AND INSTINCT

In recognition of the child's immediate and cummulative history of aggressive experiences, it may be asked whether aggression is inevitable. Some theories of human behavior have advocated this conclusion, while others have offered a less fatalistic perspective. Psychoanalysis and ethological theory each hold the former view. They see aggression as an inherent characteristic of human behavior founded upon innate etiological circumstances. However, each theory differs in its account of events leading to the display of aggression. Psychoanalysis views aggression in terms of Freud's (1959) concept of Thana-

tos, viz., the death instinct. Through this instinct, Freud proposed that the human organism releases tension and accumulatins of undischarged energy, a necessary pursuit in establishing homeostatic (i.e., physiological) balance among competing life support systems. As such, Freud saw aggression as serving a "cathartic" function in which the individual drained or purged themself of excessive, potentially destructive accumulations of energy. To illustrate, the young child may be observed (and according to psychoanalysis, should be encouraged) to release excessive energy through vigorous activity. Working within this framework, which serves an inherently determined function, psychoanalysis argues that meaningful decisions concerning how and to whom as well as where such activity may be directed can be made. Such decisions, according to this point of view, allow for the effective intervention and monitoring of aggression. Specifically, Freud reasoned that potentially destructive activity may be channeled or sublimated (i.e., direct toward innocuous or inanimate objects rather than actual persons), accomplishing its purging task without perpetrating injury upon others. Yet, unfortunately, this solution to aggressive management has not proven effective. In numerous studies in which children and adults have been exposed to film-mediated aggressive models, vicarious participation in aggressive activity (e.g., viewing a fight film) has been found to lead to an increase, rather than a decrease in subsequent aggressive behavior among viewers, as opposed to non-viewers of aggressive film content (Bandura & Walters, 1963b).

While it is likely that the draining of energy (under adult supervision) probably does aid the child in releasing tension, the value of such action is limited, being confined principally to those physiological effects (viz., fatigue) associated with the performance of high amplitude response patterns. Under these circumstances the child's behavior will indeed bear witness to a reduction in general activity level, often leading to the cessation of the aggressive response. This effect upon the course of behavior development, however, is usually of short duration since physiologically, the child is an active energy system continuously converting input to outgo. Moreover, it may be noted that by facilitating catharsis through encouraging the child to participate in vicarious aggression, the adult exposes the child to living models of the very behavior that it is hoped will be inhibited. Given these observations, we need consider whether the rerouting of aggression to safe objects may serve, contrary to the catharsis hypothesis, to strengthen the aggressive response, perhaps to be performed later, in the absence of applied adult directives and/or effective monitoring of potentially destructive behaviors.

Ethological theories have also considered aggression to be innate in origin. According to this view, interspecies (i.e., between species) aggression in humans and animals is a biological response possessing natural adaptive-survival value. Intraspecies (i.e., within species) aggression, in contrast, is maladaptive. Yet, while in most species intraspecies aggression has been curtailed by the development of evolutionary based inhibitory mechanisms (which limit the potential destruction of the species), comparable inhibitions have not characterized human evolution; man's capacity for faceless aggression, which has evolved in the absence of proper inhibitory safeguards, is cited as evidence that the human ascent up the evolutionary scale has been incongruous and nonadaptive.

The ethological position offers scant optimism for other than partial subordination and control of human aggression.

In accord with psychoanalytic proposals, ethologists advocate the employment of catharsis and sublimation as suggested safeguards against the expression of unbridled aggression. In addition, Lorenz (1966) has suggested the need to curtail aggression through the promotion of personal acquaintance and bonds of friendship among individuals of different ideology and national affiliation. However, Lorenz notes that the development of environmentally induced friendship bonds, while a necessary short-range step, would not prove sufficient in curtailing aggression over time without the emergence of some new instinctually based inhibitory mechanism.

THE LEARNING OF AGGRESSION

Psychologists concerned with the development of aggression in children have proposed alternative views of the origins of aggression. From studies which have focused on the identification of specific conditions leading to the acquisition and performance of aggressive responses a large body of research data has accumulated which supports the notion that aggression is a learned rather than innate response. These findings emphasize that the conditions responsible for the instigation, learning, and maintenance of aggressive responses are environmentally determined, a conclusion which supports the belief that environmental intervention can be an effective means of control, as well as a source for the acquisition of behavioral alternatives to aggression.

One of the most fruitful research approaches to the study of aggression in children has been directed by Bandura and his associates (Bandura, 1960, 1963, 1965, 1967, 1971, 1973; Bandura & Houston, 1961; Bandura, Ross, & Ross, 1961, 1963; Bandura & Walters, 1959,

1963a, 1963b). From these studies, conducted over the last decade, a number of important findings surrounding the learning and performance of aggression, and correspondingly its control, have emerged. One important conclusion that has been drawn from this research is that aggression forms a complex behavioral mosaic that needs to be examined in terms of those components associated with its acquisition as distinguished from those conditions which appear instrumental to its performance. This distinction appears to be an especially important one, particularly in explaining why aggression is so easily acquired across all ages, as among both sexes, but is generally performed with fewer inhibitions among younger children and among boys, than in older children and girls.

The acquisition of an aggressive response is closely associated with observational learning principles; by viewing models performing aggressive actions, the child readily acquires similar behavioral responses. This finding may be offered as suggestive in explaining the relative ease and speed with which aggressive responses are acquired across different age groups, particularly among young children with restricted experiential backgrounds and limited conceptual capacities. For the young child, observational learning appears to be a particularly effective mechanism for the acquisition of aggressive response patterns, especially since the child learns how to be aggressive at a developmental period when perceptual learning is favored over conceptual learning.

While observational learning principles may account for the acquisition of aggressive behavior, differences in the performance of aggression across varied age groups, as well as among boys and girls, may be more readily explained in terms of experienced reinforcement and situational

sanctions surrounding the exhibition of the aggressive response. Performance is dependent upon the child's cognitive awareness of the consequences of behaving aggressively, as well as the child's exercise of deliberate choice in the display of such behavior. For the young child the consequences of behaving aggressively, are often not clearly defined by socialization agents or may be inconsistently applied, leading to the child's frequent misuse of aggression. Added to these difficulties, the young child is also restricted in his command of behavioral alternatives to aggression; the relative absence of other high amplitude behavioral alternatives to aggression may prohibit the adoption of more conciliatory behavior patterns.

Among boys and girls differences in the frequency of performed aggression, as well as its structural expression (i.e., physical versus verbal aggression), reflect disparate cultural expectations and applied sanctions surrounding the performance of aggression. Among boys, cultural sanctions in support of physical aggression are quite prominent. On a behavioral level, aggressive responses are generally supported or encouraged. For girls, however, cultural expectations for the performance of aggressive acts and reinforcement surrounding such activity are more circumspect. While girls are discouraged from exhibiting various forms of physical aggression, they are permitted to display verbal or indirect forms of aggression (e.g., gossip, tattling).

Differences in the frequency and style of aggression displayed by boys and girls are of particular interest, since they highlight the role and authority of cultural conditioning and social sanctions in the performance and control of aggression. These factors, traditionally, have received less attention as explanatory concepts in the development of aggression than the empirical evidence warrants. Unfortunately, socio-cultural conditions have assumed subsidiary status to biological factors which have emphasized sex differences in general activity level and endocrine functioning as causative elements in the development of aggression. However, there is increasing evidence which suggests the need to revise our assessment of these conditions in the development and control of aggression.

From anthropological studies, such as Mead's (1950) historical account of *Sex and Temperament in Three Primitive Societies*, we have learned that culture, rather than gender, determines which behaviors will be acquired and performed by men and women, respectively. From these studies of geographically isolated tribal units it was found that the performance of aggression and other behaviors, sex-typed within our culture, may be performed by either sex along lines which contrast with those which incorporate our standards of masculinity and femininity. Among the Arapesh, Mead found that both sexes exhibit behavior which resembles our concept of femininity, while among the Mundugamor both men and women demonstrate behavior patterns, including the extensive employment of aggressive, competitive, and hostile-related actions, which approximate our concept of the masculine image. In contrast, the Tchambuli exhibit a form of role reversal, relative to our sex-role standards, in which the females display "masculine" and the males perform "feminine" behavior patterns.

Ascription to biological explanations of aggression founded upon endocrinological origins, also requires revision. Traditionally, it has been argued that differences in the secretion of androgen (the hormone responsible for the production of testosterone in males) and estrogen (the hormone

associated with the production of progesterone in females) are responsible for the occurence of aggression and sexuality in males and females. However, recent evidence indicates that both boys and girls secrete androgen and estrogen prior to puberty. Moreover, in both sexes the secretion of these hormones, previous to the onset of adolescence, appears too negligible to account for alleged differences in aggression particularly since behavioral differences in aggression among the sexes become prominent long before the child reaches puberty (Rossi, 1974). Correspondingly, it appears reasonable to conclude that cultural conditioning and applied social sanctions form two critical dimensions in the development of aggression.

Children's exposure to aggressive models has also been associated with behavioral consequences supplementing those involved in the learning of a new response pattern. Bandura and Walters (1963) have suggested that the child's observation of aggressive models may be closely tied to several alternative outcomes. Once such consequence is the production of an inhibitory (i.e., suppressing) or, alternatively, a disinhibitory (i.e., releasing) effect upon behavior. In this context, previously acquired aggressive responses, similar to those observed by the child, are either unexpressed or, conversely, are performed in accord with the child's observation of the modeled behavior. Indeed, the model's performance of aggression may function as either a positive or negative sanction for the child's imitation of displayed response patterns. Extending these observations, Bandura and Walters (1963b) also report an eliciting effect associated with aggressive modeling. In this situation exposure to a model may produce aggressive responses not previously subject to normative restraint or control; exposure to violence serves to stimulate similar responses toward expression (i.e., matching of behavior) as a function of the child's observation of related behavior in others. This latter effect was described by Redl and Wineman (1957) in highly aggressive delinquent boys. In these youngsters, Redl and Wineman refer to this response pattern as illustrative of behavioral contagion; they report that among individuals with poorly defined or deficient ego controls there is often a rapid infectious spreading of high amplitude response patterns, such as aggression, from one individual to another without apparent restraint or the exercise of effective monitoring through the implementation of internal control devices. As Redl and Wineman suggest from their observations, "Sometimes the mere visualization of acted-out behavior itself becomes the stimulus that gives intensity to a previously dormant urge or throws the ego's watchfulness overboard, or does both." (1957: 87) This observation, however, is certainly not restricted to the behavior of youngsters displaying poor impulse controls. In nondelinquent children, exposure to aggressive film content (e.g., *The Three Stooges*) is often accompanied or followed by comparable slapstick behavior of an aggressive nature. Similarly, adults have been observed in naturalistic and laboratory settings to demonstrate readily intense emotional reactions, many of which are behaviorally expressed through aggression, upon exposure to real or simulated violence. In sum, as reported by Bandura (1973), modeling influences can function as teachers, instigators, inhibitors, disinhibitors, stimulus enhancers, and emotion arousers of aggression. These eliciting conditions, combined with external sanctions or reinforcement, foster the enactment of aggressive behavior in children and adults.

THE PERFORMANCE OF AGGRESSION

As reported in the preceding section, children are frequently exposed to a variety of modeling influences leading to the acquisition of aggressive response patterns which become part of their behavioral repertoire. These acquired response patterns, however, are generally not performed as often, or at all ages, or among both sexes, at frequency levels comparable to the person's experienced observation of aggressive modeling. Obviously, exposure to aggressive models is a necessary condition for the learning of aggression, but not a sufficient cause for its performance. This observation suggests that those conditions associated with the learning of aggression differ from those principles affecting its performance. Partial confirmation of this distinction is offered by Bandura (1965, 1973). He states that the learning of an aggressive response is most closely associated with the contextual framework within which such responses are observed. For example, some models, viewed in terms of their similarity to the observer, or through their exercise of power, status, or control over desirable resources, are more likely to be imitated than models who do not possess these attributes. The performance or maintenance of aggressive behavior, in contrast, appears to be tied to reinforcement which the child experiences following the exhibition of aggressive behavioral choices (Becker, Thomas, & Carnine, 1969). According to Bandura, "Aggressive modes of response, . . . can be induced, eliminated, and reinstated by altering the effects they produce." (1973: 230)

Consequences associated with the performance of aggressive behavior may be either positive (i.e., rewarding) or negative (i.e., punishing). These effects, however, need be viewed as separate from each other since reward serves to enhance the performance of aggression, while punishment is generally associated with somewhat more complex and less predictable outcomes. Several studies which support this conclusion may be cited. Lovaas (1961) in an earlier study, trained children to exhibit verbal aggression against dolls (e.g., "bad doll," "doll should be spanked"), demonstrating that such training can result in significant increases in verbal and physical aggression. In a series of studies conducted by Walters and his associates (Cowan & Walters, 1963; Hops & Walters, 1963; Walters & Brown, 1963) comparable findings were obtained. Children reinforced for hitting a large inflated plastic doll were found to exhibit significant increases in aggression under a variety of experimentally imposed schedules of reinforcement. In one such study (Walters & Brown, 1963), the effects of reinforcement were examined in terms of the child's subsequent peer interactions. It was found that children intermittently reinforced for aggression directed toward the doll demonstrated significant transfer of displayed aggression to other children in a subsequently encountered competitive game situation.

In the natural environment the child finds equivalent support for the performance of aggressive behavior. This support, it may be noted, supplements the child's experience of observational learning opportunities discussed earlier. Reinforcement contingencies in the child's environment are established by parents and peers (Bandura & Walters, 1959; Cohen, 1971). Initially, through interactions with parents, the child may observe a variety of aggressive responses directed toward other adults and children; these observations, as they apply to children, may reflect interpersonal standards for behavior or disciplinary practices employed by the parent

in relation to siblings or the child. In the former situation, as reported by Bandura and Walters (1959) in their study of adolescent boys, parents of highly aggressive children, while often nonpermissive of aggression directed toward family members, may actively condone and encourage aggressive behavior outside the home. Among younger children, as Sears, Maccoby and Levin (1957) suggest, the parent in the role of disciplinarian, often conveys to the child this message. However, the parent in his/her direct relations with the child, may at the same time vitiate his/her effectiveness in the parental role by attempting to control the child's aggression by acting in a manner contradictory to parental aspirations regarding the child's behavior. To illustrate, as disciplinarian, the aggressive-punishing parent may serve as a living model for the learning of aggression at the same time the parent may be attempting to control or monitor aggression in the child. Child rearing practices characterized by the parents' use of aggression, unfortunately, not only aid in the acquisition of aggressive responses, but may also produce unwanted side effects. These subsidiary effects may, in turn directly or indirectly reinforce the performance of aggression. Physical punishment, for example, may motivate the child to behave aggressively by generating anger or anxiety. Correspondingly, the parents' action may foster the formation of an anger-aggression, emotional-behavioral tie which closely approximates observations of parental behavior directed toward the child. Moreover, a parent's use of corporal punishment may underscore its legitimacy as a viable means of conflict resolution. The parent who employs physical punishment as a primary strategy of child management sanctions the use of aggression (by virtue of his/her control over the child) as a preferred mode of social interaction in situations where the child (as the parent in parent–child relations) is stronger or bigger than an adversary. Finally, as the parent resorts to the use of aggression in conflict situations, this choice of action may negate the child's efforts at seeking alternative means (e.g., cooperation, compromise, conciliation) of conflict resolution.

Peers, like parents, exert a significant influence over the child's acquisition and performance of aggression. In a study conducted by Patterson, Littman and Bricker (1967) among nursery school children, patterns of aggressive peer interactions and their consequences were carefully recorded. In viewing these observations from a dyadic perspective, in which the interactions of the victim and the aggressor are analyzed, a number of interesting findings emerged. Among them was that the aggressor, as well as the victim of aggression, is affected by the frequency, form of attack, and response to aggression displayed in aggressor–victim interactions. Among passive children, who were often victimized, the effectiveness of their counteraggressive reaction was highly predictive of subsequent aggressor–victim interations; those children who exhibited successful counterattacks were found to be less often aggressed against in subsequent aggressive episodes. Moreover, in the course of such transactions both passive and moderately aggressive youngsters demonstrated significant increases in aggression. As concluded by the authors, "There is little doubt that the contingencies provided by the nursery school have a significant effect upon assertive-aggressive behaviors for some passive and moderately passive children." (Patterson, Littman & Bricker: 23) As was evident from this study, peer interactions may have substantial influence in enhancing children's per-

formance of aggressive behavior as a function of the quality, effectiveness, and consequences of such relations.

The role of peers in the development of aggression is evident among older as well as nursery school children. Specifically, peers may provide motivational impetus, models for imitative learning, opportunities for the rehearsal of acquired responses, and positive reinforcement in support of aggression (Jenkins, 1961; Clausen & Williams, 1963; Campbell, 1964; McCandless, 1969; Cohen, 1971a). In one related study conducted among elementary school boys (Cohen, 1971b), the relative significance of parents, teachers, and peers as modeling and normative influences in the development of aggression was compared. It was found that peers above all other primary socialization sources considered were most frequently associated with the child's exposure to aggressive models and reinforcement for aggression.

THE MODIFICATION OF AGGRESSION

Can the course of children's aggression be altered? While research leading to the control of aggression has proceeded less rapidly than the study of conditions enhancing aggression, recent evidence supports the belief that aggression, viewed as an acquired response, is subject to modification. The implementation of this goal, however, is multifaceted, requiring both environmental and behaviorally oriented approaches to intervention.

Environmental intervention

The concept of environmental intervention asks what changes in the life circumstances (viz., aggression-inducing experiences) affecting children need be modified in order to delimit learning opportunities and performance factors associated with the display of aggression. As a general solution it may be proposed that as aggression becomes a less pervasive occurrence in the child's surroundings, its behavioral display should diminish in frequency and likelihood of expression.

Can aggression be accountable to environmental controls? While it is evident that restrictions imposed upon the widespread portrayal of violence may be associated with a reduction of aggression, a complete prohibition of aggression is probably unattainable and perhaps is undesirable. Yet current evidence suggests that aggression may be altered through the imposition of select environmental controls. Research studies (Bogart, 1972; Comstock, 1972; Liebert, Neale & Davidson, 1973) surveying the influence of mass media upon children's behavior clearly indicate that the aggression-inducing effects of repeated exposure to violence can be curtailed through the reduction and modification of viewed film content. Moreover, the present evidence suggests that as we reverse or more properly monitor conditions instrumental in the acquisition and particularly the performance of aggression, the likelihood of aggression serving as a dominant response to conflict resolution should decrease in prominence. Empirical evidence in support of this proposal is provided by several research findings. In an investigation of children's response to violence conducted by Drabman and Thomas (1973) it was found that children who viewed an aggressive cowboy film were less likely to summon help in response to observed conflict involving others. Moreover, children viewing the aggressive film appeared to tolerate all but the most violent physical aggression and

destruction by others before seeking help. In a related study, Steuer, Applefield and Smith (1971) examined the effects of repeated exposure to aggressive film content over a period of eleven days. They found that children who viewed aggressive television programs were significantly more aggressive in interpersonal relations than subjects who viewed nonaggressive programs. These studies independently demonstrate the harmful effects of exposure to excessive violence.

As reviewed in the preceding discussion, as the child bears witness to aggressive models, he/she acquires similar responses, congruent with our knowledge of the effects of observational learning upon behavioral adoption. In terms of performance, where aggressive responses are already part of the child's existing behavioral repertoire, research studies further indicate that continued exposure to violence can lower inhibitions prohibiting aggression and may even elicit aggressive behavior. In summarizing studies of the aggressive-inducing effects of exposure to violence Berkowitz (1973) reports that aggression is enhanced under conditions where violence is perceived as justified, where the aggressor does not anticipate being punished for his/her actions, when strong inhibitions against aggression are not evoked, and where the target of aggression is seen as bearing resemblance to the observed object of aggression. These findings indicate a need to limit our copious provision of aggressive models for behavioral adoption. Moreover, they suggest that rather than reducing aggression, exposure to violence increases the probability that the child will behave in a comparable manner. Observed violence demonstrates how aggression may be performed, as well as provides sanctions which reinforce the view that aggression, performed under circumstances described above, is morally permissible.

Behavioral intervention

The control of aggression mandates behavioral as well as environmental approaches to intervention. Indeed, the modification of children's aggression needs to be prefaced by the implementation of behaviorally oriented solutions, supplementing changes in the child's environment.

Viewed from a behavioral perspective, several solutions to the modification of children's aggression may be proposed. One prerequisite to solution, as indicated earlier in this discussion, is the need to teach children to distinguish more clearly from among competing response classes (e.g., competition, dominance, assertion) those forms of aggression or derivatives thereof that are permissible from those behaviors that are not. Supplementing this concern, the child's performance of aggression needs also to be tempered by the application of uniform behavioral standards governing the form and expression of his/her anger. For example, social agents need to decide whether some forms of aggression (e.g., verbal aggression) shall be accepted, while alternative responses (e.g., physical aggression) are to be prohibited. Similarly, it needs to be decided whether aggression shall be sanctioned in some situations but prohibited or punished in others. These and related issues require resolution prior to the implementation of effective behavioral controls.

Currently, while some forms of aggression (e.g., assertive behavior) are encouraged, other response classes (e.g., unprovoked physical aggression) appear to warrant restraint. Uncontrolled aggression can prove harmful or injurious to others.

Correspondingly, from an instructional perspective the behavioral and social consequences of aggression need to be more clearly taught to children. Contrary to current practice, the socialization of children's aggression needs to be redefined in many cases in order to assist the child in recognizing that, aside from its immediate gains, aggression may not only alienate others in terms of its social consequences but also is likely to lead to greater restraint or confinement of the aggressor.

Complementing instructional objectives, the effective control of aggression will also require the encouragement of prosocial behaviors, allowing for social consequences antithetical to those usually associated with the child's expression of anger. As children are encouraged to esteem others, aggression should become a less likely behavioral occurrence (Staub, 1971). Similarly, through the fostering of affiliative motives in social interaction, with correspondingly diminished support for attempted violation of social bonds through the exercise of aggression, violence should prove a less likely behavioral outcome.

Complementing the fostering of social bonds, efforts directed toward the modification of aggression need to focus on assisting children in recognizing behavioral alternatives to conflict resolution (Sherif & Sherif, 1969). From the literature on aggression two proposals directed toward this goal may be suggested. First, it appears imperative that children be provided with modeling opportunities that allow for the acquisition and performance of behavioral alternatives to aggression. Second, we need to provide more viable support, in the form of social sanctions and positive reinforcement, for the child's employment of behavioral alternatives to aggression.

The exercise of aggression is neither an indigenous nor capricious characteristic of human nature. Aggression is a behavior which can, with proper guidance, come under the domain of social control and the long range aspirations of society.

REFERENCES

Bandura, A. Relationship of family patterns to child behavior disorders. Stanford University, Research Grant M-1734, United States Public Health, Progress Report, 1960.

Bandura, A. Behavior theory and identification learning. *American Journal of Orthopsychiatry,* 1963, **33,** 591-601.

Bandura, A. Influence of model's reinforcement contingencies on the acquisition of imitative responses. *Journal of Personality and Social Psychology,* 1965, **1,** 589-595.

Bandura, A. Modeling processes and aggression in children. In *The young child: reviews of research.* Washington, D.C.: National Association for the Education of Young Children, 1967.

Bandura. A. Analysis of modeling processes. In A. Bandura (ed.), *Psychological modeling.* Chicago: Aldine, 1971.

Bandura, A. Social learning theory of aggression. In J. F. Knutson (ed.), *The control of aggression.* Chicago: Aldine, 1973.

Bandura, A., & Huston, A. C. Identification as a process of incidental learning. *Journal of Abnormal and Social Psychology,* 1961, **63,** 311-318.

Bandura, A.; Ross, D.; & Ross, S. A. Transmission of aggression through imitation of aggressive models. *Journal of Abnormal and Social Psychology,* 1961, **63,** 575-582.

Bandura, A.; Ross, D.; & Ross, S. A. Imitation of film-mediated aggressive models. *Journal of Abnormal and Social Psychology,* 1963, **66,** 3-11.

Bandura, A., & Walters R. H. *Adolescent aggression.* New York: Ronald Press, 1959.

Bandura, A., & Walters, R. H. *Social learning and personality theory.* New York: Holt, Rinehart and Winston, 1963 (a).

Bandura, A., and Walters, R. H. Aggression. In *National Society for the Study of Education 62nd yearbook.* Part I. *Child Psy-*

chology. Chicago: The National Society for the Study of Education, 1963 (b).

Becker, W. C.; Thomas, D. R.; & Carnine, D. *Reducing behavior problems: An operant guide for teachers.* Urbana, Ill.: National Laboratory on Early Childhood Education, 1969.

Berkowitz, L. Control of aggression. In B. M. Caldwell & H. N. Ricciuti (eds.), *Review of child development research.* Vol. 3. Chicago: University of Chicago Press, 1973.

Bogart, L. "Warning, the surgeon general has determined that TV violence is dangerous to your child's mental health." *Public Opinion Quarterly,* 1972, **36,** 491-521.

Campbell, J. D. Peer relations in childhood. In M. L. Hoffman & L. W. Hoffman (eds.), *Review of child development research.* Vol. I. New York: Russell Sage Foundation, 1964.

Clausen, J. A., & Williams, J. R. Sociological correlates of child behavior. In *National Society for the Study of Education 62nd yearbook.* Part I. Chicago: National Society for the Study of Education, 1963.

Comstock, G. *Television violence: Where the surgeon general's study leads.* Santa Monica, Cal.: The Rand Corporation, 1972.

Cowan, P. A., & Walters, R. H. Studies of reinforcement of aggression. I. Effects of scheduling. *Child Development,* 1963, **34,** 543-551.

Cohen, S. The development of aggression. *Review of Educational Research,* 1971, **41,** 71-85 (a).

Cohen, S. Peers as modeling and normative influences in the development of aggression. *Psychological Reports,* 1971, **28,** 995-998 (b).

Cohen, S. *Social and personality development in childhood.* New York: The Macmillan Company, 1976.

Drabman, R. S., & Thomas, M. H. Does media violence increase children's toleration of real life aggression? *Developmental Psychology,* 1974. **10,** 418-421.

Freud, S. *Beyond the pleasure principle.* New York: Bantam Books, 1959.

Hicks, D. J. Imitation and retention of film-mediated aggressive peers and adult models. *Journal of Personality and Social Psychology,* 1965, **2,** 97-100.

Hops, H., & Walters, R. H. Studies on reinforcement of aggression. II. Effects of emotionally arousing antecedent conditions. *Child Development,* 1963, **34,** 553-562.

Jenkins, R. L. Delinquency as failure and delinquency as attainment. In P. T. Hountras (ed.), *Mental hygiene.* Columbus, Ohio: Charles Merrill, 1961.

Liebert, R. M.; Neale, J. M.; & Davidson, E. S. *The early window: Effects of television on children and youth.* Elmsford, N. Y.: Pergamon Press, 1973.

Lorenz, K. *On aggression.* New York: Harcourt Brace Jovanovich, 1966.

Lovaas, O. I. Effect of exposure to symbolic aggression on aggressive behavior. *Child Development,* 1961, **32,** 37-44.

McCandless, R. R. Childhood socialization. In D. A. Goslin (ed.), *Handbook of socialization theory and research.* Chicago: Rand McNally, 1969.

Mead, M. *Sex and temperament in three primitive societies.* New York: Dell, 1969.

Patterson, G. R.; Littman, R. A.; & Bricker, W. Assertive behavior in children. A step toward a theory of aggression. *Monographs of the Society for Research in Child Development,* 1967, **32,** (113, No. 5).

Redl, F., & Wineman, D. *The aggressive child.* New York: Free Press, 1957.

Rossi, A. S. The missing body in sociology: Closing the gap between physiology and sociology. Paper presented at the Eastern Sociological Society meeting, Philadelphia, 1974.

Sears, R. R.; Maccoby, E. E.; & Lewin, H. *Patterns of child rearing.* New York: Harper & Row, 1957.

Sherif, M., & Sherif, C. S. *Social Psychology.* New York: Harper & Row, 1969.

Staub, E. The learning and unlearning of aggression: The role of anxiety, empathy, and prosocial values. In J. L. Singer (ed.), *The control of aggression and violence.* New York: Academic Press, 1971.

Steuer, F. B.; Applefield, J. M.; & Smith, R. Televised aggression and the interpersonal aggression of preschool children. *Journal of Experimental Child Psychology,* 1971, **11,** 442-447.

Walters, R. H. On the high-magnitude theory of aggression. *Child Development,* 1964, **35,** 303-304.

Walters, R. H., & Brown, M. Studies of reinforcement of aggression, III: Transfer of responses to an interpersonal situation. *Child Development,* 1963, **34,** 563-571.

18.

Susanne Sandidge and Seymour J. Friedland

SEX-ROLE-TAKING AND AGGRESSIVE BEHAVIOR IN CHILDREN

INTRODUCTION

Sarbin (1968), in discussing role expectations and role enactment, states, "In role enactment an individual is expected to 'behave in particular ways' in the sense that the behavior is predictable; more important however . . . in the sense that others believe he ought to do so" (1968: 501). It is quite early in development that the "ought" aspect of role determined behavior is apparent, and particularly in respect to sex-related behaviors. (Kagan, 1964). However, what is valuable about a role approach is the proposition that development includes not only a knowledge about what is appropriate for one's own behavior but also what is appropriate for individuals occupying other social positions and categories with which one interacts. A method of explicating such knowledge is that of role-taking. "Role-taking in its most general form is a process of looking at or anticipating another's behavior by viewing it in the context of a role imputed to that other (Turner, 1966: 152)." A role-taking task can then demonstrate knowledge of role expectations in young children and the effects of role

prescriptions on responses in particular social situations.

The present study looks at the role-taking process with respect to aggressive behavior and sex roles. There are many studies that have been concerned with comparing differences in aggression between the two sexes. Oetzel (1966), in summarizing the literature on sex differences in aggression, indicated that in forty-four of fifty-three studies examined males were found to have higher aggression scores. There have been numerous theories that have attempted to explain this relationship between sex-role development and aggressive behavior (see Bronfenbrenner, 1960). In general, the emphasis is on how a child comes to function within the expectations for aggressive behavior held for his sex or the process of learning whereby certain aggressive behaviors are reinforced for members of one sex but not for another. Our interest in the present study is the degree to which children are sensitive to prescriptions for aggressive behaviors for members of the opposite sex, as indicated by the way in which these prescriptions determine their responses in a social situation. It is hypothesized that children quite early have such a sensitivity to cross-sex expectations, and therefore that both boys and girls will display more aggressive responses when taking the role of a boy; and further, that more aggressive behavior will be shown when the role partner is a boy. Finally, it is expected that the strong influence of role-taking should

Source: *Journal of Genetic Psychology*, 1975, **126**, 227-231. This paper was presented at the Society for Research in Child Development Meetings, Philadelphia, March 1973. It is based on a thesis submitted by the first author to Tufts University in partial fulfillment of requirements for the Master's degree. The authors wish to extend their thanks to Drs. Evelyn Pitcher and Ethan Pollack for their help.

minimize the effect of sex differences between subjects.

METHOD

Subjects

Subjects were twenty boys and twenty girls from a housing project in Boston. All subjects were white and were nine or 10 years old. Most came from families on welfare and could thus be designated as of low socioeconomic class. These children were used because of the numerous findings indicating that lower-class children conform more closely to traditional sex-role standards than do middle-class children. Children over the age of eight were used because of the expectation that such children would have relatively developed role-taking skills (Flavell, 1968).

Materials and procedure

Each subject was shown nineteen cards, each containing a schematic cartoon. Each card involved two major figures in a particular situation. One figure is shown speaking; this figure is termed the "Object Figure." There is a second figure for whom the subject must make a response, termed the "Identification Figure."

The nineteen cards included four initial warm-up cards and fifteen test cards. Scoring was based only on the fifteen test cards. For each card there was a specific statement, aggressive in content, attributed to the Object Figure. A pilot study provided the means for assessing the effectiveness of the content of most of these statements. Examples of statements are as follows: "I ought to sock you for that," "You're a chicken," "What a dummy you are." The subject was required to respond as the Identification Figure would respond to the statement provided. For half of the subjects the Object Figure was male, for half female. For half of each of these groups

the Identification Figure was male, and for half female. Thus, there were eight groups divided on the basis of sex of subject, sex of Object Figure, and sex of Identification Figure.

Each child was tested individually. Instructions, provided by a prerecorded tape, were as follows:

We're going to show you some pictures of two kids. Something is happening between them. I'll tell you what one of them is saying and you tell us what the other one is saying.

A taped male voice was used for those groups for which the Object Figure was a boy, and a taped female voice was used for groups for which the Object Figure was a girl. The four warm-up cards, which had been found in a pilot study to elicit relatively neutral responses, were given first, one at a time. The aggressive statement for each card was given, and the tape was stopped between cards to allow the subject time to respond. If the subject's response was unclear or perfunctory, he was asked, "Does he say anything else?" This procedure was used for all the cards.

At the end of the testing each subject was allowed to take a candy bar from a large bag of candy.

To make for a finer distinction between responses, two categories similar to those used by Sears, Rau, and Alpert (1965) were used. That is, each response was scored as either an antisocial aggression response or as a neutral-prosocial aggression response. These categories were defined as follows:

a. Antisocial aggression—Any action or verbal response indicating overt destructive behavior or wishes toward the other in the sense of physical harm or any statement that was provocative in the sense of making a challenge to the other or indicating refusal to compromise or resolve differences.

b. Neutral-Prosocial aggression—Highly

subtle and subdued expression of aggression with obvious intent not to escalate aggression; responses that indicated no aggression or were wholly unclear as to the presence of aggression.

A subject's score was the number of statements scored as antisocial aggression. Thus, a subject's score could range from zero to fifteen. The reliability of scoring was examined by having a second judge score the protocol of a subject, selected randomly, in each condition. Interrater agreement of 87% was found.

RESULTS

Results were analyzed by means of a $2 \times 2 \times 2$ analysis of variance, with the following variables: sex of Object Figure, sex of Identification Figure, and sex of subject.

1. Sex of Identification Figure was found to be significant ($F=13.41$, $df=1$, $p<.01$). This finding supported the hypothesis that subjects would give significantly more antisocial aggression responses for boy Identification Figures than for girl Identification Figures (see Table 18.1 for specific means).

2. Sex of Object Figure reached only the .06 level of confidence. Though not significant the means were in the direction predicted. That is, subjects produced more antisocial aggression responses directed toward boy figures than toward girl figures.

3. A significant interaction was found for Identification Figure × Object Figure ($F=4.52$, $df=1$, $p<.05$). Means were tested by the Duncan Multiple-Range Test

(Duncan, 1966). The boy Object Figure/boy Identification Figure combination was found to elicit greater aggressive response than any other. None of the other means differed significantly from each other.

4. No significant difference was found for sex of subject.

Results thus supported the hypothesis that subjects would give more antisocial aggression responses for boy Identification Figures than for girl Identification Figures. The hypothesis that subjects would give more antisocial aggression responses in conditions showing boy Object Figures was confirmed, but only at the .06 confidence level. The boy Object Figure/boy Identification Figure condition was found to elicit significantly more aggression than any other condition.

DISCUSSION

The results of this study support the proposition that children have good knowledge early of the behaviors associated with roles other than their own, and that such knowledge can determine the responses they give in social situations. Subjects of both sexes appeared to share common expectations in regard to sex-appropriate behavior.

Particularly important was the absence of significant differences between male and female subjects for responses categorized as antisocial aggression, along with the finding that all subjects manifested more of such aggressive responses when taking the role of a boy. These results indicate the limitations of viewing

TABLE 18.1. Mean Scores on Antisocial Aggression

Object and Identification Figures	Boys Condition	Boys Mean	Girls Condition	Girls Mean	Combined Mean
Boy object/boy identification	I	10.0	V	10.0	10.0
Boy object/girl identification	II	3.6	VI	6.6	5.1
Girl object/boy identification	III	7.0	VII	7.6	7.3
Girl object/girl identification	IV	6.2	VIII	5.8	6.0

aggression purely in terms of the gender of a person without regard to the role being enacted. Adherence to the expectations associated with a particular role seem to be strong even in young children.

It has already been noted that a particular subject population was used in this study because of its strong adherence to traditional sex-role standards. Findings with other groups might differ from those obtained in this study. Secondly, further study is necessary to examine whether similar results would be obtained with measures based on overt actions rather than purely verbal responses. However, the effectiveness of the role-taking task used indicates a valuable procedure for examining many of the differences attributable to sex.

REFERENCES

Bronfenbrenner, U. Freudian theories of identification and their derivatives. *Child Development,* 1960, **31,** 15-40.

Duncan, D. B. Multiple-range and multiple-F tests. *Biometrics,* 1966, **11,** 41-58.

Flavell, J. H. *The development of role-taking and communication skills in children.* New York: John Wiley and Sons, 1968.

Kagan, J. Acquisition and significance of sex typing and sex role identity. In M. Hoffman & L. Hoffman (eds.), *Review of child development research.* New York: Russell Sage Foundation, 1964.

Oetzel, R. M. Classified summary of research sex differences. In E. E. Maccoby (ed.), *The development of sex differences.* Stanford, Cal.: Stanford University Press, 1966.

Sarbin, T. Role theory. In G. Lindzey & E. Aronson (eds.), *The handbook of social psychology, Vol. I.* Reading, Mass.: Addison-Wesley, 1968.

Sears, R. R., Rau, L., & Alpert R. Identifications and child rearing. Stanford, Cal.: Stanford University Press, 1965.

Turner, R. Role-taking, role standpoint, and reference group behavior. In B. Biddle & E. Thomas (eds.), *Role theory: Concepts and research.* New York: John Wiley and Sons, 1966.

C. SEX-ROLE DEVELOPMENT

19.

Janet S. Chafetz

THE BRINGING-UP OF DICK AND JANE

A baby is born knowing nothing, but full of potential. The process by which an individual becomes a creature of society, a socialized human being reflecting culturally defined roles and norms, is complex and as yet imperfectly understood. It is evident, however, that most individuals eventually reflect societal definitions more

Source: Janet S. Chafetz. *Masculine/Feminine or Human?* Itasca, Ill.: F. E. Peacock, 1974. Chapter 3.

or less well; most males born and raised in America will someday think and behave like other American males in many important ways and not, for instance, like their Japanese counterparts. Through the socialization process humans come to more or less completely internalize the roles, norms, and values appropriate to the culture and subculture within which they function. Cultural definitions become personal definitions of propriety, normality, and worthiness. Because internalization of cultural definitions is less than total for most people, social control mechanisms are brought to bear by some individuals and social groups to encourage others to conform to expectations. Control mechanisms range from such severe forms as physical punishment inflicted by the state (imprisonment and even execution), to social ostracism or unwillingness to hire job applicants, to such mild forms as ridicule.

Underlying both the socialization process and the concomitant use of social controls is the assumption that people learn to conform by the application of sanctions. Sanctions may be positive, in which case they are known as "rewards," or negative, when they are known as "punishments." Generally, people learn more completely and retain things longer when rewards rather than punishments are employed. By their nature, however, social control mechanisms utilize largely negative sanctions, and therefore they function as relatively ineffective teaching techniques. The socialization process itself is typically comprised of a mixture of both types of sanctions. The proportion of rewards to punishments during this process varies according to such factors as ethnic subculture and social class, as well as the personalities of the individuals involved. Thus the extent to which individuals will internalize social norms and roles varies, although the fact that rewards are normally utilized to some extent helps to ensure substantial success for the process.

Human interaction is crucial to the process of personality development. A newborn infant has no concept of self. By the time a child enters school, it has begun to develop a fairly coherent picture of who it is and what the appropriate behaviors are for that identity. The process of developing this picture is probably never-ending, but by adulthood it is usually subject to relatively less change than it was earlier.

The classic explanation for how an individual's identity emerges is that offered by the symbolic interactionists, dating back a half century or more to George Herbert Mead (1934) and Charles H. Cooley (1909), among others. Through interaction with "significant others," primarily parents and, later, peer groups, children come to form an idea of self consisting of "three principal elements: the imagination of our appearance to the other person; the imagination of his judgment of that appearance, and some sort of self-feeling such as pride or mortification" (Cooley, 1909: 152). Cooley called this the "looking glass self." In developing this approach further, Mead emphasized the key role of language in the interaction process. He believes children first develop a sense of "I," namely, a basic awareness of self as actor and organism. Later the "me" develops, which consists of an understanding and internalization of how others perceive the child. The "me" is the social component of the personality; it entails the internalization of roles, norms, and values presented by society and is in many ways similar to Freud's superego. It is learned by the child through role-playing—taking the role of the other in negotiating human interactions. This is only possible through the manipulation of symbols, that is, language. In this way the child eventually learns the organized attitudes and expectations of larger social groupings, called by Mead "the generalized other." Stated in its simplest form, children learn who they are and internalize what they are expected to be by trying to put themselves in the place of others and experience themselves as others perceive them. This is possible only through the use of symbolic communication.

Two other related concepts are relevant

to a discussion of the socialization process. W. I. Thomas's (1923) renowned concept of the "definition of the situation" entails recognition of the fact that if human beings define a situation as real, then, regardless of objective reality, the fact of defining it in that way has real social consequences. If, for instance, a boy is told that "boys are athletic," regardless of the truth of this assertion, it will have a real impact on that child's behavior and expectations of himself. Robert K. Merton (1957) was essentially noting the same phenomenon when he developed the notion of the "self-fulfilling (or defeating) prophecy." Merton's concept applies to those cases where the act of predicting something helps to ensure that the phenomenon in question will (or will not) occur. Thus, for instance, the girl who is told she will never be strong (because girls aren't) will probably take no steps by which she could become strong. When later she lacks strength, a self-fulfilling prophecy will have been realized.

THE CAPTIVE AUDIENCE: CHILDHOOD

The first crucial question of the parents of a newborn baby is "What is it? a boy or a girl?" Only later will they be concerned with any other attribute of the infant, even its physical condition; the first priority is to establish its gender. Indeed, almost immediately, gender identity is permanently stamped on the child by the name it is given.

When the proud new father lifts his infant he might jostle it just a little if it's a boy; he will pet and cuddle it if it is a girl. In the months that follow mother will speak to the infant more if it happens to be female—and later everyone will wonder why it is that young girls show greater linguistic skills than boys (Lewis, 1972:

54). Father will continue to play a bit rough with the infant if the child is male. Both parents will discourage a male toddler from "clinging"—but not his sister. Indeed, recent research shows that up to six months of age male infants receive more physical contact from their mothers than do female babies (probably because they value a male child more), while after that males are more quickly and totally discouraged from such contact than females (Lewis, 1972: 56). The parents will tell little Dick, but not little Jane, that "big boys don't cry." They will devote hours to combing *her* hair and putting decorations in it and will bedeck *her* with jewelry, but they will look with horror on *his* games with mother's lipstick or clothes. Jane will soon be attired in dresses and told not to get dirty and not to do anything that will let her "underpants show"; Dick will be in trousers with no such restrictions—and later everyone will say that girls are innately less physically coordinated and strong than boys. And so begins the life and training of these new human beings.

The description of the early treatment of infants can provide useful insights in terms of the concepts developed above. First, from birth the nature of the interaction between parents and children differs markedly according to the gender of the child. If, indeed, the interaction process is crucial to the development of a self-image, it is clear that those of males and females will eventually be quite different. The parents of the little girl relate to her as a breakable object to be carefully tended, protected, and beautified; the little boy's parents treat him as self-reliant, physically active, even "tough" and not very emotionally expressive. These images are undoubtedly learned by the children. In addition, they are verbally instructed and sanctioned for doing or refraining from certain things according to gender. Finally, these restrictions and encouragements serve to "define reality" for the children in self-fulfilling ways. If little Jane is assumed to be weak, in need of protection, and an ornamental thing, she will be clothed in apparel reflecting these attributes and informed not to do anything out of keeping with her attire. Unable to swing on the jungle gym and still live up to her parents' image of her and the strictures they impose, she will most certainly fail to develop her muscles; ultimately, she will indeed be weak, in need of protection, and engrossed in her own appearance.

In taking a closer look at the process by which young children are thought to internalize their gender-relevant sex roles, David Lynn's excellent short text *Parental and Sex Role Identification* (1969) is useful. . . .

Lynn begins by asserting that both male and female infants usually establish their initial and principal identification with the mother, an identification that neither gender ever loses entirely (pp. 21-23). This is predicated on the assumption, true in the majority of cases in this society, that the mother functions as the infant's chief caretaker. It is important to note that any change of that norm would invalidate this proposition. At any rate, having established this identity, the female child can continue it and, in so doing, learn the "appropriate" sex role behavior. To the extent that "identification" strongly entails imitation, young Jane need only copy her mother to be rewarded. In this way she quickly begins to internalize the feminine role behavior expected of her.

Little Dick, however, faces a serious problem. Given the relative absence of male figures during his waking hours, the male toddler is hard pressed to find out what he is supposed to do. Early in life his mother begins to sanction him negatively

for imitating many of her ways. In this society the father is absent so often the child cannot imitate him, and when he is present, he joins the mother in punishing the boy for being "too feminine." Indeed, he usually surpasses the mother in this, perhaps because of his own sex role insecurities and a resulting fear of homosexuality. The result is that where Jane identifies easily with her mother, Dick must identify with a cultural definition of masculinity that he pieces together from peers, media, a series of don'ts from his parents, and so on (Lynn, 1969: 23-26). In fact, according to Lynn, peers are more important in shaping the identity of males than females (p. 92). The boy finds out that "boys don't cry," "boys don't cling," and so on, but often on the basis of negative sanctions from parents and peers. Given the lesser efficacy of punishments compared to rewards in the socialization process, it is not surprising that males have greater difficulty establishing their sex-role identities than females. They also fail in this endeavor more frequently, are more anxious about it throughout their lives, and are more hostile toward the opposite sex (Lynn, 1969: 57-64).

The ramifications of this duality are everywhere. Male fear of and hostility toward homosexuality finds little parallel among females, nor does the hang-up of "proving one's masculinity." Girls are far less concerned about the label "tomboy" (and, in fact, often wear it with pride) than boys are about "sissy." Undoubtedly, too, there is a relationship between this phenomenon and the kinds of problems presented by school-aged boys.

There are other implications of the two rather radically different methods of early sex-role learning. Jane, it will be recalled, learns by imitation and positive reinforcement. Dick, on the other hand, has to make a mental effort to comprehend what he is supposed to be, and he more frequently receives negative sanctions. One result, according to Lynn, is that throughout their lives females rely more on affection, or demonstrate a "greater need for affiliation," than males. Males develop greater problem-solving abilities because of this early mental exercise. Moreover, they become more concerned with internalized moral standards than females, who in turn rely more on the opinions of others (Lynn, 1969, chap. 4).

It is important to bear in mind that this duality is predicated on the relatively constant presence of the mother and, conversely, the relative absence of the father. This is certainly the typical (although hardly necessary) American pattern. If this pattern were reversed, all of the traits discussed as common to one or the other gender would need to be reversed as well. In examining the relationship of family structure to sex-role learning, Lynn offers a series of other arguments (Lynn, 1969, chap. 5). The "normal" family is assumed to consist of a close mother and *moderately* distant father. A moderately distant father is close enough to provide some model for the young boy, as well as the motivation to use that model, but sufficiently remote to require the mental effort on the part of the boy that was discussed above. Boys with either very close or very distant fathers will not develop analytical skills superior to those of the average girl. In the first case, the boy will directly imitate the father, much as the girl does the mother. In the second, the intellectual effort (and lack of motivation) may be just too great to cope with. Conversely, girls with more distant mothers and/or fathers as caretakers will develop analytical skills commensurate with those of the average male. Certainly, the assumption made by many that the best way to bring up any child, regardless of gender, is with a

constantly present mother must be open to serious question.

In our society males have considerably more prestige, power, and freedom than females. Little children are not oblivious to this fact. Thus, again according to Lynn (1969: 65-78), although boys experience initially much greater sex role identity problems than girls, as time goes on they become more firmly identified with the masculine role. Females, however, do not do so with reference to the feminine role. Indeed, a larger number of girls show preference for the high prestige and powerful masculine role than boys do for the feminine role, as witnessed by the relative numbers of "tomboys" and "sissies." Pushing this logic a step further, it is likely that given the higher prestige of the masculine role, homosexuality and sissyishness may appear as a kind of betrayal, while lesbianism and tomboyishness may appear as more or less understandable imitations of a superior status role. This would help to explain the far greater social antipathy to the former than the latter (see Progrebin, 1972). Similarly, feminine fashions often "ape" masculine ones, but the opposite rarely occurs. The whole notion of transvestism basically applies to males only; no one blinks an eye at a female in jeans, a shirt, and boots or sneakers, much less suggests that she is a transvestite, but a male in a skirt (unless he is Scotch or an ancient Roman) is a different matter.

It is clear that parents play a major role in the process of socialization in general and the communication of sex role identity and behavior in particular. Moreover, it is clear that children have established a firm notion of their sex role by about age 3, if not earlier. By this age, little Dick is already objecting to certain things because they are for girls, and Jane is happily imitating mother with her dolls and tea parties. However, a view of human development that claims that any identities or behavior patterns are irrevocably set for life by that age seems to me to be myopic. Life for most humans *is* change, to a greater or lesser degree. If such changes are slow relative to those occurring in the first years of life, they nonetheless exist and, cumulatively, may sometimes acquire substantial dimensions. Any such changes away from patterns established by parents must logically be initiated from some source outside the home environment. If society at large provides strong, even coercive supports for identities and behaviors learned early in life from parents, they will be further reinforced rather than changed. This seems, by and large, to be the case with reference to sex roles,

inasmuch as most parents reflect stereotypical sex role definitions.

REFERENCES

Cooley, Charles H. *Social organization.* New York: Scribners, 1909.

Lewis, Michael. Culture and gender roles: there's no unisex in the nursery. *Psychology Today,* May 1972, pp. 54-57.

Lynn, David B. *Parental and sex role identification: A theoretical formulation.* Berkeley, Cal.: McCutchan Publishing Corp., 1969.

Mead, George Herbert. *Mind, self, and society.* Chicago: University of Chicago Press, 1934.

Merton, Robert K. *Social theory and social structure.* 2nd ed. Glencoe, Ill.: Free Press, 1957.

Thomas, W. I. *The unadjusted girl.* Boston: Little, Brown & Co., 1923.

20.

Henry B. Biller

SEX-ROLE LEARNING: SOME COMMENTS AND COMPLEXITIES FROM A MULTIDIMENSIONAL PERSPECTIVE

What is sex-role development? Why is it important to study sex roles? These are related questions. A general definition of sex role is that it includes the different patterns of behavior that a society expects for males and females along with certain of the individual's perceptions of himself, others, and sex-typed objects. When we study sex-role development we are basically examining how boys develop masculine behavior and girls develop feminine be-

havior. Of course, what is masculine or feminine may vary greatly from society to society, or even among different subgroups in a particular society. This is not to say that sex-role development is just a simple learning process for a multitude of biological, familial, and sociocultural factors are involved in the process by which a child comes to manifest "boyish" or "girlish" behavior.

At a juncture in history when so many people are questioning the meaningfulness of sex roles and differential treatment of males and females, it may be asked why we should even study sex-role development. Is there any justification in labeling certain

Source: Paper presented at the annual meeting of the American Association for the Advancement of Science, Washington, D.C., 1972.

behaviors masculine or feminine? Are such distinctions just anachronisms? One could point out that every society has had some sex differentiations above and beyond recognition of basic biological characteristics.

However, some even argue that there is nothing basic or fundamental in human biology that necessitates sex-role distinctions. Some take the position that sex roles are just another form of stereotyped prejudice perpetuated by vested interest groups and an outmoded economic system. On the other hand, one can emphasize evidence indicating that sex roles are of some functional value in the distribution of tasks within a society, even if they are not biologically linked. But even if one holds the position that sex roles, or at least most manifestations of them, are not necessary, and should be abandoned, this does not mean that they are not worthy of study.

If we found that so-called sex-role behaviors had no consistent relationships to other behaviors, then one might justifiably abandon research in this area. Sex-role behaviors would have questionable scientific value if they were just labels for superficial characteristics that could not generate predictions about an individual's behavior. In fact, sex-role behaviors have very frequent and important links to various facets of personality development. An individual's feelings about himself, his interaction with others and his skills and abilities are in many ways often associated with his sex-role development. Certain experiences during infancy and childhood relate in a consistent way to the adult's sex-role development. We can learn much about child development by studying what types of factors influence sex-role behaviors. Different aspects of sex role are influenced in complex ways by interactions of biological, familial, and sociocultural

variables. The study of sex-role development may indeed give us a general impression of the way in which the personality development process takes place.

We also often find that irregularities or conflicts in sex-role development are highly related to various types of adjustment difficulties and psychopathology. Some would say that this is only because our society is too rigid and does not tolerate deviations. There is certainly some validity to this statement. However, even if we fully take this point of view, we cannot ignore the pervasive connections between sex-role inadequacies and personality malfunctioning.

A behavioral scientist may feel uncomfortable or comfortable with the sex-role distinctions that his society manifests. But, in either case, he has a responsibility to objectively evaluate what influence sex-role factors have in personality development. The issue of "what should be" may not always be the same as "what is." I am often struck by the fact that students and researchers frequently have difficulty in separating out these issues. Sex role can be a particularly personal issue. Sex role also has many social implications. At times it is extremely difficult to distinguish our wishes and conflicts from our observations. No doubt there are other areas of inquiry that also trigger feelings of defensiveness on the part of the student and investigator but it is doubtful, at least in our society, if any area can consistently bring out stronger emotions.

ASPECTS OF SEX-ROLE DEVELOPMENT

Sex-role development encompasses an exceedingly complex cluster of variables. In everyday conversation such terms as masculine, feminine, sissy, tomboy, homosexual are often used to convey observations related to sex role. A difficulty is that these terms often mean different things to different people.

We talk of an individual's being masculine or feminine in his behavior and appearance. When we examine such statements more carefully we often find that a person is called masculine when exhibiting aggressive or assertive behavior and called feminine when emitting more passive or dependent behavior. Such labels are not very precise but are frequently used and have a pervasive reality for many people.

Expected sex-role behaviors in a given society are based on beliefs as to what are fundamental differences between the sexes. Behaviors labeled masculine are those expected for males; behaviors labeled feminine are those expected for females. Because males are usually larger and stronger in adulthood than females, it is easy to see why aggressive, assertive, and dominant behavior may be labeled as masculine. Of course, as a society becomes less dependent on purely physical strength and endurance for survival, one might expect that such sex differences would become less important. Similarly, as there is less need to reproduce to insure survival, the sex differences in the reproductive system and related capabilities may play less of a factor in defining social roles. Moreover, there are tremendous individual differences among members of each sex. The existence of individuals whose sex is difficult to determine on the basis of biological factors and the fact that many biological sex differences are not directly related to sex role differences further complicates the issue. Nevertheless, when we compare groups of males and females, even in infancy, there are a number of biological sex differences above and beyond reproductive system differences, which may predispose some of the be-

haviors that we describe as sex-role related. It is particularly striking that we are constantly learning more about *both* the influence of subtle biological factors and environmental variables, and their complex interactions. In one sense, both biology and learning are much more important at earlier stages in development (prenatally and in infancy) than we might have once supposed.

SEX-ROLE PREFERENCE

One aspect of sex role has to do with an individual's preferences for certain activities and objects. Males and females often differ tremendously in the kinds of things they do and the types of objects they prefer: for instance, boys and girls typically play with different types of toys and engage in different kinds of games. Men and women usually differ in their hobbies, in the books they read, and their preferences for occupational activities. There are many individual differences among members of a given sex and the individual who had a wide range of interests may best maximize his or her potential.

In many ways sex-role preferences change most with the times. Fads in hairstyling and clothing make for sometimes more obvious or less obvious distinctions between the sexes. But such changes are often misleading and may not accurately reflect the influence of sex-role differentiation in a particular society. For example, just because men and women may dress in a similar fashion doesn't mean that they will behave in a similar manner in their social interactions. On the other hand, there is no doubt that at least among the highly educated in our society, there is more between-sex permeability in interest patterns and many attitudes are much less sex-linked than they were previously. There is much more equality in sexual behavior, and a growing respect for the role of the female by members of both sexes. Despite this, it would be very unrealistic to generalize from a college and/or upper-middle-class population as to the degree of sex-role change in our society. In most of our society, including the lower and working classes, there has been relatively little change from some of the traditional sex-role expectations, and this is evident in terms of sex-role preferences as well as in other aspects of sex-role behavior.

A problem with much of the research on sex-role development is that it has been restricted to measurement of sex-role preference. In itself, an individual's sex-role preference does not appear to be a particularly valid indicator of his overall masculinity or femininity and much more attention needs to be given to other aspects of sex-role functioning. A related problem concerns the frequent confusion, or assumed isomorphism, of the awareness of social norms relating to sex-role behavior with sex-role preference. The knowledge of culturally expected sex-role differences does not mean that the individual personally prefers or makes same sex choices.

SEX-ROLE ADOPTION

Sex-role adoption relates to the individual's functioning in social and environmental interaction. Aggressiveness, assertiveness, independence, and competence in physical activities, all seem much associated with what is generally thought of as masculine behavior in our society and in many others. With increasing technology an ability to understand, design, build, and repair objects also has come to be part of what we think of as masculine characteristics. Certain types of intellectual expertise, particularly when they are enmeshed in practical uses and a problem-solving context are considered quite mas-

culine. It is interesting to note that middle-class individuals are more likely to associate intellectual prowess with masculinity whereas working class individuals emphasize physical competence.

Possibly because many societies put a higher value on "masculine behaviors," definitions of femininity sometimes seem more difficult. Femininity has often been associated with the lack of masculine characteristics. Sometimes it is defined as the opposite of masculinity. More frequently it is defined in a negative manner. Passivity, dependency, and timidity are often considered feminine behaviors. However, a general skill in interpersonal relations, an ability to express a variety and intensity of emotions, and the expression of nurturant behaviors seem highly associated with what we often speak of as femininity. Sensitivity, understanding, empathy, the ability to mediate, to verbally communicate feelings and attitudes, to soothe and to comfort seem in the forefront when we speak of the positively feminine woman.

Of course such positive characteristics can also enhance the male's personality, as can the ability to be assertive and independent make for a more effective female. In fact, the most actualized individuals possess both positive masculine *and* feminine qualities, regardless of their sex.

To be viewed as masculine, a male can possess a high level of interpersonal sensitivity, as long as he also manifests a pattern of typically masculine behaviors. A female will not lose her femininity if she is assertive and independent as long as she retains her feminine expressive abilities.

Generally it is the whole gestalt of a person's behavior that we react to, at least when we know the individual well. For example, it does not make much sense to label a man as unmasculine because he occasionally cries or likes to openly express his affection to others. If he is also masculine in appearance, and assertive and aggressive we may even perceive him as more masculine because of his seeming sensitivity and gentleness.

I am emphasizing positive facets of sex-role behavior. The position that I am taking relates to the fact that there are certain sex-role related behaviors that can be considered to be very meaningful in the sense of self-actualization while others are related to a lack of competency. For example, assertiveness and independence have been traditionally considered to be hallmarks of the masculine role and certainly in *most* contexts are indices of competency. On the other hand, masculinity has often been associated with aloofness and insensitivity to others' feelings. Such characteristics can be generally viewed as manifestations of interpersonal incompetency.

The feminine role has more consistently been equated with incompetency, such characteristics as timidity and dependency being seen as very salient dimensions. Nevertheless one can extract such personality traits as nurturance and sensitivity from definitions of femininity. Again, the focus is on the development of positive masculine characteristics such as assertiveness and independence and positive feminine characteristics such as nurturance and sensitivity. A basic assumption is that, although there may be biological factors predisposing some degree of overall sex differences, both males and females can be judged as more competent if they possess both positive masculine and positive feminine characteristics.

SEX-ROLE ORIENTATION

The most important and perhaps the most stable aspect or component of sex-role behavior appears to be related to the individual's self perceptions. Sex-role orientation refers to how the individual perceives

himself in terms of his sex-role adequacy.

We have discussed how others perceive the individual's sex-role behavior in social and environmental interactions (sex-role adoption), how the individual perceives sex-typed opportunities in his environment (sex-role preference), and now we are considering how the individual perceives himself in relation to his sex-role functioning (sex-role orientation).

A very basic dimension of the individual's sex-role orientation is how he views his body. Satisfaction with one's body and its related reproductive capacity is very important. The acceptance of one's biology is very critical for a positive self-concept development. Factors such as physical appearance and perceived attractiveness to the opposite sex can be very important in the individual's overall psychological adjustment.

Sex-role orientation includes both the individual's perception of his relative masculinity and/or femininity and how he or she feels about himself in this regard. Such perceptions are not necessarily consistent with his sex-role preference or sex-role adoption. An individual may be very masculine in his preference and adoption but feel very uncomfortable about such behavior. He may feel that his behavior is very inappropriate. He may be conforming to social pressures. On the other hand, he may be manifesting culturally inappropriate behavior and desire more self-congruence. (There is a great need to study the antecedents and correlates of different sex-role patterns.) There may also be a more subtle discrepancy in which anxiety or defensiveness is exhibited but the individual is not clearly aware of the source of his problem. This is a rather frequent occurrence in individuals coming for counseling or psychotherapy. Researchers are beginning to untangle some of the complexities in the sex-role development process and to delineate the various antecedents and correlates of various sex-role patterns. A thorough understanding of the sex-role development process demands a consideration of such factors as the child's constitutional predispositions and inter-actions with siblings and peers as well as adults.

PARENTAL BEHAVIOR

I shall deal briefly with two of the many problems in socialization related to the rigidity of our conventional sex-role stereo-types. The first has to do with expected parental behaviors and the second the typical "feminization" of pre-primary and elementary school education. In a sense, these are very related issues in that in both the early socialization process in the family and in the beginning stages of our educa-tional process, there is often an exaggera-tion of feminine influence and marked paternal deprivation. These issues also relate to the tremendous need for male liberation as well as female liberation (and the need for males and females to work together cooperatively as both parents and teachers).

Men have been judged as good fathers if they economically provide for their family, but the quality of father–child interactions has not been given enough attention. The maternal role has been seen as the key process by which children become social-ized. It has been argued that child rearing is an essential dimension of the adult feminine role but definitions of masculinity have usually not encompassed fathering activities. Males receive relatively few opportunities to become experts in dealing with young children, particularly on a feeling level.

Sex-role distinctions are very much linked with the way in which we define father and mother roles. The mother in most societies is expected to be nurturant and sensitive, to be an expert in family communications and in dealing with intra-familial tensions while the father is sup-posed to be most competent in dealing with environmental exigencies and in solv-ing problems which require a knowledge of the non-social environment. Aside from some expected tutelage of the son by the father in some societies there often seems to be little concern for the quality of father–child interactions, especially in infancy and early adulthood.

We have some preliminary observations which indicate that well-fathered boys *and* girls are likely to possess both positively masculine and positively feminine be-haviors. Young children whose fathers are actively and warmly involved with them, salient in family interactions, and en-courage interpersonal competency and problem-solving skills are likely to be nurturant and sensitive as well as assertive and independent. They are also likely to feel very comfortable about their bodies and basic sex role orientations. The father's positive acceptance of himself as a male and his acceptance of his child's sex are important.

Children who are both well fathered and well mothered are likely to have positive self-concepts and a comfort about their biological sexuality. They feel good about being male or female and have a pride in their basic sex-role orientation. They are comfortable with themselves and their sexuality but yet are able to be relatively flexible in their interests and responsivity to others. Security in sex-role orientation gives the child more of an opportunity to develop in an actualized way. On the other hand, children who are uncomfortable with their basic sexuality are more likely to take either a defensive posture of rigid adherence to cultural sex-role standards or to attempt to completely avoid expected gender-related behaviors.

Given the way males and females have been socialized in our society, it is likely that, over and above constitutional predispositions, fathers and mothers will have different ranges of competencies and interests. For example, fathers are more apt to have assertive and independent characteristics whereas mothers are more likely to have a high level of interpersonal sensitivity and ability to communicate feelings. We can argue that the optimal situation for the child is to have both an involved mother and involved father. The child is then exposed to a wider degree of adaptive characteristics. If parents participate in a cooperative way, a better balance for the child can be achieved. Similarly, school situations which give children the opportunity to interact with competent teachers of both sexes may help facilitate the child's development.

TEACHER BEHAVIOR

Female teachers all too frequently react negatively to assertive behavior in the classroom and seem to feel much more comfortable with girls who are generally quieter, more obedient, and conforming. Boys seem to perceive that teachers are much more positive in responding to girls and to feminine behavior and interest patterns. Unfortunately, the type of "feminine" behavior reinforced in the classroom is often of a very negative quality if one is using self-actualization as a criterion. For example, timidity, passivity, dependency, obedience, and quietness are usually rewarded. The boy or girl who is independent, assertive, questioning, and challenging is typically at a great disadvantage. Even though girls generally seem to adapt more easily to the early school environment, such an atmosphere is not conducive to their optimal development. Girls need to learn how to be independent and asser-

tive just as much as boys do. There is accumulating data that the quality of father–child interactions can have much influence on the cognitive functioning and academic achievement of both boys and girls. Furthermore, our observations have suggested that competent male teachers in pre-elementary and elementary classrooms can have a very facilitating effect on learning and overall classroom atmosphere. Paternally deprived children seem to be especially responsive to male teachers. It is interesting to note that our research suggests that adult male influence can have particularly profound effects in the first few years of life, a time at which females have traditionally been considered to be the sole socializing agents.

With respect to this all too brief consideration of sex role issues in the family and school, it seems relevant to emphasize that the problem of lack of communication and understanding between males and females may be more than an issue of sex differences. Our society segregates males and females in many ways, both physically and psychologically. A general lack of ongoing and positive male–female peer interactions during the developmental process makes for difficulties that are not necessary. In terms of predispositions, males and females may differ in their areas of competency but such variation does not necessitate misunderstanding if mutual respect has been encouraged. More specifically, some of the negativism directed toward sex-role differences has been due to the lack of valuation for the female and her usual areas of competence as much as, if not more than, to the fact that males and females usually behave differently. An expectation of mutual respect and equal status for males and females appears much more realistic and closer at hand than a total obliteration of sex-role differences.

21.

Paul E. McGhee

TELEVISION AS A SOURCE OF LEARNING SEX-ROLE STEREOTYPES

This symposium is concerned with influences on children's sex-role behavior beyond those operating within the nuclear family. If you exclude the child's interaction with the mother and father, it's almost certain that the greatest influence on the acquisition of sex role development is to be found in the various mass media. Children spend incredible amounts of time watching television, reading books, and going to the movies. Among these various media, it has become pretty clear that television is capable of having a great impact on the child's development. Even if you make a very conservative estimate that the average child watches TV sixteen hours per week, this means that by the age of only ten the child has already viewed over 6,000 hours of TV. That also includes about 220,000 commercials.

It has been known for some time now that children can acquire a broad range of behaviors, attitudes, and emotional reactions by observing either live or symbolic models. While I don't have time to go into that research literature, I bring it up simply as a means of suggesting that there is every reason to assume that children will acquire sex-role stereotypic behavior and attitudes if those stereotypes are depicted in TV programming. If the observation of models presented on TV does have a

significant impact on children's learning of sex-role stereotypes, then children who watch highly sex-role stereotyped programs should acquire these stereotypes more readily than children who watch programs with low amounts of stereotyping. On the other hand, if it can be shown that most TV programming is highly sex-role stereotyped, we would then only need to show a relationship between amount of TV viewing time and degree of acquisition of knowledge of sex stereotyped behavior. So, let's examine the behaviors and attitudes exhibited by male and female TV models.

There have now been quite a number of analyses of the amount of aggression depicted in different types of television programming, but very few attempts have been made to determine the amount of sex typing depicted. At this time, I know of only two studies which analyze the nature of role models present in TV programs intended for children. One of these was completed by Sternglanz and Serbin (1974). They had several judges rate male and female role models in ten different children's programs on twelve different behavioral categories. The programs included "Popeye," "The Harlem Globetrotters," "Superman," "Bewitched," "Sabrina the Teenage Witch," "I Dream of Jeannie," "Archie's TV Funnies," "Scooby-Doo," "Josie and the Pussycats," and "Pebbles and Bamm-Bamm." The first thing they found out was that a number of the most popular children's programs couldn't even be included in the study because they didn't have a single

Source: Paper presented in a symposium on "Environmental aspects of sex-role behavior: Studies beyond the nuclear family" (Beverly Birns, Chairperson) at the meeting of the Society for Research in Child Development, Denver, 1975.

female character. Of those programs that were studied, 67% of the characters were males and 33% were females. Also, the characters playing bad-guy roles were almost always males; females rarely had evil characteristics. They found that males were significantly more likely than females to be depicted as aggressive, instructive, and succorant, while females were more likely to be depicted as being deferrent and as being punished for being very active. Females' behavior also tended to have no real environmental impact or consequence. In the other study, Streicher (1974) had judges rate the Saturday and Sunday morning cartoons over a 9-week period in 1972. In this study she was only interested in the female role models presented. In general, she found that cartoon females were less numerous than males, and they also made fewer appearances when they were present. They had fewer lines, played fewer roles, were less active, occupied many fewer positions of responsibility, were less noisy, and were much more juvenile than males. Mothers in these cartoons tended to work only in the house, and males did not participate at all in the housework.

The two most thorough studies of sex typing in TV programming were based on an analysis of prime-time television programs. In one of these studies, Gerbner (1972) observed 762 leading characters in dramatic programs over a 3-year period between 1967 and 1969. In the other, Tedesco (1974) analyzed the amount of sex typing occurring in non-cartoon prime-time programs over a 4-year period between 1969 and 1972. Together, these studies indicated that:

(1) Only one-quarter of all the leading characters were female.
(2) Female characters were much younger than males.

(3) Females were more likely to be depicted as married, or "about to be" married.
(4) Women were most likely to be cast in a leading role when some kind of family or romantic interest was central to the plot. In most cases some suggestion of sex was present.
(5) Males were more likely to be cast in serious roles, while females were more likely to be cast in comic or light roles.
(6) Generally males were more likely to initiate violence, but females were more likely to be victims. When females did engage in some form of violence, they were much less likely than males to get away with it.
(7) Almost two-thirds of all females were unemployed in contrast to only one-third of all males. Of those that were employed some form of professional employment was most characteristic of both sexes. But the males who were employed tended to be fairly equally distributed across such employment areas as entertainment, business, government, health and education, while over 50% of the females were employed in some kind of entertainment area.
(8) Finally, data obtained on the personality profiles of the leading characters, using a semantic differential type scale, indicated that females were depicted as being more attractive, more happy, warmer, more sociable, more fair, more peaceful, and more useful. Males were rated as being more rational, smarter, more powerful, more stable, and tolerant.

One final study is especially relevant to the data I will present shortly. Courtney and Whipple (1974) investigated the male and female role models that were provided on TV commercials between 1971 and 1973. They found that over 85% of the voice-overs in the commercials studied were men. Women were, however, just about as likely as men to be seen in the role of product representative. But the limits of this equality can be seen in the types of products that were represented by males and by females. They found that women were seen in a much more limited variety of occupations than they actually participate in. In one of their studies, they found that 75% of the advertisements using women as models involved products found in the kitchen or the bathroom. So, "The world for women in the ads is a domestic one, where women are housewives who worry about cleanliness and food preparation and serve their husbands and children. Seldom is a woman shown combining out-of-home employment with management of her home and personal life" (pp. 116-117). Men, on the other hand, tended to be shown as beneficiaries of women's work inside the house rather than making some contribution to household work. Male product representatives were usually portrayed as being more dominant, as advice givers, and as demonstrators. They were depicted in a much broader variety of occupations, while women were usually depicted in some kind of home occupation or in the family.

So from the limited data that have been obtained, it appears that traditional sex-role stereotypes are present in most aspects of television programming; this includes cartoons and other programs for children, dramatic prime-time programs, and commercials. Since this is the case, it follows that the greater the overall amount of TV watching by the child, the greater should be his acquisition of knowledge of those stereotypes. An analysis of the specific programs watched is not really necessary, since most programs are highly stereotyped. Although, of course, if individual programs were rated for the amount of sex typing depicted, we would expect children

who watched a greater proportion of highly sex-typed programs to learn traditional stereotypes most readily.

In our first attempt to examine the relationship between TV watching and the learning of sex-role stereotypes, one of my colleagues (Terry Frueh) and I obtained groups of heavy and light television watchers at different ages. We sampled both boys and girls in grades kindergarten, 2, 4, and 6. To obtain groups of high and low television watchers, we constructed a TV watching survey form on the basis of the *TV Guide* for the preceding week in the local St. Louis viewing area. A list was made of all programs for all six channels available for the preceding 7 day period. The list included the name and time of the show, along with the channel on which it was shown. Children in the two older groups (grades 4 and 6) completed the survey form in class, but children in the two younger groups took the form home, and it was completed by their mothers. In completing the form, children (or their parents) were asked to check each program that was watched during the previous week, and to estimate both the number of hours the child usually watched per week and the typicalness of the previous week's viewing. Out of a total of 300 forms initially handed out to children at the 4 grade levels, 95% were returned. Out of those subjects who returned the survey forms, groups of high and low TV watchers were formed by retaining those whose viewing time for the previous week was 25 hours or more, or 10 hours or less. This was how we operationally defined high and low TV watchers. Five males and five females at each grade level were randomly chosen out of these high and low TV watching groups to be included in the balance of the study. This provided 20 subjects at each grade level and a total sample size of 80. A subject was kept in the study only if his (her) previous week's viewing was estimated to be typical of usual viewing habits and amount of viewing time. These subjects were then individually administered the It test (Brown, 1956). The It test is actually a measure of sex-typed toy or activity preferences. The child is presented with a series of pairs of pictures depicting various toys or activities which are traditionally associated with either masculine or feminine sex roles, and is asked to indicate which of the two a "stick figure" called "It" would prefer. Those of you who are familiar with this test are aware that the It figure, which is supposed to be neutral with respect to its gender, actually has a male bias. However, since this bias should be operating similarly for both high and low TV watchers, the It test provides a good means of determining children's awareness of stereotypes operating with respect to various toys and other activities. Findings using this instrument indicate that children begin to demonstrate stereotyped preferences as early as the third or fourth year. That is, the boys begin to show preferences for traditionally masculine activities, while the girls begin to show preferences for traditionally feminine activities. These trends increase as the child gets older.

We computed a three-way analysis of variance on the children's It test scores; this included four levels of grades, two levels of sex, and two levels of viewing time. We found no significant interaction effects, but there were significant main effects for all three independent variables. We found that older children were more sex typed in their preferences than younger children, $F(3, 64) = 4.2$, $p < .01$. But this was an expected finding and of no interest for the present study. We also found that boys appeared to be more sex typed in their preferences than girls, $F(1, 64) =$ 31.2, $p < .01$. But again this finding may be accounted for by the fact that the It figure probably has a masculine bias and is not really a neutral figure. The most important finding for our present concerns was that high TV watchers had significantly higher scores on the It test than did low TV watchers, $F(1, 64) = 193.6$, $p < .001$. That is, children who watched TV 25 or more hours per week were significantly more likely than children watching 10 hours or less per week to say that the It figure preferred activities associated traditionally with sex-role stereotypes of their own sex. The difference in mean It scores were very striking. Out of a maximum score of 84, the mean score for high TV watchers was 72, while the mean for low watchers was only 51. So these findings suggested to us that television watching does play an important role in determining the extent to which children learn information regarding sex-stereotyped behaviors and attitudes. The lack of any interaction effects in our data suggests that this learning process is operating equally strongly for both older and younger children, and for both sexes. We were surprised by the lack of any interaction with grade level, since we assumed that as heavy TV watchers get older, they should become increasingly aware of sex-role stereotypes.

Of course, the problem with such data is that the order of influence operating could actually be the opposite of the one we would like to assume is operating. Or, some third variable which is highly correlated with amount of TV viewing time might be the key variable which accounts for the relationship between TV viewing time and stereotype of sex-role preferences. For example, social class differences might account for the data obtained. However, all of the subjects tested were drawn from the same middle-class suburban St. Louis area. There was not sufficient range in social class for this variable to account for the findings. While we cannot draw any final conclusions about causality here, the frequently demonstrated power of observational learning makes it very difficult *not to* conclude that the acquisition of such sex-typed toy and activity preferences among both boys and girls is strongly influenced by the heavily sex-typed behavior exhibited by male and female sex-role models present in virtually all aspects of television programming.

We have just recently replicated this study using the same set of subjects used in the first study. We wanted to compare the degree of sex typing in the current toy and activity preferences among children who remained heavy TV watchers and those who remained very light TV watchers over the 15-month period. We found that 80% of our original sample retained their original classification 15 months later. .Eighty-five percent of the heavy TV viewers remained heavy viewers, and 75% of the light viewers remained light viewers. There was also no appreciable difference between grade levels or the two sexes in their consistency in viewing time across this 15-month period. Information was obtained by the same experimenter on TV-watching habits and sex-role preferences (using the It test) using the same procedures adopted in the first study.

An ANOVA computed on their Time 2 It scores provided pretty much the same picture provided by the initial study. That is, high TV watchers were significantly more sex typed in their activity and toy preferences on the It test than low TV watchers, $F(1, 48) = 138.7$, $p < .001$. Similarly, older children were more sex typed than younger children, $F(3, 48) = 7.8$, $p < .001$. The sex difference present in the first study did not appear at Time 2. Again, there were no significant interac-

tion effects. We then computed a repeated measures ANOVA on subjects' It test scores. The nonrepeated factors were TV viewing time, sex of subject, and relative grade level (I say relative because all subjects were a grade higher at the time of the replication study; of course, the relative difference in grade levels was the same). The repeated factor was subjects' It scores at Time 1 and Time 2. We expected to find that all subjects became more sex typed in their preferences over the 15-month period (this positive relationship with age increase is usually found), but that children who were heavy TV watchers at both testing times would have increased at a more rapid rate than children who were light TV watchers at both testing times. In fact, however, we found the opposite order of change. In spite of the fact that high TV watchers showed more sex-typed toy and activity preferences at both Time 1 and Time 2, low TV watchers showed a significantly greater increase in the amount of sex typing in their preferences than did high TV watchers $F(1, 48) = 25.49$, $p < .001$. That is, while both high and low TV watchers became more sex typed in their preferences at Time 2, low viewers showed more of a change than high viewers. While this outcome is in the opposite direction of the findings we expected to obtain, an examination of the initial It scores obtained by these two groups of subjects made it clear what was happening here. The mean It scores at the initial testing were 72 for the high viewers, and 51 for the low viewers. Since the maximum score on the It test is 84, there was clearly a ceiling effect operating here. That is, because of their initial very high It scores, high viewers had less room to show an increase in sex typing at the time of the second testing. (Similarly, older children had less room to increase than younger children, and males had less room to increase than females.) So, the one thing which did become clear in this replication is that some measure other than the It test is necessary to show the progressive influence on the acquisition of knowledge of sex-role stereotypes that the heavy viewing of highly stereotyped TV programs probably has. A longitudinal study of this type with younger children could make satisfactory use of the It test as a measure of the acquisition of sex-role stereotypes, but if the study is begun with children as old as those used in our study, the heavy TV viewers will already have become so stereotyped in their preferences that there will not be sufficient room on the scale to reflect changes in knowledge of sex-role stereotypes that must actually be occurring. I have just begun such a study using children attending the Fels nursery school. The It test should reflect any changes in sex role preferences over time with a sample of children this young. In this preschool study, we will also video tape children's free play behavior and rate the amount of sex typing occurring in their overt behavior, as well as their stated activity preferences. This will give us the first data I know of relating TV viewing patterns both to children's knowledge of sex-role stereotypes, and to the amount of stereotyping demonstrated in their overt behavior.

One of the difficulties with using the It test is that it is restricted to a measure of the amount of stereotyping in children's stated preferences for concrete types of activities. The concreteness of the test accounts for the ceiling effect that occurs by the sixth grade and makes it inadequate to test many aspects of a child's knowledge of sex-role stereotypes. We were also interested in children's expectations about how males and females differ along more abstract dimensions, such as more complex psychological characteristics. There was

one measure that we came across which was designed to accomplish this end. It was developed by Bennett (1973) at Wake Forest University. Bennett used an approach similar to that used in the It test, but she used full bodied figures of a male and female rather than a stick figure. Subjects are told a number of two- or three-sentence stories and are then asked to point to the figure that the story is about. An example of one of her items is "One of these people is a shy person. They are quiet and afraid to talk to others. Which is the shy person?" Another item is "One of these people is very sure of themself. They know they will do well in their new job. Which person is sure of themself?" In total, there are twenty-four such items. Twelve of these tap such male stereotypes as assertiveness, self-confidence, ambitiousness, independence, dominance, etc.; the remaining twelve tap such female stereotypes as gentleness, emotionality, talkativeness, meekness, etc. Categorization of these adjectives as being associated with a male or female sex stereotype was based on college subjects' judgments of a much larger group of adjectives as being typical of males or females.

This Sex Stereotype measure was also administered to children following the second administration of the It Test. So, while we only had data for this measure at Time 2, it did allow us to see whether the findings obtained with the It test extended to more abstract psychological characteristics associated with the two sexes. Also, since there are separate subtests for knowledge of male and female stereotypes, we were able to relate TV watching patterns to awareness of stereotypes associated with each sex. Three $4 \times 2 \times 2$ ANOVAs were completed on subjects' stereotyped responses on male items, female items, and all items combined. The findings were very similar to those obtained using the It test. A TV watching main effect was obtained for all three analyses. That is, children who watched 25 hours or more of TV a week both initially and 15 months later gave more frequent stereotyped choices than children who watched 10 hours or less a week on both occasions on both the male items [F (1, 48)$=$22.7, $p<.001$], the female items [$F(1, 48) = 61.9$, $p<.001$], and of course on items combined [F (1, 48)$=$ 96.8, $p<.001$]. A very interesting Grade $\times$ TV watching interaction effect was also obtained on the male stereotype items. While high TV watchers made progressively more frequent stereotyped choices on the male items with increasing age, low TV watchers actually showed a linear decrease in frequency of stereotyped choices with increasing age. This suggests that children who are low TV watchers more readily learn as they get older that so-called "masculine" characteristics may actually be associated with either sex. Since heavy TV watchers probably see these masculine characteristics being depicted regularly on the TV screen, their sex stereotypic perceptions are maintained—and even strengthened.

While these findings consist of only correlational data, they are highly suggestive that heavy TV viewing by children can play a significant role in their acquisition of knowledge of sex-stereotyped behaviors, attitudes, and other complex psychological characteristics. Given the growing concern in this country with protecting children from development along stereotyped lines, it may be time to give sex typing in TV programs the same attention we have recently given to TV aggression.

REFERENCES

Bennett, S. M. Children's recognition of male and female stereotypes: A developmental analysis. Unpublished Master's thesis, Wake Forest University, 1973.

Brown, D. G. Sex-role preference in young children. *Psychological Monographs,* 1956, **70** (14), Whole No. 42.

Courtney, A. E., & Whipple, T. W. Women in TV commercials. *Journal of Communication,* 1974, **24,** 110-118.

Gerbner, G. Violence in television drama: Trends and symbolic functions. In G. A. Comstock & E. A. Rubinstein (eds.), *Television and social behavior.* Vol. 1. *Media content and control.* Washington: Government Printing Office, 1972, pp 28-187.

Sternglanz, S. H., & Serbin, L. A. Sex role stereotyping in children's television programs. *Developmental Psychology,* 1974, **10,** 710-715.

Streicher, H. W. The girls in the cartoons. *Journal of Communication,* 1974, **24,** 125-129.

Tedesco, N. S. Patterns in prime time. *Journal of Communication,* 1974, **15,** 55-64.

D. MORAL DEVELOPMENT

22.

Nancy Eisenberg Berg and Paul Mussen

THE ORIGINS AND DEVELOPMENT OF CONCEPTS OF JUSTICE

There is a vast variety of definitions of justice among the cultures of the world and, even within Western culture, there is no generally agreed upon conception of the basic nature of justice. The common core of all definitions is the concept of fairness, whose meaning varies not only among individuals but among cultures, civilizations, and historical eras. The fact that children conceive of fairness in terms that are different from adults is of central concern in this paper, which presents some major theories and empirical data about the origins and development of children's conceptions of justice. Our primary emphasis is on changing ideas about fair and just resolutions to interpersonal conflicts, the application of rules, rewards, punishments, and sanctions regulating interpersonal relationships, and most importantly on the reasons and motives underlying conceptions of justice and just behavior.

The origins and development of concepts of justice are reviewed from the points of view of three influential theories in contemporary developmental psychology—social learning, psychoanalysis, cognitive developmental theory. In our opinion, cognitive developmental theory, particularly the versions of Piaget and Kohlberg, has contributed by far the most to

our understanding of the problem. Before looking at this theory in detail, we will sketch briefly the social learning and psychoanalytical approaches to the study of the origins of concepts of justice.

SOCIAL LEARNING THEORY

Stated in grossly oversimplified terms, social learning theory is concerned with the learning of complex processes, including the acquisition of personal characteristics and social behavior, through reinforcement, modelling, or imitation. Since the primary emphasis is on overt observable behavior, the formation of concepts such as justice or fairness is generally neglected. Just or fair responses are likely to be interpreted as the results of previous rewards, approval or reward-seeking, or fear of reprisal or punishment for unfair behavior, rather than of internalized principles of justice. Concepts of justice and moral opinions can be altered through rewards, punishments, or imitation (Bandura & McDonald, 1963).

Morality is generally defined by social learning theorists as conformity to cultural norms, learned by means of reinforcement, punishment, and modelling which promote internalization of parental and societal standards. Such concepts hardly seem adequate to explain the development of principles of justice, for these are ordinarily generated when there is a conflict between two or more internalized cultural roles or norms.

Some classical learning theorists at-

Source: *Journal of Social Issues,* 1975, **31**, 183-201. Preparation of this paper was supported by a grant from the Grant Foundation.

tempt to explain justice exclusively in terms of rewards and punishments. Thus Skinner regards justice simply as the judicious use of rewards and punishments. "The issue of fairness is often simply a matter of good husbandry. The question is whether reinforcements are being used wisely" (Skinner, 1971: 106). Reinforcement patterns can be manipulated to create an individual's sense of justice or a more just society.

In learning theory terms, conscience is sometimes viewed as a "conditioned anxiety response to certain types of situations and actions" (Eysenck, 1960: 13), formed by pairing certain stimuli (such as aggressive feelings) with punishments or other aversive stimulation. This conditioning— and generalizations of it—is said to produce conflicts between the desire to satisfy internal feelings or needs immediately and discomforts from anxiety.

PSYCHOANALYTIC THEORY

In psychoanalytic theory the superego, the internalized moral arbiter of conduct, is one of the three major systems of personality. Morality is seen as an outcome of identification with parents. Through this mechanism the child incorporates parental rules and prohibitions as well as the capacity to punish himself—to experience guilt feelings—whenever he violates a rule or prohibition. According to most psychoanalytic writers, conscience formation is accomplished by about five or six years of age, with some later modifications based on demands of authority figures.

Freud regarded the child's sense of justice as a reaction formation against his envy of other children who share his parents' love and care. Since he cannot maintain a hostile attitude toward these others without damaging himself, he identifies with them and unconsciously reacts against his own hostility by demanding equal treatment for all. Moreover,

social justice means that we deny ourselves many things so that others may have to do without them as well, or, what is the same, they may not be able to ask for them. This demand for equality is the root of social conscience and the sense of duty. (Freud, 1955: 121).

The ego, another major system of the personality, functions to bring rationality and prudence into the individual's behavior, to plan means to achieve ends, and to consider the various possibilities and the best ways to interact with the environment. According to some analysts, the irrational superego gradually becomes dominated by the rational, adapted ego and, as this occurs, the individual's morality changes from one based on sanctions and rewards imposed from without to one based on reason and internalized principles of morality. As insight, understanding, knowledge, and scientific attitudes increase, the individual deals with frustration less emotionally, less with moral anger and condemnation; he begins to disapprove of the sin instead of the sinner. Related to this changing sense of justice are shifts from autism to realism, from moral inhibition to spontaneous goodness, fear to security, aggression to tolerance and love, and from the unconscious to the conscious (Flugel, 1945). Unfortunately, the processes underlying these trends are not delineated nor are empirical data to support these clinical observations provided. Nevertheless, the theorizing is important because it represents a psychoanalytic departure from the simplistic notion that the superego alone explains morality, and it clearly focuses attention on the role of the ego in moral development.

The ego psychologists, psychoanalysts who have modified and elaborated Freud's conceptions of the ego, also assert that internalization of parental values cannot adequately account for mature moral judgments and concepts of justice. They stress cognition and ego processes, explicitly recognizing that ideas about morality and justice are not completely formed in childhood but continue to develop and change during adolescence and adulthood (Bieber, 1972; Esman, 1972). These psychologists do not deal directly with the concept of justice, but their view of mental structures differs from the orthodox and allows for some consideration of autonomous moral judgments and rational conceptualizations of justice.

THE COGNITIVE DEVELOPMENTAL APPROACH

Piaget's three-stage sequence

Piaget was the first psychologist to examine the developmental sequence and structure of children's concepts of justice both theoretically and empirically. *The Moral Judgment of the Child* (1948), one of his earliest books, describes his intensive interviews with children, using simple questions and stories as stimuli, dealing with rules, punishments, authority, evaluation of transgressions, equality, and reciprocity among individuals—ideas he considered essential to concepts of morality and justice. Analysis of children's responses led Piaget to conclude that there are three major stages in the development of respect for rules and a sense of justice.

The first, labelled *heteronomous morality, moral realism,* or *morality of constraint,* is characteristic of children younger than seven to eight. During this stage, the child is morally realistic, that is, he regards duty (and the value attached to it) as "self subsistent and independent of the mind, as imposing itself regardless of the circumstances in which the individual may

find himself" (Piaget, 1948: 106). Rules, obligations, and commands are regarded as givens, external to the mind, inflexible, and unchangeable. Justice is whatever authority (adults) or the law commands, whatever rewards or punishment authorities give. The good is obedience and wrongdoing is judged according to the letter, not the spirit, of the law.

Other significant characteristics of this stage are the belief in immanent justice (the belief that nature will punish transgressions) and absoluteness of the values held—everything is totally right or wrong, and the child thinks his judgments are shared by all. Acts are assessed right or wrong on the basis of the consequences rather than on the basis of the actors' intentions or motivations. Expiatory, painful, arbitrary punishments are favored; the more serious the consequences, the greater the punishment.

According to Piaget, moral realism has two basic sources, the child's cognitive structure and his experiences. The cognitive factors are his general egocentrism, reflected in his assumption that everyone's views of events are the same as his, and the realism of his thought, that is, his tendency to reify psychological phenomena (e.g., thoughts, rules, dreams) and conceive of them as physical, thing-like entities. The environmental or experiential factors are adult control and constraint, and the inherently unequal relationship and unilateral respect between children and parents.

The second stage in the development of the concept of justice, according to Piaget, begins around the age of seven cr eight and is related to the child's increasing interactions with peers, his more equalitarian, give-and-take-relationships. A sense of autonomy and equalitarianism becomes more highly developed when beliefs in immanent justice and expiatory punishments are superseded by ideas of reciprocal punishment (punishment fitting the crime). In matters of distribution, equality takes priority over authority.

The third, most mature stage in the development of the concept of justice, the stage of *autonomous morality*—also called *moral relativism* or *morality of cooperation*—generally emerges at about 11 or 12 years of age. Now equity plays a greater role in the child's thinking about justice, and extenuating circumstances, motivations, and intentions are heavily weighted in making moral judgments. Equalitarian concepts of distributive justice begin to prevail, while arbitrary, expiatory punishments, immanent justice, moral absolutism, and blind obedience to authority are rejected. The child is now loyal to his peers and, consequently, conformity to their norms and expectations assumes great importance. Rules are perceived as products of social interaction and therefore changeable; ideals of justice are espoused independently of external pressures.

The achievement of mature, autonomous concepts of justice is to a large extent the product of cooperation, reciprocity, and role-taking among peers. Since there are no absolute authority figures in the peer group, ideas of equality of individuals and of group solidarity emerge. These in turn discourage unilateral respect and foster participation in rule making. Equality and cooperation among peers require the individual to try to take others' views—to take roles—and at the same time stimulate discussion and criticism among equals. Thus the child's egocentrism is diminished and his realism is counteracted; concern for others' welfare and rights increases.

Piaget presents a hierarchical sequence through which most individuals progress. Individual rates of progress vary, depending on opportunities for peer cooperation and reciprocal role-taking, moral educa-

tion, home life, and other environmental factors, as well as on cognitive development. Some, particularly those in transition between stages, may manifest "mixed stages"; for example, an adolescent may be autonomous in some but not all of his concepts of justice.

While Piaget generally focuses his attention almost exclusively on changes in cognitive capacities, his discussion of the development of concepts of justice emphasizes cultural and social determinants. For example, he points out that young children in primitive non-Western cultures experience less constraint than Western children do, but older children are more severely subjected to tribal traditions and the rules of their elders. For this reason, members of such cultures may never attain moral autonomy and may even manifest more heteronomous judgments as they grow older.

Research on Piaget's Theory. Aspects of this theory have been subjected to empirical test, and, in general, hypotheses about the cognitive sources of moral development have been confirmed. An age-related developmental sequence from heteronomous to autonomous conceptions of justice, at least in Western cultures, is apparent among subjects of both sexes and from a variety of nationality and races, socioeconomic classes, and intelligence levels (Abel, 1941; Bandura & McDonald, 1963; Barnes, 1894; Boehm, 1962; Cowan, Langer, Heavenrich, & Nathanson, 1969; Grinder, 1964; Harrower, 1934; Jahoda, 1958; Johnson, 1962; Lerner 1937a, 1937b; Liu, 1950; MacRae, 1954; Magowan & Lee, 1970; Medinnus, 1962; Schallenberger, 1894; Stuart, 1967; Whiteman & Kosier, 1964).

There is also research support for the central assumption of Piaget's theory, that changes in concepts of justice reflect developments in cognitive capacities. Mental age is more closely related than chronological age to such aspects of morality as moral relativism (as opposed to moral realism), distributive justice (as opposed to restitutive justice), and restitutive justice (as opposed to expiatory justice) (Cudrin, 1965). Among 10- to 12-year-olds IQ and analytic cognitive style are related to level of moral judgment, IQ being more highly correlated (Caring, 1970). As Piaget predicts, mature concepts of justice are also associated with the development of logical skills and abstract reasoning ability (Stuart, 1967; Lee, 1971).

There is little support for Piaget's hypotheses about the experiential antecedents of mature concepts of justice, however. For example, Piaget suggests that authoritarian parental control produces immature concepts of justice while equalitarian child-rearing techniques promote more mature ones. Empirical tests do not support these relationships (Johnson, 1962). Among the six measures of boys' relationships with parents and peers used in another study, only two showed that strict parental control was associated with rigid conformity to adult-dictated regulations and with lack of influence by the obligations of friendship and peer-group membership (MacRae, 1954).

Nor is there any systematic evidence that peer orientation and an emphasis on reciprocal, cooperative relationships are necessary for the development of autonomous concepts of justice or mature moral judgments. According to the data of one study, children primarily oriented to peer expectations and norms do not manifest greater degrees of moral relativism than those who submit to adult authority (Boehm & Nass, 1962). Israeli kibbutz-reared children, growing up in a communal peer-oriented environment, are not more mature in their ideas of justice than urban children raised in nuclear families;

indeed the opposite tendency has been found (Kugelmass & Bresnitz, 1967). Nor are high standings in peer group cooperation and reciprocity, measured sociometrically, closely related to maturity of the moral judgments of children between the ages of 6 and 16 (Eibl, 1968). Peer "isolates" make more use of reciprocity in their judgments about justice than do more popular children (Kohlberg, 1963b), and maturity of thinking about intentionality and reciprocity are not associated with peer group participation (Kohlberg, 1964).

Transition Between Stages. Piaget does not deal explicitly with the mechanisms accounting for progress from one moral stage to the next, but he believes it to be the product of an interaction between the organism and the environment. The child cannot advance from less mature to more mature concepts of justice until he has sufficiently developed cognitively to grasp the new concepts involved in the higher stage. Advancement to the next stage requires the assimilation of new concepts and principles into his cognitive structures so that these can be generalized. New stages are not attained all at once; rather, the child's moral judgments may be mixed between stages during transitions. When cognitive conflict is induced, that is, when the child becomes aware of conceptual contradictions, he experiences a kind of disequilibrium that energizes and motivates him to attempt to restructure the situation by changing his form of thought to a higher level (accommodation). In the higher stages, there is greater equilibrium, harmony, and integration in the individual's thinking and in the relationship between him and his environment.

Two basic methods have been used in investigations of the mechanism underlying transitions from one stage to the next. In the first, the subject is trained through reinforcement or modelling to respond at a level different from that which he spontaneously uses and it is then determined whether he subsequently applies the newer level of reasoning. In the second method, cognitive conflict is induced in an attempt to modify the child's level of moral judgments.

The first method is illustrated in a study in which boys between five and eleven years of age observed an adult model who was reinforced either for expressing moral judgments more advanced than the child's or for expressing less mature judgments. Posttests showed that modelling can produce immediate changes, both progressive and regressive, in the maturity of children's moral judgments (Bandura & McDonald, 1963), and shifts, particularly toward more advanced reasoning, have been found to last at least two weeks (Cowan *et al.,* 1969). Adolescents' progress from moral realism to moral relativism, following modelling, lasted as long as three months, but regressive changes were not enduring (Le Furgy & Woloshin, 1969).

Inducing cognitive conflict may also result in changes in young children's justice concepts. Some of the kindergarten children in one study were reinforced for mature responses to stories, that is, for considering intentions rather than simply consequences in making judgments. Others had their attention directed toward intentionality and discussed this after they heard stories. In posttests ten days later, children in both reinforcement and discussion groups gave more mature responses than a control group, and their explanations showed that more of them really understood the underlying principles of intentionality. The discussion group, the group that experienced greater cognitive conflict, was superior to the group that had simply been reinforced for correct responses (Jensen & Larm, 1970).

It is difficult to evaluate whether training or inducing cognitive conflict in these experiments produced real changes in the children's mental structures or simply provided them with specific new moral responses. The basic question, still unanswered, is whether on the basis of these experiences new, more mature concepts or principles of justice can be assimilated, understood, and generalized.

Kohlberg's theory of moral development

Another cognitive development theory of moral development, which extends Piaget's developmental stage sequence, has been presented by Kohlberg (1963a, 1964, 1971). The schema is based on analyses of interviews with boys ranging from 10 to 16 years of age. These interviews are centered on a series of moral dilemmas, told in story form, in which acts of obedience to laws or to the commands of authority conflict with the welfare or interest of the actor or other people. The subject is asked whether the hero of the story should act in ways obedient to the law or to rules, on the one hand, or in accordance with his own or other people's needs, on the other. The subject is then asked a series of questions (probes) about the thinking underlying his responses. The stories tap a variety of ways of judging obligations and values, a variety of principles of justice, and the principles are applied to a number of different kinds of issues and institutions (social norms, civil liberties, contracts and promises, punitive justice, property, personal conscience, issues of authority, and democracy).

The sequence of moral development described by Kohlberg consists of six stages ordered into three levels of moral orientation. The schema is more complex and extensive than Piaget's and it deals with changes in moral reasoning that occur not only through middle childhood and adolescence but during the mature years as well. In fact, the highest stages of moral reasoning, the principled ones, are achieved only by a relatively small proportion of mature adults. The stages are viewed as being invariant in sequence, hierarchical, universal, and intrinsic to the species, although any particular individual's development may cease at any given stage. Each stage is qualitatively different from the others in modes of cognition and each constitutes a structured whole, a comprehensive, organized way of thinking.

Kohlberg deals much more explicitly than Piaget with the development and application of principles of justice in a variety of areas. In fact, justice is the cornerstone of his theory.

The principle central to the development of moral judgment . . . is that of *justice.* Justice, the primary regard for the value and equality of all human beings and for reciprocity in human relations, is a basic and universal standard. (Note 1, p. 4)

Each of Kohlberg's stages is viewed as "a justice structure which is progressively more comprehensive, differentiated, and equilibrated than the prior structure" (Kohlberg, 1971, p. 195). That is, each successive stage represents a different, increasingly more mature application of the principles of justice, the principles for deciding between competing claims of individuals.

The nature of the individual's sense of justice is a critical criterion in assessing his stage of moral development. To illustrate, at Stage 1, justice does not involve reciprocal equal exchanges between individuals but is defined in terms of differentials in power, status, and possessions, similar to Piaget's stage of heteronomous morality or moral realism. At Stage 2, however, justice consists of either equal exchange of goods or acts or, where the needs of persons conflict, what the actor

desires for himself. Among children approximately 10 years of age, these first two levels of moral thinking are the most common. At Stage 3 (the modal stage at age 13) justice is conceived as the "golden rule" ideal of reciprocity rather than strict exchange and characteristically linked with positive interpersonal relationships. During Stage 4, which develops in adolescence and remains the predominant mode of response for many adults, justice involves relationships between individuals and the social system to which they belong. Equality in application of the laws, recognition and reward of merit (equity), and the maintenance of the rules of the society are all aspects of justice. At the highest stage (6) justice is conceptualized in terms of a universal ethical principle orientation which assumes that each human life is of unconditional value. It is "the right of every person to an equal consideration of his claims in every situation, not just those codified into law" (Kohlberg, 1971, p. 210). Stages 5 and 6 do not usually appear until an individual is in his twenties, if ever (Kohlberg, 1973).

Justice may be considered "a form of equilibrium between conflicting interpersonal claims" (Kohlberg & Gilligan, 1971), and a just solution to a moral dilemma "is a solution acceptable to all parties considering each as free and equal" (Kohlberg, 1971—adapted from Rawls, 1971). Arriving at a just solution requires taking the roles of all individuals involved in a moral conflict, perceiving the situation from all points of view in an unbiased objective way. Both welfare and justice concerns are incorporated in each moral stage, becoming increasingly more differentiated, integrated, and universal at each successive stage. Justice assumes the character of a principle at the highest stage and then takes precedence over all other considerations, including welfare.

In this theory, as in Piaget's, progress

from one moral stage to the next is seen as the result of the interaction of the maturation of the organism and experience (environmental events). The development of cognitive capacities is critical because making judgments about right and wrong is primarily an active cognitive process. Indeed, each successive moral stage is seen as a different, more advanced "structured whole," a new and more coherent cognitive organization of moral thinking. Furthermore, the sequence of stages is presumably based on a universal logic and intimately related (or even parallel) to Piaget's general cognitive or logical stages (Kohlberg, 1971).

The experiential or environmental factor that has the greatest impact on moral development according to Kohlberg is social role-taking which enhances the individual's ability to empathize with others and to perceive things from the point of view of the "generalized other" in resolving moral conflicts. Furthermore, role-taking provides opportunities to become aware of conflicts or discrepancies between one's own judgments and actions and those of others. As the individual progresses from role-taking to the resolution of conflicts between points of view, he arrives at principles of justice, and higher moral stages are said to have a more stable equilibrium than lower ones.

Research Evidence. A number of the critical aspects of Kohlberg's theory have been tested empirically and supported. For example, there is evidence of the universality of the moral stages: Subjects from Taiwan, Yucatan, and Turkey progress through the same sequence of stages as children in the United States do. In some cultures subjects apparently move through the sequence more slowly, and very few of them gave evidence of principled reasoning (Kohlberg, 1969).

Central in Kohlberg's theory is the notion that maturity of moral judgment or of concepts of justice depends upon cognitive development; the attainment of a particular stage of logic, thinking, and reasoning is a necessary although not sufficient condition for the achievement of a parallel stage of moral judgment. There is considerable empirical support for this idea. Thus, among children ranging in age from 5 through 17 years, thinking and reasoning at the level of concrete operations was found to be associated with a decrease in authority-oriented moral judgments, while reasoning at the higher, formal-operations level was related to an increase in Stage 5 moral thinking (Lee, 1971). Similarly, in another extensive study (Kuhn, Langer, Kohlberg, & Haan, in press), a broad range of subjects, aged 10 to 30 and 45 to 50 responded to several Piagetian tests as well as to the Kohlberg stories. Cognitive capacities at the concrete operations level were associated with Stage 3 or lower moral judgments and formal operations abilities appeared to be necessary for the emergence of principled moral judgment (Stages 5 or 6) or the consolidation of Stage 4 moral reasoning. Level of cognitive development and moral judgment were positively and significantly correlated, even with IQ held constant.

As Kohlberg's theory maintains, role-taking ability is significantly correlated with maturity of moral judgments and concepts of justice. The ability to take the role of another in a perceptual task is related to reciprocity in moral judgments (Lee, 1971) and reciprocal social role-taking (taking another's role and realizing that the other is also role-taking) is positively correlated with conventional (Stage 3 or 4) moral judgments in 8-, 9-, and 10-year-olds (Selman, 1971).

Transitions Between Stages. Like Piaget, Kohlberg maintains that disequilibrium created by cognitive conflict is the most significant incentive to progress in moral judgments. This was tested by Turiel (1966) in a provocative experiment in which seventh-grade boys whose moral levels had been assessed by Kohlberg stories experienced cognitive conflict produced by the experimenter's presentation of arguments for and against particular lines of action. Some heard arguments involving moral concepts one stage above their own position, some two stages above, and for a third group, the arguments were one stage below. Posttesting showed that arguments one stage advanced above the child's own level were accepted most frequently and assimilated most readily into the moral thinking of the child; next most influential were the arguments two levels advanced, and the least influential were the arguments below the child's level. These findings support the hypothesis that progress in moral reasoning is limited by what the subject can assimilate, which is reflected in his present stage of moral reasoning. Reasoning two stages above the subject's own level is apparently too advanced for ready assimilation (Turiel, 1966).

Other studies have also demonstrated that when presented with statements illustrative of different levels of moral reasoning, children prefer those above rather than those below their own level. Comprehension decreases as the statements get progressively more advanced and further above the subject's own level. From this, it may be inferred that the successive moral stages are in fact increasingly more complex, integrated, and differentiated. Moreover, the most advanced level of moral judgment and concepts of justice that the child can achieve as a result of experiencing cognitive conflict are limited by his initial (pretraining) level (Rest, Turiel, & Kohlberg, 1969; Kuhn *et al.,* in press).

Classroom discussions about mature solutions to moral dilemmas, one hour a week for 12 weeks, were used in Blatt's (1969) study to create cognitive conflict among 12-year-olds. Most of the children showed some advance in moral reasoning and justice concepts as a result of these sessions, and those who made moderate gains maintained these gains over the one year period. However, those who showed advances of more than one stage tended to regress somewhat by the end of the year. Apparently, cognitive conflict can help accelerate moral development, but unusually large gains are not likely to be maintained for a long time. This is consistent with the assumption that Kohlberg's stages form an invariant sequence.

REFERENCES

Abel, T. Moral judgments among subnormals. *Journal of Abnormal Psychology,* 1941, **36,** 378-392.

Bandura, A., & McDonald, F. J. Influence of social reinforcement and the behavior of models in shaping children's moral judgments. *Journal of Abnormal and Social Psychology,* 1963, **67,** 274-281.

Barnes, E. Punishment as seen by children. *Pedagogical Seminary (Journal of Genetic Psychology),* 1894, **3,** 87-96.

Bieber, I. Morality and Freud's concept of the superego. In S. C. Post (ed.), *Moral values and the superego concept in psychoanalysis.* New York: International Universities Press, 1972.

Blatt, M. *The effects of classroom discussion upon children's level of moral judgment.* Unpublished doctoral dissertation, University of Chicago, 1969.

Boehm, L. The development of conscience: A comparison of American children of different mental and socioeconomic levels. *Child Development,* 1962, **33,** 575-590.

Boehm, L., & Nass, M. L. Social class differences in conscience development. *Child Development,* 1962, **33,** 565-575.

Caring, L. C. *The relation of cognitive styles, sex, and intelligence to moral judgment in children.* Unpublished doctoral dissertation, New York University, 1970.

Cowan, P. A.; Langer, J.; Heavenrich, J.; & Nathanson, M. Social learning and Piaget's cognitive theory of moral development. *Journal of Personality and Social Psychology,* 1969, **11,** 261-274.

Cudrin, J. M. *The relationship of chronological age, mental age, social behavior, and number of siblings to the Piagetian concept of moral judgment development.* Unpublished doctoral dissertation, University of North Carolina, 1965.

Eibl, J. F. *Moral judgments of children in need of parents.* Unpublished doctoral dissertation, Indiana University, 1968.

Esman, A. H. Adolescence and the consolidation of values. In S. C. Post (ed.), *Moral values and the superego concept in psychoanalysis.* New York: International Universities Press, 1972.

Eysenck, H. J. The development of moral values in children: The contribution of learning theory. *British Journal of Educational Psychology,* 1960, **30,** 11-21.

Flugel, J. C. *Man, morals, and society.* London: Duckworth, 1945.

Freud, S. Group psychoanalysis and the analysis of the ego. In J. Strachey (ed.), *The complete psychological works of Sigmund Freud,* Vol. 17. London: Hogarth Press, 1955.

Grinder, R. E. Relations between behavioral and cognitive dimensions of conscience in middle childhood. *Child Development,* 1964, **35,** 881-891.

Harrower, M. R. Social status and moral development of the child. *British Journal of Educational Psychology,* 1934, **4,** 75-95.

Jahoda, G. Immanent justice among West African children. *Journal of Social Psychology,* 1958. **47,** 241-248.

Jensen, L. C., & Larm, C. Effects of two training procedures on intentionality in moral judgments among children. *Developmental Psychology,* 1970, **2,** 310.

Johnson, R. C. A study of children's moral judgments. *Child Development,* 1962, **33,** 327-354.

Kohlberg, L. The development of children's orientations toward a moral order: Sequence in the development of moral thought. *Vita Humana,* 1963, **6,** 11-33. (a)

Kohlberg, L. Moral development and identification. In H. Stevenson (ed.), *Child psychology: 62nd yearbook of the National Society for the Study of Education.* Chicago: University of Chicago Press, 1963. (b)

Kohlberg, L. Development of moral character and ideology. In M. L. Hoffman & L. W. Hoffman (eds.), *Review of child development research,* Vol. 1. New York: Russell Sage Foundation, 1964.

Kohlberg, L. Stage and sequence: The cognitive-developmental approach to socialization. In D. Goslin (ed.), *Handbook of socialization theory and research.* Chicago: Rand McNally, 1969.

Kohlberg, L. From is to ought: How to commit the naturalistic fallacy and get away with it in the study of moral development. In T. Mischel (ed.), *Cognitive development and epistemology.* New York: Academic Press, 1971.

Kohlberg, L. Continuities in childhood and adult moral development revisited. In P. B. Baltes & K. W. Schaie (eds.), *Life span developmental psychology.* New York: Academic Press, 1973.

Kohlberg, L., & Gilligan, C. The adolescent as a philosopher: The discovery of self in the postconventional world. *Daedalus,* 1971, **110,** 1051-1086.

Kugelmass, S., & Bresnitz, S. The development of intentionality in moral judgment in city and kibbutz adolescents. *Journal of Genetic Psychology,* 1967, **111,** 103-111.

Kuhn, D.; Langer, J.; Kohlberg, L.; & Haan, N. The development of formal operations in logical and moral judgment. *Genetic Psychology Monographs,* in press.

Le Furgy, W. G., & Woloshin, G. W. Immediate and long term effects of experimentally induced social influence in the modification of adolescents' moral judgments. *Journal of Personality and Social Psychology,* 1969, **12,** 104-110.

Lee, L. C. The concomitant development of cognitive and moral modes of thought: A test of selected deductions from Piaget's theory.

Genetic Psychology Monographs, 1971, **83,** 93-143.

Lerner, E. *Constraint areas and moral judgment of children.* Menasha, Wis.: Banta, 1937. (a)

Lerner, E. The problem of perspective in moral reasoning. *American Journal of Sociology,* 1937, **43,** 249-269. (b)

Liu, C. H. *The influence of cultural background on moral judgment of children.* Unpublished doctoral dissertation, Columbia University, 1950.

MacRae, D., Jr. A test of Piaget's theories of moral development. *Journal of Abnormal and Social Psychology,* 1954, **49,** 14-18.

Magowan, S. A., & Lee, T. Some sources of error in the use of the projective method for the measurement of moral judgment. *British Journal of Psychology,* 1970, **61,** 535-543.

Medinnus, G. R. Objective responsibility in children: A comparison with the Piaget data. *Journal of Genetic Psychology,* 1962, **191,** 127-133.

Piaget, J. *The moral judgment of the child.* Glencoe, Ill.: Free Press, 1948.

Rawls, J. *Justice as fairness.* Cambridge, Mass.: Harvard University Press, 1971.

Rest, J.; Turiel, E.; & Kohlberg, L. Level of moral development as a determinant of preference and comprehension of moral judgments made by others. *Journal of Personality,* 1969, **37,** 225-252.

Schallenberger, M. A study of children's rights as seen by themselves. *Pedagogical Seminary (Journal of Genetic Psychology),* 1894, **3,** 87-96.

Selman, R. The relation of role-taking to the development of moral judgment in children. *Child Development,* 1971, **42,** 79-91.

Skinner, B. F. *Beyond freedom and dignity.* New York: Bantam/Vintage, 1971.

Stuart, R. B. Decentration in the development of children's concepts of moral and causal judgment. *Journal of Genetic Psychology,* 1967, **111,** 59-68.

Turiel, E. An experimental test of the sequentiality of developmental stages in the child's moral judgments. *Journal of Personality and Social Psychology,* 1966, **3,** 611-618.

Whiteman, P. H., & Kosier, P. Development of children's moralistic judgments: Age, Sex, IQ, and certain personal experiental variables. *Child Development,* 1964, **35,** 843-851.

23.

Nancy Wadsworth Denney and Diane M. Duffy

POSSIBLE ENVIRONMENTAL CAUSES OF STAGES IN MORAL REASONING

INTRODUCTION

Kohlberg has described three distinct stages in the development of moral reasoning (1969). In the first or preconventional stage, there is an orientation toward the physical consequences of an act (e.g., rewarded acts are good and punished acts are bad) and toward deference to superior power. In the second or conventional stage, there is an orientation toward pleasing others and maintaining social order (e.g., obeying the rules set forth by the family or school). In the third or postconventional stage, the orientation is toward autonomous moral principles which are independent of other people or groups.

Kohlberg has suggested that the developmental changes which take place in moral reasoning occur as a result of internal changes in the child's cognitive structure. He contends that cognitive stages, such as those observed in moral reasoning, do not result from environmental influences alone. The following exemplifies his reasoning:

In contrast, if structural stages do define general ontogenetic sequences, then an interactional type of theory of developmental process must be used to explain ontogeny. If the child goes through qualitatively different stages of thought, his basic modes of organizing experience cannot be the direct result of

adult teaching, or they would be copies of adult thought from the start. If the child's cognitive responses differed from the adult's only in revealing less information and less complication of structure, it would be possible to view them as incomplete learning of the external structure of the world, whether that structure is defined in terms of the adult culture or in terms of the laws of the physical world. If the child's responses indicate a different structure or organization than the adult's, rather than a less complete one, and if the structure is similar in all children, it is extremely difficult to view the child's mental structure as a direct learning of the external structure (Kohlberg, 1969: 354).

Kohlberg seems to be assuming that the "external structure" remains the same for children of all ages. He implies that adults try to teach children of all ages the same things and in the same ways. However, at least with respect to moral reasoning, parents probably do not teach children of different ages the same things. It seems unlikely, for example, that parents would expound upon their own moral reasoning to a four-year-old child. It seems more likely that with respect to moral situations, parents treat children of different ages very differently and, thereby, imply different types of moral reasoning to children of different ages. For example, it is not too surprising that one of the first stages in the development of moral reasoning is that of an orientation to the physical consequences of an act and deference to superior power. How often does one hear a parent saying something like the following to a very young child: "If you hit your sister one more time, you'll come into the

Source: *Journal of Genetic Psychology,* 1974, **125,** 277-283. This research was partially supported by funds from the National Science Foundation Institutional Grant Awards Program in conjunction with the State University of New York College at Buffalo.

house!" The parent in this example is implying that the child should not hit his sister *because* of the consequences of the act. It is not surprising that children who are frequently given "explanations," such as the above, would be oriented toward punishment and authority. The parent in this case is teaching the child a preconventional type of reasoning. Surely not all parents who make such statements are, themselves, in the preconventional stage. Rather, for some reason, they are not exposing their children to their own moral reasoning. From this example, it is clear that parents are capable of implying types of moral reasoning to their children that may be very different from their own type of moral reasoning.

It seems likely that the level of moral reasoning that is implied by parents would increase with the age of their child. If this is indeed the case, then the stages that occur in the child's thinking may simply occur because the child is learning these types of thinking from his parents. Thus, it is possible that the observed stages may really originate in the external environment rather than in internal changes in the child's cognitive structure. The purpose of the present study was, first, to determine whether parents actually do imply different moral principles to children of different ages and, second, to determine whether there is a relationship between the type of moral reasoning that the parents imply and the level of moral reasoning used by the child.

METHOD

Subjects

The subjects were seventeen six-year-olds, seventeen ten-year-olds, and seventeen fourteen-year-old students at the campus school of the State University of New York College at Buffalo and their mothers. The age ranges of the three groups of children were from 6 years and 2 months to 6 years and 11 months, from 10 years and 3 months to 10 years and 10 months, and from 14 years and 1 month to 14 years and 11 months. Due to the lottery student selection employed by the campus school, the students came from a variety of racial and social class backgrounds. Approximately half of the subjects were male and half, female.

Procedure

The children and their mothers were interviewed separately. Neither was told that the other was being interviewed.

Child Interview. The children were brought individually from the classroom to the experimental room. The experimenter spent a few minutes talking with the children in order to establish rapport before beginning the interview. The children were then asked eleven questions, each of which demanded a moral judgment. Examples of such questions are as follows: (*a*) "Kathy's parents told her that if she didn't do well in school, she would be punished. On the next big test Kathy didn't know many of the answers. When the teacher wasn't looking Kathy copied someone else's answers. Kathy got a good grade on the test. Kathy's mother was so happy that Kathy got a good grade on the test that she took her out for an ice cream sundae. Was Kathy right to copy the answers? Why?"; and (*b*) "A woman had an accident on the highway. One man saw the accident and just kept on driving. Another man saw the accident and stopped to help the lady. He lifted the injured lady into his car and drove her to the hospital. There the doctor told the man that by moving the lady he had made her injuries worse. Which man did the best thing—the man who drove by or the man who stopped to help? Why?" After the child's response to each question, a number of probing questions were asked to determine why he answered the way he did.

The answers to all of the questions were tape-recorded so they could be scored at a later time. The responses were divided into Kohlberg's three main stages—preconventional, conventional, and postconventional.

Mother Interview. The mothers were interviewed individually during school hours. They were presented with fifteen questions that were intended to get at the moral principles that the mothers convey to their children by the way they respond to their children's behavior. Examples of such questions are as follows: (*a*) "If you found out that (*child's name*) had stolen something from a department store but did not get caught, what would you say or do to (*child's name*)?"; (*b*) "If you asked (*child's name*) to clean up the dishes because you had to go to a meeting right after dinner and he (she) said 'no', what would you say or do?"; and (*c*) "let's say that (*child's name*) came home from school and said that someone at school had told him that if a person was in great pain and dying of cancer, the doctor should just kill him. What would you say to him (her)?"

The mothers' responses were also tape-recorded so they could be scored at a later time. The mothers' responses were scored according to which of Kohlberg's stages of moral reasoning their actions would imply to the child. For example, if, in response to the first question cited above, the mother said that she would spank her child and tell him that if he ever stole something again he would get another spanking, she would be given a preconventional score. In this case the mother is implying to the child that the reason for

not stealing is so that he will not get spanked. Thus, she is stressing to the child that the consequences of the act are what make it either good or bad. Likewise, the mother who says that she would tell her child that he should not steal because, if he got caught, the owner of the store might call the police would get a preconventional score.

Examples of responses that would be categorized into conventional stages are: "What would Mr. Jones think if he found out that you were stealing from his store? Do you want people to think that you are a thief?" and "It's against the law to take something that doesn't belong to you so we are going to have to return it to the store."

Examples of responses that would be classified as postconventional are "I know I wouldn't feel right if I stole something. I wouldn't want other people to take things that belong to me, so I wouldn't take things that belong to other people." or "Do you think it's right for people to just go take whatever they want? What would happen if everyone just went around taking whatever they wanted no matter who it belonged to?"

RESULTS

All of the mothers' responses and all of the children's responses were categorized into either the preconventional, conventional, or postconventional category of moral reasoning. Then the most frequent category used by each mother and each child was taken as that mother's or that child's overall score. All of the analyses were performed on these overall scores.

Interrater reliability was established on both the children's and the mothers' overall scores by the first author and another rater who was unfamiliar with the project. The two raters independently categorized the protocols of twenty-five randomly selected mothers and the protocols of twenty-five randomly selected children. The interrater reliability obtained on the mothers' protocols was .89 and the interrater reliability obtained on the children's protocols was .85.

All of the data analyses were performed on the first author's categorizations of the data.

Mothers' responses

The frequencies of the mothers' implied levels of moral reasoning for the 6-, 10-, and 14-year-old children are presented in Table 23.1. There was a significant relationship between the age of the child and the level of moral reasoning implied by the mother in her treatment of the child, $X^2(4)=14.43$, $p<.01$. The older the child, the higher the level of moral reasoning the mother implied in her treatment of the child.

Children's responses

The frequencies of the 6-, 10-, and 14-year-old children's levels of moral reasoning are also presented in Table 23.1. There was a significant relationship between the age of the child and his level of moral development, $X^2(4)=16.06$, $p<.01$.

The older the child, the higher the level of moral reasoning he used.

Relationship between the mothers' and the children's responses

The correlation between the mothers' and their children's responses was $+.59$ which was significant at the .01 level. This is not too surprising in light of the fact that both the mothers' implied level of moral reasoning and the children's level of moral reasoning increased with the age of the child. However, even with age partialed out, the relationship between the mother's implied level of moral reasoning was significant, $r=.51$.

DISCUSSION

The results of the present study indicate that (*a*) the older the child the higher the level of moral reasoning he employs; (*b*) the older the child, the higher the level of moral reasoning his mother implies; and (*c*) even with age partialed out, there is a significant positive relationship between the level of moral reasoning implied by the mother and the level of moral reasoning employed by her child.

If one can assume that the mothers' responses to the hypothetical situations presented reflect the way in which they

TABLE 23.1. Levels of Moral Reasoning Implied by Mothers and Displayed by Children

Children's age	Preconventional	Conventional	Postconventional
		Implied by mothers	
6	12	1	4
10	5	4	8
14	2	7	8
		Displayed by children	
6	15	2	0
10	7	9	1
14	5	8	4

ordinarily treat their children, then the results indicate that the mothers do, indeed, treat children of different ages in ways that imply different types of moral reasoning.

Thus, it appears that there is at least one environmental factor—how the parent treats the child—which could be responsible for the stages that have been observed in the development of moral reasoning. Consequently, environmental factors should no longer be quickly dismissed as possible causes of the stages observed in young children. The environment is simply not the same for children of different ages, and thus, environmental factors should be considered as possible causes of developmental changes in the child's thinking.

Of course, the results of the present study do not prove that the stages observed in the development of moral reasoning are a result of external, adult teaching rather than a result of internal changes in cognitive structure. Because the present study was correlational, causality cannot be established. One could always argue that the mothers simply tailor their explanations to what they have found, through experience, to be understandable for the children. Thus, the children might be causing the stages in the mothers. In order to establish the direction of causality, noncorrelational research will have to be done. Until that time, one can at least conclude that environmental factors should not be discounted as possible causes of the stages in the development of moral reasoning.

REFERENCE

Kohlberg, L. Stage and sequence: The cognitive-developmental approach to socialization. In D. A. Goslin (ed.), *Handbook of socialization theory and research.* Chicago: Rand McNally, 1969.

24.

Martin L. Hoffman

TOWARD A DEVELOPMENTAL THEORY OF PROSOCIAL MOTIVATION

I would like to present some notions about the development of prosocial motives that I have been working on for some time but only recently put together into some semblance of a coherent scheme.

First, a few words about the prevailing view in psychology, which has long been that prosocial behaviors are not intrinsically motivated. They either derive from selfish motives—as in Anna Freud's view that altruism is a reaction formation against hostility—or they are produced by reinforcement, like any other behavior. Even motivation theorists like Maslow who deal with higher motives such as self-fulfillment, either ignore or give lip service to the prosocial. What could be *less* prosocial or altruistic than the continued search for peak experiences.

My assumption is that in man's evolution there has been selection for prosocial

Source: Paper presented at the National Institute of Child Health and Human Development Workshop, Elkridge, Maryland, 1972.

as well as individual motivation, since at least in the early periods of human existence some form of cooperative activity was necessary for survival. There is every reason to assume, therefore, that prosocial motives are as likely to be intrinsic as individual or selfish motives, however fragile they may appear to be in our highly individualistic society. And what I am trying to do is answer the question: If intrinsic prosocial motives do exist, what are they like, and how do they develop in the individual? My presentation will consist of a summary of several concepts that together provide the outline of a possible developmental theory of prosocial motivation. These concepts, which all rest ultimately on the human capacity to take the other's role, are: empathic distress, sympathetic distress, personal guilt, and existential guilt. My discussion will be sprinkled with anecdotal data, not as evidence but to clarify and illustrate the concepts in such a way as to suggest possible avenues for operationalizing them.

The first, empathic distress, is by no means a new concept, nor is the process by which it is acquired a complex one. The child cuts himself, feels the pain, cries. Later on he sees another child cut himself and cry. The sight of the blood, the sound of the cry, or any distress cue from the other child associated with his own prior experience of pain, can now elicit the unpleasant affect that was initially a part of that experience. This affective response to the distress cue is the empathic distress.

Even the very young child has the necessary neural capacity for this response, and he has it long before developing a sense of self or a sense of the other. As a result of this lack of self–other differentiation it is unclear to him who is experiencing the distress, and he will often behave as though he were experiencing it. A graduate student recently described two incidents with

his young son, which are beautifully illustrative. In one, the father felt depressed and looked downcast. The boy, who was 14 months at the time, noticed this and his immediate response was to move quickly to his mother to be comforted. In another, the boy, now 18 months old, was hitting his father, at first playfully but with increasing ferocity. It began to hurt and the father doubled up in mock pain. The child immediately stopped the hitting, doubled up, put his thumb in his mouth, and put his head in his father's lap— exactly the pattern used when he is experiencing pain.

Developmentally this is obviously a primitive response. We may use the word empathy but the child is obviously not putting himself in the other's place. His response is rather a passive and involuntary one, based on the "pull" of the cues emitted by the victim which are perceptually similar to cues associated with his own past painful experiences. We may also note that the resulting behavior appears to be *hedonistically* motivated, that is, designed to reduce the child's own distress rather than distress in the other. Nevertheless, it is relevant to prosocial motivation since the child's distress is contingent not on his own, but someone else's actual painful experience.

The first important developmental advance, for our purposes, occurs when the child is able to distinguish between self and other. When confronted with another person in pain he continues to have the empathic distress reaction, but because of this new cognitive capacity, he will know that it is the other person, and not he who is experiencing the actual distress. The synthesis of empathic distress with the recognition that the other is actually experiencing the discomfort constitutes what I will call sympathetic distress. The child now feels "sympathy for" rather than "sympathy with" the victim—a reciprocal rather than a parallel affective response. There are four levels of sympathetic distress, each dependent on further advances in the child's cognitive capacity.

At the first level, although the child has acquired a sense of the other, he as yet fails to distinguish between the inner states (thoughts, perceptions, feelings) of the other and of himself. Thus while he knows the other person is the victim, his assumptions about the other's feelings are based on sheer projection of his own feelings. This is evidenced in his efforts to relieve the other's distress, as illustrated again with the child of a student. A boy aged 19 months is playing in the same room as another child the same age. The other child starts to cry. The boy brings his own mother to the child, instead of the latter's mother who is also present. In another incident several weeks later, the same boy gives up his beloved Teddy to another child who is crying because his parents have left him for several days. This incident is particularly interesting because the boy's parents reminded him that he would miss his Teddy if he gave it away. He nevertheless insisted—as if the sympathetic distress he was experiencing was greater than the anticipated unpleasantness of not having the doll, which is possibly indicative of the strong motivational potential of sympathetic distress.

In many ways, this first level of sympathetic distress is as primitive as the empathic distress described earlier—a passive involuntary response to cues perceptually similar to those associated with his own past painful experiences. The overt response, however, appears to be the first instance of truly prosocial behavior. That is, the child's *aim* is to relieve the other's distress—even though his behavior will often be misguided owing to its being based on the assumption of identity be-

tween his own and the other person's inner states.

At the next developmental level of interest the child knows that the other's inner states are different from his own, that he has a different perspective based on his own needs and interpretations of events, although he is uncertain as to what that perspective is. This is largely the result of the child's cognitive development, together with experiences in which his expectations based on projection have proven to be wrong. His efforts to help now become more sophisticated. Consider this example. A boy struggles with a friend over a toy. The friend cries. The boy pauses, lets go so that the friend has the toy, but the friend keeps crying. The boy gives the friend his Teddy, but the friend keeps crying. The boy then runs to the next room, gets the friend's security blanket, and offers it to the friend, who then stops crying.

This type of response is obviously less primitive than the previous ones. The affective portion may still be similar, to be sure, and the child very likely continues to project his own needs to the victim. He is aware of the guesswork involved, however, and tries to use his knowledge about the other, as well as benefit from corrective feedback received in the situation. The projected content is just one of many inputs contributing to his response. For the first time in our developmental account the child makes active cognitive inferences about the other person's inner states. He tries, in Piaget's sense, to "construct" the other; to put himself in the other's place; to take his role.

At a still more advanced point the child becomes not only aware of the other's inner states but of his separate existence beyond the immediate situation. He is then capable of responding to the other's *general* state or plight. This third level of sympathetic distress, then, consists of a synthesis of the empathic distress reaction to the other's feeling in the immediate situation, and a more active cognitive construction of the other's general level of misfortune. Further, if the cues of the immediate and the general are contradictory, the individual has the capacity to rise above and resist the pull of the immediate and respond primarily to what he imagines are the other's general life conditions and prospects—his general level of deprivation or fulfillment. If this image diverges from his conception of an acceptable normal happy existence, a conception which he has also acquired by this time, he responds with sympathetic distress.

In a final cognitive extension the individual acquires the capacity to comprehend the plight not only of one person but entire groups or classes of people—such as those who are economically impoverished, politically oppressed, socially outcast, victimized by war, or mentally retarded. He may not have had any distress experiences quite like those of the victimized group, but it seems reasonable to assume that he has had his difficult moments and that all painful experiences have some affective aspects in common—therefore that he has the affective base for a generalized empathic distress response. The synthesis of this generalized empathic distress with the awareness of the plight of an unfortunate group constitutes this final level of sympathetic distress.

Thus far I have mentioned nothing about the individual's perception of himself as the cause of the other's distress or misfortune. This becomes a possibility once he acquires the capacity to recognize the consequences of his own action for others and the fact that he has choice over his behavior. The synthesis of sympathetic distress and awareness of being the cause of the other's distress is what I call *guilt,*

since it has both the affectively unpleasant and the cognitive self-blaming components of the guilt experience. *Personal* guilt may be experienced directly as the result of specific acts of commission, or of omission—things he might have done to help the other but didn't.

The person may also feel culpable not because of any specific action or inaction but because of his sheer *existence in a relatively advantaged position* with respect to others. While one's relative advantage may be a necessary condition for sympathetic distress—since preoccupation with one's own troubles may prevent having feeling for the other—it may at times become salient, and the primary basis for what I shall call *existential guilt.* The individual is consumed with the fact that he is enjoying what others cannot; or that others suffer misfortunes that he does not—a recognition difficult to avoid in an age of mass communications. An obvious example exists among today's affluent American youth where additional contributing factors to existential guilt are the prevalent acceptance of equalitarian social norms— all people have equal worth—and a lack of justification for their own relative advantage, since it was inherited, not earned. For some, existential guilt can shade into an exquisite form of personal guilt—a "sense of individual complicity"—should they gain an understanding of the larger matrix of social forces and social causation which enables them to see the contribution of their own reference group to the plight of the victimized groups. This may be a far more powerful motivating force than the simpler form of personal guilt mentioned earlier, since it may call for ceaseless activity in the service of social change rather than a discrete act of restitution. If I am right about this, we may have to add something to Maslow's need hierarchy. Though an individual's deficiency needs are satisfied, the person may not be able to search for fulfillment when the deficiency needs of large groups of others in society remain unsatisfied.

In discussing the development of the white middle-class radicals of the 1960's, Keniston very neatly captures the essence of the existential guilt response (although he does not call it "guilt") and the role of seeing oneself as relatively advantaged, when he states that they

. . . stressed their shock upon realizing that their own good fortune was not shared . . . and their indignation when they "really" understood that the benefits they had experienced had not been extended to others. (pp. 131-132)

Perhaps the following quotes, one from a Keniston interviewee and the other from a college student working in the summer as an "intern" for U.S. Representative Morris Udall, illustrate even more sharply the potentially important role of the perception of relative advantage in motivating prosocial behavior,

"It seemed to me completely obvious that these kids were smarter than I was, they were quicker, they were faster, they were stronger, they knew more about things. And yet, you know, I was the one that lived in a place where there were fans and no flies, and they lived with the flies. And I was clearly destined for something, and they were destined for nothing. . . . Well, I sort of made a pact with these people that when I got to be powerful I might change some things. And I think I pursued that pact pretty consistently for a long time." (p. 50)

. . . these people feel guilty that they have had the highest standard of living ever. They feel guilty because while they are enjoying this highest standard of living, American Indians are starving and black ghettos are overrun by rats. What they see is that in America, home of that "glorious dream," all sorts of people are *starving.* This goes on while they eat steak every day. Their sense of moral indignation can't stand this; and they realize that the blame rests on the shoulders of their class (*The New Republic,* Nov. 29, 1970, p. 11)

The concept of existential guilt also encompasses the survivor guilt found in wartime and so well documented by Robert Lifton in his study of the survivors of Hiroshima. Despite being maimed, disfigured, and at times half dead themselves, these people felt guilty because they lived and others had died. Lifton suggests that

. . . survivor can never, inwardly, simply conclude that it was logical and right for him, and not others, to survive. Rather he is bound by an unconscious perception of organic social balance which makes him feel that his surviving was made possible by others' deaths: If they had not died, he would have had to; if he had not survived, someone else would have. Such guilt . . . may well be that most fundamental to human existence. (p. 56)

In discussing the idea of "radiation of guilt" Lifton highlights the significance of the sense of relative advantage,

. . . the survivors feel guilt toward the dead; ordinary Japanese feel guilt toward survivors; and the rest of the world feels guilt toward the Japanese. Proceeding outward from the core of the death immersion each group internalizes the suffering of that one step closer than itself to the core which it contrasts with its own relative good fortune. However invisible these patterns may be at the periphery, they can be observed in the behavior of the members of one group toward those of another . . . (p. 499)

Lifton also confirms the connection between existential guilt and action when he states that many of the survivors, though themselves maimed and having barely enough strength to save themselves and their families, "felt accused in the eyes of the anonymous dead and dying of wrongdoing and transgression for not helping them, letting them die . . . for selfishly remaining alive and strong" (p. 36). That even under these extreme conditions existential guilt could function as a motive to prosocial action—in this case, praying for the souls of the dead—is illustrated by the survivor who said,

"In the midst of the disaster I tried to read Buddhist scriptures continuously for about a week, hoping that my effort would contribute something to the happiness of the dead. It was not exactly a sense of responsibility or anything as clear as that. It was a vague feeling—I felt sorry for the dead because they died and I survived. I wanted to pacify the spirits of the dead . . . in Buddhism we say that the souls wander about in anxiety, and if we read the scriptures to them, they lose their anxiety and start to become easy and settle down. So I felt that if I read the scriptures, I could give some comfort to the souls of those who had departed." (p. 375)

I would submit that the three types of sympathetic distress are potential bases for altruistic behavior—which I am defining as behavior aimed at helping others in distress—and the two types of guilt, for reparative behavior. When confronted with others in distress the individual experiences one or another type of sympathetic distress—or guilt if he feels responsible for the distress—which predisposes him toward behavior designed to alleviate the other's distress or to make amends for damage he may have done. Whether or not the behavior is actually exhibited depends on the strength of these motives, which is a function of the individual's prior socialization experiences, and the strength of competing motives aroused in the situation. The initial response tendency is to act—either altruistically or reparatively as called for; and in the absence of action, for whatever reason, I would expect the person either to continue to experience the distress or the guilt, or to cognitively restructure the situation so as to justify inaction, for example, by finding something in the situation to justify or deny his relative advantage, attribute motivation to the other which is consonant with his circumstances, or attribute blame to some other agent.

In this connection, Lois Murphy, in her study of sympathy in preschool children of forty years ago, reported that the child's most natural response was to help the other child in distress and that if he couldn't do this, his affective response was prolonged. We found something similar in fifth and seventh grade children's completions of stories in which the central figure commits a transgression. The vast majority of the completions involved guilt, and most of these also included some form of reparative behavior when this was permitted by the story conditions. When reparation was impossible, the guilt response was more prolonged and intense. The relation between guilt and action is also shown in several recent studies in which college students in whom guilt had been induced experimentally engaged in various prosocial acts, like volunteering to be subjects in other research and donating blood, to a greater degree than the control subjects. Finally, the motivational properties of witnessing others in distress have been shown by Tilker, who found that college students exposed to pain cues of the victim in a Milgram-type experiment were often impelled to interrupt the experiment. And by Berger and Di Lolli, also in a shock experiment, who found the victim's distress cues led to decreased reaction time by the subject.

Clearly I have not dealt with the full range of moral—or even prosocial behavior—but only two aspects of it: the response to a person in distress when one has not been, and when one has been, the cause of that distress. The first is the essential condition that calls for altruism and second, for reparation or restitution.

VI. Child-Family Relations

The family unit has long been accepted as the foundation of Western society. More than any other factor, it is the family, through its influence on its progeny, that will shape the future of society. Society and the family are intimately bound to one another. Society and one's culture often direct the pattern of family life. The family, however, is a subunit on which society rests and, therefore, through which children are introduced to their culture (McCandless, 1967). It is the family which provides the child with the "learning opportunities" needed to function within its culture (Cohen, 1976).

The Child and the Family

To discuss the child's development apart from the family would not only oversimplify, but distort the developmental process. Each child is born with a set of inherent capabilities and capacities; the family is the subunit which enhances and augments these capabilities so that the child can survive. Through the family the child is introduced to the "adaptive techniques" which his particular society has developed for dealing with the environment.

The family is an essential derivative of man's biological make-up for it is the basic social system that mediates between the child's genetic and cultural endowment and provides for his biological needs while instilling societal technique, stands between the individual and society, and offers a shelter within the society and against the remainder of society. (Lidz, 1970)

The family *is* the child's society, the microcosm in which he/she learns the ways of survival so that he/she is prepared to deal with the macrocosm. The child's experience here will set the tone for his/her involvement in society in the future. Complications arise, however, since the family is not simply a child-bearing or child-rearing institution. Its functions are certainly more complex. In addition to being the prime agent for the enculturation of children, the family serves to fulfill many needs of adults within a marital relationship. Marriage in and of itself is a complex relationship between two people seeking to form a bond in which each other's security and well-being are of mutual importance. This need remains in spite of the introduction of a child. Now, however, the relationships can no longer be reviewed as simply dyadic but rather as taking on the properties of a small group. Each member, including the child, has an effect on the other members. Each dyad (father–mother, father–child, mother–child) forms a subunit within the family with its own separate structure and function; yet each remains a part of the whole (Minuchin, 1970). These groupings themselves remain in flux primarily as a result of growth characteristics of each of its members. The reactions of the family to a one-month-old child must of necessity change when that child is 1 year of age, 5, 15, etc. The needs of each child change dramatically as he/she progresses developmentally. So, too, do the parents' needs and reactions shift as they experience their own developmental process. Child rearing within the family must be viewed from a dynamic rather than static viewpoint.

The family does not simply exist to satisfy the needs of the child, but must also concurrently serve the needs of parents and of society. No wonder, then, that there is great concern being focused around the "decline" of family life. This decline is seen by many in increases in the divorce rate, in the number of runaway children, in the increase in the number of families where both parents work. All are taken as signs that family life as it has been known in Western society is changing, presumably for the worst. There are others who are more optimistic, however, seeing the changes as an evolution to a new type of family which is healthier, smaller in size, better off economically, and more in contact with the world (Anthony, 1970).

Whether the family is in decline or dramatically altering its structure, there is little doubt that parenting has become more difficult. Couples often feel overwhelmed by their parental responsibilities. The very process of deciding to have children has become more complicated. In the past having children was an accepted and expected function of a couple; currently the decision of whether or not to have children is a legitimate and worrisome factor in many marriages. Once having made this decision, however, parental consternation is not at an end. "When" becomes a viable question. These issues are evident even before the child is conceived: How to raise the child brings other concerns as parents exhibit a growing self-consciousness about this role in a changing society.

Society is in the process of making parenthood a highly self-conscious, self-regarding affair. In so doing, it is adding heavily to the sense of personal responsibility among parents. Their tasks are much harder and involve more risks of failure when children have to be brought up as individual successes in a supposedly mobile, individualistic society rather than in a traditional and repetitious society. Bringing up children becomes less a matter of rule of thumb, custom and tradition, more a matter of acquired knowledge, of expert advice. More decisions have to be made because there is so much more that has to be decided, and as the margin of felt responsibility extends, so does the scope of anxiety about one's children.[1]

As society changes in composition, questions pertaining to the child's place in the family, how children should be raised, and what role society shall have in relation to the family become more complex.

Questions of Parenthood, Family and Society

Yarrow's paper discusses how scientists have looked at child rearing and what we can learn from the results of these efforts. In looking at the effects of early experience, the determinants of behavior, and the child's influence on its own development, she explores the need to arrive at some balance between our research findings and the practical dissemination and application of those results. Taking a different approach to child rearing, Baumrind discusses the results and implications of her research on patterns of parental authority. With care and caution, she presents her views on permissive, authoritative, and authoritarian approaches to child management.

Not all families fit into the mold of father, mother, and 1.5 children. Over 3.5 million famlies have only a single parent. What are the implications of this for child rearing? Brandwein's paper explores what we know about the effects of divorce on family functioning, especially in relation to women as heads of one-parent households. Hetherington's research on father absence discusses problems of divorce and readjustment, concentrating on the family as a unit and how divorce transforms and restructures this unit.

The view of the family as owning their child and therefore as having complete control over policies affecting the child is explored by Van Stolk in reference to child abuse. The familial factors discussed include the parents' personality and the effect of modeling.

The legal implications of removing a child from a family which is judged to be neglecting or mistreating the child is brought into question by Wald. Research has not provided enough clear answers for any definitive policy. Kramer's review of the Freud-Goldstein-Solnit book offers an approach towards protecting the child caught in family problems and dissolution.

References

Anthony, E. J., & Koupernik, C. *The child in his family.* New York: John Wiley and Sons, 1970.

[1]Titmuss, R., *The Family.* National Council of Social Service Publication, British National Conference on Social Work, National Council of Social Service, 1954.

Cohen, S. *Social and personality development in childhood.* New York: Macmillan, 1976.

Lidz, T. The family as the developmental setting. In E. J. Anthony & C. Koupernik, *The Child in His Family.* New York: John Wiley and Sons, 1970.

McCandless, B. *Children: behavior and development.* 2nd Ed. New York: Holt, Rinehart & Winston, 1971.

25.

Marian Radke Yarrow

RESEARCH ON CHILD REARING AS A BASIS FOR PRACTICE

Surely there is no more significant scientific goal than to understand human development and, with such understanding, to come closer to the realization of human potentialities and well-being. Research in child rearing is engaged in this endeavor. It is our purpose here to discuss how well the field has lived up to the promise: how substantial it is as a basic science, able to offer knowledge that can reliably be used in policies and practice, both to foster desired outcomes and to prevent or repair problems.

We shall examine a half century of research and attempt to draw some "practical" conclusions. This is a selective, not a complete analysis which inevitably reflects my own research interests and experience. The analysis is made with a deep commitment to and respect for behavioral science, although I shall at times be critical and impatient. Toward the public, the source and the user of child rearing research, I feel equal respect and impatience.

Before evaluating the contributions, I should like to provide some background perspective on this field by identifying some of the factors within and outside the science that have influenced its history and that now influence the current scene of child rearing research.

Source: Paper presented at Society for Research in Child Development, Section I of the annual meeting of the American Association for the Advancement of Science, Philadelphia, Pennsylvania, 1971.

FACTORS INFLUENTIAL IN SHAPING THE SCIENCE

Consider first the basic assumption on which the discipline proceeds: It is that the experiences of childhood have vital importance in shaping not only the present state of the child, but also in influencing the future behavior and personality of the individual. This position does not discount the role of constitutional factors in behavior; there is nothing behavioral that is not also biological. Within the general assumption there are wide variations in emphasis and theories. Historically, child-rearing research has meant the study of parent–child relationships, especially the mother–child relationship. More recently psychological research has taken a broader view of the upbringing processes to include other social institutions and influences.

Throughout its history, the research community has been organized to advance basic understanding of developmental processes, and it has been reluctant to do research on applied problems. Further, scientists have often left to others the task of making their findings useful. Advice literature to parents often proceeds without or beyond scholarly research documentation. There have been exceptions, of course. But generally, because the core of knowledge is small and not always reliable, scientists have been uneasy when pressed on questions such as *how* to rear children. At this particular point in twentieth-century America, however, the concerns of society are pressing hard. (What is adequate help for children and families who have failed? What kinds of remedial experiences can benefit the "culturally deprived?" Does the high rate of aggression, alienation and turmoil of older children and youth have roots in the rearing institutions of our society?) Child research has now become very visible outside academic halls. Increasingly it has moved to the sites of society's "hurts" and fears. This has brought changes in working styles, in methods of obtaining data, even in concepts and variables. Very important is the fact that the social pressures have broadened the rearing variables to which scientists attend. The in-life settings of research have dramatized the need to extend attention beyond formulations of intrafamilial variables (such as parent discipline, identification, Oedipal resolution, etc.) to encompass the entire behavioral and attitudinal context in which children are reared: Contexts of parents' work, poverty and riches, ethnicity, politics, all impinge closely on the family and, therefore, are inseparable from rearing conditions. Society rears its children in many ways and forms outside the family. Rearing analyses need to be made with full recognition of these contexts.

Historically, the content of child-rearing research has rather lopsidedly emphasized the harmful and undesirable rearing conditions and the developmental wounds: The rearing side has been dominated by such issues as maternal deprivation, family disorganization, parental over-indulgence, and hostility; the child side, by cognitive deficits, learning disabilities, neuroses, aggression, delinquency. This represents a reciprocality of society's needs and psychological theories. There have been fewer concerted efforts aimed directly at understanding the optimally enabling rearing conditions. (What are the rearing supports for individual trust, creativity, happiness, humanitarianism, responsibility?)

As a final background note, I want to call attention to the raw data of child-rearing research. By definition, an enormous segment of rearing is in the family. But because the family is a private domain, systematic, reliable data are not easily obtained. Research has coped in several ways: (a) It has relied on indirect evidence such as interviews. (b) It has utilized circumstances in which there is diminished family privacy, as in circumstances of crisis or pathology. Likewise, families are less private about infancy. (c) Research has been granted entry for observations by a limited number of families. (d) Experimental designs are used in which investigators attempt to simulate specific aspects of rearing in the laboratory and to measure the immediate influences on child behavior. These, in combination, are the methods of the field. With a moment's reflection, it is apparent that another kind of inaccessibility plagues childrearing research: namely, rearing and its effects takes place over time—a generation, a decade. This requires, therefore, very long-time human studies or retrospective studies, or animal studies that can provide birth to adulthood data in more manageable time periods. No one method or approach now dominates in child rearing research, and, fortunately too, there is theoretical eclecticism.

This, then, is the background against which we will look at research and its implications for practice. I have attempted this objective under four questions: (1) What is known concerning the early forerunners of the individual's later development and behavior? (2) What has research learned regarding the environmental determinants of child behavior? (3) How can research cope with or conceptualize the totality of rearing influences? (4) Is there a hopeful course for a working union of science and society?

The early experience hypothesis

There is a pervasive hypothesis in the folklore and science of human development which holds that in infancy and early childhood are laid down some of the basic determinants and directions of the individual's personality and potentialities. This is a very crucial hypothesis, one that has long been a belief, supported for a long time by folk and clinical evidence. In research on rearing this is a fundamental area of investigation, but one in which the answers are arrived at with great difficulty, and the answers come in small pieces. One piece of evidence comes from retrospective studies of disturbed adolescents and adults. In the histories of these cases there are high frequencies of early rearing deficits (such as lack of mothering, neglect, mistreatment, institutionalization, stresses of many kinds). Although this is significant evidence, it does not establish the inevitability of the later pathology or identify the processes by which early rearing influences development. Other naturalistic studies fill in some of the needed information. An example is found in follow-up studies of infants and young children whose families have been wartime casualties and who have had their early rearing under varying non-mothered conditions. From these studies we learn that later developmental problems do not always follow in the wake of early stresses. Such ambiguities press hard for more definitive research which will identify critical rearing experiences and will furnish information regarding what it is in particular children or in the developmental timing that makes for greater or lesser vulnerability.

Research on animals and direct observational studies of infants contribute evidence along this way. Harlow's now well-known experimental work with monkeys supplies a link. It achieves a research design with control over infant rearing as well as control and measurement in childhood, adolescence, adulthood, and eventual parenthood. In a very solid way, this work demonstrates profound effects of early mothering. Infant monkeys reared with their mothers and those in various ways deprived of normal mothering differed measurably, not only in infancy, but later, in emotionalism, confidence, intellection, social relationships, and physiology. Adult inadequacy in mother-deprived monkeys included sexual inadequacy and the inability to mother a next generation with affection. These are powerful suggestions as to the validity of the early experience hypothesis, even if one preserves a healthy conservatism with respect to direct and easy extrapolations from infrahuman to human development. It would seem unnecessary to comment that there are implications regarding the care of young children.

Direct study of human infants offers more information. This is a vigorous and extensive research enterprise, and it is difficult to condense its findings to a few paragraphs. These investigators, wisely I believe, have placed heavy emphasis in their work on discovering the *nature* of the infant organism and on analyzing the rearing environment in immediate and detailed terms. They ask: What is the infant's equipment; to what kinds of stimuli is he sensitive; and how do his sensitivities and abilities change? The modal type of study is an experimental one, involving control of limited segments of the infant's experience (auditory or visual stimulation, contact and handling, and so on), giving stimulation or training, and measuring specific responses. (We should note happily that in these studies investigators have turned to stimulation and enrichment.)

The many experimental studies add up to firm confirmation of young infants' receptivity, modifiability, and vulnerability. Infants' abilities to organize perceptual phenomena, to be conditioned, to discover and test out the surroundings, and to be socialized have been demonstrated. Almost immediately a strong degree of control by the rearing environment is in play. More than that can be concluded: Not all kinds of presumably enriching stimuli, administered at any time, effect changes. (There is probably a corollary of this statement: not all presumed harmful experiences, occurring at any time, adversely affect the infant.) The moderating influence of the developmental state of the organism appears to be critical. The influences of the experiences depend on how they are geared to the infants' emerging interests and rapidly changing abilities.

Further evidences of infant rearing influences come from field studies. Some of these have made use of naturally occurring circumstances of maternal absence or separation. It is important to observe that the findings are very different, depending on what fills in for the mother's absence. Hospitalization and institutionalization, when dehumanized, characteristically result in deteriorative responses, depression, and impairment. On the other hand, separations from mother (whether for hospitalization or group day care) when the psychological needs of contact, stimulation, and attentive care are provided, do not appear to affect behavior or development adversely. In other naturalistic studies it is demonstrated that the environment and behaviors of infants and toddlers are subject to enrichment. This has been done with children living in homes that are wanting in cognitive and affective stimulation. Such stimulation employed sensitively and naturally has brought encouraging improvements.

To summarize what has been learned for the infant research we will borrow Hunt's conclusion that:

> The best way to rear an infant is to be knowledgeable about his rapidly changing abilities and interests and to arrange his environment and schedule so as to provide sequences of experiences that are suitably matched to those developing characteristics, starting immediately at birth.

I think one can read the beginnings and the gaps in knowledge in this area of research. We do not yet have complete evidence on the hypothesis of early influences. There is more than enough evidence, however, to indicate the tremendous receptivities and vulnerabilities of very young children, enough to know that experiences do affect immediate developments, the foundations for later experiences and later developments. There is an obvious gap in the field concerning the progression of effects forward into the child's development. And we need to wait for further research.

DETERMINANTS OF BEHAVIOR

My second question—What are the environmental determinants of behavior?—attempts to organize the research relating to rearing influences in another way. It underplays the child's history, and it emphasizes the contemporaneous physical and social environments in which behavior takes place and the processes of learning. How does learning take place? How does the child learn prohibitions? How does he become dependent, independent, aggressive, and so on? How does he learn the values and mores of society? How does he come to reject them? What are the rearing experiences that contribute to his attitudes about himself and his response to the needs of his fellows? How does he learn control of his impulses? What kinds of rearing facilitate cognitive and intellective growth, creativity? The list does not stop. These are the kinds of questions to which we, all of us, parents, educators, politicians, want answers.

A very considerable research effort, extending from the mid-1930's through the 1950's, was directed to many of these questions. The studies have dealt with rearing and with child behavior as general traits or dispositions. Rearing is characterized in terms such as maternal "warmth" or love, permissiveness, parental power assertion, and methods of discipline—physical punishment, reasoning, etc. Children of three to six years were the usual subjects. An amalgam of psychoanalytic and learning theories has provided the conceptual underpinnings. I am slighting somewhat the advances made by this work, but in general the harvest of these many studies has been only tenuous and unstable relations between *single rearing traits* and child characteristics. To illustrate: Mother's warmth seemed sometimes to be an asset in the child's social learning. Aggressive behavior in the children was sometimes related to parents' rewarding of aggressions, sometimes to parents' use of physical punishment. Sometimes severe punishment of aggression was associated with low frequencies of aggression. Permissiveness, but also authoritarianism, were associated sometimes with child tyranny and sometimes with compliance. It seems quite clear that simple rearing variables measured as general traits have little predictive power concerning child behavior.

What are the problems with the research? Are there no predictable relations between rearing and behavior? This seems not the correct conclusion. Rather, it became evident that a trait formulation, an interview method of assessing rearing, and a single-variable analysis did not get at the many concurrent influences that are interlocked in the transactions between parent and child. This research approach was not one that efficiently isolated and extracted the effects of any one parental variable or dealt adequately with the joint or interactive effects of several variables on child behavior. These conclusions are important to consider in relation to the varying messages that have been sent to the public.

Many investigators have turned to a different strategy in the search for understanding of child behavior. By taking the research out of the rearing setting, isolating a specific segment of behavior and manipulating it in the laboratory, directing detailed examination to the effects of immediate, specific environmental events on the child's responses, investigators are attempting to elucidate general *principles* of behavior. Before reviewing this body of evidence, I want to preface it with the caveat, that this is a necessary step for research, but one that must be followed by strategies and methods that return to in-life rearing research before we can confidently apply research findings.

Two directions of experimental research are particularly relevant in our discussion. One is the work based on reinforcement theory or operant conditioning analyses. And the second concerns observational learning by children. The general principles of reinforcement theory have become familiar: Behavior that receives reinforcement is acquired or strengthened; behavior for which reinforcement is not forthcoming eventually drops out of the child's repertoire. There is unquestionable experimental evidence of the powerful effects of reinforcement procedures on many simple and not so simple kinds of child behavior. Under controlled laboratory conditions, that are in some respects abstractions of the kinds of adult–child interactions comprising rearing, adults have developed and changed child behaviors by regulating the giving and withholding of social reinforcements (affection, praise, attention). Children have been made more self-confident, less bullyish, less fearful, more able to accept adult authority, less antisocial in behavior, more persistent. It is interesting to compare this kind of analysis with the earlier investigations of parental rearing traits. An example must suffice. Let us imagine two mothers who are equally warm and nurturing (to use a general trait). A reinforcement analysis might lead to enlightenment as to why these mothers have brought forth very different children. The child of the first mother is tyrannical; the child of the second mother is considerate. To make the analysis overly simple, we find that the first mother has given a nonconditional kind of love regardless of the child's behavior, whereas in the second mother we observe a patterned giving and withholding that has shaped the child's behavior toward more adaptive social responses.

While reinforcement analyses identify significant processes determining behavior, there is also much room for misinterpretation and misapplication. The procedures of reinforcement are themselves complicated; the results depend on the schedule or frequency or spacing of reinforcement and on finding the right reinforcers for given children. The effectiveness of positive reinforcement and of withholding reinforcement depends on the experience and history and the nature of the child (on his cognitive development, for example). It depends, too, on the nature of the adult giving the reinforcement. It is *not* a simple recipe that can be applied with guaranteed results. There is not now *a* formula for regulating child behavior, a thought that frightens and enrages many people. We will return to these questions in considering the total environments of children.

Most investigators would agree that not all of child rearing can be put in reinforcement terms, which brings us to consideration of a second investigatory direction, research that is concerned with observational learning. It is hardly a discovery of science to find that children imitate and copy, yet the processes involved do not yield easily to understanding. We need to decipher what is involved. Which of the potential models surrounding the child are significant in his learning, and which of their behaviors and feelings are adopted by the child; which are ignored or rejected?

Careful experimental work makes it clear that learning from models occurs at all ages and that it begins very early. A great variety of behaviors can be acquired in this way: Seeing aggression can increase aggression; seeing the punishment of aggression can inhibit aggression; seeing kindness, generosity, cruelty—all can be increased by this process. But exposure does not automatically lead to learning. The adoption of modeled behaviors is influenced by what the child observes the consequences to be for the model: Is the model rewarded or punished for his behavior? The direct consequences for the child may also be important. Interestingly, the old wheel-horse of maternal rearing virtues, nurturance of the model, often facilitates observational learning, but it is often not a necessary condition for learning. Research has shown that observed behaviors which become part of the child's behavior need not have been modeled by real, live persons; films and dramas are exceedingly effective. Very important is this finding, for enter now the TV and movie producers, the toy manufacturers, and even the news reports as child-rearing agents in a massive sense. (As an aside, it would be extremely enlightening to analyze the total input from the media, regarding the media as rearing agents, analyzing as we would a parent's input into a child's life, and predicting the outcome for society's children.)

To summarize the contributions of research on reinforcement and on the influence of models, I believe we can say that it begins to build some solid bases for rearing principles. The laboratory work on these management techniques has unmistakably demonstrated the modifiability and vulnerability of older children. That hypotheses of *later* experience must be given equal attention to those of *early* experience in practices of child rearing is probably one of the important ideas to carry away from this research.

THE TOTALITY OF REARING

It would be a pity in assessing research to overlook the contributions it has made to an understanding of child rearing by its having identified and conceptualized the many sources of influence that comprise rearing—even though research does not at present offer a nearly complete theory of development, and it is not able to handle adequately the interactions among the various behavior determinants. In summary, it may be well to remind ourselves of the various levels of influence: In the analyses of rearing presented here, adult "management" aspects of rearing have been stressed—as if the child were a passive recipient. But let us remember that the child also *acts on* environments and *on* the adults. The child, by his characteristics and by his reactions, partly creates his own environment. *His* behavior and *his* awareness also shape his environment. This is important to keep in mind when one is

concerned about the dire possibilities in principles of behavior modification (principles which research has discovered, not invented). So, among the ingredients of behavioral determinants are the reciprocal influences of the various simultaneous environments of family and society in which the child is reared, and the child's own unique contributions to his own rearing at every point in his development.

As indicated earlier, the pressures for research utilization in a culturally diverse society have had the healthy effect of breaking into the exclusive reliance on the traditional individual and individual family model of development. Only to illustrate this issue—developmental theories of individual behavior often do not deal with some of the most salient matters in the lives that children and parents share with each other. For example, a parent's neglect or hostility toward his child may stem not so much from a quirk in his own development of impulse control as from the weight of intolerable and immediate pressures on him of poverty, social injustices, and dehumanized living. Under these circumstances, the child's defiance may be too much overload of anxiety and frustration. To attempt to interpret child upbringing, to advise on rearing practices, or to make rearing interventions within a family or society apart from social and cultural realities invites failure. Research on rearing is working hard to catch up to social realism. Applications of research findings must be made, and are increasingly being made, with great care being taken to ponder the meanings of the findings in the contexts in which they are to be practiced.

THE MEETING OF
SCIENCE AND SOCIETY

If a report on the advances in child rearing research meant the unveiling of a set of discoveries that could then simply be adopted by the public, I would not now be concerned with relations between scientists and consumers. But there are reasons for concern, recognizing that not infrequently, in one form of another, the public and the scientist are at war, or are at least distrustful of one another. Nonbehavioral scientists, politicians, parents, and children turn an acid intolerance toward the findings of research. The origins of difficulty lie on both sides. Let me try to convey what seem to me to be some of the reasons: Findings on the effects of child rearing conditions are unstable on many issues. This is particularly the case when a specific treatment or variable is singled out for evaluation. The effects of a given condition on child behavior will differ as research subjects vary (preschool children or adolescents), social context differ (urban poverty or urban affluence), methods of data-gathering vary (surveys or observations), *and* as social times change (a fearful, anxious, unsettled climate, or a hopeful, prosperous one). Specific rearing events can have a weak impact on child behavior or a strong impact or no impact at all, depending on the systems or contexts of which they are a part (constitution of the child, psychological history of the child, current matrix of influences in the physical and social environments). There is no room for simplistic answers in child rearing issues.

This *tentative* and qualified nature of knowledge places a responsibility on investigators (which they have not always taken) carefully to discuss the qualifications and generalizability of their results. Consumers, on the other hand, see this as hedging and double talk. They are frustrated by less than absolute answers. Consumers have a responsibility to expect and act within the framework of *probabilities* regarding given environmental-behavioral

relations. They need education about science.

Research in developmental psychology has impressive quantities of hard research data on the nature of the child and on the influences and interaction of internal and external influences on his behavior. This evidence, however, exists in very large part as discrete pieces of knowledge, often small pieces, in laboratory settings, on unique samples of subjects, and addressed to conceptual questions, not in the form of the questions that are in the public mind.

But this is the nature of behavioral science. In order to harness these disparate pieces of understanding, to make them relevant to social problems and the bases of dependable, practical recommendations, the very best skills and the most scholarly efforts of the scientific community are needed. This has not been a general commitment by scientists, although it is now more in the nature of "becoming." For, just as a good clinician, as a delicate mix of scientist and artist, can succeed with his patient without all the facts being in, so too seasoned investigators with insightful practitioners can work out solutions together.

In this paper I have attempted to give some conception of a research field, how it operates, what it has learned, how its learning can contribute to a sadly in-need society. I would like to conclude on a reflective note.

In "quieter" times, parents and educators seemed to be relatively clear about their rearing tasks and goals, about the conditions for which they were training their children, about the accepted values by which they expected their children to live. These are hardly the rearing realities of today. The variety of major fault-lines and changes in society—environmental and human crises and tensions, social upheavals, widespread devaluation of old values—cannot help but affect child rearing and children. Parents today discover that the circumstances and psychology of their childhood often are not applicable to the present day, that many of the experiences that their children are encountering or will encounter have no close parallels in their own upbringing, that they themselves are changing and are less certain about many formerly "settled" issues regarding rearing. Further, child rearing institutions have a visibly altered form from twenty-five years ago: *Non*family rearing agents (group day care, mass media, schools) have entered the lives of more children earlier and longer, while at the same time other traditional rearing agents are missing from the scene, at least in the small urban family. The very valuable close adults other than the parents (older sibs, aunts and uncles, grandparents, neighbors) are no longer available as significant rearing agents, as aides, as buffers, as supports to parents, especially important in middle and later childhood and adolescence. Today's children are reared by *more influences* and by *fewer personal persons*. I suspect there is not only more diffusion of rearing influences, but also greater disharmony among the influences. The task has increased in complexity for the scientist and consumer alike. But objectives are worth the effort. In the better rearing of children there is a chance for an improved quality of life.

26.

Diana Baumrind

SOME THOUGHTS ABOUT CHILDREARING

INTRODUCTION

I want to speak with you today about my research findings relating patterns of parental authority to dimensions of competence in young children and to share with you the conclusions I draw from those findings.

There are a few points I want to make before I discuss the findings themselves:

As many of you know, last week the newspapers and other mass media summarized their version of my research

Source: Paper presented at the Children's Community Center, Berkeley, California, 1969.

findings. I want to stress, especially to those of you who participated in the present study, that the news reports were based on findings from two completed studies in which the data were collected some six and one-half years ago. The data of the present study were collected last year and have not yet been analyzed in any systematic way, although I have impressionistic findings. The contents of the news stories (although not the headlines) were reasonably accurate, if extremely oversimplified. Such headlines as "THE BEST PARENTS ARE AUTHORITATIVE," "AUTHORITATIVE PARENTS DO LEAST DAMAGE," or "KIDS THRIVE IN STRICT HOMES," are meaningless at best, and at worst suggest that I think I know the *best* way for you to raise *your* children. However, no research on children could justifiably come to the conclusions which these headlines suggest (although they do reflect in oversimplified form my personal judgments) for the following reasons:

1. First, there is no such thing as a *best* way to raise children. Each individual family's total life situation is unique. A generalization which makes sense on a probability basis must be tailored to fit an individual family's situation, if indeed it fits at all. It is each parent's responsibility to become an expert on his own children, using information in books or parent effectiveness encounter groups or, best of all, by careful observation and intimate communication with the child.

2. Secondly, the generalizations which I make have a reasonable probability of being true for a particular sample, but the extent to which that sample is representative of a population, say eight years later, remains in question. Moreover, the extent to which any individual family is similar to the families in the sample affects how relevant the findings are for that family. In addition, the relationships found are not strong enough to predict for the individual family.

3. Third, to have any social meaning at all, research findings must be *interpreted* and integrated. Yet the interpretations I make of my findings may well be disputed by other equally expert investigators. I will speak *strongly* for my interpretations because I am that sort of person. But each of you must evaluate the relevance to your own family of what I say, and you must do so in the light of your personal value system and experience.

I should tell you that my *subjective* assurance about what I say rests as much upon my personal experience as a parent,

as on my research findings. I have three daughters whose ages are eleven, thirteen, and fifteen. My theories and my practice coincide rather well (I think), and I am subjectively satisfied with the effectiveness of what I call "authoritative parental control" in achieving my *personal* aim. I will generalize to say it is possible, if parents wish to—IF parents wish to—to control the behavior of children, even of adolescents, and to do so without suppressing the individuality and willfulness of the child or adolescent. What gets in the way of most parents who *do* wish to control the behavior of their children more effectively is lack of *expertness* as parents, *indecisiveness* about the application of power, *anxiety* about possible harm resulting from demands and restrictions, and *fear* that if they act in a certain way, they will lose their children's love. Nowadays I think more parents are concerned about maintaining the approval of their children than vice versa, and, indeed, many parents become paralyzed with indecision when their authority is disputed, or their children are angered by discipline.

Now I will tell you something about my research.

RESEARCH VARIABLES

For the past eight years my staff and myself have been gathering data on the behavior of preschool children in nursery schools and in structured laboratory situations. Each child studied has been observed for at least three months. These data were related to information obtained about the parent–child interaction, and about the parents' beliefs and values. We made two home visits to each family between the difficult hours of five to eight in the evening, then subsequently interviewed the mother and father separately. So far more than 300 families have participated in the study, most of them middle-class, well educated families.

Child variables

I think it is important to tell you what kinds of behavior we were looking for so that you will know what I mean by such general terms as "competence" when speaking of the child, or "authoritative parental control" when speaking of the parent.

In all correlational studies of children's social behavior, at least two dimensions are revealed. One dimension may be called *Responsible versus Socially Disruptive Behavior.* The other dimension may be called *Active versus Passive Behavior.* These two dimensions are independent of each other—that is, a socially responsible child can run the gamut from very active and self-assertive to very quiet and socially passive. Or, a socially disruptive child may be an active terrorist or he may be sullen, passive and detached from other children.

When we call a child *socially responsible,* we mean that relative to other children his age, the child takes into account the ongoing activities of other children enough not to disrupt them—he will facilitate the routine of the group; he does not actively disobey or undermine the rules of the school; he can share possessions with other children; he is sympathetic when another child needs help; he does not ·try to get another child into trouble, and so on.

When we speak of a child as *active,* we are referring to the independent, self-motivated, goal-oriented, outgoing behavior of the child. When we call a child highly active, he is relative to other children his age likely to go after what he wants forcefully, to show physical courage, and to be a leader, to feel free to question the teacher, to persevere when he encoun-

ters frustration, to show originality in his thinking, and so on.

Seventy-two very explicitly defined items were used by the raters to describe each child in relation to these two dimensions.

When I report my findings to you later on and I speak of the most *competent* group of children, I am speaking about children who were rated by the observers as being very active and very responsible. I am comparing these children to other children who are less competent in the sense that raters judged them to be lacking in self-assertiveness and self-control, or to be socially disruptive.

Clearly, any definition of competence makes certain tacit assumptions about the proper relationship of the individual to society. The child is *competent* to fulfill himself and succeed in a given society. The same qualities might not be as effective in a differently organized society. To the extent that an investigator believes that successful accommodation to the ongoing institutions of a society defines competence, he will stress the *social responsibility* dimension of competence. If an investigator believes in revolutionary change, he may reject social responsibility as a criterion to competence. To the extent that an investigator values thrust, potency, dominance, and creative push, he will stress *activity* as a dimension of competence. If, by contrast, he believes in an Eastern ideal—such as Zen Buddhism—an investigator may reject dominance and push as criteria of competence, emphasizing instead receptivity, openness, egolessness, and unwilled activity. My definition of *competence* assumes the importance both of accommodation to social institutions and of self-assertive and individualistic action in relation to these institutions. In the preschool years, I regard the development of *social responsibility* and of *individuality* as equally important for both sexes, although I suppose that our society, at least in the past, has placed the emphasis in adulthood on activity and individuality for boys and on responsibility and conformity for girls.

Parent variables

Now I would like to tell you about what we were looking for when we observed parents with their children. Our focus has been upon facets of parental authority which might conceivably predict dimensions related to competence in young children. More specifically, we measured dimensions such as the following:

1. *Directive versus nondirective behavior*—that is, the extent to which the child's life is governed by clear regulations and the parent in charge sets forth clearly the daily regimen for the child.

2. *Firm versus lax enforcement policy*— the extent to which the parent enforces directives, resists coercive demands of the child, requires the child to pay attention to her when she speaks, and is willing to use punishment if necessary to enforce her demands.

3. *Expects versus does not expect participation in household chores*—we measured the extent to which parents require the child to help with household tasks, to dress himself, to put his toys away, and to behave cooperatively with other family members.

4. *Promotes respect for established authority versus seeks to develop an equalitarian, harmonious relationship with child*—here we sought to measure what is generally thought of as authoritarian control and its opposite, i.e. the extent to which the parent assumes a stance of personal infallibility on the basis of her role as parent rather than on the basis of her specific competencies and responsibilities, and requires of the child that he defer to her without question.

We also measured such variables as:

1. The extent to which the parent encourages self-assertion and independent experimentation.

2. The extent to which the parent uses reason and explanation when directing the child.

3. The extent to which the parent values individuality in behavior and appearance by contrast or in addition to social acceptability.

METHODS USED
TO STUDY PARENT
ATTITUDES AND BEHAVIOR

In studying parental attitudes and practices we used a variety of methods. As I have already indicated, we visited the home on two occasions between the hours of five and eight, and took complete notes on the interactions which transpired. We then interviewed the mother and the father separately, discussing with each the possible ways in which the presence of the observer might have affected the behavior witnessed during the home visit. We talked with parents about their general position on childrearing, their attitudes towards permissiveness, directiveness, and the use of reason, what their ideals were for their child, and so on.

Some parents have asked how we thought the presence of the observer in the home affected the interactions we witnessed. Our general conclusion is that while most families censored some behavior (such as intense emotional shows of love or anger), the interactions we observed and rated with regard to the variables we were measuring predict pretty well how parents interact with their children. We may think about the information we obtain from home visits somewhat as we do about on-the-job tests for a prospective employee. An employer can predict the typing efficiency of a prospective employee from a five-minute typing test on standardized material. While the typist will not handle all kinds of typing tasks in the same way that she does the typing test copy, her handling of the test copy will predict pretty accurately her general speed, her knowledge of format, and her ability to spell. Under the kind of pressure that preschoolers produce during the hours of five and eight, parents generally become sufficiently involved with their customary tasks so that they fall back upon their most practiced responses, modifying these perhaps in accord with their ideals. Very few parents sought consciously to disguise this customary behavior. Since our focus is upon conscious childrearing practices and values, the observational situation is reasonably successful in providing relevant information about parental practices and values. If we were concerned primarily with incidents of highly charged emotional events, direct observation in the home would probably not have provided us with the needed information. Most studies of the effects of childrearing practices in the past have used less valid data than home visits. They have relied upon psychological tests, or self-report, or experimental observation in the laboratory setting. With all its drawbacks, then, we found that the combination of direct observation in the home setting, with interview and self-report, gave us relatively valid information of the kind we were seeking.

CONCLUSIONS FROM THE STUDY

These are the general conclusions which we drew from our data about the child-rearing antecedents of *responsible versus irresponsible behavior* and *active versus passive behavior.*

In the middle-class group we studied, parental practices which were intellectually stimulating and to some extent tension-producing (e.g., socialization and maturity demands and firmness in disciplinary matters) were associated in the young child both with self-assertion and social responsibility. Techniques which fostered self-reliance, whether by placing demands upon the child for self-control and high-level performance, or by encouraging independent action and decision-making, were associated in the child with responsible and independent behavior. Firm discipline in the home did not produce conforming or dependent behavior in the nursery school. For boys, especially, the opposite was true. Firm, demanding behavior on the part of the parent was not correlated with punitiveness or lack of warmth. The most demanding parents were, in fact, the warmest.

These conclusions concerning the effects of disciplinary practices are consistent with the findings of a second study we conducted (Baumrind, 1967). In that study, a group of nursery school children who were both responsible and independent were identified. These children were self-controlled and friendly on the one hand, and self-reliant, explorative, and self-assertive on the other hand. They were realistic, competent, and content by comparison with the other two groups of children studied. In the home setting, parents of these children were consistent, loving, and demanding. They respected the child's independent decisions, but were very firm about sustaining a position once they took a stand. They accompanied a directive with a reason. Despite vigorous and at times conflictual interactions, their homes were not marked by discord or dissensions. *These parents balanced much warmth with high control, and high demands with clear communication about what was required of the child.* By comparison with parents of children who were relatively immature, parents of these highly mature children had firmer control over the actions of their children, engaged in more independence training, and did not reward dependency. Their households were better coordinated and the policy of regulations clearer and more effectively enforced. The child was more satisfied by his interactions with his parents. By comparison with parents of children who were relatively unhappy and unfriendly, parents of the mature children were less authoritarian, although quite as firm and even more loving.

A POSITION ON CHILDREARING

I would like now to move from a report of research findings into a presentation of some of my conclusions about childrearing. I want to make clear that experts in the field disagree just as parents do. The meaning I derive from my research findings is affected by my personal values and life experience, and is not necessarily the meaning another investigator would derive.

I was quoted in the newspapers as opposing permissiveness, and to a certain extent that is true. I would like to describe my position on permissiveness in more detail. I think of the permissive parent as one who attempts to behave in a nonevaluative, acceptant, and affirmative manner toward the child's impulses, desires, and actions. She consults with him about policy decisions and gives explanations for family rules. She makes few demands for household responsibility and orderly behavior. She presents herself to the child as a resource for him to use as he wishes, not as an ideal for him to emulate, nor as an active agent responsible for shaping or altering his ongoing or future behavior. She allows the child to regulate his own activities as much as possible, avoids the exercise of control, and does not insist that he obey externally defined standards. She attempts to use reason and manipulation, but not overt power, to accomplish her ends.

The alternative to adult control, according to Neill, the best known advocate of permissiveness, is to permit the child to be self-regulated, free of restraint, and unconcerned about expression of impulse, or the effects of his carelessness. I am quoting from *Summerhill* now:

Self-regulation means the right of a baby to live freely, without outside authority in things psychic and somatic. It means that the baby feeds when it is hungry; that it becomes clean in habits only when it wants to; that it is never stormed at nor spanked; that it is always loved and protected (1964: 105, italics Neill's).

I believe that to impose anything by authority is wrong. The child should not do anything until he comes to the opinion—his own opinion—that it should be done (1964: 114, italics Neill's).

Every child has the right to wear clothes of such a kind that it does not matter a brass farthing if they get messy or not (1964: 115).

Furniture to a child is practically nonexistent. So at Summerhill we buy old car seats and old bus seats. And in a month or two they look like wrecks. Every now and again at mealtime, some youngster waiting for his second helping will while away the time by twisting his fork almost into knots (1964: 138).

Really, any man or woman who tries to give children freedom should be a millionnaire, for it is not fair that the natural carelessness of children should always be in conflict with the economic factor (1964: 139).

Permissiveness as a doctrine arose as a reaction against the authoritarian methods of a previous era in which the parent felt that her purpose in training her child was to forward not her own desire, but the Divine Will. The parent felt that since the obstacle to worldly and eternal happiness was self-will, that the subduing of the will of the child led to his salvation. The authoritarian parent of a previous era was preparing his child for a hard life in which success depended upon achievment and in which strength of purpose and ability to conform were necessary for success. With the advent of Freudian psychology and the loosening of the hold of organized religion, educated middle-class parents were taught by psychologists and educators to question the assumptions of their own authoritarian parents. Spock's 1946 edition of *Baby and Child Care* advocated the psychoanalytic view that full gratification of infantile sucking and excretory and sexual impulses were essential for secure and healthful adult personalities. The ideal educated, well-to-do family in the late 40's and 50's was organized around unlimited acceptance of the child's impulses, and around maximum freedom of choice and self-expression for the child.

However by 1957 Spock himself changed his emphasis. He said, in the 1957 edition of his famous book, "A great change in attitude has occurred, and nowadays there seems to be more chance of a conscientious parent's getting into trouble with permissiveness than with strictness."

I would like now to examine certain of the assumptions which have been made in support of permissiveness, most of which, when examined in a research setting, have not been supported.

1. One assumption previously made was that scheduled feeding and firm toilet training procedures have as their inevitable consequences adult neuroses. This apparently is not so. Unless the demands put upon the infant are unrealistic—as might be the demand for bowel training at five months—or the parent punishes the infant cruelly for failure to live up to her demands—scheduled feeding and firm toilet training do not appear to be harmful to the child.

2. A second assumption, that punishment, especially spanking, is harmful to the child, or not effective in controlling behavior, is also not supported by recent research findings. On the contrary, properly administered punishment has been shown by the behavior therapists to be an effective means of controlling the behavior of children. This hardly comes as a surprise to most parents. Brutal punishment *is* harmful to the child. Threats of punishment not carried out are harmful to the child. A parent who threatens to punish must be prepared to deal with escalation from the child by prompt administration of punishment. She cannot appease. Otherwise the threat of punishment will actually *increase* the incidence of undesirable behavior, since it is just that undesirable behavior which will cause the parent to cancel the punishment, in an attempt to appease the child.

While *prompt* punishment is usually most effective, it is important for the parent to be certain that the child knows exactly why he is being punished, and what kind of behavior the parent would prefer and why. While extremely rapid punishment following a transgression works best in training a rat or a dog, a human child is a conscious being and should be approached as one. It should not be enough for a parent, except perhaps in critical matters of safety, to *condition* a child to avoid certain kinds of behavior by prompt punishment. The parent's aim is to help the child control his own behavior, and that end requires the use of reason and the bringing to bear of moral principles to define what is right and what is wrong conduct.

Properly administered punishment, then, provides the child with important information. The child learns what it is his parent wants, and he learns about the consequences of not conforming to an authority's wishes.

3. A third assumption that advocates of permissiveness have made is that unconditional love is beneficial to the child, and that love which is conditional upon the behavior of the child is harmful to the child. I think that the notion of uncondi-

tional love has deterred many parents from fulfilling certain important parental functions. They fail to train their children for future life and make them afraid to move towards independence. Indulgent love is passive in respect to the child—not requiring of the child that he become good, or competent, or disciplined. It is content with providing nourishment and understanding. It caters to the child and overlooks petulance and obnoxious behavior—at least it tries to. The effect on the child of such love is often not good. Once the child enters the larger community, the parents are forced to restrict or deprive. Accustomed as the child is to immediate gratification, he suffers greater deprivation at such times than he would if he were accustomed to associating discipline with love. He does not accept nor can he tolerate unpleasant consequences when he acts against authority figures. Such a child, even when he is older, expects to receive, and is not prepared to give or to compromise. The rule of reciprocity, of payment for value received, is a law of life that applies to us all. The child must be prepared in the home by his parents to give according to his ability so that he can get according to his needs.

The parent who expresses love unconditionally is encouraging the child to be selfish and demanding while she herself is not. Thus she reinforces exactly the behavior which she does not approve of—greedy, demanding, inconsiderate behavior. For his part, the child is likely to feel morally inferior for what he is, and to experience conflict about what he should become. I believe that a parent expresses her love most fully when she demands of the child that he become his best, and in the early years helps him to act in accordance with *her* image of the noble, the beautiful and the best, as an initial model upon which he can create (in the adolescent years) his own ideal.

On the other hand, I do believe that to the extent that it is possible, a parent's *commitment* to the child should be unconditional. That is, the parent should stay contained *in* the experience with the child, no matter what the child does. Parental love properly expressed comes closest in my mind to the Christian notion of *Agape.* The parent continues to care for the child because it is her child and not because of the child's merits. Since she is human, the quality of her feeling for him depends upon the child's actions, but here interest in his welfare does not depend upon his actions and is abiding. This abiding interest is expressed not in gratifying the child's whims, nor in being gentle and kind with him when he is being obnoxious, nor in making few demands upon him, nor in approval of his actions, nor even in approving of what he is as a person. Unconditional *commitment* means that the child's interests are perceived as among the parent's most important interests, and that (no matter what the child does) the parent does not desert the child. But the love of a parent for a child must be demanding—not demanding of the unconditional commitment it offers—but rather demanding of the reciprocal of what it offers. The parent has the right—indeed, the duty—to expect obedience and growth towards mature behavior, in order that she can discharge her responsibilities to the child, and continue to feel unconditional commitment to his welfare. (Only parents are required, as an expression of love, to give up the object of that love, to prepare the object of love to become totally free of the lover.)

AUTHORITATIVE VERSUS AUTHORITARIAN PARENTAL CONTROL

Now that I have discussed the concept of permissiveness in childrearing, I would like to explain the distinction which I make between *authoritarian* and *authoritative* parental control.

I think of an *authority* as a person whose expertness befits him to tell another what to do, when the behavioral alternatives are known to both. An authority does not have to *exercise* his control, but it is recognized by both that by virtue of his expertness and his responsibility for the actions of the other, he is fit to exercise authority in a given area.

By *authoritative parental control* I mean that, in relation to her child, the parent should be an authority in the sense just defined.

1. *In order to be an authority, the parent must be expert.* It seems to me that many parents and teachers have come to the conclusion that they are not expert on matters which pertain to the young people placed in their charge. Therefore, since they are not expert, they abandon their role as authorities. I think instead that they should become more expert. Parents often do need more information about children of all ages than they have, in order to be expert. But much of what a parent needs to know she can learn from observing her child and listening to him. A parent must permit her child to be a socialization agent for her, as well as the other way, if the parent is to acquire the information about the child and his peer group that she needs in order to make authoritative decisions about matters which affect the child's life. Unlike the authoritarian parent, the authoritative parent modifies her role in response to the child's coaching. She responds to suggestions and complaints from the child and then transmits her own more flexible norms to her child. In this way, by becoming more expert, the parent legitimates her authority and increases her effectiveness as a socializing agent.

2. *In order to be authoritative, the parent must be willing and able to behave rationally, and to explain the rationale for her values and norms to the child.* The parent does not have to explain her actions all the time to the child, especially if she knows that the child knows the reason but is engaging in harrassment. But a parent does need to be sure that she herself knows the basis for her demands, and that the child also knows, within the limits of his understanding, the reasons behind her demands.

In authoritarian families the parent interacts with the child on the basis of formal role and status. Since the parent has superior power, she tells the child what to do and does not permit herself to be affected by what he says or does. Where parents do not consult with children on decisions affecting the children, authority can only rest on power. As the child gets older and the relative powers of parent and child shift, the basis for parental authority is undermined. Even the young child has the perfect answer to a parent who says, "you must do what I say because I am your mother," and that answer is, "I never asked to be born." The adolescent can add, "Make me," and many say just that when parents are unwise enough to clash directly with an adolescent on an issue on which the adolescent has staked his integrity or autonomy.

3. *In order to be authoritative, the parent must value self-assertion and willfulness in the child.* Her aim should be to prepare the child to become independent of her control and to leave her domain. Her methods of discipline, while firm, must therefore be respectful of the child's actual abilities and capacities. As these increase, she must share her responsibilities and prerogatives with the child, and increase her expectations for competence, achievement, and independent action.

I believe that the imposition of authority even against the child's will is useful to the child during the first six years. Indeed, power serves to legitimate authority in the mind of the child, to assure the child that his parent has the power to protect him and provide for him.

The major way in which parents exercise power in the early years is by manipulating the reinforcing and punishing stimuli which affect the child. What makes a parent a successful reinforcing agent or an attractive model for a child to imitate is his effective power to give the child what he needs—i.e., the parent's control over resources which the child desires, and his willingness and ability to provide the child with these resources in such a manner and at such a time that the child will be gratified and the family group benefitted. Thus, practically as well as morally, gratification of the child's needs within the realistic economy of the family, is a precondition for the effective imposition of parental authority. An exploited child cannot be controlled effectively over a long period of time. The parent's ability to gratify the child and to withhold gratification legitimates his authority. The child, unlike the adolescent, has not yet reached the level of cognitive development where he can legitimate authority, or object to its imposition, on a principled basis.

By early adolescence, however, power based on physical strength and control of resources cannot and should not be used to legitimate authority. The young person is now capable of formal operational thought. He can formulate principles of choice by which to judge his own actions and the actions of others. He has the conceptual ability to be critical even though he may lack the wisdom to moderate his criticism. He can see clearly many alternatives to parental directives; and the parent must be prepared to defend rationally, as she

should to an adult, a directive with which the adolescent disagrees. Moreover, the asymmetry of power which characterizes childhood no longer exists at adolescence. The adolescent cannot be forced physically to obey over any period of time.

When an adolescent refuses to do as his parent wishes, it is more congruent with his construction of reality for the parent simply to ask him, "why not?" Through the dialogue which ensues, the parent may learn that his directive was unjust; or the adolescent may learn that his parent's directive could be legitimated. In any case, a head-on confrontation is avoided. While head-on confrontation won by the parent serves to strengthen parental authority in the first six years, it produces conflict about adult authority during adolescence.

Although a young person need feel no commitment to the social ethic of his parents' generation, he does have, while he is dependent upon his parents, a moral responsibility to obey rational authority, i.e., authority based on explicitly, mutually-agreed-upon principles. The just restrictions on his freedom provide the adolescent with the major impetus to become self-supporting and responsible to himself rather than to his parents.

THE RELATIONSHIP OF INDIVIDUAL FREEDOM TO CONTROL

To an articulate exponent of permissiveness in childrearing, such as Neill, freedom for the child means that he has the liberty to do as he pleases without interference from adult guardians and, indeed, with their protection. Hegel, by contrast, defines freedom as the appreciation of necessity. By this he means that man frees himself of the objective world by understanding its nature and controlling his reactions to its attributes. His definition equates the concept of freedom with power to act, rather than with absence of external control. To Hegel, the infant is enslaved by virtue of his ignorance, his dependence upon others for sustenance, and his lack of self-control. The experience of infantile omnipotence, if such he has, is based on ignorance and illusion. His is the freedom to be irresponsible, a very limited freedom, and one appropriate only for the incompetent.

For a person to behave autonomously, he must accept responsibility for his own behavior, which in turn requires that he believe the world is orderly and susceptible to rational mastery and that he has or can develop the requisite skills to manage his own affairs.

When compliance with parental standards is achieved by use of reason, power, and external reinforcement, it may be possible to obtain obedience and self-correction without stimulating guilt reactions. To some extent the parent's aggressiveness with the child stimulates counter-aggressiveness and anger from the child, thus reducing the experience of guilt and of early internalizations of standards whose moral bases cannot yet be grasped. When the child accepts physical punishment or deprivation of privileges as the price paid for acts of disobedience, he may derive from the interaction greater power to withstand suffering and deprivation in the service of another need or an ideal and, thus, increased freedom to choose among expanded alternatives in the future.

Authoritarian control and permissive noncontrol both shield the child from the opportunity to engage in vigorous interaction with people. Demands which cannot be met or no demands, suppression of conflict or sidestepping of conflict, refusal to help or too much help, unrealistically high or low standards, all may curb or understimulate the child so that he fails to achieve the knowledge and experience which could realistically reduce his dependence upon the outside world. The authoritarian and the permissive parent may both create, in different ways, a climate in which the child is not desensitized to the anxiety associated with nonconformity, nor willing to accept punishment for transgressions. Both models minimize dissent, the former by suppression and the latter by diversion or indulgence. To learn how to dissent, the child may need a strongly held position from which to diverge and then be allowed under some circumstances to pay the price for nonconformity by being punished. Spirited give and take within the home, if accompanied by respect and warmth, may teach the child how to express aggression in self-serving and prosocial causes and to accept the partially unpleasant consequences of such actions.

The body of findings on effects of disciplinary practices give provisional support to the position that authoritative control can achieve responsible conformity with group standards without loss of individual autonomy or self-assertiveness.

27.

Ruth A. Brandwein, Carol A. Brown
and Elizabeth Maury Fox

WOMEN AND CHILDREN LAST: THE SOCIAL SITUATION OF DIVORCED MOTHERS AND THEIR FAMILIES

In the United States today over 3.5 million families with children are headed by a single parent; over 85 per cent of these parents are women (U.S. Census, 1970: 402). While extensive literature exists concerning the absence of the father in female-headed families, little attention has been paid to the remaining parent, the mother. This review, then, will focus on the mother-and-family unit which remains after the father leaves, with particular emphasis on the consequences to the unit of being headed by a woman.

A woman may become a single parent through one of several circumstances: (1) bearing children out of wedlock; (2) becoming separated or divorced; (3) becoming widowed. We wish to focus primarily on the legally separated and divorced mothers, since unwed mothers and widowed mothers have somewhat specialized and more well-defined statuses. However, since studies often fail to differentiate among the types of female-headed families, we have reviewed a number of studies which included all types.

We were struck by the paucity of research on divorced mothers; our search of recent psychological, sociological, and social welfare literature reveals very little

about these women. The older "multi-problem family" literature and juvenile delinquency studies concentrate primarily on presumed pathological effects of single mothers upon the children, rather than on the mothers themselves. Father absence rather than mother presence continues to be a major area of interest for researchers.

Related to the paucity of studies on mothers is the assumption throughout the literature that the female-headed single-parent family is deviant and pathological (Glasser and Navarre, 1965). Such families are called "broken," "disorganized," or "disintegrated" (see, e.g., Cavan, 1964), rather than recognized as widespread, viable alternative family forms (Sussman, 1971; Billingsley & Giovannoni, 1971). Both father absence studies and literature on single mothers in poverty reflect this deviance or pathology model.

Josephson (1969:274) offers the following argument: "Proof [sic] that fatherless families are regarded as abnormal lies in the considerable efforts which their victims [sic] and society make to provide father substitutes." Hence, by direct inference, any family but that with two parents must be "abnormal" and its members "victims." The deviance is twofold—not only is there one adult rather than two in the family constellation, but the family head is female rather than male. Not only is the type of family deviant, but the mother herself is assuming a deviant gender role.

This is stigmatization—the labeling of these families as deviant and the assump-

Source: *Journal of Marriage and the Family,* 1974, Aug., 498-514. Copyright © 1974 by National Council on Family Relations. Reprinted by permission. This research was partially supported by the Russell Sage Foundation. Author's names are listed in alphabetical order.

tion of negative effects on family members.[1] Evidence of stigmatization and the effects of negative sanctions upon women single parents and their children will be an underlying theme of this paper.

Stigmatization is multifaceted. Stigma is ascribed to divorced and separated women for their presumed inability to keep their men. The societal myth of the gay divorcee out to seduce other women's husbands leads to social ostracism of the divorced woman and her family. There are expectations of neighbors, schools and courts that children from broken homes will not be properly disciplined, will have sex role confusion, and will be more likely to get into trouble. The mothers themselves may incorporate society's attitudes, feeling insecure and guilt-ridden regarding their childrearing abilities. They may seek solutions in attempting the "superwoman" role, or in fleeing to remarriage.

Further evidence of negative social attitudes towards these families is the virtual absence of social supports such as public provisions for day care and housekeeping services. The major exception, Aid to Families with Dependent Children (AFDC), provides only minimal financial assistance at the price of further stigma and loss of dignity.

This review will attempt to evaluate critically the scattered findings on divorced women as single parents and on the family units they head, and to re-examine effects of stigma on these families, as seen both in societal attitudes and in professional writings about female heads of families. In Section I, we will consider how family functions are fulfilled in the single parent family, and in Section II, using the father-absence literature as an illustrative exam-

ple, we will explore some of the methodological problems with current conceptualizations of the single-parent family as a grouping under stress, and how that stress changes as a function of time and other factors. In the summary we will suggest directions for further research based on our analysis.

I. FAMILY FUNCTIONS

We will attempt to review two interrelated areas of research. The first area is research on changes in family organization and behavior which take place when the family structure and resources change. The four major areas of family functioning[2] we will consider are (1) economic functions, (2) authority, (3) domestic responsibilities (child care and housework), and (4) social and psychological supports. (1) *Economic functions:* The family must obtain enough money, goods, and services to provide for survival of its members. (2) *Authority:* The family's interests must be represented to those outside it, and the person representing the family must be acknowledged by the others. Power for decision-making within the family must also be allocated. (3) *Domestic Responsibilities:* The household must provide for the physical safety and emotional well-being of the children and must be physically maintained through cleaning, cooking, repairs, and other tasks. (4) *Supports:* The members need to give and receive a certain amount of caring and involvement towards one another and usually require a modicum of positive support from persons outside the family.

The second area of research that we will

---

[1] Goffman defines a stigma as "an attribute that is deeply discrediting" in the eyes of others. He notes, "We tend to impute a wide range of imperfections on the basis of the original one" (Goffman, 1963:5).

[2] The use of the term "functions" should not be taken to indicate a theoretical functional analysis. These are simply the four types of activities and relationships that we consider most important and problematic for a single parent.

be reviewing concomitantly with the first is research on societal factors—structures and values outside the family—that force families into certain molds, that influence the ability of the divorced mother and her family to carry out family functions. These factors include the forms of sex discrimination affecting a female head of family, societal assumptions about the importance and legitimacy of the two-parent nuclear family which work against a one-parent family regardless of the sex of the head-of-family, as well as social supports available to aid families in carrying out their functions.

Family functions are frequently assumed by social scientists and by society to be the proper role of one sex or the other. Earning the income and assuming authority for the family are ascribed to men; housework, child care, and emotional support are said to be for women (*cf.* Parsons, 1942; 1959). These assumptions affect the opportunities available to the solo parent. Since most solo parents are women, the economic and authority functions might be anticipated to be the most problematic. Given the need for income, the single parent is often forced to become the bread-winner (*i.e.,* assume the traditional male role). Assuming this function requires that accommodations in child care and housekeeping tasks occur. When we look at these domestic tasks, we find that they admit of as little flexibility and pose as many problems as the problem of obtaining money. (A British study of single-parent fathers by George and Wilding [1972] shows that single-parent fathers experience difficulties similar to single-parent mothers in this regard.)

Economic functions

Divorce and poverty are intimately related. The poorer a family is, the more likely the parents are to divorce (Goode, 1948;

Carter & Glick, 1970). The adverse effects of poverty on marital stability are even greater than the divorce statistics indicate, since poor people often separate without obtaining a legal—and costly—divorce.

Yet are divorced mothers poor only because they were poor *before* divorce, or does poverty also *follow from* divorce? Research indicates that poverty of the female-headed family may also result from divorce. Winston reports a study of divorced mothers receiving AFDC payments which shows that their ex-husbands' occupations, and apparently their ex-husbands' incomes, were not concentrated in low-income categories, but paralleled the occupational distribution of men as a whole (1971).

In 1969 the median income of families with children headed by woman aged 25 to 44 was $4,000 a year, compared to a median for all two-parent families of $11,600 (Stein, 1970). The discrepancy between these women and the two-parent family is greater for whites than non-whites, in part due to the greater poverty of nonwhites in any marital status. In 1969 the percentage of all male-headed families who were poor was 6% for whites, 20% for nonwhites. Among female-headed families the rates were 32% for whites, 58% for nonwhites (Ferris, 1971). Looking at the other end of the income distribution, only 9% of female-headed families of all races had incomes over $10,000, while 55% of two-parent families had this or more (Stein, 1970). The higher income of two-parent families results in part from the fact that both parents may be working. This economic strength of the two-parent family is denied both single mothers and single fathers.

Goode's (1948) research found that 8% of wives had incomes below $40 a week before divorce, while after divorce and before remarriage the percentage rose to 22%. Whereas 33% had $60 a week or more before divorce, after divorce only 20% had this much. While weekly incomes have increased, the pattern has persisted. Kriesberg's (1970) study of mothers in poverty shows that "among the mothers who are husbandless due to separation or divorce . . . whether or not they are poor is not related to their socio-economic origins. . . . The economic fortunes of a husbandless mother are largely determined by contemporary circumstances" (p. 177). These findings indicate that in addition to the poverty of many mothers prior to divorce, a large number of previously non-poor wives and families suffer downward economic mobility following divorce.

Much of the downward economic mobility among divorced mothers can be viewed in terms of economic discrimination against women. A mother at every class and income level is expected to depend for the major part of her and her children's support on the income of her husband, and economic opportunities for a woman without a husband are limited as a result. Women are given less job training, and are concentrated in low income, insecure occupations (Bluestone *et al.*, 1971). They are less likely than men to have jobs at all. Of persons with no money income of their own, 84% are women, most often non-employed wives (Ferris, 1971). Even working wives have to depend on their husbands for the bulk of family income—the median proportion of family income contributed by the wife's earnings was 27% in 1970 (Waldman & Gover, 1972). Thus the departure of the husband usually means the departure of the main financial contribution to the family. (Only at the very lowest income level, where the husband may not be making a financial contribution, might his departure mean in economic terms merely the loss of another mouth to feed.) Following divorce, the

mother must take responsibility for providing the income either through her own paid employment or by finding a source outside the family to substitute for the economic role of the husband.

Solutions to Economic Problems. The most common solution of the problem is for the mother to begin (or continue) working. Goode (1948) found that some mothers began working while they were married in anticipation of the divorce. The labor force participation rates for women with *pre-school* children in 1971 is as follows: married mothers, 30%; separated mothers, 41%; divorced mothers, 62% (Waldman & Gover, 1972). The rates for all married versus all divorced women were 41 and 70% respectively (Waldman & Gover, 1972).

Women regardless of marital status do not earn the incomes men can earn. Median earnings of full-time, full-year employed women average 55% of men's earnings both for the labor force as a whole and within the same occupational categories. Twenty per cent of men and 60% of women earn less than $5,000 for full-time work, while 28% of men but only 3% of women earn over $10,000 a year (Women's Bureau, 1971). The assumption that women do not or should not support a family provides justification for these low wages. Low wages in turn make it extremely difficult for most mothers alone to support a family (see Kreps, 1971).

In addition, taking a job usually conflicts with the functions of child care and homemaking. Stein found that the presence of children and the lack of reliable child care often limited female heads of families from fulltime, full-year work. Whereas 70% worked at some time during the year, only 38% of female heads of household in his study were able to work full time, full year. Sources of income which would enable the mother to remain at home, such as child support payments from the ex-husband, welfare, and assistance from relatives, usually provide even less income than working.

Although legally men are required to support their children following divorce, and in some instances their wives as well, evidence shows that the majority of men do *not* continue to provide support. Goode (1948) showed that one-third of men are not even ordered to make payments, 40% who are ordered to pay never or rarely made the payments, and an additional 11% made them only irregularly. A more recent study showed that a majority of judges in a nationwide sample award less than 35% of husband's income to the wife and family (Citizens' Advisory Council on the Status of Women, 1972). Kriesberg (1970) in the early 1960's found that among ex-husbands earning $4,000 a year or more, only 39% contributed at all to their ex-families; if earnings were under $4,000, only 20% contributed. Husbands at all income levels contributed to their ex-wives and children in only one-third of the cases. A Wisconsin study in the late 1960's showed that "within one year after the divorce decree, only 38% of the fathers were in full compliance with the support order. . . . Forty-two per cent of the fathers made no payment at all" (p. 8). By the time four years had passed 67% of fathers had ceased providing any money (Citizen's Advisory Council, 1972). The Uniform Desertion and Non-Support Act valid in most states allows a criminal complaint to be made against the father only if the family is "in destitute or necessitous circumstances." The courts are generally apathetic or opposed to taking legal action against men for nonsupport (Women's Research Center of Boston, 1972). Thus men may have the obligation to support their families, but there is little consistency in enforcing it. The Act is largely used by welfare departments; in some states, women must file criminal complaints against their husbands before becoming eligible for welfare.

Another institutionalized form of outside income available to divorced mothers, besides husbands' support payments, is public welfare (Bell, 1965). In this case the state replaces the husband in regulating the wife's activities, her work, sexual behavior, etc. (Chase, 1971; Bernard, 1964). Since welfare benefits are calculated to provide only minimum subsistance income, benefits do not raise families out of poverty. Average payments nationally in January, 1973 were $168 a month or $2,016 a year for a mother and 2.5 children. The state with highest payments, New York, gave only $284 a month, or $3,408 for such a family (HEW, 1973).

How many divorced mothers turn to welfare is difficult to determine. Goode (1948) found that 26% of his sample felt that public and community agencies were the main source of financial aid during economic difficulties. In 1970, "about three-fifths of the 3.4 million families with children headed by women received welfare assistance" (Stein, 1970). Divorce, separation, and desertion are the major reasons why families with children are headed by women, but the relative contribution of divorce, separation, and desertion to the welfare rolls is not ascertainable from current statistics. Bernard (1964) found that many poor female-headed families do not seek or obtain aid from public welfare.

In some cases, the wife's own family appears to be an important source of assistance. In Goode's (1948) study, 57% of divorcees reported their families as the main source of financial aid during crisis.

Marsden (1969) in England found many mothers depending on relatives for regular income or special gifts. Bernard (1964) found that barely one-third of low-income mothers reported substantial assistance from kin, although most had some help from kin or friends. These findings may suggest that financial aid from the family is more common and more substantial in middle-class divorce. It appears that support for mothers and children often continues to be a family responsibility, the main change being that relatives, rather than the husband, provide the funds.

Summary. In sum, economic discrimination against women, and the reluctance of ex-husbands or outside agencies to aid mothers in supporting themselves and their children, often forces the families of divorced mothers to suffer severe economic hardship. Since women usually keep the children following divorce, the parent least able to support them is left with the major economic responsibility. Even when the father keeps the children, however, his expenses, like those of the divorced mother, may increase, as assistance in child care and housekeeping must often be paid for (George & Wilding, 1972).

The effect of downward income mobility among divorced mothers is similar to the effects among any family. Lowered income means not only a drop in consumption within the home, but often a change in housing to poorer accommodations in a poorer neighborhood (Carter & Glick, 1970). Moving is itself a stress (Weissman & Paykel, 1972), in this case often compounded by problems of reduced personal safety, higher delinquency rates, and poorer schools. A rapid change in socioeconomic status is associated with anomie (Glasser & Navarre, 1964), adding to the problems of emotional support to be discussed later. Some of the correlation between multi-problem families and divorced parents has been explained in terms of

lowered SES and poorer housing (Willie, 1967).

Authority

The social conditions to which women as a whole are subject affect the divorced mother and her family not only with respect to her economic resources, but also in terms of the authority and respect she commands.

Men are accorded the right to be "head of the household." Holmstrom points out that it is legally impossible for a woman to head the family if the husband is present, regardless of her relative income, power, or status.[3] Mothers and children are expected to be under the protection of, and dependent upon, the man of the family. Sociologists reflect this attitude by routinely measuring a divorced woman's status in terms of her ex-husband or her father, thus denying that she has any status of her own (see Nye, 1964). Female heads of a family are therefore considered deviant because they are not attached to a man, which a woman "should" be, and because they head a family unit, thus usurping a status "properly" reserved for men. It can be anticipated that society will resist recognizing or accepting women in this independent and authoritative status.

The head of the family acts as gatekeeper between the family and the larger society, representing society to the family and the family to society. In addition, the head is often expected to provide authority and discipline within the family. The loss of a father, according to this analysis, leaves the family without status (Winch, 1971), without organization (Rainwater and Yancy, 1967), and without power.

---

[3]The authors know of one couple threatened with federal arrest for giving false information because they listed the wife as head of household on their Census form.

We have uncovered little empirical evidence to document the extent of discrimination against women as heads of families in their roles as gatekeeper and authority. However, there is evidence that women in general are taken less seriously and are respected less than men (Andreas, 1971; Millett, 1970; Goldberg, 1968; Hacker, 1951). We could anticipate that the female family head would receive less community prestige and status than a man at the same economic or educational level, and probably less status than a married woman who takes her status from her husband. Her reduced status might diminish prestige for the family as a whole, and make the family less powerful via-à-vis community institutions.

Evidence is accumulating concerning financial discrimination that in effect denies "head of household" status to divorced mothers (Smith, n.d.). Credit granting institutions, in keeping with policies toward married women, will often refuse credit to a divorced woman, or grant it only in her ex-husband's name. Banks frequently deny mortgages or other loans to a divorced woman, sometimes insisting that the ex-husband or the woman's father sign for her and thus partially control her property (U.S. House, 1970). Landlords may refuse to rent to families without adult males, with the result that a woman as head of household may have to pay more than a man for equivalent housing. In general, not only does the female-headed family have fewer economic resources because the head is female, but because of lack of recognition and reduced bargaining power vis-à-vis the community the family gets less with the resources it has.

Marsden (1969:109) notes that female-headed families were often shown little respect by neighbors, who, for example, borrowed things without permission. "To regain their position in some of the communities where they lived, mothers and children now had to be that bit tougher than their neighbors." We have not found any studies determining whether providers of services respond differentially to men and women. On the one hand, they may respond more quickly to women out of charitable motives; on the other hand, they may respond more slowly because they have less respect for women's demands.

We can conjecture that solo mothers, but not solo fathers or mothers with husbands, might have to deal with the attitudes and actions of men concerning sexual exploitation of a woman who "doesn't belong to anyone" and who therefore, in their minds, has no protection (Firestone, 1970). The sexual innuendos toward their solo mothers might well affect the children.

The mother may also lack the training and ability for the role of authority, protector, and counselor for the children (Bem & Bem, 1971). Certainly her competence is questioned by the larger society, Smith (Grollman, 1969) found that juvenile authorities were less likely to remand children in their mother's custody than in their father's (see also Arnold, 1971). To the extent that social institutions *give* the woman less authority over her children, she *has* less. Smith (1970) found that parents with little expertise or low perceived "legitimate right to exert influence" were listened to less by their children. These criteria are frequently fulfilled in a female-headed, single-parent family. Female role socialization also plays its part. Nye (1957) and Marsden (1969) noted the difficulties that many women heads of family had in aiding their children with advice about the world, because of their own insufficient knowledge.

However, the mother's ability to take the authority role should not be underestimated. Hansen and Hill (1964) point out that the single parent remaining with the family must take the authority role responsibly or the family will disintegrate. Although most single-parent families do not disintegrate (hence some semblance of authority is maintained), Marsden (1969) and others suggest that the quality of authority and its outside supports are altered. Kriesberg (1970) found that husbandless mothers were likely to assert more "direct controls and imposition of parental will" on their children than married mothers. The Gluecks' work on juvenile delinquency showed that mothers' supervision was more critical in predicting delinquency than the presence or absence of the father, indicating that mothers not only can but do play the authority role effectively within the family. Concerning the nature of the mother's authority in the single-parent family, Kriesberg (1970) found on the whole "no general tendency for husbandless mothers to differ from married mothers in values, beliefs and conduct that adversely affect the children."

However, Marsden (1969) found that mothers worried about how to be both authoritative and loving, *e.g.,* both mother and father (see also Glasser & Navarre, 1971). One solution was for aspects of the authority role to be taken by an older child or by a relative living nearby.

As a final point, the powerlessness of divorced mothers should be seen in proper perspective. Married mothers do not have that much power either (Gillespie, 1971). There is evidence that many divorced mothers perceive the divorced state as an increase in power and independence. Both Marsden (1969) and Goode (1948) found that one-third or more of mothers' primary complaints against ex-husbands centered on excessive domination or physical violence. "The women were not allowed to run things their own way or to make decisions as they chose, and instead had to cater to their husbands' wishes" (Goode, 1948, : 122). Cavan (1964) found that remarriage rates were higher among lesser educated women, indicating that women may be pushed into remarriage by their inability to support themselves without it, rather than drawn in by its positive attractions.

When Jacobson (1952) compared married and divorced couples on their attitudes towards women's equality, he found that divorced men were most in favor of the husband's right to dominance while their ex-wives were most in favor of the wives' right to equality within marriage.

Thus it would appear that a substantial proportion of divorced mothers do not enjoy acceding to the male head of household in his role as authority. A woman may have more power as a female head of household than she had as a female dependent of a male head of household.

Domestic functions

Two major internal domestic tasks have to be performed—housekeeping and child care. American social structures tend to require that these be the full-time job of a wife and that they be incompatible with earning a living for the family (Glasser & Navarre, 1964). Holmstrom (1972) points out that work is organized on the implicit assumption of a male worker with a wife at home. Although this assumption is increasingly unrealistic (43% of the labor force are women), familial needs still tend to be ignored in structuring conditions of employment. The nine-to-five day and the lack of part-time opportunities typify the rigidity of the system (Holmstrom, 1972).

The physical isolation of the nuclear family increases domestic work and child care for the mother, and decreases the opportunity for labor sharing (Goode, 1963). Housing and land use patterns also restrict alternatives to nuclear family living arrangements. In less than 15% of cases do married couples have an older parent living with them (Reiss, 1971), and a government study on housework found that "relatively few households included a non-employed adult woman in addition to a working mother" (Hedges and Barnett, 1972). Even ignoring its implication that only a woman would help with housework, these studies point to the isolation of the mother in her domestic tasks.

Nonfamilial assistance in the form of maids and babysitters is rare. The ratio of private household workers to all women workers declined from .169 in 1940 to .052 in 1970 (Hedges & Barnett, 1972). Day care centers are virtually nonexistent, with only 6% of children of working mothers in group care (Low & Spindler, 1968; see also Perry, 1961). Additional mothers might work if good day care were available. In a survey of welfare mothers, 40% of those not working believed that under present circumstances their children would be inadequately cared for if they went to work (Hedges & Barnett, 1972).

Housework and child care must be performed whether the single parent is a man or a woman. However, the same outside supports may not exist for both sexes. In Washington D.C., the welfare department at one time provided free homemaker services to a single father, but permitted equal services to a single mother only if she were mentally incompetent, chronically ill, or physically disabled. Since most housework is viewed as a female responsibility, informal evidence suggests that relatives are quicker to provide help to men than to women. Additionally, a single father's income may permit him to buy services that a single mother cannot afford.

Helping women with the task of child care is not generally seen by policy makers as a valid reason for creating day care programs. Programs are usually justified in terms of developing the child's potential, removing the child from a poor home situation, or providing workers to industry (Ruderman, 1968; Roby, 1973). Social institutions have traditionally made little effort to solve the problems of aiding women with child care. Instead, their policies have often had the effect of keeping women at home. With 67% of divorced mothers in the work force, schools do perform a major child care function, yet the reluctance of many school systems to implement the recent federal law requiring lunches to be available at school exemplifies institutional unresponsiveness to child care needs. Day care advocates have been successful in creating some governmental and private changes in day care policies and programs, but as yet the changes have affected only small numbers of families (Women's Bureau, 1973).

The lack of child care options feeds back on economic deprivation. Without child care, the mother may not be able to work, thus eliminating an important source of family income; if the mother does work, her children may be inadequately cared for. If child care must be paid for, this expenditure further reduces an already decreased income. The uncertainty of day care resources is reflected in employers' reluctance to hire mothers of young children (Oldham, 1971).

Removal of the free labor contribution in housework and maintenance of either spouse can lead to a decreased standard of living, regardless of income. The work may now have to be purchased or remain undone. Husbands spend an estimated 11.6 hours a week in household chores whether the wife is working or not (Hedges & Barnett, 1972). At a pay rate of $2.00 an hour, the contribution is worth over $1,100 a year. Working wives contribute an estimated 34 hours a week of household labor; nonworking wives, 57 hours. At the same pay rate, this is worth $3,500 to $6,000. Housewives do not receive such salaries for their work, but the absence of such unpaid work does affect the family's standard of living.

Little evidence is available concerning what, in fact, happens to housekeeping functions in female-headed single-parent families. The loss of a husband's housework might be anticipated to increase the burden on the children, since working mothers are totaling 63–66 hours of paid work and housework already (Hedges & Barnett, 1972). Although single parents could conceivably purchase services, most families are not rich enough to do so. They may simply let things go. Nye found that the main difference between two-parent and solo-mother households was that the solo mother's home tended to be more messy. This finding would indicate that housekeeping has a lower priority than other functions assumed by the mother.

Husbands are a major source of baby-sitting services for working mothers. Ruderman (1968) found that 23% of the arrangements for the care of children under 12 were for in-home care by their fathers. The divorced mother is without this aid. Teaching the children how to take care of themselves at a young age seems to be one solution to the problem of child care. Kriesberg (1970:247) found that "insofar as any relationships were found, they all indicated that employed husbandless mothers tended to hold values and beliefs and conduct themselves in ways that presumably would promote the independence of their children."

The amount of child care a divorced mother uses to permit social activities is not known. Marsden (1969) and Goode (1948) indicate that the women in their samples simply do not get out of the house for social activities as often as they had when married.

While pressures to maintain the mother in her isolated domestic role remain strong, alternatives can be found. Apartment houses with built-in services make neighborly sharing more convenient. Communes may be a counter trend to the isolation of nuclear family units (Kantor, 1972; Francescato, 1973). As yet, however, many communes exclude children (Kinkade, 1973; Francescato, 1973). Other types of informal organizations such as baby-sitting cooperatives and play groups may make up some of the gap. Furthermore, the isolation of the nuclear family has recently been discovered to be less total than was once assumed. Although relatively few older parents live with their married children, the majority of older parents do live within 30 minutes of a married child and see the child at least once a week (Reiss, 1971). There is no reason to believe that they do not also offer services, advice, and assistance. Relatives have also been found to be the most frequent source of day-time child care, second only to schools (Low and Spindler, 1968). The doubling up of households sometimes found among divorced mothers may ease the strain also. Bernard (1964) found that one-third of low-income female-headed households in his sample shared their quarters, most usually with the woman's own adult children.

However, limitations of housing continue to make extended cooperation difficult. Few apartments, for example, have space suitable for day care centers. The U.S. Office for Child Development refused to fund one such center in a proposed housing development for single parents, on the grounds that the mothers might become too dependent on such housing (Gershenson, p.c.).

Emotional supports

The function of emotional support is not as amenable to precise analysis as the other functions. The kinds of supports family members provide or need cannot easily be quantified. We can speak only generally about social factors that provide a favorable or unfavorable psychological climate for family living.

Social Climate. Goode's seminal work (1948) found that the divorced woman has no clearly defined status. She and her family exist in a social limbo. Negative attitudes toward divorced mothers and single-parent families are common. Despite the prevalence of the mother-headed single-parent family, the unit continues to be regarded as a deviant form (Staples, 1971).

Single-parent families headed by women are blamed for many social problems (*e.g.,* the research drawn upon in the Moynihan Report, as well as the attitudes expressed in it [Rainwater & Yancy, 1967]). Glasser and Navarre (1965) and Goode (1948) stated that the women involved believe society sees them as abnormal, and they themselves accept the label. The divorced mothers also believed that they might be inadequate parents (see Goffman, 1963). Otto Pollak (1964) in a discussion of broken homes as a social problem explained the difference between unmarried and divorced mothers as the inability of the first to "get a man" and of the second to "keep her man." Writers have observed that the difference in payments to widows and to divorcees under programs for mother-headed families reflects the value policy-makers place on the relative worthiness of the mothers (Segalman, 1968;

Wynn, 1964; Bernard, 1964; Cole, 1969). Further evidence of negative attitudes to the mother for failure to keep the family together has been advanced by Herzog and Sudia (1971), Chase (1971), and LeMasters (1971). Ober (Grollman, 1969) found that neighbors would not let their children play with children of divorced mothers (see also Marsden, 1969), and that colleges discriminated against such children in admissions policies. Landis (1960) found that 20% of children in his sample felt shame about their parents' divorce, and 10% lied about the whereabouts of the absent parent.

Both Goode (1948) and Marsden (1969) found that women they interviewed were ashamed of being divorced and denied that the divorce was their fault. Marsden (1969) also found an order of prestige among female heads of families, with widows considering themselves highest and unwed mothers lowest. Carter and Glick (1970) suggest that the frequency of moves by recently divorced families may be related to shame in dealing with neighbors and a desire to make a new start where their situation was not known.

Interpersonal Support. On the positive side, the attitudes of friends and relatives, especially the mother's family, and the amount of personal support they offer is important. Goode (1963), Sussman (1971), and Winch (1971) agree that the family network serves to protect and support individuals in industrial society. Goode (1948) found that half of the divorcees studied kept their old friends and the remainder were on the whole satisfied with the new friends they made. Marsden (1969) found that for one-third of families studied the impact of father absence was softened by a relative, friend, lodger, neighbor or boyfriend. Bernard found that none of his respondents were without some assistance from kin, however minimal. However, he also found that regardless of relative economic circumstances, women who seemed to handle their daily affairs "cheerfully and with humor" had a network of friends and relatives to draw upon. "Supplemental assistance, such as money or clothing, was vital, but having people who could give advice, encouragement and understanding was even more central to the respondent's morale. Without it, the women seemed to feel isolated, depressed, and worn out with the struggle to maintain their families" (Bernard, 1964:37-38).

Formal institutions and agencies appear unwilling and unable to provide emotional support. Weiss found that when low-income solo mothers turned to social service agencies, hospitals, churches, and guidance clinics, "they there found service to be accompanied by actions or comments injurious to their self-esteem, and support and guidance to be virtually unobtainable" (Weiss, 1973:327).

A social network also provides information to the mother that enables her to carry out her child care responsibilities, such as learning what virus is going around and what treatment is recommended (Glasser & Navarre, 1964).

Dating activities and boyfriends are an important part of the divorced mother's social relations. Sexual relations are a form of emotional support rarely studied. Data from 1956 reported by Gebhard (1971) show that sexual relations are common among divorcees of all ages and that their rate of enjoyment is higher than that of wives.

While the existence of a social network of support appears crucial in the divorced mother's life, the extent to which such a network may be the source of negative sanctions as well as positive supports is not known.

The importance of positive emotional support from other people cannot be over-emphasized when children are a 24-hour responsibility. As Glasser and Navarre (1964) have pointed out, children cannot provide emotional support—their love is demanding of the parent, rather than supportive. A great, and often overlooked, strength of the two-parent family is the presence of two *adult* members, each providing the other with aid in decision making, psychological support, replacement during illness or absence—someone to take over part of the burden. The solo parent not only has to fulfill all family functions, but has no relief from her or his burden (Glasser & Navarre, 1964).

Lewis states: "Some psychologists hold that, during the first two years of a child's life, the father's presence is more important for his psychological, physical, and economic help to the mother than for his direct effect on the child's well being (this assumes, of course, that he does give such support)" (Rainwater & Yancy, 1967). Much more research is needed to carefully define exactly how parents in a two-parent family do provide emotional support and working relief to each other. However, the indirect evidence cited above suggests that the resources available to the mother for sharing the family responsibilities and the daily griefs and joys of family life with other adults (not necessarily the father) may be critical to the survival of the family unit.

II. FATHER ABSENCE

So far, we have made no direct mention of a large body of literature purportedly dealing with single-parent families. This is the group of studies on father absence. These studies encompass a number of disciplines and research areas, but share the common theme of trying to trace father absence as a causative factor in childhood pathological behavior such as juvenile delinquency or "acting out," inadequate sex-role identification, lowered school achievement, or poor personal adjustment.

Many professionals, especially those working with single-parent families, have tended to view studies on father absence as synonymous with studies on the single-parent family and to draw rather simplistic conclusions concerning the pathogenic qualities of the single-parent family from these studies.

A paramount difficulty with the father absence studies has been their failure to consider the changed position of the mother following divorce, both with respect to society and within the family. This blind spot in the literature has both methodological and substantive implications. Methodologically a serious error is made in comparing father-absent to father-present families without taking into account the differences in functions, roles, and relationships assumed by the parents in each case. The two are not readily comparable. An additional bias enters the research since stigma against the single-parent family is not taken into account.

Father absence studies largely focus on what happens to *boy* children growing up in a fatherless home. The studies in which girls are the primary focus, or in which girls are considered separately from boys are practically nonexistent (Herzog & Sudia, 1971). A recent article by Hetherington (1973) is a notable exception. The preeoccupation with boys rested on the assumption, recently brought into serious question, that father absence has more impact on boys than on girls, and partly from clinical findings which seemed to show disproportionate numbers of father-absent boys turning up in juvenile court, at child guidance clinics, and in school psychology referrals. Having once defined the question, however, many researchers have failed to consider other variables

which may be concurrent with father absence, or if they acknowledged their existence, have failed to control adequately for their effects. Thus, Herzog and Sudia in a comprehensive review of the father-absence literature, in which they uncovered over 400 references, found only 60 (15%) which they felt were "methodologically sound," even by admittedly rather generous criteria (see also Walters & Stinnett, 1971). In most cases, a study was included if it made any attempt to compare the father-absent group to a father-present group of similar characteristics. The problems with their "core group," as they labeled the 60 studies, as well as those discussed by Billingsley and Giovannoni (1971) in their review article, range across a number of methodological issues.

We will discuss these issues in terms of analysis of family functions.

Economic Functions. In keeping with the psychodynamic emphasis of most father-absence studies, economic conditions in the father-absent families have often been overlooked or inadequately controlled. The difficulty in establishing adequate controls has been particularly acute in assessing the relative weightings of father absence versus poverty as causative factors in juvenile delinquency, school failures, etc. (see Caldwell, 1970; Willie, 1967). Herzog and Sudia (1971:27) conclude:

Even if no other questions were raised with regard to study findings in this area, doubt concerning SES controls alone would be a sufficient basis for suspecting that evidence is not yet adequate for an unqualified answer to questions about the effects of father absence.

In addition to the issue of poverty as a confounding variable, the father-absence literature takes the current economic status of the family as a given, failing to consider the psychological impact of downward mobility, which, as we have pointed out, seems to be common following the parents' divorce or separation. Another variable, somewhat outside the scope of this paper, linking family attitudes with economic stability, is the perceived legitimacy of the father's absence—in cases of "legitimate" separation, such as death or military service, the family, in effect, continues to benefit from its past association with the father as his economic functions are carried on with approval by societal agencies, whereas in the case of "illegitimate" separation, which includes divorce, the family is punished financially and socially for existing apart from the father. Since father-absence studies rarely compare groups differing along the dimension of legitimacy, there is almost no way to sort out the confounded economic/psychological effects of this variable (Rose, 1970).

Authority. In general, father-absence literature assumes that the mother will have difficulty asserting authority within the family while failing to consider her low power vis-à-vis the community at large. However, as we have noted above, her lower status in the community may reduce her ability to be seen within the family as the authority. Other factors bearing on her effectiveness as an authority remain confounded and unexamined. For example, we know very little about the way authority is used in two-parent families and the degree to which modifications must occur following divorce. As Herzog and Sudia (1971) point out, the familiar instrumental-expressive dichotomy is of little heuristic assistance.

. . . it is likely that both the maternal and the paternal roles are segmented with regard to expressive and instrumental functions. During the early years of childhood, the mother's role is strongly instrumental and the father's is largely expressive. To conceive of either one as

typically expressive or instrumental is too far from reality to be acceptable even as a schematization.

The extent of the father's involvement in within-family decision making has not been assessed. One of the few studies in which father involvement has been systematically varied (Blanchard & Biller, 1969) suggests that the behavior of father-absent boys (both for long and short periods of separation) and boys with low father-presence (present in the family but not much involved in its activities) looks similar, but significantly different from that of boys whose fathers appear to be highly involved with the family. Even when fathers are present, there is evidence that they tend to ignore their daughters (Josephson, 1969). These data suggest that, for some families at least, the switch from two-parent authority to one-parent authority may represent a less radical shift than has been thought.

Another little-explored issue has been the extent to which the father retains decision-making power for the family after the divorce has taken place. An illuminating study by Westman *et al.* (1971) suggests that decision-making conflict following divorce affects the children's behavior adversely. They found, using records from divorce courts and from child guidance clinics, that children from one-parent families appeared to be stressed only (1) where relations between the parents continued to be turbulent following the divorce, or (2) relations with the parent not in the home were forbidden the child. No children from families in which the divorced parents had mutually agreed upon and followed arrangements for finance and child care turned up in the child guidance clinic sample.

Child Care and Housekeeping. Father-absence studies have usually been concerned with the father as role model and as authority, and have not inquired into the father's actual responsibilities for child care. When we examine the literature carefully, two conclusions emerge: (1) in contrast to the extensive observations and careful documentation of mothers' interactions with young children, practically no studies report direct observations of fathers' behavior with their children (Kotelchuck, 1972); (2) in the occasional assessments of fathers' involvement in daily care of children, the typical amount of involvement has been extremely minimal, at least for small children. Rebelsky and Hanks (1971), for example, found that fathers typically spent less than one minute a day verbalizing to their infants. Kotelchuck (1972), in questioning a group of highly educated, professional fathers about their daily caretaking activities of children between six months and two years, found that fully 75% reported that they took no routine role in child care. Granted that quality of time spent with a parent may count for more than quantity, these data suggest that children's views about fathers and male models may, by necessity, depend more on cultural stereotypes, the mothers's attitude, and the children's fantasies than on extensive interactions with a flesh-and-blood father. Studies by Kohlberg (1966) and Aldous (1972) support this view.

A further implication of the father's absence from childrearing in the two-parent home is that in the single-parent family, the child may be stressed not by the father's absence but by the mother's absence. If they have depended largely upon her to fulfill their needs, and if she must now spread her energies further (whether she takes a job or not), the children may, in effect, be maternally deprived rather than paternally deprived. Perhaps the appropriate comparisons should be made along the dimension of maternal deprivation, assessing the variables which would interfere with or enhance the mother's abilities to provide adequate mothering. Immediately we are plunged back into the intricate connections between social networks, societal attitudes, and economic conditions which have been apparent all along.

Emotional Supports. Although we have little formal evidence, the discussion up to this point suggests father absence studies might be more instructive if they focused on how the father's absence affected the mother psychologically, rather than on how it affected the children. We propose to treat some of the general aspects of this issue in the following section.

One component of father absence and divorce literature has been the assumption of psychological damage to the children. Yet several studies have shown that the damage, if present, is much less than has been popularly assumed. Burchinal (1964), Nye (1957), Goode (1948), Landis (1960), Despert (1953) and others have found that a happy one-parent family is certainly no worse than, and may be better than, an unhappy two-parent family. Burchinal (1964) found no significant differences in emotional health between children of one-parent and two-parent families. Langner and Michael (1963) found that mental health among adults was more dependent upon the subject's current situation than on childhood variables such as parental divorce.

The belief in necessary psychological damage to the child appears to be based on a mistaken assumption concerning stress. Implicit in much of the literature is the idea that since divorce itself is a stressful experience and the separation of the parents causes disequilibrium in the family, therefore the ongoing state of being divorced or fatherless is a permanent condition of distress and disequilibrium.

This argument tends to ignore the time dimension. We propose that the family of divorce should be looked at as in a state of process over time.

Typically stress theory describes a change from equilibrium to disequilibrium when stress has occurred, followed by re-equilibration in which new relationships are developed and stress gradually subsides. Hansen and Hill (1969) categorize divorce as one type of stress. In assessing the amount of potential psychological damage, it is necessary to take into account how much of a stress the divorce actually is, as well as the factors leading to reequilibrium following the divorce.

The literature often refers to divorce as *family* breakdown, *family* dissolution, or *family* disorganization, rather than more correctly referring to it as *marital* dissolution. Since a family is defined as at least one adult and one or more children under 18, as long as the children remain with one of the parents following the marital dissolution, the family has not been broken. Rather what has occurred is a change in the family constellation so that where previously there were two adults and one or more children, there is now one adult. The family has not broken down, but has changed as the interrelationships within the constellation are altered by the removal of one of its members.

How much of a stress the actual divorce or uncoupling process will be depends on a variety of measurable factors. Several authors (e.g., Goode, 1948; Rosenberg, 1965) have found that the "divorce trauma" for the wife, that is, extreme stress during the period of the divorce, was related to her age, her religion, whether she or her husband most desired the divorce, how long a period of anticipation she had, and the attitudes of friends and relatives. If the period prior to divorce was one of conflict and hostility, or if the

marriage was chronically unhappy, the divorce may actually be a relief from stress rather than a stressful event. It is not surprising that researchers have found that a conflict-ridden home and an unhappy or "empty shell" family create more psychological problems for a child than a divorce. It would appear then that more attention should be paid to factors leading to the successful establishment and equilibration of a one-parent household. Most authors assume that the only form of re-equilibrium possible is remarriage; e.g., that without the "proper constellation" there can be no equilibrium. Yet several researchers (Despert, 1953; Rosenberg, 1965; Josephson, 1969) have found that remarriage appears to be worse for the child psychologically than the mother remaining divorced. As we have discussed earlier, the period immediately following divorce is a time in which family functions have to be reassigned; the level of functioning is affected by a variety of social factors in an environment which does not provide extensive supports or may actually be hostile to the single-parent family. If the difficulties of making the change are overwhelming, or if the subsequent resources are insufficient for family functioning, the family may in fact become broken if the mother can no longer cope and the children must be removed from the home.

Hansen and Hill (1964) cite literature on disasters which suggests that in times of extreme stress, people act more mature and responsible and draw closer to each other. Applying this to the situation of the mother alone with her children, it may be hypothesized that she must now become more responsible, and that she and her children will become emotionally closer to each other. Hansen and Hill (1964) have also found that people's self-concepts change according to the roles they must assume (see also Merton). As the single mother assumes more responsibility and has to act more independently, she may in fact become more mature and thus more able to deal with the problems presented to her. The same may be true of her children.

Thus it becomes evident that father absence alone is not an adequate variable for predicting family viability or children's adjustment. Prior and current demographic status, events during the divorce process, and the presence or absence of social supports for the mother and family following divorce may be much more significant factors in the family's continued viability and in the psychological adjustment of the children.

SUMMARY AND CONCLUSIONS

Over 10% of families in the United States are headed by one parent. Nearly 90% of these single parents are women. While there are a number of categories of single-parent families with children under 18, the most prevalent and increasing is that of divorce and permanent separation. Divorce by couples with children is a rapidly increasing phenomenon.

With the growth of the women's liberation movement has come an increasing body of literature cataloging discrimination against women in employment, education and income, and describing the differential socialization of the sexes for, and access to, positions of leadership and competence. However, little of this research has been applied to the situation of women who have responsibility for heading a family.

Scattered in various disciplines we have found studies comparing socioeconomic status for married and divorced women, studies of the effects of father absence on children—particularly boy children, studies of roles with and without sex-role

stereotyping, and the effects of stress upon families. Yet we found little attention paid to the husbandless mother or to the female-headed family as an operating social system following divorce. Little or no attempt has been made in the social science literature to integrate these various pieces of knowledge into an understanding of how women cope in the single-parent situation, what effect various constraints have upon them, and what variables determine women's abilities to overcome these constraints.

Over and over the literature assumes that the single-parent state is temporary. Although many women, especially those under 30, do remarry, a greater proportion, especially after the age of 30, remain divorced (Carter & Glick, 1970). Divorced men are more likely to remarry than are their ex-wives. Because of the assumption that divorcees will remarry, society does not feel obligated to provide supports for single parents. Because societal supports are largely unavailable, husbandless mothers come to view remarriage as the only viable alternative to a difficult situation. The situation will remain difficult as long as policies are based on these circular assumptions.

We are dealing with a large and growing population of adults and children living in single-parent families. Before intelligent action can be taken by or on behalf of single-parent families, the gaps in our knowledge, as demonstrated in this paper, must be filled in. Following is a summary of research questions that need to be further explored in studies of single-parent families, particularly those caused by divorce.

Questions for further research

Economic. What expectations about their future economic problems do women who are contemplating divorce have? How do their expectations affect their willingness or unwillingness to stay married? What implications does a choice of downward mobility have in a society valuing upward mobility? After divorce, how does the family react to downward mobility and the lessened resources available? What changes can be made in welfare policy, job training policies, and child-support policies to maintain family income? How can work and living arrangements be changed to enable the mother to support a family?

Roles and Functions. In a female-headed family, how are functions formerly performed and roles formerly filled by the husband redistributed? How are the mother's roles redistributed? What are the effects of this re-allocation on the family and on its individual members? What external factors aid in the redistribution and the level of functioning?

Authority. Under what conditions are women able to play the authority role within the family and to represent the family to the outside world? How do women who are single parents establish and define their position in society? Which aspects of her authority are within the mother's ability to determine, and which require change in attitudes and policies of social institutions?

Stigma. Do women heading families feel they or their children are being stigmatized or discriminated against? If so, what is their reaction to perceived stigma? What long-term social changes and short-term situational factors increase or decrease the presence and perception of stigma? E.g., how is stigma related to community values, housing patterns, available services, policies of local institutions, attitudes and behavior of "helping professionals," neighbors, family, and friends?

Other Issues. Under what conditions can patterns of stress be predicted and thus changed? What factors lead to the re-establishment of stable family patterns following divorce? What circumstances lead women to remarry rather than to remaining single parents? To what extent is the phenomenon of moving associated with divorce, and what positive and negative consequences flow from this?

We raise these questions within the context of an urgent need on the part of women as single parents for adequate understanding of their situation. Women single parents remain victimized by the current distortions and inadequacies of the data, both in their interactions within their families and in the larger society. Present assumptions about and treatment of single-parent families are based upon insufficient and often incomplete information. At best present practice and policies are based on ignorance; at worst, upon misleading and biased half-truths reflecting the general discrimination faced by women in our society. Further research directed at the issues and questions raised in this paper can provide single parents with a more realistic (and less stigmatized) appraisal of their situation, and can aid policy-makers in creating a more equitable milieu for all single parents and their families.

REFERENCES

Aldous, Joan. Children's perceptions of adult role assignment: father absence, class, race, and sex influences. *Journal of Marriage and the Family,* 1972, **34,** 55-56.

Andreas, Carol. *Sex and caste in America.* Englewood Cliffs, N.J.: Prentice Hall, 1971.

Arnold, William. Race and ethnicity relative to other factors in juvenile court dispositions. *American Journal of Sociology,* 1971, **77,** 211-227.

Bell, Winifred. *Aid to dependent children.* New York: Columbia University Press, 1965.

Bem, Sandra L., & Bem, Daryl J. Training a woman to know her place: the power of a non-conscious ideology. In Michele Hoffnung Gaskov (ed.), *Roles women play: read-*

ings toward women's liberation. Belmont, Cal.: Brooks/Cole Publishing, 1971. Pp. 84-96.

Bernard, Jesse. No news, but new ideas. In Paul Bohannan (ed.), *Divorce and after.* Garden City: Doubleday Anchor, 1964. Pp. 3-32.

Bernard, Sydney. Fatherless families; their economic and social adjustment. Papers in Social Welfare Number 7. Waltham: Florence G. Heller Graduate School for Advanced Studies in Social Welfare, Brandeis University, 1964.

Billingsley, Andrew, & Giovannoni, Jeanne M. One parent family. In Robert Morris (ed.), Encyclopedia of social work (16th Issue). Vol. I. New York: National Association of Social Workers, 1971. Pp. 362-373.

Blanchard, R., & Biller, Henry B. Father availability and academic performance among third-grade boys. *Developmental Psychology,* 1971, **4,** 301-305.

Bluestone, Barry; Murphy, William; & Stevenson, Mary H. *Low wages and the working poor.* 2 Volumes. Detroit: Institute of Labor and Industrial Relations. University of Michigan—Wayne State University, 1971.

Burchinal, Lee. Characteristics of adolescents from unbroken homes and reconstituted families. *Journal of Marriage and the Family,* 1964, **26,** 44-51.

Caldwell, B. M. Rationale for early intervention. *Exceptional Children,* 1970, **36,** 717-726.

Carter, Hugh, & Glick, Paul C. *Marriage and divorce: A social and economic study.* Cambridge: Harvard University Press, 1970.

Cavan, Ruth S. Structural variations and mobility. In Harold T. Christensen (ed.), *Handbook of marriage and the family.* Chicago: Rand McNally, 1964. Pp. 535-581.

Chase, Janet. The dynamics of institutional oppression: the AFDC mother as a victim. *Public welfare revision study.* Boston: Boston Model Cities Administration, 1971.

Citizens' Advisory Council on the Status of Women. Memorandum: The Equal Rights Amendment and alimony and child support laws. Washington, D.C., 1972.

Cole, Blanche. *Perspective in public welfare.* Washington, D.C.: U.S. Department of Health, Education and Welfare, 1969.

Despert, J. Louise. *Children of Divorce.* Garden City: Doubleday and Company, 1953.

Ferris, Abbott. *Indicators of trends in the status of American women.* New York: Russell Sage Foundation, 1971.

Firestone, Shulameth. *The dialectic of sex.* New York: William Morrow, 1970.

Francescato, Donata. Children in urban communes. *Progress report.* New Haven: Foundation Funds for Research in Psychiatry, 1973.

Gebhard, Paul. Post marital coitus among widows and divorcees. In Paul Bohannan (ed.), *Divorce and after.* Garden City: Doubleday Anchor, 1971. Pp. 89-106.

George, Victor, & Wilding, Paul. *Motherless families.* London: Routledge and Kegan Paul, 1972.

Gillespie, Dair. Who has the power? the marital struggle. *Journal of Marriage and the Family,* 1971, **33,** 445-458.

Glasser, Paul, & Navarre, Elizabeth. Structural problems of the one-parent family. *Journal of Social Issues,* 1964, **21,** 98-109.

Glasser, Paul, & Navarre, Elizabeth. The problems of families in the AFDC program. *Children,* 1965, **12,** 151-157.

Glueck, Sheldon, & Glueck, Eleanor. *Family environment and delinquency.* Boston: Houghton Mifflin, 1962.

Goffman, Erving. *Stigma: Notes on the management of spoiled identity.* Englewood Cliffs, N.J.: Prentice Hall, 1963.

Goldberg, Phillip. Are women prejudiced against women? *Trans-action,* 1968 (April), 28-30.

Goode, William J. *After divorce.* Glencoe: The Free Press, 1948.

Goode, William J. *World revolution and family patterns.* New York: The Free Press, 1963.

Grollman, Earl. *Explaining divorce to children.* Boston: Beacon Press, 1969.

Hacker, Helen. Women as a minority group. *Social Forces,* 1951, **30,** 60-66.

Hansen, Donald A., & Hill, Reuben. Families under stress. In Harold T. Christensen (ed.), *Handbook of marriage and the family.* Chicago: Rand McNally and Company, 1964.

Hedges, Janice Niepert, & Barnett, Jeanne K. Working women and the division of household tasks. *Monthly Labor Review,* 1972, **95,** 9-14.

Herzog, Elizabeth, & Sudia, C. E. Family structure and composition. In R. R. Miller (ed.), *Race, research and reason; Social work perspectives.* New York: National Association of Social Workers, 1969. Pp. 145-164.

Herzog, Elizabeth, & Sudia, C. E. *Boys in fatherless families.* Washington, D.C.: U.S. Department of Health, Education, and Welfare, Children's Bureau, Number (OCD) 72-33, 1971.

Hetherington, E. Mavis. Girls without fathers. *Psychology Today,* 1973, **6,** 46-52.

Holmstrom, Lynda L. *The Two Career Family.* Cambridge: Schenkman, 1972.

Jacobson, Allvar Hilding. Conflict of attitude toward the roles of the husband and wife in marriage. *American Sociological Review,* 1952, **15,** 146-150.

Josephson, E. The matriarchy: myth and reality. *Family Coordinator,* 1969, **18,** 268-276.

Kantor, Rosabeth M. *Commitment and Community.* Cambridge: Harvard University Press, 1972.

Kinkade, K. Commune: a Walden Two experiment. *Psychology Today,* 1973, **6,** 71-82.

Kohlberg, Lawrence. A cognitive-developmental analysis of children's sex-role concepts and attitudes. In Eleanor Maccoby (ed.), *The development of sex differences.* Stanford: Stanford University Press, 1966. Pp. 82-172.

Kotelchuck, Milton. *The nature of the child's tie to his father.* Unpublished doctoral dissertation, Harvard University, Cambridge, Mass., 1972.

Kreps, Juanita. *Sex in the marketplace: American women at work.* Baltimore: Johns Hopkins Press, 1971.

Kriesberg, Louis. *Mothers in poverty.* Chicago: Aldine, 1970.

Landis, Judson. The trauma of children when parents divorce. *Marriage and Family Living,* 1960, **22,** 7-13.

Landis, Judson. A comparison of children from divorced and non-divorced unhappy marriages. *Family Life Coordinator,* 1962, **2,** 61-65.

Le Masters, E. E. The American father. In Jacqueline P. Wiseman (ed.), *People as partners.* San Francisco: Canfield Press, 1971. Pp. 247-264.

Lewis, R. L. The unmarried parent and community resources. *Child Welfare,* 1968, **47,** 487-614.

Low, Seth, & Spindler, Pearl G. *Child care arrangements of working mothers in the United States.* Washington, D.C.: U.S. Department of Health, Education and Welfare, Children's Bureau. Number 461, 1968.

Marsden, Dennis. *Mothers alone: Poverty and the fatherless family.* London: Allen Lane, The Penguin Press, 1969.

Millett, Kate. *Sexual politics.* New York: Doubleday, 1970.

Minturn, Leigh, & Lambert, W. W. *Mothers of six cultures.* New York: John Wiley & Sons, 1964.

Nye, F. Ivan. Child adjustment in broken and in unhappy, unbroken homes. *Marriage and Family Living,* 1957, **19,** 356-361.

Nye, F. Ivan. Field research, In Harold T. Christensen (ed.), *Handbook of marriage and the family.* Chicago: Rand McNally and Company, 1964. Pp. 247-274.

Oldham, James C. Questions of exclusion and exception under Title VIII—"sex plus" and the BFOQ. *The Hastings Law Journal,* 1971, **23,** 55-94.

Parsons, Talcott. Age and sex in the social structure. *American Journal of Sociology,* 1942, **7,** 608-614.

Parsons, Talcott. Social and cultural perspectives on the family. In Marvin B. Sussman (ed.), *Sourcebook in marriage and family.* Boston: Houghton Mifflin, 1959. Pp. 36-42.

Perry, Joseph B. The mother substitute of employed mothers: an exploratory inquiry. *Marriage and Family Living,* 1961, **23,** 363-367.

Pollack, Otto. The broken family. In Nathan E. Cohen (ed.), *Social Work and Social Problems.* New York: National Association of Social Workers, 1964.

Rainwater, Lee, & Yancy, William L. *The Moynihan Report and the politics of controversy.* Cambridge: Massachusetts Institute of Technology Press, 1967.

Reiss, Ira L. *The family system in America.* New York: Holt, Rinehart and Winston, 1971.

Rebelsky, F., & Hanks, C. Fathers' verbal interaction with infants in the first three months of life. *Child Development*, 1971, **42**, 63-68.

Roby, Pamela. *Child care—Who cares? Foreign and domestic infant and early childhood development policies*. New York: Basic Books, 1973.

Rose, Lawrence. The broken home and male delinquency. In M. Wolfgang, N. Johnson, & L. Savitz (eds.), *The sociology of crime and delinquency*. New York: John Wiley & Sons, 1970.

Rosenberg, Morris. *Society and the adolescent self-image*. Princeton: Princeton University Press, 1965.

Ruderman, Florence. *Child care and working mothers*. New York: Child Welfare League of America, 1968.

Segalman, Ralph. The Protestant ethic and social welfare. *Journal of Social Issues*, 1968, **24**, 125-142.

Schlessinger, B. *The one-parent family: Perspectives and annotated bibliography*. Toronto: University of Toronto Press, 1969.

Smith, Marjorie. Money: where credit is due. *Ms.* 1972 1(4), 36-37.

Smith, Thomas. Foundations of parental influence upon adolescents: an application of social power theory. *American Sociological Review*, 1970, **35**, 860-873.

Staples, R. Toward a sociology of the black family: a theoretical and methodological assessment." *Journal of Marriage and the Family*, 1971, **33**, 119-138.

Stein, Robert L. The economic status of families headed by women. *Monthly Labor Review*, 1970, **93**.

Sussman, Marvin B. Family systems in the 1970's: analysis, policies and programs. *Annals*, 1971, **396**, 40-56.

Thomas, M. M. Children with absent fathers. *Journal of Marriage and the Family*, 1968, **30**, 89-96.

U.S. Bureau of the Census. *Census of the Population: General Social and Economic Characteristics*. Washington, D.C. PC(1)-C1, 1970.

U.S. Department of Health, Education and Welfare. *Public Assistance Statistics, January 1973*. Washington, D.C. Number SRS 73-03100 NCSS Report A-2, 1/73.

U.S. House of Representatives, Committee on Education and Labor, Special Subcommittee on Education. *Discrimination against Women. Hearings*. 2 Volumes. Washington, D.C., 1970.

U.S. Women's Bureau. *Underutilization of Women Workers*. Revised. Washington, D.C., U.S. Department of Labor, 1971.

U.S. Women's Bureau. *Day Care Facts*. Washington, D.C.: U.S. Department of Labor. Pamphlet 161 Rev., 1973.

Waldman, W. E., & Gover, K. R. Children of women in the labor force. *Monthly Labor Review*, 1971, **94**, 19-25.

Waldman, W. E., & Gover, K. R. Marital and family characteristics of the labor force. *Monthly Labor Review*, 1972, **95**, 4-8.

Walters, J., & Stinnett, N. Parent–child relationships: a decade review of research. *Journal of Marriage and the Family*, 1971, **33**, 70-111.

Weiss, Robert S. Helping relationships: relationships of clients with physicians, social workers, priests and others. *Social Problems*, 1973, **20**, 319-328.

Weissman, Myrna, & Psykel, Eugene. Moving and depression in women. *Society*, 1972, **9**, 24-28.

Westman, J.; Cline, D.; Swift, W.; & Kramer, D. The role of child psychiatry in divorce. *Archives of General Psychiatry*, 1971, **70**, 405 ff.

Willie, Charles V. The relative contribution of family status and economic status to juvenile delinquency. *Social Problems*, 1967, **14**, 326-335.

Winch, Robert F. *The modern family*. New York: Holt, Rinehart and Winston, 1971.

Winston, Marian P., & Forsher, Trude. *Nonsupport of legitimate children by affluent fathers as a cause of poverty and welfare dependence*. Santa Monica: Rand Corporation, 1971.

Women's Research Center of Boston. *Who rules Massachusetts women*. Cambridge, 1972.

Wynn, Margaret. *Fatherless families*. London: Michael Joseph, 1964.

28.

E. Mavis Hetherington, Martha Cox, and Roger Cox

BEYOND FATHER ABSENCE:
CONCEPTUALIZATION OF EFFECTS OF DIVORCE

The incidence of children raised in homes with single parents is accelerating at a dramatic rate. In 1974 it was estimated that one out of every six children was living in a home with a single parent. In 95% of the cases the single parent is the mother. This increase in single-parent families is largely attributable to a rising divorce rate, particularly in families with young children (Bronfenbrenner, 1975).

The psychological research on single-parent families has usually involved comparative studies of the development of children in intact homes or homes with fathers absent. Although the findings are complex and not altogether consistent, they can be summarized by saying that early divorce seems to have more deleterious effects on children than later divorce, and that these effects differ for boys and girls with the most marked effects occurring in boys. Disruptions in sex-role typing, cognitive development, moral development and self-control have been reported in children with absent fathers (Biller, 1974; Hetherington & Deur, 1971; Lynn, 1974). If you read this literature, you will be struck by how little we know about factors that may mediate differences found between children in intact homes and those reared by a divorced mother. These differences are usually attributed to the lack of a father to serve as an adequate male model and as a disciplinarian with boys.

Undoubtedly the lack of a male model

and the controlling influence of the father are important factors in the development of these children; however, there may be less direct but equally powerful ways in which divorce and the relative unavailability of a father affects children.

Following a divorce in which custody has been granted to the mother, the mother–child relationship may become more intense and salient. The father is infrequently present to moderate or mediate in the interaction. The mother must most of the time take over parenting roles assumed by both the mother and father in intact families, and this often imposes considerable stress on the mother. There are fewer time-outs in the parenting game in one-parent families. In intact families it has been demonstrated that a supportive father facilitates good mothering in their wives (Pederson & Robson, 1969).

In addition to pressures associated with lack of paternal support in child rearing following divorce, the divorced mother has other stresses to cope with. The lack of the paternal support system is also felt in economic needs, maintaining the household, emotional support, needs for intimacy and sexual gratification, restrictions in social and recreational activities and contacts with adults. How she copes with these stresses will impact on the development of the child.

It would be just as unfortunate to view the effects of father absence solely in terms of the effects of absence of a father on mothers and their related effects on children, as it is to lean too heavily on modeling as an explanation for these

Source: Revision of a paper presented at the Society for Research in Child Development, April 1975.

effects. Divorce affects the whole family system and the functioning and interactions of the members within that system. To get a true picture of the impact of divorce, its effects on the divorced father living out of the home and on the mother and children must be examined. Because of space limitations, this presentation will be restricted to a discussion of changes in functioning of mothers and fathers following divorce. Our findings on changes in the behavior of children following divorce will not be presented although this was a main focus of our project. Many of the stresses imposed on the parents following divorce and alterations in their life style mediated how the children adapted to the divorce, and in turn the children responses modified the parents' behavior.

The findings to be reported are part of a two-year longitudinal study of the impact of divorce on family functioning and the development of children. The goals of the study were first to examine the response to the family crisis of divorce, and patterns of reorganization of the family over the two-year period following divorce. It was assumed that the family system would go through a period of disorganization immediately after the divorce, followed by recovery, reorganization and eventual attainment of a new pattern of equilibrium. The second goal was to examine the characteristics of family members that contributed to variations in family processes. The third goal was to examine the effects of variations in family interaction and structure on the development of children.

The original sample was composed of thirty-six white, middle-class boys and thirty-six girls and their divorced parents from homes in which custody has been granted to the mother, and the same number of children and parents from intact homes. The final sample was twenty-four families in each of the groups, a total of ninety-six families on which complete data

were available. Sample attrition was largely due to remarriage in the divorced families, to families or a parent leaving the area, to lack of cooperation by schools which made important measures on the child unavailable, and to eight families who no longer wished to participate in the study. Families with stepparents were excluded, since one of the interests in the investigation was seeing how mothers and children functioned in father-absent homes and how their functioning might be related to deviant or nondeviant behavior in children. In the analyses to be presented in this paper, six families were randomly dropped from groups to maintain equal sizes in groups.

When a reduction in sample size occurs from 144 families to 96 families, one immediately becomes concerned about bias in the sample. On demographic characteristics such as age, religion, education, income, occupation, family size, and maternal employment there were no differences between subjects who dropped out or were excluded from the sample and those who remained. In addition when a family was no longer included in the study, a comparative analysis was done of their interaction patterns and those of the continuing families. Some differences in these groups will be noted in the course of this presentation. In general, there were few differences in parent–child interactions in families who did or did not remain in the study. However, there were some differences in the characteristics of parents who remarried and how they viewed themselves and their lives.

The study used a multimethod, multimeasure approach to the investigation of family interaction. The measures used in the study included interviews and structured diary records of the parents, observations of the parents and child interacting in the laboratory and home, behavior checklists of parent–child interaction kept by the parents, and a battery of personality scales on the parents. In addition, observations of the child were conducted in nursery schools; peer nomination and teacher ratings of the child's behavior, and measures of the child's sex-role typing, cognitive performance and social development were obtained. The parents and children were administered these measures at two months, one year, and two years following filing for divorce.

In this presentation the discussion will be restricted mainly to the findings based on parent interviews and the observations of the parent and child in an interaction situation in the laboratory, although I will occasionally refer to related findings on other measures. Therefore only these two procedures will be presented in detail.

As was found by Baumrind (1967, 1971), using some similar measures, the parent–child interaction patterns in the home observations and in the laboratory sessions and as reported in the interviews showed considerable congruency. For example, parents who were nurturant, made high use of positive or negative sanctions, or had good control over their children tended to be so across situations. Children

who were compliant, oppositional, or affiliative with parents also tended to maintain these behaviors across situations. These behaviors, of course, vary when the interactions involve different people such as parents, teachers, or peers.

Parents were interviewed separately on a structured parent interview schedule designed to assess discipline practices and the relationship with the child, support systems outside the family household system, social, emotional, and heterosexual relationships, quality of the relationship with the spouse, economic stress, family disorganization, satisfaction and happiness, and attitudes toward the self. The interviews were tape recorded. Each of the categories listed in Table 28.1 was rated on scales by two judges. In some cases the category involved the rating of only a single 5- or 7-point scale. In others it represents a composite score of several ratings on a group of subscales. Interjudge reliabilities ranged from .69 to .95 with a mean of .82. The interviews were derived and modified from those of Baumrind (1967, 1971), Sears, Rau, and Alpert, (1965), Martin and Hetherington (1971), and others.

TABLE 28.1.

Control of Child	Problems in Running Household
Maturity demands of child	Relationship with spouse
Communication with child	Emotional support in personal matters
Nurturance of child	Immediate support system
Permissiveness–restrictiveness with child	Social life and activities
Negative sanctions with child	Contact with adults
Positive sanctions with child	Intimate relations
Reinforcement of child for sex-typed behaviors	Sexuality
Paternal availability	Number of dates
Maternal availability	Happiness and satisfaction
Paternal face-to-face interaction with child	Competence as a parent
Maternal face-to-face interaction with child	Competence as a male/female
Quality of spouse's relationship with the child	Self-esteem
Agreement in treatment of the child	Satisfaction with employment
Emotional support in child rearing from spouse	Conflict preceding divorce
Economic stress	Tension in divorce
Family disorganization	

TABLE 28.2. Interacton Coding

Parent Behavior	Child Behavior
Command (positive)	Opposition
Command (negative)	Aversive opposition
Question	Compliance
Nonverbal intrusion	Dependency
Ignore	Negative demands (whin-
Affiliate (interact)	ing, complaining,
Positive sanctions	angry tone)
Negative sanctions	Aggression (tantrum,
Reasoning and	destructiveness)
explanation	Requests
Encourages	Affiliate
Dependency	Self manipulation
Indulgence	Play
Opposition	Ignore
Compliance	Cry
Encourages	
independence	

Each parent was observed separately interacting with the child in the laboratory in a half-hour free-play situation and in a half-hour structured situation involving puzzles, block building, bead stringing, and sorting tasks. The interaction sessions with the mother or father were on different days, separated by a period of about a month. Half of the children interacted with the mother first and half with the father first. Behavior was coded in the categories in Table 28.2. The coding procedure was similar to that used by Patterson and his colleagues where the observation period is divided into thirty-second intervals and an average of about five behavior sequences of interactions between the subject and other family members were coded in the 30-second interval. However, in order to improve reliability, a tone sounded every six seconds during the recording interval. Two raters rated all sessions. Interjudge agreement on individual responses averaged .83.

In changing to a new, single life-style, what kinds of stresses are likely to be experienced by members of a divorced couple? How might these be related to parent–child relations?

Greater economic stress in divorced couples was apparent in our sample. Although the average income of the divorced families was equal to that of the intact families, the economic problems associated with maintaining two households for divorced couples led to more financial concerns and limitations in purchasing practices in divorced couples. It has been suggested by Herzog and Sudia that many of the deleterious effects of father absence on children could be eliminated if economic stability was provided for mothers with no husband in the home. However, in our study the number of significant correlations was not above chance between income or reported feelings of economic stress and parents' reported or observed interactions with their children or with behavior of the child in nursery school. It may be that in our middle-class sample with an average family income of about $22,000 the range is not great enough to detect the effects of economic stress. In a lower-class sample, the greater extremes of economic duress might be associated with variations in parent–child interaction or the development of the child.

A second area in which stresses are experienced by divorced couples are in social life and in meaningful, intimate interpersonal relationships. Divorced adults often complain that socializing in our culture is organized around couples and that being a single adult, particularly a single woman with children, limits recreational opportunities. Both the interview findings and the diary records kept by parents indicate that social life is more restricted in divorced couples and that this effect initially is most marked for women. Divorced mothers report having significantly less contact with adults than do the other parents and often commented on their sense of being locked into a child's world. Several described themselves as prisoners and used terms like being "walled in" or "trapped." This was less true of working than nonworking mothers. Many nonworking mothers complained that most of their social contacts had been made through professional associates of the husband and that with divorce these associations terminated. In contrast, the employed mothers had contact with their co-workers and these relations often extended into after-hour social events. Although the employed women complained that it was difficult to get household chores done and of their concern about getting adequate care for their children, most felt the gratifications associated with employment outweighed the problems. Although social life for our total sample of divorced women increased over the two-year period, it always remains lower than that of married women.

Divorced men had a restricted social life two months after divorce, followed by a surge of activity at one year and a decline in activity to the wife's level by two years. Divorced men and women who had not remarried in the two years following divorce repeatedly spoke of their intense feelings of loneliness.

Heterosexual relations play a particularly important role in the happiness and attitudes toward the self of both married and divorced adults. Happiness, self-esteem, and feelings of competence in heterosexual behavior increased steadily over the two-year period for divorced males and females, but they are not as high even in the second year as those for married couples. It should be noted, however, that the subjects who later remarried and were shifted from this study of divorce and father absence to a stepparent study, scored as high on happiness although lower on self-esteem and feelings of competence as did parents in intact families. Frequency of sexual intercourse was lower for divorced parents than married couples at two months, higher at one year for males and about the same frequency at two years. Divorced males particularly seemed to show a peak of sexual activity and a pattern of dating a variety of women in the first year following divorce. However the stereotyped image of the happy, swinging single life was not altogether accurate. One of our sets of interview ratings attempted to measure intimacy in relationships. Intimacy referred to love in the Sullivanian sense of valuing the welfare of the other as much as one's own, of a deep concern and willingness to make sacrifices for the other, and strong attachment and desire to be near the other person. It should be understood that this use of the term intimacy is not synonymous with sexual intimacy although, of course, the two frequently occur together. Intimacy in relationships showed strong positive correlations with

TABLE 28.3. Correlations Between Frequency of Sexual Intercourse and Happiness in High and Low Intimacy Divorced Groups

| | High Intimacy | | Low Intimacy | |
	Male (N = 24)	Female (N = 24)	Male (N = 24)	Female (N = 24)
Two months	+.40*	+.43*	−.09 (N.S.)	−.42*
One year	+.49**	+.47**	−.41*	−.46*
Two years	+.54**	+.52**	−.48**	−.57**

*p <.05
**p <.01

happiness, self-esteem, and feelings of competence in heterosexual relations for both divorced and married men and women. Table 28.3. shows that in the divorced but not in the married sample if subjects were divided into those above and below the median in terms of intimacy in relationships, happiness correlated negatively with frequency of intercourse in the low-intimacy group and positively in the high-intimacy group. The same pattern held for self-esteem. This was true for both divorced males and females. The only nonsignificant correlation was for low-intimacy males immediately following divorce. Many males but few females were pleased at the increased opportunity for sexual experiences with a variety of partners immediately following divorce. However by the end of the first year both divorced men and women were expressing a want for intimacy and a lack of satisfaction in casual sexual encounters. Women expressed particularly intense feelings about frequent casual sexual encounters, often talking of feelings of desperation, overwhelming depression, and low self-esteem following such exchanges.

Thus far we have been focusing mainly on changes in the divorced partners in the two years following divorce. We will now look at differences in family functioning and in parent–child interactions as measured both in the interview and in direct observations in the laboratory situation.

One of the sets of interview scales was family disorganization, which dealt with the degree of structure in proscribed household roles, problems in coping with routine household tasks, and the regularity and scheduling of events. The fathers' scales dealt with similar problems but focused on those in his life and household. The households of the divorced mothers and fathers were always more disorganized than those of intact families, although this

disorganization was most marked in the first year following divorce and had significantly decreased by the second year. Children of divorced parents were more likely to get pick-up meals at irregular times. Divorced mothers and their children were less likely to eat dinner together. Bedtimes were more erratic and the children were read to less before bedtime and were more likely to arrive at school late. These results were found both in interviews and in the structured parental diaries.

The interaction patterns between divorced parents and children differed significantly from those in intact families on almost every variable studied in the interview, and on many of the parallel measures in the structured interaction situation. On these measures the differences were greatest during the first year and a process of re-equilibration seemed to be taking place by the end of the second year, particularly in mother–child relationships. However, even at the end of the second year on many dimensions parent–child relations in divorced and intact families differed. Some of the findings for fathers must be interpreted in view of the fact that divorced fathers become increasingly less available to their children over the course of the two-year period. Although at two months divorced fathers are having almost as much face-to-face interaction with their children as are fathers in intact homes who are often highly unavailable to their children (Blanchard & Biller 1971), this interaction declines rapidly. At two months about one-quarter of the divorced parents even reported that fathers in their eagerness to maximize visitation rights and maintain contact with their children were having more face-to-face contact with their children than they had before the divorce. This contact was motivated by a variety of factors in the different fathers. Sometimes it was based on a deep attachment to the child or continuing attachment to the wife, sometimes it was based on feelings of duty or attempts to assuage guilt, often it was an attempt to maintain a sense of continuity in their lives and unfortunately it was frequently at least partly motivated by a desire to annoy, compete with, or retaliate against the spouse.

The results of the interview findings and laboratory observations relating to parent–child interaction will be presented in a simplified fashion and where possible presented together.

Divorced parents make fewer maturity demands of their children, communicate less well with their children, tend to be less affectionate with their children, and show marked inconsistency in discipline and lack of control over their children in comparison to parents in intact families. Poor parenting seems most marked, particularly for divorced mothers, one year after divorce which seems to be a peak of stress in parent–child relations. Two years following the divorce, mothers are demanding more autonomous mature behavior of their children, communicate better and use more explanation and reasoning, are more nurturant and consistent, and are better able to control their children than they were the year before. A similar pattern is occurring for divorced fathers in maturity demands, communication and consistency, but they are becoming less nurturant and more detached from their children with time. In the laboratory and home observations, divorced fathers were ignoring their children more and showing less affection.

The lack of control that divorced parents have over their children, particularly one year following divorce, was apparent in home and laboratory observations. When the percentage of times the child complied to various types of parental demands was examined, the lack of compliance espe- cially to the divorced mother at one year with a marked increase in successful commands at two years is dramatic. These results for the laboratory situation are presented in Table 28.4. Some divorced mothers described their relationship with their child one year after divorce as "declared war" a "struggle for survival," "the old Chinese water torture," or "like getting bitten to death by ducks." It can also be seen in Table 28.4 that boys comply less to parental demands than do girls and that children are more compliant to their fathers' than their mothers' commands in spite of the fact that mothers usually give about twice as many commands as fathers.

The interviews and observations showed that the lack of control in the divorced parents was associated with very different patterns of relating to the child for mothers and fathers. The divorced mother tries to control the child by being more restrictive and giving more commands which the child ignores or resists. The divorced father wants his contacts with his children to be as happy as possible. He begins by initially being extremely permissive and indulgent with his children and becoming increasingly restrictive over the two-year period, although he is never as restrictive as fathers in intact homes. The divorced mother uses more negative sanctions than the divorced father does or than parents in intact families do. However by the second year her use of negative sanctions is declining as the divorced father's is increasing. In a parallel fashion, the divorced mother's use of positive sanctions increases after the first year as the divorced father's decreases. The "every day is Christmas" behavior of the divorced father declines with time. The divorced mother decreases her futile attempts at authoritarian control and becomes more effective in dealing with her child over the two-year period.

Effectiveness in dealing with the child is

Table 28.4. Percentage of Compliance to Parental Commands (Positive)

	Intact				Divorced			
	Girl		Boy		Girl		Boy	
	Father	Mother	Father	Mother	Father	Mother	Father	Mother
Two months	60.2	54.6	51.3	42.6	51.3	40.6	39.9	29.3
One Year	63.4	56.7	54.9	44.8	43.9	31.8	32.6	21.5
Two Years	64.5	59.3	57.7	45.3	52.1	44.2	43.7	37.1

Percentage of Compliance to Parental Commands (Negative)

	Intact				Divorced			
	Girl		Boy		Girl		Boy	
	Father	Mother	Father	Mother	Father	Mother	Father	Mother
Two months	55.7	49.3	47.5	36.4	47.0	34.8	35.6	23.4
One Year	59.2	51.5	50.3	38.8	39.1	27.2	28.3	17.2
Two Years	60.5	54.6	53.6	39.0	49.9	39.7	39.7	31.8

Percentage of Compliance to Parental Reasoning and Explanation

	Intact				Divorced			
	Girl		Boy		Girl		Boy	
	Father	Mother	Father	Mother	Father	Mother	Father	Mother
Two months	49.1	43.4	41.0	31.1	41.3	29.2	29.6	18.4
One Year	55.4	48.0	46.2	34.5	26.3	23.1	24.5	14.1
Two Years	62.3	58.1	58.1	47.6	50.3	42.5	41.4	36.9

related to support in child-rearing from the spouse and agreement with the spouse in disciplining the child in both divorced and intact families. When support and agreement occurred between divorced couples, the disruption in family functioning appeared to be less extreme and the re-stabilizing of family functioning occurred earlier, by the end of the first year.

When there was agreement in child-rearing, a positive attitude toward the spouse, low conflict between the divorced parents, and when the father was emotionally mature as measured by the California Personality Inventory socialization scale and the Personal Adjustment Scale of the Adjective Checklist, frequency of father's contact with the child was associated with more positive mother–child interactions. When there was disagreement and inconsistency in attitudes toward the child, and conflict and ill will between the

divorced parents, or when the father was poorly adjusted, frequent visitation was associated with poor mother–child functioning and disruptions in the children's behavior. Emotional maturity in the mother was also found to be related to her adequacy in coping with stresses in her new single life and relations with children.

Other support systems such as that of grandparents, brothers and sisters, close friends, or a competent housekeeper also were related to the mother's effectiveness in interacting with the child in divorced but not in intact families. However, they were not as salient as a continued positive relationship of the ex-husband with the family.

In summary, following divorce the family system is in a state of disequilibrium. Disorganization and disrupted family functioning seem to peak at one year and be re-stabilizing by two years following the divorce. Stresses in family functioning following divorce are reflected not only in parent–child relations but in the changes in life-style, emotional distress, and changes in attitudes toward the self of the divorced couple. These changes in the parents may be mediating factors in changes in the child's behavior. A want for intimacy seems to be a pervasive desire for both males and females and the attainment of intimate relations seems to be associated with positive adjustment and coping behavior.

Since this study only lasted two years, it is impossible to state whether the re-stabilizing process in the divorced family had reached an asymptote and was largely completed at two years or whether this readjustment would continue over a longer period of time until it would ultimately more closely resemble that in intact families.

It should be remembered that the results reported in a study such as this represent averages and that there are wide variations in coping and parenting within intact and divorced families. There are many inadequate parents and children with problems in intact families. A conflict-ridden intact family is more deleterious to family members than a stable home situation in which parents are divorced. Divorce is often a positive solution to destructive family functioning. However for most family members divorce is a stressful event involving adapting to new problems and different life-style. Our ultimate goal in this study is not to condemn divorce but to be able to identify factors associated with constructive parenting and coping following divorce and to use these findings to develop means of modifying or eliminating the deleterious sequelae of divorce.

REFERENCES

Baumrind, D. Child care practices anteceding three patterns of preschool behavior. *Genetic Psychology Monographs,* 1967, **75,** 43-83.

Baumrind, D. Current pattern of parental authority. *Developmental Psychology Monographs,* 1971, **41** (1) part 2.

Biller, H. B. *Paternal deprivation.* Lexington, Mass.: Lexington Books, 1974.

Blanchard, R. W., & Biller, H. B. Father availability and academic performance among third grade boys. *Developmental Psychology,* 1971, **4,** 301-305.

Bronfenbrenner, U. The changing American family. Paper presented at the Meeting of the Society for Research in Child Development, Denver, 1975.

Hetherington, E. M., & Deu, J. The effects of father absence on child development. *Young Children,* 1971, **26,** 233-248.

Lynn, D. B. *The father: His role in child development.* Monterey, Cal.: Brooks Cole Publishing Company, 1974.

Martin, B., & Hetherington, E. M. Family interaction and aggression, withdrawal and nondeviancy in children. Progress Report, 1971, University of Wisconsin. Project no. M.H. 12474, National Institute of Mental Health.

Pederson, F. A., & Robson, K. S. Father participation in infancy. *American Journal of Orthopsychiatry,* 1969, **39,** 466-472.

Sears, R. R.; Rau, L.; & Alpert, R. *Identification and child rearing.* Stanford: Stanford University Press, 1965.

29.

Mary Van Stolk

WHO OWNS THE CHILD?

Physical abuse of children is the intentional, nonaccidental use of physical force, or intentional, nonaccidental acts of omission, on the part of a parent or other caretaker interacting with a child in his care, aimed at hurting, injuring, or destroying that child.[1]

A recent conference on the battered child, sponsored by the Canadian Department of National Health and Welfare, recognized that at present, in Canada, only a portion of child battering is correctly diagnosed and that, in addition, many children suffer because of failure of family, neighbors, teachers, physicians, and others to report. The conferees expressed the belief that reporting, diagnosis, and treatment could be improved through education and an interdisciplinary approach to the problem. They emphasized that battering is the discernible tip of a much larger question, and on that basis advised the government that child battering should be recognized as but part of the serious overall problem of abused children in Canada.[2]

THE ROOTS OF ABUSE

Diagnosed physical injuries to children are the visible signs of a problem that, in its hidden forms (neglect, abandonment, emotional abuse), can be equally serious and costly to the child, the family and the society. One hidden portion of child abuse was pointed out recently by Dr. Karl Evang, Director-General of Health Services of Norway, who reported to the World Health Organization that an increasing number of Scandinavian children have been wrongly diagnosed as mentally retarded when their condition was actually the result of deprivation of love.[3] Undiagnosed brain damage is another part of the hidden problem of child abuse. The number of children who suffer brain damage as a result of battering can be statistically tallied, but the number who suffer brain damage as a result of physical abuse that is never diagnosed is probably much higher.[4,5]

Identifying the abused

Identification of incidences of child battering usually rests on a diagnosis of the injuries, which most frequently are broken bones, simple and compound fractures, concussions and skull fractures, internal

Source: *Childhood Education,* 1974, **50,** 259-265. Adapted from a presentation to the American Orthopsychiatric Association at its Fiftieth Annual Meeting, held in New York City (May 1973). By permission of the Association. Reprinted by permission of Mary Van Stolk and the Association for Childhood Education International, 3615 Wisconsin Avenue, N.W., Washington, D.C. Copyright © 1974 by the Association.

[1]David G. Gil, *Violence Against Children.* Cambridge, Mass.: Harvard University Press, 1970, p. 6. Reprinted with permission of the publisher.

[2]Workshop on Child Battering, Feb. 1973. Sponsored by Canadian Department of National Health and Welfare, Ottawa, Ontario.

[3]Karl Evang, Report to the World Health Org., 1973.

[4]A. Winter, *Trauma* 5 (3).

[5]R. E. Helfer. Foreword. In M. Van Stolk, *The Battered Child in Canada.* Toronto/Montreal: McClelland and Stewart Ltd., 1972, p. vi.

injuries, bruises, multiple welts, swelling, split lips, blackened eyes, lost teeth, and burns.

Sometimes only one child is singled out as the recipient of these crippling, maiming, or lethal assaults. However, all the children in these families are witnesses to the actions, and hence grow up with abuse as the dominant childrearing method taught in the home. The abused and battered child and the abusing parent are thus locked in a cycle of destruction, which too often renews itself in each succeeding generation.[6]

Most deaths occur under the age of five. However, the prognosis for battered children, even when they are removed from the home, is not good. A study reported to the American Academy of Paediatrics, by Gregg and Elmer, points out that of those children who suffered multiple skeletal trauma inflicted by abusive parents early in life, only about 10% fully recovered. The remaining 90% are still marked by physical, mental and emotional scars as they approach adolescence. Few of the children studied gave promise of becoming self-sufficient adults.[7]

The nature of abusers

Information on abusing parents has primarily centered around those who have severely injured their children in a physical sense; and studies of their backgrounds indicate that abuse is cyclic, in that these parents seemed to be carrying out the kind of violent childrearing methodology they themselves experienced at the hands of their own mothers and fathers.[8] Because

abusing parents have almost always suffered brutalization in some form, failure to recognize *all factors* of abuse as harmful may not succeed in protecting the next generation.

Boisvert suggests a typology to give researchers and others some concept as to what kinds of personalities batter children.[9] His first classification is the *psychotic* personality. Perhaps 10% of battering parents are psychotic and, in these cases, abuse is always unpredictable and uncontrollable. Second, the *inadequate* personality, where the abuser is immature, irresponsible and impulsive, and has a very low tolerance for frustration. Third, the *passive-aggressive* personality, where the abuser shows hostility and anger at having to meet expectations of others. Fourth, the *sadistic* personality, where the abusive parent has a history of sadistic behavior, usually including frequent beatings or even killing of animals. Finally, the *controllable abuser*, where abuse is a result of displaced aggression and the locus of the problem is usually a marital conflict.

Whatever their pattern of personality disorder, these people give adult confirmation of Gregg and Elmer's study of children who were mistreated and who evidence, in adolescence, inability to recover to the stage where they could be expected to be self-sufficient adults.[10]

The importance of modeling

Researchers, such as Helfer and Kempe, Steele and Pollock, point out that nurtur-

---

[6]Gil, *Violence Against Children*, p. 122.

[7]G. S. Gregg and E. Elmer, Battered Child's Trauma Found To Be Lasting, *R.N.* **30**, 28.

[8]J. E. Oliver and Audrey Taylor, Five generations of ill-treated children in one family pedigree, *British Journal of Psychiatry,* 1971, **119**, 473-80.

[9]M. J. Boisvert, The battered child syndrome, *Social Casework,* 1972, 475-80.

[10]B. F. Steele and C. B. Pollock, A psychiatric study of parents who abuse infants and small children. In R. E. Helfer & C. H. Kempe (eds.), *The Battered Child.* Chicago and London: University of Chicago Press, 1968, p. 109.

ing is learned, and that the inability of battering parents to mother or father, hence nurture, children comes from the lack of nurturing these parents experienced in their own childhood.[11] As children, battering adults did not receive the kind of nurturing they needed in order to become parents who in turn have the capacity to nurture. Rather, what they learned was a methodology which taught how not to mother or father, how not to protect and, in fact, to often feel great anger and resentment toward a child who makes a plea for nurturing.[12]

Studies on modeling and aggression, by Bandura, Walters, and others, support the concept of modeling in the family as the dominant factor upon which all other learning rests.[13,14] This concept is based on the assumption that the primary process of family education and learning is that of example; the getting or giving of information is a secondary process. Children learn to walk because they see others walk, to talk because they hear others speak, not because they are taught to walk or speak. The child mimics and models his speech patterns after the adults around him. The child also models his behavior, emotional responses, cues to laughter, tears, rejection, fears, hostilities, pleasures, or compassion, and imitates the adults and children he sees.[15]

In the area of child abuse, the most important factor is what the child sees, hears, feels, and experiences in his home environment. That is, child abusers are created by exposing children to the model of abuse. Good parents are made by exposing children to the model of good parents.

The ability to nurture is part of the earliest, hence primary, learning process. Not surprisingly, therefore, studies of cultures where the parental model is nurturing show little or no child abuse. Nurturing cultures hold philosophical and religious beliefs about the rights and privileges of children that create and support the parental desire to fulfill the needs of the child. In these cultures it is considered shameful to strike a child, or inappropriate to treat children as anything other than welcomed guests in one's house.[16,17]

ANTHROPOLOGICAL AND HISTORICAL PERSPECTIVES

The work of anthropologists such as Jules Henry and others documents that North America is a punitive childrearing culture.[18,19] Cultural beliefs and traditions about the rights of children play a large role in maintaining attitudes toward family life and the position of the child in the North American home. Delsordo wrote in

[11]*Ibid.*
[12]R. E. Helfer & C. H. Kempe, *Helping the battered child and his family.* Philadelphia and Toronto: J. B. Lippincott Co., 1972. Pp. 5, 41, 57.
[13]A. Bandura, D. Ross & S. A. Ross, *Journal of abnormal and social psychology,* 1963, **66,** 3-11; A. Bandura, *Journal of personal and social psychology,* 1965, **1,** 589-95.
[14]R. H. Walters & E. I. Thomas. Enhancement of punitiveness by visual and audiovisual displays, *Canadian Journal of Psychology,* 1963, **17,** 244-55.
[15]M. Van Stolk, *Man and woman.* Toronto/Montreal: McClelland & Stewart Ltd., 1968. Pp. 22-23.

[16]Wm. N. Stephens, *The family in cross-cultural perspective.* New York: Holt, Rinehart & Winston, 1963. Pp. 370-76.
[17]Ruth Benedict. Continuities and Discontinuities in Cultural Conditioning. In Patrick Mullahy (ed.), *A study of interpersonal relationships—new contributions to psychiatry.* New York: Grove Press, 1949. Pp. 320-23.
[18]Jules Henry, *Culture against man.* New York: Random House, 1963. Pp. 127, 147, 322.
[19]C. Bay, *The structure of freedom.* New York: Atheneum Press, 1965; C. Hampden-Turner, *Radical man, the process of psycho-social development.* Cambridge, Mass.: Schenkman Publishing Co., 1970.

1963, "To undertake a study of the entire problem of abused children is obviously bigger than any one profession. Satisfactory results may be obtained only through joint professional endeavor."[20]

It is increasingly important that professionals heed the words of Delsordo, and introduce into the study of child abuse not only the anthropologist and his study of cultures that are nurturing of children, but also the historian to shed light on our own historical beliefs and concepts regarding the rights and ownership of the child.

Children as property

In *The History of Western Philosophy,* Bertrand Russell outlines the philosophical and historical foundation of our attitude towards parental rights: "Aristotle's opinions on moral questions are always such as were conventional in his day. On some points they differ from those of our time, chiefly where some form of aristocracy comes in. We think that human beings, at least in ethical theory, all have equal rights, and that justice involves equality. Aristotle thinks that justice involves, not equality, but right proportion, which is only a 'sometimes' equality.

"The justice of a master or a father is a different thing from that of a citizen, *for a son or slave is property, and there can be no injustice to one's own property.*"[21]

The Patria Potestas endowed the Roman father with the privilege to sell, abandon, devour, kill, offer in sacrifice, or otherwise dispose of his offspring. Even in adulthood, when the children were in the father's house, they could be sold into bondage, tortured, or killed. "In the Forum, the Senate or the camp, the adult son of a Roman citizen enjoyed the public and private rights of a person; in his father's house he was a mere thing, confounded by the laws with the movables, the cattle, and the slaves, whom the capricious master might alienate or destroy without being responsible to any earthly tribunal."[22]

The belief that there can be no injustice to one's own property still allows and sanctions the abuse of children under the guise of punishment. Today, society says that a man or woman who strikes a child is committing an assault if the child is not their own, but rarely interferes in the assault of a child carried out as punishment by a parent.

Parental "rights"

Another link between societal attitude and the battering or abusive parent is confirmed by the lack of protection for the battered child by family members. A large portion of battering incidents occur with the knowledge of family members who have been aware of the abusive treatment of the child, often over a long period of time.[23] Their failure to protect the child supports the theory that, at least in part, members of the family defer to the treatment of the child out of cultural confusion over parental rights.

In North America, another dominant factor in childrearing practices is a belief in the need and parental right to use a high degree of force to punish disobedience. "It is unfortunate what my wife does, but she is the mother." "My husband may be a bit

[20] J. D. Delsordo. Protective Casework for Abused Children. *Children,* 1963, **10,** 213-18.
[21] Bertrand Russell. *History of western philosophy.* London: George Allen & Unwin Ltd., 1969, p. 186. Reprinted with permission.

[22] E. Gibbon. *The decline and fall of the Roman Empire.* New York: Peter Fenelon Collier, 1899. Pp. 352-53.
[23] Gil, *Violence against children,* pp. 122-28.

too strict, but he is the father, and we don't want spoiled children." These comments are from parents who stood by, aware of the most terrible injuries being inflicted on the child.

Society's overall tendency to insist upon the maintenance of discipline, attendance to rules, and obedience from children at all costs is mirrored by the removal of corporal punishment from prisons and correctional institutions, but not from the schools, and is legally upheld in Section 43 of the Canadian Criminal Code, which states that:

Every school teacher, parent or person standing in the place of a parent is justified in *using force* by way of correction towards a pupil or child, as the case may be, who is under his care, if the force does not exceed what is reasonable under the circumstances.[24]

and in the United States, in states such as Massachusetts, where

The Massachusetts Supreme Judicial Court has laid down the law for children who talk back and refuse to obey their parents.

The state's highest court, upholding a 317-year-old law, declared unanimously on June 7th, 1971, that children "have no right of dissent" when it comes to obeying the reasonable and lawful commands of parents. The law also applies to children under the supervision of adults other than parents. Known as the "Stubborn-Child Law," it was originated in 1654 because too many Colonial-era children were behaving disrepectfully, disobediently, and disorderly toward parents and guardians.

The law was recently challenged as unconstitutional by attorneys for a 17-year-old girl in a home for wayward children at Fall River.

In upholding the law, the court found the girl guilty of being stubborn. She was placed on probation in custody of the Youth Service Board.[25]

The sanction of rules

A large segment of North American society apparently still believes in the need to abuse and terrorize children, and is firmly convinced that all manner of paddles, belts, wooden spoons, fly swatters, and electric cords are permissible standard equipment for the job. These forms of abuse are often interspersed with threats of one kind or another. "You will be taken to the police station if you are not good." "The boogy man will get you." "You will be put in the cellar, in the alley, in the closet." Terror and solitary confinement, as well as physical abuse, are used to break the spirit and to ensure obedience. These routine, culturally sanctioned punishments, spankings, slaps, shakings, screaming sessions, and threats are not legally classified as child abuse. Often, however, the only difference between the battering home and the so-called normal home, whether it be rich or poor, is the degree of physical or emotional abuse used to enforce rules.[26]

Gil, in *Violence Against Children,* points out that lack of vacations, of play schools, of babysitters, and the stress of economic need all contribute to a higher level of general child abuse within the lower-income groups. The poor and under-privileged do not have the money to relieve the pressures of childrearing that the rich do.[27] That fact does not mean that abusive parents, whether rich or poor, do not "love" their children. They do. They want, as their parents wanted from them, love in the form of obedience, conformity, and respect. Abusive parents love in that they want the best manners, the best marks,

---

[24]Section 43, Criminal Code of Canada.
[25]*National Enquirer* (Lantana, Fla.), Aug. 15, 1971, **5** (50), 24. Reprinted with permission.

[26]Wm. J. Goode. Force and Violence in the Family. *Journal of Marriage and the Family,* 1971, **33,** 624-35.
[27]Gil, *Violence against children,* p. 144.

the best behavior from their children. They want their children to grow up to be perfect, and hence a credit to them. They love their children as they were taught to love by their parents.

To the battering and abusive parent alike the rules are all important, and the child is seen in relation to the rules. How does the child live up to the standard of the rules? Is the child's attitude one of submission to the rules? Differences over the kinds and number of rules and levels of attendance and obedience to rules cause one parent to beat or punish a child if one set of rules are broken, while another only beats or punishes to enforce a different set of rules.[28] The battering parent simply takes North American "normal child-rearing practices" to the furthest point.[29]

Because of the warped belief in the need for absolute obedience, many deaths and permanent injuries occur. "He would not stop wetting his bed so we had to beat him," goes the rationale. "She would not stop crying so I threw her across the room to show her I meant business." "I told him not to touch the stove but he would not obey, so I took his hand and held it over the burner. Next time I say don't touch, he'll obey."

CHALLENGES TO ABUSE

The child as animal

Although today the state attempts to protect the child who is grossly assaulted, only a short time ago the state gave parents the right to beat children without any interference at all. One of the first legal challenges in North America to the absolute rights of parents over children occurred in New York City in 1870. While visiting a tenement house, a church worker learned that a child was being beaten daily by her parents, and that the child was also seriously malnourished and neglected. After appeals to protective agencies including the police and the district attorney's office proved useless, the church worker appealed to the American Society for the Prevention of Cruelty to Animals. In the courts it was pointed out that this child was being treated as an animal and was certainly a member of the animal kingdom. On this basis the Society for the Prevention of Cruelty to Animals won the action, which resulted in the child's removal from her parents.[30] One year later, in 1871, the New York Society for the Prevention of Cruelty to Children was organized. Pathetic is the historical comment that the persistence and tenacity of an unnamed church worker and the S.P.C.A. were required to instigate action in one of the first recorded cases of a battered child.[31]

Why society fails to protect

The sad reality of society's failure to protect children is that a child who grows up in a battering or abusive household runs a high risk of growing up to batter or abuse in turn.[32] The link between an abusing university professor with an IQ of 150 and an abusing mother with a grade six education and an IQ of 100 lies in the physical and emotional brutalization they experienced in their childhood. Abuse,

[28]*Ibid.*, p. 126.

[29]Steele and Pollock, A psychiatric study of parents, p. 104.

[30]V. J. Fontana, *The Maltreated child. The maltreatment syndrome in children.* Springfield, Ill.: Charles C Thomas, 1964.

[31]A. Allen & A. Morton, *This is your child: The story of the National society for the prevention of cruelty to children.* London: Routledge & Kegan Paul, Ltd., 1961, p. 16.

[32]E. Erikson. *Gandhi's truth.* New York: W. W. Norton & Co., 1969, p. 234.

therefore, occurs in all walks of life and in all combinations of social and religious backgrounds.

Failure to protect a child who has once been severely battered means exposing that child to a high risk of death or permanent injury.[33]

Yet society has consistently failed to protect the child, a fact evidenced by the poor reporting rates of child abuse both in the United States and Canada, not only on the part of family, neighbors, and teachers, but more alarmingly on the part of physicians and other medical personnel.[34]

In examining the reasons why society has failed to protect the child, it becomes apparent that there is more than just a reluctance to become involved, but rather an unwillingness to break an old and cherished belief with regard to the rights of parents over children. North American society has yet to recognize that the child is not the property of the parents, but a citizen in his own right.[35] This concept of parental ownership is mirrored by physicians who fail to report a battered child out of loyalty to the physician–parent privilege; that is the belief that the parent is his patient and hence to be protected, rather than the child.

Need for preventive action

The wisest protection is that which not only protects but prevents. Care for the child and the parent is essential, but before help can be offered, the diagnosis of child abuse must be made. Ever since the Battered Child Syndrome was first recognized, it has been apparent that the major protection for the child could only come through early diagnosis and treatment, which hinge directly on the physician's reporting and his willingness to support his diagnosis by medical testimony in court.[36]

Each discipline has a vital role to play in the protection of the child. Society, represented by family members, neighbors, teachers, nurses, physicians, and others, must report to a protective agency all suspected cases of abuse. Social agencies must investigate these reports with a high degree of skill and competence, and seek diagnosis from medical practitioners who understand the diagnostic techniques available to them in assessing the extent of injury sustained by the child. Lawyers and magistrates must then appraise this information, not from the position of parental rights, but from the primary concept that a safe environment is the legal right of all children, and on that basis decide the relative safety or lack of safety of the child's environment. If at any point one discipline fails to maintain its responsibility in the chain of events from the original report to final legal assessment, the opportunity to protect the child and help the parents may be lost.

SUMMARY

In summary, child battering appears to be a symptom of a major problem, child abuse. No matter what emotional or personality disorders abusers exhibit, they are evidencing an adult response to their own abusive childhood experience.

[33]R. E. Helfer. The responsibility and role of the physician. In R. E. Helfer & C. H. Kempe (eds.), *The Battered Child*. Chicago and London: University of Chicago Press, 1968, p. 51.

[34]M. Van Stolk, *The battered child in Canada*. Toronto/Montreal: McClelland & Stewart Ltd., 1972. Pp. 58-65.

[35]Van Stolk, *Man and woman*, pp. 71-76.

[36]M. G. Paulsen. The Law and Abused Children. In R. E. Helfer & C. H. Kempe (eds.), *The Battered Child*. Chicago and London: University of Chicago Press, 1968, p. 176.

The ability or lack of ability to nurture is learned; the child models his behavior after the parents or other dominant models. Nurturing parents produce children who grow up with an ability to nurture. Violence breeds violence.

Child abuse is an interdisciplinary problem. Anthropologists point out that North American childrearing practices are punitive, and give evidence of other cultures that recognize the needs and rights of children. History exposes the basis of our concept of the ownership of children, and the belief that one can do what one wants to one's own child.

Western society is still mirroring cultural beliefs of the past, as evidenced by its reluctance to interfere with the ownership rights of parents, even when the child's human rights are obviously being violated.

30.

Michael S. Wald

LEGAL POLICIES AFFECTING CHILDREN: A LAWYER'S REQUEST FOR AID

Every year the parents of nearly a million children in this country get divorced (U.S. Department of Health, Education, and Welfare, 1970, tables 2-9).[1] The legal system has rules regulating divorce and rules for determining child custody—that is, how children are distributed after a divorce. Each year a million children are brought into the legal system as delinquents for committing crimes, acts that would result in criminal prosecutions if they were adults, or for committing acts illegal only for children, such as truancy, incorrigibility, running away, or "being in danger of leading an immoral or dissolute way of life" (U.S. Department of Health, Education, and Welfare 1973, pp. 6-7, tables 5-8).[2] The legal system must decide what to do with these children.

In addition, approximately 150,000 children are brought each year into the legal system as neglected or dependent (U.S. Department of Health, Education, and Welfare 1973, p. 13, table 2). These are children who, according to some legal standard, as interpreted by social workers and judges, are in families that have failed to maintain minimum standards of care for their children. Therefore the state intervenes coercively to provide protection for the children and to better their well-being. There are also between 100,000 and 200,000 children adopted each year (U.S. Department of Health, Education, and Welfare 1972). The legal system has rules, again interpreted by social-work agencies,

Source: *Child Development*, 1976, **47**, 1-5. © 1976 by the Society for Research in Child Development, Inc. This is an abridged version of a speech presented at the President's Symposium, "Child Development and Public Policy: Juvenile Justice," at the annual meeting for the Society for Research in Child Development, Denver, 1975.

[1] The figure is probably higher now than in 1970, given the increasing divorce rate.

[2] These are figures for children actually brought into the court system. Another million are handled "informally" by police, community-based programs, and probation departments.

for deciding which of the many applicants for these children will get them.

In all of these areas the legal system tries to further the "best interests" of the child. In fact, there are other goals as well—protection of public safety, concern over parental interests—but the major stated purpose of the law is to promote the child's interests. Unfortunately, inadequate resources, poorly trained personnel, or clearly unwise laws often result in actions contrary to a child's interest.

In large measure, however, the most significant problem facing those drafting legal policy is the absence of data about the consequences of adopting one policy or another. In deciding issues involving child custody, treatment of delinquents, and care of neglected children we just do not have the data to tell us what is the "right" policy. Yet, decisions have to be made. We have to determine how children shall be distributed at the end of a divorce. We have to determine whether or not we are going to arrest children for committing offenses and what we are going to do with them afterward. We have to determine who is permitted to adopt a child. We have to determine when parental care is so "poor" that state intervention is necessary.

Each of these questions cannot be answered solely through research or data. Their resolution ultimately rests on value judgments regarding questions such as what kinds of qualities we wish to further through child placement, what kinds of behavior we wish to foster through intervention, and from what kinds of harms we wish to protect children.

However, research can have a great influence on how these decisions are made. Research is critical in order to know the consequences of alternative policies. For example, research can tell us what kinds of impact child abuse has on both the short-run and long-term development of the abused child. Moreover, lawyers need the insights and expertise of persons doing research on child development in order to decide what the goals of legal policy should be. We need to have the best possible guidance in defining the term "best interest."

I will briefly describe the way the legal system currently handles two issues, child custody and intervention on behalf of neglected children, to give some idea of the type of problems that exist in current practices. I emphasize the more negative aspects of the system in order to illustrate the need for action on the part of other disciplines. However, I must emphasize that even when the system is working at its best, without obvious bias or clearly unwise policies, current laws may not be based on adequate understanding of a child's needs or on adequate knowledge of the impact of the legal policy.

The law generally encourages divorcing parents to decide themselves the issues of visitation and child support. In contested custody cases, however, the legal system gives a judge the authority to decide custody on the basis of the "best interests" of the child. How does a judge determine what is the best interest of the child? In most cases these decisions are made on the basis of the judge's biases, his own background, and his folk psychology. Often these decisions are based on moral value judgments, with custody being denied an adulterous or promiscuous parent or a parent with unpopular views. In such instances, of course, data may be irrelevant to a judge, who assumes that it harms the child to be with such parents.

However, even in cases when the courts turn to psychology they may perform poorly. A recent Iowa case involved a custody dispute between a child's father and grandparents. The child's mother died when he was 4 years old. The father, unable to care for the child, asked the grandparents to care for the boy temporarily. When the boy was 6, the father asked for the child's return. The grandparents refused. The trial court awarded custody to the father, and the grandparents appealed. The Iowa Supreme Court had to decide what was in the best interest of the child. They made the following calculation: "The father is an artist who is also a member of the ACLU and has lived in a number of different cities and worked for various newspapers. The father's home would be unstable, unconventional, arty, bohemian, and probably intellectually stimulating. The grandparents provided stable, dependable, conventional, middle-class, midwest background. We believe security and stability in the home are more important than intellectual stimulation in the proper development of the child."

You may agree or disagree with that conclusion of the court. The critical question is whether developmental psychology provides us with data for deciding when a child should go with one person or another. What criteria does it offer to determine the child's "best interest" with regard to custody decisions following a divorce? Do we even know the probable consequences of one type of placement or another?

Similar problems mark the legal system's treatment of child neglect. All states permit coercive intervention to protect children if parents are neglecting or abusing them. However, the terms "neglect" and "abuse" are never specifically defined in the statutes. Generally, statutes allow coercive state intervention where a home is "unfit, unsuitable, or where the parents are immoral, depraved, or failing to provide adequate supervision." As a result, much state intervention occurs in a manner directly contrary to what we know about

child psychology. Moral judgments often predominate. For example, children have been declared neglected solely on the basis that their parents were not married, even though the parents had a stable union and the children were developing normally.

Vague law facilitates intervention based on the cultural biases and moral values of those given decision-making authority. In order to limit such abuses, it is necessary to draft specific statutes defining when a child is "neglected." Again, the definition of neglect ultimately involves value judgments. However, there are very few data available to guide those making such judgments. What are the consequences of various types of "neglectful" behavior, for example, physical abuse, sexual intimacy among family members, inadequate affection, or parental rejection? What types of harms should we be concerned about? Without guidance and data on these issues, persons drafting neglect laws cannot decide when or why intervention is necessary.

There is also good reason to believe that the legal system is failing those children identified as neglected. Many such children are removed from their homes. They often are placed in institutions for periods ranging from several days to years. In one county I know, the person who runs the children's institution believes that because all of the children who come into the institution will eventually be returned to their parents or placed in foster care, the children should not develop any attachment relationships. She believes that it is bad to develop strong attachments which will later be disturbed. Accordingly, she turned down an offer by a group of senior citizens to serve the children as foster grandparents, by visiting a specific child each day, because this would establish such an attachment relationship.

Many other welfare or probation departments refuse to allow parents to visit children in placement. They argue that visitation interferes with the child's adjustment to foster care. I think there is reason to suspect from theoretical work in child psychology that both the institution and visitation policies are not in a child's "best interest." However, without research this cannot be determined, and such policies will not be changed.

One further aspect of the treatment of neglected children is especially relevant to those interested in child development. Studies show that as many as 50%–80% of the children in placement are never returned home. Fewer than 5% of children in long-term foster care are adopted, in large part because of the difficulty of terminating parental rights. As a result, they remain in a "limbo" status, often being placed in three or more foster homes. Many psychologists claim that multiple placements are harmful to children. Yet without more data on the specific impacts of multiple placements, legislators are reluctant to liberalize termination laws, believing parental rights inviolate.

These are just two of many areas in which we are not certain about proper policies and, as a result, have adopted vague laws easily subject to abuse. I will not describe the others, since I want to outline specific kinds of research that I see as critical. I have tried, in choosing research areas, to pick some which involve questions of important theoretical concern to those interested in child development. It is my belief that just a change in the focus or setting of much current research would produce findings with important theoretical as well as policy implications. Therefore, I describe the proposed research in the context of more "theoretical" issues.

There is a substantial body of research now being done examining "attachment" behavior in children. Questions about the importance of attachment are also critical in developing sound legal policy regarding child custody and state intervention on behalf of neglected children. Lawyers are aware of the evidence that separation is traumatic for children. In fact, legal policies often start with an assumption that we should try to avoid breaking attachments. Many statutes are prefaced with a presumption for maintaining families.

However, existing research does not provide us with adequate guidance in deciding how much weight to place on preserving attachments when we are dealing with "neglected" children. Are beaten children, rejected children, attached to their parents, and if so, should we worry about breaking these attachments? What are the consequences in terms of the child's long-term emotional well-being? Is there a difference in the nature, the quality, and the implications of an attachment of a child who is from an abusing family and other kinds of attachments that psychologists are concerned with?

The significance of attachment is also critical in deciding how to treat the over 300,000 children currently in foster care and those children who will be entering foster care. We know little about the impact of the separation on these children. We do not know whether the impact varies if a child is placed in a relative's home instead of in a foster home, if teenagers are placed in group homes instead of foster homes, or if we use institutions instead of homes. We know little about how the children can be best prepared for such separations, although the research by Robertson and Robertson (1971) in England gives some ideas of what procedures to follow.

We also need to know the relationship between attachment and visitation when children are in placement. Are the social workers correct who claim that allowing visitation will disrupt the child's adjustment to foster care and thereby impair the possibility of eventual return home? Under what kinds of conditions do we want to allow visitation? Does this vary by age, reason for placement, or by other factors?

Perhaps the most difficult questions involve the relationship of attachment to termination of parental rights. It is clear that most children removed from their homes remain in an out-of-home placement for long periods of time. Some are subjected to numerous moves from one foster home to another. As I have indicated, there is increasing pressure to make termination of parental rights easier when children are in foster care in order to facilitate adoption or permanent placement of these children. However, we know very little about when it is in a child's interest to have parental rights terminated. Are there some children who are so attached to their natural parents that termination will cause them to suffer permanent emotional harm? What types of harms do children suffer if left in long-term foster care?

Do we damage children by returning them to their natural parents after they have been in foster care for a period of time? In a recent book, Goldstein, Freud, and Solnit (1973) advocate giving custody to the child's "psychological parent." They argue that this can be a foster parent instead of the natural parent. But do we know under what kinds of conditions a child changes its attachment from the natural parent to a foster parent so that the foster parent becomes the "psychological parent"? Does it vary with the child's age or with the child's previous care? If a child is placed out of home, should there be varying periods of time, depending on the age of the child, at which parents could not reclaim the child? Re-

search projects can be designed to explore these questions. Such research would not only provide data important to legal policy, it should also help our understanding of the meaning and importance of attachment.

There is also substantial concern in child-development literature with the impact of a child's early home environment on his or her development. In particular, research has focused on the impact of early home environment on the development of cognitive skills. The impact of a home environment also is critical to determinations of when a child is neglected. There has been increasing pressure on the legal system to recognize, and to incorporate into the law, the fact that children can be emotionally as well as physically neglected. But how do we define emotional neglect? What is the relationship between a home environment and the child's "emotional" health, however that term is defined?

The absence of research on these issues makes it extremely difficult to write legal standards regarding emotional neglect. All legal standards are applied by judges and social workers who rarely have the training to make sophisticated decisions on a case-by-case basis. I believe that we will not in the foreseeable future have available highly trained clinicians to evaluate whether intervention is needed on behalf of a given child. Therefore, we need as specific guidelines as possible to tell decision makers how categories of cases should be treated. We need developmental psychologists who are willing to participate with lawyers in facing the hard questions involved in drafting a specific statute. They must be willing to apply existing data to help define those conditions that justify state intervention. Moreover, they must be willing to do the additional research needed to provide answers to the questions we cannot answer at present.

We also need research designed to develop guidelines for judges and child-care workers who have to decide what type of treatment to order if a child is neglected. For example, we need to know what is the outcome in child-abuse cases of providing day-care services to the child. What is the outcome if we intervene by removing the child from the home and placing the child in a foster-care setting or institution? Presently such decisions are largely made by guesses about outcome. We have no research evaluating the outcome of different types of placements for different types of children.

A third area of both theoretical and practical importance is the relationship of age to a child's emotional and cognitive development. Many commentators now urge adoption of a children's bill of rights. From a legal perspective, children's rights inevitably mean children's participation. What do we know of the child's ability to participate meaningfully in a legal proceeding? For example, state laws now vary as to whether a child between the ages of 10 and 14 has a right to be heard in a divorce proceeding. Some states allow children at 10, 11, 12, or 13 years of age to decide which parent they will live with. We need research to tell us the implications to the child of being asked to make this kind of decision. Will they feel guilty if they make the decision? Will they adjust to the divorce situation better?

There are many other issues involving a child's cognitive and emotional decision-making capacity that are of concern to the legal system. Children are being given the right to request abortions, to obtain medical care, to use birth control without parental permission. We need guidance as to what are the consequences to children of different ages of having these powers.

On a more personal note, I have often wondered, when I was representing a child in a delinquency or neglect proceeding, what it meant for me to go up to a 9- or 10-year-old and say, "I'm your lawyer. Here I am; tell me what to do. What do you want me to do in representing you?" What do the children think of me? What do legal rights mean to them? What are the long-term consequences for a child of being told you have a lawyer, you have rights, and we are going to defend you in court. Does this give children a sense of self-esteem, of controlling their own fate, a sense of powerfulness? Or does it leave them bewildered? How are children different who have gone through such proceedings?

There are many other research areas of great importance, such as the treatment of delinquents, which I cannot cover here. In a few areas a substantial amount of research has begun, but in most areas of concern to the legal system there is little or no work that I am aware of.

This is research that can be done. There are lawyers who are anxious to work with behavioral scientists in framing the questions and doing the research. Local courts and child-welfare agencies often provide ideal research settings. Many judges and social-work personnel recognize that they need to know much more about what they are doing. They are receptive to experimentation because they know they cannot do any worse than at present. Moreover, the haphazard treatment given most children in the legal system creates natural field experiments, probably with random distribution of children into different programs, which lend themselves to study.

I do not mean to minimize the problems in doing such research. Not all variables can be controlled. At times changes in agency policies undermine an entire project. Definitive answers may be impossible to get. Numerous other problems could be cited. However, the benefits are worth the costs. For without the active participation of those interested in child development the legal system will not and cannot improve its treatment of the millions of children it affects each year.

REFERENCES

Goldstein, J.; Freud, A.; & Solnit, A. *Beyond the best interests of the child.* New York: Free Press, 1973.

Robertson, J., & Robertson, J. Young children in brief separations: a fresh look. In *Psychoanalytic study of the child.* Vol. **26.** New York: Quadrangle, 1971.

U.S. Department of Health, Education, and Welfare. *Marriage and divorce statistics, Public Health Service: vital statistics of the United States 1970.* Vol. **3.** *Marriage and divorce.* Washington, D.C.: Government Printing Office, 1970.

U.S. Department of Health, Education, and Welfare. *Adoption statistics, Social and Rehabilitation Service: adoptions in 1972.* DHEW Pub. No. (SRS) 75-03259.

U.S. Department of Health, Education, and Welfare. *Office of Youth Development: juvenile court statistics 1973.* Washington, D.C.: Government Printing Office, 1973.

31.

Rita Kramer

THE "PSYCHOLOGICAL PARENT" IS THE REAL PARENT

By now it is axiomatic in the field of child development that healthy emotional and intellectual growth—the ability to relate to others and to learn—depends to a great extent on the establishment very early in life of a mutually gratifying, continuing relationship with a mothering figure who cares for and stimulates the infant. It is in this relationship that the child begins to develop security and trust—a good feeling about himself and a sense that the world is worth moving out into and exploring. Psychologists have come to believe that if you start with these feelings, you don't need much of anything else, and that without them, it doesn't much matter what else you have.

The key word here is "continuity." Where this kind of relationship never gets established (children who grow up in crowded institutions) or when it is interrupted (by the disappearance or replacement of the mothering adult for whatever reason—death, divorce, hospitalization) very young children withdraw, regress, become depressed, sometimes even retarded.

This premise is the starting point for a soon-to-be-published book—"Beyond the Best Interests of the Child"—which applies what psychoanalysts have learned about child development to a new area: the law as it affects children. It is written by the daughter of Sigmund Freud, joined by two other distinguished scholars, and it may well become as controversial among judges, lawyers, legislators, social workers and even psychiatrists as Freud's writings were to the medical and psychological establishment of his day.

Anna Freud, who is based at the Hampstead Child Therapy Clinic in London, is probably the foremost living authority on the emotional lives of children, a subject she explored in depth among children separated from their families during World War II. Her co-authors are Joseph Goldstein, a professor of law, science and social policy at Yale who specializes in the application of psychoanalysis to law, and Dr. Albert Solnit, director of the Child Study Center at Yale and a professor of pediatrics and psychiatry. This formidable threesome believes that while the law recognizes the need to protect a child's physical well-being, it has failed to make provisions for safeguarding his psychological well-being. Although our present child-custody laws are supposed to protect "the best interests of the child," the authors argue that they more often serve the emotional needs of parents or the convenience of the courts and the social-welfare agencies. What Freud-Goldstein-Solnit want to do is shift the focus of the laws to the needs of children. To accomplish this, "Beyond the Best Interests" suggests a new set of guidelines for adoption, foster-care placement, and divorce proceedings.

Freud-Goldstein-Solnit call the adult who provides day-to-day affection and stimulation "the psychological parent," and they insist that a child's relationship with his psychological parent, whether or not he or she is the child's natural parent, should never be interrupted. What counts in such a relationship is the child's degree of attachment and whether he feels wanted and needed—needed for himself, not for some financial advantage or to score against a warring spouse in a divorce or to fulfill some fantasy or replace some loss.

The book suggests replacing the old thinking in terms of "the best interests of the child," which promises so much more than it can deliver, with the idea of "the least detrimental alternative," the placement that provides the child with the best chance of being raised by his "psychological" parents.

A "real" mother or father (in the biological or legal sense) who is not around on a day-to-day basis while the child is growing, feeling, learning, is not psychologically speaking a parent at all but a stranger. A "natural" mother or father who has abandoned his or her child for any reason whatever would have no right to reclaim the child on the basis of birth or blood ties, under the book's thesis. It would be irrelevant to establish his or her fitness as a parent (character, level of education, or income), or lack of blame for the circumstances that interrupted the relationship and made him a stranger to the child (illness, business, hospitalization—even war). The only relevant questions are who is the child used to, fond of, connected with by daily experiences, related to through memories, learning from through identification? Whom is he used to coming to with his questions, finding at home when he gets there, being tucked in by at night, and trying to act like? Who gives him his bottle, eventually teaches him how to make a sandwich or throw a ball, who reads to him, whom does he wind up wanting to "be good" for so they'll go on loving him?

Freud-Goldstein-Solnit think the law has not only tended to favor biology over psychology, but has failed to understand the child's sense of time: "Unlike adults, who measure the passing of time by clock and calendar, children have their own built-in time sense, based on the urgency of their instinctual and emotional needs." What seems like a short wait to a grownup can be an intolerable separation to a young child, to whom a week can seem like a year; a month, forever. A 6-month-old who doesn't see the mother he's used to has no clear idea that she still exists. At 2 he still has no certainty that when she goes out, she will return. And two years after that he still can't understand exactly how many breakfasts or bedtimes away "six weeks" is.

Putting together the child's need for continuity in his relationship with his psychological parents and the special way in which he experiences time, Freud-Goldstein-Solnit draw these conclusions about parents, children and the law:

• The adoption decree should be made final and unconditional from the moment a child is placed with a family, as final as a birth certificate and no more subject to review (except, as in the case of the birth certificate, in cases of gross neglect or abuse). Adoption should—with absolute finality—cancel out the legal right of biological parents.

• Adoption should take place as early as possible—even before birth where this can be arranged—and with no trial periods, since a succession of temporary placements means the interruption of early attachments that is so destructive for the young child, as well as uncertainty for the adoptive parents, who may hesitate to make a full emotional commitment to the child. Expectant parents who plan to put their child up for adoption should make a firm decision before the birth, and adopting parents should be selected in advance. "If anyone is to be kept waiting, it should not be the child."

• Foster-care arrangements are usually made with the understanding that the child is placed in a home on a temporary basis and that the placing agency retains the legal right to remove the child at any time. This can lead to a lack of emotional involvement on the part of the foster parents and a feeling of insecurity on the part of the child. Freud-Goldstein-Solnit see this as a particularly silly arrangement, one which, since it tends to work against establishment of the psychological-parent/wanted-child relationship, defeats the whole purpose of replacing institutional care with family care. They suggest instead that when foster parents have truly become psychological parents, they should be considered "common-law adoptive parents," and that the courts should recognize this new category and the right it gives the foster parents to become adopters. Up to now this right has often been withheld by the courts in the face of objections by social agencies, either on their own behalf (rules and policies) or on behalf of the biological parents (who, while unable to care for their children themselves, may be unwilling to give them up for adoption).

• As in the case of adoption, custody decrees in divorce and separation proceedings should be final. One parent should be given custody and that parent—and not the court—should make all decisions about the child's life, including the right of the other parent to visit with the child. Freud-Goldstein-Solnit go so far as to suggest that two equally acceptable psychological parents should draw lots as the most rational process for resolving a hard choice.

This is the most controversial point made by the authors. They base it on the belief that (1) visiting arrangements may in themselves be sources of discontinuity in the child's experience; (2) children often have difficulty relating to two psychological parents who are not in positive contact with each other; and (3) a visiting or visited parent has little chance of being a psychological parent, since this role depends on his being available on an uninterrupted, day-to-day basis.

• In order to avoid the psychological injury caused by a sense of loss and uncertainty, all child-placement decisions should be considered by agencies and treated by the courts as psychological emergencies to be given priority on court calendars, decided—and, where necessary, reviewed—as rapidly as possible. The period for appeal should be no more than a week or two, and final decision should be given within a few days of the close of that hearing. As things stand today, decisions can drag out over weeks and months because of overworked social administrators, understaffed agencies, crowded dockets, overcautious judges and lawyers who demand postponements. On the other hand, when the *physical* well-being of a child is endangered by delay—for instance, when parents who are Jehovah's Witnesses have refused on religious grounds to authorize a blood transfusion for a deathly ill child in a hospital—the courts have shown they can move with speed and flexibility, sometimes in a matter of hours.

• The longer a child has been in the custody of an adult, the less chance there should be for another party to gain custody. Abandonment and neglect should be redefined in terms of a child's sense of time. The younger the child, the shorter the period in which a psychological tie is broken and a new one formed.

Once a child becomes the subject of a custody dispute, Freud-Goldstein-Solnit feel it can no longer be assumed that his parents are best suited to safeguard his interests. Even the social agencies involved may have policies which conflict with the child's needs—and many judges are unaware of those needs or unwilling to consider them seriously because they don't fit their common-sense view of the matter, or even threaten some personal notion of what is decent or moral. Then who represents the child? Certainly not the lawyers

of the disputing parents. Freud-Goldstein-Solnit insist that a child is being deprived of his rights in any legal proceedings concerned with his future unless he is represented by a lawyer of his own who has no other goal than to determine what is the least harmful alternative for his child client.

This suggests a whole new legal specialty —lawyers trained in psychoanalytic child development and specializing in child-custody cases. Judges and lawyers I talked with reacted to this idea in terms ranging from "impractical" (because it would cost so much and require so much additional training) to "ridiculous and unnecessary." Few of them were aware that a "child-advocacy" bill, that would make it a legal requirement for any child involved in a custody case to be represented by counsel, has been introduced in the New York State Assembly, where it is now under consideration.

In one chapter of the book Freud-Goldstein-Solnit take up an actual placement decision by Justice Bernard Nadel of the New York Supreme Court and then rewrite the decision according to their guidelines. The case is that of Stacey, an 8-year-old foster child whose mother gave her infant daughter to a child-care agency for temporary care in 1964 when she voluntarily entered a mental hospital. The agency had placed Stacey with a foster family. In 1969 the mother was released, and from then until the time of the decision in 1971 had been living with her parents, holding a job as an executive secretary, taking an active part in community affairs, and seeking to regain her child.

Justice Nadel ruled that the agency had failed to demonstrate that the rehabilitated mother was unfit to care for Stacey. He held that the lack of a parent-child relationship between them was caused by the agency's failure to encourage contact between them, and ordered the return of the child "to her natural mother" after a period of transition. Freud-Goldstein-Solnit insist that the fitness of the mother is not the issue. Here are some quotes from their reworking of the decision as they think it might better have been written:

"The real question is: Does Stacey need to have a parent assigned to her by the court? In the absence of such evidence, the law must presume that Stacey is a wanted child well settled in a reciprocal relationship with her custodians. . . . Stacey has been psychologically abandoned by her biological mother. Seven years have elapsed since their last contact. . . . Painful as it must be for this well-meaning woman, whatever the cause, whoever may feel responsible, the psychological fact, which the law acknowledges, is that Stacey does not now recognize her as a parent. . . . It is the real tie—the reality of an ongoing relationship—that is crucial to this court's decision and that demands the protection of the state through law. The court must not, despite its sympathetic concern for the petitioner, become party to tearing Stacey away from the only affectionate parents she knows."

The outcome of the real decision shows what can happen to a child caught in the legal process. Stacey was so antagonistic to her mother that the court modifed its earlier judgment and, instead of returning the child to her, gave custody to the agency, which placed her in a residential center. Five psychiatrists chosen by the various parties involved testified that she was depressed and that the mere mention of being returned to her natural mother brought on misery and tears. Even the psychiatrist called by the mother agreed that it would be harmful to return Stacey to her.

A schedule of visits was decided on to develop a gradual rapport, but it was a complete failure. Stacey rejected all offers of affection by her mother. In her frustration, the mother began to yell at her and reproach her, and the child would return upset, tearful, sometimes hysterical. In a second decision a year later, Justice Nadel decided that Stacey was one of the "exceptions to the rule of the primacy of parental custody," and that under the circumstances it would endanger her mental and emotional well-being to return her to her mother. He reversed his original order.

Not all their colleagues would agree with all the points set forth by Freud-Goldstein-Solnit. Experts I talked with, several of them divorced and with children themselves, made their sharpest attacks on the guidelines for settling custody in divorce cases—particularly the notion of allowing the parent awarded custody to make all decisions affecting the child, including the other parent's visitation rights. This could result in the noncustodial parent never being allowed to see the child at all.

One experienced child analyst asks, "Is the anxiety caused by conflict really more damaging than the anxiety caused by permanent loss? We know, from the work of Anna Freud herself, among others, that where there are two involved parents, as there are in most divorces, the loss of one parent is irreparable for the child—and this is true right up into adolescence. We have to ask ourselves what it would mean in an already unsettled society like ours—with separation, divorce, remarriage and even no marriage so common—to encourage further weakening of the ties between children and parents—even part-time parents. A father who comes once a week and hugs you and takes you for a walk in the park and asks about your report card is better than a father who never comes at all."

Despite such criticisms, "Beyond the Best Interests of the Child" is an important book, a manifesto on behalf of the rights of children that suggests new ways of looking at family relationships. Just as women until recently were chattel—the property of first their fathers and then their husbands—children have been regarded by the law as the property of their biological parents. But children, unlike any other social group, are unable to fight for their own rights.

The authors insist the law's first obligation should be to protect the child's need for continuity, and they acknowledge the anguishing decisions that are implicit in such a principle. As an extreme example, they cite the Dutch Jews who returned from concentration camps after World War II to reclaim the children they had left with non-Jewish families; many of the children had by this time become strongly attached to their foster parents. The Dutch Parliament ruled that the children should be returned to their natural parents. Freud-Goldstein-Solnit disagree. They feel that "the choice in such tragic instances is between causing intolerable hardship to the child who is torn away from his psychological parents, or causing further intolerable hardship to already victimized adults who, after losing freedom, livelihood and worldly possessions may now also lose possession of their child. . . . Harsh as it is, and as it must seem to the biological parents, their standing in court is no greater than that of a stranger."

Grown men and women have feelings too, and needs, and they suffer no less than children. Perhaps the only answer is that as with so many other social problems—like breaking the poverty cycle—a start must be made somewhere. As Freud-Goldstein-Solnit conclude: "By and large society must use each child's placement as an occasion for protecting future generations of children by increasing the number of adults-to-be who are likely to be adequate parents. Only in the implementation of this policy does there lie a real opportunity for beginning to break the cycle of sickness and hardship bequeathed from one generation to the next by adults who as children were denied the least detrimental alternative."

VII. Child-School Relations

Education and the school are major vehicles contributing to the child's development. From the age of five to sixteen, the American child will spend a major portion of his life centered around school—learning how to master its goals, how to survive it intact, or how to avoid it as much as possible. How relevant this compulsory experience is depends largely on the kind of environment the school provides and the place it has in the surrounding community.

Schools of Yesterday

The function of school has changed over the last 300 years. In the early years of this nation, most citizens were illiterate. The role of elementary education was to provide children with the basic skills of reading and writing. The "why" was made clear in the Massachusetts law of 1647:

It being one chief point of that old Deluder, Satan, to keep man from knowledge of the Scriptures, as in former times, by keeping them in an unknown tongue, so in these times . . . it is therefore ordered that every township in this jurisdiction, after the Lord has increased them to the member of fifty householders shall then forthwith appoint one within their town to teach all such children as shall resort to him to read and write.

The clear purpose of schooling, then, was to save the child's soul.

As the country grew, emphasis shifted to the child's future place as a citizen. History, geography, and arithmetic became the reading matter of the school child. Art and music were later added to broaden the educational experience and round off the child's personality. Education was aimed at making the child a cultured and enlightened citizen. "The mind is an instrument, you first sharpen it and then use it" (Whitehead, 1929).

This assumption remained unchallenged in education until the emergence of Progressive Education in the 1920's and 1930's. "The mind is never passive. . . . You cannot postpone its life until you have sharpened it" (Whitehead, 1929). The emphasis shifted to the relationship between various subjects and the necessity of viewing the child as an active, experiencing organism. The reaction on the part of schools was to reclassify the content areas of learning: history and geography become social studies; reading, writing, and speech became language arts (Cohen, 1971). In addition, children began to be grouped by ability, and teachers became specialists in varied subject areas. The child became the consumer of facts and skills.

In the late 1950's America became concerned with its failure to produce enough scientists and engineers to meet its advanced technological needs. Modern man was not being properly introduced to modern sciences. A group of scientists and educators met at Woods Hole in 1961 to work out the best ways to increase the interest and enthusiasm students had for learning the sciences. Yet, a solution was not reached. "Producing curriculum turned out to be not quite as we academics had thought" (Bruner, 1971). Educational reform had centered on curriculum reform. Deeper doubt as to how the schools were treating all children began to develop. It was asked whether a more fundamental restructuring of the entire educational system was in order (Bruner, 1971).

Questions of Today

These doubts today remain. The divergent, yet steady growth of programmed instruction as well as open schools reveal a widening gap between two approaches to the purpose of schools. School and society are interrelated. Society itself is caught between advancing technology and renewed interest in human values. The view of the child as a learner encompasses approaches which range from that of a passive recipient to an active participant (Cohen, 1971).

The place that schooling has currently in the life of the child and society is being called into question. The emergence of the open school, the movement back to home-educated children, the reappearance of the one-room school-house, and the birth of the freedom schools bring to the foreground the need to reexamine what schooling adds to the child's development and how education shall influence development.

One unique way of answering this issue is to look at children and see what we as adults can learn from them. In seeing the value of early childhood, we can begin to shape the kinds of intervention that is appropriate for the child's development. Education is a process of learning both for the child and the adult and that process must be one that preserves as well as expands the child's inherent value, that holds precious the things of value that pass with each age. This is the approach Elkind takes in looking at early childhood education.

As adults we may learn from children and structure our approaches to intervention around their needs. Yet, the question remains as to when the child is most ready for what Elkind refers to as formal education. Shall emphasis in readiness be placed on the cognitive, psychomotor, or affective domain? Shall we stress the child's motor coordination, emotional maturity, or thinking ability when we decide that it is time to introduce the child to school? The effect on such decisions can be profound. If experience is necessary for readiness, then schools need to begin to explore which experiences best serve to prepare the child. If it is a matter of maturation, then delayed admissions may be the best answer. Or is there a third alternative—to change the concept of school so that it is more adaptable to the child? Again, this is still more of a question than an answer. Kulberg's paper addresses this issue.

In school, what is it that leads to the success of some and failure of others? Viernstein and Hogan explore some of the factors which may lead to high achievement motivation. They find that it may not be any particular set of childrearing practices that motivates a child toward achieving, but rather the nature of the parental modeling to which a child is exposed. The school is not an isolated facet of the child's life, but one which plays an integral part in the community. If education wishes to produce motivated individuals, then its impact may have to be on the greater community and not just on the youth attending its sessions.

Achievement continues to be a theme as we look at the other end of the spectrum—at children failing in school. John Holt, C. E. Silberman, and others have indicated that our schools produce academic defeat. The effects of this process on the child are devastating, particularly among children with special needs. Forness explores the implications of the movement to change the present system of labeling these children as deficient to one which centers on meeting the child's individual needs. This change is difficult since it involves the system looking at itself and asking how it can adapt itself to the child instead of how it may adapt the child to fit it.

Ayllon, Layman, and Kandel further explore alternative approaches which schools might employ with children—in this case, with the nemesis of all teachers—the hyperactive child. Often, such a child is placed on medication which in many ways controls the problem the child has in school—it makes him/her more docile. However, we need ask whether the system can be more adaptive to the needs of the child rather than necessarily relying on methods which adapt the child to the system. Ayllon *et al.* suggest one such approach.

School provides a child with an important milieu in which to develop. Independent of the child's home, with different models to follow, the school offers the child an opportunity to master skills, acquire pride in work, persevere in solving problems, and establish more extensive and meaningful relationships with peers (Mussen, Conger, & Kagan, 1974). To do this, the school must be sensitive to the child's developmental needs and be willing to adapt to individual differences.

References

Bruner, J. The Process of Education Revisited. In Torrance, E. P., & White, W. F. *Issues and advances in educational psychology,* 2nd Edition. Itasca, Illinois: F. E. Peacock, 1975.

Cohen, D. H. *The learning child.* New York: Vintage, 1973.

Mussen, P.; Conger, J.; & Kagan, J. (eds.), *Child development and personality,* 4th Edition. New York: Harper & Row, 1974.

32.

David Elkind

THE EARLY YEARS: THE VITAL YEARS

For the past decade and a half, early childhood education in America has been the subject of considerable controversy and debate. In the early 1960s, early education programs were touted as panaceas for most of the nations ills from educational underachievement to racial prejudice. Today, however, opinion has moved to the other extreme and early childhood programs at their best are being described as "doing children no harm." Where once the early childhood years were regarded as "critical" for future growth, contemporary opinion more and more regards them as "trivial" with respect to later life.

Both these exaggerated positions about the value of early childhood education are clearly wrong. So too are the correlated opinions about the significance of early childhood for later growth and development. As far as children are concerned, the early years are neither critical nor trivial, but they are simply *vital* in the sense of being a period of active growth and development. Likewise, early childhood education programs were never meant to produce geniuses nor are they merely perfunctory. The aim of quality early childhood education is and always was the facilitation and enhancement of the child's growth.

It seems worthwhile, then, in view of these wide swings of public opinion, to reassert the values of early childhood, the vital years. In doing this, however, I want to reverse perspective and to look at early childhood in terms of its contribution to adult thought and feeling. That is to say, I believe that these years are as vital to adults as they are to children. Perhaps if we focus upon what we have to learn from children, instead of what we do or do not have to teach them, we can begin to get some recognition, from outside the field, of the true value of the early childhood years.

THE VALUE OF DIFFERENCES

One of the most important lessons young children teach is that differences can be valued as well as evaluated. Young children think differently than we do and literally see the world differently than older children and adults. And children try to make sense out of the world in the best way that they can. A child who says "underbrella" is trying to make sense of his verbal knowledge. Such a concept is not wrong, it is just different. Likewise, a child who calls socks and stockings "stocks" has created a concept that encompasses both his father's and his mother's footwear.

These examples are commonplace but illustrate how the child's world differs from our own. It differs in other ways as well. Young children believe that events that happen together cause one another. A teddy bear that a child clings to in a moment of fear and which is associated with a pleasant feeling, comes to be regarded as "causing" the child to feel safe. Similarly, the child who asks, "If I eat spaghetti, will I become Italian?" is

Source: Paper presented at the Rhode Island Conference for Early Childhood Education, Cranston, Rhode Island, 1976.

expressing a very special view of causality. It would be a mistake, however, to call these ideas wrong and try to correct them. They express the child's view of the world at the time and need to be valued as such rather than as "errors" that have to be eradicated.

Children also differ from adults in their capacity to process information and stimulation. When my sons were small, I once took them to a three-ring circus. During the performance I again and again tried to draw their attention to one or another of the rings where all sorts of exciting activities were going on. In one ring a man was riding a unicycle. In another a lady in a pink dress was riding a pony standing up. In another a juggler had a cane and three silver balls balanced on his nose. But my efforts were to no effect. What captured my boys' attention was the men in the aisles who were selling hot dogs, peanuts, and cotton candy. Going home I was sure the whole trip had been a failure. Indeed, I began to doubt my own childhood memories of the circus which I recalled as a tremendously new and fascinating experience.

Some weeks later, however, the children quite spontaneously began to talk about the circus at the dinner table. To my amazement, they had noticed the man on the unicycle, the lady in the pink dress, and the juggler. But it took them longer than it did me to process the information. By the way, we all have limitations in these regards. After about three paper sessions at a psychological convention I am ready for a fresh brain because the one I have is simply too full to take in any more information. Again, the child's slow pace in processing information is something to value, and to appreciate; it is not something to be overcome.

Please understand, I am not saying that these differences, which are to be valued in

their own right, must never be challenged or overcome. Most of the ideas children hold about the world that are different from adult conceptions are eventually transformed as the child interacts with the physical world and with other young people. But it is one thing to try and change something that you value and quite another to try and change something for which you have no regard. It is an important lesson that we can learn from children but which has much broader implications. Consider an Indian policy which tries to change a tribe's eating practices which happen to be nutritionally unsound. A program based on respect for the tribe's cultural investment in certain eating practices is much more likely to be effective than one that is not. In the same way, an early education program which respects the young child's unique view of the world is much more likely to be successful than one that is not. Children, no less than adults, are more willing to change if their views are understood and respected than if they are not.

Because young children are far removed from adults in their modes of thinking, they have much to teach us in the domain of valuing differences. If we can look at young children's ideas as interesting and different and not necessarily right or wrong, or bad or good, we have learned something of great value with implications far beyond the early childhood classroom.

THE VALUE OF GROWTH

Another phenomenon we can learn to value from working with young children is growth and development. Too often I am afraid, growth and development are seen as simple increases in amount. It is assumed that the child's mind matures as his body does, in quantity not in quality. But this is a false analogy, and children's thinking goes through a truly remarkable transformation between the ages of four and six. Attention to these transformations leads to enormous respect and wonder at the miracle of human development.

One way of looking at the developmental changes that occur during early childhood, is to think of this period as one of *structure formation.* The structures being formed are those which Piaget calls "concrete operations" that take their final form about the age of six or seven. Concrete operations enable school-age children to perform many mental feats they could not perform as young children. They can follow rules imposed from without, reason in syllogistic ways, and understand space, time, and causality in quantitative terms.

These structures are formed during the preschool years in part as a matter of growth, but also as part of the child's own activity. It is in this regard that the miracle of growth becomes apparent. When structures are in the process of formation, there is an intrinsic motivation to enhance this formative process. In effect, during this period children seek out all sorts of stimuli and activities to nourish their growing abilities. Because concrete operations feed on quantity relations, young children seem obsessed with counting, with size, and with "who has more."

Montessori clearly recognized the young child's need for stimuli to nourish their growing mental abilities. And she intuited that these were "sensitive periods" for certain kinds of learning. But she erred in attributing too much to the value of stimuli and too little to the ingenuity of children. Young children need stimuli to nourish their mental abilities, but they can transform almost any and all materials to this end. Indeed, the very effort of bending materials to their own needs provides important nourishment for mental growth. The way in which young children trans-

form pots and pans, boxes, clothespins, and much more into play materials is vivid testament to the motivational force of structures in the process of formation.

One can observe the same growth forces at work in the evolution of children's language. Without formal instruction of any sort, children not only learn to speak and to comprehend, but also to master an elaborate syntax and generative grammar. These abilities, it must be stressed, do not simply unfold but reflect the child's active involvement with the environment. The child's language skills, like his or her mental abilities, reflect both growth processes and the characteristics of the environment.

One aspect of growth is particularly important to emphasize, namely, individual differences. Children vary tremendously in their rates of growth. Some children seem to have growth hiccups and to change in fits and spurts. Other children change gradually. Rates of growth also vary tremendously. Some children who are behind suddenly catch up quickly while other children who seem to be ahead suddenly get stalled. Although individual differences are present throughout the life cycle, they are particularly marked during periods of structure formation. That is why it is so dismaying to me to hear of kindergarten programs in which young children are already in lockstep programs.

Once children attain concrete operations, the intrinsic motivational forces that directed children to interact with all sorts of materials are dissipated. This means that children are no longer intrinsically motivated to interact with materials and to learn new skills. At the school-age level, children enter a *structure utilization* period when the motivation to use mental abilities is social or derives from the satisfaction of a skill well learned. The concept of the school-aged child intrinsically motivated to learn to read and to do math is a myth that lays heavily on the conscience of teachers. In grade school, children learn to read and do math because the adults to whom they are attached encourage and reward such behavior. Academic achievement is socially, not intrinsically, motivated.

Observing young children can then, teach us great respect for the processes of growth. This does not mean, however, that we stand by and do nothing. Rather it forces us to ask ourselves just what sort of intervention is appropriate for this phase in the growth cycle. Clearly, it is a time for providing children with an environment rich in materials to observe and to manipulate. And it is important to provide children guidance in the handling and manipulation of some materials. Children do need help in how to hold a gerbil or a kitten. On the other hand, it is not a time to get children to utilize their still incompletely fixed mental structures in the attainment of academic skills. In effect such skill training (particularly formal reading instruction) amounts to a kind of pruning during the growth season. Much better to let the child grow a little bit free and to trim him or her back a bit during the dormant period, the middle childhood period.

Close observation of children during the early childhood years can teach us to respect and to admire the processes of growth. Hopefully too, such observation will make us courteous and thoughtful about our own interventions. But a respect for growth, gleaned from observation of young children, should not stop there. It should extend to people at all stages in life. In a recent study college students treated as elderly began to act senile. If we respect the capacity of people to grow at all age levels, we will continually ask the question: Will this intervention help or hinder this

person's growth towards a fuller and richer life? It is a question we have to ask, not only with respect to the children we teach, but also with respect to our own children, our students and not least of all, ourselves.

VALUE OF INFORMAL EDUCATION

It is a very human tendency to think in terms of either/or, of absolutes, of blacks and whites. This seems particularly true in the case of education. Somehow many people tend to think of education as a unitary entity, a body of information and practices all of one piece. From this standpoint, there is only one kind of education, the inculcation of skills and information to the young by means of specified practices of which the major one is repetitive drill. This concept of a kind of homogeneous entity of education has probably done early childhood education more harm than any other single concept.

It is, of course, not true and the idea that there are many different forms of education is one of the most important insights we can glean from the observation of young children. The children described so dramatically by Maria Montessori were engaged in informal education, an education in which the materials were self didactic. Recall Montessori's description of the little girl so involved in her work that she could not be disturbed by children circling her work table and clapping. Such activity is informal not so much because it is self didactic, as much as because it is *structure forming.*

In effect we have to distinguish activities which nourish the child's emerging cognitive structures and those which require their exercise. An analogy may help to make this point a bit more concrete. When a bodily structure, such as the heart or lungs, is in the process of formation, the processes in play are quite different than those which operate once the structure is fully formed. The beating of the heart is of a very different order from the processes which led to the heart's construction. In the same way, in education, we have to distinguish between activities related to structure formation and those which are related to structure utilization.

In this discussion, I propose to call those activities utilized for the purpose of structure formation *informal education* whereas those activities that require the utilization of mental activities, I propose to call *formal education.* Clearly, the distinctions are not always easy to make. But during a period of rapid mental growth, such as the preschool years, informal education dominates, whereas formal education is the dominant activity in the school years.

It should be apparent from the foregoing discussion that both informal and formal education are important to the full development of the child. Perhaps it is also apparent that different types of education are appropriate to different levels of development. Informal education, activities geared to the formation of mental structures, is most appropriate during the early childhood years. Formal education, geared to the utilization of mental structures, is best suited to the elementary school years. I should say, tangentially, that this approach suggests informal education for early adolescents and formal education for young people in middle and late adolescence.

How does one distinguish between informal educational activities and those which are formal? Although it is not always easy to do this, there are a few criteria that can help in making a rough discrimination. First, those activities that are generated or initiated by the child are likely to be structure-forming activities. Activities suggested or initiated by the teacher are likely to be structure-utilization activities. Secondly, activities on which children persist for long periods without external reward are likely to be structure-forming. Those which are undertaken and maintained for external rewards are most likely to be structure-utilization activities.

What I want to emphasize here is that by and large, informal education is most appropriate for the early childhood years. I wish I knew some way to shout this point from the rooftops so that everyone would hear. The idea that formal education is appropriate for young children is so widespread in this country that I wonder if we can ever turn the situation around. It stems, or so it seems to me, from the monolithic conception of education as all of a piece. All education is formal education, and if we are to teach young children, they too must be taught in a formal way.

And yet, if we look at young children we see that they learn much more from their self-regulated activities than from teacher-regulated activities. To be sure, the early childhood educator may introduce an activity such as finger painting, or block building, but the children regulate the activity. In contrast, young children learn little from a program in which they are shown materials but have no opportunity to interact with them at first hand. Formal education at the preschool level is, to me, a very sad mistake. It assumes that there is only one kind of education and deprives young children of the kind of education best suited to their developmental needs.

VALUES OF BEING HUMAN

At the end of a lecture which I gave to the parents of a suburban school system, I received an interesting question. You will not be surprised to learn that I was advocating a child-centered approach to discipline and that I was urging parents to try and see things from their children's point of view. The question I received was: Do you think there is such a thing as a "naughty" child? I am afraid I didn't answer the question very well at the time and said something to the effect that I believed children should be punished if they disobeyed rules that have been clearly and explicitly laid down.

I have been thinking about that question for quite some time and wish now that I could answer the man, having had some time for reflection. If I could answer the question now I would say that children are human and that they make mistakes for any number of reasons, just as adults do. And I believe that if those mistakes are injurious to others, then children should be punished. To call children "naughty" or "bad" or "hostile" seems to me to be a mistake. It suggests that somehow the child is outside the pale, inhuman and basically evil.

In effect we are all human. And as far as I have been able to determine, no children have committed crimes anywhere of the magnitude or cruelty as those committed by adults. Somehow it is much easier for me to accept the minor mistakes of children as human error than it is the major mistakes of adults. I have to wonder whether our treatment of children as evil-doers, rather than as humans who make mistakes, doesn't contribute more to the creation of adult "monsters" than does an understanding heart.

In this regard we have another important lesson to be learned from children. I have seen children fighting so hard that they could have killed had they been able. And I have seen one child bite through another's leather jacket hard enough to break the skin of the wearer's arm. And yet, but a few short hours later the same

children are playing peaceably with one another. The hatred and acrimony of the earlier dispute was forgotten. Children do not bear a grudge.

To be sure, children are not practicing forgiveness in the adult sense. But in another sense they are. Children do not bear a grudge because they do not attribute abiding character traits to others. Because they cannot intellectually construct the concept of an "evil" person who is always that way, they accept other children and adults on the basis of current behavior, not on the basis of past aberrations. In a very real sense, children are situationalists, who relate a person's behavior to the immediate situation rather than to abiding personality traits.

Children, in their situationalism, are probably extreme and might do better if occasionally they ascribed more abiding traits to others. But the capacity of young children to forgive, particularly their parents, is a charming and an endearing trait. Adults, in contrast, probably go to the opposite extreme and attribute almost all of an individual's behavior to abiding character tendencies. Accidental statements and actions are immediately ascribed to abiding attitudes and motives.

Perhaps what we can learn from children is to take a somewhat more moderate stand. Sometimes behavior upsetting to ourselves can be the result of inattention, carelessness, etc., rather than bad motives. Young children do not always knock over their milk "on purpose" and hostile remarks made in conversation can sometimes be inadvertent. Observation of young children can thus help us to recognize that we are all human, that we all make mistakes, and that at least some of these mistakes are unintentional. Young children in their failure to attribute long-lived bad traits to individuals provide a model of humanness that could be a very positive example to adults.

CONCLUSION

I began this paper with the observation that public opinion regarding early childhood and early childhood education has swung from viewing this age period as critical to one which now sees it as trivial. Both positions are incorrect and fail to do justice to the early childhood period. Underlying both extreme positions is a lack of understanding about the nature of young children and the kinds of educational programs most suited to them. In this paper I have tried to stress some aspects of early childhood and of early childhood education that have relevance for adults and for education at all age levels. I have tried to stress how much we have to learn from young children and what a great loss it is if we blind ourselves to the insights these age periods can provide.

Somehow we must learn to communicate the value of early childhood to the public. It is not an easy task, particularly for early childhood educators. The reason, paradoxically, stems from the very same source as our openness to learning from young children. We in early childhood tend to see children as active learners who can make choices and take responsibility for their own learning. Consequently we tend to take a more passive, observing, facilitating role. While such a role is beneficial when dealing with children, it may not be when we are dealing with administrators and legislators.

Indeed, consider the stance of those who view children as passive, as capable of learning anything at any time if it is only taught in an appropriate and an honest way. Such people tend to be active not only in their interactions with children, when they dominate the educational scene, but also with administrators and with legislators where their views, opinions, and interests often prevail. Presently, for example, child development legislation is in jeopardy because of an avalanche of letters to congressmen from a biased but active minority.

I believe that it is time that we in early childhood education become more active in our dealings with administrators and legislators. We have to recognize that our facilitative stance with respect to children is ineffective in administrative and political arenas. We must begin to be more active educationally and politically while retaining a certain passivity with respect to children. It is time that those who know and appreciate the values of early childhood and early childhood education make themselves heard.

As I have tried to indicate here, young children teach us the value of differences, of growth, of informal education, and of humanness. What we need to communicate to the general public is that early childhood is vital not only to children, but to adults as well. The early years are one of our few remaining sources of moral insight. In a very real sense, young children are an endangered species today, and it is only through our efforts that this rich repository of human values has a hope of survival.

33.

Janet M. Kulberg

HERE THEY COME, READY OR NOT!*

The issue of school failure is a prominent concern of parents and educators. A number of children of average and above intellectual ability often fail to meet the requirements of kindergarten. These children are usually judged "immature" by their teachers and may be asked to either repeat kindergarten or enter a less rigorous "transitional" first grade program. Some, as borderline cases, are promoted into first grade, increasing probable failure in later school years. Often, in retrospect, both teachers and parents question if such children were ready to start in the first place, and wonder if they would have been better off to wait another year before entering school.

In an age where positive prevention is seen as more desirable than remediation, efforts are being made to identify "high risk" children prior to school entry. Schools are more frequently asking for preschool evaluation of children, and in some states, preschool screening programs are now mandated by law. Critics of these procedures question whether it is possible to predict who will fail, and some have suggested that readiness is another, not too subtle, form of discrimination.

The concept of readiness, defining when learning is most appropriate, has been of considerable concern to teachers and educators. Yet it remains today an area of both complexity and controversy. There is general agreement that readiness can be defined as having requisite skills necessary for undertaking new learnings. However, what those requisite skills are and how they come to be is subject to differing concepts of preparedness. At one extreme, Bruner (1960) holds the position that "the foundations of any subject may be taught to anyone at any age in some form" (p. 7) and thereby suggests that some degree of readiness is always present. Others hold that school readiness is dependent almost exclusively upon the experiential background of the learner or a matter of accumulated knowledge. Ilg and Ames (1965), from a maturational perspective, believe that learning can take place only as the child reaches an appropriate level of biological preparedness, suggesting that inner forces rather than external stimulation form the basis for educational probing.

Based on the wide separation of opinion on how it comes about, what to do about school readiness also takes rather divergent directions. Concern is most pronounced when a child is judged immature or unready to undertake certain educational tasks. Environmentalists see the answer in compensatory education, making up for what has been missed. Followers of Bruner's position would suggest that the school's strategy should be one of finding appropriate instructional techniques to meet the child where he is. A postponement of instruction until the child matures is the usual recommendation based upon a maturational model of readiness.

The concept of readiness implied a

*Much of the thinking for this paper has developed out of collaborative research with Elaine S. Gershman, Assistant Professor of Psychology, University of Maine at Orono. Recognition of her contribution is hereby acknowledged and appreciated.

number of assumptions about its nature, its amenability to training, and the adaptability of the schools. In order to understand the issues surrounding readiness, one must ask several additional questions: What constitutes readiness? That is, what trait or traits are critical for success in school? Are these few or many in number? Can they or their precursors be identified prior to school entry? If the child lacks particular dimensions of readiness, can they be taught, or must we wait for readiness to develop? Where should change be expected to occur—in the child, in the school? This paper addresses itself to these questions, drawing implications for our understanding of human development and its interface with school practice.

THE NATURE OF READINESS

The concept of readiness assumes that certain traits, skills, attitudes, and motivations are an essential foundation before specific learning can occur. For example, readiness to read is thought to be dependent upon certain levels of visual and auditory discrimination, vocabulary knowledge, ability to concentrate, and interest in school tasks. Each of these is thought, in turn, to have its own set of precursors, arranged hierarchically, and necessary to develop before the next level of organization can occur.

Though many educators subscribe to the idea of this kind of hierarchical arrangement, few can provide more than a skeleton of the necessary prerequisites to formal learning. In place of a well-worked-out theory, backed by empirical support, we have varying opinions, based on much conjecture and little data. Our current knowledge of what constitutes readiness for school is much like the blind men's description of an elephant. The point of view is dominated by the particular part of the beast that the theorist has touched. However, before we throw the elephant out, let's look at what has been suggested as elements in the school readiness puzzle.

When we ask teachers why children fail, we get one set of answers. Hindsight would suggest that children who subsequently bog down or fail are not a unitary or homogeneous group. Instead they show immaturity in a number of areas. Teachers identify a wide variety of symptoms: inability to stick to a task, easy frustration or upset, dependence, difficulty in completing tasks, poor motor control, distractability, babyishness, inability to play with others, uncooperativeness. A closer look at what teachers are saying suggests that their primary emphasis is on factors that could be classified as social/emotional, with psychomotor skills running a strong second. Less attention is given, overtly, at least, to cognitive function.

Research, on the other hand, has dealt primarily with the latter. In the past, concern about school readiness has centered on predicting reading readiness from a variety of physical and cognitive traits: general intelligence, lateral dominance, visual and auditory acuity, knowledge of basic concepts. These efforts resulted in identification of mental age as the single best predictor of reading readiness and the development of readiness tests that were highly cognitive in nature.

But dissatisfaction arose with recognition that good mental ability, and thereby good potential for reading, might be a necessary condition for success in school but it clearly was not a sufficient condition. Many children with good mental ability were not succeeding in school. It must be that other traits also come into play.

More recent research efforts have concentrated on specific skills rather than more global abilities. Satz and Friel (1974), have been following a large sample of children tested at school entry. They have identified three specific skills as predictors of school success: alphabet recitation, finger localization, and visual discrimination. Hess (1974) established high predictive validity with an eight-minute assessment of intellectual readiness, and the Metropolitan Readiness Test (MRT), known for its ability to identify children who are likely to encounter reading difficulty (Anastasi, 1976). The MRT consists of a number of cognitive and psychomotor subjects. It is interesting to note that most research success has been in the cognitive and psychomotor domain, while little research attention has been paid to the things teachers say are important: social/emotional and psychomotor skills. This is possibly because social/emotional characteristics are so difficult to define, objectify, observe, and study.

From these efforts we get some hints as to what readiness might be. It seems to take some mixture of cognitive skills, including general mental ability, past learning (alphabet recitation), psychoneurological organization (finger localization), psychomotor skill (copying and drawing), and social/emotional maturity (cooperativeness, frustration tolerance, achievement motivation). To what degree and in what combination, however, is yet to be determined accurately. Our own research (Kulberg & Gershman, 1973) gives most weight to cognitive factors, while affective and psychomotor variables are also related but with less strength.

If there is uncertainty and disagreement about what makes up readiness, the debate is heightened when we ask how it comes about. In many ways, this boils down to the age-old nature/nurture controversy. Tyler (1964) in an extensive review of issues related to school readiness, warned against getting caught in the trap of endless debate and suggested a more

empirical approach involving attempts to build for readiness. If, indeed, readiness is a result of inner forces, deliberate efforts to train for readiness should have an effect no greater than that of waiting for readiness to evolve. If, on the other hand, nurture is the dominant force, deliberate effort should have a clear and demonstrable effect. Some research of this type has occurred in areas tangential to readiness which shed light on factors thought to constitute readiness.

If we can agree that the evidence cited above points to cognitive, psychomotor, and affective factors in readiness, we can look at what the literature says about the course of development of each for cues to the course of development of readiness. With the exception of a few, notably Gesell and his followers, (Ilg and Ames, 1965) who see a strong maturational base to all facets of development, there is general agreement that each area may develop differently. Maturation and learning may affect different traits differently, and, further, may affect a particular trait differently at different times or states of development.

Consider first the course of cognitive development. Although far from settled, it seems that few behavioral scientists remain who doubt the possibility of significantly altering the course of cognitive development through variations in experience. Further, Bloom (1964) provides strong evidence that periods of maximum growth are most fruitful times for environmental stimulation. He suggests, therefore, that the preschool years are the most critical for cognitive development. Research now centers on what kinds of experiences are most relevant to full development of intellect and under what conditions of timing and duration their effects are maximized.

Early psychomotor skills seem to be dependent on maturation. The age expectancies are fairly well delineated and attempts to speed up these skills have resulted in a temporary advantage to the child, often outweighed by the amount of effort required to train. Later psychomotor skills may be more amenable to training than earlier ones.

There is increasing evidence that many behaviors in the area of affective development are influenced, if not controlled, by environmental effects. Development in this area seems dependent upon variations in handling and experience and appears highly subject to training.

It is apparent, then, that the course of development of readiness is dependent on the weight given to each of the above factors. If readiness is primarily psychomotor in nature, its development will depend heavily upon maturation. If it is cognitive or affective, experience could have a significant influence.

ASSESSING READINESS

If there is confusion on what constitutes readiness and how it comes about, the issue is further compounded by attempts to measure it. If we could agree on a package of traits or characteristics that constitute readiness, measuring them efficiently and reliably would still present many problems. Preschoolers are known to experience rapid change and are extremely variable in performance. To obtain consistent measures on any traits at this age is a problem well known to test constructors. Setting out to design a test of readiness is filled with pitfalls.

Another dimension of the testing problem is anchoring our test at the far end. Before we can determine whether tests of readiness do indeed predict success in school, we must establish what success in school is. That is as elusive as defining readiness. Is success in school a matter of having been passed to the next grade level? Of making all A's and B's? Of being judged successful by the teacher? Of parental satisfaction? Of self-concept? All of these have been suggested as possible criteria, and, as is often the case in prediction studies, results vary depending on the criterion selected.

It is clear that we need ways of working with multiple predictors (traits) and multiple criteria (outcomes). Yet, these complex statistical techniques have seldom been used in the development of readiness tests. Let's take a look at what has been done.

In the past five years, there has been a flood of readiness tests reaching the market. No less than fifty published tests can be counted, and the literature refers to innumerable "experimental" and homemade surveys. This burgeoning interest reflects the coming together of several concerns. Some tests have grown out of preschool programs for the culturally deprived, such as Head Start, in an attempt to assess program effectiveness and at the same time predict chances of success in school. Thus, designed as achievement tests, they have also been used for prognosis. The IQ test ban in New York City has spurred development of more culture-fair readiness batteries. Legislators have raised concern about early identification of handicapped children, and, in many cases, their legislation has been extended to include the more subtle "high risk" kinds of handicap. General recognition of the importance of the preschool years, especially for cognitive development, has contributed to this movement. And, finally, retrospective analysis of children who fail has led to attempts at preventing failure before it occurs.

Because of the increasing demand for tests of readiness, many of the instruments on the market have not been put through the rigorous demands of good test con- struction. In many cases, there is neither a clear rationale nor a firm empirical base for selection of the items. Instead, items appear to be selected on the basis of some prior notion of what makes up readiness, with little follow-up to determine if these items do predict success.

Tests range in content from single- faceted to multi-faceted, reflecting the theoretical biases of their authors. Many of the more heterogeneous tests are heavily weighted toward one favored dimension. Thus, they can be classified by their emphasis on cognitive (Boehm, MRT, Hess), psychomotor (Gesell, Preschool Screening Survey), or affective dimensions. Some directly test the child, while others rely on teacher ratings (Rhode Island Pupil Identification Scale), parent re- ports (Vane), or physicians' observations (Sprigle). Most are designed as screening instruments, reporting a single general index of readiness, while some attempt to be diagnostic, with several subtest scores (STAR, CIRCUS). The shortest takes eight minutes to administer, longer ones may take more than an hour of testing, scattered over several sittings. From this, it is quite obvious that what is obtained on one test of readiness is quite different from another.

The variety of approaches would not be so disturbing if each demonstrated its usefulness by providing evidence that chil- dren who score high do succeed in school on some criterion, while children who score low do not. Little of this kind of validity is presented with the tests or in the literature.

IMPLICATIONS FOR SCHOOL

If we can assume that the necessary traits for school success can be identified and measured prior to school entry, we are left with the problem of knowing what to do about the children who do not measure up. Schools that have initiated screening pro- grams often are uncertain about how to handle the immature children they iden- tify. Action has generally taken one of two forms. Either specialized remedial, or compensatory, programs are recommend- ed to make up for deficiencies noted in the children, or a better fit between child and school is sought through delayed admis- sion or grade repetition. Once again, we see the nature/nurture issue lurking in the shadows, and the question reduces to: Can readiness be taught?

The proponents of each side of this question argue strongly for their position, but neither side offers very convincing support in the form of well-controlled studies.

In recent years and in support of grade repetition, Chase (1968) cited teacher and parent satisfaction when children were retained on the basis of immaturity. Scott and Ames (1969) used teacher judgment and school marks as criteria and came up with the same conclusion. Confidence in these results would increase with sup- portive studies that use control groups for comparison as well as objective criteria of achievement and adjustment.

Reports on attempts at school program modification for immature children are scarce in the literature. Although encour- aged by the results of such modification with culturally deprived children, Spollen and Ballif (1971) were unable to demon- strate superiority of a specialized curricu- lum over regular kindergarten attendance for children with developmental lag. They suggest the need for a longitudinal ap- proach and more specific, sequential pro- grams in the area of perceptual–motor skills and language development.

This latter recommendation of Spollen and Ballif may be the key to the whole puzzle. If it turns out that readiness is composed of several factors, and if these various factors are differentially affected by maturation or learning, it would be logical that some kinds of readiness would respond best to delayed admission, while others would best be taught. Some preliminary findings by this author and associate have taken exactly that form (Kulberg and Gershman, 1973). Comparing matched groups of immature children who participated in one of three types of schooling—delayed admission, experimental readiness class, or traditional kindergarten—it was apparent that training was relatively ineffective for psychomotor skills, but effective in the cognitive and affective domains. Waiting, on the other hand, was an advantage for those who were immature in the psychomotor sphere. Further exploration of even more specific traits seems warranted and promising from these preliminary findings.

But both of these methods—delayed admission or remedial education—place the locus of change with the child. That is, in both cases, the child must come up to some kind of predetermined standard. There is yet another alternative, not often considered in the educational planning for immature children. Why not place the locus of change with the school? Is it possible for schools to be developed which could meet each child wherever he is and teach him at his own pace and by his own style? Bruner (1960) suggests that it is not only possible, but is the responsibility of the school to do so. The child is ready, there is nothing to wait for, it is the school's job to find the way to teach him.

CONCLUSION

As is true in many areas of human development, school readiness raises more

questions than it answers. The need for more research in the area is the obvious conclusion to be drawn. Fortunately, that effort is underway. Meanwhile, however, children will continue to enter school, ready or not, and schools will continue to make their best efforts to work with them. Hopefully, the above will aid in identifying where the points of controversy lie and will impress upon us the necessity for proceeding cautiously in making decisions about children's lives. *Caveat emptor!*

REFERENCES

Anastasi, A. *Psychological testing, 4th ed.* New York: Macmillan, 1976.

Bloom, B. S. *Stability and change in human characteristics.* New York: John Wiley & Sons, 1964.

Bruner, J. S. *The process of education.* Cambridge: Harvard University Press, 1960.

Chase, H. A study of the impact of grade retention on primary school children. *Journal of Psychology,* 1968, **70**, 169-173.

Hess, R. J., & Hahn, R. T. II. Prediction of school failure and the Hess School Readiness Scale. *Psychology in the Schools,* 1974, **11**, 134-135.

Ilg, F. L., & Ames, L. B. *School readiness.* New York: Harper & Row, 1965.

Kulberg, J. M., & Gershman, E. S. School readiness: studies of assessment procedures and comparison of three types of programming for immature 5-year-olds. *Psychology in the Schools,* 1973, 410-420.

Satz, P., & Friel, M. S. Some predictive antecedents of specific reading disability: A preliminary two-year follow-up. *Journal of Learning Disabilities,* 1974, **7**, 437-444.

Scott, J., & Ames, L. B. Improved academic, personal and social adjustment in selected primary school repeaters. *Elementary School Journal,* 1969, **69**, 431-439.

Spollen J., & Ballif, B. Effectiveness of individualized instruction for kindergarten children with a developmental lag. *Exceptional Children,* 1971, **38**, 205-209.

34.

Mary Cowan Viernstein and Robert Hogan

PARENTAL PERSONALITY FACTORS AND
ACHIEVEMENT MOTIVATION IN TALENTED
ADOLESCENTS

INTRODUCTION

Highly intelligent children vary considerably in their occupational aspirations.
Prior explanations of these differences
have appealed primarily to childrearing
tactics and subsequent learned achievement motivation. The best-known work on
the subject is that of McClelland *et al.*
(1953), who explain achievement motivation as the product of a particular set of
childrearing tactics that in turn derive
from certain parental expectations. Rosen
and D'Andrade (1959), for example,
found that parents of sons with high need
Achievement scores set higher "levels of
aspiration" for their sons' performances in
a series of difficult tasks than did the
parents of sons with low need Achievement. Further, the mothers of high need
Achievement sons were encouraging during performance tasks, and reacted affec-
tionately to their accomplishment. On the
other hand, fathers of low need Achievement boys reacted with irritation and
tended to give specific directions to a son
who was not performing well.

Another explanation of differences in
achievement motivation is implicit in the
work of Duncan *et al.* (1968). They note
that the rated socioeconomic status of

occupations is correlated highly both with
psychologists' concept of the intelligence
demands of each occupation and with the
general public's concept of the prestige or
social standing of an occupation. According to Duncan *et al.* (1968), " 'intelligence'
is a socially defined quality [which] . . . is
not essentially different from that of
achievement or status in the occupational
sphere. . . ." They conclude that "what we
now *mean* by intelligence is something like
the probability of acceptable performance
(given the opportunity) in occupations
varying in social status" (pp. 90-91). Thus
Duncan *et al.* explain achievement, and by
implication level of occupational aspiration, in terms of intelligence.

Finally, Weiner and Kukla (1970) account for achievement motivation in terms
of attribution theory: individuals high in
achievement motivation "are more likely
to approach achievement-related activities
. . . because they tend to ascribe success to
themselves. . . . [They] persist longer given
failure . . . because they are more likely to
ascribe the failure to a lack of effort, and
less likely to attribute failure to a deficiency in ability. . . . [They] choose tasks
of intermediate difficulty . . . because performance at those tasks is more likely to
yield information about one's capabilities
than selection of tasks which are very easy
or extremely difficult" (p. 19). Thus for
Weiner and Kukla achievement motivation
reflects a self-image that leads to persistence and a disposition to choose tasks
which maximize evaluative feedback.

Source: *Journal of Youth and Adolescence,* 1975,
4, 183-190.

Work on this paper was supported by a grant from
the Spencer Foundation, Chicago, Illinois.

In contrast to the views described above, this paper suggests that achievement motivation is a function of the personality styles of the adult models that children are exposed to during socialization.

METHOD

The subjects of this study, 234 girls and 150 boys, were selected from a larger sample of 707 seventh and eighth graders who took part in a verbal talent search at The Johns Hopkins University. All subjects scored at or above the 98th percentile on a standardized measure of verbal achievement given in their own schools. The subjects were white and primarily middle-class. Each student completed the Scholastic Aptitude Test (SAT) and a questionnaire listing the occupation and education of both parents and his or her own occupational aspiration. Occupations were coded according to their relative status and prestige using the system described by Shuy *et al.* (1968). Occupational levels ranged from professional workers (level 5) to jobs requiring no training (level 1). To rate level of education, parents who had not graduated from high school were assigned a score of 1, high school graduates were scored 2, parents with some college education 3, college graduates 4, and parents with more than a college education 5.

Students who aspired to an occupation one or more levels above their fathers' were assumed to have high achievement aspirations. Those choosing an occupation at the same level or lower than their fathers' were assumed to have low achievement aspirations. Thus the level of a child's occupational choice relative to the father's actual occupational level is our index of aspiration or achievement motivation. Students whose fathers were at level 5 were omitted since by definition they could not be high aspirers. The final group of 234 girls and 150 boys contained 165 high-aspiring and 69 low-aspiring girls and 105 high-aspiring and 45 low-aspiring boys.

Personality types of children and parents were obtained by applying Holland's classification (Holland *et al.*, 1972) and Viernstein's extension of the classification (Viernstein, 1972) to the first occupational choices of the children and to the present occupations of their parents. Holland's theory describes people in terms of six personality types: Realistic, Investigative, Artistic, Social, Enterprising, and Conventional. In Holland's system every occupation can be designated by an ordered set of three letters. These letters are the components, in order of importance, that describe people in a particular occupation. For example, a physicist is primarily Investigative, secondarily Artistic, and thirdly Realistic, and is designated IAR. This three-letter Holland occupational code, IAR, denotes a personality type. Composite personality profiles for each of the four groups, i.e., for the high- and low-aspiring girls and the high- and low-aspiring boys and for parents of these groups were obtained using the three-letter Holland codes, with scores assigned to each letter. To assign scores, a code of ESA, for example, was assigned an Enterprising score 3, a Social score 2, an Artistic score 1, and Realistic, Investigative, and Conventional scores of 0. The resultant mean scores for the six types represent the group personality profile. Differences in these composite personality profiles were evaluated by *t* tests.

The congruency of the parents' personalities, defined in terms of Holland's typology, was also assessed using a Levels of Consistency Table (Holland, 1973, p. 22). The first letter of the mother's

Holland code was compared with the father's for all mother-father pairs. For example, an S code for the mother and an R code for the father yields an SR congruency code. Codes with the same letters are the most congruent; they were assigned a score of 4. Less congruent codes were assigned scores of 3, 2, and 1, according to Holland's High, Medium, and Low consistency code combinations. Congruency scores were assigned for parents, and χ^2 tests were then used to evaluate the differences in the congruency scores for the high- and low-aspiration groups.

RESULTS

Table 34.1 presents a comparison on our classification variables between children with high aspirations and those with low

aspirations. In Table 34.1, comparing the high- and low-aspiring boys, little difference is found in their SAT scores, or the levels of the fathers' and mothers' educational levels, or the fathers' occupational levels. The same is true for the girls, with the exception that the low-aspiring girls tend to have mothers with high occupational levels. As expected for both low-aspiring girls and boys, the fathers' educational levels tend to be higher, and significantly so for the girls. This was expected because the selection process was based on the occupational level of the fathers, which is strongly correlated with educational level. The mean values of the fathers' occupational level and the students' occupational choice are given in Table 34.1. The results of the statistical tests show that the high- and low-aspiring groups seem to be different.

TABLE 34.1. A Comparison of High and Low Aspirers on SAT Scores and Other Variables

	Girls				Boys			
	High Aspirers (N = 165)		Low Aspirers (N = 69)		High Aspirers (N = 105)		Low Aspirers (N = 45)	
	Mean	SD	Mean	SD	Mean	SD	Mean	SD
SAT verbal	432	93.4	431	107.0	435	87.2	447	85.2
Mothers' educational level	2.9	1.2	3.1	1.2	2.8	1.2	3.2	1.2
Mothers' occupational level	3.4 (N = 79)	0.9	3.8^a (N = 32)	0.7	3.5 (N = 53)	1.4	3.5 (N = 23)	0.8
Fathers' educational level	3.1	1.2	3.5^a	1.2	3.1	1.4	3.5	1.3
Fathers' occupational level	3.1	0.9	3.8^c	0.4	3.2	0.9	3.6^b	0.6
Students' occupational choice level	4.6	0.6	3.6^c	0.5	4.8	0.4	3.4^c	0.7

^{a} $p < 0.05$.
^{b} $p < 0.01$.
^{c} $p < 0.001$.

TABLE 34.2. Percentage of Personality Types of High and Low
Aspirers and Their Parents Using Holland Codes

	Children		Mothers		Fathers	
	High Aspirers	Low Aspirers	High Aspirers	Low Aspirers	High Aspirers	Low Aspirers
Girls	($N = 166$)	($N = 69$)	($N = 166$)	($N = 66$)	($N = 166$)	($N = 69$)
Realistic	7.6	9.0	1.4	1.3	19.5	7.2^a
Investigative	34.4	13.3^a	4.7	6.6	14.7	12.4
Artistic	24.3	22.6	23.6	23.7	2.7	3.9
Social	24.6	36.9^a	43.9	44.8	20.3	21.8
Enterprising	8.4	12.1^c	17.2	14.0	27.8	35.8^b
Conventional	0.1	6.2^a	9.0	9.7	15.0	19.0
Boys	($N = 105$)	($N = 45$)	($N = 103$)	($N = 45$)	($N = 105$)	($N = 45$)
Realistic	12.7	20.9^b	3.0	1.9	16.7	12.7
Investigative	40.9	20.5^a	2.3	5.4^c	13.7	17.8
Artistic	19.6	14.9	22.1	24.1	2.9	5.9^c
Social	17.1	24.1^c	41.7	45.2	21.4	21.0
Enterprising	7.4	12.1^c	22.3	15.4^c	31.2	27.7
Conventional	2.4	7.6^a	8.8	7.7	14.2	15.0

$^a p < 0.001$.
$^b p < 0.01$.
$^c p < 0.05$.

Table 34.2 presents the distributions of personality codes in the four groups of children and their parents. From Table 34.2, high and low aspirers of both sexes are distinctly different: the dominant code of high aspirers is Investigative, while the dominant code of low aspirers is Social. Mothers of high-aspiring boys are much higher on the Enterprising component than mothers of low-aspiring boys ($p < 0.05$). Girls with low aspirations have a profile more similar to their mothers', both notably high on Social, while those with high aspirations most resemble their fathers, who are lower than the mothers on Social and higher than the mothers on Investigative. Both high- and low-aspiring boys have profiles resembling more closely their fathers' than their mothers'.

Table 34.3 shows the average scores of congruency of personality codes of the parents. High-aspiring boys and low-aspiring girls have parents whose personalities are significantly more congruent than those of low-aspiring boys and high-aspiring girls. A X^2 test revealed that these differences were significant ($p < 0.05$).

DISCUSSION

A consideration qualifies the results presented here: The subjects are very bright

TABLE 34.3. Comparisons of the Parental Congruency
Scores of High and Low Aspirers

	High Aspirers			Low Aspirers		
	N	Mean	SD	N	Mean	SD
Girls	163	2.52	0.95	66	2.74^a	0.70
Boys	104	2.79	0.93	45	2.69^a	0.96

$^a p < 0.05$.

children from a poorly defined population. Thus one must be cautious in generalizing interpretations of results. However, the significance of the effects found despite the noise of the data suggests that the effects are real.

Five interesting points are contained in the foregoing results.

First, SAT scores for the group were on a par with those of college-bound high school juniors, indicating that the subjects were overall quite talented.

Second, the personality profiles of high aspirers clearly differ from those of low aspirers. The high-aspiring groups can be characterized as Investigative while the low-aspiring groups appear to be Social. In the Holland model, this indicates that the high-aspiring youngsters are introspective and prefer "creative investigation of physical, biological, and cultural phenomena in order to understand and control such phenomena; and . . . [have] an aversion to persuasive, social, and repetitive activities" (Holland, 1973: 14). On the other hand, the low aspirers prefer "activities that entail the manipulation of others to inform, train, develop, cure, or enlighten; and an aversion to explicit, ordered, systematic activities involving materials, tools, or machines . . . [and have] human relations competencies such as interpersonal and educational competencies and . . . a deficit in manual and technical competencies" (Holland, 1973: 16).

Third, girls with high aspirations have profiles more similar to their fathers' profiles, whereas the low aspirers more closely resemble their mothers. Low aspirers shun the vocations of their fathers and select socially oriented careers. It appears, then, that the high-aspiring girls may model themselves after their fathers. In contrast, the low aspirers do not.

Fourth, the boys in the high-aspiring group have enterprising mothers, which suggests that their mothers may influence their achievement motivation. High vocational aspirations are characteristic of the enterprising type; such persons are ambitious and value political and economic achievement. Moreover, an enterprising person has "a preference for activities that entail the manipulation of others to attain organizational goals for economic gain . . . and leadership, interpersonal, and persuasive competencies" (Holland, 1973: 16). Thus the high-aspiring boys seem to be positively influenced by both their mothers and their fathers.

Fifth, relative to the low-aspiring boys, the high-aspiring boys come from families in which the parents' personalities are consistent with one another. Thus the high-aspiring boys live in familial environments where, in comparison with the low-aspiring boys, there is less likelihood of interpersonal tensions between the parents. For the high-aspiring girls, however, the situation is precisely reversed; it is the parents with the less congruent personalities who produce the upwardly aspiring girls.

Bearing in mind the restrictions in generality entailed by our highly selected sample, these findings suggest a tentative formulation of the childhood origins of achievement motivation. Boys with high achievement motivation are intellectually self-confident and come from supportive, fairly stable family environments in which the mother is likely to be economically and socially ambitious. High achievement motivation in boys can be explained in terms of effective socialization to norms of achievement in which the desire to achieve is enhanced by a stable, harmonious home environment supplied by parents with similar values, by the presence of an acceptable paternal model, and by the extra encouragement provided by an achievement-oriented mother. Thus parental models and a harmonious home environment rather than a discrete set of childrearing tactics *per se* may be critical for the development of achievement motivation in boys. Douvan and Adelson (1958) present evidence for a theory of the personality determinants of mobility in adolescent boys that is consistent with this description. The picture of the high-aspiring girl is quite different. She more often models after her father than her mother and comes from an environment in which the parents have inconsistent personalities; according to Holland (1973), she is thus "likely to develop an inaccurate picture of [her] self and the world, inconsistent values, inconsistent interests and competencies, and little self-confidence." This often leads to personal ineffectiveness and instability (Holland, 1973: 43). Thus a female with high achievement motivation may be conflicted and insecure. One can surmise that she is also not well socialized —that she is in conflict with the norms of her family and social group. This interpretation is consistent with the view that women in our society are role-conflicted, that professional women may be even more so (*cf.* Stein and Bailey, 1973), and that adolescent girls with high occupational aspirations are incompletely identified with their mothers (*cf.* Douvan and Adelson, 1966; Lansky *et al.,* 1961). In summary, achievement motivation in boys may be explained in terms of exposure to dynamic, ambitious, achievement-oriented mothers, to an acceptable paternal model, and to parents with similar values. In contrast, achievement motivation in girls may arise from exposure to parental conflict, and from modeling after the parent of opposite sex. In both cases, achievement motivation may be a function of modeling rather than experience with a particular set of childrearing practices designed to foster independence and self-esteem. It follows that unambitious, disaffected, anergic parents may have considerable difficulty producing upwardly mobile children.

ACKNOWLEDGMENTS

The authors wish to thank Catherine Garvey, John Holland, and Roger Webb for their helpful comments concerning this paper.

REFERENCES

Douvan, E., & Adelson, J. The psychodynamics of social mobility in adolescent boys. *Journal Abnormal Social Psychology,* 1958, **56**, 31-44.

Douvan, E., & Adelson, J. *The adolescent experience.* New York: John Wiley & Sons, 1966.

Duncan, O. D., Featherman, D. L., & Duncan, B. Socioeconomic background and occupational achievement: Extensions of a basic model. Final Report, Project No. 5-0074 (EO-191), U.S. Department of Health, Education, and Welfare, Office of Education, Bureau of Research, Washington, D.C., 1968.

Holland, J. L. *Making vocational choices: A theory of careers,* Englewood Cliffs, N.J.: Prentice-Hall, 1973.

Holland, J. L., Viernstein, M. C., Kuo, H., Karweit, N. L., & Blum, Z. D. A psychological classification of occupations. *Journal Supplement Abstract Service,* 1972, **2**, 84.

Lansky, L. M., Crandall, V. J., Kagan, J., & Baker, C. T. Sex differences in aggression and its correlates in middle class adolescents. *Child development,* 1961, **32**, 45-58.

McClelland, D. C., Atkinson, J. W., Clark, R. A., & Lowell, E. L. *The achievement motive,* New York: Appleton-Century-Crofts, 1953.

Rosen, B. C., & D'Andrade, R. G. The psychosocial origin of achievement motivation. *Sociometry,* 1959, **22**, 185-218.

Shuy, R. W., Wolfram, W. A., & Riley, W. K. *Field techniques in an urban language study.* Washington, D.C.: Center for Applied Linguistics, 1968.

Stein, A. H., & Bailey, M. M. The socialization of achievement orientation in females. *Psychological Bulletin,* 1973, **80,** 345-366.

Viernstein, M. C. The extension of Holland's occupational classification to all occupations in the Dictionary of Occupational Titles. *Journal Vocational Behavior,* 1972, **2,** 107-121.

Weiner, B., and Kukla, A. An attributional analysis of achievement motivation. *Journal of Personality and Social Psychology,* 1970, **15,** 1-20.

35.

Steven R. Forness

IMPLICATIONS OF RECENT TRENDS IN EDUCATIONAL LABELING

Special educators have historically tended to consider each category of exceptional children as homogeneous, containing *one* kind of child requiring *one* kind of educational approach. Such an approach was generally conceived as being distinct and separate from other approaches required in other categories. Thus a child with a "learning disability" may have been treated rather differently from a child with "emotional problems" or a child with "mental retardation." Each may have been assigned to separate special classes with teachers prepared exclusively to teach in one specialty but not in others. Under this system, considerable emphasis was placed on etiology, diagnosis, and classification.

It is now clear that special education is undergoing a transformation in the use of categorical labels. There is a decided shift away from traditional labels with readily defined and mutually exclusive categories, a trend which would seem to have serious implications for the way in which children with learning problems are both managed and taught in school settings. There have been successful attempts to group the learning disabled, mildly retarded, emotionally disturbed, and children with other types of handicaps together in the same classrooms with teachers who have been prepared to deal with a wide variety of learning and behavior problems (Taylor *et al.,* 1972). A child with the symptoms of dyslexia, under this system, may work in a classroom side by side with retarded children or children with psychiatric problems. He may be taught with materials and techniques devised previously exclusively for

Source: *Journal of Learning Disabilities,* 1974, **7,** 445-449, © 1974 by the Professional Press. Preparation of this paper was supported, in part, by grants to the UCLA Child Psychiatry and Mental Retardation Program from the U.S. Office of Education (OEG-0-72-3974 (603)) and NICHD (HD-04612, 00345 and 05615).

these children. In terms of instruction, traditional distinctions between himself and other exceptional children are being increasingly diminished.

ORIGINS OF DISENCHANTMENT WITH LABELS

Nowhere has the trend away from a categorical label been more obvious than in the field called "mental retardation." Historically, classes for severely retarded children were located in separate special schools or institutional settings. Subsequently, classes for mildly retarded children were organized in regular public schools. Under the latter model, the school was considered the primary agent for labeling exceptional children (Robbins *et al.*, 1967). Ordinarily, after having failed academically in the regular classroom, a child was referred for placement in a special classroom where he remained for most of his school day—segregated almost completely from normal peers and, for that matter, from other exceptional children. Many states began to mandate such classes during the late 1940's, and the accompanying educational regulations resulted in a "calcification" of the label for children so identified. There are, however, several problems with such classes—problems which led some people to question seriously the relevance of labels such as "mental retardation."

For example, research has failed to show conclusively that special class placement is any more beneficial for certain children than simply leaving them in a regular classroom in competition with normal peers (Forness, 1972; MacMillan, 1973). Other evidence has shown that a child who is labeled mentally retarded may behave as he does in academic situations not necessarily because he is intellectually

retarded, but because the label contributes substantially to a teacher's expectation of his academic progress (Beez, 1971; Elashoff & Snow, 1971). For a more complete review of labeling issues, the reader is referred to Jones (1972). While none of this work is conclusive, it nonetheless suggests that *some* children who have been labeled in the past as mentally retarded actually fulfill the role of a retardate only when certain social conditions (i.e., the special class) are imposed upon them. It should be mentioned that this notion of culturally referenced mental retardation in the field of education is a social development which runs historically parallel to a similar notion of mental illness in the field of psychiatry, in which the diagnosis of mental illness is seen as a function of local norms and cultural needs (Rosenhan, 1973; Szasz, 1970). It should also be noted that there has been little parallel inquiry into the effect of other commonly used labels—for example, "hyperkinesis" or "learning disorder."

The widespread use of behavior modification as an approach to educational problems has also contributed substantially to the present disenchantment with categorical labels. Since behavior modification tends to minimize use of labels and concentrate instead on performance, it is perhaps no accident that analysis of the effects of labeling emerged as a serious form of inquiry at the same time that behavior modification grew as an educational technique.

Accumulated dissatisfaction with labeling began to coalesce in the late 1960s. While reasons for abandoning the cherished notion of special class placement had long been evident, an article by Dunn (1968) was the first serious suggestion that the time had come to do so. It was also at about this time that a series of class-action lawsuits were brought against several school districts across the nation on behalf of parents whose children had been either misdiagnosed or misplaced in special classes for the mentally retarded (Ross *et al.*, 1971). Such cases, commonly but not invariably, involved minority-group plaintiffs who had either been unfairly tested for intellectual potential or who had been placed in special classes for the retarded even though, strictly speaking, they did not meet the standards for admission to these classes. Redress was sought mainly through injunction to return such children to regular classes, with supplementary services as necessary to help them maintain satisfactory educational progress in the regular grades. School administrators found themselves suddenly on the defensive and momentarily lost the initiative in educational decision-making to the courts.

It was also in the late 1960s that a project was initiated which eventually demonstrated that children previously separated in special classes for the mentally retarded, the emotionally disturbed, and the learning disabled could be effectively grouped together in a single school setting (Taylor *et al.*, 1972). Developed in a California public school system, this was essentially a method whereby handicapped children were assigned to a "learning center" on the basis of their educational or behavioral deficits irrespective of their previous special education labels. These deficits were defined with reference to the child's readiness for regular classroom functioning, and every child in the program spent as much time as was individually possible in a regular classroom that was regarded as his primary assignment. Emphasis was on the settings, tasks, and incentives necessary to move the child toward full participation in a regular classroom. Hence, administrative emphasis

began to shift from categorical *labels* to categorical *needs*.

IMPLICATIONS

One of the first responses toward *formally* divesting the field of its traditional categorical labels has already come in California. The master plan for special education in that state declares that a single category of special education will henceforth exist, this category to be called "children with exceptional needs" (California State Department of Education, 1973). It further allows a variety of administrative arrangements for such children, ranging in degree from placement in special centers or special classes to full-time placement in regular classrooms with only occasional direct or indirect assistance from a special education resource person as needed. Thus several types of exceptional children will be given equal access to a variety of educational arrangements; and, as indicated in the master plan, even so-called normal children with *occasional* problems in learning or behavior will be eligible for such special education. While the California plan does not represent the final word in delabeling, it does represent a significant acknowledgment of change.

It is important to point out that administrative modifications alone do not necessarily eliminate labels. Simply reassigning children into different grouping patterns will not guarantee their decertification from a specific category. The tendency will certainly remain, at least in the transitional phase of decategorization, to use labels as convenient shorthand. This will undoubtedly be the case as children currently in special education are reshuffled into new arrangements. It is interesting to note, in this regard, that the California plan retains at least a vestige of certain labels, but only for accounting and reporting purposes. The "learning center" concept, referred to earlier, also employs a labeling system; but these labels are now connotative of a child's readiness for regular classroom functioning—e.g., "pre-academic" vs. "academic," and thus imply a sense of movement toward a goal. This is quite uncharacteristic of traditional labels.

Ways must be found to reconceptualize not only the way such children are grouped but the very ways in which professionals think about them. The traditional labeling stimuli associated with what a child is must be dropped and he must be perceived in relation to what he needs in order to achieve his optimum school progress. This should come more easily as new, previously unlabeled children enter the system for the first time, and any professional's preconceptions have had increasingly less chance to operate on his individuality.

The full implication of these changes for education of children called learning disabled, however, is not yet clear. At least part of the rationale for self-contained programs for any category of exceptional children was that these children require special materials and approaches not found in regular classes or in other special programs. Just as parents and professionals seem recently to be achieving a measure of success in the organization and funding of special classes for learning disabled children, the framework of services for all special children is being modified. Separate provisions based on traditional diagnostic distinctions will no longer be the rule. While this approach would seem to benefit some types of exceptional children (*e.g.,* those labeled as mentally retarded), is there any compelling reason to think that those children now labeled as learning disabled will benefit as well?

One clear advantage will be a breakdown of traditional barriers between educators working in various categories. Advances in one area of exceptionality have traditionally been slow to permeate other areas. Behavior modification techniques, for example, were historically developed and refined with severely disturbed and retarded children. Such techniques have been relatively slow to be adopted by teachers of learning disabled and hyperkinetic children, not because of limited applicability, but because of the field's early preoccupation with supposed underlying neurological mechanisms. Until recently, the heavy neurological emphasis over-shadowed serious consideration of motivational components of learning disability or hyperkinesis (Keogh, 1971).

A review of educational practices with exceptional children reveals many more similarities than differences across categories (Hewett, 1974). Yet, there remains a proliferation of separate teacher training programs, specialty textbooks, and specialized consultants—a decidedly inefficient use of manpower and resources. Consolidation of these limited resources would seem much more likely under a noncategorical system. The same inefficiency is obvious in a system which spends an inordinate amount of time in classifying and diagnosing children for eligibility for special classes or learning disability groups. This practice has often led to uncertainty in making a decision as to whether a child diagnosed as dyslexic with accompanying behavior problems was better placed in a learning disability group or in a class for the emotionally disturbed, or whether a hyperkinetic child with borderline intelligence was better served in a class for the retarded or in a class for the educationally handicapped. While such pigeonholing inevitably deprived some children of needed services, the noncategorical system enables a variety of services to be rendered to each child. It also frees certain resources that might otherwise be tied up in providing full-time special placement to a child who needs only limited services in one area, e.g., perceptual training.

Traditional roles which ancillary professionals now fulfill with learning disabled children are also quite likely to be affected. There continues to be doubt that the intellectual and perceptual testing ordinarily performed by psychologists is of any direct use in remediation (Camp, 1973). This criticism is certain to be intensified under a noncategorical system, and modality-based treatment programs based on such testing are also certain to be modified (Lilly & Kelleher, 1973). One is even led to wonder if school psychologists, as their training is presently constituted, will continue to have a function under the present scheme. Likewise, pediatricians and other medical specialists may find that specialty clinics organized around medical aspects of "hyperkinesis" or "learning disability" tend to become outmoded as educators become relatively less preoccupied with questions of diagnosis and etiology and more concerned with optimal curriculum materials and motivational approaches. The physician's present consultative role to school districts is also likely to be transformed for the same reason.

While ancillary professionals can survive these changes, teacher training programs and teachers in existing categories are likely to need extensive and somewhat taxing rejuvenation. As with most trends, transition can be expected to proceed quite unevenly at state, local, and federal levels. Federal monies for teacher training programs in the Bureau of Education of the Handicapped, U.S. Office of Education, continue to be funneled through categorical channels. There is as yet no clear conceptualization of content needed for training programs to prepare "generic"

special education teachers. Target dates for implementation of much of the California noncategorical plan are set for late 1975; yet it is doubtful that preservice programs will have any appreciable numbers of "generalists" available by that time. In-service efforts to broaden the training of categorically prepared teachers already in the field may have to bear the brunt of personnel preparation efforts. This approach to the problem could create considerable variability in credentialing and standards, not only from state to state but from district to district.

While such tactical problems can easily be solved and are not mentioned here as criticism of the noncategorical strategy, the transitional phase is certain to interrupt the momentum of professionals in the learning disability area. The field of learning disabilities, historically one of the more recently developed areas in special education, has avoided many of the pitfalls of other specialties. For example, programs for learning disabled children have not necessarily adhered to a one-dimensional, special-class model but offer a wide range of options for delivery of services, including integrated special classes, resource teachers, learning disability groups, and diagnostic classrooms. Along with these options, an impressive cadre of specialists is available, within and ancillary to the field of education. It is possible, at least in the transitional phase of moving toward a "generalist" orientation, that the field will be less able to afford the type of precise specialization in which a professional deals exclusively with one type of handicapping condition. Such a loss, however transitory, to the field of learning disabilities is obviously a gain for the field at large, since the learning disabilities model, if one can call it that, is in fact very similar to the model required for delivery of services under a no-label system.

It is conceivable that the specialized, well delineated, perceptual-motor training programs (many of which have been used in the learning disability field) will be broadened and adapted to fit a wide variety of disabled children, including those now regarded as retarded or sensory handicapped. It is likewise conceivable that these expanded approaches will, in circular fashion, return to use with learning disabled children, with adaptations derived from other areas including the social learning and motivational contexts recently characteristic of education for the retarded.

It remains to be determined whether placing children who are now in learning disability classrooms in programs with children traditionally regarded as mentally retarded or emotionally disturbed will be disadvantageous in areas as yet unforeseen. While the effect of a "no-label" system may be advantageous to some children (e.g., those labeled mentally retarded), it is by no means certain that either teachers or other children *outside* the system will treat exceptional children as a group any differently. It is, further, conceivable that the same misconceptions and biases that the layman now reserves for emotional disturbance and mental retardation might generalize to learning disabled children as well. As mentioned earlier, however, there is no evidence to guarantee that similar expectancies are not already generated by present programs and labels for learning disability children. Indeed, emphasis on individualized programming, which is necessitated under the new system by immediate focus on each child's educational needs, gives one reason to be hopeful that all children will be better served. The time is here for professionals in various specialty areas to come together in serious consideration of these possibilities.

REFERENCES

Beez, W. V. Influence of biased psychological reports on teacher behavior and pupil performance. In M. W. Miles (ed.), *Learning in social settings.* Boston: Allyn & Bacon, 1971.

California State Department of Education. Master Plan for Special Education (1st Draft). Sacramento, 1973.

Camp, B. W. Psychometric tests and learning in severely disabled readers. *Journal of Learning Disabilities,* 1973, **6**, 512-517.

Dunn, L. M. Special education for the mildly retarded—is much of it justifiable? *Exceptional Children,* 1968, **35**, 5-22.

Elashoff, J. D., & Snow, R. E. *Pygmalion reconsidered: A case study in statistical inference.* Worthington, Ohio: Charles A. Jones, 1971.

Forness, S. R.: The mildly retarded as casualties of the educational system. *Journal School Psychology,* 1972, **10**, 117-126.

Hewett, F. M., with Forness, S. R. *Education of exceptional learners.* Boston: Allyn & Bacon, 1974.

Jones, R. L. Labels and stigma in special education. *Exceptional Children,* 1972, **38**, 553-564.

Keogh, B. K. Hyperactivity and learning disorders: Review and speculation. *Exceptional Children,* 1971, **38**, 101-109.

Lilly, S. M., & Kelleher, J. Modality strengths and aptitude treatment interaction. *Journal Special Education,* 1973, **7**, 5-13.

MacMillan, D. L. Issues and trends in special education. *Mental Retardation,* 1973, **11**, 3-8.

Robbins, R. C., Mercer, J. R., & Meyers, C. E. The school as a collecting-labeling system. *Journal School Psychology,* 1967, **5**, 270-279.

Rosenhan, D. On being sane in insane places. *Science,* 1973, **179**, 250-258.

Ross, S. R., DeYoung, H. G., & Cohen, J. S. Confrontation: Special education placement and the law. *Exceptional Children,* 1971, **38**, 5-12.

Szasz, T. *The manufacture of madness.* New York: Dell, 1970.

Taylor, F. D., *et al.:* A learning center plan for special education. *Focus on Exceptional Children,* 1972, **4**, 1-7.

36.

Teodoro Ayllon, Dale Layman, and Henry J. Kandel

A BEHAVIORAL-EDUCATIONAL ALTERNATIVE TO DRUG CONTROL OF HYPERACTIVE CHILDREN

Hyperactivity or hyperkinesis in the classroom is a clinical condition characterized by excessive movement, inpredictable behaviors, unawareness of consequences, inability to focus on and concentrate on a particular task, and poor academic performance (Stewart, Pitts, Craig, & Dieruf, 1966). It is estimated that about 200,000 children in the United States are currently receiving amphetamines to control their hyperactivity (Krippner, Silverman, Cavallo, & Healy, 1973).

Drugs such as methylphenidate (Ritalin) and chlorpromazine have been shown to control hyperactivity in the laboratory and applied settings. The evidence from the laboratory is based on recording devices actuated by the child's movements (Hollis & St. Omer, 1972; Sprague, Barnes, & Werry, 1970; Sykes, Douglas, Weiss, & Minde, 1971). In the classroom, children have been rated by their teachers along various dimensions to determine the effectiveness of stimulants on their behavior. Comly (1971) found that of forty hyperactive children, whose behavior was rated twice weekly by teachers, those children receiving stimulants were rated as having better listening ability, less excitability, less forgetfulness, and better peer relationships. In a similar study, Denhoff,

Davis, and Hawkins (1971) showed that teachers rated hyperactive children on dextro-amphetamine (Dexedrine) as improved on measures of hyperactivity, short attention span, and impulsivity. In addition, global ratings by parents, teachers, and clinicians have shown that drugs such as methylphenidate (Ritalin) and dextro-amphetamine decreased children's hyperactivity in school and at home (Conners, 1971).

While there is still some conflicting evidence on drug effectiveness (Krippner *et al.*, 1973), as well as a growing ethical concern for the morality and wisdom implied in administering medication to children (Fish, 1971; Hentoff, 1970; Keogh, 1971; Ladd, 1970), drugs are commonly used to control hyperactivity in the classroom.

Because the often-implied objective behind the use of drugs for the hyperactive child is that of enabling him to profit academically, it is surprising that few data directly support this belief. Most studies have measured the effect of medication on component skills of learning, *e.g.*, attention, concentration, and discrimination. For example, Conners and Rothschild (1968), Epstein, Lasagna, Conners, Rodriguez (1968), Knights and Hinton (1968) tested drug effects on general intelligence test performance. Sprague *et al.* (1970) studied children's responses of "same" or "different" to pairs of visual stimuli presented on a screen. Conners, Eisenberg, and Sharpe (1964) studied the effects of methylphenidate (Ritalin) on paired-asso-

Source: *Journal of Applied Behavior Analysis,* 1975, **8**, 137-146. The cooperative spirit of the parents and teachers of the children in this study is gratefully acknowledged. Special thanks go to Dr. E. Ensminger for his unflagging interest and encouragement.

ciate learning and Porteus Maze performance in children with hyperactive symptoms. Others (Conners, Eisenberg, & Barcai, 1967; Sprague & Toppe, 1966), concentrated their efforts on the effects of drugs on the attention of hyperactive children to various tasks. These laboratory studies investigated the effects of drugs on component skills related to learning, but they did not measure academic performance *per se* (*e.g.,* math and reading) in the classroom.

Sulzbacher (1972) experimentally analyzed the effects of drugs on academic behaviors of hyperactive children in the classroom. Measures of correct solutions and error rates were taken in arithmetic, writing, and reading in three hyperactive children. In addition, measures were taken of the children's rates of talk-outs in class and their rates of out-of-seat behavior during class. The children were successively given a placebo, then 5 mg of dextro-amphetamine (Dexedrine), and finally 10 mg of dextro-amphetamine. The results showed that medication of 5 mg improved the children's academic responses; however, there was wide variance in academic performance when the children were administered 10 mg. The results for social behavior also varied. Of two children, one showed less hyperactive classroom behavior (talk-outs and out-of-seat behavior) at a dosage level different than the second child. However, the placebo had more effect on controlling the third child's behavior than did medication. The author's conclusion was that stimulant drugs "can effectively modify disruptive behaviors without adversely affecting academic performance in the classroom." Drug effects on academic performance, however, were highly variable.

Since Sulzbacher's major interest was in determining the role of drugs on hyperactivity and academic performance, he did not pursue behavioral alternatives to the control of hyperactivity. Yet, there is at present, a body of established findings indicating that such alternatives may be available. For example, O'Leary and Becker (1967) found that when children were rewarded for sitting, making eye contact with the teacher, and engaging in academically related activities, their misbehavior was virtually eliminated. Ayllon, Layman, and Burke (1972) showed that misbehavior may be also reduced, not by rewarding the child for good conduct, but by imposing academic structure in the classroom. This structure involved giving academic assignments with a short time limit for their completion. Ayllon and Roberts (1974) found that another behavioral technique to eliminate classroom misbehavior is to reward children for academic performance only. These findings suggest that disruptive behavior can be weakened by reinforcing incompatible academic performance. Using this method, the child performs well both academically and socially without treating the disruptive behavior directly.

The children in the above studies were disruptive, not hyperactive. Although the topography of the response is similar, hyperactivity differs from distruption in its magnitude, duration, and frequency. Illustrations of this difference are well documented, indicating that hyperactive children are in constant motion, fidget excessively, frequently enter and leave the classroom, move from one class activity to another, and rarely complete their projects or stay with one particular game or activity. Their academic performance is typically poor (Campbell, Douglas, & Morgenstern, 1971; Freibergs & Douglas, 1969; Stewart, Pitts, Craig, & Dieruf, 1966; Sykes, Douglas, Weiss, & Minde, 1971).

Two questions arise:

Can behavioral techniques used to decrease disruptive behavior be at least as effective as drugs in controlling an extreme form of classroom misbehavior such as hyperactivity? At the same time, can such techniques help the hyperactive child to grow educationally? The present study attempted to answer these questions.

METHOD

Subjects and setting

Three school children (Crystal, Paul, and Dudley), clinically diagnosed as chronically hyperactive, were all receiving drugs to control their hyperactivity.

Crystal was an 8-yr-old girl. She was 47 inches (118 cm) tall and weighed 76 pounds (34.2 kg). She had an I.Q. of 118 as measured on the WISC. She was enrolled in a learning-disabilities class because of the hyperactive behavior she displayed before taking medication and because of her poor academic work. She had been on drugs since she was 5 years old, when her doctor felt that her behavior was so unpredictable that he prescribed 5 mg of methylphenidate q.i.d. to calm her down.

Paul was a 9-yr-old boy. He was 53 inches (133 cm) tall and weighed 65 pounds (29.2 kg). He had an I.Q. of 94 as measured on the WISC. He had been enrolled in the learning-disabilities class for 2 years before the study and had been taking 5 mg of methylphenidate b.i.d. for 1 year to control his hyperactive behavior.

Dudley was a 10-yr-old boy. He was 55 inches (138 cm) tall and weighed 76 pounds (34.2 kg). He had an I.Q. of 103 as measured on the WISC. He was enrolled in a learning-disabilities class for 2 years before the study and on the advice of his doctor had been taking 5 mg of methylphenidate t.i.d. for 4 years.

In addition to their drug treatment,

Crystal and Dudley were under the care of a child psychiatrist and a pediatrician during the study.

The three children attended a private elementary school. They were enrolled in a self-contained learning disability class of ten children and one teacher. The children and the teacher remained together throughout the school day in the same room. Other personnel during the study consisted of two observer-recorders: one of the authors and an undergraduate student.

Response definition

Hyperactivity and academic performance across two academic periods, math and reading, were measured.

Math. Math was defined as addition of whole numbers under 10. The teacher wrote ten problems on the board at the beginning of each class. The children were given 10 minutes to complete the problems. Problems were taken from Laidlaw Series Workbooks, Levels P and 1.

Reading. Reading was defined as comprehension and was measured by workbook responses to previously read stories in a basal reader. Each child had 20 minutes to complete a ten-question workbook page per day. The books were Merril-Linguistic Readers - 3. In both math and reading, the written response served as a permanent product from which the percentage of correct answers could be determined.

The academic assignments in both math and reading increased slightly in difficulty as the child progressed through the work.

Hyperactivity. Since hyperactive behavior has overlapping topographical properties with other deviant behaviors, hyperactive behavior was defined using the same response definition as presented by Becker, Madsen, Arnold, and Thomas for deviant behavior in the classroom (1967). To define and record deviant behavior, Becker and his colleagues used seven general categories of behavior incompatible with learning. These included gross motor behaviors, disruptive noise with objects, disturbing others, orienting responses, blurting out, talking, and other miscellaneous behaviors incompatible with learning. In the present experiment, the behaviors of the hyperactive children most often fell into the following four categories: gross motor behaviors, disruptive noise, disturbing others, and blurting out. The most frequently recorded category for these hyperactive children was gross motor behaviors, which included running around the room, rocking in chairs, and jumping on one or both feet. Disruptive noise with objects included the constant turning of book pages and the excessive flipping of notebook paper. Disturbing others and blurting out included the constant movement of arms, resulting in the destruction of objects and hitting others, screaming, and high-pitched and rapid speech. Categories that were not recorded with any consistency included orienting responses and talking, as in a conversation with another person. Thus, although the response definition for deviant behavior was used, the actual recording was heavily weighted on those behaviors described by Stewart *et al.* (1966) as being typical of hyperactive children.

Observational and Recording Procedure for Hyperactivity. Initially, six children were identified by the school director as being hyperactive and receiving medication for it. These children were observed across two class periods: math and reading. The duration of each class period was 45 minutes. Each child was observed in successive order on a time-sample of 25 seconds. At the end of each 25-second interval, the behavior of the child under observation was coded as showing hyperactivity or its absence. At that time, the observer marked a single slash in the appropriate interval, on a recording sheet, if one or more hyperactive behaviors occurred. If no hyperactive behaviors were observed at that time, the appropriate interval was marked with an "O." The number of intervals of hyperactivity over the total number of intervals for each child gave the observer the per cent of intervals in which each child was hyperactive. Each of the six children was observed a total of seventeen times per 45-minute class period. Using this recording procedure, it was possible to determine, during baseline, that the most chronically hyperactive children were Crystal, Paul, and Dudley. By dropping observations on the less-severely hyperactive children it was possible to increase the number of observations for the chronically hyperactive ones. Recording hyperactivity from one child to the next was now sampled about every 18 seconds in the manner described above. Each child was now observed approximately fifty times each class period throughout the remaining phases of the experiment.

Observer Agreement on Academic Performance and Hyperactivity. The percentage of correct math and reading problems was checked by the teacher and one of the authors each day and the obtained agreement score was 100% on each occasion for each child.

Reliability checks for hyperactivity were taken by one of the authors and one of three undergraduate students in Special Education. The student was given the list of deviant behaviors described by Becker *et al.* (1967) one day before the reliability check to become familiar with the responses. The students were not told of the purpose of the study or of the changes in experimental conditions. Each observer during the reliability check used a watch with a sweep second hand. In addition, a prepared sheet showed the observers the sequence in which the children were to be sampled and the intervals at the end of which each observer was to look at the subject and record whether or not the behavior was occurring at that instant. Each observer sat on opposite sides of the room to ensure unbiased observations.

The percentage of agreement for hyperactive as well as nonhyperactive behavior was calculated by comparing each interval and dividing agreements in each by the total number of observations and multiplying by 100. Reliability checks were taken to include the baseline period under medication (Blocks 2, 3, 5, and 6; in Figures 1, 2, and 3), the period when medication was discontinued and no reinforcement was available (Blocks 7 and 9), and the final period when reinforcement was introduced in both math and reading (Block 11). Reliability scores for hyperactivity for each child were always more than 85% with the scores ranging from a low of 87% to a high of 100%. The average reliability score was 97%.

Check-Point System and Back-Up Reinforcers. A token reinforcement system similar to that used by O'Leary and Becker (1967) in a classroom setting was used. Children were awarded checks by the teacher on an index card. One check was recorded for each correct academic response. The checks could be exchanged for a large array of back-up reinforcers later in the day. The back-up reinforcers ranged in price from one check to seventy-five checks, and included such items and activities as candy, school supplies, free time, lunch in the teacher's room, and picnics in the park.

Procedure

Each subject's daily level of hyperactivity and academic achievement, on and off medication, were directly observed and recorded before the behavioral program. In addition, using a multiple-baseline design, the relative effectiveness of the motivational system on (*a*) hyperactivity, and (*b*) academic performance in math and reading was evaluated. This type of design allowed each child to serve as his own control, thereby minimizing the idiosyncratic drug-behavior interactions that have the potential for confounding the interpretations and even the results when comparing one subject with another. This design is particularly useful in the study of the effects of discontinuing drugs on behavior, since as Sprague *et al.* (1970) and Sulzbacher (1972) have pointed out, the inherent problem in assessing effects of medication lies in the fact that each child reacts to the presence or absence of medication on an individual basis.

The design of the study included the following four phases:

Phase 1: *on medication.* Crystal, Paul, Dudley were observed for 17 days to evaluate hyperactive behavior when they were taking drugs. Academic performance in math and reading was also measured.

With the full cooperation of the children's doctors and their parents, medication was discontinued on the eighteenth day, a Saturday. An additional two days, Sunday and Monday (a school holiday) allowed a three-day "wash-out" period for the effect of medication to disappear. It is known that these stimulant drugs are almost completely metabolized within one day. No measures of hyperactivity or academic performance were obtained during this weekend period.

Phase 2: *off medication.* Following the three-day "wash-out" period, a three-day baseline when the children were off medication was obtained. Time-sampling observations of hyperactivity were continued, as well as measures of academic performance. This phase served as the basis against which the effects of reinforcement on hyperactivity and academic performance could later be compared.

Phase 3: *no medication; reinforcement of math.* During this six-day period, the children remained off drugs while the teacher introduced a reinforcement system for math performance only. Observations of hyperactivity continued and academic performance was measured.

Phase 4: *no medication; reinforcement of math plus reading.* During this six-day phase, the children remained off drugs while reinforcement was added for reading and reinforcement of math was maintained. Observations of hyperactivity and measures of academic performance were continued.

RESULTS

When Ritalin was discontinued, the level of hyperactivity doubled or tripled its initial level. However, when reinforcement was systematically administered for academic performance, hyperactivity for all three children decreased to a level comparable to the initial period when Ritalin chemically controlled it.

Figure 36.1 shows that hyperactivity for Crystal during the drug phase in math averaged about 20%, while academic performance in math was zero. When Ritalin was discontinued, hyperactivity rose to an average of 87% and math performance remained low at an average of 8%. When math was reinforced, and Crystal continued to stay off drugs, hyperactivity dropped significantly from 87% to about 9%. Math performance increased to 65%. Hyperactivity in math was effectively controlled through reinforcement of math performance. However, the multiple-baseline design shows that concurrently Crystal's hyperactivity during reading class

remained at 90% before reinforcement was introduced for correct reading responses.

At the same time measures were taken in the area of math, hyperactivity and academic performance were also measured

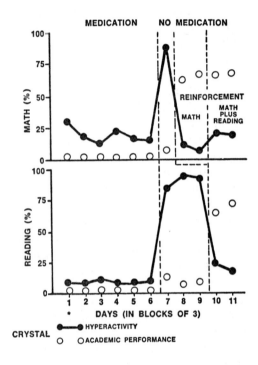

Figure 36.1. Crystal. The percentage of intervals in which hyperactivity took place and the per cent of correct math and reading performance. The first and second segments respectively show the effects of medication, and its subsequent withdrawal, on hyperactivity and academic performance. A multiple-baseline analysis of the effects of reinforcement across math and reading and concurrent hyperactivity is shown starting on the third top segment. The last segment shows the effects of reinforcement on math plus reading and its concurrent effect on hyperactivity. (The asterisk indicates one data point averaged over two rather than three days.)

in the area of reading. Crystal's hyper-activity during reading class averaged approximately 10% under medication. Academic performance in reading was zero under medication. When Crystal was taken off drugs, hyperactivity rose dramat-ically from 10% to an average of 91%. Academic performance remained low at approximately 10%. Only when reinforce-ment was administered for reading was hyperactivity in this area reduced from 91% to 20%. Reading performance in-creased from 10% to an average of 69%.

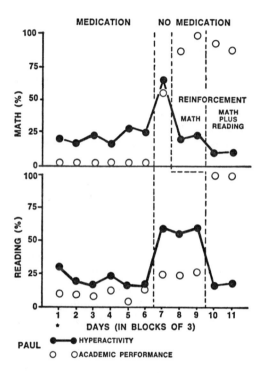

Figure 36.2. Paul. The percentage of in-tervals in which hyperactivity took place and the per cent of correct math and read-ing performance. The first and second seg-ments respectively show the effects of medication, and its subsequent with-drawal, on hyperactivity and academic performance. A multiple-baseline analysis of the effects of reinforcement across math and reading and concurrent hyperactivity is shown starting on the third top segment. The last segment shows the effects of rein-forcement on math plus reading and its concurrent effect on hyperactivity. (The asterisk indicates one data point averaged over two rather than three days.)

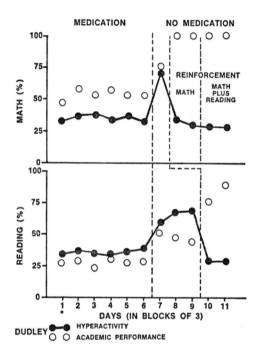

Figure 36.3. Dudley. The percentage of intervals in which hyperactivity took place and the per cent of correct math and reading performance. The first and second segments respectively show the effects of medication, and its subsequent with-drawal, on hyperactivity and academic performance. A multiple-baseline analysis of the effects of reinforcement across math and reading and concurrent hyperactivity is shown starting on the third top segment. The last segment shows the effects of rein-forcement on math plus reading and its concurrent effect on hyperactivity. (The asterisk indicates one data point averaged over two rather than three days.)

Similar results were found for Paul and Dudley, as can be seen in Figures 36.2 and 36.3.

Figure 36.4 shows the pre and post measures of hyperactivity and academic performance for Dudley, Crystal, and Paul as a group. It can be seen that when the children were taking drugs, hyperactivity was well controlled and averaged about 24% during math and reading. When medication was discontinued and a reinforcement program was established to strengthen academic performance, the combined level of hyperactivity was about 20% during math and reading for the three children. This level (20%) of hyperactivity matched that obtained under medication (24%).

During the period when the children were taking drugs, their per cent correct in math and reading combined averaged 12%. When medication was discontinued and a reinforcement program was estab-

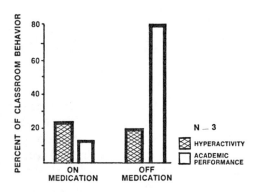

Figure 36.4. Average per cent of hyperactivity and academic performance in math and reading for three children. The first two bars summarize findings from the 17-day baseline under drug therapy. The last two bars show results for the final six-day period without drug therapy but with a reinforcement program for both math and reading performance.

lished, their average per cent correct in both academic subjects increased from 12% to 85%.

DISCUSSION

These findings show that reinforcement of academic performance suppresses hyperactivity, and they thus support and extend the findings of Ayllon and Roberts (1974). Further, the academic gains produced by the behavioral program contrast dramatically with the lack of academic progress shown by these children under medication.[1]

The multiple-baseline design demonstrates that token reinforcement for academic achievement was responsible for the concurrent suppression of hyperactivity. Indeed, while this control was demonstrated during math periods, the children's concurrent hyperactivity during reading remained at a high level, so long as the reinforcement procedure for reading was withheld. Only when reinforcement was introduced for both math and reading performance did the hyperactivity for all three children drop to levels comparable to those controlled by the drug.

The control over hyperactivity by the enhancement of academic performance was quick, stable, and independent of the duration and dosage of the medication received by each child before the program. One child had been under medication for as long as 4 years, another child for 1 year. Despite this extreme difference in history of medication, the behavioral effects were not differential to that history.

When medication was discontinued, hyperactivity increased immediately and to a high level in all three children. The effectiveness of medication in controlling

---

[1]For a systematic replication of this study see Layman, *unpublished.*

hyperactivity, evaluated through direct observations of behavior, supports the data of earlier studies using recordings based on instrumentation (Hollis *et al.,* 1972; Sprague *et al.,* 1970; Sykes *et al.,* 1971).

During the few days of no medication, hyperactivity became so severe that the teacher and parents freely commented on the gross difference in the children's behavior in school and at home. Their reports centered around such descriptions as "He's just like a whirlwind," "She is climbing the walls, it's awful," "Just can't do a thing with her . . ." "He's not attending, doesn't listen to anything I tell him," and others. It was only with a great deal of support and counselling that the teacher and parents were able to tolerate this stressful period. It was this high level of hyperactivity shown by all three children that allowed the opportunity to test the effectiveness of a reinforcement program for academic performance in controlling hyperactivity.

Since both hyperactivity and academic performance increased concurrently, as soon as medication was discontinued, it might be construed that these two dimensions are compatible. This may be an unwarranted conclusion, however, because the slight increments in academic performance concurrent with increments in hyperactivity may only reflect the type of recording method used in this study. For example, measures of the behavior of the children show that once they had finished their academic assignments, they became hyperactive. Thus, academic performance and hyperactivity could take place sequentially. When the time limit for academic performance had expired (*e.g.,* after 10 or 20 minutes, depending on the subject matter) the child could engage in hyperactivity for the rest of the class period.

It usually took only one session for each

child to learn that academic performance was associated with reinforcement while hyperactivity was not, suggesting that in the absence of medication these children react to reinforcement as normal children do. The classroom with reinforcement procedures now set the occasion for academic performance, rather than hyperactivity.

The present results suggest that the continued use of Ritalin and possibly other drugs to control hyperactivity may result in compliant but academically incompetent students. Surely, the goal of school is not to make children into docile robots either by behavioral techniques or by medication. Rather, the goal should be one of providing children with the social and academic tools required to become successful in their social interactions and competent in their academic performance. Judging from the reactions and comments of both parents and teacher, this goal was achieved during the reinforcement period of the study. The parents were particularly relieved that their children, who had been dependent on Ritalin for years, could now function normally in school without the drug. Similarly, the teacher was excited over the fact that she could now build the social and academic skills of the children because they were more attentive and responsive to her than when they were under medication.

On the basis of these findings, it would seem appropriate to recommend that hyperactive children under medication periodically be given the opportunity to be drug-free, to minimize drug dependence, and to facilitate change through alternative behavioral techniques. While this study focused on behavioral alternatives to Ritalin for the control of hyperactivity, it is possible that another drug or a combination of medication and a behavioral program may also be helpful.

This study offers a behavioral and educationally justifiable alternative to the use of medication for hyperactive children. The control of hyperactivity by medication, while effective, may be too costly to the child, in that it may retard his academic and social growth, a human cost that schools and society can ill afford.

REFERENCES

Ayllon, T., and Kelly, K. Effects of reinforcement on standardized test performance. *Journal of Applied Behavior Analysis*, 1972, **5**, 477-484.

Ayllon, T., Layman, D., & Burke, S. Disruptive behavior and reinforcement of academic performance. *Psychological Record*, 1972, **22**, 315-323.

Ayllon, T., & Roberts, M. Eliminating discipline problems by strengthening academic performance. *Journal of Applied Behavior Analysis*, 1974, **7**, 71-76.

Becker, W., Madsen, C., Arnold, C., & Thomas, D. The contingent use of teacher attention and praise in reducing classroom behavior problems. *The Journal of Special Education*, 1967, **1**, 287-307.

Campbell, S., Douglas, U., & Morgenstern, G. Cognitive styles in hyperactive children and the effect of methylphenidate. *Journal of Child Psychology and Psychiatry*, 1971, **12**, 55-67.

Comly, H. Cerebral stimulants for children with learning disorders. *Journal of Learning Disabilities*, 1971, **4**, 484-490.

Conners, C., Eisenberg, L., & Barcai, A. Effect of dextro-amphetamine in children: studies on subjects with learning disabilities and school behavior problems. *Archives of General Psychiatry*, 1967, **17**, 478-485.

Conners, C., Eisenberg, L., & Sharpe, L. Effects of methylphenidate (Ritalin) on paired-associate learning and Porteus performance in emotionally disturbed children. *Journal of Consulting Psychology*, 1964, **28**, 14-22.

Conners, C. & Rothschild, G. Drugs and learning in children. In G. Helmuch (ed.), *Learning disorders*, Vol. 3. Seattle: Special Child Publications, 1968.

Conners, K. Recent drug studies with hyperkinetic children. *Journal of Learning Disabilities*, 1971, **4**, 476-483.

Denhoff, E., Davis, A., & Hawkins, A. Effects of dextro-amphetamine on hyperkinetic children: a controlled double blind study. *Journal of Learning Disabilities*, 1971, **4**, 491-499.

Epstein, L., Lasagna, L., Conners, K., & Rodriguez, A. Correlation of dextro-amphetamine excretion and drug response in hyperkinetic children. *Journal of Nervous and Mental Disease*, 1968, **146**, 136-146.

Fish, B. The "one child, one drug" myth of stimulants in hyperkinesis: importance of diagnostic categories in evaluating treatment. *Archives of General Psychiatry*, 1971, **25**, 193-203.

Freibergs, V., & Douglas, V. Concept learning in hyperactive and normal children. *Journal of Abnormal Psychology*, 1969, **74**, 388-395.

Hentoff, N. The drugged classroom. *Evergreen Review*, December 1970, 6-11.

Hollis, J., & St. Omer, V. Direct measurement of psychopharmacologic response: effects of chlorpromazine on motor behavior of retarded children. *American Journal of Mental Deficiency*, 1972, **76**, 397-407.

Keogh, B. Hyperactivity and learning disorders: review and speculation. *Exceptional Children*, 1971, **38**, 101-109.

Knights, R., & Hinton, G. Minimal brain dysfunction: clinical and psychological test characteristics. *Academic Therapy*, 1968, **4**, 265-273.

Krippner, S., Silverman, R., Cavallo, M., & Healy, M. A study of hyperkinetic children receiving stimulant drugs. *Academic Therapy*, 1973, **8**, 261-269.

Ladd, E. Pills for classroom peace? *Saturday Review*, November 1970, 66-83.

Layman, D. *A behavioral investigation: the effects of medication on disruptive classroom behavior and academic performance.* Unpublished doctoral dissertation, Georgia State University, 1974.

O'Leary, K. D., & Becker, W. C. Behavior modification of an adjustment class: a token reinforcement program. *Exceptional Children,* 1967, **33,** 637-642.

Sprague, R., Barnes, B., & Werry, J. Methylphenidate and thoridazine: learning, reaction time, activity, and classroom behavior in disturbed children. *American Journal of Orthopsychiatry,* 1970, **40,** 615-628.

Sprague, R., & Toppe, L. Relationship between activity level and delay of reinforcement. *Experimental Child Psychology,* 1966, **3,** 390-397.

Stewart, M., Pitts, F., Craig, A., & Dieruf, W. The hyperactive child syndrome. *American Journal of Orthopsychiatry,* 1966, **36,** 861-867.

Sulzbacher, S. Behavior analysis of drug effects in the classroom. In G. Semb (ed.), *Behavior analysis and education,* University of Kansas, 1972.

Sykes, D., Douglas, V., Weiss, G., & Minde, K. Attention in hyperactive children and the effect of methylphenidate (Ritalin). *Journal of Child Psychology and Psychiatry,* 1971, **12,** 129-139.

VIII. Conclusions

Yes, we do like children. More is known today about children and their development than ever before. Publications and discussions centering around children, childrearing, and the developmental process have proliferated. Research has recorded statistics regarding children's physical growth and detailed the physiological changes which accompany the various stages of childhood. The intellectual functioning of children has been examined in relation to the development of separate functions as well as the unfolding of various levels and stages of cognitive abilities. The language of children has been viewed as having properties separate from that of adult speech and examined as to its own semantic and syntactical applications to the child's world. The development of morality and the concept of justice has been examined in relation to the child's emerging cognitive abilities. Yes, we do like children!

Or do we? Bronfenbrenner (1975) talks about the progressive isolation and fragmentation of the American family in regard to its childrearing role. One third of married women with children under six are now working mothers. One of every six children under 18 is living in a single-parent family; 90% of these are independent families where the single parent is the head of the household and therefore most likely working.

All this has reduced to two the average number of adults present in the home who care for children. This is especially true among younger families with younger children across all strata of society.

Concomittant with a reduction in influence on the part of the family, Keniston states that the United States is an underdeveloped nation in terms of comprehensive support systems for children and their families. The United States is fourteenth among nations in combating infant mortality, with this standing dropping steadily. The rate of infant death for nonwhites is twice that for whites. Child abuse has increased, especially in single-parent families where the mother is twenty-five years of age (Bronfenbrenner, 1975). Yet there have been drastic reductions in funds for day care support facilities. Crimes by children have increased over 200% since 1964. In his article, Wald points to the dilemma of the juvenile courts: What is to be done with the numerous children who come before the courts in a variety of situations? Not enough adequate answers are available to ensure the child's welfare. Kramer, in her review of *Beyond the Best Interests of Children,* indicates that the child's physical well-being is protected, but not its psychological well-being.

It is often said that children are the future of our society. Yet training for parenthood is neglected. Our school systems are finding less and less money while taking on more and more functions. When budget cutbacks force program reductions, the "non-essentials" are the first to be dropped: counselors, special education, fine arts, speech therapists, aides. The prime emphasis is placed on achievement. Programs are developed for socially deprived youngsters and are judged by their success in improving IQ and achievement scores. Do we like children? Yes. The question is what do we want for and from them.

Children of Tomorrow

Children are the future. The future is built on the present. If our commitment is towards the future, it must be made now in the present. Which aspects of our various cultures should we homogenize with the rest of society? Which need to be emphasized? Can we teach children to perform the variety of academic functions expected of them without turning them off to thinking? What are the qualities we want to see exemplified in the future adults of our society, and what are we willing to do to help ensure their development?

Rheingold's paper views the question as one of values. What are our values and which of them do we want our children to have? If children are the future of our country, we must commit ourselves to that future *NOW.*

Reference

Bronfenbrenner, U. The next generation of Americans. Paper presented at the Annual Meeting of the American Association of Advertising Agencies, Dorado, Puerto Rico, 1975.

37.

Harriet L. Rheingold

TO REAR A CHILD

Every social ill of our times arises from behavior. Yet we treat each ill as though divorced from behaving persons. Reasonable as it may seem to work toward the amelioration of the ills, we shall not succeed until we learn how to prevent them. We can prevent them only when we learn how to rear a child properly.

My general concern starts with the behavior of the child who becomes the man. No person will disagree when I state categorically that children are our greatest natural resource. Yet, the world behaves as though they were no resource at all. The land, the water, the air—all are to be conserved, for they support life. What after all does the child contribute? How shortsighted we are—the child conceived tonight will be the adolescent of tomorrow and the adult of the day after. Nothing is more important than the person that child becomes; he alone holds the key to future life. We need ask only what can a man contribute to know that society has no greater resource. How shall we rear the child to become the man he can be?

My particular concern stems from the shallowness of current attempts to improve the rearing of the young child. Let me start with an activity now popular among child

Source: *American Psychologist*, 1973, **28**, 42-46. © 1973 by The American Psychological Association. Reprinted by permission.

Based on a paper presented at The David Shakow Symposium at the National Institutes of Health, Bethesda, Maryland, 1971. I thank Lorna S. Benjamin for directing my attention to the *Dictionary of Occupations* and my colleagues for editorial comments.

psychologists, that of increasing stimulation for the infant in his cradle. This activity is advanced as a solution for the poor intellectual status of the disadvantaged child. What recommends this practice? The effects of early experience on deprived laboratory animals? But no human child in any environment resembles the cage-raised laboratory rat or monkey. Or, does the fact that every middle-class infant has a mobile over his crib recommend the practice? But I cannot accept middle-class rearing as an optimum standard, nor yet as the best to which we can aspire. Are not our social ills the ills of middle-class rearing? No, increased stimulation is too simple a panacea, and a mobile over the crib is not enough.

I find shortsighted also the gauging of such worthy activities as Head Start by the number of IQ points they produce. Are a few IQ points a sufficient goal or even a proper goal? May it not be as important to gauge Head Start by improved social behavior?

I question too the push to set up more and more day care centers—not for the release they may provide a mother from duties she cannot or wishes not to carry out, or for the physical care they may provide a child, but because day care centers and even nursery schools do not necessarily improve the rearing of a child. Group care need not be harmful, but neither do we have evidence that it is consistently beneficial.

Here and there, too, we now see attempts to train parents as substitutes for such stimulation as day care centers or Head

Start might provide. Attempts to train parents of the ghetto are not new; first it was the immigrant parent, now it is the black and "inner-city" parent. These efforts, however, are still few, isolated, and fragmentary. But, once again, what I protest is that the standard to which the parents are to be trained is but middle-class rearing.

Furthermore, who speaks for the gifted child? A humane society accepts as a moral imperative the needs of its less able children. Should the more able not get at least as much attention? Can we be satisfied if their rearing is less than the best possible? Do not these, our future leaders, also need advocates?

The present small attempts to improve the rearing of children—each worthy but woefully limited—fall short of the demands of the times. When all of the poor children have IQs of 100, what then? These attempts are not yet addressed to the higher human needs of all of our people.

THE ILLS OF OUR TIMES

What are the demands of the times? The social ills have been enumerated so often they roll off our tongues like a litany: war, the poverty of fifty million people, their poor housing and health, crime, brutalizing treatment of prisoners, destruction of the environment, educational funds under pressure, cities desperate for help—I could go on. As a people we live at levels beyond the dreams of our fathers. Dissent is still tolerated, and political freedom has survived. Yet what marks our times is the painful awareness of not knowing what to do. We seem to drift in lethargy, bewilderment, and near-despair, and we feel powerless to alter events. We believe our leaders and our politicians, when reason plainly shows that their shifting contradictions only reflect our own. We are unable to foresee—let alone plan for—the consequences of decisions and actions until they reach catastrophic proportions. We consume whatever technology breeds, and blame science. We are not really honest nor yet an honorable society. We pride ourselves on being ungovernable. We live complacently with injustices and barbarities, with irrational hates and fears, and show a meanness of mind and spirit that ill becomes any great people.

We set up series of paper programs and endless conferences, commissions, and committees, and then pass some of the finest laws in the world, but we do not implement them if the cost falls on the privileged. As Hacker (1970) commented,

If the merest hope of survival were to be granted to millions of black children, they would have to have care and attention costing many times what even the most prosperous of suburbs give to their own sons and daughters (p. 107).

We are irresponsible in blaming our troubles on civilization, on the transformation of the economy by technology, on military-industrial domination, on the need to contain an opposing political ideology, on television, science, pollution, or overpopulation. All of these are man-made; all of these are men and women behaving; none are the givens of life itself or of the environment. Intelligence, foresight, imagination, responsibility, and concern could have foreseen the consequences of our behavior, as indeed some of our thinkers did foresee.

The tasks that confront us now will yield only to a study of man's behavior, and to the rearing of a new generation of children. It is time to live up to man's promise.

A PROGRAM OF ACTION

To insure the good society, to rear a new generation, I propose a program of action far beyond our present fragmented and limited efforts. I propose no less than a major mobilization of the resources of this nation, of men and women, of time and money. Are we a people who can commit all of our resources only for war—for killing and not for living?

De Jouvenel (1962, orig. publ. 1945) wrote,

The war through which we have just lived has surpassed in savagery and destructive force any yet seen by the Western World. This force has been generated by the unparalleled scale on which men and materials have been thrown in. Not only have armies been raised to the number of ten, of fifteen, of twenty millions of men, but also, behind the lines, whole populations have been conscribed that these armies might not lack the latest and deadliest weapons. Every inhabitant of a country with breath in him has served war's turn, and the non-essential tasks which sweeten life have come to be tolerated at all only so far as they have been thought necessary to sustain the spirit of the one vast instrument of war into which whole peoples have been forged (p. 1).

During those war years, we as a nation commandeered the service of sixteen million men and spent $330 billion—that is, 1940 dollars. Again, I ask: Are we a people who can commit that much only for destructive purposes? I ask for no less effort and no less money to raise men and women, to rear children, to a new level of humanness.

How shall we start? First, we declare a national emergency. The enemy is hatred, bigotry, selfishness, privilege, and stupidity. Next, we commandeer talent. We can volunteer or be drafted. We pay our fellow man and the future of mankind by a year or 2 or even 3 of every 10 years of our lives.

Who shall be commandeered? We need every kind of talent—writers, artists, scientists, critics of the social order, laymen, politicians, lawyers, educators. What

shall characterize the men and women who start the task? Long ago Emerson said it well:

Of no use are the men who study to do exactly as was done before, who can never understand that today is a new day. . . . We want men of original perception and original action, who can open their eyes wider than to a nationality—namely, to consideration of benefit to the human race—can act in the interest of civilization; [We want] men of elastic mind . . . who can live in the moment and take a step forward.

Let me add: and women, too.

What shall be their assignment? There are several, and for each assignment we need many groups, groups that work sometimes independently, and sometimes together. The first task shall be to enunciate the values that the new generation should be taught to honor, those values that shall guide the rearing of children.

SETTING THE VALUES OF REARING

Once we ask how should a child be reared, we face the larger question: the nature of the human being the rearing is to create. Without preamble we are plunged into the problem of values. For the traits we aim to create, the goals of rearing, will depend on our values.

It is just at this point that the scientist by nature and training stops. Our sophisticated society, too, becomes apprehensive at the very idea of setting values. Values are old-fashioned and suspect and we shy away from them. Values carry the flavor of dictatorship. But the fact that totalitarian and communist societies have set the values for their societies should not deter us from setting values for our own society. It is not the setting of values that we should object to, but the nature of the values.

We have just come through a period when we have been taught—and as psychologists we have taught—that everything is relative and that goodness may compensate for and even cloak evil intentions. As a result, in our time we have substituted alibis for moral standards, and seem to have preferred chaos to order. Parents have hesitated to convey values to their children, and the past few generations have seen a steady abdication of parental authority. Thus, officially we drift valueless.

But it is with values that we must begin. Once we have declared the values, we can set the goals of rearing. We can then ponder how they can be translated into behavior.

The values must be designed not just to eliminate the problems facing us but must go far beyond. Can we not now imagine a new order of behavior? Behavior to counteract the degradation of life? To preserve the humanity of man? To control our own evolution?

Many of our most sensitive, creative, and concerned citizens must devote their genius to the setting forth of the values that shall be the goals of rearing. Theirs will be a long and arduous task, but one to which many mature and responsible persons today, and many in the past, have given thought. In my own catalog of values I place first the brotherhood of man, and then, almost as corollaries, a concern for the environment, and the opportunity for each person in our society to realize his own potential for development. I propose these only as examples and not at all as a definitive or exhaustive catalog. That I do not present an entire, perfected, and unassailable set of values in no way detracts from my proposal. Rather, it must be seen that the task demands the efforts not of one person but of task forces of men and

women of "original perception and original actions . . . of elastic mind."

REARING THE CHILD

Each of the values then must be translated into traits and behavior that honor the values. How does a child or an adolescent or adult behave when he is *responsive* to the needs of his fellows? When he is *responsible* for the needs of others? And in the varieties of situations in which he may find himself? What are the behaviors that index a concern for the environment in 2-year-olds, in 10-year-olds? And so we can go down the list, and for each question we need rosters of workers. The task is not yet finished, for now still other groups of scientists, artists, laymen, and the rest must decide how children should be reared so that they behave in accord with the values of the society.

I do not see why one assignment need be completed before another. All can be weighed and debated at the same time. We should not be deterred because interdisciplinary effort still comes hard. We should not be put off by anyone's asking when does one begin to rear a child. We used to say that the first five years of life were the most important for later development; that span of time has been shrinking, until now some say the first two years of life. I would change that to say every day, any day, *now*, is the most important time in the life of a child; and I would start on Day 1 of his life. I shall not be put off, either, by the disclaimer that surely every child is an individual and must be reared differently. I admit it.

One last charge remains, the training of those who rear children. The most difficult, the most important task in the world—the rearing of a child—at the present time is judged by our society to require no training at all. We behave as though the ability to conceive and bear a child, as though the acts of conception and birth automatically confer on a mother or a father knowledge on how to rear that child. Fortunately, most children are born robust and with enough good sense that we do not end up with a population of incompetents—inexperienced and inept though their parents may be.

The child is by nature active, alert, spirited, curious, and happy. After years of observing children at home and in the laboratory, I continue to be impressed with how avidly the child seeks new experiences, how ceaselessly he strives to be independent. He is friendly, generous, and affectionate. Above all, he can learn. What happens to that nature? He need not grow up fearful, selfish, dependent, dishonest, and unruly. Our social ills begin with parents themselves fearful, selfish, and hostile.

To teach a child to read and write requires four years of collegiate education, special courses, practice teaching, and a diploma. To teach a handicapped child requires even more training. But, as matters now stand, we still consider that to rear a human being requires none.

Nor are day care centers and nursery schools the answer. Living in families has much to offer, and rearing outside the home, as in the home, will be only as good as the people who care for the children. And here I do criticize the solution now receiving support in many quarters: of entrusting the rearing of children to paraprofessionals. Of course, I applaud training people to nurture children, but I criticize the belief, given what little knowledge of good rearing we now possess, that a few months of training are sufficient to make adolescents, the rehabilitated, the retired, and otherwise unemployable people, good rearers of children.

Let me digress to show the low opinion our society now holds of child care. In the *Dictionary of Occupational Titles* (United States Department of Labor, 1965), both a child care attendant and a nursery school teacher receive a rating of 7 on their relationship to people. The category 7, next to the lowest on the list, is classified as serving. At the top we find 0 for dealing with individuals in terms of their total personality, 2 for instructing, 4 for amusing others, 6 for talking with others to convey or exchange information (I skip over the intermediate numbers), and finally 7, the lowest, for attending to the needs of people or their wishes.

Thus, the child care attendant and the nursery school teacher are judged not to deal with children in terms of their total personality, not to exchange ideas with children, not to instruct or train through explanation, or even to amuse, but simply to attend to needs or requests. The requirements for these occupations are listed as:

a combination of patience and sympathy for the problems of others; the ability to relate to people; stability under pressure; attentiveness and the ability to pay attention to detail; clean personal habits; freedom from communicable diseases; and some degree of manual and finger dexterity and motor coordination (p. 479).

What training does the *Dictionary* specify? A "general . . . acceptance and successful execution of domestic responsibilities and such casual work experience as babysitting . . . (p. 479)." I find this frightening. To care for children is to rear them, and to rear them is more than babysitting and cleaning house.

But perhaps I misread the dictionary, and 7 is after all a proper rating. No, because I find that 7 also classifies a rest room attendant and a parking lot attendant. Surely a parking lot attendant and a nursery school teacher are a world apart.

Obviously, we have not begun to understand what is needed. We must set out at once the specifications for a new profession; I shall name it Scientists of Rearing. They shall be scientists who devote themselves to acquiring and testing knowledge on the rearing of children, and to discovering how successful different practices are in achieving the behaviors that index the values society will now espouse, and how successful in eliminating destructive, self-defeating, and mean behaviors. These scientists will also teach those who will teach the parents and all those who care for children. This new profession must be accepted as the highest in the land.

Next, parents must be taught how to rear their children. Although this cannot be done in a single generation, we can begin now with those who are parents. But we must also teach those who will be parents. We will teach children in grade school and high school how to be parents. We teach it in college. Parents-to-be must be certified as to their competence, and a practical examination is better than a paper one. We must take an examination to obtain a license to drive a car. The child deserves no less; the good of the country demands much more.

CONCLUSIONS

My tone has been evangelical, it is true; but to me, it falls short of the fervor the subject deserves. I will be the first to admit that I have not supplied practical details, but I will defend my proposal against a matter sure to concern many persons: the specter of utopianism. I do not object if my proposals seem utopian in the sense that they are desirable but impractical or unrealizable, because I think they are not only realizable but necessary. I do object if you use the term to mean that I am proposing to create a perfect society in which perfection is defined as just harmony. I have in mind no attempt to rear uniform children, forever at peace, all virtuous without effort. If the science of human behavior has taught us one thing, it is that rearing, training, and teaching can be imposed on no one. The recipient is a partner, and his uniqueness ensures the richness of diversity. Even if we wish it, pure harmony is not the human condition. Rather, in Walt Whitman's words, "It is provided in the essence of things that from any fruition of success, no matter what, shall come forth something to make a greater struggle necessary."

To draw these remarks to a close, I offer a recent letter of a father to the editor of the journal of an honorary society. He wrote,

Could you organize . . . a series of articles indicating the type of environment, both in the home and outside, which a child, from birth on, should be exposed to so that he may grow up to be a thinking, understanding, human being?

Who today can answer this poignant plea?

The rearers of children are entrusted with the care and training of our most precious resource. It must be clear to any government that the present state and future of that nation depend on its people. From them come the leaders. Upon them depends obedience to the laws; upon them, and not the experts, come the acceptance or rejection of social values. The dreamers and the idealists only point the way; upon the people depends the following of any way. An educated and responsible citizenry is a country's greatest asset.

The time is propitious. It is a time when despite its many imperfections the level of human welfare is higher than ever before and recognized for the first time as the legal responsibility of government. Man glimpses a new image of himself. Yet the removal of each injustice reveals still another, and we become troubled, impatient, and doubtful.

The rearing of a new generation can provide that voice of moral assurance in an era of bitter doubt. A responsible people, free of prejudice, concerned for the quality of human life, will be able to revise our economic and political institutions so that at last they become responsive to human hopes.

My proposals immediately would have a salutary effect on the nation. No longer would we drift; no longer would we patch. Instead we would consecrate ourselves to a task of high purpose. We would begin to behave like a great people who have

promises to keep and pledges to redeem. In rearing children, we write the future history of the world. We could start now to make that history a shining affirmation of what it means to be human.

REFERENCES

De Jouvenel, B. *On power, its nature and the history of its growth.* (Trans. by J. F. Huntington.) Boston: Beacon Press, 1962.

Hacker, A. *The end of the American era.* New York: Atheneum, 1970.

United States Department of Labor, Manpower Administration. *Dictionary of occupational titles.* (3rd ed.) Vol. 1, *Definitions of titles.* Washington, D.C.: United States Government Printing Office, 1965.

Name Index

Subject Index

261; research questions in, 276; sex-role stereotypes of, 206
Pavlovian learning, role of language in, 128
passive-aggressive personality, and child abuse, 290
peer group: and moral reasoning, 217–28; as a socialization agent, 5
perceptions, organization of and language, 142. See also cognitive maps
perceptual constancy. *See* object constancy
perceptual experiences, measurement of, 31–32
permissiveness: assumptions of, 254–55; origins of, 253; results of, 255
personal guilt, 233
personality characteristics: and occupation, 326–27; and test performance, 85–87
phonemic contractions, 131
pivots, 137–39
play, and intellectual competence, 38
postconventional stage of moral reasoning, 226
poverty: extent in U.S. of, 4; and divorce, 261–64; and female-headed families, 8, 261–63; and overstimulation of infants, 21–22. *See also* cultural deprivation
predicative construction of children's statements, 139
predictive validity of tests, 81–82
pregnancy, anxiety over and parent-child interaction, 44–45
prelingual stage of language development, 143–44
preoperational stage of cognitive development: activities for children in, 94; characteristics of, 89
preschool programs: attitude toward, 312; need to recognize child's cognitive structure in, 312–13; need to recognize individual differences in, 314. *See also* intervention programs
Preschool Screening Survey, 323
principle of bounded rationality, 87
principle of contextuality, 79
process variables, vs. status variables in measures of achievement, 53–54
projection, and prosocial behavior, 232
prosocial behavior: developmental theory of, 230–36; and situationalism of children, 317–38
proximity-avoiding behaviors, 166, 169–70
proximity-seeking behaviors, 166, 169
psychological parents, 300, 303
psychoanalytic theory, on moral reasoning, 216–17

psychomotor skills, and readiness, 320–22. *See also* coordination, psychomotor
psychotic personality, and child abuse, 290
punishment: in moral realism stage of moral development, 217; and social class, 54

racial differences, study of: and cultural relativism, 54–59; process variables vs. status variables in, 53–54
random articulation stage of language development, 143–44. *See also* babbling
readiness: assessing, 322–23; defined, 319–20; hierarchial arrangement of skills in, 320–21; implications for school of, 323-24; problems of tests of, 323
Receptive Language and Spatial Abilities test, 37
relative advantage, and guilt, 233
remarriage: likelihood for males vs. females, 275; and stress in divorce, 274
retardation: definitional changes of, 73–74; effects of labeling on, 332
Rhode Island Pupil Identification Scale, 323
Ritalin (methylphenidate), 337
rites of passage, 1–2
role play: measurement of, 32; and motor-empathy, 77
role taking: and moral reasoning, 222; and prosocial behavior, 232; and sex-role identification, 197; study of, 100–104

sadistic personality, and child abuse, 290
SAT scores, and achievement motivation, 327
scapegoating, 44, 290
schizophrenia, and infant capabilities, 25–26
schools: "feminization" of, 207; historical purpose of, 308; and intellectualization of children, 6–8; labeling of students in, 331–36; measures of success of, 8; modern purpose of, 309–10; as opportunity equalizers, 5; sex-role socialization in, 207
search behavior, 167, 168–69
self, elements of, 197
self-expression, measurement of, 32
self-other distinction: and language acquisition, 145–46; and prosocial behavior, 231
sensorimotor stage of cognitive development: activities for children in, 94; characteristics of, 89; cognitive maps developed during, 90–91
sensory thresholds: and childhood psychosis, 25; and colic, 19, 23; and fantasy life, 19. *See also* infants

THE BOOK MANUFACTURE

Child Development: Contemporary Perspectives was set at Fox Valley Typesetting, Menasha, Wisconsin, and printed and bound at R. R. Donnelley & Sons Company, Crawfordsville, Indiana. Cover design was by Jane Rae Brown, internal design by the F. E. Peacock Publishers, Inc., art department. The type is Times Roman.